Designing a New America

A VOLUME IN THE SERIES

Political Development of the American Nation
Studies in Politics and History

Edited by
Sidney M. Milkis and Jerome M. Mileur

Designing a New America

THE ORIGINS OF

NEW DEAL PLANNING,

1890–1943

Patrick D. Reagan

University of Massachusetts Press
AMHERST

Copyright © 1999 by
The University of Massachusetts Press
All rights reserved
Printed in the United States of America
LC 99-30717
ISBN 1-55849-230-5
Designed by Jack Harrison
Set in Adobe Bembo by Graphic Composition, Inc.
Printed and bound by Sheridan Books

Library of Congress Cataloging-in-Publication Data
Reagan, Patrick D., 1953–
Designing a new America : the origins of New Deal planning, 1890–1943 / Patrick D.
    Reagan.
        p.   cm.—(Political development of the American nation : studies in politics and
    history)
    Includes bibliographical references and index.
    ISBN 1-55849-230-5 (cloth : alk. paper).
    1. United States—Economic policy—1933–1945.
    2. New Deal, 1933–1939.
    3. United States.   National Resources Planning Board.   I. Title.   II. Series: Political
development of the American nation.
    HC106.3.R36   2000
    338.973′009′043—DC21   99-30717
                                                                                CIP

British Library Cataloguing in Publication data are available.

To Reilly for everything

Contents

Acknowledgments

While writing is a solitary endeavor, research is a collective one. Bringing the two processes together creates communities of scholars, colleagues, friends, and family that we all wish could be found everywhere. While engaged in this project, I received encouragement, suggestions, and helpful criticism from a number of people. Their assistance has made this a better book. I did not always follow the proffered advice, so where mistakes exist they are mine alone.

Scholars cannot work without the courteous, professional, and quietly effective labors of librarians and archivists. At the Department of Special Collections of the University of Chicago Library, Michael Ryan and the staff of Delena Little, Susan Rugh, Albert Tanner, and Betty Teleky offered friendly assistance with a touch of humor. Jeri Nunn and Elizabeth B. Mason guided me through the Columbia Oral History Collection, while archivist Kenneth A. Lohf of the Rare Book and Manuscript Room of the Butler Library at Columbia University led the way through manuscript collections and cataloged letters. At the Harvard University Archives, Dr. Clark Elliott and Kathy Miller not only assisted with research in the Hansen papers, but also tracked down student and alumni records for Frederic Delano, Henry Dennison, and Charles W. Eliot II. At the Harvard Graduate School of Business Administration Archives, Florence Bartoshesky located company histories and filled in gaps in the correspondence of Henry Dennison, while engaging me in thoughtful conversation. Archivists at the Herbert C. Hoover Library assisted me in working through the Hoover and Hunt papers. The Library of Congress staff professionally eased research in the Harold Ickes and John Merriam collections. Richard Crawford and Karen Paul of the Legislative and Natural Resources Branch of the Civil Archives Division at the National Archives went beyond the call of duty in locating materials. Their heroic work under trying conditions is proof that government employees are among the most underrated laborers in our national vineyard of liberty. Joseph Ernst and J. William Hess of the Rockefeller Archive Center proved excellent guides through the fascinating records now open to researchers at that important depository. William R. Emerson arranged for me to meet with archivist Curtis J. Clow who graciously allowed access to the private archives of the Messrs. Rockefeller to research materials available nowhere else, while Peter Johnson gave insight on the Rockefeller family history. Many of these records are now open to researchers at the Rockefeller Archive Center. At the Franklin D. Roosevelt Library, everyone was helpful but most especially William R. Emerson, Don Schewe, and Joe Morgan. The staff at the FDR Library went out of their way to help at every turn. Librarians Karyl Winn and Janet Ness at the University of Washington Libraries helped in locating material from the George Yantis papers. At Tennessee Technological University, Linda Mulder showed, more times than I can count, what a superb interlibrary loan librarian can do. Oral history interviews were kindly granted by Dr. Eveline M. Burns, James T. Dennison, Elizabeth D. Dunker, and Charles W. Eliot II.

Scholars and colleagues have given advice, criticism, and leads that were invariably on the mark, although I have not followed all their suggestions. No one has been more steady in providing a model of what a scholar and friend can be than Ellis W. Hawley, who has spoken, argued, cajoled, and ministered to me over many years. Robert H. Bremner, Austin Kerr, and Warren Van Tine at Ohio State University gave sound counsel, personal support, scholarly admonition, and, at a difficult time, shelter in a storm. Guy Alchon read an earlier version of the work offering pointed, astute criticisms that have made it a better book while offering the chance to exchange ideas in a variety of professional forums. Martin Bulmer shared research ideas about Beardsley Ruml and intellectual currents at the University of Chicago in the 1920s, while, in the midst of a busy schedule, Barry D. Karl listened patiently to my ideas about Charles Merriam and national planning. Kim McQuaid drew on his unparalleled knowledge of business-government relations to pass on research materials from the Ralph Flanders papers along with the most witty, charming, and incisive letters. Colleagues at Kenyon College listened to ideas, read chapters, and gave me a model for good teaching. As my teacher, mentor, and colleague, Roy Wortman has given more than I could ever expect or hope from a friend. Colleagues in the Department of History at Tennessee Technological University have supported my endeavors, not only through the leadership of the late B. F. Jones and

William J. Brinker, but also with the day-to-day fellowship of a diverse, humane set of people only rarely found in today's academy so often riven by ideological and personal agendas. Ballard Campbell, Peter Field, Larry Gerber, Alonzo Hamby, David Hamilton, Richard Jensen, Kim McQuaid, Judith Sealander, and Margaret Weir discussed key ideas at various points in the project. Friends and colleagues in the H-Net network, especially Ballard Campbell, Bob Cherny, Kriste Lindenmeyer, and Michael Pierce of H-SHGAPE, continue to show the value of creating and maintaining a community of scholars through the emerging medium of the Internet.

Scholars need financial support as well as intellectual guidance. Ohio State University provided not only a university fellowship, but also research grants from the graduate school, the Graduate Student Alumni Research Awards program, and the Foster Rhea Dulles Memorial Fund of the Department of History. Frances Seeber of the Eleanor Roosevelt Institute and William Emerson of the Franklin D. Roosevelt Library smoothed the way for two research grants at the Roosevelt Library. Warren Van Tine unselfishly provided shelter as well as a mentor's guidance. Tennessee Technological University's Faculty Research Committee granted research funds over a period of years, while the Non-Instructional Grant Committee provided a semester off for writing and revision. The National Endowment for the Humanities program for summer stipends made possible my attendance at a summer seminar, "The New Rationality: Planners and Politicians in Wartime and Interwar America, 1917–1945," at the University of Iowa directed by Lawrence E. Gelfand and Ellis W. Hawley, as well as research at the Hoover Library. Gelfand and Hawley led one of the most intellectually challenging, personally enjoyable, and professionally rewarding experiences possible in the community of scholars that NEH monies support.

Sidney Milkis and Jerome Mileur expressed an enthusiasm about this work reflective of the spirit of scholarly exchange. They carefully read and considered the argument, invited me to participate in an exciting conference on the New Deal at Brandeis University, and selected superb readers for the work. Jerry Mileur's meticulous editing dramatically improved the final book, reconfirming his reputation as a master of his craft. At the University of Massachusetts Press, senior editor Clark Dougan was friendly, professional, and expeditious in moving from acquisition through publication. Managing editors Pam Wilkinson and Ella Kusnetz handled details superbly in an understanding, patient way. Catlin Murphy and other members of the press's staff were courteous, skilled, and professional. Craig Noll did an excellent job copyediting the work and saved me from some detailed mistakes. Alonzo Hamby and an unnamed reader for the press gave thoughtful readings, made constructive criticisms, and led the author to recast the work, making for a more effective, clear, and significant interpretation. I had the pleasure to meet and discuss comments and exchange ideas personally with Lon Hamby thanks to our meeting at the New Deal conference arranged by Sid Milkis and Jerry Mileur. Few authors can be so lucky as to have such a rewarding experience throughout the publication process.

I would like to thank *Newsweek* magazine for permission to reprint the photographs of Frederic Delano and Charles Merriam from the March 22, 1943, issue. The photograph of Wesley Clair Mitchell appears courtesy of Columbia University. James T. Dennison not only agreed to speak with the author about his father, Henry Dennison, he also provided the photograph and permission to publish it here. Alvin Ruml graciously provided the 1947 photograph of his father, Beardsley Ruml, which originally appeared in the March 1951 *Dartmouth Alumni Magazine*. Dartmouth College Library granted permission to publish it here. Thank you to editor Eileen McMahon, who allowed for publication of parts of chapter 4 which originally appeared in a different form in "From Depression to Depression: Hooverian National Planning, 1921–1933," *Mid-America: An Historical Journal* 70 (1988): 35–60.

Friends and family have given support, food, shelter, and encouragement at each step in the path. V. Antonio Aniñao, John Graham, Kathy Reagan, Mike Reagan, Warren Van Tine, and Stu Wegener gave generously of their time, hospitality, congeniality, and friendship. Matt Winkler and his father, Robin Winkler, were warm, gracious, charming, cultivated, and challenging hosts—their love of history and human compassion show that hope and good cheer remain alive. Matt and Robin gave me memories of New York City and the Hudson River Valley that will last a lifetime. Guy Alchon, Chris Anderson, Barbara Ellis, David Hamilton, Ellis Hawley, Austin Kerr, Warren Van Tine, and Roy Wortman showed that scholarship and friendship are best experienced in tandem. Thomas Jefferson once said that the land belongs to the living. Those of us in the current generation keep memory and hope alive in our hearts and minds. All these people helped this author to understand the communities of librarians and archivists, scholars, colleagues, friends, and families more than any one of them realizes. Finally, to my wife, Reilly, librarian and teacher, I owe the joys of a life fully lived, sharing everything involved in publishing a book while teaching, advising, and caring for our families, friends, and furry fellows. To Reilly, I dedicate this work with love, admiration, respect, and gratitude.

Designing a New America

1

The Origins of
New Deal Planning

ORGANIZATIONAL CHANGE AND PUBLIC-POLICY MAKING IN MODERN AMERICA

We do not have to suppose; we know that these speculations will be met by a superior smile of incredulity. The funny thing about it is that the groups are actually beginning to form. As yet they are scattered and amorphous; here a body of engineers, there a body of economic planners. Watch them. They will bear watching. If occasion arises, join them. They are part of what H. G. Wells has called the Open Conspiracy.

Why should Russians have all the fun of remaking a world?

—STUART CHASE, *A New Deal*

IN JULY 1933 President Franklin D. Roosevelt appointed the first and only national planning agency in U.S. history. Over the next ten years, Roosevelt's planners used their individual experiences, professional expertise, and institutional connections to engage in one of the most revealing episodes in the history of American public-policy making. In a short historical span of one decade, FDR's planners created a bank of public-works projects that could be drawn upon as a countercyclical tool in response to downturns in the business cycle. This early economic policy was expanded in the debate over the adoption of compensatory spending policy in the late 1930s that is usually credited to Keynesian economists. The New Deal planners established regional planning boards in New England and the Pacific Northwest, founded state planning boards in a majority of the states, and engaged in some of the most extensive land-use planning experiments in the nation's history. By the late

1930s they participated in New Deal policy debates over the best ways to respond to the recession of 1937–38 and to implement executive-branch reorganization to streamline the growing number of agencies gathered in the New Deal's alphabet soup. During mobilization for World War II, New Deal planners and their small technical staff conducted numerous industrial plant site-location studies, established the Roster of Specialized and Scientific Personnel to use human resources appropriately during war, and began the process of postwar planning for domestic America. Postwar planning reports suggested that economic growth, a society of abundance, and social welfare reforms could help to win the peace after defeat of the fascist powers. Both the federal income withholding tax and the famous GI Bill of Rights grew out of these wartime planning efforts. In 1943 the planners came under severe criticism in Congress, lost a key appropriations battle, and fell victim to a counterattack by the legislative branch on what was perceived as the inordinate growth of executive-branch power as a result of New Deal reforms and wartime mobilization.

For most of the planning board's history, a small group of key people served at the pleasure of the president in a planning organization set within the executive branch of the federal government. Its work proceeded through a governmental agency that changed its name several times from National Planning Board (1933–34) to National Resources Board (1934–35), National Resources Committee (1935–39), and finally National Resources Planning Board (1939–43). Although the name, structure, and scope of the New Deal planning board changed over time, there was remarkable continuity of personnel at the top. Between 1933 and 1943 five prominent people served as Roosevelt's planners: Frederic A. Delano, Charles E. Merriam, Wesley Clair Mitchell, Henry S. Dennison, and Beardsley Ruml. FDR's five planners viewed national planning as an ongoing process rather than a set of preconceived blueprints to be implemented by an all-powerful state. These New Deal planners brought to their work considerable experience over a longer time span than that of the immediate crisis years of 1929–32.

Born into an almost aristocratic Hudson River Valley family, Frederic A. Delano attended Harvard College before entering the railroad industry and making a reputation as a skilled business manager and then city planner in Progressive-Era Chicago.[1] Following wartime work in France, in the 1920s Delano moved beyond his position as head of the American Railway Association to direct the Regional Plan of New York and Its Environs, as well as the national movement that created the National Capital Park and Planning Commission in Washington, D.C. During the 1930s and 1940s this regional planning group led the way for creation of a range of new federal buildings and the famous Memorial Parkway in the nation's capital city. In 1933 President Franklin D. Roosevelt appointed Delano, his uncle, as head of the New Deal planning board. Delano, a lifelong Republican (except for brief support of Wilson in 1912), had a distinguished reputation in business management and was a leader in the nascent city and regional planning movement.

Charles E. Merriam grew up in comfortable surroundings in Iowa, attended Columbia University, became the first political scientist at the new University of Chicago, and started a career as a nationally known political scientist and urban reformer in Chicago before World War I. After service during the war with the Committee on Public Information, Merriam widened his professional contacts by sponsoring cross-disciplinary research at the University of Chicago, leading the American Political Science Association, and founding the Social Science Research Council (SSRC).[2] Following service on various Hooverian committees in the 1920s, Merriam sat between 1929 and 1933 as vice chair with Wesley Clair Mitchell on the President's Research Committee on Social Trends. In July 1933 Merriam's old Chicago mayoral campaign manager, Republican Progressive Harold L. Ickes, then secretary of the interior and head of the Public Works Administration, selected Merriam to serve with Frederic Delano on the New Deal planning agency. Progressive reform between 1901 and 1918, social science research, personal political loyalties, and associational experience in Hooverian efforts of the New Era from 1921 through 1932 brought these two independent Republicans together under the aegis of a liberal Democratic president on the country's first national planning board.

Wesley Clair Mitchell entered the new University of Chicago with the first class in 1892 to study economics. Over the course of a distinguished career as a professional economist, Mitchell worked at the University of California at Berkeley, Columbia University, and the University of Chicago. By 1914 Mitchell had a reputation as the nation's leading institutional economist with expertise on the business cycle. During the 1917–18 mobilization, he served as head of the Price Section of the War Industries Board under former Harvard Business School dean Edwin F. Gay. In 1920 Mitchell and Gay founded the National Bureau of Economic Research (NBER), which conducted much of the economic research for a number of the Hooverian committees growing out of the 1921 President's Conference on Unemployment. In 1927 Mitchell succeeded Merriam as head of the SSRC and, in 1929, headed the NBER's effort in producing the Hoover-sponsored report *Recent Economic Changes* (1929). As director of the President's Research Committee on Social Trends (1929–33), Mitchell wrote the summary recommendation for establishment of a national planning agency. Not surprisingly, when President Roosevelt created that agency in July 1933, Mitchell was selected to work with fellow planners Delano and Merriam.[3]

Henry S. Dennison, son of a successful Boston manufacturer, attended Harvard before taking over the family firm in Framingham, Massachusetts.[4] As head of the Dennison Manufacturing Company, he restructured the firm, pioneered in a range of business reform efforts in Massachusetts during the Progressive Era, and won appointment as organizer of planning and statistics for the U.S. Shipping Board and the War Industries Board during World War I. In the 1920s Dennison experimented with welfare capitalist reforms at his firm, streamlined part of the U.S. Postal Service, advocated scientific management through the Taylor Society, participated in the *Recent Economic Changes* study, and established contacts with Hooverian activists and business reformers at the Harvard Business School. His associational work as cofounder of the Twentieth Century Fund philanthropy (1920), originator of the Boston-area Manufacturers' Research Association (1922), founder of the American Management Association (1923), and creator of the stillborn Business Research Council (1929) also served Dennison in good stead. By 1933 a disillusioned Dennison—who had voted Republican until 1932, with the exception of supporting Woodrow Wilson in 1912 and 1916—proved willing to accept appointment to the Industrial Advisory Board, a business advisory component of the National Recovery Administration. Thereafter, a pro-New Deal stance and prior contact with other planners led to his appointment in 1935 to the planning agency as a replacement for the resigning Wesley Clair Mitchell.

Beardsley Ruml, son of an Iowa physician, originally studied the emerging field of psychology while a student at the University of Chicago. Work with a former faculty mentor in the first industrial psychology department in the nation at the Carnegie Institute of Technology led directly to Ruml's appointment as test maker for the War Department in World War I. After the war he quickly left the field of industrial psychology for more challenging work as assistant to another former mentor, now serving as president of the Carnegie Corporation philanthropy. This move gave entrée to the newly opened directorship of the Laura Spelman Rockefeller Memorial, one of four major Rockefeller philanthropies, and de facto participation in the formative years of the Social Science Research Council. During the New Era, Ruml became one of the most

important philanthropic managers in the country, responsible for under-
writing the development of the social sciences at such prestigious schools
as Merriam's own University of Chicago, partnership with Merriam in
the SSRC, financing of most of the Hoover committees that grew out of
the 1921 Unemployment Conference, reorganization of the Rockefeller
Foundation, which absorbed the LSRM, and founding of the Spelman
Fund of New York, which under the direction of Ruml and his successor
Merriam funded much of the new research in the field of public administration.[5] From his positions as dean of the University of Chicago's new
Social Science Division and as treasurer of the New York City–based
R. H. Macy's department store chain, Ruml played a key advisory role
in the early New Deal. Recognition came in 1935 with his appointment
along with Dennison as representative of the business community to replace Mitchell on Roosevelt's New Deal planning board.

Longtime fellow Republicans, social science research advocates, and
experienced associational activists, Delano, Merriam, Mitchell, Dennison, and Ruml served as FDR's New Deal national planners. Drawing
upon their own background in such key institutions as the railroad industry, city and regional planning, professional social science, institutional
economics, business firms, and philanthropic foundations, Roosevelt's
planners created a historically distinct form of national planning to fit
the American setting. As such, they were participants in a broader debate over the making of modern liberalism that transformed the older
nineteenth-century ideology of classical liberalism into one more appropriate to the changed conditions of urban-industrial America in the
twentieth century.[6] Still, they sought to combine what they considered
the best of that older liberalism, their own intellectual development and
institutional connections in modern America, and changing economic,
political, and social conditions to formulate a new, twentieth-century liberalism. Their lifetime of work came to constitute a new public ideology
of liberalism that contained an important place for national planning in
the public sector as a way to address lags between economic growth, the
social consequences of that growth, and the relationship between public-
policy advisers and the American democratic process. Within the voluntarist circumstances of a two-party political system, an industrial capitalist
economy dominated by private-sector activity, and a broader culture
with a long-running tradition of antistatist values based on distrust and
fear of centralized governmental power, New Deal planning proved considerably more voluntarist than purely statist when compared with other
nations' experiments in planning.

Rather than assuming a priori that FDR's planners advocated a statist-oriented style of command economic planning in response to the crisis of the Great Depression, which many studies suggest, their history between the 1890s and the 1940s suggests that the story of New Deal planning is a much more complicated and ambiguous one.[7] FDR's planners acted in the context of changing values, an evolving set of institutions, shifting political and economic circumstances, and the ebb and flow of planning opportunities to create a distinctly national, American form of planning. As such, the planners left a historical record that may be examined in light of the broader changes in modern America. They were part of a wide-ranging national debate over how to create a new society based on modern institutions that grew out of developments in the business community, the urban environment, the rise of professionalism and its attendant associations in the social sciences, the recognition of the need for a new kind of twentieth-century liberalism, and the building of new interconnections among business, government, social science research, and philanthropic management. Neither they nor others held a monopoly on this national debate. The history of New Deal planning must be seen in the context of the broader transformation of twentieth-century American political economy, which raised issues such as the appropriate role of the executive branch in organizing governmental response to change, the proper use of economic policy to respond to changes in the business cycle, and the utility of social scientific expertise in dealing with major questions of public policy.

In effect, FDR's planners eventually created an American tradition of national planning based on their experiences, the nation's specific historical circumstances, and the complicated operations of a federalist political culture that engendered tension between the president and the Congress, competing political parties, and Jeffersonian ideals and Hamiltonian methods. Building on the past, the planners also were harbingers of the future postwar mixed economy built on both long-term economic growth and a peculiarly conservative and restricted welfare state. Their history belies any simple attempt to paint them as radical collectivists bent on destroying the American system of mature industrial capitalism by taking opportunistic advantage in the crisis atmosphere of the Great Depression. New Deal planning, like other chapters in the history of modern America, is best understood in the historical framework of the long view rather than only as a Depression-born phenomenon. Unlike national planning in the communist Soviet Union, fascist Italy, Nazi Germany, or a militarized Japan, New Deal planning was not based on the traditional model of command and control planning led by the state to formulate blueprints intended to create a new kind of economy, society, and polity. From a historical vantage point, New Deal planning differed from its counterparts in other nations as a result of both different national and historical settings and the personal background, ideas, institutional networks, and political environment encountered by planners in the American arena. In a sense, American planning took an exceptional national form different from its counterparts elsewhere in the 1930s because it was built on a very different history than the planning efforts of other nations.

In two short articles and the more comprehensive *Toward a Planned Society: From Roosevelt to Nixon* (1976), historian Otis L. Graham, Jr., argued that the evolutionary course of national planning in the United States made possible the acceptance of planning by both major political parties.[8] Graham implied that President Richard M. Nixon, in saying, "We are all Keynesians," might also have said, "We are all planners." Graham's work remains the only truly comprehensive history of modern American national planning. Graham's thesis, however, about the shift of attitudes toward planning was based in the assumption common to all previous histories of planning—that it began in the 1930s as a response to the Depression. Rather than asking who the planners were and what they did, Graham asked what happened to the *idea* of planning over the period 1933–72. The perspective is an important one, but it misses part of the historical picture. National planning under the New Deal had its roots in the pre-1933 period in the evolving ideas and institutional connections of the people who became FDR's planners.

To understand how Roosevelt's New Deal planners thought and acted requires kinds of historical understanding rarely achieved by contemporary commentators in the 1930s or by scholars since. The public debate over planning that emerged between 1929 and 1933 often focused on either the practical efforts by business leaders, who assumed the utility of the corporate model for public-policy making, or the more abstract planning ideals discussed by intellectuals and academics, who often assumed a bipolar choice between the voluntarism of laissez-faire policies or the statist path of governmental coercion, with no other choices in between. Students of the 1930s planning debate have centered their discussion on those people who commented publicly about or openly advocated some form of rigidly statist, command-style economic planning, while institutional histories of New Deal planning have focused on the governmental programs for industrial recovery (the National Recovery Administration), agricultural recovery (the Agricultural Adjustment Administration), and regional planning (the Tennessee Valley Authority) that instituted partial, sectoral planning later ruled unconstitutional by the Supreme Court or compromised by the complexities of Depression-era politics.[9]

Yet in modern America there were thousands who discussed policy options between these ideological opposites, but later scholars have not always delineated who these people were, what they thought, how they institutionalized their ideas, and what policy alternatives they offered in differing contexts. New Deal planners were part of a broader discussion about ongoing changes in the nature and direction of modern America. Between the 1890s and the 1940s, these American planners joined a burgeoning national debate over how to transform the nineteenth-century tradition of classical liberalism into a modern, twentieth-century liberalism that could take into account the many changes in the United States since the onset of industrialization and the attendant changes marked by the huge movement of millions of people from abroad to America, from small towns to cities, and from cities to industrial metropolitan centers. The economic, social, political, and cultural consequences of industrial growth, human migration, and increased urbanization as the nation moved into the twentieth century challenged the older ideals of individualism, laissez-faire in business-government relations, voluntarist cooperation among individual citizens, the democratic viability of the two-party system, the distinction between private- and public-sector activity, and the relationship between national leaders and the mass public. This historical transition from classic to modern liberalism is the focus of a growing body of scholarly research found in the work of historians of the organizational society, political scientists interested in the nature of state capacity to formulate public policy, and historical sociologists seeking to understand the relationship between state and society over a broad sweep of time.

Within the last forty years historians have tried to understand the emergence of modern America in terms of the growth of "the organizational society," built on the bedrock of group response to socioeconomic change. These scholars emphasize the importance of understanding the national response to urbanization and industrialization in the late nineteenth and early twentieth century. Most of these accounts center on the Progressive Era of 1901–18 as the key period in modern U.S. history. But gradually the insights of this school have been applied into the twentieth century to argue that the modern "search for order" continued through the era of Progressive reform, the wartime mobilization efforts of the

Great War, the redefinition of voluntarism in modern organizational terms in the 1920s, and the New Deal response to the Depression and World War II. Beyond 1945 the focus blurs.[10]

At the center of the debate about the emergence of modern America lies the question of the range and impact of corporate thought and action. Historian Alfred Chandler, Jr., has shown that national business corporations of the late nineteenth century pioneered in building the quintessential modern American institution—the hierarchical, bureaucratic, administrative structure built around functional operating divisions responsible for different areas in the production, distribution, and consumption processes.[11] Other historians have extended Chandler's insights into all aspects of American life—labor unions, farmer organizations, political parties, foreign policy, and mass culture. Those individuals and groups left out of the institutional network created by the rise of the organized society have until recently been ignored by many historians, but the rise of the new social history has corrected that oversight in part.[12] Behind this new set of institutions that crossed the lines of a more distinct separation of private- and public-sector lines in the political economy of nineteenth-century America lay a broad-ranging debate over how to preserve the classic liberal values of individualism, private property, upward social mobility, and the positive value of political diversity. Over the longer sweep of the first half of the twentieth century, Roosevelt's planners modified the corporate model based on an upper-class vision of what America could and should be to build an institutional network that they would draw on once they became New Deal planners.

As the United States industrialized under the leadership of business elites, using the institutional mechanism of the national and international business corporation, other groups loosely defined such as farmers, workers, immigrants, blacks, and women found themselves less influential in the emerging political economy of the modern era. Yet business leaders were not the only actors in this national debate over how best to shape the economy, polity, and society. While corporate managers may have organized first, others followed in their wake, including a variety of increasingly well-educated members of the academic professions who proved willing to establish connections in public-policy making by working through such key institutions as municipal and regional planning agencies, social science professional groups, voluntary reform associations, and coordinating bodies intended to bring together various organized groups to create a nexus of national policy-making institutions.[13]

Scholarly investigation into the origins of the organizational society has tended to focus on periodization, seeking to identify what have been variously called turning points, watersheds, pivotal eras, transitions, and key decades. One can read a vast literature that encompasses the period 1890–1945 trying to sort out competing intellectual claims without coming to any definitive conclusion as to just when the United States entered the modern age. To date, the mass of serious investigations has centered on five periods: the Progressive Era of 1901–18, World War I, the New Era capitalism of the 1920s, New Deal reform in the 1930s, and World War II. But none of the many studies of Progressive reform in response to the depression of the 1890s, Wilsonian mobilization to meet wartime exigencies of 1917–18, Hooverian associational efforts during the New Era of the 1921–32 years, New Deal responses to the Great Depression, or a second period of wartime mobilization in the 1940s has shown any one period or crisis as the single critical episode in the emergence of modern America. Taken collectively, this body of scholarship suggests that the process of institutional change proved at once more gradual and more complicated than traditional accounts suggest. Study of the rise and decline of New Deal planning can help in making sense of this broader historical transformation of American public-policy making during the first half of the twentieth century.

One group of scholars has suggested that Progressive reformers emerged from the part of the population that realized, in the wake of the depression of the 1890s, that the nation faced a growing number of problems and needed to do something to address these problems before the country split apart. Yet there is little consensus among historians of Progressivism as to just who the reformers were, what issues were their central concern, how they proposed to deal with those issues, and what they achieved and failed to achieve in their efforts to come to grips with the consequences of economic, social, political, and cultural change.[14] Among these Progressives were five individuals just starting their careers who later ended up on the New Deal planning board.

Another set of scholars has suggested that national crises such as wars and depressions have marked the major changes in modern American life. Some have argued that the brief wartime mobilization of 1917–18 built on the Progressive Era precedents of placing more emphasis on the voluntary associational responses to economic, social, and political change seeking to bring together both private- and public-sector actors and institutions to create a new kind of intergroup cooperation on the national level that various scholars have termed "corporate liberalism," "corporatism," "the associative state," "the war welfare state," or the "parastate."[15]

During the wartime mobilization, these new kinds of public-policy actors and organizations experimented with business–government cooperation through such agencies as the War Industries Board, the National War Labor Board, and the Food Administration. They also created the first truly national government propaganda agency in the Committee on Public Information and sought to use new scientific and social scientific tools in such venues as the U.S. Shipping Board, personnel testing for the U.S. Army, and founding of the National Research Council as an umbrella group to coordinate the emerging concerns of professional scientists creating their own associations.[16] The people who ended up on Franklin D. Roosevelt's planning board in the 1930s all served on various wartime boards in 1917–18 as part of this broader process of organizational change in modern American life.

The institutional innovations of the war years, however, failed to outlive the arrival of peace in 1919, leaving many of those who had been involved in the mobilization experience dissatisfied with the incomplete and haphazard nature of these emergency experiments. Many of the veterans of the Great Crusade on the home front carried their work over to different settings in the postwar period and into the New Era political economy best represented by Secretary of Commerce Herbert C. Hoover, who brought assistants from the Commission for the Relief of Belgium, the Food Administration, and the American Relief Administration into both the Department of Commerce and a range of working groups stemming from the Unemployment Conference of 1921. Among these Hooverian policy actors were a diversity of business leaders, heads of trade associations, members of the Taylor Society (which promoted scientific management), philanthropic managers, and social scientists in search of economic stability, gain, efficiency, an ordered approach to research, and professional legitimacy.[17] Among these New Era actors were the five people Franklin D. Roosevelt selected to sit on the New Deal's National Planning Board in July 1933.

Many scholars have argued that the New Deal response to the Great Depression stemmed directly from the atmosphere of national emergency and crisis reminiscent of the 1917–18 years, but this literature does not adequately account for how this earlier mobilization experience was translated into the very different economic and political conditions of the 1930s.[18] With the onset of depression in 1929, the Hoover administration drew upon the recommendations of both the Unemployment Conference of 1921 and the committee and conference system created in response to the forgotten depression of 1920–21 to design public policies to deal with the more serious and systemic problems of the later depression of the 1930s. Yet a burgeoning body of scholarship suggests that the movement from the New Era to the New Deal may not have been quite so dramatic as previous histories of New Deal reform argued.[19] FDR's planners provided a direct connection between Hooverian voluntarist planning efforts of the 1920s and the New Deal statist planning of the 1930s.

What changed in the 1930s was the context of planning. In the wake of worldwide economic collapse, Republican congressional losses in 1930 and 1932, Democratic congressional victories in 1930, 1932, 1934, and 1936, which culminated in the rise of strong executive leadership under Democratic president Franklin D. Roosevelt, a new majority political coalition was born. Under FDR and his New Deal reformers, the nation recognized that Hoover's voluntarist approach would not resolve the pressing issues of the Depression. The New Deal represented the rise of governmental efforts at economic recovery, unemployment relief, and a raft of reform legislation, including the first public planning board in American history.[20] Yet statist policies did not replace voluntarist ones wholesale, as seen in the case of New Deal planning. Between 1933 and 1939 FDR's planners gradually expanded the scope and nature of national planning, eventually instituting what might be called a Third New Deal between 1937 and 1943 centered on fiscal economic policy and executive-branch reorganization that moved beyond the Second New Deal of 1935–37, which emphasized social welfare and labor reforms.

In the wake of U.S. entry into World War II, the nation faced the challenge of creating what Roosevelt termed "the Arsenal of Democracy." Scholars still debate whether that wartime mobilization marked a dramatic turning point in modern U.S. history.[21] Not surprisingly, the war years engendered tremendous political debate over the role of the federal government and private businesses in promoting economic growth, what should be done to achieve a smooth transition from war to postwar peace, and whether the war agencies should be demobilized and the country returned to its traditional limited state policies. The planning agency's very existence came under question; angry conservatives in Congress cut its funds and destroyed the most significant experiment in national planning that the United States had ever seen. But New Deal planning left a broad legacy for the postwar years that set much of the liberal agenda for the next thirty years.

Recent scholarship has tried to grapple with the complexities of this new political economy over the broad sweep of time between the depression of the 1890s and the wartime mobilization of the 1940s. While arguments are made that a particular era is the key transitional period, no scholar or interpretive school of researchers has been able to make a persuasive case for a critical period. Marxist scholars have moved beyond the older notion of the secondary importance of ideology and the state to formulate sophisticated theories of the role of the state in promoting economic growth and social stability, without remaining beholden to the concept of an hegemonic ruling class of capitalists.[22] Public-policy advocates acted from within the state to create viable national policies, but they had to work within the constraints of a tradition of limited state action, the predominance of private voluntary institutions in the economic realm, changes in the nature of the two-party political system, and periodic confrontations between executive, legislative, and judicial branches of the federal government, as well as the complicated network of the federal system that blurred lines of authority among federal, state, and local governments. Another group of scholars in political science, historical sociology, and political history has reinvigorated the study of state-society relations in modern America by insisting on "bringing the state back in" to political and historical analysis.[23] Study of the making of New Deal planning can contribute to this broader discussion over the nature, scope, and impact of changes in private (voluntary), public (statist), and private-public (cross-sectoral) responses to economic change, the usefulness of social scientists as policy experts, and interrelationships between political conditions and planning efforts over the entire period from Progressivism, through mobilization for the Great War, the associational efforts of the New Era, the New Deal reaction to the crisis of the Great Depression, to the wartime mobilization for World War II. The lifetime experience of FDR's planners influenced what they did on the New Deal planning agency, while the socioeconomic context in which they planned revealed the limits of modern American liberalism and the strength of a political economy that by the postwar years was no longer either purely voluntarist or purely statist.

Between the 1890s and the mid-1940s the policy implications of social science research were worked out by a diversity of professionals, business managers, academics, philanthropists, and staff members of new research centers in public and private universities, private research centers, and business and governmental agencies. FDR's planners proved key players in this ongoing debate, which brought thousands of individuals together into an emerging organizational nexus, part of which involved the possibility of creating an American variant of national planning that was neither fully voluntarist in the nineteenth-century sense of the term nor wholly statist in the Depression-era sense of collectivist planning. The lost history of New Deal planning can be recovered by placing FDR's planners in the midst of the ongoing debate over the redefinition of twentieth-century American liberalism rather than caricaturing them as utopian dreamers best left relegated to the sidelines of the debate. Roosevelt's planners were neither collectivists intent upon destroying industrial capitalism nor puppets of a ruling capitalist class. They are best understood through their backgrounds, educations, values, institutional connections, and policy positions as viewed through a historical lens and not through preconceived notions of planning that may explain planning in other countries but are not very helpful in understanding the national planning of the New Deal.

Scholars have been loathe to probe the history of modern American national planning. Existing studies focus on specific examples of piecemeal planning during such national emergencies as the Great War or the Great Depression, suggesting a discontinuity in public-policy making over time. The standard interpretation of New Deal planning has been that Americans—only once in the 1930s, and then only as a reaction to the crisis of the Great Depression—seriously considered *national* planning as a viable alternative to the extant system of corporate managerial capitalism. Some scholars note that the origins of the American planning ideal came from late nineteenth-century intellectuals. Reform Darwinist Lester Frank Ward argued that governmental intervention was the natural result of societal evolution. Using the rational construct of the human mind as evolved over generations, reformers could employ the national state as a positive tool to build a dynamic and just society. Similarly, economist Simon N. Patten argued that the notion of economic regulation of the private sector by the public was not only possible but increasingly more likely. In *The Promise of American Life* (1909), liberal journalist Herbert Croly employed Hegelian logic and Hamiltonian precedent to argue that a new nationalism directed by a powerful reform executive might resolve the tensions of an America torn by the conflicts of the urban-industrial age. The unorthodox economist Thorstein Veblen went one step further to argue that a soviet of technicians might create the new society through consciously planned social and economic choices. Despite the visions of Ward, Patten, Croly, and Veblen, the technocracy of the intellectuals never appeared.[24]

In its stead, America saw the establishment of the corporate society based on the idea that organized groups might build a new order through voluntary intergroup cooperation. As historians usually write the story, the corporate revolution in business triumphed over sporadic attempts at reform sponsored by city, state, and national governments and a host of liberal and radical social movements. But these alternatives such as populism, a farmer-labor alliance, urban liberalism, socialism, and communism were unattractive to the mass citizenry, who did not seriously consider challenging the new order until the collapse of the national economy as symbolized by the stock market crash of October 1929. The ensuing Great Depression brought declining production and prices, rising unemployment, deepening distress, and widespread loss of confidence in the nation's economic system and its political leaders. In 1932, the story continues, Democratic governor Franklin D. Roosevelt of New York entered the presidential race against his opponent, Herbert Hoover, the Great Engineer. Democracy's aristocrat, Roosevelt, replaced the man responsible for the creation of tar-paper ghettos called Hoovervilles. Most historians today would grant that Roosevelt's New Deal initiated the first experiment with national planning. But the caveat is always entered that the New Deal as a whole was not really planned; rather, it stumbled from program to program, searching for solutions to problems that traditional theories could neither explain nor resolve. Standard histories of the New Deal mention the existence of the National Planning Board, created in July 1933, but these works say little more than that the board was an adjunct to the Public Works Administration created under Title II of the National Industrial Recovery Act of 1933.[25]

We know that in the period 1931–33 numerous social commentators publicly discussed precedents for national planning in the far-off Soviet Union. Public debate centered on how to apply the lessons from the Soviet experiment to the American scene. Popular economist Stuart Chase argued that America must receive a "New Deal" that would tread the narrow road between an outmoded system of free enterprise and the regimentation of the Soviet Gosplan. Political scientist Charles A. Beard gathered together various suggestions on planning into a volume entitled *America Faces the Future*. During the 1932 election campaign, Democratic presidential candidate Franklin D. Roosevelt favorably noted the growth of city and regional planning in the United States. Some scholars suggest that FDR's transition team may have engaged in a kind of planning process that brought intellectuals into public service in a way unlike any since the Progressive Era. While specialists still wrangle over the role and significance of Roosevelt's Brain Trust, most historians would agree that Adolf A. Berle, Raymond Moley, and Rexford Tugwell had ideas about economic policy that included some place for considering national planning. The focus usually centers on controversial adviser Rexford G. Tugwell.[26]

Tugwell became the best known of America's early New Deal planners. He also became the most reviled. Yet as historian Bernard Sternsher has shown, Tugwell was well within the mainstream American economic tradition. Using his background in institutional economics as a base, Tugwell argued that voluntary cooperation with some prodding by the federal government might bring about economic balance in the basic industries through the National Recovery Administration (NRA). To complement this work, Tugwell argued that American agriculture must also seek balance through the domestic allotment system created under the Agricultural Adjustment Administration. Tugwell's planning ideas began with the notion that the search for economic stabilization must include balance at center stage.[27]

Historian Ellis W. Hawley draws out the implications of this idea of balance for the group he designates as planners after the NRA had been declared unconstitutional by the Supreme Court in its famous 1935 "sick chicken" case: "On the whole, the planners regarded most of the New Deal measures as grossly inadequate; yet the majority of them were not socialists in the generally accepted sense of the term. Their economic and political ideology sprang from such men as Thorstein Veblen, Simon Patten, and Herbert Croly, not from Karl Marx. Their heroes were the engineer, the technician, and the ultimate consumer, not the factory worker. Their central concepts stressed economic balance and unified cooperation, not class struggle and the rule of the proletariat."[28] Hawley's point should be well taken, yet scholars for the most part have not pursued it. Hawley's analysis of the antitrust tradition, the business commonwealth tradition of industrial self-government, and New Deal economic policy suggests the need to ask some fundamental questions about the history of New Deal planning. Who were FDR's planners? What do we know about their intellectual development and institutional connections? What paths did they take to the New Deal planning board? What part did they see for national planning in the development of modern American liberalism? What did they propose and accomplish between 1933 and 1943? Why did Congress abolish the planning board in 1943? What kind of legacy did FDR's planners leave for postwar America?

Existing accounts provide us with only the beginnings of answers to important questions about the history of New Deal planning. Few secondary works go beyond mentioning the names of the planners and say next to nothing about their socioeconomic background, family life, education, intellectual development, or early careers. Published works assume an internalist perspective, thus implying that the planners were an isolated set, a few individuals so busy thinking up utopian visions that they were divorced from the broader changes transforming modern America. Since these studies adopt an institutional approach, another presupposition is that planning neither existed nor mattered until creation of the National Planning Board in 1933 in direct response to the crisis of the Depression. None devotes much attention to the historical roots of planning in the years before the New Deal. No scholar has examined the planners from a biographical, historical, or comparative perspective in order to understand the origins of New Deal planning. Most of the secondary literature assumes that American national planning in the 1930s began with the European model of state, command-style economic planning. This static application of a changeless model applied across national and historical cases does not historically account for why planning emerged in modern America, what form it took in the 1930s, and what the planners proposed and accomplished. The extant scholarly works by historians, political scientists, sociologists, and policy analysts cross-cite secondary accounts, while none have studied the historical records left by FDR's planners.

The time has come to examine carefully the origins of New Deal planning through the lives of those who served on the planning board from 1933 to 1943. Five people who were among the most prominent, reputable, and respectable in their chosen fields sat on FDR's planning board. The sole remnant of historical knowledge today about Frederic Adrian Delano is that he was President Roosevelt's uncle and received the nickname Uncle Fred from friends and critics alike. Courtesy of Barry Karl's biography, we know much more about Charles E. Merriam, who served as chairman of the Political Science Department at the University of Chicago.[29] Karl's definitive study of Merriam remains the only full biography of an American planner to date. Columbia University economist Wesley Clair Mitchell, as head of the National Bureau of Economic Research, pioneered in studying the statistical complexities and wavelike undulations of the business cycle. NBER publications and esoteric studies note the significance of Mitchell's work, but the closest work to a biography is a 1953 memoir by his wife, Lucy Sprague Mitchell, and a few short articles by professional economists who were Mitchell's colleagues and friends.[30] Massachusetts business leader Henry Sturgis Dennison is the subject of one thoroughly researched article, while philanthropic manager Beardsley Ruml appears as a minor player in two articles but has received no extensive attention by scholars.[31] Beyond knowledge from these limited published works, the lives, thought, and institutional work of FDR's planners are little known.

Planner Charles E. Merriam left some publications about the planning board that indicate its roots in city, state, and regional planning. His scholarly interests led him to trace the names, forms, and institutional evolution of the board in two articles published during and immediately after the board's existence. Economist Allen Gruchy agrees with historian Ellis Hawley that Veblenian ideas permeated the work of planners on the board's Industrial Committee such as Wesley Clair Mitchell, John Maurice Clark, Gardiner C. Means, and Mordecai Ezekiel. Those few studies of the planning board—most of which remain unpublished works by graduate students—stress the institutional history of American national planning. While several general histories of American planning had earlier sketched the outlines of planning history, these works went into considerable, but narrowly focused, narrative detail.[32]

Institutional histories of the planning board all rely on the same implicit assumptions and research methodology.[33] Each presumes the institutional impact of the planning board during the New Deal period through review of its organizational records. So thoroughly do these works accept the working assumptions of the organizational society that the narrative centers on detailed depiction of "facts," committee reports, and internal administrative records. In abolishing the board in the spring of 1943, conservatives in Congress hoped to bury the past of national planning in the dusty rooms of the National Archives in Washington, D.C. Since then a small group of enterprising students has dredged diligently through the institutional remains to flesh out the narrative story of national planning without providing broader interpretive analysis. Writing in 1960, public servant Norman Beckman accurately summarized the state of national planning history in saying, "It is evident that history has passed by NRPB's government-wide approach to federal planning organization."[34]

Yet hidden in relatively unknown and little-consulted journals lie a small number of very insightful articles about the history of American national planning. In 1939 Clifford J. Hynning traced the origins of national planning to the Progressive Era, including the work of the Hooverian committees during the 1920s. Historian Byrd Jones wrote an insightful case study of the evolution of the National Planning Board's "Plan for Planning" included in its *Final Report* of June 1934. That document held the key to planning history with its idea of advisory national planning by a small, part-time group of social science research experts giving advice to the president, with final policy decisions always made by elected representatives in the president's office and the Congress. Historian Philip Funigiello used the planners' efforts at urban reform planning during World War II as a case study of national planning and its impact on the local level. The dean of planning historians, political scientist Albert Lepawsky—a onetime Merriam student and member of the planning board's western regional office—remains the only scholar who asked the most significant questions: who were the planners, and what did they do? In a series of short, insightful articles, Lepawsky tried to revive the forgotten story of New Deal planning. As a policy analyst, however, he was more concerned with learning the "lessons" of earlier planning experience than with gaining historical understanding.[35]

Merriam biographer Barry D. Karl provides the most challenging discussions of planning in a broad national context. Karl first became interested in Merriam through his study of executive reorganization plans by the President's Committee on Administrative Management (1936–37), of which Merriam had been a member. Karl then studied the evolution of the study *Recent Social Trends* (1933), directed by Wesley Clair Mitchell and Charles E. Merriam. Karl argued that the President's Research Committee on Social Trends sponsored by President Herbert Hoover proved a turning point in the politicization of social science research work for the federal government. In more recent articles, Karl suggested the connections between managerial elites and democratic society in the modern age, seeing the work of Merriam and the New Deal planners as part of the broader debate over the ongoing tensions between national public-policy making and the American democratic ideal.[36]

In light of the last generation of work by historians, political scientists, and historical sociologists, we can begin to suggest how the history of New Deal planning between the 1890s and the 1940s was part of the broader story of the emergence of modern America. Roosevelt's planners came of age amid an expanding organizational nexus marked by Progressive reform, the wartime mobilization of 1917–18, New Era efforts to stabilize the business cycle, and the crisis atmosphere engendered by the Great Depression. Between the late nineteenth century and the Progressive Era, each of the planners created his own niche in the new organizational society by dint of fortunate birth, comfortable upbringing, privileged education, and early career development. Mobilization for total war in 1917–18 brought them to the realization of limitations in their own and their nation's capacity to respond rationally to rapid economic and social changes. Participation on wartime boards sparked a search for a new way of ordering their experience in hopes of serving themselves and their professions, class, and country. The decade of the 1920s brought these hopes to fruition in the institutional practices of associational activity involving cooperation between functionally organized groups at the center of American life—business management, city and regional planning bodies, professional associations, social research institutes, business corporations, trade associations, philanthropies, and the federal government. In bringing together such groups, these planners and their thousands of colleagues sought to transform and to reinvigorate the liberal tradition in order to stabilize national life around the center of intergroup cooperation rather than the older nineteenth-century individualist ideal.[37]

To build the associational network desired, advocates of the new liberal order had to meet certain conditions—what might be termed prerequisites for national planning. Relying on the experience, influence, and growing power of trained professionals called for an emphasis on detailed research, presupposing a rational, tested method of formulating public policy. This research could prove productive only if it brought together a number of people acting as a cooperating team willing to integrate diverse information. Integration in turn required coordination of the work of specialists through the use of administrative, hierarchical bureaucracies of varying purpose, funding, and complexity. At the top of the coordinating agency or agencies, innovative leaders had to assume direction of the efforts on a national level. Such leadership necessitated sponsorship by influential people in the federal government along with financial support from interested philanthropies. In the process, new kinds of institutions were created that crossed boundaries between private and public sectors, Republican and Democratic Party loyalties, professional and political interests, and intellectual and democratic ends. FDR's planners were among these people creating innovative private/public institutional linkages that were sometimes capable of lasting over relatively long periods of time while adjusting to changing economic, political, and social circumstances. These new kinds of organizations, which could be termed *cross-sectoral institutions,* centered on like-minded people who came together initially because of common membership in a particular firm, industry, city, region, academic discipline, profession, research institute, foundation, or government agency. Recognizing the need for rational collection, analysis, distribution, and use of knowledge, they moved into the arena of national policy-making bodies often during an immediate crisis. When the specific catalyst passed, they joined into increasingly more formal institutions that refused to heed older distinctions between strictly separated "private" and "public" bodies. Over time, these new policy makers created institutions with members, funding, structure, and missions that blurred, crossed, recrossed, and mixed what had been considered distinct spheres of private, voluntary, entrepreneurial activities and public, statist, managerial activities. Often working within a setting unseen or unknown by the broader public, these policy actors were establishing links that led to a new kind of institution that remained outside the consciousness of most Americans. While hardly the sole group of these kinds of policy makers, who sometimes acted in a private setting with government sponsorship and philanthropic funding, the five people who became first Hoover's, then FDR's, planners were part of a larger process of historical evolution that does not seem recognized by much of the scholarly literature except in individual case studies, usually in the form of unpublished works or short articles.[38]

Building the associational network proved a time-consuming, frustrating, and imperfect task. America's state-building capacity proved weak and halting in the face of the resistance from those enamored of antistatist values carried over from the nineteenth century. Yet under the leadership of Secretary of Commerce Herbert Hoover, various proponents of associational cooperation worked deliberately throughout the 1920s to accomplish their work. Employing the cumulative experience and knowledge gained from individual research projects, trade association work, professional organization, and philanthropic management, these people learned to work together. The professional associations served as coordinating agencies under the direction of federal officials working in Hoover's Department of Commerce. Managers in such organizations as the Rockefeller philanthropies, the Carnegie Corporation, the Twentieth Century Fund, and the Commonwealth Fund proved willing to support a wide range of research projects that would take America into the New Era.

Between 1917 and 1933 thousands of people participated in this associational network building. The five who became FDR's planners in 1933 served as activist leaders helping to build these new institutional networks. Associational work in the 1920s resulted in each of these planners moving beyond the realm of immediate self-interest and professional gain into the national arena of a newly emerging form of public-policy making. Between the 1890s and 1933 each planner followed a complicated path to New Deal planning that involved taking up active roles in shaping the lessons of Progressive reform, wartime mobilization, and the associational-state actions of New Era America. The roots of New Deal planning lay in the people, ideas, and institutional links of the five men who became FDR's planners.

The confluence of people, ideas, and events brought these five together gradually in the associational efforts of the New Era, which in turn paved the way for entry into New Deal planning. Just as important as the individuals, however, were the institutional networks within which they worked. During and immediately after the mobilization experience of the Great War, a number of social research institutions were founded to study national issues, including the National Research Council, the National Bureau of Economic Research, the Twentieth Century Fund, and Robert Brookings's Institute for Government Research and the Institute of Economics, and the umbrella Social Science Research Council, led and inspired by Merriam and Ruml. These arose out of the need for accurate information as a possible basis for the formulation of public policies.[39]

Herbert Hoover, the new secretary of commerce, called on these private institutes, as well as academic centers such as the University of Chicago, for help in dealing with the postwar depression of 1920–21. In 1921 Hoover organized the President's Conference on Unemployment with the help of an Economic Advisory Committee consisting of trade association officials, social scientists, academic economists, and his own Economic Committee in the Department of Commerce. Among the advisers were Edwin F. Gay, Wesley Clair Mitchell, and Henry S. Dennison, who were fresh from wartime mobilization work in statistical data collection and analysis. Using economic data and analysis provided by Mitchell and the NBER staff, conference delegates made recommendations favoring economic stabilization and regularization, drawing upon statistics gathered by private institutes, trade associations, and the federal government. Further recommendations presaged the Hooverian program for using the conference and committee system as a kind of associational national planning network for the rest of the decade, drawing on the social scientific expertise of the NBER and the SSRC. Not only did the Department of Commerce gather economic statistics for distribution to trade associations, but Hoover also now considered innovative measures in case of future cyclic downturns. Conference participants called for detailed study of economic trends, including studies of business cycles and unemployment, and established ongoing subcommittees to this end. The delegates advocated the creation of a permanent federal agency to prepare long-range plans for public works during prosperous years that might serve as an economic balancing wheel in times of recession.[40]

The Unemployment Conference of 1921 established a number of important precedents in public-policy making. The call for further economic and social research led directly to the federally sponsored, privately funded studies on business cycles, seasonal unemployment, and the nation's first national economic and social inventories, summarized in the landmark volumes *Recent Economic Changes* (1929) and *Recent Social Trends* (1933). It also led to greater emphasis on voluntary relief efforts, first employed in 1921 and later adopted by President Hoover's Emergency Committee for Employment (1930–31) and Organization for Unemployment Relief (1931–32), and to consideration of public works planning, which culminated in the establishment of the Federal Employment Stabilization Board in 1931. Each of these efforts involved one or more of the five planners, provided testing grounds for their policy ideas, and brought their organizations into an evolving interwar planning nexus that could be transformed into a national planning body in the event of a major crisis and changed economic circumstances. Seen as individual projects, these research efforts might appear as only sporadic efforts by interested individuals. Viewed as a conscious response to the depression of 1920–21 that later expanded into a more full-blown institutional effort after 1929, they laid the foundation for American national planning under the New Deal.

Hoover asked each of the planners at some point to perform governmental service. Initially each declined, but eventually they participated, if only for a limited time, in the various policy research projects growing out of the 1921 conference subcommittees, thereby expanding their own personal, professional, and institutional networks. Cooperation among government officials, business executives, philanthropic managers, trade association representatives, labor leaders, economic researchers, and policy-oriented social scientists revealed the organizational presuppositions behind Hooverian voluntary associational national planning. Hoover asked his assistant Edward Eyre Hunt to contact an appropriate public or private leader, establish a committee representing the various organized groups, and then seek funds from a private philanthropy while insisting on public recognition of federal sponsorship of the project. The emerging pattern set the stage for some later New Deal programs; at key points, however, Hoover often drew back from emphasizing the positive role of government-led action. Voluntarist principles and a long-running anti-statist political tradition acted as constraints on the Hooverian associative state, which left only ad hoc planning networks of a temporary nature in place to pioneer new forms of public-policy making. The culmination and turning point came with Hoover's appointment of the President's Research Committee on Social Trends in the crisis period of 1929–33. Significantly, over time the Hooverian program broadened its reach, moving from a kind of crude economic determinism into the wider realms of social research that documented what social scientists such as William F. Ogburn and Charles E. Merriam saw as an increasing gap between technological skill and social cooperation, which they identified as the problem of "cultural lag."

In the course of the 1920s these associational linkages became increasingly more formal. At the same time that Merriam, Mitchell, and Ruml formed the SSRC as a national umbrella group for the social sciences to match the work of the National Research Council (NRC) in the physical sciences and the American Council of Learned Societies in the humanities, Hoover assistant Hunt talked with John C. Merriam, Charles Merriam's brother and head of the Carnegie Institution, about the new SSRC conducting a study in regard to labor disputes for one of the Unemployment Conference's follow-up studies. Charles Merriam declined in the interest of getting the SSRC on its feet, but only a short time later he agreed to work jointly with the NRC Committee on the Scientific Problems of Human Migration. Merriam and Mitchell agreed that the NBER would conduct the study under the auspices of the SSRC with monies from the Laura Spelman Rockefeller Memorial (LSRM), then headed by Beardsley Ruml. The project proved fortuitous in several ways. It put Merriam in touch with Ruml and Mitchell, paved the way for LSRM support of the infant SSRC, and enhanced the reputation of Mitchell's NBER.[41]

The growing links between people, ideas, and institutions regarding the usefulness of social scientific research as a tool for addressing national issues led finally into the planning programs of the early New Deal. The making of New Deal planning took place within the broader context of changes that affected individuals, groups, professions, and organizations in different ways. Yet the fact that these five people ended up as FDR's planners cannot be explained as either total coincidence or planned conspiracy. Rather, New Deal planning calls for historical explanation in the context of how these five New Deal planners emerged from a complex organizational nexus at the center of modern American life.

Chapters 2–6 explain the paths that each of the planners took in arriving at membership on the New Deal planning agency. Business manager Frederic A. Delano, imbued with an ethic of social responsibility because of his social background, developed a national reputation in city and regional planning that led him from Chicago and New York to Washington, D.C. He became the father of New Deal planning. Political scientist, urban reformer, and social science manager Charles E. Merriam became the theorist of New Deal planning. Institutional economist Wesley Clair Mitchell, the nation's leading business-cycle expert, pioneer in developing new economic statistical studies, and founder of the NBER, became Secretary of Commerce Herbert Hoover's social science researcher par excellence and served on the New Deal planning agency for two years until professional interests and political uncertainty about its direction led him to resign late in 1935. He was replaced by two representatives from the business community, Henry S. Dennison and Beardsley Ruml. Business manager Dennison reorganized his corporation, instituted new managerial and welfare capitalist reforms, and expanded his intellectual horizons both geographically and socially to move into social welfare reform, business research, and participation in business-government cooperation in both the New Era and the early New Deal. As director of the Laura Spelman Rockefeller Memorial, philanthropic manager Beardsley Ruml supported his friends Merriam and Mitchell in their social science research efforts throughout the 1920s, helped to create a national research network funded by a private-sector foundation, and moved into the arena of public-policy making by financing the Hooverian studies of the New Era and then joining the early New Deal as an informal policy adviser.

Chapter 7 explains how, during the interwar period, the planners' interests and institutional connections converged gradually in the process of building, expanding, and using these new cross-sectoral institutions to participate in associational planning under Hoover that became transformed into the New Deal planning board as the nation's economic, social, and political conditions changed because of the crisis of the Great Depression. Unlike Hoover, they proved willing and able to move from the New Era to the New Deal when they joined together as FDR's planners with the support, financing, and institutional mechanisms of the state. Between 1933 and 1943 they acted in concert to build an advisory national planning process under the executive authority of President Franklin D. Roosevelt. Between 1933 and 1937 they expanded the planning process of both the federal and state governments from narrowly focused physical and natural resources to include broad-based economic and social planning that exacerbated tensions within Roosevelt's cabinet and between the president and the Congress.

Chapter 8 details how, between 1937 and 1943, FDR's planners participated in a series of policy debates that some scholars have begun to refer to as the Third New Deal, centered on how to respond to the recession of 1937–38, how to rationalize newly created New Deal agencies through executive-branch reorganization, how to plan for wartime needs, and how to prepare for peacetime through postwar planning. This process culminated in a series of postwar reports that placed the planners in the middle of executive-congressional tensions, which undermined further New Deal reforms in the midst of World War II.

The epilogue analyzes the 1943 debate over the future of the New Deal planning board, examines the detailed politics of the wartime period that led to the board's abolition, and discusses the various postwar legacies such as the federal income withholding tax, the GI Bill of Rights, the Employment Act of 1946, and the host of postwar planning groups, some of them cross-sectoral institutions, which emerged to revive the more voluntarist efforts in the immediate postwar years.

Unlike planners in other nations more accustomed to a fully statist mode of planning, the American planners hoped to preserve the system of mature industrial capitalism through a combination of monetary, fiscal, and welfare policies that would increase American productivity and wealth without redistributing power. In that sense, their vision remained ultimately conservative in promoting social and economic stability in the name of American democracy, which they distinguished from the authoritarian dictatorships that America and its allies fought against in World War II and would come to fear in the form of communist aggression in the postwar period. The planners' democratic rhetoric encompassed the noblest ideals of a changing tradition of modern American liberalism confronted not only by the short-term challenges of global depression and a second world war but also by the longer-term consequences of economic and social changes brought about by industrialization and urbanization, the rise of private managerial power and the broader influence of the corporate institutional model, and the emergence of interest-group politics in the course of two world wars, a depression, the threats of fascism and communism, the example of strong executive power set by FDR, and shifts in the balance of executive and congressional power during the New Deal and mobilization for World War II. Unconcerned with the secondary layers of American group life, FDR's planners, like other modern liberals, overlooked—to their discredit—the unequal distribution of wealth, income, and power that remained a fact of American life throughout the period and that undermined the older national tradition of Jeffersonian individualism.

To make sense of the history of New Deal planning, one must begin with a historical examination of those who planned. Such a study must identify who the planners were, what ideas they developed about liberalism, planning, and the utility of social science research, and account for the institutional resources and experience they brought to New Deal planning. To explain the shift from Hooverian New Era planning to Rooseveltian New Deal planning requires understanding how economic, social, and political conditions changed between 1929 and 1933 as the Depression worsened. To make sense of the evolution of New Deal planning in the decade between 1933 and 1943, one must look at the planners' ideas, the institutional support they received from FDR, and the growing conflict between President Roosevelt and conservatives in the Congress. While the eventual end of the planning experiment in 1943 can be partially explained by analysis of this conflict, the angry, passionate, and ideological resistance in Congress that greeted the postwar planning reports of that year suggest a deeper, less rational explanation based on a long-running Jeffersonian fear of centralized state power mixed with distrust of any Hamiltonian means such as the planners' reliance on executive branch leadership, monies, and political support.[42] Scholars—ever faithful to a rational worldview—remain understandably loathe to examine human weakness, political blundering, and seemingly irrational political debate over major social and economic issues within outmoded ideological frames of reference as occurred throughout the 1933–45 period. Hence, this study of New Deal planning begins with an insistence that we must make the effort to see this history within a longer time frame than usual. We must see New Deal planning as having emerged as part of a broader historical process—that is, we must understand the *making* of New Deal planning. To do so means we must see the planners as individuals with identifiable lives, as historical actors working within specific institutional contexts, as policy actors advocating a new, modern liberal ideology, as political participants—citizens—both shaping and reacting to changing conditions, and, finally, as Americans, who like millions of others, were caught up within the more sweeping transformation of American life in the first half of the twentieth century. New Deal planners were not isolated utopian visionaries reacting to the crisis of the Great Depression; they were part and parcel of the making of modern America.

Frederic A. Delano, Father of New Deal Planning

UPPER-CLASS DUTY, MANAGERIALISM, AND CITY AND REGIONAL PLANNING

THE CORPORATE REVOLUTION in business in the late nineteenth century, the city planning movement of the Progressive Era, the wartime mobilization of 1917–18, and the associational activities of the city and regional planning movements of the 1920s were the breeding grounds for national planning.[1] As chairman of Franklin D. Roosevelt's planning agency between 1933 and 1943, Frederic A. Delano acted as father to New Deal planning. Delano embarked on a distinguished career from the advantage of an upper-class family background that paved the way for his rapid rise up the managerial ladder of the railroad industry. During the Progressive Era, Delano brought his practical business experience to bear on the famous city plan of Chicago. Moving easily between business and civic roles, Delano early transcended traditional distinctions between private and public sectors when he was appointed to the staff of the director of transportation with the American Expeditionary Force in France in 1918. Throughout the 1920s he engaged in a variety of associational activities in city and regional planning that included temporary government service. By the late 1920s Delano garnered a reputation as a respectable, civic-minded businessman and philanthropist willing to work with voluntary groups within and outside of government. After his nephew Franklin D. Roosevelt won election to the presidency, Delano accepted the post as head of the National Planning Board. Delano directed the research, coordination, and advisory work of the only comprehensive governmental planning agency in American history.[2]

M. L. Wilson, a Washington associate, later observed that Delano was "the kind of personality that would be produced by a high-grade cultured family of the last century." Delano proudly traced his family heritage to the early colonists at Plymouth and Boston in the 1620s and 1630s. In the early nineteenth century the Delano family and other Boston merchants built the clipper-ship trade with China. Between 1833 and 1846 Warren Delano II, Frederic's father, made the family fortune through his partnership in Russell & Company, the leading commission house in Canton, dealing in tea and the growing Chinese market for Indian and Turkish opium. In 1843 Warren returned home and met and married Catherine Robbins Lyman, the youngest daughter of a prominent Northampton judge. In 1846, after three years in Canton, China, the Delanos returned to set up magnificent homes in the scenic Hudson River Valley north of New York City.[3]

In 1851 Warren bought a sixty-acre estate just north of Newburgh, New York, rebuilt it, and named it Algonac, an Algonquian name meaning "hill and river." He invested profits from the China trade in dock property in New York City, coal mines in Pennsylvania, copper lands in Tennessee, and iron ore mines in Maryland. Caught without liquid assets in the panic of 1857, Warren went back to China to recoup his fortune in the renewed tea and opium trade out of Hong Kong, now carried on by modern steamships operated by the old Russell & Company firm. On September 10, 1863, Frederic A. Delano was born into this prosperous, upper-class family at its Rose Hill home in Hong Kong. After a tour of Europe, the Delanos returned to the United States to raise their large family. Frederic, the fourth son and eleventh child, grew up in secure Delano family households at Fairhaven, a thirty-three-acre summer estate in New Bedford, Massachusetts, and at Algonac, the new sixty-acre winter residence.[4]

Nurtured in the wealthy, cultured, aristocratic Delano family, Frederic grew up knowing he had a place in the world that few Americans could match. Through his career as a China trader and investor in industrial properties, Warren Delano provided his family with security, social prestige, and the self-assurance such privilege made possible. From his father, Frederic learned to value both individual character and a broader sense of social responsibility: "[Father] appreciated his duty to his Maker, to society and to his family, and felt keenly that he must do nothing to sully that good name. His attitude to the traditions of ancestry was normal and natural. If he felt proud of the name he bore, there was no spirit of brag or ostentation in his attitude. While he never discussed the subject with me, I gathered from what he let fall at different times, that the motto of the ancienne noblesse of France ('Noblesse Oblige') truly expressed his point of view; not that he claimed to have been born to any special privileges, but rather that whatever unusual opportunities he had enjoyed, or talents he might have inherited, all laid upon him the duty of making that much more of his life."[5] This paternal notion of noblesse oblige was one part of the upper-class world of the Hudson River Valley elite in which the Delanos lived. Two of Frederic's sisters married China traders; Sara married James Roosevelt and bore their son Franklin. His brother Warren III took over family properties and ultimately became "the largest owner and operator of coal properties in the United States."[6] These social values informed Frederic's career in railroad management, city planning, regional planning, and government advisory work.

After attending prestigious Adams Academy in Quincy, Massachusetts, Frederic entered Harvard College in the fall of 1881. While at Harvard, he engaged in the proper elite social activities, with membership in the Delta Kappa Epsilon fraternity, the A. D. Club, and Hasty Pudding. He studied natural history, topography, geology, engineering, and government, leading to graduation cum laude in the spring of 1885. Over several summer vacations, Frederic worked in the family coal mines. His father reported that Fred was "as black and grimy as the district union there—and apparently enjoys the experiment."[7]

Following graduation, Delano joined a relative and business colleague of his father's on a topographical survey near Milton, Massachusetts, which led to a three-month trip as a member of a Chicago, Burlington, and Quincy (CB&Q) Railroad geological survey for a potential route between Denver and Salt Lake City. Turning down an offer from his uncle to finance a trip to Europe to study new engineering techniques, Delano joined the CB&Q as a machinist's apprentice in its shop at Aurora, Illinois. He explained his decision to accept this low-level engineering job to his uncle in terms of his wish to advance quickly into the managerial ranks: "On the [CB&Q] Railroad the same system of advancement as on the Pennsylvania is used and I know quite a number of Harvard fellows already connected with the road. By doing this—although I may later conclude not to stick to railroading—I will not lose time and the experience which I gain cannot but be of direct use in securing me another position."[8]

Delano entered the railroad industry at a propitious moment. Between 1865 and 1900 the railroads expanded rapidly to create both a national transportation system and a vast national marketplace in an industrializing

America. Railroads pioneered new kinds of business leadership, acting within the innovative structure of the national business corporation.[9] At the start of Delano's managerial career in railroads, the CB&Q had emerged as a major transportation link between Chicago and the growing West. When founder Charles Murray Forbes retired in 1881, the CB&Q stretched across four states, ran 2,924 miles of track, collected $21 million in revenues, and paid dividends of 8 percent.[10] In 1885 the CB&Q reached Denver and sought to move even farther west, as reflected by the Denver-Salt Lake City route survey Delano had joined.

Frederic moved a step beyond the earlier career pattern of his father, Warren II. Along with upper-class friends and business associates such as John Murray Forbes, Warren made the family fortune in the China trade, invested that money in railroads such as the CB&Q and other industrial properties, and now consolidated those gains in national corporations. President Charles E. Perkins of the CB&Q developed his own principles of business administration in order to create a corps of loyal corporate managers. By October 1885 Delano had moved into the managerial corps from his initial position as an apprentice machinist.[11]

Delano entered the managerial hierarchy because of class advantage, willing service as a strikebreaker, engineering skill, an opportune marriage, and administrative experience. As early as 1885–86 he served as a strikebreaker during the railroad industry's Great Upheaval.[12] His father denounced the Knights of Labor, but Frederic took a somewhat more genteel view: "We have had a good many strikes this Winter and Spring and some have come pretty near the house. Very recently the Socialists in Chicago and Milwaukee have done atrocities which fills every one with horror.—Notwithstanding all I think we have less of such troubles in store for us here than they have abroad.—Here where every possible liscence is given to the press and to socialist meetings the law abiding citizens are in such majority that the feeling of anarchy is better suppressed than when kept down by the hand of monarchical power.—At present there is a freighthandlers strike in Chicago and I am going in daily to do my share of the work until things are settled and new men employed."[13] The "labor question" remained a constant in Delano's thought for the rest of his life.

In April 1887 Frederic became acting engineer of tests in the CB&Q's Bureau of Rail and Rail Joints at Aurora. After studying the strength and durability of steel rails, Delano presented the results of his research to the American Society of Mechanical Engineers convention. CB&Q managers were so impressed that they promoted Delano in July 1887 to head of the Bureau of Rail and Rail Inspection Tests and Records at Chicago.[14] His work in Chicago garnered Delano appointment as private secretary to CB&Q president Charles E. Perkins and a select party of the company's executives and their relatives. In early 1888 Delano once again used strikebreaking service as a way to advance by driving locomotives through strikers' lines. That spring he became engaged to Matilda A. Peasley, daughter of CB&Q first vice president James C. Peasley, whom he had met while secretary to President Perkins. As a wedding present, Warren Delano II gave the couple $10,000 to buy a new home in Chicago.[15]

In April 1889 Frederic became assistant to CB&Q second vice president Henry B. Stone. A year later, he moved up to superintendent of Chicago terminals in charge of freight-handling operations at one end of the CB&Q's line. By 1890 Delano had turned class advantage, engineering skill, strikebreaking, marriage to the boss's daughter, and corporate expertise into a lucrative career as one of the managerial leaders of the CB&Q railroad. Yet the 1890s were a hard time for young Frederic Delano. Though he had begun a promising career, he remained somewhat discontented. With the CB&Q experiencing setbacks because of the depression of the 1890s, Frederic thought seriously about leaving the railroad industry. Taking a short trip to Europe with his wife, Tillie, Delano studied the European railroad system and evaluated his own life. By late 1894 he began investing $30,000 in various stocks to consolidate his wealth from family and job. In early 1896 his mother, Catherine Delano, died from cancer, followed two years later by his father's death from bronchial pneumonia. Frederic decided to invest some of his money in a new venture by his brother, Warren III, the Coke Oven By Products Company, as well as the family's New Boston Coal Company. In late 1896 Frederic was elected a director of the Union Mining Company, another of the family's varied speculative interests.[16]

Torn between his "ambitions to rise in the CB&Q line" and his desire to stay in close touch with his family, Delano became restless with corporate life. Speaking with CB&Q president Perkins, Frederic noted his desire to "be more foot loose and free to go away on personal business." Retaining his ideal of noblesse oblige, Delano wrote his brother, "Unless I change as I grow older, I shall want to live simply all my life and spend what surplus income I have in encouraging those pursuits and vocations which seem to me most permanent and best worth encouraging." Speaking like the manager he had become, Delano worried about promotion in the CB&Q which he saw as entertaining "a disposition to be very consid-

erate, at times almost too considerate, of once faithful but now super-
annuated officers—. . . . [though] I stand well with every officer of the
company."[17]

Delano's fortunes soon changed. With the death of his father in February 1898, he inherited between $30,000 and $40,000, which he then invested in a number of family interests. At the CB&Q he developed a
new design for a faster locomotive for the Chicago-to-Omaha mail run.
Competitors stole the design and forced Delano into a long legal battle
that finally netted him patent rights and a $5,000 settlement. By February
1899 he rose to the position of superintendent of motive power, machinery, and cars at the Chicago office—a promotion that "was more expected a year ago than now, but none the less grateful." In July 1901
Delano received his final promotion in the CB&Q to general manager
at Chicago. He probably exchanged his patent rights for the improved
locomotive for the usual one dollar and the new managerial role. By 1902
Frederic was well established in the corporate hierarchy, making $18,000
per year.[18]

Like other managers of his day, Delano did not live in a social vacuum.
The railroad industry not only modeled the new corporate institutional
structure, but it also became an arena of social debate regarding the issues
of governmental regulation and settlement of labor disputes. Delano's solutions to these issues stemmed from his conception of noblesse oblige
and served to presage his later activities during the Progressive Era.

In 1887 the Interstate Commerce Commission began its work to control abuses in railroad rate making. By the 1890s Delano had to face the
implications of this regulation. President Perkins of the CB&Q remained
vehemently opposed to any kind of government interference.[19] In con-
trast, Delano argued for an adjustment of corporate thinking that later
served as the model for many of the regulatory reforms of Progressives.
Looking back on his role as manager, he summarized his views on regulation: "I frequently took the position that if the railroads would recognize
some of their own faults and endeavor to clean house, they would avoid
unfriendly and unfavorable criticism and eventual legislation; but I was
always in a hopeless minority of men who thought the only way to save
our faces was to fight every inch of the way, and while we undoubtedly
postponed reforms by that method, the reforms when adopted by Congress were very much more drastic than I think they would have been if
the railroad officials had shown a willingness to meet public demands at
least half way."[20] Delano argued that, with the growth of large corporations and consequent government regulation, managers had to learn

to adjust to new social realities. He realized that regulation could serve as a way to deal with "ruinous competition" and to unite corporations, workers, and the government in what he termed "a community of interest." He carried this view through in dealing with workers on the CB&Q and the family coal properties.[21]

He held ambiguous ideas about "the labor question." He argued that miners working in the family coal mines ought to be given steady work to foster employee loyalty. Workers ought to cooperate in promoting the new system of a "community of interest" between corporatist-minded groups, including business firms, the government as watchdog, and workers. From his position as general manager at Chicago, Delano had to recognize the inequalities of power between these groups.[22] Yet in writing to brother Warren about the coal strikes of 1900 and 1902, Frederic thought that "unions are getting more aggressive and arrogant." His own position remained that of a manager forced to deal with economic matters first and foremost. In a 1903 letter to Warren, Delano admitted, "I am unfortunately pushed into a rather prominent place as Chairman of the Executive Committee of our General Managers' Assn—we are getting together with other large Employers for a strong stand and we shall either avert a fight by our firmness or have one which will clear the air for some time to come."[23] Opposing the "Popocratic platform" of the Democrats in 1896, Delano followed in the political footsteps of his father, a lifelong, respectable Republican. Only later, in the 1912 campaign of Woodrow Wilson, did Delano temporarily shift to the Democratic column.

In January 1905 Delano faced a turning point in his career. The CB&Q had been purchased by the James Hill railroad system, which wanted to bring in its own manager. Frederic wrote in shock to his brother: "I can't tell you what a wrench it is to give up associations of nearly 20 years.—Just what I shall do I have not figured out but I think I shall begin by taking two or three months vacation and then come back and see what offers for I can't be held idle.—I feel the disappointment keenly because I thought my record was without reproach."[24] Though he could have stayed idle, Delano soon found himself back in railroad work. In mid-April 1905, Delano took a position with George Gould's Pittsburgh-Wabash Terminal Railroad as first vice president and as president of the Wheeling and Lake Erie Railroad. By October he moved up to the presidency of the Wabash. Between 1905 and 1911 he worked to salvage the financial solvency of the Wabash, hard hit by the panic of 1907. But Delano failed. In 1913 and 1914 Delano served as president of the Chicago, Indianapolis and Louisville (Monon), which brought his long business career in railroad management to an end.[25]

During this rather hectic period in his life, Delano had consolidated his position as a respectable businessman and member of the Chicago social elite. In April 1905 Secretary of War William Howard Taft appointed Delano as consultant to the War Department's railroad construction project in the Philippines. Delano served as chairman of the Board of Directors for the Metropolitan West and South Sides Elevated Railroad Company of Chicago, director of the Hamilton Bank of Chicago, and director of brother Warren's Union Mining Company of Maryland. By 1908 Delano's business reputation had spread so widely that he was elected president of the American Railway Association, the industry's trade group. His social credentials soon matched those plaudits. In 1908 Delano could claim membership in many of Chicago's leading business associations, social clubs, and voluntary associations.[26]

Yet perhaps his greatest pride came from his election in June 1908 as an overseer to Harvard University. Less than a year after his election, Delano spoke before the students of the newly established Harvard Graduate School of Business Administration, summarizing his railroad management career in light of his own view of noblesse oblige: "[Railroading as a profession] means enthusiastic devotion to a work for the work's sake, without regard to the money consideration. Taken in this sense, railroading may, I think, be classed as a profession. It is work worth doing; it is in a sense public service, something to which the community are interested in seeing well done." He went on to note that "railroads have become so large, so complex, and so highly centralized, that the work in different departments has become specialized."[27] Delano had gone through a key period of corporate development—the transition from small, locally oriented, family- or partnership-operated businesses to the large, national, bureaucratic, and managerially run corporations. In the process, like many Americans, he learned to adjust to the impact of industrialization and economic growth led by the large-scale corporate organizations pioneered in the railroad industry. In the future, such growth would occur at the behest of managers trained in specialized fields of knowledge. Delano carried this ideal of managerial expertise into his next field of endeavor, the Chicago City Plan, one of the most widely known examples of the new field of urban planning in the Progressive Era.

Memorializing Delano upon his death in 1953, members of the Commercial Club of Chicago drew attention to his linking railroad management concerns with civic consciousness: "Because of his railroad experience it was natural that he took particular interest in the intricate problem of reconciling the public interest and that of the railroads entering Chicago from the east and south."[28] Membership in the elite Merchants Club, a younger rival to the more established, conservative Commercial Club, led Delano into the city planning movement. Both clubs had supported building Chicago's Great White City for the 1893 World's Fair. Elected to the Merchants Club in late 1902, Delano had already "given a good deal of thought to the matter of coordinating the railway terminals of the City" and "realized that it had a bearing on the whole question of *City Planning*." He talked with Charles D. Norton, a prominent insurance executive and Merchants Club member, about the club's hiring architect Daniel Burnham to develop a city plan that would incorporate Delano's views on consolidating the city's railroad terminals. President Walter Wilson of the Merchants Club contacted Burnham, who expressed interest but noted that he had commitments to the rival Commercial Club, which was working up similar ideas.[29]

Temporarily blocked, in September 1904 Delano distributed a brochure on railway terminals and a city plan, using drawings from Burnham's office to members of both clubs. By the fall of 1906 Norton, newly elected as president of the Merchants Club, chaired that group's City Plan Committee, with Delano as secretary. Norton and Delano continued talks with Burnham, noting that "while the Commercial Club had emphasized the importance of the Lake Front and the desirability of making the city more attractive, our study—and mine particularly—had been in the direction of planning railway terminals, and so forth, and that not only was there no conflict between the two ideas, but they were properly parts of the one big problem."[30] In 1907 the two clubs merged as the Commercial Club, reorganizing the City Plan Committee in the form of a new, expanded Executive Committee that promoted preparation of the Chicago Plan under Burnham's direction.[31]

Delano recalled that "fundamentally, what these men had in mind was highly and essentially practical—that a great city, like any other corporate undertaking, must plan ahead for its future."[32] Burnham's famous Chicago city plan, paid for with $85,000 from the Commercial Club, resulted from the kind of systematic survey that lay behind so many other Progressive Era reforms. Burnham and the City Plan Committee consulted with "the governor, the mayor, almost all the aldermen, the park commissioners, army and navy engineers, railroad and traction engineers and officials, harbor and drainage experts, property owners' associations, committees from the Chicago Association of Commerce, newspaper men, members of the State Legislature, congressmen, and many others."[33] Significantly for both Delano and the city planning movement, these consultations did not involve discussions with residents of immigrant, black, and working-class sectors of the city.[34] President Emeritus Charles Eliot of Harvard University accurately noted that "the promoter of this great work is an organization of business men, who naturally have in view chiefly the manufacturing and commercial interests of the city. . . . [The Commercial Club] maintains that the execution of the Plan would stimulate the increase of Chicago's wealth not in an exaggerated and transient way, but in a rational, steady, and permanent way. . . . all men can learn from this remarkable Plan how much good city-planning has to do with the conservation of human health, intelligence, and morality, natural resources which are quite as well worth considering as forests, water-powers, waterways, and mines."[35] One historian of city planning summarized Burnham's 1909 Chicago city plan as "an essentially aristocratic city, pleasing to the merchant princes who participated in its conception but not meeting some of the basic economic and human needs."[36]

Now one of the "merchant princes" in his own right, Delano would have agreed in part with this assessment. His primary interest in the plan lay in implementing his developing notions of cooperation, efficiency, and public service. He later wrote his New Deal planning colleague Charles E. Merriam that "from my long experience in Chicago, I am still of the opinion that great competition between railroads for terminal facilities was very wasteful, and it would have been better for the railroads and better for the country if all these railroad resources, some of them representing huge expenditures of money, had been pooled for the general good."[37] Delano rejected the contention by some that the Chicago Plan could be termed "Chicago Beautiful,"—an outgrowth of the English garden city ideal—for him it was a business proposition that included his ideas for stabilizing the railroad terminal situation through corporate cooperation with the city government.[38]

Promotion of the Plan of Chicago bore out Delano's view. Shortly after the Commercial Club received the plan in February 1908, it presented Burnham's work to the city as a gift. Mayor Fred Busse recommended to the city council that it establish a Chicago Plan Commission of 328 respectable citizens. The council quickly approved Busse's appointments in November 1909. In 1910 the new commission hired Walter L. Moody, general manager of the Association of Commerce, as managing director in charge of promoting the plan. Using another $200,000 provided by the Commercial Club, Moody conducted a huge public-relations campaign that included pamphlets, slide shows, and a special manual for use in children's classrooms. Delano, Norton, and Charles Wacker, a prominent merchant, aided Moody in the effort.[39] While complete implementation of the plan took several decades, as Roy Lubove has noted, the plan saw the emergence of a new breed of city planner: "Increasingly . . . the professional planner evolved into a technician who minimized normative goals—structural or institutional innovation—and became the prophet of the 'City Scientific' or 'City Efficient.' Technical matters relating to zoning, law, finance, capital expenditure, and transportation became his province."[40] Delano helped to manage this transformation during the 1920s.

Delano's involvement in the Chicago City Plan pointed the way to his participation in national Progressive reform and hinted at the direction his career would take for the next thirty-five years. Delano now moved in on the ground floor of the city planning movement. The Chicago Plan resulted from the instigation of respectable businessmen—Delano, Norton, and Wacker—consulting with the planning expert, architect Daniel Burnham. Unlike other business leaders, Delano viewed business-government cooperation through city planning and interest-group politics as a progressive development. To Delano, older ideas about strict separation between private and public sectors no longer made any sense in urban-industrial America. Rather, cooperation among groups, albeit the most powerful ones, could build what he called a "community of interest." In Chicago, Delano saw just such cooperation among railroad corporations, commercial firms, local and state governments, and, in his view, all Chicagoans. Yet Burnham's staff of experts consulted only those citizens organized into groups wielding economic, political, and social power. While most of the Chicago Plan involved physical planning—streets, parks, buildings, and transportation systems—the process could be expanded over time. According to Delano, the people to head this expansion would be those who accepted the necessity of responsible social duty from their position in organized groups. The organized group-oriented ideology, which both crossed and blurred distinctions between the private and public sectors, continued to influence Delano in later endeavors.

Delano carried this ideology over into his thinking on such Progressive Era issues as government regulation of railroad rates, the labor question, and reform of the banking system. Reluctant to abandon completely his railroad experience, Delano gradually moved away from a strict managerial, business-oriented approach to social issues. Speaking to the Chicago Literary Club in 1910, he suggested balancing managerial methods and social responsibility:

> In the last hundred years, and particularly in the last twenty-five, there has been an immense development of corporations. Corporations have grown so much in the magnitude and scope of their operations that it has necessitated the development of the corporate organization to a high state of perfection and because of the much greater flexibility in all such matters, man's ingenuity has had much freer play than in the development of Governmental organization. One thing which has been learned perhaps more clearly than any other in the development of corporate methods has been the working out in a very clear and complete way of all questions of authority and responsibility. Anyone familiar with corporate methods knows that there are few things more important than defining the limitations of authority and fixing the responsibility in like proportion. In corporation management we find no hesitation in placing a great deal of authority in the hands of single individuals, but with the authority, there is necessarily imposed strict responsibility and accountability for results.[41]

During the Progressive Era, Delano carefully steered a middle course between the older tradition of laissez-faire and the newer tradition of positive governmental regulation. Developing an approach to associational activity via private groups seeking cooperation with government, Delano set the pattern for his work in both the wartime mobilization for World War I and the New Era of the 1920s.

Recognizing Delano's reputation, President William Howard Taft offered him positions as a member of the Interstate Commerce Commission and as minister to China. Delano declined in order to travel around the country making numerous speeches on rate regulation. Taking a middle course between more conservative managers opposed to any form of regulation and more liberal proponents of strict regulation, Delano served as a moderating voice. Appearing before the Interstate Commerce Commission, Delano supported the railroads' case for increased freight rates, using the arguments of cost efficiency and the need to promote harmony between employers, shippers, employees, and consumers.[42] Delano summarized his view of regulation:

> Many say that it is a short step from the supervision of prices by the government to the control of all business by the government, or what might be termed "State Socialism." To my mind, however, there is a very wide gulf between private ownership and operation with public supervision and public operation. And yet private ownership is successful only so long as the

incentive of a fair margin of profit exists. This incentive is a valuable aid to efficient methods, and, when the possible excesses of human greed are held in check by publicity and supervision, represents to my mind almost ideal conditions. . . . The remedy is not in finding how to evade this law, however bad it is, but a united effort to get an honest, sincere law which decent men can and will live up to. If business men believe this, why should we not come out in the open and discuss it?. . . let us insist on getting governmental methods a little nearer to the efficiency of ordinary business methods.[43]

Delano's regulatory ideas resembled those of the early Herbert Croly and Walter Lippmann.[44] Arguing that industrial development resulted in the creation of huge corporations, Delano accepted the inevitability of such growth, which had to be regulated in the public interest, though never to the detriment of fair profits. Garnering a reputation as a fair-minded arbitrator in labor disputes, he now moved into the mainstream of Progressive reform. In late 1912, while on the Executive Committee of the American Railway Association, he was asked to submit names for railroad representatives on the Commission on Industrial Relations. Secretary Charles Nagel of the Department of Commerce and Labor turned to Delano as that representative, President William Howard Taft backed the idea, but the 1912–13 lame duck session of Congress refused to approve any of Taft's nominations. In early 1913 newly elected president Woodrow Wilson appointed Delano to the commission.[45]

In this temporary government advisory work, Delano again took the middle road, arguing for the need to arbitrate labor disputes, while he insisted that managers must retain final control of their labor force. The most liberal member of the commission, Chairman Frank P. Walsh, saw Delano as "my bulwark of strength" who had "splendid judgment and tact." Counsel William Thompson agreed in seeing Delano as "a real pillar of strength in shaping the final conclusions of the Commission." Florence Harriman, another business member, viewed Delano as "a delightful and cultivated gentleman, greatly in the confidence of both railway owners and railway employees. He had a real restraining influence on our Chairman, and it was after his departure . . . that Walsh's 'truculence' became so marked." Delano approved of the commission's use of a research staff, consultation with key groups, and the assumption by Presidents Taft and Wilson that it could arrive at a social consensus akin to Delano's "community of interest." Before the final deliberations of the commission, Delano moved on to become a vice-governor of the newly created Federal Reserve Board. Chairman Walsh and Counsel Thompson expressed regret on Delano's leaving, but Delano explained that he "could not honorably decline" the new position, even though the commission's work was "so important and constructive."[46]

Twenty-one years later, Delano recalled that his career changed direction with his acceptance of the Federal Reserve job: "I gave up my railway career of thirty years to enter the Government service, and while I haven't been in direct Government service all the time since, I have been closely associated with it since August 1914." When asked why he left the railroad industry, Delano replied, "Early in life I decided to work hard and if possible to establish myself independently by the time I was 50, then get the most out of life by doing what I wanted." From the Progressive Era forward, Delano shifted back and forth between voluntary associational work and government advisory work.[47]

Delano first began to think about money and banking issues during the 1896 presidential campaign, when he had supported the Republican candidate William McKinley. He stuck with the Republican Party through the Roosevelt and Taft administrations but in 1912 shifted to the Democratic candidate, Woodrow Wilson. In response to the panic of 1907, Delano and other members of the Commercial Club of Chicago founded the National Citizens League to promote reform of the banking system. The league helped prepare the ground for bills that resulted in passage of the Federal Reserve Act of 1913. Delano rightly saw the creation of the Federal Reserve system as a compromise measure that provided centralized supervision and regional, if not local, control of banking. He approved of the system's intended goal of stabilizing the monetary system, decentralizing reserves, and providing for flexible, yet sound currency.[48] He saw the Federal Reserve Board as providing a way to make governmental supervision of the banking system administratively responsible, much as business managers did for private-sector corporations. Yet he also interpreted the new system as bringing diverse elements together into associational contact that merged private and public functions: "In defining the Federal Reserve System as a central bank I think there are two points that might be stressed somewhat. One is that the word 'federal' is not used only in its sense as a synonym of *national,* but in its sense of *federated.* In other words, the Reserve System is superimposed on our existing National and State banking systems, and aims to *federate* those banks together, or at least, by federating their reserves and centralizing their supervision, to bind them into one system. The other point is the oft-quoted phrase that the Reserve System is a 'bank of banks.'"[49]

By 1916 Delano had grown disenchanted with Wilson as a result of

U.S. intervention in Mexico, Wilson's unwillingness to stand up to Germany on the issue of submarine warfare, and particularly over Wilson's failure to arbitrate in the 1916 railroad dispute, which led to passage of the Adamson Act. In 1916 he voted for the Republican candidate, Charles Evans Hughes. With American entry into the Great War, Delano again put social duty above income and sought a more active role. In June 1918 he resigned from the Federal Reserve Board to take a major's commission in the Army Engineering Corps. He joined the staff of Brigadier General William W. Atterbury, former vice president of the Pennsylvania Railroad, at the Director General of Transportation Office in Tours, France.[50]

Delano's wartime mobilization work highlighted his engineering skills, his corporate managerial experience, and his ideas for the Chicago City Plan in coordinating and centrally supervising a transportation system. In October 1918 Lieutenant Colonel Delano became director of transportation for the American Expeditionary Force, headquartered in Paris. He helped standardize French rail gauge and centralize the chaotic *chefs-de-gare* system. By May 1919 Colonel Delano aided in settling AEF accounts in France and demobilizing the wartime transportation administrative structure. Discharged in October 1919, Delano received the Distinguished Service Medal from the U.S. government and the Legion of Honor from the French state.[51]

While in Europe, Delano rejected several offers that presaged later work. Food Administrator Herbert Hoover tried to enlist Delano in postwar reconstruction efforts to serve in labor arbitration in the Teschen coalfields on the Czechoslovakian-Polish border, on the Danube River navigation board, and in financial advising to the new Polish government. Delano declined on the grounds that he must consult with his wife, Tillie, and that no guarantee seemed forthcoming from the "financial interests" involved. Hoover later succeeded in gaining Delano's service in the early stages of the Great Depression.[52]

On his return to the United States, Delano declined an offer to become executive manager of the American Railway Association (ARA), serving as "the connecting link between the railroads of the country and the Government" in the transition period after passage of the Transportation Act of 1920, because the Supreme Court had already appointed him the receiver in the Texas-Oklahoma boundary dispute over the Red River. In turning down the ARA job, Delano urged railroad executives to join together in a strong voluntary association to promote cooperation among owners, managers, workers, and the public—though "of course, the railway managers must be in control." To justify this position, Delano unwittingly pointed toward his own future concerns: "You may think these views radical and communistic, but the reason for them is that it is my firm belief that, unless the Railway Executives suggest something constructive in the way of unifying railway policy on the larger public questions, the Interstate Commerce Commission or Congress will feel compelled to do it."[53]

While acting as receiver in the Red River boundary case from 1920 to 1925, Delano served notice that his idea of associational action precluded a strict dividing line between private and public sectors. Throughout the 1920s he enlarged his own associational work, which he saw as all of a piece. Perhaps trying to make up for the family's earlier gains from the China opium market, Delano accepted the urgings of Secretary of Commerce Hoover in late 1926 and early 1927 to head the League of Nations Commission of Enquiry into the Production of Opium in Persia. Delano recommended that Persia develop its internal transportation system, improve its agricultural and irrigation systems, and set up a protective tariff.[54]

In establishing his official residence in Washington, D.C., Delano also joined a variety of social clubs, voluntary organizations, and philanthropies. Carrying over ideas and activities learned in Chicago, Delano moved into city and regional planning, bringing with him a sense of social duty and managerial efficiency. He played key roles in founding the National Capital Park and Planning Commission and directing the Regional Plan of New York and Its Environs. Like many Americans involved in voluntary associational activities in the 1920s, Delano sought cooperation among various interest groups and branches of government. His efforts in city and regional planning set the stage for his appointment to the National Planning Board.[55]

Since 1913, Delano had been a member of the American Civic Association (ACA), a voluntary associational group interested in promoting civic consciousness and planning. In 1922 the ACA decided to promote a national educational plan to revive L'Enfant's plan for Washington, D.C., as modified by the Senate MacMillan Commission Report of 1909. The group developed contacts with a number of business organizations such as the U.S. Chamber of Commerce and its local branches, as well as civic-reform groups favoring the "City Beautiful" ideal and professional organizations of architects, landscape architects, planners, and others. Using his influence with the Washington, D.C., Board of Trade, Delano headed the Committee of One Hundred for the Federal City, the Washington-based branch of a larger movement dedicated to planning a rebuilt capital city. Bringing together commercial, civic, and planning groups, the committee conducted a campaign to convince Congress to establish a planning commission for Washington, D.C.[56]

In 1924 Congress created the National Capital Park Commission (NCPC) to plan the extension of the city's parks under the direction of skilled professionals. The ACA's Committee of One Hundred lobbied for broadening of the commission's functions. Along with the renaming of the agency as the National Capital Park and Planning Commission (NCPPC) in 1926 came expanded authority to plan for parks, highways, new federal buildings, and development of the mall in front of the capitol building.[57]

President Coolidge appointed Delano as one of four public members to the new NCPPC in recognition of his work with the ACA Committee of One Hundred and the earlier NCPC's City Planning Committee. The leading scholar of planning for Washington, D.C., notes that "in the early years the leading figures were commission members Frederic A. Delano and Frederick Law Olmsted, Jr., and staff member Charles W. Eliot, II." Delano directed expansion of the commission's work to include new parks and highways for regional areas in Virginia and Maryland. Eliot, grandson of the famous president of Harvard University and representative of the new profession of landscape architecture, was hired as a professional city planner on the basis of his work in the field with various Massachusetts cities and Olmsted's firm.[58] In 1929 Delano took over as chairman of the NCPPC to begin work on updating the earlier plans of L'Enfant and the MacMillan Commission. He emphasized the physical planning of roadways, parks, and buildings, with a small unsuccessful effort at slum housing reform. While Delano acted as the policy-making manager, city planner Eliot became Delano's operating executive. Together they soon moved on to Franklin D. Roosevelt's National Planning Board.[59]

During these years Delano also participated in the early stages of regional planning, expanding his ideas from city planning in Chicago and Washington, D.C., to regional planning in New York. His work with the Regional Plan of New York and Its Environs (RPNY) reinforced his stress on voluntary associational activity, while setting precedents for later work in national planning.[60] The RPNY grew out of the promotional efforts of Charles D. Norton, Delano's colleague in the earlier Chicago Plan. In 1920 Norton, a newly elected member of the Board of Trustees of the Russell Sage Foundation, took his proposal for New York to the foundation. He argued that the committee on the RPNY was "directed and authorized to organize, develop and publish a Plan of New York which shall embody and record the best thought and vision of our engineers, our artists and architects, our public servants and social workers, and our far-seeing business men." With Delano's help, he was a trustee of the foundation, Norton succeeded in convincing the Russell Sage Foundation to support the plan.[61] One scholar has noted that "this privately sponsored project promised to be the most significant planning venture in the twenties, as much because of the caliber of the planners and other experts participating in it as because of the scope of the undertaking."[62] Norton appointed his friend and colleague Delano to investigate New York's harbor and railroad terminal situation—the same initial job he had performed for the earlier Chicago Plan.

Delano's role remained limited at first, but following Norton's death in March 1923, he took over as head of the Russell Sage Foundation Committee on the Regional Plan of New York and Its Environs. Over the next few years the committee received over one million dollars but eventually became independent of the foundation. As had the earlier Chicago Plan, the RPNY illustrated the increasing reliance on professional experts in new fields such as architectural planning, landscape architecture, and city planning and the growing interdependence of voluntary associations acting in concert with governmental agencies, as city planning expanded into the broader scope of regional planning.

In 1923 the committee hired a veteran of the English garden–city planning movement, Thomas Adams, as general director of surveys and plans. Over the next nine years Adams and a huge professional staff, including veterans of the earlier landmark Pittsburgh Survey, consulted with interest groups, specialized planning experts, and politicians before publishing ten survey volumes and two volumes presenting the regional plan for the New York metropolitan area.[63] Announcing the onset of work in 1922, Secretary of Commerce Herbert Hoover noted that "the action of the Trustees of the Russell Sage Foundation in providing for the survey by engineers and other experts of the economic and social situation, and the preparation of the comprehensive plan for the development of New York City and its Environs deserves the highest commendation."[64] Following the precedent set in Chicago, the plan was presented to the public as a gift on May 27, 1929. That same day a new voluntary association, the Regional Plan Association, started its promotion of the plan to convince local governments and interest groups to adopt whole parts of the plan.

With publication of the various volumes, the RPNY gained numerous plaudits; however, several perceptive critics noted weaknesses in the plan. As early as 1926 Charles A. Beard drew attention to the over-whelming problems of interest-group opposition to sections of the plan. By 1932 social critic Lewis Mumford attacked specific assumptions behind the plan, the conduct of the surveys, and the lack of social vision inherent in all the plan volumes: "Until the planner has a guiding notion as to what the good life in his generation is, how it is expressed in communities, what organs must be created for it, his elaborate surveys and his vast engineering projects will remain disoriented—disoriented and wasteful." Even though tempering Mumford's criticism, one recent scholar finds his indictment accurate in noting that "the plan was in many respects conservative, and in none more so than in its treatment of the housing problem."[65]

Delano managed to avoid confronting such criticism when the committee disbanded in late April 1932, but he did learn a number of lessons from the RPNY experience. In accepting the voluntary associational organization that led to creation of the RPNY, Delano had built on the earlier work of the Chicago Plan. Like-minded associationalists of the 1920s, many of them working with Secretary of Commerce Hoover, were engaged in parallel efforts. Delano managed to transform his corporate experience through the prism of his ideal of noblesse oblige into an ideal of public service that would serve him well in the context of New Deal national planning.[66] One recent description of the institutional structure of regional planning sounds much like the later structure of New Deal planning: "The regional plan committee was an independent organization with six special divisions, four advisory committees of architects, a large advisory engineering committee, an advisory legal committee, and dozens of special consultants. On its staff served men who later would hold important positions in the National Resources Planning Board, the National Capital Park and Planning Commission, the New York City Planning Commission, and countless other planning agencies."[67] The New Deal planning agency used exactly these techniques: specialized administrative divisions, project advisory committees, a technical research staff, and part-time expert consultants. Perhaps most important, the limitations of social vision noted by critics such as Beard and Mumford plagued the New Deal board throughout its history.

Delano expanded his efforts at voluntary organization in other ways during the 1920s. In 1925, as head of the American Civic Association and at the suggestion of Herbert Hoover, he spearheaded efforts to create an umbrella group named the Federated Societies on Planning and Parks and garnered financial support from such organized philanthropies as the

Russell Sage Foundation and the Laura Spelman Rockefeller Memorial. Like Merriam at the Social Science Research Council and Mitchell at the National Bureau for Economic Research, Delano in these city and regional planning groups of the 1920s relied upon voluntarist ideology, professional expertise, philanthropic funding, business-community support, and interest-group politics to implement his planning ideal. In 1929 at a conference chaired by Delano, and as a by-product of the RPNY, Harvard University founded a new Graduate School of Design. By the 1930s Charles W. Eliot II, a 1923 graduate of the first Harvard class trained in landscape architecture and later Delano's assistant, was joined by a number of new professionals in city, regional, and national planning.[68] By the end of the 1920s Delano had refined his conception of voluntary association through practical experience in civic groups, his position as director for the Richmond Federal Reserve Bank, and the city and regional planning movements in Chicago, Washington, D.C., and New York.

With the onslaught of the Depression, Delano carried on his proclaimed role as social steward with even more associational work that crossed back and forth between private and public sectors. In the spring of 1930 President Herbert Hoover appointed Colonel Arthur Woods to head the President's Emergency Committee for Employment (PECE) with a host of prominent appointees, including Frederic Delano.[69] Employing the now widely accepted New Era voluntarist philosophy of cooperation between business corporations, trade associations, civic groups, and branches of local, state, and federal government, PECE chairman Woods interpreted his organization's role as "based upon the idea that the primary responsibility for meeting the emergency lay with the states and local communities, and that the Federal Government would supplement their activities."[70] Working through local and national committees dedicated to treading the middle ground between laissez-faire and the reform activism of the positive state, the PECE hit upon the idea of limited public works projects to aid in overcoming massive unemployment. Public criticism followed and led to the failure of the PECE, after which Hoover turned to the similarly oriented President's Organization for Unemployment Relief. That effort also failed, but the precedent for public works planning by the federal government in response to depression had been set.

Delano also participated in local efforts to deal with the unemployed in Washington, D.C. Arguing that the Depression stemmed from excessive speculation, overproduction, and underconsumption, he turned to voluntary efforts to restore public confidence. As head of the District of Columbia's Committee on Employment, Delano explained that it had "not set up anything new" but rather had "endeavored to make use of existing utilities and make the most of them."[71] Yet despite contributions from the Washington Chamber of Commerce, the Marine Corps, and the Coast Guard, the committee did not have enough money to reduce the number of unemployed significantly. Delano proposed the creation of a "volunteer industrial army" based on the experience of voluntary cooperation from the mobilization of 1917–18. Delano resigned from the committee in distress, having lost his own Washington home in October 1931 in the economic crunch.[72]

The day before his resignation, Delano wrote in a letter to a friend at his old firm, the Wabash Railroad, "I am not one of those who believes that those who disagree with me are therefore Bolsheviks. However, I would be sorry to see our country abandon the idea of personal liberty. I am a great believer in voluntary cooperation, but I am not quite ready to say that cooperation shall be compulsory."[73] Shortly thereafter, he wrote the editor of the *New York Times* summarizing his own personal evolution to the idea of national planning: "Governments should act like enlightened individuals and corporations. They should build up reserves against a rainy day when times are good, and so be in a position to aid their citizens in bad times rather than increase their burdens by taxation. . . . What we need is to rely on intelligent and disinterested guidance which comprehends the facts and is willing to state their real implications."[74] For the next twenty-two months, Delano fleshed out the implications of this view, moving from traditional nostrums of cutting back federal expenditures and balancing the federal budget toward a form of national voluntary cooperation modeled on corporate welfare capitalist programs, the mobilization for the Great War, and the associational activities of the 1920s.[75]

Perhaps his experience as president of the Stable Money Association between March 1929 and the spring of 1933 best revealed the nature of Delano's move toward voluntarist national planning. In a speech to the association's members—industrialists, bankers, economists, and other interest-group leaders—Delano voiced his unease in accepting the post, "not because I had any doubt that the problem it has undertaken is worthy of my effort, but because I wondered whether the time had really arrived when men of affairs are willing to take hold of it in an endeavor to find a solution."[76] His continued discomfort with the "men of affairs" eventually led to his resignation from the association.[77]

Increasingly dissatisfied with both Hoover's policies and the abdication of social responsibility by the "men of affairs," Delano turned at last to the Democratic Party and its presidential nominee, his nephew Franklin Delano Roosevelt. In a series of letters and articles from the summer of 1932 to the spring of 1933, Delano detailed his loss of hope in Hoover and the Republican Party, both of which he held responsible for the excesses of big business in the preceding decade that led to the "debacle" of 1929.[78]

Family ties, concern for "making haste slowly" through renewed associational ties between the federal government and private groups, and recognition of the need to do something led Delano to support Roosevelt. Writing to his sister Kassie, Delano voiced his faith in his nephew: "I believe in Franklin implicitly, but more important I am something of a *fatalist*. It seems to me he was picked for the job and that he will not and cannot fail."[79] Delano's shift in political loyalty from the Republican administrations of the 1920s to the Democratic one of the 1930s resulted more from Delano's sense of social responsibility, which he saw embodied in his nephew Franklin Delano Roosevelt, than from either opportunism or a change of heart. He later inaccurately made the claim that he was a lifelong Democrat.[80] Yet as he wrote the head of the Brookings Institution, the times called for both caution and change: "It appears evident to me that a radical, or let us say an advanced liberal, in a conservative party carries forward far more advanced social and economic legislation than a similar type of man in a liberal party. . . . So it seems to me we were due in 1932–33 for revolution *if* a leader having the public confidence had not been willing to try some of the *new ideas*."[81]

Several months later, Delano accepted the position as head of the Brookings Institution following the death of its founder, St. Louis businessman Robert Brookings, in light of the fact that the organization "kept constantly in mind the importance of a close relationship of business methods and practical considerations with the facts of scientific research."[82] As the institution moved in a conservative direction under Harold Moulton, who was increasingly critical of Roosevelt's New Deal, Delano became uncomfortable. He finally resigned in May 1937 to devote his time to work for the planning board. Roosevelt must be supported in these times, he insisted, while Moulton and other Brookings staffers disagreed, especially in their criticism of plans for executive-branch reorganization.[83]

Early in 1933 Delano began to generate ideas for the new administration. Not surprisingly, he drew on his own experiences in railroad management, city planning, wartime mobilization, regional planning, and associational activity to propose measures for cooperation among interest groups under the voluntary guidance, rather than statist compulsion, of the federal government. Delano consulted with Bernard Baruch, famous head of the War Industries Board (WIB) during the Great War, about the usefulness of his idea of an industrial reserve army. With Baruch concurring, Delano sent a memorandum to one of Roosevelt's aides calling for revival of the WIB, extension of Hoover's Reconstruction Finance Corporation, and consideration of national planning for land use and public works through expanded agencies such as the National Capital Park and Planning Commission. Delano argued that restabilization of manufacturing industries producing capital goods could produce a ripple effect all down the industrial line.[84]

Having established his reputation as a business manager, civic leader, and planner, by 1933 Delano had access to national leaders in various fields, an institutional network of voluntary groups in the private and public sectors, and, to a limited extent, the ear of his nephew, President Franklin Delano Roosevelt. Building on what historian William Leuchtenburg has termed the analogue of war, extending that model to city and regional planning, and seeing some of his own ideas come to fruition through passage of the National Industrial Recovery Act, Delano lived near the center of political power.[85] His idea for voluntary cooperation among interest groups regulated by the federal government led him to support such New Deal agencies as the National Recovery Administration (NRA), the Agricultural Adjustment Administration, the Securities and Exchange Commission, and the Tennessee Valley Authority.[86]

Delano's interest in the idea of industrial self-government as found in the NRA was not disinterested. Since the mid-nineteenth century, the Delano family had invested heavily in coal properties in Pennsylvania and Maryland. As early as 1922 Frederic Delano had written to Secretary of Commerce Herbert Hoover proposing a kind of voluntary planning in the coal industry. He suggested that more efficient mines be allowed to push competitors under so that productivity could increase, miners could work shorter hours, and consumers could pay lower prices. He suggested the same idea during the early months of the Roosevelt administration. NRA codes, however, proved a mixed blessing. Delano's own mortgage bonds were invested in some of the same small coal companies that he now saw as hindered by the NRA coal code. By the late 1930s Delano retained the faith that an "impartial" coal administrator could hasten the end of "ruinous competition" through the Bituminous Coal Commission, but he had lost much faith in the actual practice of industrial self-government.[87]

Over the course of his own service on the New Deal planning board, Delano experienced similar disappointments, while overlooking inconsistencies in his own thought. Attempting to preserve voluntarism, fair competition, and protection of the public interest through statist action proved more difficult in practice than in theory. On July 7, 1933, Delano became operative head of the National Planning Board, created under authority of Title II of the National Industrial Recovery Act. Delano's assistant from the Washington, D.C., planning commission, Charles W. Eliot II, took the job as executive officer of the new planning agency.[88]

Critics later claimed that Delano received the appointment solely because of the blood relation to Roosevelt. Friends, critics, and journalists henceforth referred to Delano as Uncle Fred. Yet clearly Delano, one of the best-qualified people in the nation for the job, deserved the appointment. His own career based on the ideal of noblesse oblige and social responsibility, his practical managerial experience in the railroad industry in peace and war, his work in city and regional planning in Chicago, Washington, and New York, and his associational work of the 1920s made him an appropriate father to New Deal planning.[89]

Franklin Roosevelt already had indicated privately, while governor of New York, that "the Federal Government has a distinct function as a fact-gatherer for the whole Nation."[90] Roosevelt's interests in conservation, land-use planning, and planned use of natural resources were well known. He was well aware of Uncle Fred's planning experience. Moreover, both FDR and Delano saw national planning in terms of a voluntary advisory agency that would collect facts through special committees and expert consultants to arrive at what they perceived as the public interest. Secretary of the Interior Harold L. Ickes knew of Delano's work through his friend Charles E. Merriam and through his deputy administrator of public works, Colonel Henry M. Waite. Personal ties assured the continuity in ideology, institutional networks, and career experience from the pre-1933 years to the New Deal.[91]

At the same time, the personal ties between Uncle Fred and nephew Franklin discomforted Delano for the next ten years. While he backed Roosevelt enthusiastically after inauguration, Delano sought to keep a formal distance between them to forestall any possible criticism. In letters to Roosevelt during 1933 Delano adopted increasingly formal terms of address, moving from "personal" through "My dear Mr. President" to "Mr. President." In private he vehemently defended his nephew's politics and did so publicly in May 1937, when he resigned from the Brookings Institution. But the ever jovial Roosevelt made the problem harder for Delano by continuing to address him as "Dear Uncle Fred" in official correspondence.[92]

Delano nonetheless took up the challenge of national planning. Shortly after his appointment to the planning board, he wrote a friend that the new agency "is purely an advisory committee, which will be consulted by the Administrators of the Public Works program, on questions of general policy, forms of instruction and general advice. It probably means that we will not pass on many actual projects, but will try to suggest principles on which these projects will be handled."[93] Over the next decade, Delano refined what he meant by national planning. He already saw many precedents for it, including Alexander Hamilton's *Report on Manufactures,* development of the public land system, various protective tariffs, and land grants to railroad corporations in the West.[94]

Frederic Adrian Delano fathered a distinctly American national planning ideal that drew upon the older tradition of voluntary association as modified by the impact of industrialization and urbanization. He had come to the idea of planning long before the crisis of the Great Depression. Delano had no need to look to a far-off Soviet Union for inspiration; rather, he looked to the America in which he had grown to maturity. Writing to a friend in late 1937, Delano summarized his view of an American national planning effort: "In spite of defects as exhibited, I am still a believer in the capitalistic system and however desirable Communism or State Socialism might be idealistic, I feel that it is contrary to human nature to find it, and until we get the 'human animal' better educated to think less of himself and more of his associates, it won't work. . . . I do not see, however, why intelligent men in the world cannot do something towards remedying the defects of the capitalistic form of government. . . . am I right in saying that some way of curing this defect in the capitalistic system must be found by the friends of that system if they want to avoid something more serious?"[95] Delano and his fellow New Deal planners spent the next ten years trying to find the remedy that would enable them to build a new tradition of planning that combined aspects of nineteenth-century voluntarism with some parts of the twentieth-century positive state that looked to a new, transformed liberalism.

Charles E. Merriam and Social Science

POLITICS, PROFESSIONALISM, AND PLANNING

HISTORICAL MEMORY plays odd tricks with human lives. To a later generation, Frederic A. Delano represented a shadowy, avuncular figure aiding Franklin D. Roosevelt in moments of crisis. Yet social circles in Chicago, New York, and Washington, D.C., saw Delano as a man of action. He brought to national planning the values of the upper class, the corporate experience of a railroad manager, the city and regional planner's concern for rationality, expertise, and efficiency, as well as real talent for voluntary associational work that crossed private- and public-sector lines. Memory has served Charles E. Merriam in like fashion. Most often remembered for his academic work, Merriam had a lifelong interest in politics. Active for a short time in Chicago reform politics, he went on to become a manager of American social science and an advocate of professional expertise in the making of public policy. While Delano served as the father of New Deal planning, Merriam emerged as its organizer and theorist.[1]

Once known as the "Woodrow Wilson of the West"—the scholar in politics—Merriam is now somewhat inaccurately remembered as the "father of behavioral political science." Over time, his students and colleagues at the University of Chicago carried out research that garnered him numerous accolades. A colleague, Leonard D. White, noted that Merriam was "an extraordinary—sometimes a baffling—combination of the scholar, the practical politician, and the statesman." Yet with the methodological advances within political science after World War II,

Merriam's work came under attack for its moral presuppositions, its failure to live up to the promise of behavioral analysis, and its reliance on a kind of nationalist faith in American democracy as the summum bonum of the political process.[2]

Close study of Merriam's career reveals key similarities to Delano's path to national planning. Delano began life within a secure family setting in the Hudson River Valley. Merriam started it in a less wealthy, yet secure family setting in a small town in the Midwest. Delano moved rapidly up the corporate ladder in the pioneering railroad industry. Merriam followed suit in the burgeoning discipline of political science at the newly founded University of Chicago. Involvement in the City Plan of Chicago altered the direction of Delano's career. Chicago politics effected changes in Merriam's life in the same period of Progressive reform. Delano expanded his institutional ties through city and regional planning agencies in Chicago, Washington, D.C., and New York. Merriam built an academic empire at Chicago that led to expanded contacts in the community, his profession, and the nation. Building on earlier ideas of social duty and associational activity, Delano moved to the center of American political life in the nation's capital. Merriam helped found the national umbrella group for the social sciences, the Social Science Research Council, which led to service on President Herbert Hoover's Research Committee on Social Trends. Work for associational committees in the 1920s ultimately brought Delano and Merriam together on the New Deal planning board.

Merriam's commitment to the organization of American public policy with professional social scientists serving as advisers to governmental leaders paralleled Delano's concerted efforts at promoting social stability. Maturing in the period of adjustment to urbanization and industrialization, Merriam sought to reformulate the American liberal tradition by professionalizing social science, using research in public-policy making, moderating his early reform efforts to theorize about maintaining a social equilibrium between various organized interests, presiding over the creation of associational networks within the social sciences, and using those networks to engage in national planning as a rational process. In this respect, Bernard Crick, one of Merriam's severest critics, concludes that Merriam "becomes the first clear example of that frequent type whose 'private' political experience is a far richer source of knowledge than his 'public' political theory, only the particular theory he held inhibited the expression of his experience."[3]

Crick's criticism goes to the core of Merriam's career as an incipient planner. Merriam biographer Barry Karl has argued that Merriam is best understood as an "academic entrepreneur." Yet he moved beyond the individualist ethos of the entrepreneur to become one of the most skilled managers of American social science, coordinating the research efforts of thousands of social scientists. Merriam began his academic career as an entrepreneur, then branched out into the arena of Progressive political reform. Following this early stage of his career, Merriam built innovative social science networks within the University of Chicago, went beyond academic walls into the streets of Chicago, and ultimately into national leadership of the American Political Science Association. By the 1920s Merriam headed a national effort to coordinate the various social science disciplines through the medium of associational activity between professional organizations, with the support of receptive philanthropic managers such as his friend Beardsley Ruml. By the time of his appointment to the National Planning Board in July 1933, Merriam represented a new breed of public-policy actor—a manager of social scientific knowledge—who sought to build active cooperation between private experts and the executive branch of the federal government. Throughout his life, friends and colleagues recognized Merriam as a leader and organizer, addressing him regularly in personal correspondence as "Chief," "The Boss," and "Captain."[4]

At one point, Merriam drafted an autobiography entitled "The Education of Charles E. Merriam." Fragments remain, but only a much abbreviated version ever saw print. The title, however, seems appropriate for a man who changed from political scientist and reformer into a social science manager and national planner. Merriam's social scientific worldview, which grew out of personal, intellectual, political, and organizational experience, evolved into a brief for American national planning. To his family, Merriam always answered to the name "Ed," but to most others he remained the more imposing "Charles E. Merriam." This division in his personal and professional personae reflected an ongoing tension between assumed values and the search for the scientific ideal of truth. That tension first emerged in his early family life and education.[5]

In 1638 the Merriam family emigrated from England to settle in Massachusetts, but they moved west before the Civil War. Charles Edward Merriam, Sr., sought to provide comfort, education, and opportunity for his family. The son of proud New England and Scottish Presbyterian parents who barely made enough to live on, Charles Sr. moved to Hopkinton, Iowa, in 1855 and fought with the Union army during the Civil War. In 1868 he married his business partner's daughter, Margaret Campbell Kirkwood, a devout Scottish Presbyterian schoolteacher. Merriam biographer Barry Karl notes that Margaret "brought to the marriage not only the first really settled home [Charles Sr.] could identify as his own, but also the sense of culture and education which he himself could no longer hope to obtain."[6] Charles and Margaret had three children: John Campbell, Charles Edward, Jr., and Susan.

Born in Hopkinton, Iowa, on November 15, 1874, Charles Jr. faced the tension created by a father's expectations, a mother's hopes, and a brother's proven achievement. Charles Sr. had established a family-run grocery store, won the postmastership, speculated in small land sales, and created what Charles Jr. later called "a family of politicos." Margaret hoped that her eldest son, John, would enter the ministry; her hope did not come true. Charles Sr. wanted Ed to become a successful politician and sought to prod him on to the proper education. While brother John went on to the University of Munich to study paleontology, Charles Jr. stayed in Hopkinton to pursue a liberal education at Lenox College, where his father served as a trustee. Biographer Karl points to the ambivalence of both sons in rejecting their parents' hopes while simultaneously accepting much of their worldview: "Both John and Ed Merriam contributed to a liberal rebellion which worked to control the excesses of economic privilege, to reshape a rigidly conceived biblical morality, and to sensitize the machinery of politics to changes in the public will. At the same time, however, both men shared their father's commitment to capitalism not simply as a historical order of economic life but as a source of social virtue, to American Protestantism not simply as one among many routes to spiritual understanding but as the most potentially liberating route, and to American government as the one closest to the 'natural' order of political life toward which all men would ultimately move."[7] Charles Jr. hoped to emulate his older brother's success in combining this assumed Protestant morality with rigorous scientific analysis in his own education. Between 1890 and 1895 Charles pursued a liberal arts education at the recently secularized Lenox College, taught for a year, and studied law at the State University of Iowa for one year. Disillusioned with the provincial nature of legal studies, he decided to escape to the East to get away from law, politics, and business. Having a classical education and an interest in science from his "No. 1 Tutor," his brother John, Charles joined other Americans in moving from small-town nineteenth-century America to the urban-industrial world of New York City.[8]

Selecting Columbia University over John Hopkins for graduate work, Merriam entered professional study at a propitious time. Between 1865 and 1910 the modern American university with specialized studies directed by scholars trained in new philosophies and using new methods of teaching and research began organizing a national network of knowledge akin to the corporate structure pioneered by big business corporations. Merriam explained, "I was interested in the organization of human affairs so that you would have outward stability of an organization and a spirit of justice." His chosen field of political science had recently emerged from a welter of social science disciplines under the tutelage of John W. Burgess, founder of the School of Political Science at Columbia University in 1880.

By the time Merriam entered in 1896, Columbia had overtaken Johns Hopkins as the center of American social science.[9] Adapting the historical-comparative method and a curriculum of elective courses, lectures based on research, and the research-oriented graduate seminar from his own training in the German scientific historical school in Berlin, Burgess created the school of political studies that Merriam carried into the next generation at the University of Chicago. Despite his conservative Hegelian metaphysics grafted onto the historical method, Burgess began the shift away from the traditional emphasis on juristic, formal political science, envisioning a synthesis of the various social sciences. By 1896 Columbia's School of Political Science, the best in the nation, included scholars such as William A. Dunning in American history and political philosophy, Frank Goodnow in administration, Munro Smith in comparative jurisprudence, James Harvey Robinson in medieval history, E. R. A. Seligman in public finance, John Bates Clark in economics, and Franklin Giddings in sociology. Merriam had access to this very talented group of teachers and social scientists.[10]

Merriam later recalled that his initial intellectual interests at Columbia had been "directed primarily to economics, but political theory emerged triumphant, although not without many a lingering glance at economics, sociology, and history." After receiving the master's degree in 1897, he served first as a fellow in political philosophy, then as lecturer substituting for his mentor, William A. Dunning, who was away on research in 1898–99. In 1899 Merriam traveled to Berlin and Paris to learn from his mentors' teachers, but he found the experience disappointing. With the completion of the doctorate in 1900 under the joint supervision of Dunning and Otto von Gierke of the University of Berlin, Merriam served notice that he would carry the work of the founding generation of American political science into the next generation. Drawing on his Columbia mentors, he was most strongly influenced by Dunning, Burgess, Goodnow, von Gierke, and Robinson.[11]

Educated in Berlin, Dunning brought the German "science" of history to Columbia, deleting Kantian and Hegelian metaphysics, to emphasize the collection of facts, the narrative description of political theories, and the relation of ideas and institutions in American history. Merriam later wrote of Dunning, "The most striking characteristic of [Dunning's work] was its dispassionate and objective quality, its detached point of view. Few men of equal ability have been able to resist the temptation to formulate an independent system and advance a dogmatic philosophy." Merriam's academic interest in research, political theory, and national unity stemmed from Dunning's influence.[12]

While Dunning emphasized factual research as "scientific" history, Burgess created "a national university out of an urban college, introducing the systematic study of politics and public law."[13] Speaking before the American Historical Association in December 1896, Burgess summarized his desire to synthesize various social science methodologies:

> Political science consists of something more than facts and logical conclusions from facts. It contains an element of philosophical speculation, which, when true and correct, is the forerunner of history. When political facts and conclusions come into contact with political reason they awaken in that reason a consciousness of political ideals not yet realized. Thrown into the forms of propositions these ideals become principles of political science, then articles of political creeds, and, at last, laws and institutions. Now while this speculative element in political science must be kept in constant truthful and vital connection with the historical component, and must be in a certain very important sense, regulated by the historical component, it is, nevertheless, the most important element in political science because it lights the way of progress and directs human experience towards its ultimate purpose.[14]

In repudiating the natural rights and social contract theories of government, Burgess took refuge in conservative Hegelian teleology to argue that nationalism, the sovereignty of the state over society, and political analysis by only the most competent persons should be the concerns of political science. Merriam never accepted the Hegelian elements of Burgess's thought; however, he continually discussed the need for systematic political theory and wrote on the subject for the rest of his professional career. Burgess helped Merriam recognize the need for a theoretical framework to complement Dunning's emphasis on factual research and nationalist faith as the solvents of American democracy.[15]

Merriam eventually gained a reputation as a practical student of politics, gleaning ideas from the work of Frank Goodnow in public administration, Otto von Gierke in municipal and legal administration, and James Harvey Robinson in New York City reform politics. Goodnow suggested that the traditional formal distinctions between the legislative, executive, and judicial branches of American government might be understood better through the distinction between *politics* ("the guiding or influencing of governmental policy") and *administration* ("the execution of that policy"). Goodnow argued that politics must control administration. Merriam refined this idea to argue that social science researchers must only advise politicians, who would remain responsible for making policy decisions. Von Gierke, head of the German Imperial Code Commission, advocated using the urban environment as a research laboratory to determine the social effectiveness of voluntary associations mediating between the individual and the state. Merriam honed this idea into his theory of the utility of social science research as a mediating influence between voluntary associations and the American state. Under the prodding of Robinson and fellow students, Merriam went into New York politics, joining in an unsuccessful 1897 campaign to elect Seth Low as reform mayor. In his doctoral dissertation, *History of the Theory of Sovereignty since Rousseau* (1900), published in Burgess's influential Columbia Series of Studies in History, Economics, and Public Law, Merriam synthesized the factual research of Dunning, the theoretical concerns of Burgess, and the practical bent of Goodnow's and von Gierke's work. Soon he took up Robinson's call to political reform in the arena of Chicago politics.[16]

With Dunning's help, Merriam secured a position as *docent* in political science at the University of Chicago that same year. Merriam's early academic career made him part of what historian Morton White has called the revolt against formalism, with its focus on historicism ("the attempt to explain facts by reference to earlier facts") and cultural organicism ("the attempt to find explanations and relevant material in social sciences other than the one which is primarily under investigation").[17] In joining this revolt, Merriam sought to modernize American liberalism by retaining his faith in the progress of American democracy, which could be complemented by the new methods and tools of modern social science. At the start of his career, Merriam seemed destined for a life of staid scholarly achievement, but that direction changed dramatically in the coming years.

Shortly after arriving at the University of Chicago, Merriam married Elizabeth Hilda Doyle, the sister of a Columbia classmate. More than his personal life took on new dimensions. Under the tutelage of President William Rainey Harper, the University of Chicago sought not only to educate the city's new middle class but also to train specialized experts for the urban-industrial age. Harper was wary of allowing his professors to engage in active political work in Chicago, whose elite donated money to the new university. Merriam's new supervisor was Harry Pratt Judson, a conservative practitioner of the traditional study of politics. A product of the new university system, Merriam would have to prove himself as the university's first political scientist. From 1900 to 1918 Merriam engaged in a variety of entrepreneurial efforts to establish himself within his department, the university, the city, the rising urban reform community, and his profession.[18]

Merriam advanced quickly up the academic hierarchy, earning promotion to associate (1902), instructor (1903), assistant professor (1905), associate professor (1907), and professor (1911). Like Delano, Merriam rose up the administrative structure of a major modern institution—the new university. For the first decade of his academic career, Merriam was uncomfortable and thought about moving to another university. Between 1907 and 1911 Chicago managed to keep Merriam only through pay raises and promotion to the deanship of the College of Commerce and Administration, predecessor to the Business School. Merriam's major scholarly work of the period, *A History of American Political Theories* (1903), extended ideas gleaned from Burgess and Dunning while hinting at Merriam's developing interest in relating ideas to their historical contexts. By 1905, Merriam later wrote, he "was well on his way toward a five-foot shelf of erudition in political science, 'historical and comparative.'"[19]

The 1903 *History* revealed Merriam's concern for combating attacks on the theory of progress and the inevitable expansion of American democracy stemming from changes wrought by industrialization. Six years before Herbert Croly's *Promise of American Life,* Merriam stated the creed that carried him into the Progressive reform fray. His own academic research took on practical overtones with study of the intricacies of political-party life and the need for institutional reforms such as the primary election. On the advice of his mentor Dunning and the political commentator James Bryce, Merriam entered the political arena. Though retaining his interest in political theory, Merriam now focused on creating ties between the university, local businesses, philanthropies, social welfare organizations, and those advocating the reform of city government.[20]

In entering the arena of urban politics as an observer-participant, Merriam sought to eliminate graft and waste and replace them with expertise and efficiency, based upon his earlier observations in Germany: "[In Berlin] I saw efficient government of a type I had not known before and I was deeply impressed by it. German militarism was absurd to me, when it was not hateful, but the science of administration the German cities especially seemed to understand thoroughly. A trained expert as mayor and a permanent staff of employees, the absence of spoils politics, I looked upon with the very keenest interest. If the democratic spirit of Iowa could be combined with the administrative efficiency of Germany the result would certainly be good. But could it be done?"[21] At the same time that scholars, philanthropists, and reformers across America turned to social science research and public administration theory to improve city government, Merriam did his part in Chicago. While his mentor E. R. A. Seligman and his later colleague Luther Gulick worked in New York City, Merriam built his own vehicles for social research by professional experts in the rapidly changing social sciences to serve as the base for municipal reform backed by the new middle class. In this respect, Merriam moved beyond the confines of the university, expanded his practical political contacts throughout the city, built his professional reputation, honed his ideology of Progressive reform, and laid the institutional base for his own political career. While the city served as a kind of social laboratory, as it did in the 1920s for his colleague Robert Park, Merriam also identified national issues with which he soon wrestled as a manager of American social science. His entrepreneurial talents developed in these Chicago years proved a solid foundation for associational consolidation in the years 1917–33.[22]

Historian Stephen Diner has shown that Merriam led the "fight for the new *system* of public administration in the city government" by working within a complex institutional reform setting: "Activist professors thus found striking compatibility of ideology and social experience with the businessmen, lawyers, social workers, physicians, and other professionals engaged in reform. All groups claimed expertise in special areas, experienced specialization and initiated advanced training programs, worked primarily in large and bureaucratic institutions and believed that professionals should serve the common good. It is not surprising, therefore, that they joined together so readily to form a highly organized and unified reform community."[23] Amid the welter of Merriam's reform activities lay a systematic approach to urban reform that not only revealed the use of social science research for partisan political purposes but also fused his nationalist faith in American democracy and his academic hopes for a science of politics. From his active membership in the Chicago City Charter Convention of 1906 through his defeat in the aldermanic primary of 1917, Merriam attempted to combine theory and practical politics.[24]

Like many urban progressives, Merriam sought (unsuccessfully, as it turned out) to gain home rule for Chicago to escape the corruption of spoils politics rampant in the downstate legislature. In 1906, under the auspices of the reform-oriented City Club, Merriam undertook a study of Chicago's taxation and revenue systems. He concluded that centralization, consolidation, and modernization of accounting methods were a necessity. He backed the establishment of the City Plan Commission in 1907, "not primarily an executive body, it was in the nature of a consulting expert." Merriam strengthened his social and political ties through election as vice president of the City Club and alderman from the Seventh Ward (Hyde Park) representing the university area and its reform allies in business, philanthropy, city planning, and social work.[25]

After election as Republican alderman to the city council in 1909, despite the initial opposition of party regulars, Merriam put to work his reform ideology of investigation, exposure, expert recommendation, and administrative follow-up. Between 1909 and 1911 he sat on three important city council commissions (Harbor Commission, Commission on City Expenditures, and Waste Commission) and two key committees (Finance Committee and Committee on Crime). At the root of this work lay Merriam's faith in the revival of democracy, his reliance on the pragmatic value of social science research and expert advice, and his hope for the rationalization of municipal government. He joined Frederic Delano on the Harbor Commission to suggest ways to coordinate plans for the new harbor, consolidation of the railway terminals, and consideration of extending the park system. Merriam and Delano met in the crucible of urban reform on the grounds of similar ideological, professional, and social interests.[26]

Merriam's reform politics led to some exposure of graft, some administrative reorganization aimed at systematizing governmental procedures, but only partially successful follow-up because of opposition by interest groups that held a different vision of urban growth and had the political power to defeat his view. His own political career followed a similar mixed pattern. In 1911, with the encouragement of urban reformers, financial support from industrialist Charles R. Crane and philanthropist Julius Rosenwald, backing from professionals and suburbanites, and political advice from his new friend and campaign manager Harold L. Ickes, Merriam ran for mayor as a progressive Republican. He had to overcome opposition from both Republican and Democratic party regulars. After winning the Republican primary by a wide margin, Merriam lost the general election to the Democratic boss, Carter H. Harrison, by the narrow margin of 17,000 votes out of a total of 367,000 cast.[27] Defeated but undaunted, Merriam and Ickes established the Illinois Progressive Party, supporting Robert La Follette in 1912, until his collapse left the presidential nomination to Teddy Roosevelt. It would not be the last time Republican progressives Merriam and Ickes took an independent tack in politics; they worked together again in the 1930s with another Roosevelt. Merriam stood for a range of Progressive reforms, including election reform laws (primary, short ballot, initiative and referendum, woman suffrage), home rule for Chicago, public regulation of utilities, and conservation of natural resources.[28]

Merriam lost his bid to succeed in practical politics; however, the next generation brought to fruition his emphasis on public administration and the advisory use of social science research. Having outpaced the older mugwump tradition of moral reform, Merriam added the modern concern for more systematic administrative efficiency, the investigatory techniques of social science, and the advisory planning potential of expertise. President William Howard Taft offered Merriam, as he had Delano, a position on the Commission on Economy and Efficiency alongside his old mentor Frank Goodnow, but Merriam declined, preferring to stay in Chicago. He joined the advisory committee of the Chicago City Planning Commission, tried to create a Department of Public Welfare modeled on the New York Bureau of Municipal Research, and founded and directed the Chicago Bureau of Public Efficiency with the financial support of the City Club.[29] For Merriam, the bureau served "merely to stimulate and support those public officials in establishing and maintaining the highest standards of business efficiency."[30] President Wilson recognized Merriam's stature, offering him a position on the Tariff Commission, but again Merriam declined, though he later opined that "this was a mistake."[31] By the late 1920s Merriam was ready to take up an advisory role with the federal government.

Merriam's life as a politician was not long lasting. He served as alderman from the Seventh Ward from 1913 through 1917, when he lost the primary by five votes. In 1915 he lost the Republican mayoral primary to the regular candidate, William Thompson. For all practical purposes, his political career was over by then, but in shifting from the entrepreneurial stage of his early academic and political career to the managerial one in the 1920s, he widened his political influence from the local urban setting of Chicago to the national arena.

Amid a welter of issues and specialized reports, Merriam gained from his Progressive reform experience a set of principles that defined his view of government. In his investigatory work, Merriam focused on three areas of public-policy making: budget, personnel, and administration. These served as the focal point of Merriam's work in Social Science Research Council committees, the New Deal planning agency, and the executive reorganization committee in the late 1930s. His concern for specialized knowledge as an advisory tool for the use of policy makers took root as the central idea in his conception of national planning. Speaking at a city planning conference in March 1917, Merriam emphasized the social science base of planning: "If I were called upon to point out the dominant characteristic of our American cities during the last ten years, I should say that the most striking feature is the tendency of our city to organize its own growth—to plan its own development. Not theory alone but grim necessity drives the city builders of our day to that painstaking study of facts and forces, that careful coordination and systematization of diverse factors which we call planning. The sanitary survey and plan, the financial survey and plan, the governmental survey and plan, the social survey and plan, and the physical survey and plan, loom large in the present day municipality."[32] He argued that city planning involved conservation of resources "to promote the common interest, improve the common efficiency and enhance the value of the individual life."[33] Merriam held a historicist conception of planning as a process rather than as a structural given that did not change over time: "We fully realize that it is impossible to establish a permanent plan which posterity cannot alter. Posterity will unquestionably be wiser than we are. Yet the broad outlines of development can now be traced. If no plans were made except upon absolute finalities, there would be neither business nor government. Cities may now make fundamental plans to and on which the present generation may build. Waste and confusion may be reduced within limits by practical planning of the future. In short, if a city cannot be made to order, there is no reason why the genius of order cannot preside over its own making."[34] Yet this ideal of planning as organizational process dependent on expert advice did have its cost in that Merriam's "rather vague notion of the new politics evokes an image of a society in which the area of political disagreement is narrowed almost to the vanishing point, and the area of scientifically-based conclusions is correspondingly widened."[35] The role of citizens in this new democracy remained to be defined.

Wartime mobilization work confirmed for Merriam the importance of bringing together social scientists, business leaders, and government officials. With American entry into the Great War in April 1917, he joined the Signal Corps to work as an examiner for the Chicago aviation board. Wanting to do more, he joined the Committee on Public Information (CPI), serving in Italy between April and September 1918 as American High Commissioner for Public Information in Rome. Acting as liaison between Italian political leaders and President Woodrow Wilson's adviser Colonel Edward M. House, Merriam promulgated propaganda to encourage Italian support for the Allied war effort. Biographer Karl shows that this war work "shocked" Merriam by adding to marital difficulties (exacerbated by a brief romantic affair in Europe), shaking his faith in the Progressive crusade, and leading directly to his defeat in the 1919 Republican Chicago mayoral primary. That the war shook Merriam's convictions cannot be denied, though how remains open to doubt. One of the major activities of the CPI's Rome office involved stemming the tide of popular support for socialism and revolution. He clearly sought to bolster Italian support for the Allied cause and may have used Rockefeller Foundation funds to swing socialist leader Benito Mussolini to a pro-interventionist stance. Ironically, Merriam may have used philanthropic money to support the leader whose fascist cause he vehemently opposed in the 1930s.[36]

Merriam began thinking seriously about the use of information as a way to educate the American electorate. In the 1920s he conducted several studies of civic education that often walked a fine line between reliance on expertise and the manipulation of public opinion. Looking back in 1950, Merriam summarized his developing ideas on political pluralism and the role of social science: "It is possible to develop—and I should think we are—a considerable number of persons with a certain amount of expertness on the technical side and a certain amount of skill on the political side, who may, from time to time, be drawn into either politics or administration. Steadily we get a wider range of interchange between business and government and the universities and now [1950], I suppose also with labor. Where a man doing government work isn't a public servant or he may not be a professor or he may not be merely in the line of business or in the line of labor, but where you get a circulation of skilled persons from one industry to another."[37]

During the 1920s and 1930s Merriam reached the zenith of his professional career. Turning away from active partisan politics after his 1919 defeat in Chicago, he moved back to the professional study of politics and built a national social science research network. Before the 1920s he had established his name in the Political Science Department, the University of Chicago, and throughout the city of Chicago. Now he worked at extending those positions, moderating his reform outlook to create the Chicago School of political science, which replaced the earlier Columbia School. He also promoted the creation of an umbrella organization for the social sciences and consolidated the pattern of interlocking associational links among social science experts, businessmen, philanthropists, and government officials.

Merriam's academic work during the 1920s signaled a turning away from reform politics toward the development of his own organizing talents. In *American Political Ideas* (1920) he moved further away from the theories of Burgess to emphasize those of Dunning that related ideas to their social contexts. This work stated Merriam's faith in the American liberal democratic view of politics, which became especially important to political scientists in the 1950s. Several years before his University of Chicago colleague William F. Ogburn coined the term "cultural lag," Merriam presented the idea of a "social lag" between political thinking and social development. Industrialization, urbanization, and immigration produced a number of important social changes, Politically, the influence of state government declined in relation to the growth of urban and national government, while the executive branch of the federal government gained over the legislative and judicial branches. Most important, American society had become a complex interplay of new interest groups that included huge business corporations, labor unions, organized agriculture, and specialized groups working for such issues as woman suffrage, prohibition, municipal reform, city planning, and conservation.[38]

Merriam noted the conflict of ideas among conservatives such as Herbert Spencer and William Graham Sumner, liberals such as Lester F. Ward, Herbert Croly, Walter Lippmann, and Teddy Roosevelt, and influential radicals such as Edward Bellamy, Henry George, and Morris Hillquit. Over time, the older tradition of laissez-faire in political economy had given way to a more modern view of the positive role of the state advocated by Progressive reformers. In effect, ideas had changed to adjust to social conditions. Implicitly, Merriam laid the groundwork for his version of liberal pluralism, which emphasized the role of private voluntary associations as well as the positive state: "While the government was being centralized and while the party system was being regulated and officialized, the unofficial voluntary organizations were springing up in other and less official types of association and action. On the whole, public opinion favored these extra legal agencies more than it did government. . . . Organizations of capital, organizations of labor, party organizations and the unofficial citizens' organizations all grew more rapidly in power than did the formal government itself. . . . These new types were not the result of conscious calculation. They were the instinctive product of political interest and activity finding expression wherever it found an open way leading to political result."[39]

Rejecting both conservative and socialist alternatives, Merriam sought a middle way through a transformed liberalism. In his next major work, *The American Party System* (1922), he looked to political parties as the agents of mediation between social groups. Defining the party "as a type of social group, primarily concerned with social control as exercised through the government," he presented the issue of American politics as having to do with the "yet unsettled questions regarding the balance between technical knowledge, political leadership, and popular control."[40] Extending his insights from his reform experience, Merriam now sought to define the role of social scientific knowledge, its subordination to political leaders (those responsible for making policy decisions), and the need for civic education of individuals through interest-group organizations and other voluntary associations. Denying the death of Progressivism, Merriam sought to redefine liberalism in modernist terms through his own roles as scholar, organizer and manager of knowledge, and financial lobbyist.[41]

Strong presidents were the key to this modern liberalism. In four lectures delivered at Amherst College in 1924, Merriam pointed to Abraham Lincoln, William Jennings Bryan, Teddy Roosevelt, and Woodrow Wilson as exemplifying the characteristics of good political leaders. Leadership required such qualities as "sensitiveness to social and industrial tendencies," quick perception of alternatives followed by "prompt action," "facility in group combination and compromise," and skilled oratory.[42] Taking strong executive leadership as almost a given, Merriam called upon his profession for better methods of study. He argued that political science should move beyond its narrowly academic focus into the realm of organized voluntary cooperation between professional experts both within each discipline and between the different social sciences. In the 1920s Merriam redefined his progressive liberalism as professional activity. In two short addresses before the American Political Science Association, in 1921 and 1926, as well as in various articles published as *New Aspects of Politics* (1925), Merriam reexamined the state of political science as both methodology and profession, exhorted his colleagues to accept the gains made by an expanding and more broadly based social science research network of professional associations, and suggested ways for political science to plan its future. This work revealed continuities in Merriam's thought, incorporated the new liberalism broached in *American Political Ideas,* and pointed the way toward his ideal of planning as an advisory process.[43]

Developing the idea of social lag presented in *American Political Ideas,* Merriam argued in *New Aspects of Politics* that the "ways and means by which the technical and professional study of politics may be improved in quality and serviceability" paralleled society's need to adjust to social change through expert research.[44] But for research to be useful, professionalization and corporate organization were necessary:

> In many ways politics has been outstripped in the race for modern equipment supplying the rapid, comprehensive and systematic assembly and analysis of pertinent facts. . . . The best equipped research man in the best equipped institution of learning hardly has machinery comparable with that of the best lawyer in his office, or of the best engineer, or the expert of the large corporation, or the secretary of the chamber of commerce, or the research department of the Amalgamated Clothiers. The truth is that he often has no laboratory equipment at all, and curiously enough in these days of large scale organization, he labors single-handed, even when he discusses this characteristic feature of our civilization. In this respect the political and social sciences have been generally outstripped by the so-called "natural" sciences—now often dropping the "natural"—which are far better supplied with the personnel and facilities for research.[45]

Rejecting earlier modes of analysis in political science—a priori prior to 1850, historical and comparative from 1850 to 1900, and the then current emphasis on observation, survey, and measurement—Merriam saw a new era emerging that would include cross-disciplinary approaches. Taking the middle road between advocating pure social "science" and Charles Beard's contemporaneous concern for humanistic analysis, Merriam proposed that the full range of modern social science methodologies be used. To understand the behavioral aspects of human nature, the social environment, and the nation's cultural heritage, he called for the use of social sciences such as statistics, social psychology, sociology, geography, ethnology, and biology.

Underlying Merriam's exhortation of his fellow social scientists was his notion of political prudence: "the conclusions of experience and reflection regarding the problems of the state." Merriam believed that social science expertise could both aid politicians in making policy decisions and provide a basis for civic education to raise the general level of political intelligence. Only in this way could he reconcile an ongoing tension among political leaders and parties, social scientists, and the democratic "mass" of the community. By promoting a new kind of political analysis emphasizing the study of behavior rather than legal structure or metaphysics, Merriam hoped to provide the electorate, legislative bodies, administrative agencies, and executive leaders with precise, informed intelligence for the purposes of "social control."[46]

Many of Merriam's ideas in *New Aspects of Politics* paralleled his own organizational activities of the 1920s. To make social science "serviceable," Merriam pointed to the need for "cooperation of the various governmental agencies, of the several institutions of higher learning, and perhaps of private research funds."[47] Paralleling the associational efforts of Frederic Delano at the same time, Merriam laid out his program for a modernized liberalism, suggested avenues for future research, and pointed to potential sources of financial support. American social science, he believed, could serve well both political leaders and the electorate by emphasizing "above everything else the crying need for organization and coordination of effort both in general method and with specific reference to the activities of our professional societies."[48] Filtering his concern for professionalization through the prism of Progressive reform and Chicago political activity, Merriam had found a way to organize social science knowledge for political purposes—to realize the very modernized liberalism he saw as a prerequisite for the preservation of democracy in a world threatened by the rise of fascism and totalitarianism. In the 1920s Merriam led an organizing effort in a dazzling array of venues that both created a national social science research network and, in effect, established a set of ad hoc planning institutions in the New Era.

Merriam started this effort with the Political Science Department at the University of Chicago. Beginning with his appointment in 1900 as the university's first political scientist, Merriam had tried to win the current president's support for expanding the department. In the 1920s he got that chance. Appointed chairman in 1923 after turning down an offer to replace his mentor, Dunning, in the Lieber Chair at Columbia University, Merriam transplanted the Columbia School to Chicago. For Merriam the department became a "community of researchers."[49] He broadened the scope of the graduate program and brought in new faculty members competent in both academic and associational settings. During this period Chicago Ph.D.s proliferated under Merriam's direction. His students moved into the department upon completion of their doctorates, among whom were Harold D. Lasswell, Harold F. Gosnell, and

Carroll D. Woody. The recently promoted scholar of public administration, Leonard D. White, became a partner in Merriam's departmental program. Building on his fusion of university research, civic education, and cooperation with interest groups and the municipal government from the Progressive Era, Merriam put into practice the idea of cooperative, team research to study political behavior. Modeling a proposed School of Politics on the Institute of Public Administration (the renamed New York Bureau of Municipal Research), he argued unsuccessfully throughout the 1920s for the creation of a regional research center at the university. He hoped that eventually this school would become "a center of conference and consultation between government officials and research men."[50]

In 1923, with the financial assistance of the Laura Spelman Rockefeller Memorial, directed by Beardsley Ruml, holder of a Chicago Ph.D. in psychology, Merriam established the Local Community Research Committee (LCRC). The committee implemented a number of Merriam's ideas, including use of the urban community as a research laboratory, emphasis on interdisciplinary methodologies, active cooperation among scholars and associational groups from both the private and public sectors, and coordination of projects at various stages of development. The LCRC published a number of influential studies by members of the University of Chicago faculty, including Merriam, White, T. V. Smith, Gosnell, Robert Park, Edith Abbott, Sophonisba Breckinridge, Ernest Burgess, and E. Franklin Frazier—many of whom were on their way to becoming leading scholars in their fields. By 1929 dedication of the new Social Science Research Building, "1126," marked the institutionalization of the Social Science Research Committee, an outgrowth of the LCRC, at the University of Chicago.[51]

Merriam continued his research and writing, but his strength lay in encouraging students and colleagues to experiment with new methodological approaches. In 1924 he and Harold Gosnell published *Non-Voting: Causes and Methods of Control,* one of the first studies to use actual electoral data to determine voting and non-voting behavior. By 1929 Merriam brought about creation of the Public Administration Clearing House (PACH) with support from the Laura Spelman Rockefeller Memorial. The PACH served as a coordinating group for new professional associations, linking private and public sectors in the new field of public administration. The clearinghouse did on the urban level what Merriam already had begun for social science on the national level. Merriam's liberal vision of active cooperation between associational groups served as a kind of professional analogue to Delano's idea of a "community of interest."[52]

Merriam organized beyond the department, university, and city. Between 1920 and 1926 he argued for professionalization of political science through equipment modernization, interdisciplinary cooperation, organization of professional associations, and ultimately creation of a national social science research umbrella organization. Beginning with talks before the American Political Science Association (APSA), Merriam carried his campaign to colleagues throughout the nation.[53] As a member of the APSA's Committee on Political Research, he had a hand in writing up recommendations for a permanent research committee, interdisciplinary cooperation among social scientists, and establishment of a national research council. Three follow-up conferences sponsored by the APSA seconded those suggestions.[54]

With his election in December 1925 as president of the APSA, Merriam reached the pinnacle of his profession. His presidential address summarized the new work in political science that he had encouraged for the last five years. His brother John Merriam, now a prominent philanthropic manager as president of the Carnegie Institution of Washington, D.C., wrote Charles that the head of the Carnegie Corporation had applauded the address.[55] That philanthropic managers would note Merriam's 1925 presidential address came as no surprise. Since his political reform days in Chicago, Merriam had built ties to organized philanthropy and extended them to the national level through his work with Beardsley Ruml of the Laura Spelman Rockefeller Memorial. These ties proved valuable assets in the 1920s, for Merriam's direction of a series of studies on civic education in Russia, Great Britain, the Austro-Hungarian empire, Italy, Germany, Switzerland, France, and the United States depended on financial support from the LSRM. Merriam hired prominent scholars in the social sciences to research and write individual volumes in the series, which was published by the University of Chicago Press with additional monies from the LSRM.[56]

In the summary volume of the civic education series, *The Making of Citizens* (1931), Merriam once again revealed his belief in American uniqueness and the strength of the nation's democratic politics. Arguing that traditional factors in civic training had declined, Merriam saw the rise of systematic efforts at inculcation of national values that might be used by various interest groups for different ends.[57] While he claimed to write a cross-national comparison of systems, Merriam's overwhelming support for the American school, political party system, and scientific understanding of politics belied the claim to objectivity. At the same time, Merriam sat on the American Historical Association's Commission on Social Studies, funded by the Carnegie Corporation and the Common-wealth Fund. Despite differences with committee members Charles Beard and George Counts, Merriam once again advocated reconciling science, politics, and democracy in *Civic Education in the United States* (1934), written for the commission.[58]

If Merriam remained ambiguous about the proper relationship be-tween social science and civic education, he did not equivocate on the organization and professionalization of the social sciences. After his turn away from partisan reform politics in 1919, he moved toward more prac-tical research and argued that research agencies should move beyond par-tisan work. As part of his ongoing attempt to reconcile politics, social science, and democracy, Merriam pursued national organization of the social sciences. Creation of the Social Science Research Council in 1923 represented the culmination of Merriam's work as a manager of social science. By concentrating on people (personnel), funds (budgets), and administration (organizational structure), he moved toward the institu-tionalization of American social science research as an ongoing, advi-sory process.[59]

Establishment of the SSRC paralleled developments in the natural sci-ences and the humanities that had led to creation of the National Re-search Council (NRC) in 1916 and the American Council of Learned Societies (ACLS) in 1920. All three groups brought together professional associations in a national umbrella group that could then seek funding, organize long-term research agendas, and coordinate the distribution and use of new knowledge to meet the challenges of modern American life. Leading scholars in research committees of the American Political Sci-ence Association (APSA), the American Sociological Society (ASS), and the American Economic Association (AEA) decided that neither the NRC nor the ACLS could serve the purpose of unifying the various so-cial sciences. Meeting jointly in December 1922 in Chicago, the APSA, the ASS, and later the AEA formed the core of the SSRC. Originally called the Social Research Council after its model, the NRC, the SSRC sought to promote the very ideas and experimentation through innova-tive methods that Merriam advocated. While Merriam hardly organized the council single-handedly, his initiative, professional reputation, skilled use of associational contacts, forceful lobbying for philanthropic monies, and leadership of the SSRC in its formative years place him at center stage of this national social science organization. In 1927 he was replaced by institutional economist Wesley Clair Mitchell; together they worked with Presidents Herbert Hoover and Franklin Roosevelt to advance advisory national planning.[60]

That its founders envisioned the SSRC at first as part of the NRC stemmed from more than coincidence. Merriam's elder brother, John, who had become a full professor and dean at the University of California, Berkeley, had served as president of the NRC in 1919 and now had wide-ranging philanthropic contacts as president of the Carnegie Institution of Washington, D.C. Charles Merriam took advantage of his brother's network to correspond with two key people, Robert M. Yerkes and Beardsley Ruml. Yerkes, a well-known behavioral psychologist, headed the Research Information Service of the NRC, on which John Merriam had served previously. Yerkes had been appointed director of a special Committee on the Scientific Problems of Human Migration of the NRC. Through personal research interests and the prodding of Mary Van Kleeck of the Russell Sage Foundation, Charles Merriam moved toward cooperation with the NRC on this project. Consulting with his brother John, Yerkes, and director Ruml of the Laura Spelman Rockefeller Memorial, Charles Merriam found personal, institutional, and financial support that got the SSRC off the ground. By the end of the 1920s the SSRC served as an autonomous professional organization for the social sciences in America while institutionally complementing the work of the NRC and the ACLS.[61]

More important for the long-range survival and growth of the council, Merriam and Ruml became close personal and professional friends, a relationship that continued for the remainder of their lives. Recognizing that Ruml's interest in promoting a planned national program of research in the social sciences sponsored by the LSRM could serve his own interests, Merriam quickly moved to cooperate with the NRC on the migration study, which was financed by the LSRM. Following the example set by the NRC's use of a $5-million grant from the Carnegie Corporation, Merriam used the initial support from the LSRM for the NRC-SSRC migration project to advocate more extensive philanthropic sponsorship of the council's work in its early years. By the early 1930s SSRC reliance on LSRM aid weakened the social science research effort, but in the 1920s this help was indispensable.[62]

The initial plan for financing the SSRC stemmed from Merriam's experience with Chicago philanthropies in the Progressive Era. The SSRC hoped to propose joint funding by the Russell Sage Foundation, the LSRM, the Carnegie Corporation, and the Commonwealth Fund for a five-year budget to cover administrative expenses. The idea worked for the first five years, but increasing involvement in an expanding program and administrative structure led the SSRC to seek most of its funds from the LSRM via the Merriam-Ruml link. In late 1927 the LSRM appropriated $1,765,000 for administrative costs, research projects, a journal of social science abstracts, and continued funding of an annual conference at Hanover, New Hampshire, on the Dartmouth University campus, Ruml's undergraduate alma mater.[63]

During the New Era, Merriam worked at various levels to achieve his hope of scientizing, professionalizing, and unifying the social sciences. He was now at the zenith of his professional career as a political scientist—appointed chairman of the Political Science Department at the University of Chicago (1923), elected chairman of the SSRC (1923), and selected by his peers as president of the APSA (1925). The SSRC consolidated its position as the national association for the social sciences bringing in not only the original core of the APSA, ASS, and AEA but also the American Statistical Association, the American Psychological Association, the American Historical Association, and the American Anthropological Association. The council forged financial links with modern philanthropy through the LSRM, began an abstracting service, created the Committee on Problems and Policy, which planned the research agenda, and started its fellowship program with additional LSRM support. Complex interlocking friendships, professional correspondence, and institutional ties built a network that Merriam used to link together private and public sector research agencies, private philanthropies, and professional associations rapidly gaining reputations for the expertise of their members. Merriam's social science research network paralleled Delano's associational city and regional planning networks of the same decade.[64]

In 1926–27 philanthropic managers led by Bearsdley Ruml of the LSRM tried to recruit Merriam as organizer of a social science research network in Europe to parallel that in the United States. After discussing the matter at length with his brother John, Merriam decided to accept the offer, but severe medical problems with ulcers, perhaps brought on by the fast-paced organizational activity of the preceding years, forestalled the effort. Declining the proffered position reluctantly, Merriam did accept special consultant status with the Rockefeller Foundation and later took control of the newly organized Spelman Fund of New York, which took over some of the LSRM's work after reorganization of the Rockefeller philanthropies in the late 1920s.[65] Begun in 1927, these reorganization plans led to abolition of the LSRM, creation of the Social

Sciences Division of the foundation, and establishment of the Spelman Fund initially headed by Ruml, who was later succeeded by Merriam. Until its own abolition in 1948, the Spelman Fund supported research and training in the field of public administration, the very field Merriam had pioneered in the Progressive Era.[66]

Despite his rhetorical disclaimers to the contrary regarding noninvolvement of social scientists in partisan policy research throughout this period, Merriam did not in fact oppose such work. For the rest of his life, Merriam advocated creating centers for research and training of public administrators.[67] His work as a manager of social science led him to an ideology of advisory planning in which social scientists would serve as a mediating force between political leaders, interest groups, and the "mass" of the citizenry. Merriam's support of such work complemented analogous efforts by such organizations as Luther Gulick's Institute for Public Administration, the Brookings Institution, Louis Brownlow's Public Administration Clearing House, and Wesley Clair Mitchell's National Bureau of Economic Research. Not surprisingly, Merriam's next social science venture brought him to public advisory work for the President's Research Committee on Social Trends (PRCST), 1929–33, sponsored by Herbert Hoover.[68]

The PRCST's massive, two-volume summary study *Recent Social Trends in the United States* and its accompanying thirteen volumes of specialized studies was the landmark social science investigation of the 1920s. Planned by a committee of the SSRC, financed by the Rockefeller Foundation with a huge grant of $560,000, researched from late 1929 to the spring of 1933, the study altered the direction and use of social science research in the United States. The President's Research Committee on Social Trends, originally called the Committee on Social Research, looked in two directions at once, serving as the culmination of New Era social science and its ad hoc associational planning institutions and also setting precedents for more statist-oriented planning in the New Deal. In its formative years from 1923 through 1929, the SSRC under Merriam's leadership had moved to expand its definition of social research. New committees arose to advise various private and public agencies on the feasibility and utility of social research, to plan long-range programs in research, to promote the idea of cooperative group research, and to move such research in the direction of studying current social problems. Merriam played key parts in initiating, financing, writing, and timing the release of the PRCST's study.

As early as the spring of 1928, Merriam had begun discussing such a study with members of the SSRC and one member of the NRC. Merriam's policy orientation arose from his concern that "one such case so determined with the aid of technical experts would go a long way toward influencing the community toward the use of similar devices in dealing with other knotty problems."[69] He discussed the idea with Robert Lynd of the SSRC and a year later raised the idea with his brother John, who concluded, Merriam later wrote, that "President Hoover would be very friendly toward any type of scientific research relating to the work of the government."[70] Broaching the topic to Arthur Woods of the Rockefeller Foundation, Merriam set the project in motion.[71]

The resulting investigation looked like a prime example of New Era social science research, bringing together Merriam and other representatives of the SSRC, managers from the Rockefeller Foundation who discussed the idea at the 1929 Hanover conference, and President Hoover's administrative assistant French Strother. After meeting with Strother, SSRC agent William F. Ogburn, a prominent sociologist who had just moved from Columbia to the University of Chicago, arranged a dinner conference at the White House on September 6, 1929. President Hoover met with Strother, Secretary of the Interior Ray Lyman Wilbur, Howard Odum of the Institute for Research in Social Science at the University of North Carolina and the SSRC, Wesley Clair Mitchell of the National Bureau of Economic Research, Merriam, and Shelby Harrison of the Russell Sage Foundation. Hoover hoped to put together a research committee to survey social problems and suggest ways to enact a reform program under the direction of Secretary of the Interior Wilbur.[72]

From the start, Hoover assistants French Strother and Edward Eyre Hunt made it clear that the president intended to use the committee's reports for practical, partisan political purposes of reform. Committee members initially agreed, although later some changed their minds. Hoover intended to rebuild the Department of the Interior employing similar techniques to those used over the past decade to reorganize and transform the Department of Commerce.[73] He envisioned public hearings, a blue-ribbon committee of cabinet officials sitting with leading social scientists, and private, voluntary philanthropic financing. The committee quickly dropped the ideas for public hearings and cabinet participation; however, discussion of financing revealed the complex interplay among government officials, social scientists, and philanthropists. In its prospectus for the study, the committee suggested three alternatives for control of funding: by a single university such as Chicago, which had offered its services; by the SSRC; or directly by the committee itself. After much discussion, committee members followed President Hoover's suggestion to leave the decision to Rockefeller Foundation representatives, who chose to leave control in the committee's hands. The SSRC acted as fiscal agent responsible for disbursing the $560,000 grant appropriated by the Rockefeller Foundation in early December 1929.[74]

Barry Karl, Merriam's biographer and historian of the PRCST, argues that over the course of the study some of the members became wary of Hoover's intention to use the reports before publication. Merriam in particular raised objections to "leaking" the reports in the depths of the Depression and the middle of the presidential election of 1932. Karl interprets Merriam's objections as an indication of his unwillingness to become involved in partisan politics. The evidence indicates, however, a more complex reason. Merriam agreed with Hoover on the purposes for the study but disagreed on the usefulness of this kind of social science research. Hoover anticipated direct application of the research results to immediate problems in the social welfare field. Merriam saw a more long-range function for the committee that was reflected in the work he did while on the PRCST.[75]

Appropriately, Merriam's essay "Government and Society" served as the conclusion to the two-volume final report of over 1,500 pages. Merriam both summarized the evolution of his own thinking of the last decade and hinted at the direction of his activities as a New Deal planner in the decade to come by drawing on ideas developed in *American Political Ideas, New Aspects of Politics,* and less well known work for the APSA and the SSRC. Beginning with the idea of social lag he had first proposed in 1920, Merriam argued that the enormous social changes wrought by the rise of national business corporations, the development of politically influential interest groups, the extension of governmental powers, the strengthening of the executive branch in relation to the legislative branch, and the full-blown emergence of the urban-industrial world of the organized society had surpassed both the ideas of political theorists and the powers of the national government to promote social control by maintaining political and social equilibrium. In the essay Merriam did not propose any solutions of either a general or a particular nature. A reading of the two-volume report suggests that Merriam had little influence on the final product as a whole.[76]

Yet Merriam played the central part in the most explosive section of the final report—the deceptively simple "Review of Findings," which introduced the published summary volumes. The editorial evolution of this section tells an interesting story. Early on, economist Wesley Clair

Mitchell, director of the study, accepted the task of writing the introductory remarks. Yet Merriam, not Mitchell, penned the initial draft introduction of June 1932. Mitchell's own first draft received a scathing review from sociologist William F. Ogburn, who suggested massive revision. When the editorial smoke cleared, Mitchell's revision of his own draft served as the published, printed version. Yet Mitchell relied heavily on an unpublished version of Merriam's draft for key sections of the final draft.[77]

This 1932 document revealed Merriam's evolving ideas on national planning that he later took into his role as New Deal planner. In the draft he used fiery prose uncharacteristic of his usual writing style. Merriam began by stating his implicit difference with President Hoover: "For the first time in the history of the United States, the Chief Executive of the Nation has called upon a group of social scientists to examine and report upon the recent social trends in this country, with a view to providing such a review of the lines of development as might serve as a basis of formulation of large national policies looking to the next period in the Nation's growth. . . . We have not construed our duty as ending with the delivery of a set of carefully prepared special reports, but have included the larger responsibility of turning public attention to new directions and to other levels of thinking."[78] He continued in noting that the committee functioned as a social research group that not only analyzed recent social trends between 1900 and 1930 but also pointed out emerging problems and stated recommendations. Presenting his own view of modernized liberalism, Merriam drew attention to the organized, institutional components of this new form of liberalism:

> Important factors in the field of institutions are the rise of the school and of scientific research, the emergence of women in industry and the accompanying weakening of the family, the fixation of interest on the welfare of the child, the growth of governmental functions and expenditures, the growth of public and private philanthropy, the weakening of labor and agriculture with the rise of economic concentrations and their dominant position in industrial life, the emergence of the metropolitan region and the decline and reorientation of the rural areas, the emergence of leisure time on a greater scale than before and the accompanying problem of recreation, the increasing growth of attention to art, the unexampled rise of medical care, the shift in social and religious attitudes, the course of organized religion, the lag in plans for integration and organization of governmental, industrial and social life. [79]

Merriam cataloged this list of emerging social problems that, he argued, had surged ahead of any attempts to deal with them. He proposed no radical solutions but, rather, insisted on the need to promote socioeconomic stability through the mechanisms of a transformed liberalism. In order to bring about "closer coordination and more effective integration," Merriam suggested "the creation of ways and means for political realization—social planning in the broadest sense of the term."[80]

What Merriam meant by such social planning is suggested in the boldest section of his draft (incorporated almost verbatim into the published version signed by Mitchell), where he proposed the creation of an "advisory National Council, representative of scientific, educational, governmental, economic and other appropriate elements" appointed by the president on the nomination of the SSRC.[81] As in the past, Merriam emphasized the need for planning at the national level as a process changing over time, advisory in nature, staffed by social scientists, and final policy decision making conducted by elected political leaders.[82] Merriam's ideal of national planning stemmed from his own personal, professional, and organizational experience in an American national context: "The type of planning now most urgently required is neither economic planning alone, nor governmental planning alone. The new synthesis must include the scientific, the educational, as well as the economic, (including here the industrial and the agricultural) and also the governmental. . . . Furthermore, it is important not to overstate the aspect either of integration or centralism in control, or of governmentalism. The unity here presented as essential to rounded social development may be achieved partly within and through the government and partly within other institutions and through other than governmental agencies."[83] Should the nation fail to adopt such measures, Merriam feared and deplored the possible alternative courses of development: "The alternative to such a type of social initiative may conceivably be a prolongation of a policy of disintegration and perhaps some automatic readjustment as time goes on. More definite alternatives, however, are urged by fascist or dictatorial planning and by communistic planning, in both of which the factors of force and violence loom large. In either of these cases the basic decisions are frankly imposed by power groups, and violence subordinates intelligence in social guidance."[84]

Merriam had arrived at a tentative definition of national planning as a kind of voluntary associationalism involving governmental action guided by the advice of the new social sciences *along with* a continuation of private organizational activity advocated by such diverse groups as those gathered around Herbert Hoover, the United States Chamber of Commerce, various business trade associations, a second generation of philanthropies adopting the corporate methods of big business, and some within the executive ranks of the American Federation of Labor. In moving one step beyond Hoover's insistence on purely private voluntarism, Merriam was ready for Franklin Roosevelt and the New Deal. His conception of national planning—reached by quite a different experience than that of Frederic Delano—emerged from his own intellectual development, professional research, political reform efforts in Progressive Era Chicago, and associational activities as a social science activist between 1917 and 1933. Yet in a broader sense, Merriam's ideal of national planning closely paralleled that of Delano. Barry Karl accurately summarizes the impact of Merriam's involvement with Hoover's President's Research Committee on Social Trends in noting that "social science entered the New Deal in a much more political form as the new experts sought to engage more actively in the political process itself."[85]

Charles E. Merriam had been a lifelong Republican, but his politics were independent and open to change. His old friend and campaign manager from the 1911 Chicago mayoral race, Harold L. Ickes, took a similar view. As Hoover retreated from the implications of his voluntarist stance in using the Reconstruction Finance Corporation and the Agricultural Marketing Act of 1929 to promote industrial and agricultural recovery in the midst of the most severe economic downturn in U.S. history, he moved forward toward the more statist programs of the New Deal. To the end of his life, Merriam credited Hoover with starting national planning, pointing to the President's Research Committee on Social Trends as an important precedent. The move into the administration of Franklin Delano Roosevelt under his longtime friends Harold L. Ickes, now the secretary of the Interior and public works administrator, and Frederic A. Delano came easily for Merriam.[86]

On July 26, 1933, President Roosevelt, on the advice of Ickes, appointed Merriam, Delano, and Wesley Clair Mitchell to the National Planning Board. Merriam had reached the center of national power and influence in the New Deal. Years later, he recalled his admiration for Franklin D. Roosevelt: "He was quite willing to discuss any matter that came along in the realm of governmental affairs. And he seemed to discuss it all in a rather relaxed way. I suppose he was relaxed because he knew we weren't going to ask him for jobs, contracts, grants-in-aid, or what not. And when he was in a relaxed mood, he let his mind play freely over the whole range of governmental responsibilities—in a sense leaving him out of the picture. I've never seen anyone who would discuss power as objectively as he would—as if he had nothing much to do with it; as if he were looking into a picture, seeing what was happening, but himself out of it. If he did, he had it skillfully concealed. There was no need of his concealing it from us—he trusted us."[87] The next ten years showed that Merriam did not understand Roosevelt as well as he later thought. His trust in executive-branch power through the office of a strong presidency led by Franklin D. Roosevelt led to heated ideological debates over national planning that gave the lie to Merriam's repeatedly stated concern for promoting social stability through a harmonious reconciliation of political leadership, social science expertise, and democracy defined as organized interest-group cooperation among voluntary associations.

Wesley Clair Mitchell and Economic Research

BUSINESS CYCLES, SOCIAL SCIENCE, AND HOOVERIAN PLANNING

AMERICA'S NATIONAL PLANNERS sought to ease the transition from the world of the late nineteenth century to that of the twentieth century. Each of the planners, however, took a somewhat different road to the New Deal planning agency. Like political scientist Charles E. Merriam, institutional economist Wesley Clair Mitchell argued that twentieth-century social science expertise could help to make for better public policy. As the nation's leading institutional economist, he specialized in researching fluctuations in the business cycle in order to move beyond crisis-oriented policies. As cofounder and research director of the National Bureau of Economic Research, which conducted many of the technical economic studies for Secretary of Commerce Herbert Hoover's committee and conference system in the 1920s, he brought a wealth of professional experience and wide contacts in the social scientific community to New Deal planning. No wonder New Deal Brain Truster Adolf A. Berle, Jr., called him "the greatest American economic scholar of the twentieth century," who "gave the best of his thought to governmental research and planning."[1]

Mitchell began his professional evolution as an economist through education at the new University of Chicago and a series of academic appointments at some of the nation's leading universities. His early work on prices, the money system, and statistical study of various parts of the business cycle led to a growing reputation in academic circles that then broadened into government work in the 1917–33 period. In the wake of his Progressive Era renown as the nation's expert on business-cycle research, Mitchell's reputation blossomed during wartime work with the War Industries Board, while his recognition of the need for a new agency that could collect and analyze economic statistics led to founding of the NBER in 1920. During and after the President's Unemployment Conference of 1921, Mitchell's NBER conducted most of the technical economic research and reporting that committees growing out of that conference used as part of Secretary of Commerce Hoover's building of the associative state. As head of the NBER, Mitchell directed these studies throughout the 1920s while cooperating with Charles Merriam, whom he succeeded as head of the Social Science Research Council, which brought together social science expertise from across many academic disciplines. Like Merriam, Mitchell came to rely on the private, voluntary network of organized philanthropies to finance New Era associational efforts sponsored by the federal government. Between 1921 and 1929, using this new kind of private-public partnership, Merriam and Mitchell helped to build the institutional infrastructure of Hooverian planning that culminated logically in the nation's first quasi-planning effort created by President Herbert Hoover in 1929. Between 1929 and 1933 they collaborated as leaders of the President's Research Committee on Social Trends, which recommended creation of a national planning board. Not surprisingly, they were two of Franklin Roosevelt's choices, along with Delano, to lead the experiment in New Deal planning from 1933 to 1943.

Mitchell used his experience in the war-mobilization agencies of 1917–18 to identify lags in the collection, analysis, and use of economic data that could be helpful in developing policies aimed at controlling the economic and social impact of changes in the course of the business cycle. In 1920 he cofounded the NBER, which became one of the most important economic research agencies in twentieth-century America.[2] Responding to the postwar boom and depression between 1919 and 1921, Mitchell and the NBER began a long-term research effort to develop new statistical series for national income. Their collective expertise led to active cooperation with Secretary of Commerce Hoover under the auspices of the President's Conference on Unemployment to lay the foundation for a voluntarist form of national planning. Hoover and Mitchell, using their respective staffs in the Department of Commerce and the NBER, learned to promote private- and public-sector cooperation between delegates to the conference representing major economic interest groups and the federal government. In the course of the 1920s

Mitchell and Hoover established what can be termed associative national planning, which brought together the executive branch of the federal government, private-sector economic-interest groups, a second generation of organizationally minded philanthropies, and newly emerging research organizations in the social sciences such as the Merriam-inspired Social Science Research Council and the Mitchell-led NBER.[3] Between 1929 and 1933 Mitchell and the NBER's work with subcommittees from the 1921 Unemployment Conference culminated in two landmark social science studies, *Recent Economic Changes* (1929) and *Recent Social Trends* (1933). As research director of the President's Research Committee on Social Trends (1929–33), Mitchell worked closely with vice chairman Charles Merriam and other representatives of the burgeoning social sciences to make the transition from the ad hoc, voluntarist planning efforts of the New Era to the more institutionalized, statist-oriented planning efforts of the New Deal by way of various cross-sectoral institutions in the Hoover network. In its final report, the committee called for the establishment of an advisory national planning agency.[4] In July 1933 Mitchell joined Delano and Merriam on the New Deal planning board. Intellectual evolution as an institutional economist, economic expertise on business cycles, leadership of the NBER, use of the expanding networks of the rapidly expanding American social sciences financed by organized philanthropy, and service on various Hooverian groups constituted Mitchell's road to Depression-era national planning.

Mitchell's path to planning had some similarities to that of Delano and Merriam. Coming from a comfortable family background, he was able to take advantage of a superb education and entrée into the institutional arena of professional economics in the nation's leading research universities.[5] Born as the second son into a middle-class family of seven children in Rushville, Illinois, on August 5, 1874, Mitchell made good as his father had not. His father, a promising physician, had served in the medical corps of the Union army during the Civil War, only to come home maimed by a war wound. Taking up farming in the Midwest, Mitchell placed his hopes in his talented son Wesley. After a brilliant four years in Decatur High School and additional college preparatory study, in 1892 Mitchell entered the first class at the University of Chicago, which became one of the finest research-oriented universities in the nation. Soon abandoning classics for economics under the tutelage of classical economist J. Laurence Laughlin, Mitchell proved an unorthodox student of economics. Broadening his interests under the stimulation of philosopher John Dewey, the father of pragmatism, and gadfly institutional economist

Thorstein Veblen, who insisted on the importance of psychology, institutions, and historical perspective as part of the economic method, Mitchell studied not only economics and philosophy but also psychology, anthropology, and history. Seeing that classical economics often stemmed from deduction, rather than careful empirical study, early in his intellectual development Mitchell focused on the institutional, historical, and, later, statistical components of economics. In 1896 he received his doctoral degree in economics, *summa cum laude,* with a minor in philosophy.[6]

After a one-year stint with the Division of Methods and Results in the Census Office in Washington, D.C., and two years as an instructor in economics at the University of Chicago, Mitchell entered a period of teaching and intense study from 1903 to 1912 at the University of California, Berkeley, interrupted only by a one-year lectureship at Harvard in 1908. His early economic research involved the history of the greenback money experiment, using statistical methods to collect and analyze fluctuations in prices, which in turn led Mitchell to investigate the statistical complexities regarding changes in wages, interest, rent, and profits over the entire period of greenback use. Following publication of his first two books, *A History of the Greenbacks, with Special Reference to the Economic Consequences of Their Issue: 1862–65* (1903) and *Gold, Prices, and Wages under the Greenback Standard* (1908), Mitchell's intellectual interests broadened as he developed a new course in economic history, realized the significance of statistical information on prices, and investigated the link between human behavior and the price system. Early on, Mitchell began addressing the gap between economic theory; the collection, availability, and utility of statistical economic knowledge; and the role of the business cycle in implementing human wants and needs. His increasing emphasis on the need to improve economic knowledge through inductive, factual, and statistical methods led to a lifetime interest in business cycles. If economists could understand the statistical specifics of the business cycle, they might one day be able to both understand and control the course of the cycle at both the microeconomic and macroeconomic levels of the firm and government policies. In his early growth as an academic economist from 1903 to 1912, Mitchell's decision to focus on the empirical study of the business cycle established his name and professional reputation. Shortly after his marriage to Lucy Sprague, daughter of a prominent Chicago grocer and first dean of women at the University of California, Berkeley, Mitchell moved to Columbia University, already a mature scholar.

In 1913 he published the seminal work, *Business Cycles,* which reoriented the study of that subject with the use of sophisticated statistical data, placed it on the map of professional economics, and made it a permanent area of study for the new NBER from the 1920s to the present. In pointing to the centrality of private business corporations and managerial decisions in seeking profit through industrial production, Mitchell focused on businesses as the most important economic institutions in modern America. Yet as an institutional economist strongly influenced by Veblen, Mitchell distinguished between the private, voluntarist efforts of business leaders and the public, socially responsible ends of industrial production in the national economy. In seeking profits above all else, business leaders sometimes engaged in socially costly behaviors such as wasting natural resources and using child labor. In 1913 Mitchell called for practical efforts to meet the challenge of understanding and dealing with the recurring business cycle through such methods as reform of the banking system, monetary stability, new government policies for spending during depression rather than prosperity, and sharing business information beyond the narrow range of business and financial leaders. Business profit-seeking could be balanced by social provision via government efforts at understanding and, perhaps someday, controlling the business cycle as it worked through alternating phases of prosperity, crisis, depression, and revival. Mitchell implicitly was moving toward a kind of planning process that went beyond a nineteenth-century economics that was voluntarist, and dominated by the private sector, but he stopped short of a full-blown twentieth-century, statist Keynesian economics. Rather than focus on the work of individual entrepreneurs and firms, he suggested coordinating economic activity among business firms and between business and government, thus balancing the private-profit motive with the public responsibility to deal with the social impact of economic change. He emphasized the need for government collection of economic statistics and cooperation with businesses to iron out peaks and troughs in the cycle that brought forth growth, prosperity, lags between production and consumption, crisis, and downturn. Once business leaders had access to accurate, reliable information via economists working with the government, they could hopefully correct for part of the cyclic impact on production, prices, consumption, and employment. Later commentators noted that Mitchell spent most of his professional career engaged in the collection and analysis of technical data, leaving the policy implications to his professional successors. Mitchell's intellectual evolution as an academic economist presaged a lifelong career in economic research, practical use of statistical data, and recognition of the growing complexity of business-government relations. In becoming the nation's leading expert on business cycles, which had disrupted the national economy since the onset of industrial cycles of boom and bust since the 1870s, Mitchell soon advocated better understanding and control of business cycles as wartime mobilizer, founder of the National Bureau of Economic Research, and Hooverian planner in the 1920s. By the eve of the Great War, Mitchell had established his intellectual reputation as one of the nation's leading economists.[7] Not surprisingly, he was called on to help with economic advising by the federal government after U.S. entry into the Great War.

Work with wartime planners Edwin F. Gay and Henry S. Dennison during the economic mobilization effort of 1917–18 led to Mitchell's appointment as chief of the Price Section of the War Industries Board (WIB). In his prewar research, Mitchell had abandoned the nineteenth-century tradition of classical economics as based on deductive and simplistic reasoning without examination of actual economic institutions and data. During the war Mitchell conducted price studies for the U.S. Shipping Board and the WIB and tried to improve government statistical services by establishing with Gay the Central Bureau of Planning and Statistics as a federal clearinghouse to coordinate the flow of economic information. Abolition of the bureau after the war appalled Mitchell, who saw even this wartime effort as too small in scale and scope, held back by the limited number of technical experts.[8]

Distraught at the small number of trained, experienced statisticians caught up in the ill-coordinated mobilization agencies of World War I, Mitchell used his presidential address to the December 1918 convention of the American Statistical Association to exhort his fellow statisticians and economists to cooperate with federal officials in the postwar era. From his work amassing economic data, constructing useful comparative statistical series, and promoting both professionalism in economics and cooperation among businesses, social researchers, and the federal government, Mitchell recognized a national need. In 1920 he joined with Gay, a German-trained economic historian and first dean of the Harvard Business School, to found the National Bureau of Economic Research. With financial aid from several private philanthropies, it promoted the scientific study of national income distribution with the help of two of Mitchell's former students at Columbia, Frederick R. Macaulay and Oswald W. Knauth, and Williford I. King, a former student and colleague of economist John R. Commons at the University of Wisconsin. Mitchell thus moved beyond the confines of Columbia University and the economics profession into a broader institutional realm connecting economic research, government sponsorship, and philanthropic assistance through the NBER at the same time that Delano, Merriam, Dennison, and Ruml were doing so in other fields. The decade of the 1920s saw Mitchell, Merriam, and Ruml join in organizing the Social Science Research Council, with Mitchell succeeding Merriam as chairman from 1927 to 1929. For Mitchell and the other planners, the 1920s brought partial fruition of their hopes for social science research and its utility in public-policy making.[9]

Between 1922 and 1924 Mitchell's NBER conducted research for subcommittees of the President's Conference on Unemployment on business cycles and unemployment and seasonal operation in the construction industries. Between January 1928 and February 1929 the NBER completed the first national economic survey of the United States, resulting in a two-volume summary work, *Recent Economic Changes.* Chaired by Mitchell, this study brought together private research institutes, trade association officials, and staff members of various government agencies, including Herbert Hoover's newly reorganized Department of Commerce. Mitchell wrote the concluding review chapter, which summarized much of the NBER's work for the Hooverian subcommittees of the 1920s. Not surprisingly, the sister study, *Recent Social Trends,* conducted between late 1929 and early 1933, brought together Mitchell as chairman and Merriam as vice chairman. Financial support for the former study came from the Carnegie Corporation and the Laura Spelman Rockefeller Memorial, headed by Beardsley Ruml, while the lion's share of monetary support for the latter study came from the LSRM and its successor, the Social Science Division of the Rockefeller Foundation. Supporting information and technical advice came from the burgeoning nexus of social science research institutions backed by support of the SSRC and the federal government.[10]

During the New Era of the 1920s, Secretary of Commerce Herbert Hoover set pre-New Deal precedents for American national planning. Drawing on his experiences as manager of the wartime Commission for Relief in Belgium and the Food Administration and postwar work as head of the American Relief Administration in Europe, Hoover set the pace for planning in reaction to the depression following the end of the Great War. Yet Hoover did not act alone; he served as symbolic leader in an evolving, yet fragile network of ad hoc, cross-sectoral planning institutions created in response to the depression of 1920–21. Mitchell, one of Hoover's planners, helped lay the groundwork for a distinctly American form of voluntary national planning that was used throughout the New

Era of managerial capitalism in the 1920s. Between 1921 and 1933 representatives of the state, social science research organizations, corporate business, and philanthropic foundations cooperated to form this planning network. By the mid-1920s Hoover and a close aide referred to these planning projects as the "committee and conference system."[11]

As secretary of commerce, and later as president, Hoover served as midwife to New Era national planning, assisted by Mitchell and the NBER. As head of the Department of Commerce from 1921 to 1929, Hoover presided over piecemeal planning for economic standardization and rationalization, stabilization of the "sick" economic sectors, promotion of emerging economic sectors, and the search for a voluntarist conception of national planning. Hoover's attempts to build what Ellis Hawley has termed the associative state reveal a picture at odds with a post-New Deal understanding of the relationship among the planning ideal, the institutional capacity for planning, and the people who planned. Contrary to the view that, by definition, national planning must inherently stem from the coercive efforts of a farseeing state working through clearly defined public-sector institutions, planning in the Hoover years was voluntarist and advisory in a form that was far more complex—and ambiguous—than a later statist view of American national planning remembered.[12]

Hoover and his expert advisers like Mitchell hoped to bridge the growing gap between nineteenth-century liberal values and the realities of the twentieth-century corporatist society. Hoover saw in American society the atomistic, self-interested individuals of Adam Smith's self-regulating world struggling to survive in the organizational context of group power permeated by the corporate model of the hierarchical, functionally oriented, administrative structure first established by national business corporations in the late nineteenth century. Hoping to preserve the liberal values of republican America—individual liberty, private property, the work ethic, socioeconomic mobility, and a stable economy dominated by private-sector activity—Hoover sought to create new institutional avenues of opportunity through the transformation of the ideal and institutional representations of voluntary association. Hooverian loyalists, social scientists, businessmen, and philanthropic managers cooperated to build the Hooverian planning network. As research director of the National Bureau of Economic Research, Mitchell worked at the center of this planning apparatus. In emphasizing a new role for organized group knowledge, power, and influence in policy making, Mitchell and Hoover with the individual and organizational help of hundreds of

Hooverian activists built what may be termed associative national planning. Never intending to create permanent public-sector bases to institute planning, they nevertheless brought together a congeries of planning groups from the public, public-private, and private sectors that moved beyond the nineteenth-century liberal distinction between separate private- and public-sector activity.[13]

Social scientists like Mitchell and Merriam—along with Hoover, his loyal aides, corporate managers, and a growing corps of interest-group leaders—acted within the historical context of America's mobilization for the Great War in 1917–18 and the subsequent postwar reconstruction debate between 1919 and 1921. In the work of the war-mobilization agencies—the Commission for Relief in Belgium, the Committee on Public Information, the War Industries Board, the Food and Fuel Administrations, and the War Labor Board—these managers qua mobilization planners sought to find hints of things to come.[14] Having erected temporary planning structures, some of Wilson's war managers tried to carry the lessons over into the period of postwar demobilization and reconstruction. Failing at that by the spring of 1919, the planners looked on as the boom of 1919–20 seemed to belie their arguments as to the need for national coordination and planning for the economic and social future of postwar America.[15]

For both Mitchell and Hoover, the postwar reconstruction period raised key issues regarding control of the business cycle and relief of unemployment that assumed increased importance following the boom and collapse of 1919–21. Between mid-July 1919 and early January 1920, the Senate Select Committee on Reconstruction and Production held hearings to determine the extent of economic dislocation in the coal and housing industries. In March 1921 the committee presented a series of recommendations to the Senate that presaged the planning effort about to begin under Hoover's tutelage. Even before his appointment as secretary of commerce in March 1921, Hoover had begun to address the problem of what he termed industrial waste. As head of the Federated American Engineering Societies, Hoover instigated the economic investigation published as *Waste in Industry* on October 29, 1921. Edward Eyre Hunt, secretary of the committee that conducted the study, wrote to Hoover that the cooperative voluntary spirit among members of the committee and use of the knowledge of engineering experts "mark an epoch." Such committee work, Hunt argued, would further the standardization drive directed by the Department of Commerce's Bureau of Standards and lay the basis for cooperation between labor and management. As a newly

appointed member of the Harding cabinet, Hoover reorganized the Department of Commerce to promote economic rationalization and stabilization. By reordering old or creating new bureaus within the department
with the help of a group of aides who had followed him from war to
postwar work, Hoover hoped to play a central role in building what later
became known as New Era capitalism. The emerging economic order
depended on the interaction of high production, high wages, and high
consumption.[16]

Before that work could start, however, Hoover and economists like
Mitchell working in groups such as the NBER faced the crisis of the
postwar depression of 1920–21. Economic collapse in the wake of the
boom of 1919–20 proved to be one of the most severe and rapid downturns of the business cycle in U.S. economic history. From the zenith of
February 1920 to its nadir in April 1921, industrial production fell 34
percent. Between July 1920 and August 1921, the wholesale price index
fell 45 percent. The Bureau of Labor Statistics index of factory employment decreased 31 percent between March 1920 and July 1921. The
money supply declined by 9 percent over the course of the cyclical downturn. The average annual unemployment rate increased from the postwar
low of 1.4 percent in 1919 to 5.2 percent in 1920 and hit the depression
peak of 11.7 percent in 1921. By 1921 almost five million people in the
civilian labor force were unemployed. At the 1921 meeting of the American Economic Association, Mitchell argued that the problem of fluctuations in the business cycle and the resulting increases in unemployment
as seen in the depression of 1920–21 called for national action.[17]

In his postpresidential memoirs Hoover drew attention to the depression, noting that "the postwar slump had deepened, and unemployment
had seriously increased."[18] In the summer of 1921, after the reorganization of the Department of Commerce had begun, Hoover conferred with
key leaders in the business community about calling a conference sponsored by the president and directed by Hoover to deal with the issue of
unemployment. The resulting President's Conference on Unemployment brought together a limited number of leaders of the business community in Washington, D.C., in the fall of 1921 to study "the unemployment situation."[19] In a telegram to the presidents of the U.S. Chamber
of Commerce, the National Association of Manufacturers, the National
Federation of Construction Industries, and the Association of Railway
Executives, Hoover explained that the conference would "endeavor to
make such constructive suggestions as may assist [the depression's] ame-
lioration during the winter and as would tend to give confidence to the

business community. . . . We will need to have some flexibility in choice [of members] so as to round out the whole conference geographically and represent the most important sectors of the community."[20]

Drawing on the staff of the Department of Commerce, representatives of the business community, experts from Mitchell's National Bureau of Economic Research, the reformist American Association for Labor Legislation, and the Taylor Society, Hoover set up an Economic Advisory Committee to plan the agenda of the Unemployment Conference. Memories of the failure of President Wilson's two industrial conferences in late 1919 and early 1920 in the wake of the steel strike of 1919 haunted Hoover, who had served as chairman of the second conference. While the advisory committee gathered, Hoover carefully selected the delegates to the conference proper so as to avoid the conflicts reflected in President Wilson's two earlier industrial conferences.[21]

In organizing the conference, Hoover brought together representatives from functional sectors of the economy, professional economists like Mitchell, various other experts, token leaders of organized labor, and "neutrals" representing the public. In early September 1921 Hoover consulted with a small group of economists from Columbia, Harvard, MIT, Cornell, and other prominent universities to determine the technical program for the public conference. The two most important of the economists were Gay and Mitchell, cofounders of the private NBER. Mitchell and his fellow economic experts at the NBER proved to be long-running players in Hoover's planning initiatives.[22]

Cooperating with the economists, the Economic Advisory Committee set the deliberative direction for the conference by calling for expert investigation and delegate discussion in committee of four major issues.

1. What was the extent of unemployment?
2. How could the conference encourage voluntary cooperation at the local level to provide relief for the unemployed?
3. Would increasing public- and private-works expenditures during this and future depressions help to stabilize the business cycle?
4. How well did economists and businessmen understand the workings of the business cycle, and could that understanding lead to control of the cycle in some way?

The conference's consideration of these questions established the framework for later national planning efforts from 1922 through 1933. Hoover hoped to use advice from business leaders and social science experts cooperating through the medium of government sponsorship. Private-sector voluntary activity with the help of the emerging social sciences could lead via public encouragement by the state to collection of accurate, scientific statistics regarding employment and unemployment. Such voluntary associative planning for immediate unemployment relief would give experience in planning for future unemployment relief. Hooverian planning also advocated the use of public works spending as a countercyclical balancing tool to even out the peaks and troughs in the business cycle. All of these efforts in turn would promote long-range economic stabilization. The planning effort focused on the need for using voluntary associational groups at the core of the planning process in order to avoid a coercive, bureaucratic state. Hoover's planners sought to employ organized institutions created by interest groups in the private sector as a means to engage in macroeconomic national planning. The role of the federal government lay in promoting these private efforts through the committee and conference system, undergirded by the research effort of Mitchell's NBER and the growing corps of social scientists now organizing under Merriam's Social Science Research Council.[23]

Functional representation of economic leaders served as the organizing principle for selection of public delegates to the conference. Hoover noted in his memoirs that "we had selected some three hundred leaders from production, distribution, banking, construction, labor and agriculture" as delegates to the Unemployment Conference, which met in Washington, D.C., between September 26 and October 13, 1921.[24] The Economic Advisory Committee determined in large part the deliberative results. Delegates accepted the experts' findings as to the extent of unemployment stemming from the downturn of the business cycle, rather than from seasonal unemployment, and their finding that most of the jobless had worked in the industrial sectors of the economy. The problem of cyclical unemployment seemed one of real concern for future investigation and planning. In regard to immediate relief, one committee member wrote that "as winter approaches every community ought to be prepared and whatever agencies—public or private—that are willing to cooperate in the relief of unemployment, should unite in a common program."[25] That program, the recommendations continued, should "consist of plans for advancing and increasing public works, of stimulating wise programs by public and private charitable and civic agencies, of strengthening family welfare agencies, of creating and directing special community and municipal activities. Most important of all is the consideration of what private employers are doing to spread employment, to undertake repairs and improvements, to manufacture wherever possible for replenishing stocks. Even the Federal Government can help in emergency measures not only through public works but in its fiscal policies in their effect upon the stimulation and revival of industry."[26]

In its final report, the conference included more extended analyses of the issues that had been posed by the Economic Advisory Committee. By September 1921, the delegates found, around three and a half million people in the non-farm labor force were unemployed. Working from the business-cycle theory developed by Mitchell in his classic 1913 work, which detailed "the rhythmical alternations of activity and stagnation so characteristic of modern business," the delegates pointed to the need for scientific collection and analysis of both cyclical and seasonal business data in order to discover ways to control or flatten out the cycle. The Committee on Public Works drew on the ideas of its chairman, Otto T. Mallery, who had developed the theory that increased public- and private works spending during economic declines in the key construction industries could help to even out the fluctuations in the business cycle.[27]

To raise immediate unemployment relief, the conference established the Civic and Emergency Measures Committee. Committee chairman Arthur Woods had worked as a businessman, the police commissioner of New York City, member of the Committee on Public Information, head of the Aviation Section of the American Expeditionary Force, and special assistant to Secretary of War Newton D. Baker in 1919 to find jobs for returning veterans.[28] The Woods Committee acted as a clearinghouse for information gathering and distribution at the state and local levels. While claiming that voluntary relief planning helped to meet the crisis of unemployment in the winter of 1921–22, the committee overlooked the facts collected by its own roving investigators. Most unemployment occurred in the industrialized cities of the Northeast, the Central Atlantic, and the Midwest. By way of President Harding's encouragement to state governors and local communities to set up governors' and mayors' committees to register the unemployed and help them find private-sector jobs, the Woods Committee hoped to avoid the European dole, reinvigorate the spirit of wartime cooperation, and preserve the national tradition of voluntary action.[29] Though the committee's public releases seemed to indicate widespread success of the relief effort, its internal records told another story. Political resistance from the mayors of New York, Chicago, and Boston prevented relief efforts in those key cities from responding effectively to the plight of the unemployed.[30] In December 1921 Mary Van Kleeck, head of the Department of Industrial Studies of the Russell Sage Foundation and delegate to the Unemployment Conference, wrote

Woods that local mayors failed to make the voluntary committees "truly representative," adding, "They are appointing business men and leaving out both labor and the social workers."[31] The foundation sponsored a study of relief efforts in fifteen cities over the winter of 1921–22, which found that local committees lacked continuity, finances, and effective relief coordination. The economic downturn of 1920–21 was too short to validate the effectiveness of this planning effort, but Hoover and veterans of the 1921 conference later assumed it had. Voluntarist unemployment relief policies from the postwar depression were carried over into the 1929–33 period, to disastrous effect.[32]

By late May 1922 Hoover concluded that "the business tide has turned," that a permanent relief administrative structure appeared to be off to a good start, and that the work of the Unemployment Conference "should all give continuing results of constructive character in dealing with these problems of the future."[33] In the aftermath of the conference, Hoover conducted a large-scale publicity campaign modeled on that of his wartime work that ignored the flaws in the committee and conference system. Still, Hoover and Mitchell took the Unemployment Conference as the starting point in their plans for "reconstruction and development," which continued throughout the New Era. The conference originally had been intended as a long-range look into the American future but had added the short-range planning perspective in response to the depression of 1920–21.[34]

Throughout his tenure as secretary of commerce, Hoover engaged in piecemeal, short-range planning aimed at stabilizing "sick" industries (such as coal and lumber) and promoting newly emerging industries (such as aviation, motion picture, and radio). These actions eventually encouraged the trade association antitrust revision movement that culminated in the New Deal's National Recovery Administration.[35] Hoover's New Era long-range planning began in 1921. In its genesis, organization, structure, deliberations, publicity, and results, the Unemployment Conference of 1921 laid the groundwork for Hoover's voluntarist form of national planning. Hoover drew a number of lessons from the planning experience of the Unemployment Conference. It confirmed his own vision of associative national planning by bringing together public-sector, cross-sectoral and private-sector organizations, as well as social science experts from universities and private research agencies such as Mitchell's NBER. Hoover loyalists provided publicity to promote voluntary cooperation rather than direct coercion by the state.

The Economic Advisory Committee assured the continuation of this planning initiative by establishing a standing committee headed by Hoover. The standing committee was authorized to appoint special committees to plan investigations of the business cycle, remedies for unemployment in seasonal industries, possibilities for unemployment insurance, and economic revival of the construction industries. Of these four potential committees, two became a reality—the Business Cycle Committee and the Committee on Seasonal Operation—both aspects of Mitchell and the NBER's long-term research program. Creation of these committees led to the committee and conference system that Hoover, his aide Edward Eyre Hunt, and his economic expert Mitchell used throughout the decade.[36]

For his associative national planning to work effectively, Hoover had to combine a number of disparate components. He needed a superb organizer loyal to his vision of cooperative planning in order to coordinate the activities of the people and organizations involved in each of the specialized planning studies. Hoover refused to seek financial support from the Congress; however, he insisted on sponsorship by the executive branch via the president, himself as secretary of commerce, or one of the newly reorganized divisions within the Department of Commerce. To finance the studies, Hoover turned to a national network of philanthropic foundations managed by a second generation of managerial trustees and directors. To conduct the technical research, he needed people like Mitchell and institutions like the NBER. As the plans shaped up, Hoover had to consider the relationship between social science expertise and policy implementation of knowledge in practical, usable form. He chose to organize each of the studies around a carefully picked coterie of loyalists who made up the sponsoring committee that directed the study, managed the policy recommendations through the deliberative process, and wrote the final report. Invariably, this committee consisted primarily of representatives of the business community, which Hoover usually equated with "the public." Under the sponsoring committee, social science experts from private-sector research organizations—often research director Mitchell of the NBER—conducted the technical investigations upon which the business delegates and the Hoover loyalists drew for final recommendations in the committee report. To promulgate information about both the investigations and the findings, Hoover relied on extensive public relations campaigns orchestrated by veterans of the Commission for Relief in Belgium, the Food Administration, the American Relief Administration, and the divisional staffers and privately hired assistants in the Department of Commerce. For implementation of the recommendations, he depended upon voluntary cooperation among private-sector businessmen, corporate managers, heads of local and state Chambers of Commerce, trade association representatives, and past and present presidents of the U.S. Chamber of Commerce and the National Association of Manufacturers. Cooperation would be elicited through personal contacts and public relations techniques.[37]

First use of this systematic approach to planning came with the Business Cycle Committee of 1921–23. Edward Eyre Hunt, a true Hoover loyalist, coordinated the actions. A former socialist from the Harvard class of 1910, which had included Walter Lippmann and John Reed, Hunt had gone to work for Hoover with the Commission for Relief in Belgium during the Great War. By 1921 he served as secretary of the Waste in Industry study, from which position he moved on to become secretary of the Unemployment Conference of 1921. Since the conference technically continued through the work of the committees appointed by the standing committee, Hunt acted as the secretary of the Business Cycle Committee. Over the course of the New Era decade, Hunt saw the work of these committees as of a single piece in the progression toward national planning. By the end of the 1920s, in correspondence with his chief, Herbert Hoover, Hunt consciously referred to the committee and conference system as "national planning."[38]

In mid-October 1921, shortly after the Unemployment Conference, Hunt wrote Hoover about the purposes of the business-cycle study. He emphasized that the work should be practical in aiming at economic stability and growth, should use the expertise of researchers in business and the social sciences, and should deal with the question of control of the cycle via dissection by economists. Mitchell and the NBER proved crucial in this regard. Hunt also wrote the proposal sent to the philanthropic foundations to fund the business-cycle investigation, using the earlier model of the Waste in Industry proposal that had been submitted successfully to the Russell Sage Foundation. At key points in the negotiations between Hoover, his philanthropic contact man, Edgar Rickard, and the philanthropic managers, Hunt stepped in to iron out any difficulties.[39]

To fund the business-cycle study, Hoover turned to three private philanthropies: the Commonwealth Fund, the Carnegie Corporation, and the Russell Sage Foundation. Following his usual practice of staying quietly out of sight, Hoover had Julius Barnes—former head of the wartime Grain Corporation, organizer and member of the Unemployment Conference, and a member of the standing committee—consult with Edgar Rickard. Rickard, a publisher of mining journals, had befriended Hoover in London in 1914, served on the executive committee of the American Relief Administration's European Children's Fund, and became Hoover's longest-tenured publicist. Rickard contacted the heads of the Commonwealth Fund and the Carnegie Corporation, sent them Hunt's memo about the study over Hoover's signature, and after denial of funding from the Commonwealth Fund, turned to the Russell Sage Foundation. The result of these complicated maneuverings brought $50,000 for the Business Cycle Committee's investigation from the Carnegie Corporation by February 1922.[40] In the midst of the negotiations, Hoover wrote Rickard about his perception of the aims of the study, perhaps unaware that his remarks would be passed on to the philanthropic managers:

> It is extremely critical that the matter should be carried out as a private undertaking under the guidance of such leading manufacturers and industrial leaders as the above mentioned. Even were it possible to obtain an appropriation from Congress for such a purpose, the character of the results would not have the weight that they will have under a committee such as this.
>
> The object of such a study is to clarify the atmosphere in the United States. There is a great under current of demand for governmental action in the matter of unemployment of the type of European countries and I believe that a careful investigation will demonstrate that such methods are not applicable nor desirable to American life but that there are constructive suggestions consonant with our own economic system that can be outlined.[41]

As secretary of commerce, Hoover, like Mitchell, sought to find an American middle way to achieve economic stabilization by way of a government-sponsored study using the economic expertise of Mitchell and the NBER. Together government officials and economists could promote macroeconomic policy making through private-sector businessmen, corporate firms, and trade associations. Voluntarist planning through state sponsorship, expertise, and business-government cooperation were well in tune with the precepts of New Era capitalism.

Hoover appointed "such leading manufacturers and industrial leaders" to the sponsoring committee on November 7, 1921, in the middle of the negotiations for financing. Owen D. Young, president of General Electric, served as chairman because of his intervention with philanthropic managers at a key point in the campaign to win support for funding the business-cycle study. The other members of the committee included Joseph H. Defrees, president of the U.S. Chamber of Commerce; Clarence M. Woolley, chairman of the American Radiator Company; Mary Van Kleeck, director of the Department of Industrial Studies of the Russell Sage Foundation; the token labor representative, Matthew Woll, of the Executive Council of the American Federation of Labor; and E. E. Hunt as secretary. All except Young had been delegates to the Unemployment Conference. Hoover appointments to the Business Cycle Committee were intended to ensure that practical use would be made of the technical study conducted by Mitchell and the staff of the National Bureau of Economic Research.[42]

While financing and committee organization proceeded, Hunt approached Edwin F. Gay and Mitchell about the NBER preparing the economic studies that would address the statistical problem of how to determine the extent and numbers of the unemployed, the relationship of unemployment to the changes in the business cycle, and the surveying of methods to prevent or dampen extreme fluctuations in the business cycle. Using a draft outline proposal written by Hunt, Mitchell worked up the final proposal, which was submitted to the philanthropic foundations and used by NBER staffers to guide research for the technical studies. They used the newly developed statistical series on production and national income developed by the NBER to calculate a range of between 15 and 20 percent differences in production between the peaks and troughs of the business cycle in recent years. In a series of policy recommendations validating his concern for the utility of economic research, Mitchell pointed to such possible methods of ameliorating the extremes of the cycle as efforts by individual firms, stabilization efforts across whole industries by trade associations, legislative proposals including monetary and banking reforms, advance planning of public works, a new system of public employment offices, forms of unemployment insurance, and upgrading of statistical services by the Department of Commerce. Not surprisingly, despite tensions between the NBER and the sponsoring committee during the spring and fall of 1922, the committee's final recommendations came very close to the ideas listed in Mitchell's proposal. Hoover and Hunt were quite pleased with the work of the Business Cycle Committee as reflected in its public report.[43] Economic historian Joseph Dorfman notes:

> The study helped to make the community business-cycle conscious; that is, that business conditions followed a recurrent pattern of boom, crash, depression, and recovery, with each phase inextricably related to the one which preceded and the one that followed. Along with this there developed an awareness of the special type of unemployment associated with the depression phase of the cycle. Prior to 1910 men thought in terms not of business cycles, but of periods of bad business and such unpredictables as money panics and

the phenomena of nature. For the most part only such unemployment as derived from seasonal fluctuations were viewed as ameliorable. The shift in emphasis from seasonal to cyclical unemployment was accompanied by a concurrent change in the attitude and requirements for ameliorative action toward the unemployed. The basis of the problem was no longer considered a matter for the affected individual but rather a subject for social (including government) action. Mitchell's work thus played a large role in the shift to this more socially meaningful and humane viewpoint.[44]

Mitchell and the NBER had brought their social science expertise to bear on the problems of depression and seasonal and cyclical unemployment that later Hoover committees continued to research. Later work by committees from the Unemployment Conference of 1921 followed up on many of Mitchell's suggestions.

Long before public release of the final report on April 2, 1923, coordinator Hunt worked at publicizing the committee's work and the value of Mitchell and the NBER's technical investigations. He had reason for concern. John B. Andrews, longtime secretary of the American Association for Labor Legislation, had advocated passage of unemployment compensation legislation at the state level since 1914.[45] In the midst of the Business Cycle Committee's deliberations, Andrews wrote Hunt that only through direct state action could "the financial burden [be placed] upon the business managers and thereby keep them thinking about this problem in good times as well as in times of business depression."[46] Shortly after publication and release of the final report, the president of the National Unemployment League wrote Hunt that "the Report is a very great disappointment to me, as it does not seem to deal so much with the suffering and plight of the unemployed and with remedial measures for their relief in times of business depression, as it does with regulating business conditions and attempting to do away with the losses there."[47] Once again, the broad social impact of unemployment in an economic downturn was underestimated by the voluntary approach to unemployment planning, which would return to haunt President Hoover in the 1929–33 period. But that was not a concern in 1923. Hunt had corresponded with Frederick M. Feiker, vice president of McGraw-Hill Book Company, who was responsible for that firm's network of trade and professional journals, about publication of articles promoting the committee's work. Hunt also arranged with Ordway Tead of the same firm's business publications division to publish the final report as part of the educational and publicity campaign. In late summer 1922 chairman Owen D. Young proposed taking a referendum among trade associations, the Chambers of Commerce, unions, the American Banking Association, and other organizations as a way to keep discussion and action about business-cycle information alive after completion of the report. Hoover aides in the Department of Commerce worked at placing articles and editorials in newspapers across the country as well as features in trade and technical journals in the hope of making the publicity campaign a success.[48]

Thinking of writing a book on the theme of unemployment in response to the increasing criticisms raised by Mary Van Kleeck and John B. Andrews, Hunt canvassed his friend and colleague Mitchell about the idea. Mitchell wrote back:

> I really don't see much in the idea of arguing the merits of any given social philosophy. You could do a most attractive and persuasive presentation of voluntary individual action; but after you had gotten done and lost the glow of the moment, you would be quite as capable, doing an equally charming and persuasive account, the rising tide of cooperative action through government. We don't know enough yet to know which philosophy is the more effective in the long run. My guess is that each is better in certain fields, and that in many fields both can be used to better effect than either alone. Anyway, that kind of discussion would run out into dialectic and you have too clear and too modern a head to feel content with the kind of writing that would have suited the generations between Bentham and Darwin. Indeed you would sink to the level, Mr. Gladstone and be praised so widely as to become a misanthrope [*sic*].
>
> It's a big task and a hard one—the kind that is really worth doing and that leaves you a stronger man for all your future years for doing it. Most people won't understand what you have in mind until you have done it. And then people will see a good deal more in your results after ten years than within the months during which the book reviews often [*sic*].[49]

Hunt—and Hoover—must not have thought much of the commentary. When Young suggested that the Business Cycle Committee meet after release of the report to consider its impact and ways to recruit converts, Hoover noted it was "a splendid idea as it will keep the pot boiling. I am rather astonished at the result the report is actually having in the conduct of business already."[50] Hunt kept faith as well. At the end of 1926 he sent Hoover a list of all the investigatory reports "directly attributable to the [Unemployment] Conference." Prominently displayed on the list was *Business Cycles and Unemployment,* the title of the committee's final report.[51]

The pattern of Hooverian associative planning with the help of the social scientists like Mitchell and institutions like the NBER continued in the other committee investigation stemming from the Unemployment Conference. As secretary of the Committee on Seasonal Operation, created in response to one of Mitchell's recommendations from the Business Cycle study, Hunt coordinated the program by obtaining financial support and suggesting ideas for the publicity campaign. He first discussed the possibility of monetary support with Mary Van Kleeck of the Russell Sage Foundation for a study of seasonal operation and unemployment intended to complement the business-cycle study of cyclical operation and unemployment. After Van Kleeck indicated that the foundation already had committed monies to the NBER for the business-cycle technical study, Hunt contacted President Henry S. Pritchett of the Carnegie Corporation to request a grant for $25,000. Ultimately, the Committee on Seasonal Operation garnered $13,000 from the Carnegie Corporation, contingent on obtaining another $5,200 from other sources, which included American Telephone & Telegraph Company, six trade associations in the construction industries, and the American Federation of Labor, which gave a small contribution.[52] While Hunt put together the financial package, Hoover appointed the sponsoring committee, which included Ernest T. Trigg, former head of the National Federation of Construction Industries and president of a Philadelphia lumber company, as chairman, along with presidents of two other national trade associations, presidents of two construction companies, two token labor representatives, one banker, two experts, his public works planning specialist Otto T. Mallery, and John M. Gries, chief of the Division of Building and Housing in the Department of Commerce.[53]

Hunt approached Harold G. Moulton of the Institute of Economics about conducting the technical study, while his boss, Hoover, raised the same point with Moulton's boss, St. Louis businessman Robert S. Brookings. After consulting with Mitchell, Hunt decided that Brookings's Institute of Economics did not have the requisite influence with important businessmen.[54] John Gries and his assistant James Taylor, both of the Division of Building and Housing in Hoover's newly reorganized Department of Commerce, were given the job of conducting the technical study for the committee. Originally the investigation included plans to examine seasonal unemployment in the bituminous coal, construction, transportation, banking, credit, and other industries. But Hoover decided to concentrate research on the construction industries, which he argued were of "strategic importance. . . . as a balance wheel, and these industries are notoriously seasonal."[55] After completing its deliberations on

March 5, 1924, the Committee on Seasonal Operation in the Construction Industries presented its recommendations: standardization of contracts and building materials should continue, statistical collection by the Division of Building and Housing should be upgraded, the outmoded custom regarding cutbacks during the winter season should be overturned, and voluntary associations should accept the idea of long-range planning of public works during boom times to prepare for depression periods. Hunt arranged to publish the final report in book form with McGraw-Hill and in a shorter pamphlet form in the Department of Commerce's Elimination of Waste Series.[56]

Even though Gries saw the report as having a decided impact via increases in winter construction, Hoover and his aides might have taken a closer look. Mitchell and Otto T. Mallery, chief proponents of legislative enactment of long-range planning of public works projects, had argued for this form of countercyclical (and counterseasonal) economic policy since their work for the Unemployment Conference and the Business Cycle Committee. Bills for direct action on this issue to promote stabilization in the key construction industries or creation of government committees to at least consider the policy had been introduced in Congress in 1922, 1923, and 1924. Similar bills were introduced in 1927 and 1928—the one in the latter year taking the title of a "Prosperity Reserve" plan. Not one of the bills passed both houses. Once again, lacking the stimulus of an immediate crisis, the short-term perspective and reliance on private, voluntary action triumphed over the long-term possibility of concerted government action that later inhibited Hooverian planning in the face of the Great Depression in the next decade.[57]

To follow up on the work of the Unemployment Conference, the Business Cycle Committee, and the Seasonal Operation Committee, Hunt and Hoover next tried to put together a study on the bases of adjustment of industrial disputes. Obviously worried about another outbreak of industrial conflict like that of 1919, they sought to use the associative planning network to arrive at a conception of peaceful adjustment of labor-management conflict through social science expertise. Between late October 1923 and mid-February 1925, Hunt and Hoover contacted Arthur Woods, now a close adviser to the Rockefeller Foundation and president of the Laura Spelman Rockefeller Memorial, and Beardsley Ruml, director of the LSRM, to ask for a grant of $100,000. The study would be conducted by Professor Joseph Willits of the Wharton School of Business at the University of Pennsylvania, a friend and professional colleague of Mitchell's. Both John D. Rockefeller, Jr., and philanthropic manager Ruml proved reluctant to fund the investigation.[58] In reporting his telephone conversation with Ruml to Hoover, Hunt noted Ruml's pronouncement of what proved to be the death knell of the study: "Mr. Rockefeller had advised [Ruml] yesterday that he is much interested in the proposed study of Bases of Adjustment in Industrial Disputes but feels that it would be unwise for him to give the entire amount or to take any action that would seem to imply his initiative in the matter. [He is willing to give 25 percent of the amount needed up to $25,000 if balance can be raised from other sources.] He wishes you to consider this as an anonymous proposition until the necessary sum is in hand."[59] Despite their efforts to procure the "necessary sum," neither Hunt nor Hoover was ever able to get this planning effort implemented.

With completion of the projected economic planning from the Unemployment Conference of 1921 by 1924, Hoover's associative national planning entered a hiatus. He had begun to carry out his system of voluntary cooperation by reorganizing the Department of Commerce and institutionalizing that organization's simplification, standardization, and stabilization plans. In the construction industries Hoover encouraged the work of the American Construction Council, founded in June 1922, under the leadership of Franklin D. Roosevelt. Both Hoover and Roosevelt hoped that the council would promote upgrading the collection of statistics in the key construction industries while simultaneously encouraging private-sector firms to participate voluntarily in a countercyclical policy of increased building during cyclical downturns with complementary cutbacks in periods of growth.[60] After 1925 Secretary of Commerce Hoover broke free of the restraining influence of other cabinet departments to promote a wide range of industrial conferences at which representatives of the trade association movement voiced their desires for antitrust revision. This movement toward industrial self-government under government encouragement culminated eventually in a partial victory through the New Deal's National Recovery Administration.[61]

While Hoover acted, Hunt and Mitchell drew back to think through the implications of the committee and conference system and increased knowledge about fluctuations in the business cycle. In 1925 Hunt published *Conferences, Committees, Conventions and How to Run Them*, a comparative study of private-, cross-sectoral, and public-sector conferences based on his own experience and reading. In private correspondence and memoranda, Hunt wrote even more openly about what he unabashedly termed "national planning." Writing to journalist Frederick Lewis Allen, Hunt noted that such work as Hoover's reorganization of the Department of Commerce would simultaneously promote American national planning and preserve private-sector incentive. Hunt now saw the Hoover committee and conference system built since 1921 with the active cooperation of Mitchell and the private-sector NBER as worthy of institutionalization in the form of national planning. As he thought about the subject, Hunt expanded his corporatist ideal of planning to include government cooperation with large corporations, national business organizations such as the Chamber of Commerce, national trade associations, state and local business groups; use of social scientific surveys; and, as a "leavening," work with some representatives of organized labor. He pointed to investigations sponsored by the American Engineering Council (a private body), the Unemployment Conference of 1921 (a private-public body), and the U.S. Coal Commission (a federal public body) to buttress his argument. While Hunt considered the broader implications of the Hooverian ad hoc planning efforts, Mitchell and NBER staffers worked on a revision of his 1913 work on business cycles in an attempt to include new statistical advances, explain the factors accounting for the economic prosperity of the period, and detail the complex interrelationships now found among businesses, government, experts, bankers, investors, and consumers. Still concerned with the incompleteness and potential misunderstanding and misuse of business-cycle information, Mitchell reemphasized the "planlessness" of business leaders, the need for ongoing statistical work, and suggestions about the growing economic function of both government and consumers.[62]

As Mitchell, Hunt, and Hoover understood the term, "national planning" involved a cooperative effort among enlightened officials in the executive branch of the federal government, social science experts like Mitchell and Merriam, business-oriented national organizations, business leaders like Henry Dennison, and philanthropic managers like Beardsley Ruml. The culmination of Hooverian associative planning came with two landmark investigations in which Mitchell played key roles as both economic expert and social science manager. Just as he and his colleagues at the NBER completed revision of his 1913 work on the business cycle, published as *Business Cycles: The Problem and Its Setting,* they were asked to lead the research effort in a national study of economic changes sponsored by Hoover. Mitchell and the NBER served for the Committee on Recent Economic Changes (1927–29) the same function that Merriam and the Social Science Research Council soon served for the President's Research Committee on Social Trends (1929–33). Hooverian planning with its emphasis on social science expertise, interest-group cooperation, private philanthropic financing, and public sponsorship now reached its zenith.[63]

In March 1927 Hoover decided to reactivate the study of business cycles in order to consider fundamental changes in the business cycle over the long term, how far the cycle's peaks and troughs had been "mitigated," where the economy stood in the current cycle, and what statistical services could be used or begun to "more clearly give warnings or indications of the position."[64] Hunt approached managers of the Carnegie Corporation and the Laura Spelman Rockefeller Memorial about funding and obtained $75,000 from each. Once again Hoover carefully selected the sponsoring committee and turned to Mitchell and the NBER to conduct the technical studies between January 1928 and February 1929. McGraw-Hill again published the resulting report, a two-volume study entitled *Recent Economic Changes in the United States* (1929).[65]

The Committee on Recent Economic Changes presented a generally optimistic outlook for the nation's economic future in the summary sections written by the sponsoring committee. The NBER's special investigations and some additional ones were included in chapters written by businessmen and social science experts in the fields of industry, construction, transportation, marketing, labor, management, agriculture, price movements, money and credit, foreign markets and credit, and the national income and its distribution. As research director of both the NBER and the committee, Mitchell wrote the lengthy final review chapter. Hunt published short articles and later a two-hundred-page popular summary of the committee's findings in hopes of publicizing the work and sparking cooperative voluntary action. The ideological basis of the report paralleled that of New Era capitalism's triad—high production, high wages, and high consumption. These legs of economic growth could be maintained through what the committee called "the technique of economic balance." The ideas behind Hooverian planning permeated the final report—the belief that the business cycle could be understood and controlled scientifically, cyclical unemployment could be ameliorated, seasonal unemployment could be overcome easily, advance public works planning could be an effective countercyclical tool, and, ultimately, reliance on voluntary cooperation among organized economic interests would preserve the traditional voluntarist American system.[66] Yet in his summary chapter, "How Matters Stand in the Spring of 1929," Mitchell added a note of sobriety.

> That we have not had a serious crisis since 1920 or a severe depression since 1921 is no guarantee that we shall be equally prudent, skillful and fortunate

in the years to come. If we are to maintain business prosperity, we must continue to earn it month after month and year after year by intelligent effort. The incomes disbursed to consumers, and to wage earners in particular, must be increased on a scale sufficient to pay for the swelling volume of consumers' goods sent to market. The credit structure must be kept in due adjustment to the earnings of business enterprises. Security prices must not outrun prospective profits capitalized at the going rate of interest. Commodity stocks must be held in line with current sales. Overcommitments of all sorts must be avoided. The building of new industrial equipment must not be overrapid. These and similar matters which might be mentioned present delicate problems of management which will find their practical solutions in the daily decisions of business executives. Perhaps errors are being kept within the limits of tolerance. Perhaps no serious setback will occur for years to come. But we are leaving 1921 well behind us, and there are signs that the caution inspired by that disastrous year is wearing thin.[67]

Already, by 1927, Mitchell was beginning to realize that the "lessons of 1921" might not apply to a later, more serious economic downturn in the business cycle, but the positive tone of the report along with a seemingly healthy short-term economic outlook left little room for doubts like Mitchell's.

The connecting link between the economic planning efforts since 1921 and broader social planning long envisioned by Mitchell came through the work of the President's Research Committee on Social Trends (1929–33). Newly elected president Herbert Hoover cooperated with his close friend Ray Lyman Wilbur, secretary of the interior, in the hope of reorganizing the Department of the Interior for social welfare planning in ways similar to Hoover's earlier restructuring of the Department of Commerce for economic planning. They saw Interior as expanding to two divisions—one for public works, the other for education, health, and recreation. In September 1929 presidential aide Edgar French Strother brought leaders of the Merriam-inspired and Mitchell-led Social Science Research Council to the White House to discuss plans with Hoover for the first national inventory of the nation's physical, biological, and social resources as a complement to the just-completed economic inventory. Sociologists William Ogburn and Howard Odum, political scientist Merriam, and economist Mitchell agreed to take part in the study. Merriam and Beardsley Ruml, director of the Laura Spelman Rockefeller Memorial, had cofounded the SSRC in early 1923 with LSRM financial support in order to create a national research network for social science paralleling that of the American Council of Learned Societies for the humanities and the war-generated National Research

Council for the physical sciences. In 1927 Mitchell succeeded Merriam as the president of the SSRC. Ruml worked to expand this social science research network to include private research bodies such as the NBER, policy-analysis organizations that blurred the lines between public- and private-sector work such as the Brookings Institution, and cooperative federal agencies interested in promoting data collection and distribution. Through this complicated organizational nexus built up since 1921, these associational planners brought forth the country's first planned social resources inventory. A massive grant of $560,000 from the newly created Social Science Division of the Rockefeller Foundation, which had taken up the Ruml-directed LSRM's work, made the two-and-one-half-year investigation possible.[68]

But this time Hoover's associative planning process revealed its flaws, just as the business cycle moved into a trough and political conditions shifted rapidly. As the president and head of the executive branch of the federal government, Hoover clearly indicated at the inception of the study that he intended to use advance copies of the committee's reports as guides for action. In the midst of the election year of 1932, that intention created tensions both within the committee proper (between the research purists and those who argued for policy application of research findings) and between Hoover's liaison Strother and the committee members. Though the two-volume summary report, *Recent Social Trends in the United States,* published by McGraw-Hill, appeared in January 1933, changing external conditions—the onset of the depression, Republican losses in the congressional elections of 1930 and 1932, and the Democratic presidential victory in 1932—buried publicity about the report.[69]

New Era capitalism proved fundamentally flawed. Structural weaknesses in the economy, failure to separate investment from commercial banking, overreliance on holding-company schemes, stock speculation, and gaping chasms in the distribution of income and wealth between social classes led to economic collapse. Underconsumption by those with the money to spend and maldistribution of income and wealth that left many consumers unable to spend (and thus unable to increase demand) brought the dream of New Era industrial capitalism crashing down into the deepest trough in business-cycle history.[70] The Great Depression struck with gale force, a "slowly sucking maelstrom," as Boston businessman Henry Dennison put it.[71] The closer social scientists such as Mitchell and Merriam got to the political and social arena, the more controversial their ideas and actions became, just as their political sponsor's credibility was undermined by changing economic conditions. This pattern recurred in the course of New Deal planning from 1933 through 1943. Never completely institutionalized because of Hoover's overweening fear of the managerial state, his national planning efforts were ill fated. Between 1929 and 1933 voluntary mechanisms were not strong enough to withstand the economic storm that engulfed the ad hoc institutions of the associative planning state. Governmental sponsorship by New Era officials, social science research by Mitchell and the NBER, financing through managerial philanthropists, deliberation by organized business leaders, and publicity by true believing Hoover loyalists engendered an overabundance of faith in the efficacy of Hooverian voluntarist, national planning by the associative state in the wake of the worst downturn in the business cycle of the twentieth century.

External events clearly delivered the death blow. With the onset of the Great Depression of 1929–41, the earlier depression of 1920–21 paled in comparison. It became "the forgotten depression." Herbert Hoover— once the American hero, now the American goat—fell victim to his own vision for, and experience with, national planning. Between 1921 and 1933 public-sector, cross-sectoral, and private-sector organizations forged associational linkages that created a distinctive style of voluntary national planning. Government officials, social scientists, business leaders, and philanthropic managers came together in an attempt to respond to the concerns raised by the depression of 1920–21. Veterans of the war-time mobilization agencies and members of Hoover's reorganized Department of Commerce moved into the Unemployment Conference of 1921 and its follow-up committees. Led by people like Wesley Clair Mitchell and Charles Merriam, social scientists from the National Bureau of Economic Research and the various professional organizations associated with the Social Science Research Council provided the expertise that undergirded Hooverian planning efforts. Each of these conferences and committees was staffed by managers of business corporations, representatives of trade associations, and leaders of such business groups as the U.S. Chamber of Commerce. Yet rather than seeking funding from the federal government, Hoover's planners sought the aid of private philanthropic managers heading such voluntary philanthropies as the Russell Sage Foundation, the Commonwealth Fund, the Carnegie Corporation, the Laura Spelman Rockefeller Memorial, and its successor, the Social Science Division of the Rockefeller Foundation.

In the crisis atmosphere of 1929–33, Hooverian associative planning shriveled in the face of global economic catastrophe, yet national planning, like the phoenix rising from the ashes, arose reborn to pave the way to the future. Included among the array of Hooverian associationalists were President Franklin D. Roosevelt's planners—Frederic A. Delano, Charles E. Merriam, and Wesley Clair Mitchell. For the moment, businessmen and business-like philanthropic managers were out of favor. At the 1936 Harvard tercentenary celebration, Mitchell summarized his own mature view about an American form of national planning, which now hung precariously between Hooverian voluntarism and Rooseveltian statism: "But the indications seem to me fairly clear that in the long run men will try increasingly to use the power and resources of their governments to solve their economic problems even in those nations that escape social revolutions. . . . Our choice does not lie between two sharply contrasted systems, private enterprise and governmental regulations; the real choices that we shall be making more or less deliberately are choices among the indefinitely numerous possible mixtures of private enterprise and governmental regulation, as applied to this, that, or the other type of activity, under different conditions of time and place."[72]

Perhaps, like Hoover, Mitchell would prove unable and unwilling to make the complete transition from New Era capitalism to New Deal reform. In late 1935 he resigned from the planning agency, citing as his reason a desire to focus on business-cycle research at the NBER. Still uncertain about the extent, reliability, and utility of economic knowledge in both short- and long-term economic policy making, he proved unwilling to take the next step into a relatively more statist form of planning. Mitchell would be replaced with two other veteran Hoover planners, Henry S. Dennison and Beardsley Ruml, more willing to make the move into New Deal reform because of changing economic, political, and social conditions of Depression-era America.

Henry S. Dennison and the Middle Way

BUSINESS, WELFARE CAPITALISM, AND ASSOCIATIONAL PLANNING

THE CORPORATE MODEL that emerged in the wake of the business revolution of the late nineteenth and early twentieth centuries had a tremendous impact on the nature of institutional life in modern America. Over time, the nature, scope, and organization of business changed to meet new needs. Individual owners gave way to more specialized managers capable of using stockholders' investments to build and maintain stable economic organizations that could survive the turns of the business cycle of an industrial economy investigated so thoroughly by Mitchell and the NBER. Reform-minded business leaders played crucial roles in bringing forth new kinds of national institutions, while some went even further in promoting cooperation with government, social science, and interest groups.[1] Few business leaders proved as farsighted or as willing to expand their strategic perspective as Boston businessman Henry S. Dennison. Practicing the new discipline of business administration through his firm, reform groups, and broad associational activities in the 1906–33 period, he emphasized the role of business managers in effecting efficiency, promoting social equilibrium, and cooperating with governmental agencies in planning to meet the ups and downs of the business cycle.[2] As one of two business representatives appointed to the New Deal planning board in late 1935 to replace Mitchell, Dennison represented a hardheaded, practical interest in national planning. Contrary to the fears of the American right and the hopes of the American left, the planning elite had room for a representative economic type—the modern business executive shrewd enough to back reform from above. Seeking a middle path between entrepreneurial capitalism and liberal Democratic reform, Dennison used his experience with his private-sector firm, growing contacts at the state and national levels, involvement in a variety of government advisory roles, and a myriad of associational efforts between the Progressive Era and the early years of the Great Depression to develop a business perspective on national planning.

Raised in an upper-class Boston family, Dennison entered the world of business leadership through the family firm. By 1917 he served as a national leader of welfare capitalist reform who then joined the economic mobilization effort. His associational activities in the 1920s included the Taylorite efficiency movement, business administration, the study of business cycles, and efforts to promote managerial professionalism that brought him into contact with Delano, Merriam, Mitchell, and Ruml. Participation in the trade association movement during the New Era led to his work with the early New Deal's National Recovery Administration. In 1936, when he joined Roosevelt's New Deal planning board, Dennison was, as economist John Kenneth Galbraith writes, "arguably the most interesting businessman in the United States."[3]

Born in Boston on March 4, 1877, Dennison entered life as the son of a second-generation business family. In 1844 his great-grandfather Andrew Dennison left the shoemaking trade because of increased competition and mechanization to found the Dennison Manufacturing Company in Brunswick, Maine. The company's history reflected that of many American businesses in the mid to late nineteenth century. Andrew Dennison made jewelry boxes for his younger son and soon went into partnership with his elder son, Eliphalet Whorf Dennison, who quickly sought to expand the business through aggressive selling and expansion of the product line. Eliphalet bought the company on credit in 1855, moving it to a new factory in Roxbury, Massachusetts, that same year. In search of new capital for expansion during the Civil War, Eliphalet went into partnership with three other men in 1863. Between 1863 and 1878 Henry's grandfather expanded sales and production, began shifting from wholesaling to retailing, and bought out or undersold the competition. Hard hit by the panic of 1873 and fires that destroyed whole factories, Eliphalet decided to take the company into another stage of corporate growth. In 1878 he incorporated with a capitalization of $150,000 to reorganize the family business into a joint company in Massachusetts. When Eliphalet died in 1886, the board of directors elected as president Henry B. Dennison, the father of Henry S. The younger Henry entered into this well-to-do Boston family at the period of initial growth when the company incorporated, sought new products and markets, and experimented with the new technique of advertising.[4]

While Henry S. Dennison began life in a prosperous family, he soon had to turn to his extended family for support. Nine days after his birth, his mother, Emma J. (Stanley) Dennison, died from heart problems aggravated by childbirth. His father, Henry B., served as works manager of the firm but faced recurring bouts of illness and alcoholism. Henry S. attended Roxbury Latin School before moving on to Harvard in 1895. His record at Harvard remained relatively undistinguished while studying philosophy with William James until choosing to major in chemistry. In June 1899, he graduated cum laude from Harvard, with honorable mention in chemistry. The next month he began work as a truck hauler in the wax department of the Roxbury plant. Not well accepted at Harvard because of his connections with "trade," he looked forward to moving away from liberal arts study to practical experience in the family business.[5]

Henry S. started his business career with important advantages. As a child, he and his two sisters had received the only shares of voting stock in the company that were held by nonmanagerial people. His Harvard education and family connections strengthened the ties of class to place him in the Dennison Manufacturing Company with an assured road up the managerial ranks. He quickly combined his assets with the healthy position of the firm, which in 1898 had opened a new factory in Framingham, west of Boston. Since sales of jewelry boxes fluctuated with the market, the company diversified its product lines into boxes and lines of stationery goods such as letter-sealing wax, greeting cards, and crepe paper to complement the main line of shipping labels. The younger Henry thus began at a propitious moment in the company's history. Since incorporation in 1878, the firm had increased sales by 329 percent, net profits by 645 percent, and capital assets by 814 percent. Henry's son later noted that by 1899 the corporation "though no industrial giant was the recognized leader in the markets for tags, crepe paper, stationery specialization."[6] Between 1898 and 1906, when Henry became works manager, annual sales increased 163 percent from $1,689,000 to $4,451,000, while investment for new machinery increased by 300 percent.[7] Dennison inherited a corporation undergoing rapid structural change at a decisive point in its economic expansion.

As had Delano at a slightly earlier point in time, Dennison moved rapidly up the corporate ladder. In 1901 he became the foreman of the sealing wax department. After developing new cost and accounting procedures while working in the front office, Henry became works manager in 1906 with the aid of his uncle, Charles S. Dennison, who had seized control of the board of directors from his rivals in the New York City sales office. In 1909 the board elected Henry as one of the directors. From 1910 through 1913 he served as purchasing agent and treasurer and by 1917 was president of the company.

The corporate reorganization Henry implemented presaged his life's work. Having built its economic growth from 1855 to 1906 around strong sales, the production end of the firm suffered from lagging invest-ment and outmoded machinery and administration. His Uncle Charles hoped to develop the production end of the business with Henry's aid. Reviving an unsuccessful 1878 plan to keep control of the company in the hands of the managers, Charles and Henry promoted more efficient production, returning control to the managers, and integrating the com-pany's operations through centralization. Henry recognized the growing trend toward accurate collection of records, functional division of labor and administration, and increasing specialization through use of divi-sional sections.[8] After returning from an inspection trip in 1900 to the National Cash Register Company in Dayton, Ohio, Henry thought that most of NCR's welfare capitalist methods would not apply to the Den-nison plants, but he did see value in the Dayton firm's various "plans." He argued that NCR's success stemmed from "keen, thoughtful planning," which encompassed welfare programs for workers, research to promote continuous rather than large profits, gradual advance, use of the military system of hierarchy, and coordination of the various departments.[9] Most important, Henry concluded, "one of the soundest features of their Plan is the absence of pure philanthropy. Wholesale, indiscriminate charity harms both giver and receiver. They have no charity beyond fair dealing between man & man. Their Plan is founded on economy, economy which looks ahead for its returns, and this is the only principle which can accomplish anything. . . . They have thus avoided the universal fate of reformers, who jump to their goal and try to pull a heavy public after them."[10]

Henry and Charles Dennison sought to rationalize the firm through executive reorganization, administrative restructuring, and implementa-tion of welfare capitalist measures for their workers. In 1906 they took matters into their own hands. Charles forced the resignation of the cur-rent president, who represented the sales faction, installed Henry as works manager at the Framingham plant, and encouraged him to begin reorganization. Though the new president came from the sales ranks, he deferred to the Dennisons. Henry created merchandising committees staffed by representatives of production, sales, and management to serve as coordinating bodies between production and sales. Between 1900 and 1917 he experimented with various reform measures such as a clinic, lunchroom, separate lounges for women (the majority of the unskilled workers), recreation facilities, a circulating library, social clubs, and a company savings fund.[11]

Dennison's central focus stemmed from the 1911 reincorporation, which marked what company historian Charlotte Heath noted as "the beginning of a more scientific approach to management, as evidenced at the factory by the beginning of functionalization, divisional control, emphasis on accounting methods, the establishment of a research department, a methods department, and the nucleus of a planning department."[12] Dennison argued that adoption of modern corporate management practices was the key to business efficiency. Though he and other Dennison managers insisted that the 1911 restructuring marked the beginning of what they called industrial democracy, the new structure clearly placed power in managerial hands. With the support of Mrs. J. P. Warbasse, daughter of a preceding president who had inherited controlling stock in the corporation, Henry implemented his Managerial Industrial Partnership Plan. The plan called for changing common stock into preferred stock and giving the new industrial partner stock to firm managers. Dennison hoped to reverse the trend toward absentee stock ownership, to place direct power in the hands of the managers, and eventually to leave voting power only in the hands of these managers. Contemporaries hailed the idea as the first experiment in profit sharing and the "democratizing" of the business. Henry saw the plan differently, arguing that responsibility must be related to ability and that reward should be connected with service to the company.[13] Above all, as he explained in the 1920s, "The motive was not a desire to share the fruits of prosperity with as many as possible, but to safeguard the future of the business by developing a stable, qualified management, and balancing of self-interests into an aggregate favorable to steady growth."[14]

After Charles Dennison's death in 1912, Henry became company treasurer. For the next twenty-seven years, he continued to integrate the firm by centralizing production, sales, and merchandising functions at the Framingham plant and by creating new divisions. In 1914 the company established an employment department that collected data on prospective employees, wrote a training pamphlet for new employees, filed annual reports on every employee, and kept track of the firm's labor turnover with Taylorite efficiency. In 1916 the firm began the first private unemployment insurance fund in the United States. These corporate innovations led to the years from 1916 to 1920 being the fastest growth period in the company's history and also gave Dennison the reform credentials he needed to broaden his experience beyond the individual firm into city, state, and national arenas.[15]

After 1912 Dennison participated in a number of significant voluntary associations, where he met people who influenced him for the rest of his life. As vice president and then director of the Boston Chamber of Commerce, Dennison met liberal businessmen such as Edward A. and Lincoln Filene, who encouraged his experiments at the company. He also made contacts with other managers and employer associations as well as beginning discussions with business-cycle economists Edwin F. Gay and Wesley Clair Mitchell. Dennison joined voluntary organizations like the American Economic Association and the moderate reform group the American Association for Labor Legislation (AALL), which promoted social insurance as a way to deal with the issues of industrial accidents, sickness, unemployment, and old age. His links with the AALL led to participation on the 1914 Massachusetts Commission on Old Age Pensions and the 1915 Committee on Unemployment. In all these groups Dennison took what he called "the middle way" between Progressive reformers and more conservative members of the business community. Already he conceived of American society as a series of interest groups that should be brought together to cooperate rather than compete with one another. His election as president of the Dennison Manufacturing Company in 1917 reflected widespread faith in his managerial abilities.[16]

As Dennison's connections to local, regional, and national associations widened, so did his interests. In 1912 and 1916 Dennison moved away from his traditional commitment to the Republican Party and voted for Democratic presidential candidate Woodrow Wilson. His business contact and friendship with Edwin F. Gay, first dean of the Graduate School of Business Administration at Harvard, led to Dennison's participation in wartime mobilization work for the federal government. In April 1917, two days after Wilson asked for a declaration of war against Germany from Congress, Arch Shaw, a Chicago publisher with close ties to the Harvard Business School, asked Gay and Dennison to join the newly formed Commercial Economy Board of the Council of National Defense. Dennison resigned his recently acquired position as director of the Boston Chamber of Commerce (seedbed of the U.S. Chamber of Commerce) to take up war work in the spirit of cooperation between private business managers and government agencies. Working as Gay's assistant in Washington, D.C., Dennison played key roles in improving cost accounting, coordinating private- and public-sector activities, and collecting and using statistics as an administrative tool by the federal government.[17]

For the next year and a half, Dennison applied his private-sector business experience as a government-sponsored war manager. He led efforts to coordinate shipping needs; to collect technical data for the Shipping Board, the War Trade Board, and the War Industries Board; and to recognize the importance of research in planning for the future. He worked with Gay at the Commercial Economy Board and its successor, the Division of Planning and Statistics of the U.S. Shipping Board. Gay and Dennison created a like-named division for the War Industries Board at the request of director Bernard Baruch, which was succeeded by the independent Central Bureau of Planning and Statistics, which reported to President Wilson through Baruch. Each of these agencies began with a practical problem, confronted that problem with analysis and statistical data, and brought new administrative tools into the federal government. Gay, Dennison, and Mitchell hoped to make the Central Bureau into a more permanent body, but bureaucratic resistance and an early end to the war left this hope unrealized. Many veterans of these groups entered into the variegated associational activities of the postwar era.[18]

As one of the famous dollar-a-year managers who worked for the government during the war, Dennison struggled to play a part in the evolution of new kinds of institutions directly affecting the making of public policy. These mobilization agencies brought together private- and public-sector actors in an attempt to meet the needs of the day with administrative techniques that had been developed in business firms like the Dennison Manufacturing Company. Yet in a voluntarist society like the United States, centralized command planning remained anathema. New organizations emerged that were neither wholly private and voluntary nor wholly public and statist. Wartime economic mobilization, according to its most insightful historian, Robert Cuff, involved a battle by businessmen and government officials to establish a new middle ground between the older modes of laissez-faire and modern forms of bureaucratic organization: "Businessmen in government groped for some middle way which would combine the traditional virtues of the free enterprise system as they understood it with the national planning required by the war. The outcome, as might be expected, was a bundle of paradoxes and contradictions which cannot be described as either free enterprise or public planning."[19] War mobilization work took Dennison beyond the boundaries of the Dennison Manufacturing Company, allowed him to develop his ideas concerning efficiency in a national context, introduced him to other national players in policy-making circles, and suggested to him the possibilities of statistical and economic research begun by business managers in both the private and the public sectors. He carried the idea of business research into his work during the 1920s while moving out of governmental service and into a variety of professional and trade association groups. Other Wilsonian war managers followed him to work with various Hooverian planning efforts in the 1920s.[20]

In the immediate postwar years Dennison began integrating his own activities in business, government, and philanthropy. During the decade of New Era capitalism, he followed a path that combined the associational work of Delano with the social science research and networking of Merriam and Mitchell. As usual, he started with the Dennison Manufacturing Company. In the spring of 1919, amid a wave of worker strikes and rising interest in the movement for industrial democracy, Dennison extended his profit-sharing plan of 1911 to encompass the loyal workers in his plants. Discussed as early as 1909, the idea of including workers in the industrial partnership stock plan had been rejected as unfeasible because of workers' ignorance of managerial aspects of the business. In 1919 Dennison began a company union—the Works Committee—to improve cooperation between labor and management, to promote industrial peace, and primarily to ensure effective management. The Works Committee enacted an Employees Industrial Partnership (EIP) plan, which would give workers with the longest service, the most loyal, a one-third share in profits after payment on preferred stock and two-thirds payment to managers under the Managers Industrial Partnership (MIP) plan. Differences between the 1911 MIP and the 1919 EIP reflected Dennison's belief in the need for managerial control from the top. MIP stock eligibility had been based on ratios of salary above $1,200 per year, while the EIP was based on length of service. MIP stock dividends came out of the remaining profits on a two-thirds basis; EIP dividends were on a one-third basis. Most important in regard to managerial control, MIP stock carried voting privileges; EIP stock specifically excluded voting rights. In sum, the new EIP clearly placed those workers who qualified above the unskilled workers and below the managerial ranks. Though touted at the time as a step toward industrial democracy, the EIP in practice served as a means of control over the work force. Yet Dennison, like other business managers employing these methods, used the rhetoric of welfare capitalist reform to argue with other employers that some forms of worker representation had to be accepted by American businesses. He went so far as to advocate a national industrial conference to promote discussion.[21]

In October 1919 Dennison became a member of the public group of representatives to President Wilson's First Industrial Conference in Washington, D.C. Wilson announced the conference the day after the National Strike Committee had set September 22, 1919, as the date for the start of the steel strike, which resulted in 350,000 steelworkers going off their jobs. The conference quickly became embroiled in the issues of the steel strike and the American Federation of Labor's search for public approval of workers' rights to organize unions and bargain collectively. Significantly, the conference structure followed the usual Progressive inclusion of interest-group representation by employers, labor, and the public. Dennison now took his war-mobilization work in hand to argue that solutions might arise from the experience of the Dennison Manufacturing Company.[22]

In public hearings, conference delegates considered resolutions introduced by representatives from various interest groups. While no resolution survived intact because of the bitter debates between groups representing employers and labor, Dennison's proposed resolutions revealed his managerial thinking. He suggested that plant committees akin to his firm's Works Committee of 1919 be established to ensure "the joint consideration by these committees and the employers of such constructive matters as methods of enlisting workers' interest, and of improving efficiency of production, which are of mutual value [for] employers and employees."[23] Dennison also proposed more extensive use of his Managerial Industrial Partnership plan of 1911 as a way to promote managerial control of corporate policy. On the central issue of collective bargaining, he chose the middle way again, arguing for the joint establishment of both company unions and trade unions, thus defending his own Works Committee while recognizing the import of independent trade unions. As he had during his wartime work for government agencies, Dennison argued for the continued evolution of the middle way.[24]

Reflecting on the conference after its breakup over the issues raised by the steel strike, Dennison deplored the self-interested stances of employers and workers bent on industrial warfare. Referring to the importance of "public opinion" in determining the collective welfare, he argued,

> The only remedy appears to be a strongly centralized government which will be more powerful than any special interest, however well organized—a gov-

ernment possessing powers of our recent war organization. I believe that wonderful possibilities exist under such a plan for eliminating waste, motion, uncertainty, distribution costs, and particularly the selling expenses now connected with industry. I can see no unsurmountable difficulty to running the entire United States as efficiently and with as little internal friction as the United States Steel Corporation or the Woolworth chain of stores is operated. Such a plan as this would probably be opposed by all individuals who possess powerful personalities as they would consider it an infringement on their chances of private initiative; but the job would surely be large enough to call forth the best brains in the country and in view of the menacing possibilities which may lurk in the future, we may have to sacrifice some of the liberty and freedom which has heretofore been an integral part of an enlightened democratic form of government.[25]

Dennison saw himself, Henry Ford, E. A. Filene, and other businessmen as the more liberal element of industrial leadership that could direct the country's policies. He further suggested that the U.S. Chamber of Commerce could set up a statistical bureau to "be able to forecast impending industrial, political, and social changes." Seeing a new kind of voluntary associational activity emerging in all areas of socioeconomic life, Dennison promoted the ideas of industrial peace, intergroup cooperation, and management by an enlightened industrial leadership. Planning based on statistical research would be another way of promoting social equilibrium. By 1919 his ideas closely paralleled those of Delano's "community of interest," Merriam's pluralistic society, and Mitchell's search for business-cycle stability through economic research.[26]

Dennison's move from the arena of the business corporation to that of governmental adviser closely matched that of Delano, but from 1919 onward he took up the concerns expressed by Merriam and Mitchell to adjust social ideas to changes within the political and economic system. Like Merriam and Mitchell, Dennison tempered advocacy of welfare capitalist reform with an emphasis on exhortation, research, and cooperation among like-minded professionals in business, the social sciences, and the federal government. Two activities in 1919 foreshadowed Dennison's work in the 1920s. Along with liberal businessman Edward A. Filene, he helped found a philanthropic organization for research into industrial democracy that later moved in the direction of more broadly based economic research. The Twentieth Century Fund, as it was renamed in 1922, endowed by Edward Filene, supported Dennison's attempts to create the International Management Institute in Geneva to study industrial management. Dennison served as a trustee of the Twentieth Century Fund until his death in 1952 and headed the Executive Committee from 1937 to 1949—the most active years for social research.[27] From 1919 to 1921 Dennison continued to promote his company's experiments as president of the Taylor Society. Throughout the 1920s he pounded away in the pages of the *Bulletin of the Taylor Society* at the need for increased efficiency in all divisions of corporate enterprise. Concerns about efficiency, the need to awaken industrial managers to their social role to control business, and an increasing emphasis on economic research came to the fore of Dennison's thinking in the period of New Era capitalism.[28]

Dennison did more than talk about efficiency. From 1921 to 1927 he served as executive director of the Service Relations Division of the U.S. Post Office. As a liberal businessman representing a leading manufacturer in a moderate-sized sector of the economy, he saw no need to pay homage to the older tradition of classical economics but argued that federal agencies ought to emphasize business-like efficiency, practice welfare capitalism with their workers, and establish divisional hierarchical bureaucracies as had national corporations.[29]

While many members of the scientific management movement of the 1920s only mouthed an ideology of efficiency, Dennison acted. Complementing the work of Mitchell and the National Bureau of Economic Research, he began to plan ways of practically dealing with fluctuations in the business cycle. Through its research department, the Dennison Manufacturing Company gathered business statistics from the weekly reports of the Federal Reserve Board, strike statistics, and figures on business failures in an attempt to forecast the operation of the cycle. Dennison's system came under test in the depression of 1920–21. In January 1920 Dennison and his company planners met to decide on means to counteract a downturn that they forecast for November 1920. The planning proved prescient. Dennison's managers took a holistic view of the firm's operations. They decided to further hone divisional work. By revising the 1917 five-year plan for the advertising department, they chose to invest in advertising during slow periods and cut back in times of prosperity. Similar measures were taken in cutting back the sales force through attrition. Production schedules were set to keep inventories between prescribed minimum and maximum levels. Not surprisingly, the company's net losses for 1921 were considerably less than if no planning had been done.[30]

While Mitchell soon addressed the problem of unemployment from a more theoretical perspective, Dennison cast his management eye on the problem of cyclical and seasonal unemployment as a problem for his own firm. Seeing the rise and fall of major business cycles every seven to ten years and minor cycles every three years, he believed that the private, voluntarist methods of the business corporation, through planning, could deal with resulting unemployment. To that end, in 1916 he set up one of the earliest private unemployment insurance funds. His firm initiated long-range stock goods planning, encouraged buyers of seasonal goods to place their orders earlier, added new product lines in slack periods, and trained employees to work in different departments. Meshing these plans with those in selling, advertising, and merchandising, Dennison now incorporated production plans. To deal with the problem of seasonal unemployment, the company increased funds in the unemployment reserve and distributed relief in the form of 80 percent of wages to those workers with dependents and 60 percent to those without dependents. The plan proved so successful that at the height of unemployment in January 1921, the company had only a 4 percent unemployment rate and an even lower rate of 0.75 percent for the entire 1920–21 period. Company plans led to a disbursement of only 0.7 percent of the total yearly payroll in 1921.[31]

As a result of the firm's experience in 1920–21, Dennison once again moved into the public arena to exhort skeptical members of the business community, consult with academic economists, and participate in governmental discussions of policy. Drawing upon the experiments of employers like Dennison as well as the work of the American Association for Labor Legislation and wartime precedents for statistical work, the new secretary of commerce, Herbert Hoover, initiated the Unemployment Conference of 1921. The planning staff for the conference included not only staffers from the Department of Commerce and his wartime colleague Gay but also business leader Dennison. The Economic Committee, which set the recommendations for the conference, included many ideas Dennison had implemented at his firm. The committee report included statistical enumeration of 3.5 million unemployed; suggestions for local voluntary relief efforts by organized charities, employers, and municipal governments; and recommendations for permanent reform such as statistical bureaus in the federal government, business planning to meet business-cycle fluctuations, and advance public works planning to complement private efforts. The day after the conference adjourned, Dennison sent summaries of its work and recommendations to all his managers.[32]

Dennison now gained prominence as a member of the liberal part of the business community that sought to promote economic stabilization efforts, to extend the knowledge gained thereby to national trade associations, and to cooperate with Hoover's reorganized Department of Commerce in promoting planned national economic policies. Throughout the 1920s such corporate liberals as Dennison, Gerard Swope and Owen Young of General Electric and Dennison's old friend Edward Filene promoted such activities.[33] In the 1930s this work culminated in such national planning efforts as the Swope Plan, the National Recovery Administration, and the Business Advisory and Planning Council of the Department of Commerce. Increasingly, Dennison's activities moved in directions analogous to those of Delano in city and regional planning, Merriam in social science research and management, and Mitchell in economic policy-advising work.

After his participation in the 1921 conference, Dennison took up the study of business cycles in earnest. The combined impact of the Dennison Manufacturing Company experiments, statistical work for the wartime governmental agencies, and renewed interest in business stabilization at the 1921 Unemployment Conference led Dennison into the heart of economic research. Like Delano, Dennison had been involved in the early discussions leading to the establishment of the Graduate School of Business Administration at Harvard. During this period he repeatedly called upon his friend and colleague Edwin F. Gay, from whom he learned the importance of business-cycle theory. He also relied on Gay and his successor as dean of the Graduate School of Business Administration at Harvard, Wallace B. Donham, to recommend Business School graduates as prospective Dennison managers. In the midst of the 1921 depression, Dennison and Donham made concerted efforts to increase popular understanding of business-cycle theory in terms of its practical advantages to business leaders. While noting the need for both governmental and private plans for depression relief, Dennison clearly favored the private, voluntary efforts like those made by his own company.[34]

Shortly after the conference of 1921, Dennison began to develop ideas about unemployment planning as a result of his own firm's experience and discussions with Mitchell regarding the operation of the business cycle. He argued that all departments of a firm should follow turns in the business cycle in order to coordinate investment, purchasing, production, selling, advertising, distribution, and credit. Businesses must learn to cut back strategically on investment, purchasing, and production before peaks in the cycle. In turn, they must learn to increase advertising, selling, credit, and planned introduction of new product lines during periods of slow growth.[35] In the 1930s this idea became the basis for a conservative kind of deficit-spending policy that sought equilibrium over the length of major business cycles. Though not recognized at the time, business thinking like this planted the seeds for a program of business-government cooperation through statistical research, the dissemination of information by the Department of Commerce, improved labor-management relations through private unemployment insurance, and creation of federal realms such as public works planning to fill in gaps left by the private sector. Keynesian economists later termed these "bottle-necks." By the late 1920s Dennison had appeared before the Wisconsin legislature and the Congress testifying in favor of unemployment relief and the creation of a "prosperity reserve" of public works.

Like other New Era capitalists, Dennison believed strongly in the use-fulness of scientific management and improved economic research by the business community. Influenced by such management experts as Mary Parker Follett and Seebohm Rowntree, Dennison argued that managers needed more education to become better managers. Professional business managers had to learn to coordinate divisional structures; to promote co-operation between investors, managers, workers, and consumers; and to model the federal government after the private-sector business corpora-tion. Dennison invoked "the social motive," by which he meant much the same thing as Delano's "community of interest," to promote team-work and harmony. Yet he never considered these ideas to be utopian in the least, always emphasizing the hard-boiled business practicality of such ideas.[36] In one of his many New Era speeches, Dennison summarized his views: "The balance of motive in Big Business has shifted in this new period from the stark self-interest of its beginnings under *laissez-faire* to the social motive which is clearly apparent. . . .The essential feature of the factory system is the voluntary disciplined coordination of group effort under competent technical direction, and this feature has only be-come more evident, as, with the growth in size of the organization, the difficulties of the human relationships involved have challenged the best cooperative spirit in the management. Successful business, under pressure from without, but chiefly from within, is no longer autocratic, but on the other hand it is not organized on the principle of Jacksonian democ-racy, nor is it likely to be."[37]

Dennison exhorted his fellow managers throughout the 1920s to orga-nize themselves as a profession, to establish improved economic research methods, and to form voluntary associations that could deal with business specialties such as statistical research, marketing, manufacturing, and distribution.[38] Dennison continued to work with various governmental bodies as well as private businesses. His work with Secretary Hoover's Coal Commission, which grew out of one of the follow-up studies of the Unemployment Conference of 1921, led to further advisory work for Hoover. With the recession of 1927 Hoover revived the work of the Business Cycle committee, bringing together a panel of experts directed by Mitchell and Gay that included Leo Wolman on labor, Edwin G. Nourse on agriculture, and Henry Dennison on management to work on the problem between 1927 and 1929.[39]

The Committee on Recent Economic Changes (CREC) grew out of the concerns of people like Dennison who had begun investigating ways to achieve economic stabilization of industry. Throughout the 1920s Hoover had created a loyal corps of planners through his ground-breaking study *Waste in Industry,* his reorganization of the Department of Commerce, the Unemployment Conference of 1921 and the subsequent committee and conference system, and his promotion of the voluntary trade association movement aimed at bringing about cooperation be-tween businesses and the federal government. Many of these people brought their experience and ideas into the work of the CREC, which focused on finding ways to iron out fluctuations in the business cycle. Financed by the Carnegie Corporation and the Laura Spelman Rockefel-ler Memorial and using Mitchell and the NBER's economic expertise, the CREC provided a national economic inventory, used the practical business experience of leaders like Dennison, and set the stage for the President's Research Committee on Social Trends.[40]

As the author of a key chapter on management in the CREC's final 1929 report, Dennison played a role similar to that filled by Charles Mer-riam several years later on the PRCST. Research director Mitchell of the NBER provided the common link between the two studies. Dennison's "Management" chapter for *Recent Economic Changes* summarized the de-velopments in business management in the 1921–27 period, though its framework included organizational changes since the late nineteenth century. Dennison included not only sections on various operational changes within different industries but also ideas that he had put into practice throughout the decade. He associated the stable prices, rising production, and increased sales volume of the New Era with the devel-opment of business management as a profession. Organizing in a number of trade associations and umbrella groups, managers used the research of private agencies, the Department of Commerce, and the newly emerging business schools in the universities to make plans for their firms. Catalog-ing the evolution of functionalization through specialized divisions,

Dennison set forth the corporate hierarchy of research, planning, staff
and line executive structures, coordination of divisional work, and the
use of new management techniques. By promoting consultation and advisory planning, executives could move toward cooperation rather than
live with outmoded ideas of competition. Such planning methods as bud-
geting and forecasting would strengthen New Era capitalism. Dennison
continued with a discussion of management innovations in manufacturing and marketing that involved increased specialization and integration
of the very same methods used at the Dennison Manufacturing Company. Revealing his own priority with management, he briefly mentioned the impact of technological unemployment and the rise of personnel management on workers. In concluding, he drew attention to the
need for more business planning, advocated more economic research,
and praised the military-like hierarchy that brought "balance" to the corporate staff.[41]

Recent Economic Changes served for Dennison the same function that
Recent Social Trends did for Merriam and Mitchell several years later: the
summation of his career in the 1920s and prologue to his activities of the
1930s. While Merriam and Mitchell managed the professionalization of
American social science, Dennison actively sought to promote managerial professionalism by bringing business leaders together in industry associations. In 1922, with the help of Lincoln Filene, he established the
Manufacturers' Research Association (MRA) to cement cooperation between Boston firms with the help of economic research by the Engineering and Business Schools at Harvard. Financed through the Twentieth Century Fund, the MRA collapsed in late 1931.[42] In like manner,
Dennison founded the National Personnel Association in 1922 with
funds from the Twentieth Century Fund to bring together line executives
for ongoing education in personnel work. Later known as the American
Management Association, the group continued its work for the rest of
the century. Dennison later extended its reach to Europe with the creation of the International Management Institute, centered in Geneva,
Switzerland.[43]

In the "Management" chapter of *Recent Economic Changes,* Dennison
looked forward as well as backward to note significantly that "several
hundred business executives are members of some national association of
the social sciences."[44] He had widened his own contacts beyond Gay and
Mitchell to include members of private research agencies, academic
economists interested in business problems, and teachers at technical and
engineering schools. Dennison participated in the Social Science Re-

search Council's Hanover summer conference at Dartmouth College and knew philanthropic managers through his work with the Twentieth Century Fund. In 1926 the SSRC elected Dennison chairman of its Advisory Committee on Industrial Relations. Meeting people such as Joseph Willits of the Wharton School of Business at the University of Pennsylvania, John R. Commons of the University of Wisconsin, and Walter V. Bingham, a leading industrial psychologist, Dennison further expanded his circle of colleagues. That circle included Secretary of Commerce Hoover, whom Dennison publicly endorsed for the presidency in October 1928. In July 1929 Dennison became a member of the Department of Commerce's advisory committee to plan the first national census on distribution of manufactured goods. The many contacts led to Dennison's most ambitious undertaking of the decade—the creation of the Business Research Council.[45]

Dennison stressed the practical importance of business research for forecasting the peaks and troughs of the business cycle. Colleagues in several associations took his exhortations to heart. In 1928 C. O. Ruggles, professor of Public Utility Management at the Harvard Business School and Dennison's friend, asked W. J. Donald, managing director of the American Management Association, to draw up plans for a group that could gather information on useful economic research from corporate leaders, business and technical schools, and private agencies for presentation at the next convention of the American Association of Collegiate Schools of Business in May 1929. The association approved the plan, which sought to merge itself, the Taylor Society, and the American Management Association into a research umbrella group modeled after the Social Science Research Council. The proposed Business Research Council (BRC) could act as a clearinghouse of information from philanthropic research projects, professional business schools, and government agencies. In the fall of 1929 the founders elected Dennison president of the council, Ruggles as vice president, and Donald as secretary-treasurer. They applied for funding to both the Twentieth Century Fund and the Rockefeller Foundation, following the path earlier taken by the SSRC. Additional members were nominated by the Association of Collegiate Schools of Business, the American Economic Association, the American Statistical Association, the American Management Association, and the American Trade Association Executives, while the American Federation of Labor and the U.S. Chamber of Commerce declined to nominate members.[46]

The original BRC officers and members hoped to achieve the active cooperation of leading corporate managers; however, several problems led to the collapse of the BRC. Internal quarrels led especially by elements of the Taylor Society, the inability to attract enough corporate leaders, the unwillingness of the SSRC to become actively involved in cooperative research, and the rejection of grant applications by the Rockefeller Foundation led to the council's gradual demise between 1931 and 1933. More significantly, the onset of the Depression and private efforts by Walter Teagle of Standard Oil of New Jersey, Arthur Woods, chairman of Hoover's President's Emergency Committee for Employment, and Joseph Willits of the Wharton School and the Rockefeller Foundation led Dennison to jettison the BRC, resigning from it in January 1935 following his work with the Business Advisory and Planning Council.[47]

Despite its ultimate failure, the BRC experiment served to highlight the convergence of ideas, people, and institutions that soon led Dennison, Delano, Merriam, and Mitchell to New Deal planning. All four stressed the value of professionalism, the need to organize national associations, and the importance of creating a national umbrella group to focus the energies of those associations. They recognized an emerging consensus on the need for organized cooperation among leaders in their respective associational groups and the federal government. Dennison's efforts on behalf of the American Management Association proved as successful as Delano's for the Washington and New York planning agencies, Merriam's for the American Political Science Association and the SSRC, and Mitchell's for the NBER and the SSRC. But Dennison's attempt to organize the BRC fell far short of the other three planners' efforts in the 1920s. In the next several years, Dennison joined the early New Deal, but he proved more hesitant than Delano and Merriam in making the transition to governmental planning. Still, his ideas on planning changed rapidly in the course of the Depression, governmental work in the early New Deal, and the collapse of business planning with the abandonment by leading business executives of both the Business Advisory and Planning Council and the National Recovery Administration.

Dennison was personally devastated by the stock market crash of 1929 and the start of the Great Depression. Having spent most of the New Era promulgating the virtues of voluntary planning sponsored by private-sector institutions, he eventually came to realize that Hooverian voluntarism was not producing results. In a national radio address on December 26, 1930, under the auspices of the President's Emergency Committee for Employment, Dennison exhorted business managers to heed the lessons of 1921. Citing the experience of the Dennison Manufacturing Company's unemployment insurance reserve fund in the depression of 1920–21, he called on executives to develop more such private plans, modified with employee contributions. He hoped that private employer plans might provide state and national governments with experimental markers. Until these were proven successful or flawed, government legislative bodies should hold up on public unemployment insurance plans. While adhering to his notions of corporate responsibility developed in the 1920s, leaving leadership to business managers, Dennison did not preclude alternatives.[48]

In a March 1930 speech before the annual convention of the American Economic Association, Dennison revealed his own ambiguous response to what he later termed the "slowly sucking maelstrom" of the Depression:

> Considering the great underlying power of publicity and the new powers which are being disclosed in expert advertising, I am inclined to think the first explorative steps of this country toward such invention were taken by the Department of Commerce seven or eight years ago in instituting their advisory conferences [following the Unemployment Conference of 1921]. This sort of governing might well be called an integration of laissez-faire and political control—a relative freedom offered in the choice of means of carrying on business, compulsory as to general direction and minimum speed.
>
> There is bound to be a steady growth of community influence on all business activities. Our fear that the community organized as a political government is not now fit, either in structure, personnel, or tradition to exercise wise "government control" has led us to a strengthening influence and control by trade associations formed within the business world itself. But this after all, exercised, in the open, as eventually it must be to succeed, is a community control. It may persist in its present form of self-control by business associations, or government personnel and structure may become adapted to its exercise, or, what is more likely, the two may federate. The possible forms are many; the practical essence is the accountability of business to the whole community.[49]

Through early 1931 Dennison brought out his business–cycle analysis of depression to argue that business had to learn to prepare for lean years during the years of prosperity. This could be done through the work of the various functional divisions of the corporation, including research, marketing, production, merchandising, sales, and personnel. According to him, those workers needing relief could use the private plan begun at his firm in 1915 and put to the test in 1921. From late 1929 through early

1931, he used the vaunted experience of New Era capitalism—increased production, higher wages, and advertising to create greater consumer demand—to prod his fellow managers to solve through voluntary means the problems created by the downturn in the business cycle.[50]

By early 1931 Dennison realized that the experiences taken from 1921 were no longer enough to stem the tide of the Great Depression. His company suffered along with Dennison's hurt pride. From peak employment of 2,800 people in the 1920s, the firm saw employment drop to 1,468 by 1932. In 1931 and 1932 the Dennison Manufacturing Company incurred net losses for the first time in its history. Though the firm continued to pay out from the unemployment reserve to the end of 1930, resources ran thin. So precarious did the financial solvency of the company become that for the first time since its inception in 1911, the Managerial Industrial Partnership plan appeared threatened with failure and the attendant loss of stock control to absentee owners unfamiliar with the firm's operations.[51] Dennison later recalled the personal impact of these developments: "One of the thousand reasons I have for a life-long bitter quarrel with the old economic system is that practically every bit of that pension idea had to be given up during the depression. . . . Nothing makes me more bitter now than to be told I did well to pull the concern through the depression. I didn't pull it through; I made thousands of people who couldn't afford to do it."[52] In January 1931 Dennison announced publicly that he favored Boston Mayor James Curley's idea for a Federal Industrial Planning Board that would work to prevent depressions.[53] He was coming around to the idea that there was indeed a role for the public sector in promoting economic recovery.

In 1931 Dennison entered the emerging debate over national planning. Two weeks after Gerard Swope of General Electric announced his national plan for industrial self-government under trade association auspices at the National Electric Manufacturers Association in New York City, the U.S. Chamber of Commerce followed suit. Its Committee on Continuity of Business and Employment, which included Henry Dennison, arrived at conclusions similar to those of Swope. Both plans argued that the downturn in the business cycle, caused by the long-range dislocations of World War I and speculation in the stock market, could be confronted only by those responsible corporate leaders acting together to stabilize production, prices, and employment through their own organizations. Both plans extended the experiences of welfare capitalism to argue for privately run systems of unemployment insurance, workmen's compensation, and retraining programs. The key element in both plans lay in provisions for cooperation with some government agency such as the Federal Trade Commission or a new National Economic Council.[54] Seen only in the short run, these ideas seemed a rigid reenactment of New Era capitalism raised to a higher degree. Yet recognition of the need for business-government cooperation did bring forth conscious, if overblown and inaccurate, memories of the War Industries Board. In the longer run, these plans revealed a gradual evolution in Dennison's thinking about national planning as a middle way between statist planning and an outmoded economic individualism.

During 1931 and 1932 Dennison reexamined his own corporatist ideas to arrive at some unusually perceptive conclusions concerning the place of business in American society, the need for a reinvigoration of corporate responsibility, the relationship between the social sciences and his own ideas for business termed "organization engineering," and the possibilities of national planning. In *Organization Engineering* (1932), Dennison more consciously than ever before discussed the implications of the corporate revolution in business with its new ideas regarding structure, industrial worker psychology, and the potential for reduction of conflict.[55] Obviously affected by the Depression, Dennison began speaking publicly about the necessity of searching out the middle way:

> A power for good and evil [competitive industrialism] cannot be abolished— or left absolutely unrestrained. It's easy for the ultra-radical to make his claim that it must be entirely eliminated—and comforting to him—but here and now ridiculous. Of much more serious import to America to-day is the call of the reactionary to bow and blindly worship it. . . . All proper regulative laws restrict the freedom of our baser motives, and give us bonds which give us freedom of the only sort worth having. Exactly this is true of economic individualism:—that we can save it only if we limit it;—allowed once more to run in flood force through such channels as it chooses it may work away foundation stones already loose and bring the whole great structure tumbling down about our heads. The most adoring of its blind idolaters are therefore its worst enemies.[56]

How did Dennison reach these tentative conclusions? Using business-cycle analysis, he argued that normal commercial and industrial factors did not abnormally distort the normal downturn of the cycle in 1929. By indirection, Dennison came to accept the underconsumptionist view of the Depression as caused by weaknesses in the economy—declining prices, agricultural stress, a weak international financial structure, rising tariffs, faltering bankers unwilling to control stock speculation, and, most important, increased wealth flowing only to the well-to-do rather than into investment channels. The prosperity of the 1920s had not reached a broad enough segment of the population to sustain growth. Dennison now admitted that one of the key tenets of New Capitalism was fundamentally flawed. What, he asked, could be done? Answers that might provide useful beginnings included international stabilization of money to control prices, regulation of the stock market, international stability, redirection of national income to the mass of Americans who would then spend money for consumer goods, guarantee of bank deposits, reassessment of tariff policies by all countries, and reexamination of unrestricted competition.[57]

By the summer of 1932 Dennison's rethinking led to a prescient discussion of national planning. In a paper entitled "A Five-Year Plan for Planning," written for a study group conducted by Edwin F. Gay at the Harvard Business School, Dennison stepped back from his immediate business experience to offer ideas similar to those of Charles Merriam. Dennison began his discussion by replying to critics of planning. Those who believed that cycles were inevitable were fatalistic and oftentimes "in relatively comfortable circumstances." He then rejected the debate over government intervention versus competition as a false dichotomy, arguing that many who rejected intervention ideologically were often those who "are eager enough for government interference when they can see it react in their own favor." To those who argued that human beings lack the wisdom to plan, Dennison responded that this critique assumed that "planning" was equivalent to "a plan"—rigid and specific. To the arguments of "the Lazy Fairies," he proposed that a test of the automatic system of the invisible hand, if truly done, would destroy the very governmental aids—protective tariffs, the Interstate Commerce Commission, the Federal Reserve Board, and taxation and government bonds—that supported the economic system.[58]

In the paper at Harvard, Dennison presented his philosophy of planning. He argued that planning must be flexible, range over the course of the business cycle, and educate the various groups in American society gradually. Economic planning, for example, could not at first be compulsory but must be advisory and educational in consultation with Congress, trade associations, and other organized representatives of the people. Planning would be a process that changed over time and did not respond to quickly changing fashions or the emergency needs of a given moment:

> Our national planning will by its nature aim at evolution not revolution. It will have to do with an organic entity, with that group of human beings,

human institutions, and human habit patterns which we call the United States of to-day; and its problem will, therefore be of organic growth, partly of emergent evolution into the fields of the new; and, hence, a vital part of its technique must be recognized as experiment. Its final objective, therefore, will be somewhat vague and general,—a statement of direction and effort rather than a goal. From the economic point of view it can, perhaps, be stated as a steadily, if slowly rising general standard of living, with the. maximum possible freedom from large and abrupt fluctuations. . . . the problem of national planning is therefore not how to jump from complete laissez-faire to complete social control. We haven't, and never have had, the one, and haven't, and probably never will have the other.[59]

In light of this flexible notion of national planning as a process involving cooperation between organized groups, Dennison argued that his proposed planning board must consist of prestigious members willing to consult with existing research agencies in business, cooperating with both the executive branch and Congressional committees, and educating the wider public. Above all, he stressed that the board must not be told specifically what to plan; they must decide for themselves on both subjects of study, the topics on which to report, and when.[60]

Significantly, Dennison saw American national planning as requiring a "plan for planning"—the first report of the National Planning Board in June 1934 used these exact words. He included a multilayered "five-year plan for planning" encompassing for each year ideas for action, for study and action, and for study. For the first year, he suggested public works planning over a five-to-ten-year period and the development of trade associations—ideas raised by Hoover's Unemployment Conference studies and his actions as secretary of commerce. The banking system must be strengthened, and single industries such as coal must be studied along with taxation policies. The rest of his cataloged suggestions seem today like an inventory of later New Deal projects: study of housing problems, distribution of commodities as well as wealth and income, statistical data gathering, improvement of antitrust laws, study of agricultural problems, creation of a permanent relief organization, analysis of labor laws and business forecasting, and oversight by the government of power production. In the last section of his paper, Dennison suggested the president, after consultation with organized interests, should appoint a small planning board of five to seven people. The board could use existing research agencies as consultants and have the authority to establish a small permanent staff complemented by ad hoc staff members. Members of the board should serve as paid, full-time staff officers coming from "professional men who have had close connection with business, and in that new and growing field of business professionalism; economists like [Bryce] Stewart; engineer-business men like [Ralph E.] Flanders; analytical accountants like [?] Ernst; highly trained trade association managers like [?] Compton; a working political scientist like [Charles E.] Merriam; and so on."[61]

At first, Dennison's approach to national planning differed somewhat from Delano's and Merriam's and was more in line with Mitchell's in placing more emphasis on the practical usefulness of private, voluntary experience from the business community. Though Dennison had served on governmental bodies, his primary experience came from his own corporation, trade association work, and the ad hoc social science research networks that grew out of the 1921 Unemployment Conference. His ideas on voluntary cooperation between business and government went farther than Hoover's, as the 1929–33 period showed, but leaned more toward business control than did Delano's. Merriam downplayed the relation of business and government to emphasize professionalism and the advisory role of social scientists acting in concert with private and public institutions. Dennison's growing commitment to careful economic research, especially on the business cycle, aimed at producing practical business results closely mirrored Mitchell's. Dennison was an appropriate replacement for the resigning Mitchell.

Yet the overall similarities between Delano, Merriam, Mitchell, and Dennison overshadowed any differences in degree. All four had reached the modern organizational view of society as ranged along lines of group interest, only the terms were different. What Delano called "the community of interest," Merriam referred to as "political pluralism." Mitchell's concern with "recent economic and social changes" paralleled Dennison's search for "the middle way." All four nascent planners argued for the necessity of cooperation among business leaders, politicians, social science professionals, and research groups as part of an advisory planning process. They favored appointment of a national planning board by the president that could serve as a national staff advisory group, leaving final decisions up to the existing political process. The planners' individual routes to planning remained distinct in particulars, but the end result was very much the same. Only the mixture of ideas, people, and institutions differed in place, time, and dominant group influence. Dennison's entry into the early New Deal, however, underscored the differences and hid the similarities. Nevertheless, in 1932 he also abandoned President Herbert C. Hoover, who had seemed so promising in the 1920s, to vote for

Franklin D. Roosevelt. He made the transition from Hooverian voluntarism to Rooseveltian New Deal reform as smoothly as Delano and Merriam and with fewer qualms than Mitchell, who felt obligated to leave the planning board in 1935.

Roosevelt's inauguration as president on March 4, 1933, coincided with Dennison's fifty-sixth birthday. Affected deeply by the weaknesses in New Era capitalism revealed by the Depression, he willingly joined the Roosevelt administration in several advisory positions. His work for the Business Advisory and Planning Council (BAPC), the Industrial Advisory Board (IAB) of the National Recovery Administration, and the National Labor Board led to his appointment to the planning agency. Work for these New Deal agencies involved application of the voluntarist ideals from his associational activities of the 1920s, expansion of companies' welfare capitalist reforms in hopes of finding a "middle way" between no union recognition and full industrial democracy to hold back the rising tide of industrial unionism, and ongoing evolution of Dennison's ideas on national planning.

The BAPC grew out of the trade association ideas of Secretary of Commerce Hoover, but it included two new ideas. Hoover's conception of voluntary association encompassed industrial self-government by trade associations guided by economic information provided by governmental agencies such as the Department of Commerce. In March/April 1933 the new secretary of commerce, Daniel Roper, called for the creation of the BAPC as a form of industrial self-government to promote active cooperation between business and the federal government. While BAPC funding came from private business sources, its offices were in the Department of Commerce building in Washington, D.C. Large manufacturing corporations and industry trade associations selected members to serve on the BAPC.[62] BAPC historian Kim McQuaid notes that members came from three groups: executives such as Gerard Swope and Walter Teagle from technologically intensive industries, some trade association executives from decentralized industries such as cotton textiles, and "innovative scientific managers like Henry S. Dennison." Moving beyond the strict voluntarist lines drawn by Hoover in the 1928–32 period, the BAPC, McQuaid notes, was "in the government, but not *of* it."[63]

In its early years the BAPC focused on making the National Recovery Administration work to effect economic recovery in the industrial sector. As the major piece of the early New Deal's recovery efforts, the NRA enacted a modified version of the New Era ideal of industrial self-government, with some concessions to government supervision and industrial workers' right to organize unions.[64] Dennison's participation in the BAPC put him at the center of this experiment in sectoral economic planning through service on various committees that dealt with both the wider implications of the NRA and the more practical advisory function of drawing up and presenting proposed industrial codes. This work led naturally to his continuing reconsideration of national planning and his advocacy of "fair competition" through codes of production, pricing, and wages for such industries as tag manufacturing, paper box producers, and sealing wax firms.

By the fall of 1933 Dennison entered the entangling world of industrial code hearings to advise his fellow business executives to accept the new world of economic cooperation through fair competition. Early in November 1933 he became chairman of a BAPC committee established to study Gerard Swope's proposal for a National Chamber of Commerce and Industry modeled on the War Industries Board, Wilson's Industrial Conferences of 1919–20, the trade association movement of the 1920s, the Swope Plan of 1931, and various plans advanced by the U.S. Chamber of Commerce in 1931 and 1932. Dennison accepted Swope's argument about the need to continue some sort of industrial self-government, but he differed with Swope in regard to what governmental agency might best carry on the work of the NRA. Expanding his earlier planning ideas, Dennison saw an integral role for the federal government in supervision and data collection. Again seeking the middle way between voluntary organization by trade associations and government compulsion, Dennison supported the idea of minor concessions to labor and consumers. Reviving his welfare capitalist view of labor relations based on his firm's experience, Dennison advocated minimum wages, maximum hours, continued abolition of child labor, gradual development of health and safety standards, and use of unemployment reserves and separation allowances for laid-off workers. The issues of the future of the NRA, labor policy, and national planning plagued the BAPC and entangled its members on the Industrial Advisory Board of the NRA.[65]

At the first BAPC meeting on June 26, 1933, NRA administrator General Hugh Johnson, Swope's boss at the War Industries Board during the Great War, asked the BAPC to appoint members to a new Industrial Advisory Board to represent employers in the policy formulation, code writing, and administration of the NRA. In theory, the business-oriented IAB was complemented by both labor and consumer boards, but in practice the IAB dominated the drafting of NRA industrial codes. Ideally, Johnson hoped to establish a three-pronged, corporatist-oriented organization consisting of the Industrial Advisory Board, the Labor Advisory Board, and the Consumers' Advisory Board to balance interest-group representation within the pluralistic system. As several studies of the NRA show, the IAB proved by far the most influential of the boards in leading the NRA toward a corporate orientation that left small businesses, workers, and consumers underrepresented and powerless. The board paralleled the BAPC in its function emphasizing general policy discussions and implementation of industry codes. Between January and April 1934 Dennison served on the IAB during the very period that saw the disintegration of consensus over the NRA's sponsorship of corporate-dominated codes, the labor provisions of Section 7a granting workers the right to organize unions, and small business support for continuation of the NRA. Experience on both the BAPC and the IAB led Dennison to expand his idea of national planning to seek the middle way between associationalism and government compulsion and to revive his welfare capitalist views on labor policy.[66]

During his tenure on the IAB, Dennison sought to mediate between employers anxious to eliminate the labor provisions of the National Industrial Recovery Act (Section 7a) and union representatives trying to push for labor's right to organize, bargain collectively, and win recognition for independent unionism. Relying on his own firm's experience and ideas from Wilson's first Industrial Conference in 1919, Dennison argued for the middle way by compromising—both company unions and independent unions should be allowed under the NRA. In a draft report regarding the proposed Wagner (National Labor Relations) bill of 1935 after the Labor Advisory Board, the National Labor Board, and other compromises had fallen through, Dennison revealed his own dependence on the welfare capitalist model, which had worked only partially in large corporations but had failed in the midst of the Depression. He ignored the growing sentiment for industrial unionism in the basic industries that would shortly lead to the creation of the Committee for Industrial Organization (CIO) within the American Federation of Labor. While taking a relatively liberal attitude within both the wider business community and the select members of the BAPC, Dennison still leaned toward corporate control of national planning in the industrial sector of the economy. For a short time, he served as chairman of the National Labor Board, but as the labor policies of the early New Deal fell apart, Dennison turned to other activities.[67]

The crux of Dennison's failure lay in his desire to bring together all interested organized groups under the voluntary harmony intended by the NRA. The limitations of this liberal pluralist model of economic reality led to problems for all of the members of Roosevelt's planning agency throughout the 1933–43 period. Yet this weakness was not self-evident in 1934. In a 1934 memorandum for the IAB, Dennison drew on his earlier "Five-Year Plan for Planning" (1932) to argue for public works planning; planning in such areas as taxation, governmental efficiency, agriculture, housing, natural resources, and business; and study of the national distribution of income. Despite efforts to convince the U.S. Chamber of Commerce, various trade association executives, and disillusioned members of the BAPC to continue with the NRA experiment, Dennison remained caught in the collapsing structure of the NRA.[68]

In another 1934 memorandum, "Suggestions for a Popular Presentation of Planning," Dennison brought together his earlier ideas on planning. Including whole sections from the 1932 paper prepared for Gay's private group at Harvard, Dennison now brought his proposals into the public arena. Significantly, he changed only one major section—that on the structure of the planning board. He suggested three alternatives: creating a national planning board of five permanent men of "integrating minds" along with nine part-time men possibly representing organized interests, developing a full-time agency under Roosevelt's National Emergency Council, or his preferred alternative of expanding the functions and funding of the currently existing National Planning Board, which included Delano, Merriam, and Mitchell. Dennison was ready to move on to government national planning.[69]

As the NRA collapsed and BAPC members wrangled over continuation of the NRA and labor policies, Dennison renewed contacts that led to the New Deal planning agency. Having known Merriam since the mid-1920s, he came to know him even better through participation in the Hanover conferences of the Social Science Research Council. In June 1934 Merriam suggested that the National Planning Board and the BAPC arrange a meeting to discuss their mutual interests. Secretary of Commerce Daniel Roper had interested both Merriam and Delano in the idea. By September 1935 Delano and Merriam were looking for a replacement for the resigning Mitchell. After consultations with Secretary of Commerce Roper, Secretary of the Interior Harold Ickes, and President Roosevelt, Delano and Merriam decided to create an advisory group representing the business community. They chose Henry Dennison and Beardsley Ruml to fill the positions. In December 1935 Dennison accepted Roosevelt's appointment and attended his first meeting of the National Resources Committee on January 18, 1936. Dennison now joined these men of "integrating minds" with whom he entertained such faith for the future of national planning.[70]

As a prominent, successful business leader who had an established track record with business reformers in the Progressive Era, wartime mobilizers of 1917–18, associationalist activists throughout the 1920s, and New Dealers in the early 1930s, Dennison was the most interesting business advocate of national planning by the mid-1930s. In March 1935 he wrote his friend Ida M. Tarbell about what might happen if nothing were done to spark recovery and reform: "If the old system comes back, I'll bet a thousand to one that it might succeed for a few years but would go into a worse tailspin than '32 ever thought of being, and would end in a revolution. Personally, I would rather try to work our way out in an evolutionary fashion than to have revolutionary results tried out on us."[71] Fearing a possible revolution, Dennison continued to seek the middle way. He rejected theories of monarchy, aristocracy, reaction, and revolution in favor of the "middle-of-the-roaders." Seeing American society as divided into organizational groups such as business, labor, and agriculture vying for influence with the federal government, Dennison advocated moderate reform often based on the corporate models of his own experience as the only way out of the Depression and its possible concomitants of reaction or revolution.[72]

With the growing alienation of many in the business community from the New Deal by 1935, Dennison and his fellow planners represented a small but significant counterpoint that might revive the New Deal's interest in national planning. By 1936 his ideas about national planning closely paralleled those of FDR's other planners. He saw planning as an ongoing process in which professional representatives of organized groups could use social science research to advise the president without becoming embroiled in political factionalism. He equated business efficiency and welfare capitalism, managerial expertise, voluntary associational activity, and economic research with a corporatist model of national planning sponsored by the federal government that sounded much like the ideas of his fellow New Deal planners. Henry S. Dennison remained committed to the industrial capitalist system and thought national planning might offer a way to preserve the economic order that he had helped to build. His commitment to New Deal planning continued despite the death of his wife in 1936, two heart attacks in 1937 and 1941, and gradually increasing detachment from the daily operations of the firm.[73]

6

Beardsley Ruml, Foundation Manager

PHILANTHROPY, SOCIAL SCIENCE, AND PUBLIC POLICY

NEW DEAL planning grew from the ideas, values, and institutions of the planners themselves, many of whom were products of a new national social science research network financed by a second generation of philanthropic managers. In the New Era of the 1920s, the future New Deal planner Beardsley Ruml was the most important of these philanthropic managers in his position as director of the Laura Spelman Rockefeller Memorial.[1] Ruml envisioned and financed the creation of a national social science research network that brought together people like Merriam, Mitchell, Dennison, Hoover, and Hunt. More important, it brought together such leading institutions as the University of Chicago, the NBER, the SSRC, the social science professional associations, and the various Hoover planning bodies that grew out of the Unemployment Conference of 1921, which in turn culminated in the Recent Economic Changes study and the President's Research Committee on Social Trends. Yet Ruml's path to the New Deal planning agency took a less direct route than had his fellow planners. His career as a philanthropic manager mirrored the rise of organized philanthropy as an underwriter of voluntarist ad hoc planning under Secretary of Commerce Herbert Hoover. Like the other planners, Ruml participated in a range of institutions that belied an older nineteenth-century distinction between private- and public-sector work.[2] As a twentieth-century man, Ruml combined philanthropy, social science, and public-policy advising in ways that are today difficult to reconstruct but that reflect the complex roots of New Deal planning.

140

The first generation of philanthropists, from the late nineteenth century, had to learn how to create, organize, and consolidate voluntary agencies that would carry on their intended work. The best of these philanthropies recruited a new generation of leaders, such as Beardsley Ruml, who could manage large capital endowments, administer sizable grants to the rapidly professionalizing research community, and begin to plan for long-term creation of scientific research programs that would not waste the social capital that the first generation of philanthropists sought to invest as stewards to urban-industrial America. Many of the second-generation philanthropic managers came out of the war mobilization experience of 1917–18 to join foundations that participated in Hooverian planning efforts in the 1920s, which brought together people like Delano, Merriam, Mitchell, Dennison, and Ruml.[3]

By the 1920s the philanthropic world was no longer centered in the earlier generation of wealthy industrialists, their friends, and class allies in politics, society, and higher education. As industrialization changed the nation, so too did philanthropy. Along with business corporations, labor unions, professional political parties, and the various academic professional associations, philanthropic foundations entered into the organizational society.[4] First came the Carnegie philanthropies endowed by the Pittsburgh steelmaker Andrew Carnegie: the Carnegie Institute of Pittsburgh (1896), the Carnegie Institution of Washington, D.C. (1902), the Carnegie Hero Fund (1904), the Carnegie Foundation for the Advancement of Teaching (1905), the Carnegie Endowment for International Peace (1910), and the Carnegie Corporation of New York (1911). Not to be outdone, Standard Oil founder John D. Rockefeller, Sr., created a series of Rockefeller-funded philanthropies: the Rockefeller Institute for Medical Research (1901), the General Education Board (1902), the Rockefeller Foundation (1913), and later the Spelman Fund of New York (1928). As each of these foundations matured, it had to find skilled managers capable of carrying the institution into the next stage of philanthropy.[5] At the center of this whirlwind was Beardsley Ruml, director of the Laura Spelman Rockefeller Memorial (1918).

Of the five New Deal planners, Ruml was the most creative, unorthodox, and private. His name became a household word only in 1943, just as the planning board came to an end. Throughout his life, Ruml gathered a host of colorful nicknames, though most friends called him simply "B." In college, classmates knew him as "Rum." Soon enough he earned the title "Big Breeze," for his volubility, which evolved into the shortened "B Ruml." Some associates called him "Brummel." Others saw Ruml as

"Dr. Johnson," for his penchant of conducting business over a good meal spiced with tasty drinks. After one of the annual Social Science Research Council's conferences at Hanover, New Hampshire, Charles Merriam referred to Ruml as "the New Machiavelli." *Fortune* magazine termed him "Buddha," for his contemplative poses among associates at the University of Chicago. His bent toward experimentation at the University of Chicago earned Ruml the name "Cuckoo." Journalists gave Ruml the name "Falstaff," for his good cheer and enjoyment of life. Opponents of Ruml's pay-as-you-go income tax plan of 1943 branded him "Rommel," after the German general. Late in his career, Merriam compared Ruml with Walter Lippmann and Stuart Chase as "the Merchant Prince." Many people in positions of influence knew Ruml, though few knew him well.[6]

In the period 1922–46, Ruml proved an astute wielder of power and influence in a public life and career now virtually forgotten. Educated in applied psychology at the birth of that profession, he joined the wartime mobilization effort of 1917–18, bringing the use of mental tests to the U.S. Army's selection of personnel to fight the war. In 1922 he switched to philanthropic management, presiding over the creation of the Social Science Research Council. Recognizing the importance of well-supported research, Ruml moved on to head the Spelman Fund of New York, just as social science came to the foreground as a potential tool with which to confront the Great Depression. With President Robert Maynard Hutchins of the University of Chicago, Ruml sought to integrate professional knowledge through curricular reform. Hutchins called Ruml "the founder of the social sciences in America."[7] As businesses fought to regain losses in the Depression, Ruml took the position of treasurer of the R. H. Macy department store in New York City. Amid the proliferation of alphabet-soup agencies in Roosevelt's New Deal, Ruml worked quietly within circles of advisory influence in ways that cannot be completely recovered today. Brought in to head the newly created Public Administration Clearing House at Chicago in 1930, Louis Brownlow thought that Ruml was "one of the most complex and comprehensive minds of modern times."[8]

Throughout his career, Ruml played the role of policy catalyst, rather than that of expert or political leader. Many friends and colleagues remembered Ruml as an "idea man" who sparked new ways of looking at old problems, initiated debate in policy circles only to move on to the next problem, and always allowed others to take credit for his ideas. Charles Merriam's view of Ruml as the new Machiavelli was echoed by

Roosevelt's secretary of labor, Frances Perkins, who saw Ruml as "very much the fox," adding that "the thing he wants is never the thing he appears to want."[9]

Ruml rivaled Delano, Merriam, Mitchell, and Dennison in importance while spreading his intellectual and institutional net more widely than any of them. Journalist Alva Johnston, in a 1945 issue of *The New Yorker,* wrote that Ruml's "career is almost geological in its mixed stratification of science, public affairs, and private business."[10] Beginning with psychological studies, Ruml seized the opportunity to move into philanthropic work as head of the innovative Laura Spelman Rockefeller Memorial. Working with a number of social scientists, the prestigious Charles Merriam principal among them, Ruml reorganized the LSRM to move in the same direction as Delano, Merriam, Mitchell, and Dennison. Arguing for the utility of social science research, Ruml briefly entered the academy in the early years of the Great Depression. But in the 1930s and 1940s he moved back into private business and governmental advisory work to become an aide in major policy decisions of Roosevelt's New Deal. In 1935 Ruml joined FDR's planning board with Dennison as a fellow representative of the business community.

Not much is known about Ruml's early life. His grandfather, Vaclav Ruml, worked as a shawl maker in a small town outside Prague in the 1860s after serving as an officer in the Austro-Hungarian cavalry. Deciding that his skill would not serve him well in a modernizing society, Vaclav gathered one hundred dollars and sailed for the United States. One among millions of new immigrants to urban-industrial America, he worked as a common laborer for the rest of his life, highly respected in the Bohemian community in Cedar Rapids, Iowa. His son Wentzle worked hard to gain an apprenticeship with the local doctor, followed by study at Northwestern University Medical School. An accomplished brain surgeon, Wentzle married Salome Beardsley, supervisor of nurses at St. Luke's Hospital in Cedar Rapids. The combination of sturdy Czech origins and Salome's durable New England Scottish-English background must have worked well. On November 5, 1894, Beardsley Ruml entered the world ready to build on the achievements of his parents. His father owned three farms, ran a successful medical practice, and garnered a reputation as a skilled surgeon. Beardsley Ruml's childhood remains unknown except for several stories he passed out to every journalist who came his way. He told all these interviewers that as a child he was frugal, developed an acute business sense, and showed a talent for mathematical calculation. Ruml was a bright, hard-working student at Cedar Rapids'

Washington High School, graduating in only three years with a 98 average.[11]

As a superior student, Ruml obtained excellent educational credentials that served him well. At Dartmouth College he briefly tried out for the football team, but his 190-pound frame and poor coordination soon led to more sedentary activities. He edited the literary paper *Bema,* acted in and wrote plays, and studied psychology and philosophy. Graduation in three and one half years with honors in both fields led to his selection for Phi Beta Kappa. Ruml's study under Walter Van Dyke Bingham proved the key to his early career in psychology, just as that field was emerging as a professional discipline.[12] Bingham obtained a postgraduate fellowship for Ruml to study psychology under Bingham's own doctoral adviser, James R. Angell, at the University of Chicago. While at Chicago, Ruml studied the relatively new field of mental testing, completing his doctoral work under the direction of the well-known and respected psychologist Angell. Angell published Ruml's Ph.D. dissertation, "The Reliability of Mental Tests in the Division of an Academic Group," in *Psychological Monographs,* a university-sponsored professional journal that Angell edited. Early contact with Angell provided Ruml with enormous advantages, as his mentor later became the dean of faculties and acting president of the University of Chicago, chairman of the National Research Council, president of the Carnegie Corporation, and president of Yale University.[13] In the summer of 1917 Ruml seemed headed for a traditional academic career in psychology. He married Lois Treadwell, a fellow graduate student and daughter of a Vassar zoology professor and soon thereafter entered the work that turned his career in a more practical direction. Though he never again actively engaged in scholarly research, Ruml's studies in mental testing and his contacts with Bingham, Angell, and Walter Dill Scott stood him in good stead.

The same year that Ruml graduated from Dartmouth, Bingham moved to the Carnegie Institute of Technology in Pittsburgh to set up the first department of applied psychology in the United States. Ruml joined his mentor as a member of the school's psychology faculty. In 1916, at the request of several prominent businessmen, Bingham established the Bureau of Salesmanship Research at the school, which led to the practical application of psychological principles from the academy to the business world. He borrowed the services of Walter Dill Scott of Northwestern University, who became the director of the bureau. Scott pioneered in the field of applied psychology based on his earlier work developing psychological tests, which aided businesses in hiring, training, and transferring salesmen.[14] Ruml's work with Bingham and Scott in Pittsburgh led directly to his entry into wartime mobilization work in 1917.

With the American entry into the Great War, Scott, Bingham, and Robert M. Yerkes of the American Psychological Association and a special committee of the recently established National Research Council sought to interest the federal government in the application of modified tests to determine the mental competence of draftees about to enter the armed forces. Yerkes proved more interested in the value of test results for professional knowledge, while Scott gained the approval of Secretary of War Newton D. Baker for a limited program for testing of candidates for Officer Training School. Scott outdid Yerkes with the founding of an expanded program through creation of the Committee on Classification of Personnel in the Army (CCPA) in the Adjutant General's Office of the War Department. Simultaneously Yerkes began application of mental testing programs through the Medical Department of the Surgeon General's Office. Eventually the work in intelligence and trade testing fused in the CCPA's activities.[15]

The CCPA carried the earlier work and most of the staffs from Scott's and Bingham's division of applied psychology and the Bureau of Salesmanship Research into the wartime mobilization effort. Committee members, including Beardsley Ruml, sought to apply the techniques of interviewing, intelligence testing, trade testing, and occupational skill classification from the business and academic areas to the problem of manpower hiring, training, and assignment in the armed services. Bringing along business employment managers and trained academic psychologists such as Angell and Ruml, Scott and Bingham organized government programs in personnel management that flourished in large corporations during the 1920s.[16] Using technical research skills, these managers performed work akin to that of other wartime agencies staffed by such men as Delano, Merriam, Mitchell, and Dennison.

Ruml had been teaching and serving as Bingham's assistant at Carnegie when CCPA directors Scott and Bingham called him to war work. At the test laboratory in Newark, New Jersey, Ruml directed reliability tests for the Test Trades Division of the CCPA, later heading that division, which developed the occupational tests to determine skill levels and work assignments for the U.S. Army draftees.[17] While it was only a brief excursion into applied psychology, this job kept Ruml in contact with Scott and Bingham and renewed his link with Angell. Seeing the value of applied research to meet the social problem of allocating human resources,

Ruml now turned away from an academic career to enter a fruitful period of philanthropic management in support of social science research.

Ruml's transition from practical psychologist to philanthropic manager was aided by his circle of associates, which included Scott, Bingham, and Angell. After the dissolution of the CCPA in the immediate postwar years, these three men took important positions in academia or business. Scott returned to teaching at Northwestern University but kept his hand in applied psychology. In 1919 he and other veterans of the CCPA formed an industrial psychology consulting firm, the Scott Company, based in Philadelphia. Scott served as president, while Ruml took over as secretary. The Scott Company was the first consulting agency in a rapidly burgeoning field that aimed at advising ways to control work forces and promote harmony between employers and workers. It prospered briefly until its key members moved on to other jobs. Scott became president of Northwestern. Ruml rejoined his patron Angell. While a member of the Scott Company, Ruml sought to encourage large corporations and the more experimental medium-sized firms, including the Dennison Manufacturing Company, to modify the wartime trade tests to suit their firms' interests.[18]

Members of the CCPA also carried on their scientific research on industrial psychology as well as practical consulting advice to businesses. The key people were on the National Research Council's Committee on Industrial Personnel Research, chaired by Robert M. Yerkes, a leading psychologist who had been involved in the wartime use of psychology as well. With interest in psychology growing, the NRC committee called for the creation of an umbrella organization that could act as a national clearinghouse for personnel research. In 1919 Bingham, Scott, Angell, and Ruml formed the Personnel Research Federation to bring together business schools and specialized research departments at the universities, large corporations such as American Telephone and Telegraph, medium-size companies such as the Dennison Manufacturing Company, and key federal agencies such as the Bureau of Labor Statistics. The federation sought funds through voluntary dues, application to wealthy individuals such as John D. Rockefeller, Jr., and contracting jobs with companies such as the White Motor Company. Bingham edited its periodical, the *Journal of Personnel Research,* and served as its head for most of the decade.[19] In the early 1920s Ruml tried to organize an umbrella research organization like the SSRC, soon to be founded by Merriam and Mitchell, but with a turn in his fortunes, Ruml's interests shifted.

Just as Charles E. Merriam used contact with his brother John C. Merriam, former president of the National Research Council, so too Beardsley Ruml used his link with James R. Angell, who in 1920 succeeded John C. Merriam as president of the NRC during its transition to peacetime. Through the efforts of founder George Ellery Hale, the NRC retained presidential approval to continue its research work but had to find private sources of support. The developing ties between research groups organized on a voluntary basis and philanthropic foundations adopting managerial leadership brought new positions for both former NRC presidents. After his tenure at the National Research Council, John Merriam moved on to head the Carnegie Institution of Washington, D.C., while Angell accepted the presidency of the Carnegie Corporation in 1921 and asked his protégé Ruml to come along as his assistant.[20]

Though Angell and Ruml remained at the Carnegie Corporation for only a little over one year, they created quite a stir among the older trustees. Within that short time they allocated almost $30 million for various projects, which kept corporation funds tied up for years. To overcome the problem, Ruml originated the idea of "income warrants," which banks would discount for a 5 percent return. One Carnegie Corporation official later suggested that the technique was akin to using Keynesian financing to plan the philanthropy's future. Ruml gained his initial experience in politicking with trustees, promoting a long-term plan for funding of projects, and revealing a penchant for managerial innovation that he would fine-tune throughout the rest of the 1920s.[21]

In 1921, when Angell moved on to the presidency of Yale University, he did not forget Ruml. Moving easily in philanthropic circles, Angell talked regularly with such people as Abraham Flexner and Raymond B. Fosdick, both close advisers to John D. Rockefeller, Jr. The younger Rockefeller wanted to invest millions in various philanthropic projects but found the job beyond the abilities of any one individual. He faced the dilemma of how to provide for the transition in leadership of the four major Rockefeller foundations from the founding generation to a second generation of skilled philanthropic managers. In 1921 Rockefeller adviser Fosdick looked for a promising young man who could conduct several surveys about possible Rockefeller contributions to the Metropolitan Museum of Art, the American Museum of Natural History, and the New York Public Library. After talking with Flexner and Angell, Fosdick decided on Ruml for the temporary job. By the end of 1921 Fosdick suggested to Rockefeller that one of the smaller philanthropies of the family, the Laura Spelman Rockefeller Memorial, ought to be reorganized. Ruml seemed to be the right man for the job.[22]

Writing to Rockefeller, Fosdick neatly captured Ruml at a turning point in his life: "Ruml is a young man—in fact, he is not quite 30—but he gives the appearance of being 37 or 38. He is quiet, thoughtful and studious, and I believe he would soon develop a grasp not only of the problems of the Memorial but of its future possibilities. He has, too, a very pleasing, friendly personality and meets people easily and gracefully. . . . He would come with the highest recommendations from all sorts of people. His mind is elastic, he has youth and wide experience to commend him, and I think he would be useful to you in many ways."[23] About to enter the most important years of his career, Ruml seized his advantage and accepted the position as director of the memorial in early 1922.

At the time of Ruml's appointment, four Rockefeller philanthropic foundations existed.[24] The Rockefeller Institute for Medical Research (1901) focused on the field of medical research and education. The General Education Board (1902) emphasized research on education. After a bitter debate in Congress, followed by the outbreak of violent industrial war at the Rockefeller-controlled Colorado Fuel and Iron Company, the Rockefeller Foundation received a charter in 1913 to expand the family's philanthropic interests.[25] Following the death of his wife, Laura Spelman Rockefeller, John D. Rockefeller, Sr., founded the Laura Spelman Rockefeller Memorial in 1918 with a grant of almost $64 million. Initially the memorial appropriated philanthropic gifts to the favorite personal causes of Mrs. Rockefeller. Finding they had a surplus of funds, trustees moved into wider concerns centered on the welfare of women and children. By late 1921 the LSRM held almost a $74 million principal, with annual funds of $4 million available for its work. Yet trustees found the LSRM's program narrow, unimaginative, and unfocused. On the recommendation of fellow Rockefeller advisers James Angell and Abraham Flexner, Fosdick convinced the younger Rockefeller, who had been given charge of the memorial, that Beardsley Ruml showed promise of being able to turn the philanthropy into a dynamic, viable organization with a definite purpose. Ruml did not disappoint Fosdick, Rockefeller, Jr., or the trustees.[26]

In the letter to Rockefeller recommending Ruml, Fosdick raised several key issues regarding the future of the LSRM. Fearing public opinion might view suspiciously the memorial's support of traditional Rockefeller personal causes, he suggested an expansion of the board of trustees, a consolidation of interests around two or three major national or international programs, and several possible fields for these new endeavors. Fosdick pointed to the problem faced by many of the philanthropic enterprises in the period that had begun as the personal creations of men who had gained enormous fortunes through the building of industrial empires in the late nineteenth century. Many operated through the good graces of the founding fathers and men of their generation, many of whom were ill equipped to face the challenges of twentieth-century problems and skeptical of the centralizing administrative structures pioneered by the new national business corporations. Ruml served as the entering wedge bringing these new methods into the memorial from which they might ripple out to the other Rockefeller boards by the end of the 1920s.[27]

Charles Merriam later said of Ruml's role at the LSRM that "Ruml was a dynamic, catalytic influence whose chief function was bringing people together, energizing and stimulating."[28] Organizing a skilled group of men interested in promoting a more active role for philanthropy in addressing current social problems so as to bring about social equilibrium, Ruml soon proved worth his salary. Hired at $7,500 per year in 1922, he won increases for restructuring the memorial that led to the munificent wage of $15,000 by the end of the decade.[29] Taking his new career in stride, he later said, "The fact is, I had Foundation trouble: a large fund, some $75,000,000 dedicated to the advancement of human welfare, but without policy or program."[30] LSRM staff came from the emerging disciplines of psychology, social welfare, and statistics, and many of them had worked on the wartime boards of 1917–18. Many moved into key positions with the Rockefeller Foundation in the 1930s and New Deal agencies in the 1930s and 1940s.[31]

Officially appointed director of the LSRM in May 1922, Ruml set to work on his first long-range plan. By October 1922 he presented a lengthy report to the board of trustees that reviewed past efforts, noted present surplus funds, provided a rationale for a new program that was set out, gave specific recommendations to implement the plan, and noted the fiscal feasibility of his plan. He suggested a reworking of the memorial's policy to concentrate on social science research as applied to contemporary social problems.[32]

Before Ruml's program, the LSRM had followed the other Rockefeller boards in supporting work in widely scattered fields, with some emphasis on public health and voluntary efforts in social welfare. From 1918 to 1923 the LSRM aided emergency relief efforts in Europe and China, various Baptist denominational organizations, and assorted social welfare groups. Noting an excess of at least $2 million per year after grants to these groups, Ruml saw resources being wasted. He argued that helping individual social welfare projects operated by diverse individuals or small charities did not help those who most needed help. Rather, a concerted effort should be made to concentrate on two or three fields over an extended period of time: "The problem of policy for the Memorial is not the problem of shaping a single year's activities; it is rather the problem of determining the work of a period of years, perhaps a decade." He continued, "It is, of course, not the intention to attempt to fix at this time the precise channels of expenditure for this vast amount."[33] While different in particulars, Ruml's ideas paralleled the contemporaneous efforts of Delano in city and regional planning, Merriam in political science, Mitchell in business-cycle studies, and Dennison in business planning and welfare capitalism. Like them, Ruml sought rationalization and coordination through planning: "It is also true that *the field chosen must not be so wide that the Memorial's influence will be lost in a scattering of efforts, coordinated perhaps, but unequal to the task. A program to be satisfactory must be broad enough, but at the same time precise enough. It must reach fundamental issues, but it must not drive too deep. It must produce results of basic importance; but it must be produce results."[34]

Ruml's rationale stemmed from his recognition of the changing role of institutions in the new organizational society and called for a synthesis of current research methodologies: *"An examination of the operations of organizations in the field of social welfare shows as a primary need the development of the social sciences and the production of a body of substantiated and widely accepted generalizations as to human capacities and motives and as to the behavior of human beings as individuals and in groups.* Under the term 'social sciences' we may include sociology, ethnology, anthropology, and psychology, and certain aspects of economics, history, political economy, and biology."[35] Ruml remained critical of a too "pure" social research that did not confront existing social problems. Research should bring practical results over the long run to meet social problems stemming from what sociologist William Fielding Ogburn at the same called the social lag between technology and values: "The need for knowledge of social forces is certainly very great. Not only is it required by social welfare organizations, but by business and industry, and by agencies of government as well. *It is becoming more and more clearly recognized that unless means are found of meeting the complex social problems that are so rapidly developing, our increasing control of physical forces may prove increasingly destructive of human values. To be sure, social knowledge is not a substitute for social righteousness: but unless we are ready to admit that the situation is utterly hopeless, we must believe that knowledge is a far greater aid to righteousness than is ignorance. . . . Here then is a field and a program—*

the development of the social sciences and the production of a body of fact and prin-
ciple that will be utilized in the solution of social problems."[36] Although social
scientific knowledge might help to solve social problems, Ruml argued
that existing research agencies did not have the trained people or the institutional base needed for such an ambitious program.

The LSRM, Ruml argued, should take up arms to build a national
social science research network. Using its enormous financial resources,
it could help to educate social scientists and build the necessary institutions. To implement his plan, he thought it best to award grants to universities, private research agencies, and, to a much lesser extent, governmental agencies to build a national network of research centers. These
centers should be permanent and institutionalized programs located in
large universities and would need scholars with the necessary research
credentials, wide-ranging interdisciplinary contacts, and a broad exposure to people, places, and research trends around the country and across
the seas.

As he explained to Raymond Fosdick, Ruml intended a social science
research plan that would be both modern and conservative. Arguing that
the previous work of the LSRM was outmoded, Ruml looked to a
"trickle down" approach with emphasis on a coordinated program in the
social sciences: "Question might properly be raised as to whether the
most rapid advance in human welfare will come though a general eleva-
tion of masses of 'backward' peoples. In education, in science, in art, the
truly significant advances are made, not by attempting to bring those of
inferior talents up to a general level of mediocrity, but rather by the intensive cultivation of opportunities for the unusually able. May it not also be
true that in attempting to improve general standards of civilization the
point of attack is the social organizations of the 'advanced' rather than of
the 'backward' peoples?. . . . I am not a historian, but is it not true that
the violent disruptions of civilized life in the past have come, not from
the invasion of barbarian hordes, but from the disorganization which had
developed within the 'advanced' societies themselves?"[37] After John D.
Rockefeller, Jr., and the LSRM trustees approved Ruml's plan, Fosdick
later reported, "Ruml proceeded with vigor and shrewdness to implement his ideas."[38]

Ruml's October 1922 memorandum called for initiatives in three major areas: social science, child study and parent education, and studies in
interracial relations. While the LSRM funded agencies in all of these for
the rest of the decade, its major grants went to the emerging centers of
social science research in the universities. Recognizing that these centers

would need help in terms of specific research projects, administrative expenses, physical plant, research assistance, and skilled personnel, the LSRM provided block grants to key universities. Universities receiving aid included Harvard, Yale, Columbia, North Carolina, Virginia, Syracuse, Stanford, Cornell, Vanderbilt, Pennsylvania, and several others. In each case, the memorial sought to aid specialized research centers that promised to become leaders in their fields. The LSRM, for example, laid the financial groundwork for Howard Odum's Institute for Research in Social Science at the University of North Carolina, which pioneered in regional and race relations studies. Sir William Beveridge of the London School of Economics and Political Science accepted huge contributions from the memorial to construct new buildings.[39]

Not surprisingly, the LSRM began its program with support for the formation of the Local Community Research Committee at the University of Chicago. Merriam hoped to promote the active cooperation of the various social science departments in order to research concrete policy proposals as well as pure knowledge. While completing his doctorate under Angell at Chicago, Ruml had worked with Merriam. By early 1923 Ruml renewed contact with Merriam, which grew into a close personal and professional friendship during the 1920s. It would be almost impossible to overstate the importance of their friendship. Together Ruml and Merriam built the University of Chicago into the leading social science research center in the 1920s, with the cooperation of such scholars as Robert Park, Leon Marshall, Leonard D. White, T.V. Smith, Harold Gosnell, Harold Lasswell, and a host of others gathered in the Local Community Research Committee. Their efforts culminated in 1929 with dedication of the LSRM-financed Social Science Research Building, known as "1126." Under Merriam and Ruml's leadership, Chicago garnered the lion's share of LSRM monies in support of social science research in the 1920s.[40]

As director of the LSRM, Ruml supported research not only at major universities but also at emerging policy centers such as Mitchell's NBER as it pursued research on national income and wealth series, the business cycle, and work for the Hooverian committee and conference system growing out of the Unemployment Conference of 1921. The memorial also provided some limited funds for the National Research Council in its research work for subcommittees of the conference that set the precedent for formation of the SSRC. Throughout the 1920s, the memorial appropriated funds for the merger of Robert Brookings's Institute for Government Research, the Institute of Economics, and the Graduate

School of Economics and Government in the form of the Brookings Institution. These three agencies grew out of the research interests raised in the war and postwar period regarding the federal budget, executive-branch organization, and business-government relations. When trustees decided to merge the three agencies in 1927, the LSRM provided grants to accomplish consolidation and centralization. While LSRM support for these private research groups did not reach the level of aid given to the centers in the universities, this financial backing proved significant in creating linkages among social scientists across disciplinary lines and between research institutions.[41]

While Ruml contemplated creating a national social science research network centered in major universities, he was also concerned with coordination of the network. In 1923 he and Merriam established the Social Science Research Council as the national, and eventually international, umbrella group tying the network together. Social scientists involved in the early years of the SSRC agreed that Merriam and Ruml put the SSRC on its organizational feet, but the exact mechanisms are little known today.[42] Merriam kept in close touch with his brother John, former head of the National Research Council, which served as the model for the SSRC, and used his brother's contacts in the philanthropic community to gain Ruml's support for the ambitious project. Initially, Ruml was skeptical about the SSRC, arguing that the NRC and the American Council of Learned Societies were already sponsoring complementary research that made the proposed SSRC redundant. By late 1923 Ruml changed his mind, concluding that the SSRC could fill social science research gaps left between the scientific research of the NRC and the humanistic work of the ACLS. Philanthropic manager Ruml ensured the SSRC's growth through a series of intricate discussions involving John C. Merriam, then head of the Carnegie Institution of Washington, D.C.; Charles E. Merriam, first head of the SSRC; and Robert Yerkes, head of the NRC's special Committee on the Scientific Aspects of Human Migration. For a time, the three seriously entertained the idea of combining the NRC and the SSRC by making the SSRC a subdivision of the NRC, which had emerged from the wartime mobilization effort of the Great War. When members of the NRC executive body proved reluctant to add the social sciences to their organization, another route had to be taken.[43]

At first, Ruml supported the SSRC only indirectly. He, the two Merriams, Yerkes, and Mitchell of the NBER set up temporary cooperating committees for the NRC's human migration study. The ensuing work went so well that other committees followed: a study of international communication in the news, Mitchell's study of the impact of the mechanization of industry as a special report for the NRC study on migration, and several other smaller cooperative studies.[44] At the same time, Edward Eyre Hunt, secretary of the Unemployment Conference of 1921 and contact person for Secretary of Commerce Hoover, tried to interest Merriam in having the SSRC conduct wage studies for the conference's subcommittees. Merriam demurred, arguing that the SSRC needed to get on its feet first. Yet this contact led to cooperation later in the decade when Hunt served as secretary for Hoover's President's Research Committee on Social Trends. The interlacing social science network drew tighter over the decade, bringing Merriam, Mitchell, Dennison, and Ruml closer to work with the federal government.

With the creation of the SSRC assured, Ruml moved on to other areas in social science. In late 1924, after conferring with Merriam, he proposed the creation of two kinds of fellowships that would assure continuity of training, institutions, and research. He set up fellowships for European students in the social sciences to come to the United States for study and, with Merriam, created SSRC fellowships for American students to study in Europe. Originally envisioned as a relatively small endeavor, the SSRC fellowship program later became a key part of its work. Through these grants, the LSRM and the SSRC provided for the next generation of social scientists, who staffed key research positions in private philanthropies and New Deal agencies in the 1930s and 1940s. The most well known was the young Swedish economist Gunnar Myrdal, author of the classic 1944 study *An American Dilemma: The Negro Problem and Modern Democracy*. According to Myrdal, Ruml convinced President Frederick P. Keppel of the Carnegie Corporation to hire Myrdal as research director for that famous study because of Myrdal's earlier work as an LSRM fellow.[45]

Perhaps the most immediately helpful steps for promoting social science involved LSRM sponsorship of the SSRC's annual summer conferences at Hanover, New Hampshire, on the Dartmouth campus. As a Dartmouth alumnus, Ruml arranged to lease rooms from his old fraternity for the initial meeting in 1925, chaired by his close friend Merriam. While the first meeting saw active participation by LSRM staff, later conferences were somewhat more independently run. These LSRM-financed meetings brought together social scientists from a variety of fields and created a truly national social science community. Since each conference was built around a particular topic, such as psychology, anthropology, social problems, economic theory, or philanthropy, those attending could talk informally within a relaxed social setting with those most up-to-date in their fields. At every meeting, the Problems and Policy Committee of the SSRC, the executive body, determined the future course of SSRC policy. Attending social scientists often advised and consulted with staff members from both the LSRM and the Rockefeller Foundation about which organizations to fund for the coming year. In effect, the Hanover conferences served as advisory councils for the growing network of social science research agencies, the professional associations connected in the SSRC, and the Rockefeller boards interested in funding such research. For people like Ruml, Merriam, Mitchell, and Dennison, these annual events consolidated an emerging body of social science institutions capable of planning future funding and research across the nation. Ad hoc national planning institutions emerged with voluntarist, philanthropic funding and a social science research base that first Herbert Hoover and later Franklin Roosevelt drew on extensively for public-policy advice.[46]

In November 1927 Edmund E. Day of the SSRC noted that "the Council as it stands today is in a very real sense the Memorial's creation."[47] Merriam's plan for financing the SSRC administrative, committee, research, and planning expenses originally sought to enlist the LSRM's support on a matching-grant basis. Other philanthropies such as the General Education Board, the Carnegie Corporation, the Julius Rosenwald Fund, the Russell Sage Foundation, the Commonwealth Fund, and several smaller funds did grant some monies to the SSRC, but by 1927 the council depended on the LSRM for its survival. The SSRC's *Decennial Report* (1934) revealed that the LSRM provided 96 percent of the council's money actually expended in the period 1923–33.[48]

If monies disbursed is a measure of success, Ruml achieved his goal of creating, funding, and institutionalizing a national program of social science research. Significantly, much of the money went to two organizations: the University of Chicago and the Social Science Research Council. Between 1923 and 1927, some 40 percent of all global LSRM appropriations for social science went to these two institutions. For the U.S. alone, these organizations received 52 percent of the funds expended.[49] Ruml and Merriam served each other, their respective organizations, American social science, and Hooverian associative planning. Together, they created a national network of social science researchers that extended its intellectual reach and policy influence over at least the 1921–45 period, if not beyond. Even after they joined the New Deal planning board, they continued to cooperate in consolidating initiatives begun in the New Era of the 1920s.

By late 1927 Ruml reached a new peak in his career. As the activist head of the Laura Spelman Rockefeller Memorial, he had wide contacts in the professional associations, the SSRC, the business community, and federal government agencies connected with Secretary of Commerce Hoover. His organization financed the nation's first economic and social inventories, *Recent Economic Changes* and *Recent Social Trends,* which brought together Merriam, Mitchell, Dennison, and Ruml and led directly to establishment of the New Deal planning board. Not surprisingly, in 1928 Merriam and Mitchell tried to convince Ruml to succeed them as chairman of the SSRC, but he declined in order to stay on at the LSRM.[50]

As director of the memorial, Ruml had a free hand to implement his plan; however, he also had to deal with the intricate administrative structures that loosely tied together all four Rockefeller philanthropies. In promoting an activist policy, Ruml came up against the traditional bent of some of the older trustees of the Rockefeller Foundation. Yet he toed the line carefully, proposing a number of policy principles in 1924 that the other boards soon adopted as their own. He argued that, to avoid public perception of the LSRM's work as scheming by the Rockefeller family, the memorial should avoid direct research, provide grants without conditions to the institutions involved, and never support organizations advocating specific legislation. The board of trustees approved these principles in 1924 and reaffirmed them in 1928.[51] Still there was a fine line between promoting social science research to serve "human welfare" and appropriating monies for policy research centers like the SSRC, the NBER, and the Brookings Institution. Ruml remained caught in this ideological trap. Like Delano's community of interest, Merriam's harmonious social equilibrium based on a plurality of interests, Mitchell's ideal of nonpartisan economic research, and Dennison's search for the middle way between voluntarism and statism, Beardsley Ruml's ideal of philanthropic management assumed that private financial support for a national program of useful social scientific research would necessarily serve a vaguely defined national interest applicable to all Americans. Like the other planners, Ruml assumed an ideological framework that could and would serve a broader public through the practical application of expert social scientific research. But who would make the choices as to what projects would be pursued, funded, and used to make policy decisions? And whose self-interest would be served by such decisions? The ideological assumption was that managers, social scientists, and politicians necessarily served a broader public interest.

As a modern philanthropic manager, Ruml also faced the dilemma of how to bring the foundation into the organizational world without angering trustees, losing his job, and undermining his program of promoting American social science. He succeeded in mollifying the trustees for most of the decade, but conflict between an older generation of nineteenth-century moralists and younger twentieth-century managers brewed beneath a surface calm. Eventually, the question of reorganizing the Rockefeller philanthropies had to be confronted.[52] In a 1926 letter to his father, John D. Rockefeller, Jr., took the side of the twentieth-century advocates of managerial philanthropy such as Beardsley Ruml:

> At the same time, as you said to me at Ormond, if you were proposing today to set aside for the well-being of mankind throughout the world the total sum of money which has been put into these foundations, you would undoubtedly combine all the activities, with the exception of the Rockefeller Institute—which ought to be an independent entity—in the hands of a single board with a charter as broad as the charter of the Rockefeller Foundation. With the soundness of that conclusion I am in complete accord. In the light of the experience of the last thirty years, I am convinced that one representative board with competent officers and staff and with departmental committees of the board to deal with the various fields, instead of the separate boards that now exist, could cover the field with ease and economy. Such a plan would result in much saving and the prevention of many overlappings in fields, in which, with the best of intention on everyone's part, duplications at least to some extent have been almost inevitable under the present set-up.[53]

During 1926 and 1927 Raymond B. Fosdick, Rockefeller family lawyer and Rockefeller Foundation trustee, put together a reorganization plan that would effect just these changes. Following the model of the national business corporation, the Rockefeller Foundation would centralize responsibility, departmentalize the new divisions of the foundation according to function, and create the modern hierarchical, bureaucratic administrative structure already familiar to Delano, Merriam, Mitchell, and Dennison. In successfully implementing his plan of October 1922 and playing a key role in the 1928–29 reorganization, Ruml's career as philanthropic manager paralleled the paths of his fellow planners.

As of January 1929 the Rockefeller Foundation encompassed five functional divisions: natural sciences, medical sciences, social sciences, humanities, and medical education. The LSRM was consolidated within the new Division of the Social Sciences under Edmund E. Day, president of Cornell University and an active member of the SSRC.[54] Ruml played a key role in convincing Fosdick to accept the principle of functional specialization along divisional lines. Some $17.5 million of the LSRM's principal went to traditional Rockefeller charitable groups. The new Social Science Division took over only the research orientation of the LSRM, while applied research for training government personnel and studying public administration went to the newly formed Spelman Fund of New York, headed by Ruml.

Having advocated the integration of social science research, private philanthropic support, and cooperation among private, public, and mixed agencies, Ruml consolidated his position during the years from 1928 to 1934. On the surface, his work seemed to dissipate into a number of unrelated activities; however, his career followed continuing interests in these three areas. Rather than concentrating on any one area, Ruml remained engaged with all three in ways that remain difficult to reconstruct. He directed the initial work of the Spelman Fund along the lines of the LSRM until trustees of the Rockefeller Foundation decided to absorb the areas of child welfare and interracial relations, leaving only public administration in the hands of the Spelman Fund.[55]

From 1928 to its dissolution in 1948, the Spelman Fund provided grants to numerous agencies concerned with public administration. The most important were the Public Administration Clearing House at the University of Chicago, the Public Administration Service also at Chicago, and the Public Administration Committee of the SSRC. Again, the Ruml-Merriam team worked together superbly. The PACH brought together in one building on the Chicago campus such professional associations as the American Legislators Association, the American Public Works Association, the Public Administration Service, the American Municipal Association, the International City Managers Association, the Municipal Finance Officers Association, the National Association of Housing, and the National Municipal League. Though Ruml resigned in December 1930, his successors, Arthur Woods and Charles Merriam, carried on his original program. Many of the people associated with PACH, Louis Brownlow being the best known, moved on to New Deal agencies on local and state levels. The SSRC committee moved its proposals into New Deal agencies that eventually led to the President's Committee on Administrative Management in 1937. The Spelman Fund also provided monies for the establishment of state planning boards under the direction of Roosevelt's national planning board.[56]

Ruml maintained his connections with academic social science through the University of Chicago. In the spring of 1928 he interviewed for the presidency of the University of Chicago, but the position went to Robert Maynard Hutchins, a friend of both Ruml and Ruml's old mentor, James R. Angell, then president of Yale University. In 1931 Hutchins, a longtime admirer of the social science programs at Chicago, brought Ruml to the university as head of the newly created Division of Social Sciences and professor of education. Ruml taught only one seminar but advised Hutchins on a controversial plan to promote divisional integration of departments aimed at promoting interdisciplinary research and improved undergraduate education. As a former manager of the LSRM, Ruml was a natural ally for Hutchins in the attempt to reorganize the university. Hutchins wanted to emphasize the graduate and research programs but met strong resistance from some of the faculty, the alumni association, and supporters of the football team, which Hutchins tried to abolish. While at the University of Chicago, Ruml played the role he liked best—that of a contemplative Buddha coming up with ideas tossed out to others for consideration.[57]

In 1934 Ruml resigned his position at Chicago to accept the job as treasurer of the R. H. Macy's department store in New York City, at an annual salary of $40,000, which within two years had risen to $70,000. He remained a trustee of the Spelman Fund and a member of the policy-making body of the SSRC, the Committee on Problems and Policy, while his work at Macy's gained him something of a reputation as both social scientist and businessman.[58]

In the early 1930s Ruml made a gradual transition from philanthropic manager to informal government adviser. Unlike Delano, Merriam, Mitchell, and Dennison, he did not enter formal service with the federal government at any point in the period between 1920 and 1933. Ruml's voluntarist focus during the New Era enabled him to make contact with a wide variety of people in both the private and the public sectors. His work as government adviser was the next step in a logical progression from that earlier work and marked his eventual move into New Deal circles. Like his fellow business representative Henry Dennison, Ruml was reluctant to take a formal job with the federal government, but he continued to avail himself of many opportunities to act as informal adviser willing to initiate ideas while allowing more publicly identified New Dealers to take the credit. Ruml used his contacts in business, academia, social science, and government to act as a behind-the-scenes adviser, mediator, and idea man. Not surprisingly in light of the LSRM's interest in social welfare policies, Ruml's participation in work for farm relief and unemployment headed the list of such activities.

Given the paucity of primary-source material on Ruml's activities as government adviser in the early 1930s, the best way to approach his work is through his role in promoting the domestic allotment plan that FDR Brain Truster Rexford G. Tugwell considered after the election of 1932. Recent scholarship suggests that the evolution of farm policy from 1920 to 1935 owed more than previously thought to the institutional strength of the Bureau of Agricultural Economics in the U.S. Department of Agriculture in the 1920s, better state capacity for agricultural than industrial planning throughout the New Era, and the voluntarist concerns of associative planning.[59] Ruml's role in the agricultural policy debate indicated that, like many of the others involved, his thoughts changed with changing economic and political circumstances.

Not surprisingly, Ruml's role in the making of farm policy in 1932 grew out of his work as director of the LSRM and adviser to the Rockefeller family.[60] Starting with a demonstration project of the Fairway Farms Corporation in the 1920s, his interest in farm policy led to support for a voluntary domestic allotment plan that was submitted to an agricultural economist hired by the LSRM to develop the plan more fully. In spring 1932 Ruml's contacts with two key people in these projects led to a discussion with Roosevelt adviser Rexford Tugwell regarding proposed plans for farm relief. Eventually this input served to initiate plans incorporated into Roosevelt's campaign speeches in the fall of 1932. From then on, the campaign for domestic allotment turned toward consultation with experts and interest-group representatives, compromise, and modifications that became the Agricultural Adjustment Act of 1933.

Ruml came to the debate through his connection with the Fairway Farms project. During the early 1920s, while studying agricultural economics at the University of Wisconsin, Henry C. Taylor, an agricultural expert who lived in Montana, experimented with the idea of scientific land-use planning on two small farms he owned outside Madison, Wisconsin. He hoped for a multilevel experiment dealing with collection of data, use of technological improvements, and provision of land ownership for able tenants lacking capital for independent farming. He soon dropped the idea and moved on to Washington, D.C., where he and Secretary of Agriculture Henry C. Wallace founded the Bureau of Agricultural Economics in the Department of Agriculture.[61]

In 1923 the LSRM hired Taylor as a consultant on a similar project begun by Milburn L. Wilson, several Montana businessmen and bankers, and agricultural experts. This group sought a solution to Montana's dry farming problem caused by decreasing wheat prices, bad weather, and overexpansion during the wartime boom for wheat. Wilson adapted Taylor's ideas for a demonstration project of eight farms that operated on a limited-profit basis to modernize farming methods, instituted an innovative owner-tenant contract providing for eventual independent ownership, and tested for the ideal size for dry wheat farming depending on local conditions. To determine if it would contribute funds, the LSRM sent Taylor to Montana to judge the feasibility of the Fairway Farms project. The LSRM gave small sums for two years, then ended its support. At the instigation of Taylor and Wilson, Ruml intervened personally as LSRM director and trusted Rockefeller adviser to convince John D. Rockefeller, Jr., to donate money personally to continue the project. As a condition of support, both Rockefeller and Ruml demanded that the project incorporate, arguing that the demonstration farms must operate in a business-like manner.[62]

The Fairway Farms experiment had mixed results. Because of bad weather, poor land, continued decreases in the price of wheat, and a limited budget, many of the tenants had at best small success. By the late 1920s agricultural economist Taylor concluded that the successes of the project were in the data collected on size, lowered labor and production costs owing to technological innovation, and the success of operating combined farm units with large acreage, corporate control, and vigorous business efficiency.[63] Under the Federal Subsistence Homesteads Division, headed by M. L. Wilson in the New Deal years, the tenant purchase contract, the model of supervised corporate management, and the idea of integrated land-use methods developed on the project served as models. In 1933 the Fairway Farms Corporation became the Farm Foundation, run by Taylor and Ruml as a voluntary demonstration project alongside the more innovative experiments of the Farm Security Administration.[64]

The significance of Ruml's work with the Fairway Farms Corporation lay in the fact that Taylor was among one of the very first of a new breed of specialized agricultural economists and cofounder of the Bureau of Agricultural Economics, which agricultural historian Richard Kirkendall says "became the central planning agency for the Department of Agriculture" in the New Deal years.[65] A social scientist, representative of the trends Ruml, Dennison, Mitchell, Merriam, and Delano applauded, Taylor mirrored the rise of expertise in policy making through his involvement in the network of businesses, private associations, universities, and governmental agencies. The Fairway Farms project saved Taylor's career, but it also gave Ruml contacts with Wilson and launched him on the idea of agricultural planning.

In 1925 Taylor lost his job as head of the Bureau of Agricultural Economics because of a press report that he had used his position to advocate passage of the McNary-Haugen two-price farm bill. At the time, Walter Dill Scott, the president of Northwestern University, asked Taylor to come to Northwestern to direct the work of Richard T. Ely's Institute for Research in Land Economics, which was moving there from the University of Wisconsin. Taylor accepted the position on the basis of a Rockefeller Foundation grant to the institute that would cover his salary. Sometime in this period at one of the summer Hanover conferences of the SSRC, Ruml presented Taylor with an idea for a voluntary domestic allotment plan. Ruml argued that the McNary-Haugen bill would raise production without addressing the real farm problem of overproduction, while an allotment system with transferable rights for governmental subsidies would raise prices and keep production down.[66]

Acting in voluntarist fashion, Ruml turned to private philanthropic support to address this troubling issue of public policy. Early in 1928 the LSRM asked Taylor to conduct a survey of the feasibility of Ruml's plan, but Taylor declined on the grounds that he lacked time. Taylor recommended John D. Black, an economics professor at Harvard University, who took on the job of surveying various plans for farm relief. The powerful American Farm Bureau Federation supported the corporate farming plan of a two-price system like that found in the McNary-Haugen bill, but President Calvin Coolidge rebuffed the congressional farm bloc repeatedly with vetoes of the measure. The National Grange, an older farm organization, advocated an export debenture program that called for the sale of surplus crops overseas so as to raise domestic prices. Both of these plans promoted dumping rather than dealing with overproduction. The more liberal National Farmers Union sought to implement a price-fixing plan that would pay farmers for the cost of production. By the late 1920s most of these plans seemed ill fated and politically unfeasible. An agricultural economist, W. J. Spillman, had raised the possibility of an allotment system earlier, but it had been ignored. Ruml revived the idea to argue that a voluntary system of allotment administered by the federal government must be considered before the problem literally destroyed the country and its farmers. Black incorporated his discussion in the LSRM survey, which he published as chapter 10 of his influential *Agricultural Reform in the United States* (1929). Significantly, Ruml and the LSRM chose to leave any mention of their support out of the acknowledgements.[67]

By 1928 M. L. Wilson had given up on the idea of scientific management of large-scale farming through land-use planning as used by the Fairway Farms project. Adhering to some elements of that earlier effort at farm relief, Wilson now publicly advocated the voluntary domestic allotment plan developed by Black for Ruml. Various elements of the farm interests were slowly coming around to the idea as well. Ruml kept in touch with Wilson, who refined the idea and trooped across the country building support for the plan. While the Hoover administration defended its efforts at price stabilization through the Federal Farm Board and voluntary efforts, Ruml, Black, Wilson, and others went beyond the confines of voluntarism to accept cooperation between farmers and the government, much as Dennison advocated cooperation between business and government.[68]

During the campaign of 1932 they got their chance to convince advisers to Democratic candidate Franklin D. Roosevelt. In spring 1932 Roosevelt assigned Brain Truster Rexford Tugwell to develop a farm relief program for the upcoming presidential campaign. Tugwell met Ruml in Washington, D.C., where Ruml informed him of Wilson's work and suggested they consult him.[69] After speaking with Wilson, Tugwell included the domestic allotment idea in drafts of Roosevelt's acceptance speech on July 2, 1932, at the Democratic convention in Chicago.[70] While the drafts went through many hands and numerous editions, Roosevelt clearly supported the idea, albeit in vague terms, which was acceptable to all the farm interests and could win passage in Congress. On September 14, 1932, Roosevelt restated these ideas in his farm policy speech at Topeka, Kansas.[71] Hedging on the differences between the various plans, he astutely attacked the Hoover administration's efforts and vaguely suggested that a Roosevelt presidency would take a more sympathetic attitude toward the nation's farmers. By spring 1933 the domestic allotment idea became reality in modified form with passage of the Agricultural Adjustment Act, one of the major pieces of early New Deal legislation.

Working behind the scenes throughout the policy-making process, Ruml had become an informal New Deal adviser. Looking for a way to raise farm prices without dumping produce overseas, Ruml hit upon the idea of cooperation between county agents supplied by the American Farm Bureau Federation and agricultural experts in federal agencies exemplified by the pioneering Taylor and carried on by the likes of M. L. Wilson. Typically, Ruml stayed out of the public eye, allowing Black, Wilson, Tugwell, and Roosevelt to take credit for his idea.[72] As Tugwell, Mordecai Ezekiel, an economist for the Federal Farm Board, Fred Lee, general counsel of the American Farm Bureau Federation, and Jerome Frank, a Felix Frankfurter protégé, drafted the agricultural adjustment bill, Ruml remained quietly in the background.[73] Yet the record shows that he had helped to develop agricultural planning in the 1920s by supporting the Fairway Farms Corporation and agricultural experts like Taylor and Wilson. In the early New Deal he initiated the idea of domestic allotment, used philanthropic monies to have it refined by Harvard social scientist Black, and helped mediate among agricultural experts responsible for the policy speeches of the 1932 presidential campaign. Like Dennison, Ruml, the New Era voluntarist, had become an informal New Deal government policy adviser.

Though quiet, Ruml remained active. In 1930 he began talking selectively about the need for government to adjust to changing economic conditions brought on by the Depression. Arguing that movements he called "federation" occurred in commerce, education, social work, and the social sciences, Ruml urged the government to make similar policy changes through research, planning, and expert technical administration of social welfare policy. In 1930 he served on Hoover's President's Emergency Committee for Employment under chairman Arthur Woods, his old friend from the LSRM. Like Dennison, Ruml was willing to move beyond a narrowly defined voluntarism that damned Hoover in the eyes of public opinion as a leader either incapable or unwilling to do anything about human suffering of the unemployed in the wake of the Depression. Ruml proposed the creation of limited-dividend housing corporations that could bring together planners, architects, businessmen, and politicians from all levels of government. Soon enough, he turned away from Hoover, disillusioned by the known failure in farm relief policies.[74]

Like fellow planners Delano, Merriam, Mitchell, and Dennison, Ruml was willing to move beyond Hooverian associative planning when economic, social, and political circumstances changed as the Great Depression deepened. Yet Ruml refused to consider himself either a liberal New Deal activist or a radical revolutionary. Throughout his life he took pride in being a registered Republican who voted Democratic to "balance things." Ruml continued to have his say in policy decisions, but the exact nature, extent, and issue orientation do not come out in the few scattered documents remaining. He had access to policy makers such as Harry Hopkins and played some part in the discussion leading up to passage of the Social Security Act of 1935. The evidence that survives indicates that Ruml sought to compromise in the interest of moderation. He approved public works programs, for example, as a kind of temporary relief program but insisted that the deflationary effect on the federal budget be balanced in the long run. Like Dennison, he thought labor must remain satisfied with company unions under the National Recovery Administration in order to preserve the "community of interest that subsists between stockholders, management and labor in any enterprise."[75]

One revealing document sheds some light on Ruml's thinking as of November 1934. Shortly after the off-year elections, Roosevelt invited an unknown individual to "bring his views to the White House." In a short memorandum to this individual, Ruml assured Roosevelt that, despite criticism of New Deal programs by the business community, the Democratic successes in the election gave Roosevelt the chance to move forward if only he showed "patience": "The country is weary of the controversy over stabilization and a balanced budget. Obviously, the President's explanation has been accepted by the voters. On these subjects, at least, he is the pragmatist; his critics are the doctrinaires. It seems to me that business generally will go along with him if he will take a leaf from his own book and encourage the practical against the theoretical, not only in the matter of currency and government spending, but also in dealing with the banking problem, N.R.A., labor, relief standards and the recently suggested plan of subsidizing business to create employment."[76] Ruml concluded, in a quiet, but authoritative way, by calling for continued use of voluntary methods for governmental response to depression conditions:

> I would urge the President to play down any talk of any broad plan of subsidizing industrial production and to talk instead about voluntary agreements to be made in industries where conditions warrant, respecting additional production at government risk.
>
> For example, the government might finance the manufacture of a million freight cars, to be leased to the railroads, if the roads want them, but not otherwise. I find it difficult to think of many industries in which increased demand arising out of larger payrolls would take care of the increased production involved in the process. One trouble is that in modern mass industry, the volume of production can be increased geometrically by an arithmetic increase in direct labor. Unless wages balance the money value of increased production, the weight of surplus stocks so produced will crash the whole structure to the ground. The point is, the administration should not publicize such ideas.[77]

Ruml's discussion of fiscal policy sounded as if Henry Dennison and the host of New Era capitalist advocates of the 1920s were speaking. Yet the idea of governmental support of the private sector through voluntary means hardly frightened Ruml and remained a definite possibility. Narrowly interpreted, Ruml rejected the idea of fiscal-spending policy; more widely construed, he hinted at the possibility of a conservative fiscal-spending policy over the long term to put business back on its feet. The idea was in germ form only, but it loomed larger in Ruml's thoughts for the rest of the decade. Between 1935 and 1943 he carried these ideas through more thoroughly as one of FDR's planners, and then as a founding member of the postwar Committee for Economic Development (1942), a successor agency to the Business Advisory and Planning Council, on which fellow business representative Henry Dennison served.

Viewed over the long term of 1917–33, Beardsley Ruml's service as philanthropic manager of the Laura Spelman Rockefeller Memorial and trustee of the Spelman Fund of New York was an apprenticeship for New Deal planning. His career suggested the possibilities of long-range benefits from a kind of social deficit spending by a modernized philanthropy such as the LSRM. Ruml learned to act in concert with social scientists such as Charles Merriam and Wesley Clair Mitchell, newly emerging institutions such as the Social Science Research Council and the National Bureau of Economic Research, the growing national network of universities, research institutes, and government agencies brought together by Secretary of Commerce Hoover, and practical business leaders such as Henry Dennison. The federal government could sponsor such national efforts as the various committees growing out of the Unemployment Conference of 1921, the Recent Economic Changes study, and the President's Research Committee on Social Trends. Private-sector philanthropies such as the Laura Spelman Rockefeller Memorial, the Rockefeller Foundation, and the Spelman Fund of New York could finance, influence, and use social science to create new public policies by voluntarist means. The lines separating private- and public-sector activity were blurring. They would blur even faster as economic conditions worsened and the Republican Party lost control of Congress and the presidency between 1930 and 1932.

By 1930 Ruml knew Delano, Merriam, Mitchell, and Dennison well. He had worked with Delano on the President's Emergency Committee for Employment and knew of his experience as city and regional planner. Between 1921 and 1933 Ruml, Merriam, and Mitchell had become close friends as well as colleagues through LSRM support for the University of Chicago, the Social Science Research Council, the NBER, Hoover's ad hoc associational planning in the committee and conference system, and the two landmark inventories of the nation's economic and social resources. By the mid-1920s Ruml knew Dennison for his welfare capitalist reforms, his support of voluntarist forms of unemployment planning, and his association with social scientists in the SSRC.

By 1935 Beardsley Ruml was ready to become a New Deal planner. In October, when Merriam wrote to Delano about a replacement for Mitchell on the planning board, he suggested Ruml, who "could be classified as a businessman formerly and still affiliated with the Rockefeller Foundation, but recognized as a bold and independent thinker."[78] Merriam called Delano's attention to Ruml's role in sponsoring the President's Research Committee on Social Trends, his membership on the SSRC's decision-making body, the Committee on Problems and Policy, his management of the LSRM, and his work on the domestic allotment plan. Delano agreed and recommended Ruml to Secretary of the Interior Harold Ickes, titular head of the planning agency, who in turn passed on the recommendation to President Franklin D. Roosevelt.[79] In his letter requesting Ruml to join Dennison as a new member of the advisory committee representing the business community, Roosevelt wrote, "I hope you will find it possible to bring to the work of the Committee the benefit of your experience."[80] Master politician Franklin Roosevelt selected one of the most wily, astute, and thoughtful philanthropic managers of the twentieth century as the last of his national planners.

The personalities, ideas, institutions, and experience of FDR's five planners shaped an institutional nexus for a new stage of national planning that went beyond Hoover's voluntarism. Yet, they were reluctant to go as far as the statist command planning on the European model practiced in fascist Italy, Nazi Germany, and the communist Soviet Union. New Deal planning grew out of the American national experience. Collectively, FDR's planners defined New Deal planning in a way that was faithful to the memory of Progressive reform, the wartime mobilization of 1917–18, and the associational efforts of Hooverians in the 1920s. The wrenching impact of the Great Depression of the 1930s could not change or negate the social background, the intellectual development, or the institutional experience of these planners. The pre-New Deal experience of Roosevelt's planners framed their approach to national planning in the 1930s and 1940s within the context of a complex institutional nexus beyond coincidence or merely personal ties, but that was far short of any sort of conspiracy. Drastic changes in the American economy, society, and the political system between 1929 and 1933 carried the actors from that nexus into the arena of New Deal planning.

7

The Organizational Nexus of New Deal Planning

FROM HOOVER TO FDR

FROM 1933 to 1943 New Deal planners tried to bring order where ideological confusion, intellectual doubt, and nostalgia for remnants of an older order had reigned. Planning came from above through the efforts of the five men sitting atop Franklin Roosevelt's planning board. While planning occurred in the midst of the Great Depression, the planners brought ideas and institutional connections from earlier experience between 1900 and 1933 in both the private and the public sectors. FDR's planners were part of a much broader and longer tradition that sought to bring together a host of experienced people, a new set of cross-sectoral institutions, and the ideological undergirding of a new set of modern liberal ideas that were worked out more fully and tested between 1933 to 1945.[1]

Between 1900 and 1933 new networks of policy actors created a range of new institutions amounting to an organizational nexus that laid the groundwork for national planning first under Herbert Hoover, then under his successor, Franklin D. Roosevelt. Partisan loyalty did not matter in this process; competency, leadership, and adept handling of these new institutions did. Building a corps of such people took time, resources, learning how to respond to changing conditions, and creating institutions that could carry on what had been learned. Delano, Merriam, Mitchell, Dennison, and Ruml did not end up as New Deal planners by accident, fate, or dire conditions resulting from the precipitous decline in the American economy. Their career lines converged toward New Deal planning in a way that made each of them logical, appropriate choices to

168

become FDR's planners. The period before 1917 encompassed an initial stage of career development that found each planner taking up personal, professional, and policy roles in the complex institutions of modern America. The limits of Progressive reform and wartime mobilization in 1917–18 made them realize shortcomings in their own and their nation's understanding of how a modern economy, society, and polity worked. Participation on various wartime boards sparked a search for a new way of ordering their experience in hopes of serving their organizations, professions, class, and country.[2]

The decade of the 1920s brought these hopes to fruition in the idea of associational activity involving cooperation between functionally organized groups at the center of American life—professional associations, social science research institutes, business corporations, trade associations, philanthropies, and the federal government. Herbert Hoover brought some of these people together in reorganizing the Department of Commerce, sponsoring the Unemployment Conference of 1921, creating the committee and conference system as a set of ad hoc, voluntary planning institutions, and using the expertise of thousands of these modern policy advisers in ways that suggested consolidation of modern institutions that combined the best of an older voluntarist tradition of decentralized power, reliance on private-sector money, and federal sponsorship of developmental activities while nurturing a twentieth-century respect for the positive state, promotion of business-government cooperation, practical use of social science expertise, and new kinds of public policies that went beyond reaction to an immediate crisis such as a war, depression, or shift in political party dominance. National inventories represented by *Recent Economic Changes* (1929) and *Recent Social Trends* (1933) represented the first step in consolidating some of these ideas, people, and institutions in order to rationally prepare policies for the longer term based on the best knowledge of the day. Though hardly a self-conscious attempt to willfully create a modern liberalism, in fact that is just what happened. By suggesting there was a role for the state in planning the best ways to respond to economic changes and their social consequences, these modern liberals had paved the way for New Deal reform. Nor surprisingly, some of them served on various New Deal agencies, including the planning board in its different guises between 1933 and 1943.[3]

The emerging mosaic of American life from the late nineteenth century to 1933 revealed a picture of national groups organizing to gain power, influence, and wealth. Leading the way were the institutions of big business in the wake of industrialism, the concentration of huge numbers of people in the nation's cities, and the massive migration of ordinary Americans to the industrial centers. The initial response to these changes came from people in the business community, who organized first, fastest, and best. Represented at first by such groups as the National Civic Federation, big businesses in the years after the Great War adopted the institutional model of hierarchical, functionally oriented, administrative bureaucracies as the way of the future. Other groups followed in the wake of the business pioneers or fell by the wayside. American farmers, skilled workers, professionals, and academics took up the banner of progress to change the national landscape. Like millions of other Americans, Roosevelt's planners tried to develop a new way of understanding how urban-industrial America operated. During the New Deal, they attempted to bring order to the public realm, using models first developed in the private sector, but in a new way by creating institutional links across private- and public-sector lines that neither reenacted nineteenth-century voluntarism nor insisted upon a full-blown, twentieth-century statism. The cross-sectoral institutions that they created proved to be important seedbeds for modern national policy making. New Deal planning sought to synthesize the best of the old and the most innovative of the new in a way that crossed ideological boundaries, just as the planners' lifelong loyalties to the Republican Party belied their work with New Deal Democrats.

FDR's planners served as proponents of an America freed from the shibboleths of an outmoded nineteenth-century liberalism based upon classical economics and its attendant values of individualism, freewheeling economic growth, and representative democracy. Moving freely between the interstices joining public and private sectors, they learned that traditional distinctions between private and public no longer made much sense. Their practical experiences with business corporations, the city and regional planning movement, professional social science, and organized philanthropy provided an opportunity to create a new kind of institution based on modifications of those with which they came into contact during Progressive reform, wartime mobilization, and New Era policy advising. After experimenting with new administrative structures in specific firms, regions, and disciplines, the planners extended their work into the national realm through planning sponsored by the New Deal. National planning matured in response to the Depression by people willing to bridge three generations of experience: the genteel world of Delano's and Dennison's youth, the professionalizing disciplines of American social science of Merriam's and Mitchell's early careers, and the transformed world of modern philanthropy managed so well by Ruml.

New Deal planners argued that the nineteenth-century distinction between public and private sectors no longer served as either a description of socioeconomic reality or a prescription for national progress. Their rationalist approach to the social order presumed both respect for the past and hope for the future. By employing people, ideas, and institutions from their own immediate past, they tried to rearrange the present order to meet the challenges posed by the trauma of depression followed later by the test of world war. They promoted socially liberal ideas of reform with politically conservative ends to preserve an America rapidly outgrowing its earlier political ideals and economic practices.

The planners brought a class vision to their work. Raised in white, middle- and upper-class American families of the late nineteenth century, they started life with definite social advantages. Childhood and education occurred in a well-ordered, comfortable, economically secure environment foreign to many other Americans. Their ideology had a conservative component stemming from their well-off, elite family backgrounds. Education at such historically prestigious schools at Harvard and newly emerging ones such as the University of Chicago and Columbia put each planner in a position to build on the early foundation of family life and social background. Delano and Dennison took advantage of their family backgrounds, contacts, and managerial experience in business to expand their understanding and make contact with reformers in such areas as business management, labor relations, civic reform, and planning groups at the local, state, and national levels. Merriam, Mitchell, and Ruml took somewhat different routes. All three came from small towns in the Midwest to study at prestigious graduate schools that had reorganized the American university curriculum and put into place programs centered on rational, functional education in the sciences and the social sciences. As political science, economics, and psychology entered a period of professionalization based on expertise, contact with like-minded scholars, and the addition of journals, national associations, and umbrella groups, they moved into the arena of public-policy debate that led to involvement in Progressive reform, wartime mobilization, and economic stabilization efforts between 1900 and 1933. While the path of academic social science trod by Merriam, Mitchell, and Ruml was different from the business route taken by Delano and Dennison, the larger pattern was the same: early career development followed by a broadening of vision beyond a specific firm or discipline that led to national prominence, growing connections with others in their field, and the founding and cultivation of institutional networks that flowered during the Great War and the New Era of the 1920s.

With the class advantage of secure family life, superior education, and career beginnings well in hand, each of the planners moved into a range of influential positions in some of America's major twentieth-century institutions. The years following education in the emerging research universities served as a time for experimentation, practical experience leading to advancement, establishment of their own families, and building institutional ties with influential friends. After establishing his career track, each planner widened his interests to engage in policy-advising bodies that broadened the circle of friends, colleagues, and supporters. Eventually each became aware of the intricate links between his profession and some form of governmental work. Some of these links were informal, temporary advisory work for a federal commission, but others were precedents for more extensive connections with federal officials that bloomed sooner or later.

The details of each planner's career remained distinct from that of the others as expanding intellectual horizons and institutional connections brought them toward converging interests. Intellectual differences existed, but they were matters of degree, not substance. Generationally, the planners' experiences were different. Delano and Merriam, most closely tied in terms of general outlook, raised larger questions regarding the evolving definition of national planning. As the most prominent political scientist and economist in the nation, Merriam and Mitchell were most interested in promoting the policy expertise of social science researchers, both within their respective disciplines and among members of the professional associations gathered in the Social Science Research Council. Dennison came from roughly the same generation as Delano and Merriam, but his practical business concerns constrained his intellectual reach, while the younger Ruml proved headstrong, experimental, and bold in not only advocating, but also funding, creation of the first national social scientific network the country had seen.

Despite these generational differences, these five planners agreed upon first principles by the time they came together on FDR's National Planning Board in 1933. Through their early work, they came to question the reigning ideology of American national life. For much of the nineteenth century, the liberal creed held that national economic growth occurred through the efforts of self-interested entrepreneurs. Individual self-reliance relegated group or national interests to the secondary realm of public life. The political corollary to the separation of public and private spheres involved rhetorical adherence to democratic principles through the institutions of representative government. For most Americans in the nineteenth century, the United States was a unique experiment, both geographically and historically. Yet the economic changes wrought by industrialization, the rise of big business, and the nationalization of the American economy called for a new description of, and prescription for, national life in light of the massive social consequences of those changes.

Americans argued widely over the appropriate replacement for the outmoded tenets of classical liberalism. People ranging across the political spectrum gave a variety of answers from conservative revival of competition to radical collectivism with a socialist bent. The most influential group lay in the middle, hoping to reorient liberalism around the idea of organizational pluralism that could encompass both institutional change and conserve the best ideas and values of the past. FDR's planners were among this middle group. Advocates of pluralism argued that the atomistic molecules of Adam Smith's self-regulating model incorrectly assumed individuals were at the center of the economy, society, and polity. Rather than individualist molecules, they argued that organized interest groups were the basic unit of the modern political economy. The problem, then, was how to regulate social and economic relations between these groups. For some, a further problem was how to open this system to emerging groups. By the start of the twentieth century, theorists such as Merriam argued that business, labor, and agriculture were the major groups. Throughout the Progressive Era, reformers debated how the government should and did fit into this new system. Should it regulate new groups as well as established ones from above? Should it share power as an equal partner competing with other groups? Or should government become merely one organization among many, a kind of broker state mediating among the others?

That debate continued over the course of the twentieth century. At times, it became more vigorous than usual during key periods such as Progressive reform, mobilization for world war in 1917–18, and the reworking of voluntarism in Hoover's associative state in the 1920s. Not surprisingly, the people that President Franklin D. Roosevelt selected to serve on the New Deal planning boards came out of those same formative experiences. What lessons the planners drew from these earlier periods directly influenced how they responded to the crisis of the Great Depression and, later, a second world war. Not unexpectedly, their ideas regarding national planning encompassed elements of the debate from each of these periods. Seen only from the vantage point of the post-1929 crisis of the Depression or the post-1933 assumption of power by FDR, the planners' ideas might appear to have emerged from a historical vacuum.

Yet when viewed over the longer sweep of modern American history from the 1890s to the early 1930s, this mix of people, ideas, and institutions mirrored the complicated turns in an ongoing debate over the nature and direction of modern American life.

By comparing the careers of the planners over time, the individual differences become less important and the similarities more striking in making sense of the history of national planning. These five people who served as FDR's national planners gradually modified and extended the institutional models they knew best and most immediately. Delano and Dennison were most familiar with the modern American business corporation, pioneered by firms in the railroad industry in the late nineteenth century, which in the 1917–33 period became national firms willing to experiment with new modes of production, distribution, sales, advertising, and firm-specific planning in response to recurrent changes in the business cycle. While Delano moved into city and regional planning in Chicago, Washington, and New York, Dennison used his firm as both business laboratory and jumping-off point in his search for ways to learn from government advisory work and business-cycle research. Merriam and Mitchell entered the rapidly changing academic professions in the emerging social sciences, represented by graduate programs at leading universities such as Chicago and Columbia, and founded such national institutions as the Social Science Research Council and the National Bureau of Economic Research, which proved vital components in Hoover's ad hoc planning groups of the 1920s. Younger, more energetic, and just as comfortable in a business as an academic setting, Ruml was a leader of the second generation of philanthropists who actively managed— planned—the future of social science research as a useful tool for national progress. Through the LSRM and its Rockefeller monies, Ruml served as a financial organizer who funded not only individuals such as Merriam and groups such as the SSRC and the NBER but also Hooverian planning efforts that grew out of the Unemployment Conference of 1921, which culminated in the landmark studies of 1929 and 1933. While evaluation of the five planners should not overstate their representativeness, the longitudinal patterns and institutional connections that led from Hooverian associative planning in the 1920s to New Deal planning in the 1930s and 1940s cannot be overlooked. By the late 1920s people, ideas, institutions, and financial needs rapidly converged, culminating in the study *Recent Social Trends* sponsored by Republican president Herbert Hoover. Recommendations coming from that body led directly to Democratic president Franklin D. Roosevelt's creating the National Planning

Board. In July 1933 Roosevelt appointed Delano, Merriam, and Mitchell as his New Deal planners. In late 1935 Dennison and Ruml replaced Mitchell, who had resigned. Planning moved from Hoover to FDR.

Delano represented the amalgamation of older ideas of paternal social duty inherited from his family and class with the newer ideas of corporate management and city and regional planning.[4] Yet Delano, the oldest of the five, was not quite a professional planner, relying on the research and advice of younger experts for the detailed work of physical planning on a day-to-day basis. Between 1909 and 1940 city planners established their own professional groups, including the National Conference on City Planning (1909), the American City Planning Institute (1917), the American Institute of Planners (1934), the American Planning and Civic Association, and the American Society of Planning Officials (1935). Beginning in 1909 with Professor Joseph Pray's course on city planning at Harvard University, planners created a professional group identity. By 1923 nineteen colleges and universities offered such courses, including Harvard's new graduate course in landscape architecture.[5] Delano's assistant at the National Capital Park and Planning Commission from 1926 through 1933, Charles W. Eliot II, was one of the first graduates of new university programs in city planning. Born into one of Boston's leading families—his grandfather was the most famous president in Harvard's history—on November 5, 1899, Eliot followed after his namesake, Charles W. Eliot, an uncle, who was a prominent landscape architect. The younger Charles received an excellent education at the Browne and Nichols School and Harvard. Serving with the Red Cross Ambulance Corps in Italy during World War I, he returned to complete his undergraduate work in 1920. After a short trip to Europe on a traveling fellowship, Eliot returned to enter Harvard's new program in landscape architecture. In the profession's early years, landscape architects took the lead in promoting city planning during the 1920s. With his grandfather's financial support, Eliot entered private practice, becoming involved in physical city planning in various Massachusetts towns. In 1926 an old family friend and landscape architect partner, Frederick Law Olmsted, Jr. a member of the NCPPC with Delano, invited Eliot to join the commission as a planner. While working with the NCPPC, Eliot often stayed with his father's old fraternity mate, Delano. By the late 1920s Eliot and Delano, now head of the commission, helped plan for the extension of Washington's parks, highways, and federal buildings. In 1933 Delano and Eliot served together as chairman and director of the National Planning Board.[6]

Merriam came to planning through the social sciences. He trod the path of specialization, functional organization of knowledge by professional field, and eventual foundation of the overarching Social Science Research Council. Between 1923 and 1926 under Merriam's leadership, the SSRC sought to create professional social science standards, publish a bibliographic abstract to aid researchers, promote national guidelines for state-sponsored social research, and integrate researchers into a national network. By the late 1920s the SSRC had built a hierarchical structure, with the Problems and Policy Committee at the top, followed by both permanent and temporary committees staffed by experts engaged in special studies. As a national coordinating body sometimes referred to as a peak organization, one of the most important of the new breed of cross-sectoral institutions, the SSRC sought to promote cooperation among private research agencies, philanthropic foundations, and the federal government.[7]

Mitchell, the most important economist of his generation, abandoned nineteen-century classical economics as based on deductive and simplistic reasoning without examination of actual economic institutions and data. His career reflected a concern with amassing economic data, constructing useful comparative statistical series, and promoting both professionalism in economics and cooperation among businesses, social researchers, and the federal government. As founder and research director of the National Bureau of Economic Research, he joined Merriam and Ruml in organizing the SSRC, succeeding Merriam as chairman from 1927 to 1929. The 1921–33 period brought academic professionals the opportunity to apply social science research by conducting public-policy advisory work for the federal government financed by private philanthropies. The Hoover committees from the Unemployment Conference of 1921 used the expertise of Mitchell and the NBER to create an associative form of Hooverian planning that culminated in the President's Research Committee on Social Trends, which recommended creating a permanent planning agency. Government sponsorship, private philanthropic funding, and academic social science proved mutually reinforcing in New Era America. Mitchell's NBER mirrored the rise of modern social science-oriented policy institutes that later were called think tanks, a specialized kind of cross-sectoral institution.

Dennison took a more practical route to planning that reflected his experience in private business and early firm-specific planning. Moving beyond the company and his home town of Boston, he entered government service off and on between 1917 and 1933. During the 1920s, he worked to build the New Era dream of a reinvigorated capitalism based on increased productivity and consumption while laying the ground-work for voluntary unemployment relief, active cooperation among businesses through the trade association movement, and an unsuccessful effort to found the Business Research Council on Merriam and Mitchell's SSRC model. Business leaders like Dennison were becoming key players in the evolution of the modern American political economy, which brought private, public, and cross-sectoral institutions together in the making of national policy that emerged in the NRA effort at industrial recovery in the early New Deal.[8]

Ruml represented a new kind of policy manager who came out of the private sector, joining other second-generation philanthropic leaders as a manager of knowledge using private funding to engage in what was really public-policy making.[9] On the heels of his leadership of the LSRM in establishing a national social science research network, he cemented ties among philanthropists, researchers, businessmen, planners, and government officials in the emerging Hoover planning efforts. Rockefeller-connected philanthropies such as the LSRM, the new Social Science Division of the reorganized Rockefeller Foundation, and the Spelman Fund of New York, all influenced by Ruml at some point, financed an institutional network of social scientists that participated not only in the Hoover studies of the New Era but also in the state and regional planning boards of the 1930s and 1940s as well as the new field of public administration. Ruml provided the financial and organizational links among an entire generation of researchers, business leaders, and policy analysts that ultimately brought five of the most important of these interwar planners together on the New Deal planning board.

To build the associational network needed to make the transition from Hoover to Roosevelt, advocates of the new order had to meet certain conditions. Relying on the experience of trained professionals in business management, city planning, social science, and philanthropy, they called for an emphasis on detailed research. This research could be productive only if it brought together a number of people acting as a cooperating team willing to integrate diverse information. Integration in turn required coordination of the work of specialists through the use of new, ad hoc institutions in order to preserve some elements of voluntarism without giving way to a potentially dangerous, all-powerful state. To build such an associative planning state, innovative leaders had to assume direction of the efforts on a national level. Such leadership necessitated sponsorship by influential people in the federal government along with financial support from interested philanthropies.

Building this network proved a time-consuming, frustrating, and imperfect process. Yet under the leadership of Secretary of Commerce and later President Herbert Hoover, various proponents of associational co-operation worked deliberately throughout the 1920s to integrate national priorities, new knowledge, expertise, and practical business experience funded with private monies to make public policy.[10] Employing the cumulative knowledge, experience, and personal connections gained from Hoover's committee and conference system between 1921 and 1929, these individuals learned to work together. The professional associations served as coordinating agencies under the direction of federal officials. Managers in such organizations as the Rockefeller philanthropies, the Carnegie Corporation, the Twentieth Century Fund, and the Common-wealth Fund proved willing to support a wide range of research projects. Ad hoc planning in the 1920s took the planners into the arena of national policy, which led them to develop an ideology of advisory national planning with a distinctly American national focus. They wanted a form of planning that was neither laissez-faire nor statist, but rather something in between. Their own intellectual development, institutional connections, and transition from local and regional voluntary groups to national public-policy forums made for an American variant of planning that was neither wholly private nor wholly public. Growing links between people, ideas, and institutions regarding the utility of social science research as a tool for addressing national issues led finally into New Deal planning as economic, political, and social conditions changed in the Great Depression.

The confluence of people, institutions, and an emerging national-policy process brought the five planners together in the associational efforts of the New Era. During and immediately after the Great War, a number of social scientific research institutions studying national issues were founded that bolstered the new university system of the late nineteenth century. Centers such as the National Research Council, the National Bureau of Economic Research, the Twentieth Century Fund, and Robert Brookings's Institute for Government Research and the Institute of Economics arose out of the concern for accurate information as a possible basis for the formulation of public policies.[11] Herbert Hoover called on these private institutes as well as academic centers such as the University of Chicago for help in dealing with the postwar depression of 1920–21.

The Unemployment Conference of 1921 established a number of important precedents in public-policy planning.[12] Its call for further economic and social research led directly to the landmark studies summarized in *Recent Economic Changes* (1929) and *Recent Social Trends* (1933), an emphasis on voluntarist relief efforts first employed in 1921 and then redeployed by President Hoover in the 1929–31 period, and consideration of public works planning culminating in the establishment of the Federal Employment Stabilization Board in 1931. Each of these major efforts involved one or more of the planners and brought their organizations into the evolving planning nexus. Seen as individual projects, these research plans might appear as only sporadic efforts by interested individuals. Viewed as a conscious response to the depression of 1920–21 that later expanded into a more full-blown institutional effort, they laid the foundation for an American national planning first under Hoover, then under FDR.

Hoover asked each of the planners at some point to perform government service. Initially each declined, but as more projects grew out of the 1921 conference subcommittees, they came together, if only for a time, in Hoover's associational planning efforts. Cooperation between social scientists, trade association executives, labor leaders, government officials, social researchers, and philanthropic managers revealed a complicated mosaic of individuals and institutions behind Hooverian planning. Hoover would ask his assistant Edward Eyre Hunt to contact an appropriate official, establish a committee representing the various organized groups, and then seek funds from a private philanthropy while insisting on public recognition of federal sponsorship of the project. The emerging pattern set the stage for the early New Deal programs, though at key points Hoover always drew back from emphasizing overmuch the positive role of government sponsorship. The culmination and turning point came with President Hoover's Research Committee on Social Trends in the crisis period of 1929–33, which revealed the weakness of Hooverian voluntarism. Significantly, over time the Hooverian program broadened its reach, moving from a kind of crude economic determinism into the wider realms of social research that documented what social scientists such as William Fielding Ogburn and Charles Merriam saw as an increasing gap between technological skill and social cooperation, what they termed cultural lag. In the course of the 1920s, these associational linkages became increasingly formal as seen in the formation of such groups as the city and regional planning bodies headed by Delano, the SSRC and NBER led by Merriam and Mitchell, the business groups led by Dennison, and the LSRM and its successors directed by Ruml.

The emphasis on direction from above through the executive branch, use of organized team research in the social sciences, and administrative structuring of the projects clearly paved the way for New Deal planning. Yet the failure of Hoover's voluntarism between 1929 and 1933 in the area of unemployment relief overshadowed these parallel efforts to create a planning process. Millions of Americans suffered while Hoover relied upon voluntarist policies from his experiences in wartime mobilization, the Unemployment Conference of 1921, and as secretary of commerce during the New Era. Relying on these earlier efforts, Hoover did not adjust his belief in the utility of voluntary association as seen by the work of the President's Emergency Committee for Employment. PECE chairman Arthur Woods, a Rockefeller Foundation official who had supervised Ruml in the 1920s, worked with other members including Ruml and Erving P. Hayes, company historian of the Dennison Manufacturing Company. Hoover loyalist Edward Eyre Hunt served as secretary of the committee, which, as in 1921, relied on local and state governments and private relief agencies at the very time when these groups ran out of money, faith, and hope.[13] In failing to allow for government action on the national level to bolster the faltering efforts of voluntary agencies and the welfare capitalist plans of large corporations, Hoover sounded the death knell of his program. But Delano, Merriam, Mitchell, Dennison, and Ruml modified Hoover's idea of voluntarism to develop a more expansive ideology of advisory national planning in the 1930s. They proved more flexible than Hoover, moving into the realm of governmental action as well as promoting simultaneous action through voluntary cooperation.[14]

The organizational nexus that developed between 1917 and 1929 shaped the planners' emerging idea of national planning that fused Hoover's voluntarism with a more positive view of government action usually associated with Roosevelt's New Deal. Between 1929 and 1933 they brought a progressive faith in the power of knowledge, an extensive network of people and institutions, and a growing faith in planning as a process to provide continuity in public policy in moving from the Hoover era to the New Deal. The immediate move was from Hoover's Research Committee on Social Trends and the Emergency Committee for Employment to Roosevelt's National Planning Board.[15]

Spurred by a draft summary written by Merriam and approved by editor Mitchell, the President's Research Committee on Social Trends recommended the creation of a National Advisory Council. It argued that the council be set up on the model of the Social Science Research Council to include "scientific, educational, governmental, economic (industrial, agricultural and labor) points of contact." The proposed council,

Merriam wrote, should "consider some fundamental questions of the social order, economic, governmental, educational, technical, cultural, always in their interrelation, and in light of the trends and possibilities of modern science."[16] Internal divisions among committee members, coupled with pressure from Hoover's liaison man, led to a dispute over the role of social scientists in the federal government. There was also a question of whether Hoover's use of unpublished draft reports during the election campaign in the fall of 1932 tainted its research with political bias. Some committee members thought so. But research director William Fielding Ogburn and SSRC members Robert T. Crane, Merriam, and Ruml thought not. In the spring of 1933 Hoover refused to formally present a copy of *Recent Social Trends,* the two-volume summary report, to President-Elect Franklin Roosevelt. Ogburn, Crane, Merriam, and Ruml went to the SSRC, which had sponsored the study and administered the philanthropic grant monies, to argue that the committee's work should continue under the sponsorship of the new administration through three special Commissions of Inquiry. After Roosevelt approved two of the projects, the Rockefeller Foundation and the Spelman Fund financed the work.[17] The cross-sectoral institutional ties—a complicated nexus among business leaders, researchers, philanthropists, and the government—moved forward into the New Deal. Some of Hoover's key New Era planners were now Roosevelt's New Deal planners.

The immediate origin of the National Planning Board was an ongoing debate over the utility of a public works policy. As early as 1917 Pennsylvania had established a state Emergency Public Works Commission under the direction of Otto T. Mallery. During the Great War, Mallery had worked with the War Labor Policies Board and then went to work with Arthur Woods, who served as assistant director to the secretary of war. Woods brought Mallery in to head the Federal Aid and Works Section of the War Department. During the Unemployment Conference of 1921, Mallery chaired the Public Works Committee and advocated the adoption of a planned public works policy as an economic balance wheel to stabilize the economy by identifying projects during prosperous years that could be implemented during depressions. Throughout the 1920s Mallery worked for the various subcommittees of the Unemployment Conference and the Department of Commerce to push for adoption of his ideas.[18]

Though the Republican administrations of the 1920s rhetorically took up the cause of public works planning on a limited basis, the idea never took hold. With the establishment of the PECE in October 1930; however, the idea gained new supporters. The PECE recommended that President Hoover ask Congress to expand public works appropriations to $840 million. Hoover balked and asked for $100–150 million. Congress granted $116.5 million. With public outcry reaching huge proportions by October 1931, Congress passed a proposal by Senator Robert F. Wagner (D-N.Y.) to create the Federal Employment Stabilization Board, which would collect economic statistics, report to the president, and plan a six-year shelf of public works. Hoover appointed an uninterested D. H. Sawyer to head the agency, which did little in its less than two years of existence. But the precedent for public works planning resulting from the policy debates and social research of the 1920s had been set. From this small beginning came the National Planning Board.[19]

Between the fall of 1928 and the fall of 1932 in the midst of presidential election campaigns, Hoover instituted programs that both set the agenda for the public debate over national planning from 1930 to the spring of 1933 and presaged the planning efforts of the New Deal. Hoover moved first in the area of federal appropriations to win increases in public works programs modeled after Mallery's work. On June 16, 1929, he signed the Agricultural Marketing Act, creating the Federal Farm Board to promote voluntary cooperation among the nation's farmers. On January 22, 1932, after the growing effects of the Depression were recognized, Hoover signed the act establishing the Reconstruction Finance Corporation to promote industrial recovery from above through economic balance in the major industries. The public debate over national planning concentrated on exactly these three areas: public works, industrial recovery, and farm relief programs.[20]

Discussing national planning under other national models—fascist Italy, Nazi Germany, and the Soviet Union—as ways to face the trauma of the Great Depression, high-profile commentators envisioned dramatic scenarios of collectivism made possible by a powerful state. Yet they oversimplified a complex national debate among influential businessmen, trade association officials, politicians, reformers, and others caught up in the interwar organizational nexus of planning. For these parties, the common thread was to find a way to promote recovery through the cooperation of key groups in a pluralist society—business, labor, agriculture, and a host of more specialized interests. All proponents of national planning agreed that harmony was required to overcome the national emergency. Differences arose as to who would control the planning apparatus, how various interests should be incorporated, and the roles that government and private businesses would play in this effort. A variety of individuals, institutions, and interest groups became involved in the debate in ways that traditional distinctions between individualism and collectivism do not explain.[21]

Hooverian associationalism and Rooseveltian reform in the arena of national planning were not so different as many accounts suggest. In late 1934, now out of office, Hoover, defined planning in a letter to Mitchell: "'National Planning' is a matter of definition of terms. My objection is to calling such stuff as NRA, PWA, CWA, TVA as 'national planning' unless, of course, one is planning Fascism or Socialism. 'National Planning' to preserve the initiative of men, etc., would be all right with me."[22] Hoover saw his efforts of the 1920s as the way to preserve the American tradition of voluntary cooperation with government encouragement. Mitchell, now a member of the National Planning Board, took the argument one step further in his response to Hoover:

> To me it seems that the appointment of a national planning board would be the easiest way for the present [Roosevelt] administration to return to what your predecessor in the presidency called "normalcy." . . . It seems to me that we need some way of focusing the intelligence of the country upon social and economic problems of the sort that Recent Social Trends revealed. The board which Delano, Merriam, and I have suggested and which the cabinet members of the National Resources Board [the successor agency to the National Planning Board] have accepted "in principle," would not be able themselves to work out practical solutions. But I think they might develop an organization with numerous contacts which, if given fair working conditions, might do a better job than can be done by our usual methods of agitation or hurried political action. Indeed, I think that some organized way of meeting the difficulties that keep turning up in the course of social evolution is the best way of avoiding violent revolution.[23]

The potential for social upheaval in the Depression years in the guise of communism, socialism, or fascism led Delano, Merriam, and Mitchell to take national planning beyond the confines of New Era voluntarism into the realm of positive state action in the New Deal.

Creation of the National Planning Board also came from earlier conservation efforts and the personal interest of Franklin D. Roosevelt, as well as the institutional precedents of the New Era. President-Elect Roosevelt had long believed in land-use planning, experimental farming, and the conservation of natural resources. As governor of New York from 1929 to 1932, he instituted a number of experimental programs in industrial recovery, farm planning, public works, and conservation with the aid of experienced administrators such as Harry Hopkins and Frances Perkins. Knowledge of Progressive Era efforts in scientific conservation by his distant cousin Theodore Roosevelt, discussions with Delano regarding the Regional Plan of New York and Its Environs, and discussions of plans for the New Deal with Brain Trusters Raymond Moley, Adolf A. Berle, and Rexford Tugwell led Roosevelt to consider national planning.[24] In the end, however, his version of national planning did not differ significantly in its ends from that of the Hoover presidency.[25]

During the election campaign of 1932, Roosevelt's Brain Trust suggested a number of policy prescriptions for industrial recovery, adjustment of agricultural production and prices, and expanded public works programming. In the course of the 1932 campaign, Brain Trusters sought with some success to educate Roosevelt on the need for creating harmony among a diversity of social groups. In December 1932 FDR summarized where his New Deal would stand in words that Delano, Merriam, and Mitchell might have written:

> The economic life of the country, representing as it does diversified population and interests, can best be brought into harmony through wise and judicious and temperate national leadership through the government at Washington. . . . The interests of labor and industry cannot be promoted at the expense of agriculture; neither can capital reach a condition of true prosperity without at the same time offering a more legitimate share to labor. Any neglected group, whether of agriculture, industry, mining, commerce, or finance, can infect our whole national life and produce widespread misery. My administration shall be devoted to the task of giving practical force and the necessary legislative form to the great central fact of contemporary American life, viz., the interdependence of all factors, sections, and interests in this great country.[26]

Roosevelt's New Deal planning thus built on the precedents of Progressive hopes for creating a harmony of national interests, on the war-mobilization efforts at business-government cooperation, and on Hoover's voluntary planning of the 1920s with the goal of a national planning agency based on a modified version of the staff and line structures pioneered by the modern business corporation. New Deal planning would promote economic, social, and political stability by control from above. Reform of the American system meant modifying rather than expunging the complex organizational networks created over the last half century. In this broader ideological sense, New Deal planning reflected the other New Deal responses to the Great Depression.[27] Rexford Tugwell, one of the original Brain Trusters, said of the early New Deal's industrial and agricultural recovery programs: "This economic order and stability, I had argued, could be reached by allowing industrial groups to reorganize and establish legalized relations with each other . . . it was an attempt to find a way to maintain pluralism within guiding rules. . . . This was indeed the heart of the National Recovery Act. . . . This industrial bill was to regularize competition in industry. The Agricultural Adjustment Act [AAA] was to perform a comparable service for agriculture."[28]

The roots of New Deal planning may have been the wartime mobilization experience of 1917–18, public policy in the postwar depression of 1920–21, and the associational visions of Hoover, but most commentators on the New Deal note that Roosevelt confused the picture. An astute politician with a patrician background, FDR managed to combine conservative and liberal ideas in ways that policy makers often found astounding.[29] That Roosevelt could tell congressional Democratic liberals, influential businessmen, trade association executives, more wide-ranging planners, advocates of labor legislation, and supporters of an expanded public works program to combine their diverse draft bills into what led to the National Industrial Recovery Act (NIRA) of June 1933 revealed how central Roosevelt's leadership would be in the New Deal. While social scientists played a key role in developing the varying plans for farm policy in the 1920s and restructured them in the midst of the campaign of 1932, Roosevelt called the final tune. The resulting double-edged planning for industrial recovery and farm relief embodied in the NRA and AAA proved a mélange of policy alternatives previously thought at odds with one another. Roosevelt's political skills made the New Deal possible and credible. He used the advice of experts, especially social scientists, more than any president since the Progressive Era, though the experts did not always agree with Roosevelt's choices. The results often revealed the confusion inherent in such use of executive power, but Roosevelt masterfully played advisers off against one another. When administrators discovered what had been done, they often found themselves without support for their policies. The course of national planning between 1933 and 1943 told the same story.[30]

The National Industrial Recovery Act of June 16, 1933, created new agencies for both industrial recovery (the National Recovery Administration) and public works (the Public Works Administration [PWA]). While sectoral industrial planning through industry codes, suspension of anti-trust laws, and code regulations for production, prices, maximum hours, and elimination of child labor came with the NRA, Roosevelt split off public works under a separate agency. He hoped to control federal spending, much as his predecessor Hoover had, by placing the PWA (technically known as the Federal Emergency Administration of Public Works) under the direction of Secretary of the Interior Harold L. Ickes. Known for his hard-nosed determination to get the most for the money spent, Ickes appointed Colonel D. H. Sawyer of the Federal Employment Stabilization Board as temporary administrator. When Secretary of Commerce Daniel Roper suggested that Sawyer had not accomplished much since 1931, Roosevelt appointed Ickes permanent administrator on July 5, 1933.[31] Two days later, Ickes appointed Frederic Delano, Charles Merriam, and Wesley Clair Mitchell to the Advisory Committee of the National Planning Board (NPB) under the authority of Title II (Public Works) of the NIRA.[32]

Originally created to serve Public Works Administrator Ickes as a planning agency to offset economic downturns through public construction, the NPB quickly moved in another direction. In the early months of their work, FDR's planners sought advice from experts in public works theory. By November 1933 Merriam convinced Delano, Mitchell, and Ickes to think in longer-range terms. The planners saw the NPB as a potential general staff agency under the executive branch that would review planning efforts around the nation. They began work on preparing a "plan for planning" that would both educate the nation and recommend creation of a permanent planning board directly responsible to the president.[33]

The planners divided responsibilities for sections of the proposed "plan for planning," which was to be part of the NPB's final report. Delano took over the areas of physical planning on city, state, regional, and national levels. Merriam developed ideas on "governmental planning," defined as efforts to bring public administration theory and practice to national planning. Mitchell focused on the idea of economic planning, using the model of business planning by large corporations to level out the business cycle. In January 1934 the NPB hired Lewis Lorwin and Arthur Hinrichs to prepare a detailed report on the history and extent of planning in the United States. By late winter/early spring 1934, board members gathered to discuss the writing of the final report and its presentation to President Roosevelt.[34]

At the same time, the NPB arranged for joint meetings with representatives from the newly formed Business Advisory and Planning Council of the Department of Commerce. Chairman Henry Dennison of the Industrial Advisory Board of the BAPC brought his close friend and colleague Morris Leeds with him to the April 23, 1934, meeting, where the draft report was discussed. Though not yet an official member of the planning board, Dennison participated in this key phase of the NPB's work. Bringing his rediscovered interest in national planning with him, Dennison joined the other planners in advocating creation of an advisory planning board under the direction of the president that would use the expertise of social and natural scientists to recommend national policies.[35] Delano and Merriam stressed that representatives from functionally oriented interest groups and professions should be included as members of a rotating panel of consultants selected by the board. Mitchell and Dennison emphasized the role that business trade associations might play in a permanent planning body.

In drafting the final report, the planners stimulated the creation of city, state, and regional planning boards around the country, as well as planning public works programming. With financial help from the Rockefeller Foundation, these subnational planning boards promoted cooperation among all levels of government, the business community, and the social science research network built in the 1920s by Merriam, Mitchell, and Ruml. The NPB also solicited help from the National Academy of Sciences (NAS) and the Social Science Research Council (SSRC) in drafting sections on the utility of research to national planning, which included a memo from John Merriam, head of the Committee on Government Relations of the NAS.[36] The SSRC appointed a special committee to draft its section. Not surprisingly, the report focused on the research network as centered in universities, private research institutes, statistical bureaus analogous to industrial laboratories such as Bell Labs and those at General Electric, government bureaus in the Agriculture, Commerce, and Labor Departments, and various professional associations and umbrella groups. At the very time that Rockefeller support for the SSRC began to dry up, new money came from the federal government. Within a year, the NPB formalized these relations by establishing advisory committees from the NAS and SSRC. By the mid-1930s Charles Merriam's brother John had become Roosevelt's scientific adviser as head of the Science Committee of the planning board.[37]

By the end of May 1934 Charles Merriam had completed his draft of "A Plan for Planning," which he saw as the core of the *Final Report— 1933–34*. In NPB meetings of June 18–27, 1934, Merriam's draft was altered considerably. While the general outlines of his draft were retained, Mitchell fleshed out sections dealing with corporate planning. Mitchell praised the efforts in business planning but noted that concern for profits, the inherent limitations of intraindustry planning, and the impact of the Depression called for modifications in the corporate model. Mitchell,

Delano, and Merriam hoped to expand governmental planning beyond narrowly economic concerns to a broader focus on the general welfare. They hoped to promote the integration of planning by business, labor, agriculture, science and technology, social welfare, and government. Merriam's own concern with the rise of communism and fascism led to a final caveat that reflected the concerns of the New Deal as a whole: "Not passive acceptance but violent explosion is the alternative if we fail to develop security and progress by rational and evolutionary methods." Clearly, the New Deal planners saw advisory national planning by experts whose recommendations would be approved or vetoed by both the president and the Congress as a way to avoid anarchy and revolution from either the left or right.[38]

As included in the NPB's *Final Report—1933–34,* "A Plan for Planning" dealt with major policy issues: the history of American planning, current types of planning in the United States, critical summaries of national planning in other countries, a definition and justification of national planning, a future vision of an abundant society made possible by planning, and specific recommendations for creating a permanent planning board. If American national planning had a bible, "A Plan for Planning" was it. FDR's planners saw national planning as a continuously changing policy-making process led by the federal government working in cooperation with other organized groups while drawing on the research expertise of social scientists.

According to the New Deal planners, planning had nationally distinct roots in American history. They reviewed the litany of planning efforts over the broad sweep of U.S. history: the constitutional convention, Alexander Hamilton's *Report on Manufactures,* a report by Albert Gallatin (secretary of the treasury under Jefferson and Madison) on internal improvements, Speaker of the House Henry Clay's "American System," land policy, public education policy, corporate planning by national businesses, government regulation in the late nineteenth century, the conservation movement led by Theodore Roosevelt and Gifford Pinchot, economic mobilization for World War I, Hooverian and trade association work in the 1920s, creation of the Federal Employment Stabilization Board in 1931, and the various plans advocated in the period 1931–33. Recognizing the preeminent influence of business corporations since the late nineteenth century, the planners called for national planning based on a modified version of corporate planning to promote economic stabilization and social peace between interest groups. They also stressed that planning already had a place at all levels of government in a variety of areas relating to national resources. The report reviewed national planning in Japan, Russia, Italy, and Germany, rejecting all of them as unsuited to America. Merriam saw the United States as dedicated to the principles of social democracy, the constitutional rule of the president and the Congress, and freedom from the class distinctions of Europe.[39]

The NPB defined planning as "the systematic, continuous, forward looking application of the best intelligence available to programs of common affairs in the public field, as it does to private affairs." New Deal planners rejected older nineteenth-century liberal distinctions between private and public sectors, arguing that private regimentation already occurred in American life without planning. Planning did not mean total governmental control, centralization of all segments of American life, or the replacement of private initiative by public fiat. Instead, planning would take place voluntarily, led by the advice of experts working in concert with elected political leaders, organized groups, and the public. Yet at the core of this definition and justification lay an important contradiction. The planners' experience with Progressive reform, wartime mobilization, and Hoover's New Era associational planning led them to a belief, a secular faith, in progress, science, and rationality. They maintained a faith in their own benevolent control and use of social scientific research, in the rational behavior of political actors in the executive and legislative branches of the federal government, in the possibility of social peace among unequally organized groups, and in smooth coordination among all levels of government in the complex federal structure of American governance. The "public" came almost as an afterthought. The planners believed sincerely that the hierarchical general staff model drawn from their work with national business corporations, trade associations, professional associations in the social sciences and their national peak association of the SSRC, and the emerging network of private and public research institutes could serve the public, with planners acting as democratic agents of gradual, evolutionary change. To avoid the political, social, and economic strife of a class-torn Europe, America must turn to the elite, upper-class ordering taken for granted by the New Deal planners.[40]

In the final section of "A Plan for Planning," Roosevelt's planners recommended the establishment of a permanent National Planning Board of no more than five members appointed by the president, along with a rotating panel of consultants selected by the board. The consultant panel would include members of "governmental bureaus, labor, agriculture, industry, the home, technical and scientific societies, and other groups concerned with the sound formulation of the lines of our national progress." The board would consist of permanent staff members, a skeletal crew of technicians, and temporary consultants. By using this staff structure and a temporary line structure, the agency would avoid the bureaucratization and overcentralization found in the business model. Above all, planning should remain advisory in nature so as to preserve the balance between political, social, and, economic power.[41]

The planners went through five drafts of "A Plan for Planning" during their meeting at Delano's Algonac estate in Newburgh, New York. On June 25, 1934, they traveled up the Hudson River to Roosevelt's Hyde Park home to present the draft report. NPB minutes noted, "The President received the group in his study, with his back to us when we came in, and turning and shaking hands with us as we entered. Mr. Delano handed him the black bound report, containing the first part of the recommendations of the Board ["A Plan for Planning"]. The President stopped in the middle of his perusal of the report to express his approval. He explained that he wanted to talk to the Board because of his promise to Congress concerning land and water plans. He stated that he wanted a report by December first, in order to tell the country about it before Congress meets."[42] Roosevelt expressed his desire to continue the planning board for another year and accepted the suggestion to rename the board the National Resources Board (NRB).

The results of this meeting, however, disconcerted the planners, who had hoped to implement their broad vision of an advisory national planning group with a small number of experienced individuals dedicated to the utility of social science research. Roosevelt's practical and short-term orientation so distressed board members that they sent a joint telegram to Roosevelt stating their objections to the narrowing of focus in the NRB. Board members wanted it to be small and directly responsible to the president. Cabinet members Harold Ickes (Interior), Henry Wallace (Agriculture), Frances Perkins (Labor), and Federal Emergency Relief administrator Harry Hopkins sought to keep the NRB under cabinet control. Roosevelt ignored the planners' telegram and had Charles W. Eliot II draft Executive Order 6777, which created the NRB under authority of the NIRA, with Delano, Merriam, and Mitchell as an advisory committee alongside the secretaries of war, agriculture, commerce and labor and the Federal Emergency Relief administrator. On July 4, 1934, the National Resources Board succeeded the National Planning Board.[43]

Behind the meeting with Roosevelt lay a host of problems that haunted New Deal planning over the next ten years. How should the planning board be organized? What would be the relation of the board to the president, cabinet members, federal agencies, and the Congress? How would the board be funded if it remained a temporary agency created by a politically shifting President Roosevelt? How would the planners implement their idea of advisory long-range planning in the face of continued pressure to engage in short-term, piecemeal planning? Would the planners remain united, or would internal conflicts exacerbate the other problems? Over the course of the next decade these questions continued to trouble FDR's planners.

By December 1, 1934, the new NRB sent Roosevelt the report on land and water planning he had requested in June. It included a shortened version of "A Plan for Planning," along with detailed analyses by the NRB's Land, Water, and Mineral Policy Committees. The planners tried to satisfy Roosevelt and themselves by giving the president the detailed physical planning reports he wanted for partisan reasons, while implementing their own long-range strategy for using social science research in an advisory planning process. Between 1934 and 1943 the planning agency prepared hundreds of reports that even today remain among the best surveys in some fields. Their idea of planning was not utopian but, rather, research oriented and open ended in recommendations.[44]

The NRB changed names twice more between 1935 and 1939. Under Executive Order 7065, the National Resources Committee was created with funding from the Emergency Relief Appropriation Act of 1935. Its administrative structure followed that of the NRB, only its source of funding changed after the Supreme Court declared the National Industrial Recovery Act unconstitutional. In 1939, under Reorganization Plan No. 1, the National Resources Planning Board became an independent agency in the Executive Office. Between 1939 and 1943 Roosevelt funded the NRPB from both emergency relief appropriations and executive emergency appropriations. The change in authorization and funding proved crucial in the debate of 1943 that ended New Deal planning. In terms of personnel, the planning agency remained remarkably stable.[45]

The only significant change in personnel came when Mitchell resigned in September 1935. Mitchell had grown increasingly skeptical about the value of what he called "piecemeal" and "emergency," or "crisis," planning. Trained as an economist, he wrestled with the problem of balancing precise knowledge and the social usefulness of national planning. In late 1935 he saw planning as needing the complete energies of full-time planners. When Roosevelt did not see the value of this kind of planning agency, Mitchell resigned. He never gave up faith in the ideal of planning but wanted to pursue work as research director of the NBER. Merriam and Delano quickly decided to bring on Henry Dennison and Beardsley Ruml as an advisory committee representing the business community.[46]

With the addition of Dennison and Ruml, the planning board's work took a new direction. Delano, Merriam, and Mitchell served as the older generation that had gotten national planning off the ground in the midst of the excited political atmosphere of the First Hundred Days of the New Deal. Their emphasis on the idea of advisory planning suited the voluntarist predilections of Dennison and Ruml. All five planners supported the development of the planning board along a modified corporate model, thus valuing the insights and practical business experience of Dennison and Ruml. Above all, they interpreted planning as a cooperative effort aimed at promoting efficient use of natural resources and rational consideration of human resources. Organization charts for the NPB, NRB, NRC, and NRPB showed clearly the bureaucratic expansion of the planning agency from a small executive staff to a modest staff and line agency by the late 1930s.[47] The board sought to carry the ideas of modern rationality, efficiency, and scientifically based policy making into the federal government, as drawn from business, trade associations, city and regional planning, professional social science, and private-public cooperation with the assistance of modern philanthropy into the policy process. New Deal planning reflected the development of modern American liberalism, as well as institution building from the Progressive Era, wartime mobilization, and the New Era.

The New Deal planners hoped to bring new public administration techniques to national planning. But they placed an inordinate faith in President Roosevelt's support for their work and evinced a certain naïveté about government jurisdictional boundaries and a blindness to an ideological opposition to planning in Congress. Franklin Roosevelt played a central role in directing the energies of the planners. Between 1934 and 1937 the planners oversaw a social science research effort that resulted in publication of an enormous number of important studies centering on natural resources planning for land use, water use, and mineral development. Assuming a value-neutral stance for science-based planning, the planners ignored the political context of New Deal planning, which became heated as the emergency conditions of the Depression passed. Roosevelt's planners often overlooked the inherent weakness of the planning board's structure as an independent agency under the president, which led to cabinet and interdepartmental rivalries, while dependence on temporary year-to-year funding under the auspices of the executive branch exposed the planners to power struggles between the president and the Congress. The rising tide of congressional opposition to creating a permanent planning board under the president led to ongoing funding problems and political conflicts that threatened the very existence of the planning agency.[48]

Between July 1934 and late 1937 the planning board created a host of specialized committees dealing with land-use planning, multiuse water planning, mineral policy, industrial resources, transportation, energy, science, population, and stimulation of city, state, and regional planning. Initially part-time outside consultants from universities, private research institutes, and governmental agencies did much of this work. But by the late 1930s the agency began using its own, more experienced technical committees, with, from time to time, special research committees. Over time, as one scholar of New Deal planning has noted, the board followed "a normal bureaucratic evolution, toward more employees and a more formal organization."[49]

President Roosevelt supported the planners' work, but he did so quietly and only so far as it served his purposes, consciously shying away from making the family connection with Delano in public while using it to full advantage in private correspondence with his uncle. Following his usual acute political instincts, Roosevelt garnered executive authority as a way of continuing the board, while shifting the source of funds when required. Though congressional liberal Democrats proposed legislation for a permanent planning board from 1936 on, Roosevelt hedged his bets.[50] New Deal planning served Roosevelt's purposes at times, but he had no real appreciation for the long-range ideas proposed by his planners. He was more interested in pet projects, such as the effort in 1937 to extend the Tennessee Valley Authority to seven other river basins, a campaign that was a dismal failure. After that fight and the loss of the Supreme Court packing plan, FDR allowed the board to take his and its own political heat.[51]

From the shift in name to the NRB in June 1934, the planners came face-to-face with the jealousies of cabinet officials and heads of governmental agencies. The best-known instance of this involved Secretary of the Interior Harold Ickes, whose attack on the idea of an independent board grew from fears that he would lose a group he considered part of his bureaucratic "turf." At the same time, Federal Emergency Relief administrator Harry Hopkins, famous for his public feud with Ickes, feared that the planners' interests in public works planning and coordination would interfere with his own efforts at unemployment relief through public works projects. Secretary of War George H. Dern meanwhile took up the cudgels of the Army Corps of Engineers and the River and Harbors Bloc in Congress to oppose multiuse water planning. Secretary of Agriculture Henry Wallace continued to seek separation of overall staff planning by the NRB from the operational planning of his research staffs in the Department of Agriculture, especially those in the Agricultural Adjustment Administration. Bureaucratic infighting had been common-place in private business corporations; government operations proved no better or worse.[52]

Congress proved even more critical of the planning board's work. The hardening coalition of Republicans and conservative southern Democrats resisted efforts to make the planning agency permanent. Not understand-ing the idea of advisory national planning grounded in the American tra-dition of voluntary cooperation, Congress criticized the planners for pro-moting European-style collectivism and centralized command economic planning. Much of the criticism of the planners also served as a way for conservative politicians to get at the politically hard-to-reach Roosevelt. Viewing the research work of the planning board as too expensive, they refused to see the broader social benefits of thinking for the long term, overlooking the advantages of what relief administrator Harry Hopkins called "spending-to-save." Fearful of "bureaucracy," conservatives in Congress condemned the planners' "duplication of effort" in both coor-dinating governmental programming and bringing rationality to New Deal policy making. Constrained by the limits of nineteenth-century lib-eralism, they failed to see that the staff and line structure of the board followed from the corporate model in business that they defended as "free enterprise." Pressure from powerful pork-barrel politicians of the Rivers and Harbors Bloc more interested in the immediate, short-term political benefits of public works led to continued attacks on the planning agency, which became seen as a competitor to their self-interest.[53]

By 1937 FDR's planners had accomplished more than any previous planning effort in American history. In response to the crisis of the Great Depression, the planners had made the transition from Hoover's volun-tary associational planning based on the precedents of Progressive reform and wartime mobilization to New Deal planning with a distinct, but hardly pure, statist orientation. Under the changed circumstances of a world depression, the repudiation of Hoover and the Republican coali-tion in Congress, the election of Franklin D. Roosevelt, and the start of a new Democratic coalition, these lifelong Republicans joined the national effort to bring economic stability, social security, rational order, and political harmony to the national policy-making process. In helping to build the interwar organizational nexus of planning, they had brought together a range of people and institutions at the national level that included business leaders, city and regional planners, skilled professional social scientists, public-policy research bodies in the private and public sectors, and a second generation of philanthropic managers. They worked within not only private and public institutions but also the new cross-sectoral institutions as well. Moving from the President's Research Committee on Social Trends to the National Planning Board and its successor agencies, they had evolved from Hooverian associationalists to Rooseveltian New Dealers. Under their direction, national planning sponsored by the executive branch of the federal government and financed by both executive emergency funds and, at times, private philanthropies had legitimated natural resources management, an immense social research effort, regional planning in New England and the Pacific Northwest, and state planning boards in a majority of the states. Important studies from the Unemployment Conference of 1921 to the Research Committee on Social Trends and the New Deal planning boards suggested that public works planning could achieve economic stabilization of the business cycle and address the related problem of cyclical unemployment. Yet between 1933 and 1937 the planners had to act within the constraints of President Roosevelt's politically oriented management style, the irrational bureaucratic rivalries and jealousies of cabinet officials and executive-branch agencies, and the rising opposition from conservatives in Congress looking for vicarious Rooseveltian targets. Between 1937 and 1943 these constraints narrowed further, leaving FDR's planners with shrinking political options in facing the problems of economic recession, executive reorganization, defense production, and postwar planning.

The Crucible of Planning

RECESSION, WAR, AND POSTWAR
PLANNING, 1937–1943

NOW THAT THEY had a strong leader in Franklin D. Roosevelt and political support from the Democratic coalition that triumphed in the 1936 election, FDR's planners appeared to be on the verge of a series of stunning planning successes that would legitimate both national planning and the new liberalism. Like FDR, they thought that new conditions made possible by the early New Deal would allow for rapid and smooth acceptance of their general welfare definition of national planning under the National Resources Committee. Roosevelt and New Deal reformers had partially restored the psychological confidence of the American people through their charisma, infectious optimism, and willingness to try new methods. By 1935–36, early New Deal pump-priming efforts had apparently paid off by jump-starting economic recovery. Voters seemed to approve as reflected by political victories in both the 1934 off-year congressional elections and the 1936 presidential election, which consolidated FDR's hold on the presidency and increased Democratic majorities in both houses of Congress. Results from the 1936 election suggested that the new Democratic majority coalition grew out of the success and popularity of such New Deal social welfare measures as the Social Security Act of 1935, the National Labor Relations Act of 1935, and the start of Harry Hopkins's work relief programs in the Works Progress Administration. The future looked bright for FDR, the New Deal, the Democratic Party, the country, and the national economy. No wonder the planners held high hopes for the future of New Deal planning as well. Between 1937 and 1943 they broadened the scope of New Deal planning beyond physical- and natural resources planning to encompass socioeconomic planning in response to the challenges posed by depression, world war, and postwar demobilization. As they moved into the arena of public policy and debate, FDR's planners expanded their reach and implemented aspects of the new ideology of modern liberalism. Yet their efforts were constrained by changing external circumstances marked by administrative confusion in the welter of New Deal alphabet-soup agencies, the recession of 1937, fascist aggression abroad, wartime mobilization, and calls for postwar planning. As the planners moved steadily into the arena of national politics, their vision for a new America included increasingly controversial issues such as new fiscal policies that were later identified with Keynesian economics, executive-branch reorganization, and an independent life for the planning agency. In this move from depression to wartime planning, they entered a heated crucible that tested their resolve and challenged them to face difficult policy questions, including preparation for building a prosperous and stable postwar America.

Recent scholars have suggested that the period from 1937 to 1943 saw New Deal reform efforts transformed from the immediate social welfare emphasis of the Second New Deal toward a "Third New Deal" intended at once to consolidate earlier New Deal gains from a reorganized executive branch and to propose a new set of policies based on the emerging idea of a full-employment economy buttressed by expanded social welfare programs made possible by wartime reinvigoration of the economy.[1] Roosevelt's planners were key players in this transformation, though their entanglement in politics ultimately ended their organizational existence. By becoming involved in these heated issues, the planners faced growing political constraints in the form of conflicts that pitted the president against Congress, permanent cabinet agencies in the executive branch against more fragile groups such as the planning board, supporters of an expanded New Deal against conservatives opposed to much of New Deal reform, wartime mobilizers seeking economic stability and social peace versus liberals hoping to use the war to spark further reform, and postwar planners who envisioned a postwar society of abundance versus mobilization administrators and military leaders more concerned with the immediate goal of winning of the war against fascism.[2] Ironically, as New Deal planning reached maturity, political, economic, and administrative constraints placed limitations on its future, including the very existence of national planning in the public sector.

Between 1937 and 1943 the planning board expanded its scope to include a variety of investigations into public works planning, natural resources conservation, the impact of technology, declining population, and the structure of the American economy.[3] While the immediate stimulus for this expansion lay in the recession of 1937–38, these efforts grew out of the planners' desire to implement planning as a continuous process. By the late 1930s FDR's planners were articulating an ideology of modern liberalism, with planning as a key component. Using the planning board as an elite group of policy advisers, a strong president such as Franklin Roosevelt could bring together the varied interest groups of the twentieth-century political economy—industry, labor, agriculture, and the professions would be the core constituencies—while acting in concert with a Democratic-led Congress to make America's future bright, rational, progressive, and prosperous. This ideology of liberal pluralism, which later evolved into interest-group liberalism, the planners argued, was vastly superior to the competing ideologies of fascism and communism that emphasized the role of dictators, single-party dominance, an omnipotent state, command-style economic planning, and limited social welfare programs for the mass public. They saw national planning as an advisory process that could and should bring together planners, government agencies, private research consultants from a number of research agencies, trade associations in the business community, and—to a much lesser extent—consultation with labor unions, farm interests, and individual members of the public. During this same period, President Roosevelt adopted an increasingly ambivalent attitude toward the planning agency as he responded to shifting political, diplomatic, and economic conditions. Between 1937 and 1939 he failed to reorganize the Supreme Court, executive-branch agencies, and the Democratic Party. Unable to purge the Democratic Party of key conservatives or forestall victories by conservative Southern Democrats and Republicans in the congressional elections of 1938, FDR and the New Deal came under increasing criticism and attack. Congressional opponents of FDR and New Deal expansion of executive-branch power focused on a vulnerable planning board as a way to attack Roosevelt indirectly. With the outbreak of World War II in Europe in September 1939, America faced the immediate task of mobilizing for total war for the second time in the century, with much of the effort concentrated on winning the war rather than worrying about the peace that would follow in the long run. At the moment of seeming triumph in leading the way for the Third New Deal, FDR's planners faced a new set of constraints that did not bode well for their future as national policy advisers. Still, in the midst of developing plans for executive-branch reorganization, a response to the recession of 1937–38, wartime production needs, and postwar abundance, none of this was obvious or predetermined as a foregone conclusion at the time.

From the outset of Roosevelt's presidency in 1933, a number of New Dealers had wrestled with the issue of government reorganization.[4] That issue had first emerged in the Progressive Era, but it became increasingly urgent as the New Deal created a plethora of agencies throughout the executive branch to combat the Great Depression. A variety of individuals and groups sought to address the issue of executive-branch reorganization. In 1936 President Roosevelt turned the problem over to his planners through the Committee on Administrative Management (CAM). The work of the CAM led to legislative recommendations that FDR introduced at exactly the same time as the famous "court packing" plan to add new justices to the Supreme Court, which ended in political disaster.[5] Over the next two years, bills intended to make the planning agency a permanent body under the president were defeated or so thoroughly rewritten that the NRC's successor agency, the newly reorganized and renamed National Resources Planning Board created in 1939, faced continuing challenges to its existence from a Congress angry with the ongoing New Deal extension of executive-branch power.

In this same period FDR's planners worked on developing responses to the recession of 1937–38. By 1937–38 the planners entered the policy debate over how to deal with the consequences of the recession: rising unemployment, declining production and prices, and the consequent dip into recession. In this debate, the planners developed a moderate version of compensatory spending policy, which they took into the post-defense crisis of 1939–41. Initially, plans for mobilizing the economy for World War II involved the planning board but soon passed it by. More significantly, FDR's planners developed a series of reports released in early 1943 that called for a postwar economy of abundance that combined the concept of a full employment economy with an ambitious set of social welfare proposals that would make the welfare state a complement to full employment. Roosevelt's shift to Dr. Win-the-War and congressional resistance to planning led to a climactic debate in the spring of 1943 that abolished the NRPB. In providing only enough money to liquidate the board's operations and mandating that its records be sent to the National Archives, Congress hoped to stamp out all vestiges of national planning by the federal government. Yet the growth of various private research agencies during the war and passage of the Employment Act of 1946 ensured the continuation of planning, albeit in more restricted voluntarist forms. The congressional debate of 1943 confused the debate over just what national planning in the United States meant. Adoption by default of Keynesian compensatory spending policy in the war and postwar years furthered that confusion. Planners tried desperately to explain that their spending policy intended to preserve the system of industrial capitalism by supporting the private sector through government spending in times of recession and depression when private investment lagged. Few members of Congress listened. When New Deal planning shifted from advocating compensatory spending as a short-term response to the recession of 1937–38 to recommending fiscal policy as an engine of postwar economic growth, full employment, and the abundant society, conservatives in Congress drew on the long-standing American tradition of antistatism to kill the planning board.[6] New Deal planning lost its institutional home, although many of the ideas developed in the Third New Deal anchored the postwar policy agenda of modern liberalism.

Three of the central issues in the Third New Deal centered on the necessity to respond to the crisis of the recession of 1937–38, the reorganization of the various executive-branch agencies created by the New Deal in order to consolidate reform, and the institutionalization of the planning board as a permanent executive-branch advisory group. Between 1937 and 1939 FDR's planners wrestled with these issues in a political context of increased opposition to New Deal policies. This part of New Deal history, often lost in traditional accounts of the fading away of New Deal reform and FDR's turn toward internationalist diplomacy, had the New Deal planners at center stage as reform liberalism was transformed by the reemergence of a fiscal policy focused on spending, executive reorganization as an attempt to deal with the administrative expansion of the New Deal state, and the reemergence of conservative opposition to reform among both southern Democrats and Republicans.

The Great Depression raised the fear that the United States might be caught up in the worldwide rise of fascism amid the indecision of Western democracies. Among the planners, Merriam and Ruml paid particularly close attention to developing the new liberal ideology as an American alternative to European fascism. All the planners saw the emerging focus of interest-group liberalism as a healthy, spirited alternative based on American history, culture, and conditions to centralized state power inherent in fascist ideology. A rational, scientific effort to deal with national problems using the expertise of NRPB staff members along with continued use of the American political system based on the separation of powers, a strong federal system of state and local power, and democratic debate would serve as an antidote to the depredations of fascism. Historians of the New Deal assume that by 1937–38 Roosevelt's program of domestic relief, recovery, and reform had come to its end.[7] Congressional opposition to the Supreme Court packing plan, the conservative shift in electoral politics in the 1938 congressional elections, and Roosevelt's rising concern with foreign policy led to compromise and the setting aside of reform measures. Once World War II began, the standard accounts suggest, FDR had to turn his attention to prosecuting the war effort, and domestic reform gave way to a national and international mobilization.[8] Yet the same period between 1937 and 1943 saw vigorous debate over the proposals of the Third New Deal, most of which came out of the efforts of planners at the NRPB. But fear of centralized power in fascist countries and conflation of fascism and Soviet communism as related forms of "collectivism" eventually tainted the planning effort and undermined the Third New Deal.

Internal policy conflict emerged over what to do in response to the sharp downturn in the economy in 1937. From its start in September 1937 to the end in June 1938, this recession proved the most rapid economic decline in U.S. history.[9] Over the course of the recession, industrial production dropped by 33 percent, national income fell by 13 percent, profits were off by 78 percent, payrolls declined by 35 percent, industrial stock averages lost 50 percent, and manufacturing employment went down by 23 percent. This sharp turn in the business cycle led to an internal crisis among New Dealers, which indicated considerable confusion over what policy to follow. One faction, conservative defenders of economic orthodoxy represented by Secretary of the Treasury Henry Morgenthau, Jr., his Treasury advisers, Reconstruction Finance Corporation head Jesse Jones, and Secretary of Commerce Daniel C. Roper, argued that the decline stemmed from the business community's lack of confidence and hence failure to invest because of New Deal reforms, which represented in business leaders' minds an attack on free enterprise through government regulatory power. According to the conservatives, the best policy lay in balancing the federal budget, revising the tax laws, and restoring the confidence of the business community through stabilizing efforts. Another faction, the antitrusters led by such New Dealers as Leon Henderson, Tommy Corcoran, Benjamin Cohen, and Robert Jackson, argued that the recession had been brought on by the continued concentration of economic power via monopoly power of large firms that engaged in what National Resources Committee economist Gardiner Means called "administered pricing." A third faction, variously known as the spenders, the liberals, or the New Dealers—best represented by Federal Reserve Board chairman Marriner S. Eccles, Secretary of the Interior Harold Ickes, and FDR's planners—argued that tight money policy by the Federal Reserve system, cutbacks in pump-priming monies by the federal government in 1937, and the deflationary impact of the start of Social Security taxes meant that fiscal and monetary policy needed to be more innovative.[10] In some accounts, the outcome of the policy debate over what one scholar terms "the struggle for the soul of FDR" led to the emergence of the "new economics" based on the policy prescriptions of advisers strongly influenced by the British economist John Maynard Keynes.[11]

Scholars differ over the impact of the economic policy debate. In 1932 Democratic presidential candidate Franklin D. Roosevelt outdid Republican incumbent Herbert Hoover in calling for a balanced federal budget. Shortly after his inauguration in March 1933, Roosevelt appointed the conservative Lewis Douglas as budget director, knowing that Douglas stood for economic orthodoxy. But the Treasury Department adopted a "dual budget" in July 1933 that distinguished between normal operating expenditures and emergency expenditures to meet the unprecedented conditions of the Depression. By 1934 Douglas resigned in defeat, thinking that Roosevelt had gone too far in adopting temporary spending policies for the Public Works Administration and the Agricultural Adjustment Administration. Like others in the Roosevelt administration, such as Secretary of the Treasury Henry Morgenthau, Jr., Douglas feared the permanent use of spending policy based on the measures to deal with "the war against the national emergency."[12]

The Roosevelt administration continued emergency spending until early in 1937, when it decided to cut back relief and public works expenditures, since the economy seemed to be rebounding. But when the economy entered another downturn in the fall of 1937, what conservatives in Congress and the business community referred to as Roosevelt's recession, New Dealers had to find a way of meeting the new crisis or, they feared, find the United States facing both a renewed depression and the possibility of radical revolution from either the communist left or the fascist right. Scholars studying this period usually see the rise of Keynesian economics as the New Deal's solution to the crisis. Yet the policy debate was not so clear-cut as a retrospective view would suggest. Much of the existing scholarly literature proceeds from the presupposition that an intellectual history of the "Keynesian revolution" need not show any direct influence by Keynes or his disciples on Roosevelt or New Deal policy makers. Most of the extant work also assumes that, if one accepts the idea that the late New Deal accepted Keynesian fiscal policy by default, then one can read the work of younger American Keynesian economists back from the wartime mobilization for World War II into the policy debate of 1937–38. Yet the roots of fiscal policy can and should be traced more precisely to some of the New Dealers themselves, most of whom were not influenced directly by Keynes or his ideas.[13]

Roosevelt did hear from John Maynard Keynes by letter in December 1933 and personal appearance in June 1934. In the United States, however, Keynes's work remained for the most part unknown. Roosevelt rejected Keynes's proffered advice, preferring the ideas from his own administrators. Roosevelt's advisers, however, could not agree among themselves, and a protracted debate ensued among the conservatives, the antimonopolists, and the spenders. Chairman of the Board of Governors of the Federal Reserve Board, Marriner S. Eccles, advocated the resumption of spending by the federal government. Secretary Morgenthau at the Treasury opposed that policy, arguing that the budget must be balanced and the Reserve Board should loosen its monetary policy to stimulate investment in the private sector. Between the fall of 1937 and April 1938 the policy crisis came to a head. The complicated turns in the debate eventually brought a new group of professional economists into the decision-making process, many of whom became convinced Keynesians.[14]

Keynesian economic ideas did come to the United States, but not directly. Few American economists had even heard of Keynes. Even fewer understood Keynesian arguments. Those few who did learned from the new dean of American economics, Alvin H. Hansen. Born into a Swedish-American family in 1887 in South Dakota, Hansen received his education at Yankton College and the University of Wisconsin. His teaching career led him to Wisconsin, Brown University, the University of Minnesota, and Harvard University. When he came to Harvard in 1937, Hansen established a graduate seminar in economics along with the more orthodox economist John Williams. In the late 1930s Hansen's seminar served as the focal point for discussion of the new economics of Keynes, which Hansen had only recently and only in part accepted. Veterans of the seminar included many economists who carried out the "Keynesian revolution" during World War II and after. Among the graduates were Paul Samuelson, G. Griffith Johnson, Walter S. Salant, and other less well known policy makers.[15] Scholars of the Keynesian revolution—assuming that the intellectual history of Keynesianism precludes more precise accounting for names, dates, and timing by specific New Deal advisers—

argue that these economists entered the policy debate in the late 1930s and emerged as the victors. Closer study reveals a more complex policy conflict within New Deal circles. The liberal/spenders faction brought together Mormon banker Marriner Eccles and key people at the Federal Reserve Board, allies from the antimonopoly group, including Henderson, Corcoran, and Cohen, and planners in the National Resources Committee. Conservatives standing for the resumption of orthodoxy were the policy intellectuals surrounding Henry Morgenthau, Jr., at the Department of the Treasury. In the middle of the debate sat little-known and now-forgotten people including planners Henry Dennison, Beardsley Ruml, and Frederic Delano.[16]

Keynesian economics triumphed only temporarily in the late 1930s and by default, rather than via a self-conscious policy revolution, during World War II.[17] Overdramatization of the 1937–38 debate as the first chapter in the Keynesian revolution not only presumes a rationally persuasive policy alternative and a consensus among New Deal advisers; it also puts Keynesian ideas in place before their real impact was felt either among professional economists or among national policy makers.[18] The debate over how to deal with the recession served as prologue to the adoption by default of Keynesian fiscal and tax policies during mobilization for World War II. Proto-Keynesian policies were specifically drawn from the experiences of individuals such as Federal Reserve Board Chairman Eccles; Works Progress Administration administrators Harry Hopkins, Leon Henderson, and Aubrey Williams; and planners Dennison and Ruml. Each of these individuals came to fiscal spending policy not through the sophisticated theories of formally educated university economists but rather through common-sense efforts to avoid social revolution in a world wracked by depression, the rise of fascism, and dramatic changes in world geopolitics. Compensatory spending policy for Dennison and Ruml came about as an extension of earlier ideas concerning business-government cooperation. Government would spend monies to fill in gaps—Keynesians came to call them bottlenecks—left by the private sector. New Deal planners argued that government spending in recession or depression could balance weaknesses in the private sector (i.e., lagging investments), which would take up the slack in prosperous times.

New Deal planners played different roles in the 1937–38 policy debate. Dennison sought to develop a very moderate form of spending policy mixed with monetary and tax policies to present to his fellow businessmen. Ruml took up the cudgels of actual policy advising that led to FDR's resumption of spending in the spring of 1938. Delano served as a kind of mediator, hoping to spark discussion and bring the Eccles-Morgenthau factions to a compromise solution. Simultaneously, Charles E. Merriam, concerned about the perception that only fascists could be efficient, tried to bring order to executive-branch administration through investigation and implementation of reorganization plans. By 1939 the planners had brought some order to the executive branch through an ambivalent acceptance of moderate spending policy, continued study of economic policy, and congressional compromise on restructuring of executive-branch administration. Seen in their separate manifestations, these efforts appear disjointed and unrelated, but they were part of the evolving process of national planning under the Third New Deal.

Henry Dennison led the way into the policy debate. Drawing on his work as a trustee of the Twentieth Century Fund and his interest in business-cycle theory throughout the 1920s, Dennison came to the New Deal with the willingness to consider new ideas. During his tenure on the Business Advisory and Planning Council and the Industrial Advisory Board of the NRA, he made contact with two liberal businessmen—Ralph Flanders of the Jones and Lamson Machine Company of Springfield, Vermont, and Morris Leeds of the Leeds and Northrup Company, an electrical firm in Philadelphia. Together with his old friend Lincoln Filene of Filene's Department Stores in Boston, they began discussions about the need to develop policies promoting full employment and a high production and high consumption economy. Along the way, Dennison sought the help of other able individuals. In 1937 he hired a young economist, John Kenneth Galbraith, to guide him through the thicket of economic theory. In the course of these discussions, Dennison moved Galbraith toward what we now call fiscal-spending policy ideas.[19]

In 1938 Dennison published the results of his work with Galbraith, Filene, Flanders, and Leeds. In *Modern Competition and Business Policy,* Dennison and Galbraith drew on the work of the Twentieth Century Fund, the National Bureau of Economic Research, and the landmark study *The Modern Corporation and Private Property* (1933), by Adolf A. Berle and Gardiner C. Means. Dennison and Galbraith argued that the rise of the modern national business corporation, the increasing concentration of economic power, and the phenomenon of administered prices led to a necessary rejection of classical economics and the need to consider new policies. They suggested a middle way between the outmoded policy of antitrust and total government control, in favoring cooperation between business and government. Industrial publicity of prices, production figures, wages and hours, assets and liabilities might bring forth the cooperative ideal first broached by trade associations in the 1920s and tried under the NRA. Supporting the idea of mild government regulation of business, Galbraith and Dennison sought to promote economic balance to stabilize the depression-racked economy.[20]

In the fall of 1938 Dennison, Filene, Flanders, and Leeds published the results of their work as *Toward Full Employment*. Probably influenced by Mitchell's critique of intra-firm business planning included in the 1934 "A Plan for Planning," they accepted a combination of spending policy over the course of the business cycle, adoption of a "flexible budget," careful use of Federal Reserve monetary policy, and modification of the income tax structure with higher taxes in prosperous times to balance the budget.[21] Though not well received by the intended audience in the business community, the work showed Dennison moving toward a moderate form of spending policy stemming from the idea of a balanced budget at high levels of employment, production, and consumption over the course of the business cycle.

From 1937 through the fall of 1938, Dennison established contacts with Alvin Hansen's Harvard economics seminar and spending advocates such as Lauchlin Currie, Isador Lubin, and Mordecai Ezekiel in federal agencies. This network of spending advocates held discussions at informal meetings of the Eccles faction in Washington, D.C., which included Harry Hopkins and Beardsley Ruml. While Dennison did publicity work aimed at the business community, Ruml worked at convincing key policy decision makers in Washington. In 1934 Ruml had resigned his position as dean of the Division of Social Sciences at the University of Chicago to accept a position as treasurer for Macy's Department Store in New York City. While at Macy's, Ruml reorganized the accounting system and instituted a new credit plan that allowed customers to buy goods through a kind of mini-deficit-spending policy.[22] At the same time, he began work with the National Resources Committee. As in the 1920s, the Merriam-Ruml collaboration again proved fruitful, with Merriam leading the charge for executive reorganization, while his old friend Ruml led the fight for the resumption of federal spending.

By late 1937/early 1938, Ruml concluded that, unless the government under the auspices of the Federal Reserve Board accepted the idea of budgetary deficits, the economic recession would place the Roosevelt administration in a situation analogous to that faced by Hoover in 1929. Arguing in private memoranda and in discussions among members of the Eccles faction that compensatory spending policy was a must, Ruml moved quietly but effectively back into the policy decision-makers' circle. At the end of March 1938, Roosevelt advisers traveled in different directions for a brief respite from the intense policy debate. Ruml joined Leon Henderson and Aubrey Williams of Hopkins's WPA in Washington for a train trip to Pine Mountain Valley, near Roosevelt's Warm Springs retreat in Georgia. While at Pine Mountain, the three drafted a key memorandum that Hopkins took to Roosevelt to convince the president to adopt spending policy through a resumption of federal expenditures. Authorship of the memo has been attributed to Henderson, but he credited Ruml as the major author. The memo laid out ideas similar to those of Dennison and, not quite fully, ideas later attributed to Keynesian economists.[23]

Ruml set forth spending policy in the best possible light to convince Roosevelt. Rather than attacking the "strike of capital" by the business community (Roosevelt's explanation for the recession), Ruml argued that the problem lay in a declining national income. Citing the figure of roughly $60 billion for the national income early in 1937, Ruml argued that private enterprise could invest only about $4 billion, while the federal government could spend between $3 and $6 billion to reach full employment. Using material from National Resources Committee reports, Ruml showed that the nation had lost $200 billion (1936 prices) since 1929 in idle men and machines—a sum "greater than the value of all physical property in the United States in 1932." Pointing out that government had always intervened to create purchasing power—witness the alienation of land in the early republic—Ruml noted that spending policy had and could again sustain "the competitive capitalist system."[24]

Ruml insisted on drawing distinctions between democratic planning and "totalitarian" planning in Russia, Germany, and Italy. European, statist planners intervened in the economy to stimulate production. The appropriate democratic form in America would be to stimulate consumption to preserve "competition," which is "indispensable." Noting the criticisms of the business community, Ruml left open the choice available in a more prosperous time, implying that government spending would become superfluous and private enterprise maintained. Not accepting permanent deficits, Ruml left open the more moderate form of spending policy openly espoused at the same time by Dennison. Several months earlier, he had suggested to Henderson that part of the federal income tax be canceled as another way of spending to promote full employment, production, and consumption.[25] The idea went nowhere in 1938, but in 1942 it resurfaced as the famous pay-as-you-go income tax plan associated with Ruml that became the federal withholding tax.[26] But 1938 was not 1942. Ruml had quietly influenced Hopkins, Henderson, and Williams, who in turn convinced Roosevelt to ask Congress for over $3 billion to stimulate income growth, jobs, and unemployment relief.

In his address to Congress on April 14, 1938, Roosevelt cited almost verbatim whole sections from Ruml's April 1 memorandum. He called for legislation appropriating over $3 billion for relief and creation of jobs to expand purchasing power. Significantly, Roosevelt took up where Ruml left off to call for the eventual creation of a $100 billion national income in the next decade, including the provision that "private funds be put to work and all of us recognize that such funds are entitled to a fair profit."[27] That same evening, Roosevelt went on national radio to explain the request in one of his famous fireside chats. In that talk, the president emphasized dangerous world trends and tied fear of world war to the need for promoting an expanding economy based on the spenders' moderate version of compensatory spending policy. Roosevelt explained that "all the energies of government and business must be directed to increasing the national income, to putting more people into private jobs, to giving security and a feeling of security to all people in all walks of life."[28] We know now that this policy did not bring the country out of depression—only spending for World War II did that. Nevertheless, the idea of a full employment economy that would stabilize the economy by increasing mass purchasing power, promote peace among conflicting groups, and build a high consumption economy had been introduced into the national policy debate. In taking up their role as social science advisers to the president, the planners injected their expertise and that of staffers on the NRC into the most important economic policy debate of the late 1930s. By implementing their modern liberal ideology through the planning process, they were engaged in what they viewed as a democratic, American process qualitatively different from the totalitarian planning of the Soviet Union, Nazi Germany, fascist Italy, and a militarized Japan. U.S. economic conditions called for a distinctly American national response based upon a healthy mistrust of state power, a desire for business–government cooperation, the use of social science expertise, and inclusion of the ordinary citizen as consumer, not just producer. In their eyes, the ideology of modern American liberalism constituted a measured response by the federal government that would be counterbalanced by private-sector investment over the length of the business cycle. This was not full-fledged Keynesianism, but it went beyond both laissez-faire economics and Hooverian voluntarism. After 1941 members of the planning board took up this program and made it the cornerstone of their postwar plan for America. In the nationalist fervor of the wartime home front, this made perfect sense to FDR's planners, but not all members of Congress understood or agreed.

The day after Roosevelt's fireside chat, Frederic Delano wrote his nephew to say, "I was greatly impressed with your speech." Quickly adopting the new policy as that of the National Resources Committee, Delano moved to broaden its impact within governmental circles.[29] On April 26, 1938, he conferred with defeated Secretary of the Treasury Henry Morgenthau, Jr., to suggest formation of a Fiscal and Monetary Advisory Board consisting of Morgenthau, Federal Reserve Board Chairman Eccles, Director of the Budget Daniel Bell, and a representative of the NRC. Acting as mediator, Delano used the idea that he had received from Ruml to create bridges between the Eccles and Morgenthau factions. After a cool reception from Morgenthau, Delano took the proposal to Roosevelt on June 6. Dennison and Delano both noted that the idea could prove a convenient way to mend fences with the business community as well as to promote continuous discussion of new economic ideas within the administration.[30] Over the next year and a half, the board met at the Treasury Building to discuss fiscal and monetary matters. Eventually the fiscal and monetary board was lost in the preparation for war, but the NRC took up the idea from 1939 through 1943.[31]

In the midst of the economic policy debate of 1937–38, the New Deal planners continued to broaden their view of national planning beyond physical- and natural resources planning to encompass socioeconomic planning. Included were the beginnings of fiscal-spending and tax policies later associated with Keynesian economists and, more significantly, a national strategy of full employment based on private-public cooperation, the creation of millions of new jobs, and mass consumption usually linked to the postwar abundant society of the 1950s. The work of the Industrial Policy Committee under the direction of Gardiner C. Means reflected this emphasis on socioeconomic planning.[32] This committee's work remained a controversial thorn in the side of congressional critics who did not understand the new economic policy. By 1939 the NRC accepted the necessity of a moderate spending policy. Dennison's contact with Alvin Hansen, later called the American Keynes, contributed to this move, but the planners' embrace of the new economics remained halting and ambivalent. They hired Hansen in 1938 as a part-time consultant for individual projects, but FDR's planners never accepted his ideas on permanent spending policy as fully their own. In the course of the post-defense and postwar planning effort, Hansen's work came into wider public view and entangled the planners in a vicious fight for survival. The emphasis on economic balance, spending to complement private enterprise while maintaining competition, and the dependence on high consumption with the possible alternative policy of tax cutting rather than direct deficit spending all indicated some reserve on the part of the New Deal planners.[33] Their growing dependence on Roosevelt's presidential authority, their inability to explain the ambivalent nature of the economic program, and their reliance on Congress for funding raised the question of how national planning could be consolidated under the Third New Deal.

While his fellow New Deal planners joined the economic policy debate, Merriam took up the battle to reorganize executive-branch agencies in order to modernize the presidency, bring about administrative rationality, and institutionalize the planning board as a permanent agency under the president. Executive reorganization had a long history, stretching back at least to the Taft administration. The Budget and Accounting Act of 1921 had established the idea of a national budget, but the act placed control in the comptroller general in the Department of the Treasury. The compromise bill of 1921, which created the position of budget director, left control in part to the Congress as well as the president. Reform advocates since 1921 had hoped to bring the office directly under the president in order to create a more centralized and accountable agency, a reorganization that Merriam championed in the 1930s.[34]

Merriam hoped to bring the planning board under the president alongside the Bureau of the Budget. In this way, the executive branch could build a staff structure to set policy and coordinate administration of the growing number of permanent and emergency agencies that made up the New Deal. The federal government could be run efficiently like a business, not like a totalitarian dictatorship. The method for promoting such a plan grew directly out of the earlier organizational nexus created in the 1920s. Merriam sought to create a more compact planning board directly responsible to the president while retaining an emphasis on advisory national planning with final decisions made by the president and the Congress.[35]

Seen within the narrow context of the President's Committee on Administrative Management (1936–39), the reorganization effort had no direct ties with the NRC. But the guiding light, Merriam, ensured that this investigatory committee kept the broader view. Shortly after the completion of *Recent Social Trends,* the Problems and Policy Committee of the Social Science Research Council had discussed ways to continue parts of that group's work. SSRC leaders asked a subcommittee consisting of Merriam, Ruml, and popular economist Stuart Chase to recommend how this could be done. That group called for establishing three temporary Commissions of Inquiry: on Public Service Personnel, American International Economic Relations, and Population Distribution.[36] Those involved hoped to enlist the financial support of the Spelman Fund of New York (then directed by Merriam, who had succeeded Ruml) and the Rockefeller Foundation. Eventually the Spelman Fund granted $57,500 for the study of personnel, while the Rockefeller Foundation appropriated $60,000 for the study of international economic relations.[37] In addition to bringing together Alvin Hansen and Beardsley Ruml, the latter committee work launched Hansen's career as a government adviser.

The Commission of Inquiry on Public Service Personnel proved especially important to Roosevelt's planners. Merriam wanted to bring the expertise and experience of the SSRC to governmental service. Part of the effort culminated in his moves to convince Ickes, Delano, and Executive Director Robert T. Crane of the SSRC to obtain Roosevelt's support for the studies. In November 1933 Roosevelt approved the studies on personnel and international economic relations.[38] Luther Gulick, head of the Institute for Public Administration at Columbia, successor agency to the Progressive Era New York Bureau of Municipal Research, with which Merriam had worked earlier, led the former committee as research director. Alvin Hansen served as the latter committee's research director, while Ruml's friend President Robert Hutchins of the University of Chicago served as its chairman. In addition to launching Hansen's government advisory career, the two projects set the precedent for the Committee on Administrative Management.[39]

In late 1933/early 1934, Roosevelt sought a replacement for the Republican appointee to the U.S. Civil Service Commission. In January 1934, after consultation with Ickes, he decided on Merriam, who declined the offer, citing his more important work for the National Planning Board. But he recommended his University of Chicago friend, colleague, and public administration scholar Leonard D. White, who accepted. At the same time, Merriam took the results of the SSRC's Commission of Inquiry on Public Service Personnel to the planning board in hopes that the work could be continued under governmental auspices. Executive Director Charles W. Eliot II underscored the importance of such a study to Delano: "If occasion arises I hope you can discuss with the President the relationship of the planning job to the budget job. The two together constitute the two major policy arms of the Executive."[40] By late 1935 Louis Brownlow, head of the new Public Administration Clearing House at the University of Chicago and head of the Public Administration Committee of the SSRC, had prepared a memorandum on the subject that Ickes presented to Roosevelt. On March 20, 1936, Roosevelt appointed Gulick, Merriam, and Brownlow to the President's Committee on Administrative Management, which became known as the Brownlow Committee.[41]

In its one-and-a-half-year study, the committee used the expertise of both private and government research agencies created in the previous twenty years, including the SSRC, the Brookings Institution, the Public Administration Clearing House, and the National Resources Committee. Roosevelt saw its work as an effort to bring order to the confusing mélange of permanent and emergency agencies of the New Deal. However, by the time executive reorganization bills were presented to Congress early in 1937, the political climate had changed. Matters were complicated by the simultaneous introduction of the Supreme Court reorganization bill. In the wake of Roosevelt's landslide reelection in November 1936, neither he nor New Dealers anticipated that administrative restructuring of the executive and judicial branches would meet with a firestorm of protest in Congress. FDR made matters worse politically by not bothering to tell his majority leaders or key members of the Democratic Party in Congress that the two bills would be introduced at the same time, and indeed almost no one knew about the judiciary bill until he announced it in public. Congressional conservatives proposed amendments to the executive reorganization bills presented in 1937, 1938, and 1939 that Roosevelt and his advisers opposed. As Merriam pointed out many times in public comments and testimony before Congress, only the addition of a renamed planning board, the National Resources Planning Board, was a totally new idea. By June 1939, when the reorganization bill finally passed, numerous compromises had been made, but the legislation did create a modernized presidency.[42]

The reorganization bill led to technical specifications for civil service reform, restructuring of the Executive Office, and allowing the president to select a maximum of six administrative assistants. Roosevelt's Reorganization Plan No. 1 incorporated the major changes, which transferred the Bureau of the Budget to the Executive Office, abolished the National Resources Committee, created a new three-member National Resources Planning Board within the Executive Office, established the Liaison Office for Personnel Management within the same office to coordinate administration of federal personnel, and created the Office of Government Reports, which was consolidated with the Office of War Information in 1942. The Executive Office became a managerial staff for the president, with control over budget, planning, and personnel. Line agencies in the various executive-branch offices were under the hierarchical supervision of the president's staff. Scholars disagree as to the long-range significance of the reorganization, but for the planners it involved major changes.[43]

The new National Resources Planning Board no longer had to contend directly with intra-Cabinet politics. Previously, Delano, Merriam, and Mitchell (replaced by Dennison and Ruml in 1935) had served as an advisory committee working with cabinet members on the board. Now they worked as independent members of the NRPB directly under the president. Reporting to the president, the planners no longer had to deal with the personal, administrative, and political jealousies of cabinet members; however, they also became more beholden to FDR for support, monies, power, and influence. Now, though, conflicts of jurisdiction between the Bureau of the Budget and the NRPB became a distinct possibility. Most important, the manner in which Roosevelt created the NRPB angered congressional critics. Until the 1935 Supreme Court decision invalidating the National Industrial Recovery Act of 1933, the board had existed under the legislative authority of Title II of that act. After 1936 Roosevelt had continued the planning agency by executive order and funded it through line appropriations under the public works and relief appropriations acts of 1936–38. From 1935 to 1939 efforts to create a permanent planning board came under increasing attack in Congress, where it was seen as an abuse of power by the executive branch. During the debate over the reorganization bill of 1939, the House of Representatives specifically excluded authorization for the planning board. In July 1939 Roosevelt had to turn once again to executive authority with Reorganization Plan No. 1 and Executive Order 8248 to create the new NRPB. Saved by the president, the board remained subject to Congress for its operating budget. Between 1939 and 1943 the NRPB underwent an annual reevaluation in congressional appropriation hearings for independent offices. In 1943 the rising executive-legislative tension came to a head with the New Deal planning board caught in the middle, and Congress abolished the board by killing its funding.[44]

In the summer of 1939 the newly restructured NRPB had a new institutional home in the Executive Office as a managerial arm of the president. New Deal planners had truly become FDR's planners. The agency developed studies that emphasized the value of moderate spending policy to raise national income, create full employment, encourage high production and consumption to preserve industrial capitalism, and stabilize the economy. Throughout the late 1930s Merriam in particular, through speeches and published works, addressed the need to preserve American society in the face of rising fascism, militarism, and totalitarian communism.[45] Both privately and publicly, he defended the planning board and modern liberalism as viable options for America to avoid being trapped in a Hobson's choice between fascism or communism. Highly critical of dictatorial power in other countries, he and the other planners saw Roosevelt, New Deal reform, a capitalist economy, the two-party system, and the American advisory national planning process as nationally and historically distinct from the statist regimes of Europe and Asia. Yet they were blind to the fact that Roosevelt, the boldest executor of presidential power to that point in American history, might one day abandon the planning board, come under attack for abusing executive-branch power, or face competing policy priorities in the midst of another national crisis such as war. Seeing themselves as rational, objective social scientists whose own interests coincided with those of the nation and the American people, they were unprepared to lobby Congress aggressively for continued political and financial support and to defend modern liberal ideology and New Deal planning's part in the policy-making process. This secular faith in rationality, science, process, and American politics would one day betray the planning board.

The creation of the NRPB paralleled the start of world war in Europe on September 1, 1939. Roosevelt's increasing preoccupation with foreign affairs and economic mobilization for war worked to the detriment of the planners. One small indication of things to come concerned the appointment of another member of the board, George F. Yantis, as called for under the 1939 reorganization. Since the fall of 1935, when Mitchell had resigned, Delano and Merriam were the only two official members of the planning board. Dennison and Ruml constituted an advisory committee of representatives from the business community that in practice took Mitchell's place. Yantis now officially took Mitchell's place. His appointment revealed Roosevelt's attitude about planning as an ad hoc, piecemeal operation subject to the political needs of the moment.

Educated as a lawyer in Washington state where he served clients in the lumber, pulp, oyster, and banking industries, Yantis had served on a number of temporary New Deal committees in Washington, including the Columbia River Basin Commission.[46] Elected as a Democratic repre-

sentative from Olympia in 1930, Yantis by 1933 sat as the speaker of the
house in his home state. Roosevelt relied on Yantis for support of the
New Deal in Washington State. In June 1937 Yantis had been appointed
as the chairman of the Pacific Northwest District of the National Resources Committee regional organization. From 1939 through 1942
Roosevelt put his political support behind other Democratic stalwarts in
Washington State for a number of positions, including the Washington governorship, although he passed over Yantis, who must have felt
slighted. Yantis's appointment to the NRPB probably served as a way to
push him out of Roosevelt's political path. Yantis was most interested
in regional power planning; his role on the NRPB remained minimal.
Roosevelt's willingness to use the planning board as a kind of holding
ground to avoid political embarrassment in Washington State while
maintaining support for the New Deal in the Northwest suggested that
his attitude toward the planners was shifting. He might not be willing to
expend much political capital to defend the planning board if circumstances got too rough. After 1939 Roosevelt gave minimal attention to
the potential difficulties faced by the planners. Ironically, as FDR's support for national planning began to waver, the planners not only retained
an enormous faith in their charismatic president but also found their organization increasingly dependent on both his authority and congressional monies. Little noticed at the time, New Deal planning became
weaker just as it became more entangled in executive-legislative politics
that boded ill as the planners addressed more controversial issues of wartime mobilization and postwar planning.

After September 1939 the NRPB turned its attention to what it called
"post-defense planning." Initially, the board focused its work on a
changed attitude toward planning of a public works shelf for a six-year
advance period. Seeing war on the horizon, the planners tried to adapt
their programs so as to help in the mobilization effort. They presented
Roosevelt with a variety of suggestions involving a productivity conference bringing together representatives from business, labor, and agriculture, but Roosevelt vetoed the idea as thinking too far ahead. After the
fall of France in June 1940, the board shifted to public education with a
series of radio programs entitled *This Is Our America,* discussing topics
such as energy, natural resources, science, transportation, health, and education.[47]

Between June and November 1940 Roosevelt began diverting some
emergency funds under his discretion for temporary defense work by the
planning agency. In November 1940 he gave a mandate to the NRPB for

wide-ranging studies to prevent a "post-emergency slump." The most immediately helpful work involved creation of the Industrial Plant Location Committee, which gathered information on physical site location, production, employment, and possible defense plant sites.[48] The other major undertaking was creation of the Roster of Specialized and Scientific Personnel, which centralized information on skilled people available for either government defense work or deferment from the Selective Service Act of 1940 for work in private industry. The major difficulty in all of this post-defense work lay in confusion over jurisdictional lines between existing and newly created agencies. Roosevelt never tried to organize a coherent hierarchy of war mobilization agencies. Similar to his earlier political tactics for domestic reform, he chose to let administrators fight it out among themselves.[49]

Roosevelt used the new Economic Stabilization Unit within the NRPB to obtain quarterly reports on economic trends. But whenever the planners tried to organize a public conference of interested groups as a way of following through on their ideology of pluralist liberalism, Roosevelt postponed any action.[50] In October 1941 Roosevelt called for a strict separation of domestic and international postwar planning. In that month the planners agreed in writing that Sumner Welles's State Department and Henry A. Wallace's Economic Defense Board would handle all international postwar planning efforts, while the NRPB would address domestic postwar planning.[51] In a March 1942 meeting Merriam, noting the shift away from direct war planning to more long-range planning for the postwar period, argued that the board must "fight with ideas" in order to complement the fighting now done with men and munitions.[52] From mid-1942 on, the planning board shifted its work to public education, paralleling efforts by corporations to advertise products no longer produced but that would be available after the war.[53]

From 1939 to 1943 the lion's share of NRPB funds from congressional appropriations and Roosevelt's war emergency funds went toward immediate wartime planning. The heated public debate that erupted in the spring of 1943 centered on the NRPB's domestic postwar planning efforts. By mid-1942 FDR's planners had taken up serious postwar planning, as reflected in the board's 1941 and 1942 reports.[54] New Deal planners hoped to use the wartime mobilization to spark further domestic reform, just as an earlier generation of Great War liberals had hoped to do in 1917–18.[55] But as had happened in the earlier wartime period, those hopes proved illusory.[56]

Planners at the NRPB mobilized social scientists from a variety of disciplines to develop postwar plans. In June 1940 the board reorganized for the last time, structuring itself into four functional administrative divisions. Reorganization Plan No. 1 had abolished both the National Resources Committee and the older, inactive Federal Employment Stabilization Board (FESB) of 1931. The NRPB took over the functions of both groups until Congress limited the board's authority to the duties of the FESB. Planners interpreted their mandate widely and reorganized into Divisions A, B, C and a Field Section. Division A took over the responsibility for economic trends research and reporting. Division B inherited planning for natural resources—land, water, energy, and transportation—and the new Industrial Location Section. Division C took over the advance planning of public works on national, state, and local levels. The Field Section administered the ten regional offices and coordinated state planning board activities built up since 1933. While the NRPB table of organization showed clear-cut division of responsibility, the board never had a large enough staff to maintain distinct areas of work.[57]

During the post-defense crisis of 1939–41, the board added new groups responsible for war and postwar planning. In February 1941 the NRPB hired Luther Gulick as post-emergency planning consultant. By June 1941, after consultation with both Roosevelt and his planners, Gulick decided on a twofold approach. The board would develop postwar plans internally, then report to the president.[58] To publicize these efforts, the NRPB began publication of a series of pamphlets dealing with postwar fiscal policy, expansion of Social Security benefits, and more wide-ranging proposals in public housing, health, education, and transportation. Between late summer 1941 and spring of 1943, the planning board distributed thousands of copies of these pamphlets to federal administrators, business leaders, labor organizations, and social welfare groups. Individual copies were sent to people who requested information on postwar planning activities. Planners kept their focus on organized groups, hoping to strike a responsive chord with the broader public.[59]

NRPB postwar planning emphasized the necessity of creating a full employment economy based on a balance of high production and mass consumption. Continuing the policy first enunciated in 1937–38, the planners argued that the key to a better postwar America lay in national economic policies that would promote a full employment economy, stimulate complementary—and compensatory—fiscal policies based on public- and private-sector investment, create harmony between organized groups, accord organized labor the rights to organize and bargain collectively, and provide a measure of economic security for all Americans.[60]

The symbolic core of the postwar planning strategy lay in what the NRPB called a Second Bill of Rights. Luther Gulick, head of the Post-War Agenda Section, summarized the ideas in a 1943 letter to Congressman Lyndon B. Johnson (D-Tex.): "In fact I am convinced that we in the United States of America will not act sensibly outside our borders in world affairs unless we have full employment here at home. If we don't plan for and achieve full employment in the United States, we will adopt all sorts of foolish and fallacious international policies and in the process help destroy the conditions of a peaceful world order. All of these things are complicated, interrelated, and hard to understand."[61] As early as August 1939 Delano had suggested to President Roosevelt the idea of expanding the Bill of Rights from the political to the social arena, to enumerate educational opportunity, health and medical care, decent shelter, the right to work, and economic security. In the summer of 1940 Delano expanded the proposal in a memo to Roosevelt. Following Roosevelt's Four Freedoms speech to Congress on January 6, 1941, the NRPB went to work refining its Second Bill of Rights under Gulick's direction.[62]

In a presentation on June 29, 1941, at Roosevelt's Hyde Park home, the planners proposed an "Economic Bill of Rights" to be presented by the president in a message before Congress. Roosevelt expressed approval of the idea and asked his planners to revise the draft for further consideration.[63] Though not widely distributed until Roosevelt's release of the NRPB's 1943 report to the Congress in March 1943, the ambitious proposal for a Second Bill of Rights represented the ideology of modern American liberalism in the guise of postwar planning. The planners' Economic Bill of Rights set out a broad vision of revived domestic reform that underlay much of the post-1945 liberal policy agenda:

1. The right to work, usefully and creatively through the productive years;
2. The right to fair play, adequate to command the necessities and amenities of life in exchange for work, ideas, thrift, and other socially valuable service;
3. The right to adequate food, clothing, shelter, and medical care;
4. The right to security, with freedom from fear of old age, want, dependency, sickness, unemployment, and accident;
5. The right to live in a system of free enterprise, free from compulsory labor, irresponsible private power, arbitrary public authority, and unregulated monopolies;
6. The right to come and go, to speak or be silent, free from the spyings of secret political police;

7. The right to equality before the law, with equal access to justice in fact;
8. The right to education, for work, for citizenship, and for personal growth and happiness; and
9. The right to rest, recreation, and adventure, the opportunity to enjoy life and take part in advancing civilization.[64]

Just as the Four Freedoms speech represented FDR's response to fascist ideology and aggression overseas, so the planners' document represented their view of domestic American liberal democracy at home. Its major points directly challenged the belief system of fascist and communist ideologies in a way that no previous planning document had quite captured. It was an expansive vision of a postwar America freed from the wreckage of the Great Depression, inspired by the possibilities of economic abundance, distrustful of centralized state power, and imbued with the American ideals of individualism. The document encompassed a set of assumptions about the meaning of life in modern America that symbolized a shift away from the economic concerns and social insecurity of the 1930s toward a strong, powerful, prosperous America that could emerge from the wreckage of World War II. The emphasis on the rights of individual Americans was based on an implicit presupposition that a full employment economy could bring the promise of decent wages, mass consumption, and the abundant society to fruition in postwar America. But the rhetoric necessary to present this new rights-based liberalism to the broader public represented a tremendous challenge to the older, nineteenth-century liberalism that permeated much of the politics, economy, society, and culture of 1940s America.[65] If Franklin Roosevelt proved unwilling to voice that new rhetoric, if the planners were perceived as advocating statist, command economic planning, and if conservative southern Democrats and Republicans who emerged victorious in the elections of 1942 made an issue of this new liberalism, the entire postwar planning vision could collapse.

At the end of May 1942 the NRPB began work on its postwar plan for inclusion in its 1943 report, which would be submitted to Roosevelt, who would in turn release it to Congress. The planners consulted with Keynesian economists in various federal departments to arrive at a mixed program of governmental timed spending to promote consumption and production at high levels of employment during recession, alongside more progressive income taxes during prosperity to control inflation, balance the budget, and provide revenue for Social Security programs. The approach finally chosen for the 1943 report included consideration of a twofold program of Social Security reform based on intensive review of relief programs during the 1930s and postwar planning for a full employment economy. Though initially seen as two separate projects, these two prongs merged in the final 1943 NRPB report.[66]

In the fall of 1939 the newly renamed NRPB had decided, with Roosevelt's approval, to conduct a wide-ranging study of New Deal work relief and relief programs under the direction of William Haber, who had been the Michigan Federal Emergency Relief administrator.[67] Haber called in Dr. Eveline Burns for advice. In 1926 Burns had received a doctorate in economics from the London School of Economics for her work on the British work relief system. That same year Burns came to the United States on an SSRC fellowship, paid for with Laura Spelman Rockefeller Memorial monies. She and her economist husband, Arthur R. Burns, accepted positions in the Economics Department at Columbia University. Eveline Burns became active in the National Consumers League and Abraham Epstein's reform group, the American Association for Old Age Security. By 1934 she had become well known enough to serve on the Committee on Economic Security, which prepared drafts of the social security bill of 1935. To implement the Social Security Act provisions, Burns led the effort to train administrators for the Social Security Board and published the first working manual on social security, *Toward Social Security* (1936). By 1939 she had worked with SSRC subcommittees and established her reputation as a leading expert in the field.[68]

Between December 1939 and September 1941 Burns served as research director of the NRPB's temporary Committee on Long-Range Work and Relief Policies. After conducting a sweeping review of social welfare programs in the 1930s, the committee recommended changes in the Social Security system that would result in a significant broadening in the number of people covered and benefits allowed. The board submitted advance copies of the committee's report, *Security, Work, and Relief Policies,* to Roosevelt on December 5, 1941, for transmittal to Congress along with a draft message for submission to Congress on December 15, 1941. Surrounding the bombing of Pearl Harbor and preparation for wartime mobilization, the report got lost in the confusion.[69] Despite repeated requests from the NRPB, it did not surface until March 1943, when it came before Congress along with the 1943 annual report. The delay brought confusion on a number of issues. The Beveridge White Paper ("the Beveridge Report') on social insurance came out in Great Britain before the American report on which it was partially modeled.[70] Presentation of the social welfare report with the NRPB's 1943 annual report led politicians in Congress to think that the NRPB was presenting a "socialistic," "cradle-to-grave" program of social reform and state command economic planning. Roosevelt's delay in submitting the report to Congress tainted the proposed changes in Social Security, implying that these recommendations would be bundled with postwar economic planning and damaging the NRPB's presentation of its case for continued funding in congressional appropriations hearings that climaxed just as the reports were submitted.

The second half of the NRPB program included discussion of fiscal policies associated with Keynesian economist Alvin Hansen of Harvard University. As part of Gulick's pamphlet series on postwar planning, Hansen had written a number of the more widely known works. In these pamphlets Hansen not only recommended a compensatory fiscal-spending policy in the immediate postwar years but also advocated a revision of the tax structure to include more progressive income taxes and elimination of more regressive sales taxes. The NRPB conducted extensive talks with Hansen and other Keynesian economists during the preparation of the 1943 report, but its public reports always consciously shied away from officially sanctioning Hansen's specific policy proposals, which involved a more permanent, statist-oriented concept of spending policy than FDR's planners were prepared to advocate. Once the report was released to Congress and the public, this subtle distinction made little difference, as the NRPB became entangled in a political fight for its very survival.[71]

The 1943 *National Resources Development Report* submitted to Roosevelt in late 1942 included three parts. Part 1 encompassed the more wide-ranging postwar program. Part 2 dealt with wartime planning for natural resources use, economic trends reporting, preparation of the six-year advance public works shelf, and regional, state, and local planning. Part 3 included the massive review of social welfare programs, *Security, Work, and Relief Policies,* written wholly by Dr. Eveline Burns, along with recommendations for reform of the Social Security system through widening of coverage, extension of benefits, and administrative handling of relief programs. The most controversial part of the plan centered on Part 1 with its postwar plan for adoption of compensatory fiscal-spending policy along with more liberal monetary and tax policies.[72]

Part 1 included plans for gradual demobilization of men and machines after the war, with provisions for education, insurance, and a possible mustering-out pay for military veterans along with dismissal wages and extended unemployment insurance for civilian war workers—hints of the very successful and popular GI Bills of Rights enacted in 1944. Government plants would be gradually turned over to private companies, while the lifting of economic controls on prices and wages would occur gradually with the aim of restoring the prewar emphasis on private enterprise. The heart of the report consciously focused on the notion of continuous economic growth through business-government cooperation and compensatory use of spending policy over the course of the business cycle to create a postwar economy based on growth, full employment, and mass consumption. In light of the experience of Delano, Dennison, and Ruml in 1937 and 1938, the recommendations showed a cautious consideration mixed with admitted uncertainty about Keynesian economic policy. In some respects, the ideas were a resurrection of New Era capitalism from the 1920s filtered through the experience of the Depression and the New Deal. While there was no explicit theoretical underpinning in the technical work of economists such as Alvin Hansen and Lauchlin Currie, a moderate form of public-sector investment to temporarily take the place of lagging private investment was more reminiscent of the ideas of the planners rather than the emerging generation of Keynesian professional economists. Qualifications about monetary and tax policy—important now that Beardsley Ruml was in the midst of advocating a massive tax cut through his pay-as-you-go income tax plan, which prefigured a postwar conservative variant of Keynesianism—suggested that, in 1943, FDR's planners remained ambivalent about accepting Keynesianism wholesale. But critics paid little attention to the planners' qualifications.[73]

Release of the NRPB's 1943 postwar planning report marked the zenith of both New Deal planning and modern American liberalism. Since 1937, FDR's planners had successfully expanded their policy-advising role, while entering the rough-and-tumble world of politics. Their ongoing efforts further articulated the ideology of modern liberalism as an American national alternative to the Depression-era ideologies of fascism and communism, which they found abhorrent. Unlike Soviet and Nazi planners, they refused to give wide berth to command-style economic planning, preferring a moderate form of compensatory spending policy that would be counterbalanced by increased private investment over the length of the business cycle, while arguing for some expansion of a limited American welfare state to deal with the social consequences of economic change. Aware of the public's perception of fascist efficiency, they recognized the need to streamline and coordinate the various agencies that had been created or expanded by the New Deal. Ruml, Dennison, and Delano had led the successful fight to convince Roosevelt to resume government spending in response to the recession of 1937–38, while

Merriam had paved the path for limited executive-branch reorganization. But the euphoria after the election landslide of 1936 led both FDR and the planners to propose a Third New Deal, which never fully got off the ground because of shifting political alliances that put conservative southern Democrats in league with Republicans after the elections of 1938. Roosevelt's Supreme Court plan, the executive reorganization bills, the attempt to purge the Democratic Party of conservatives, and the effort to create a permanent planning board had either been defeated or severely compromised. FDR had been shown to be politically vulnerable. By extension, so were the New Deal planners. The outbreak of World War II gave them new life in regard to wartime mobilization and the possibility of preparing ambitious postwar plans. Wartime mobilization led to economic recovery, an increased need to promote business-government cooperation, and growing political conservatism in the Congress. Yet their increasing reliance on FDR's patronage and financial support left his planners in a precarious position, subject to growing tension between the president and the Congress. At the very moment of their seeming triumph, symbolized by the wide-ranging 1943 report that called for institutionalizing a modernized American liberalism that, they hoped, would lead to a prosperous, harmonious, and peaceful postwar America in the wake of the Great Depression and World War II, the planning board would be abolished. America's first and only experiment with government national planning was about to end.

Epilogue

THE ABOLITION AND LEGACY
OF NEW DEAL PLANNING

AMERICAN NATIONAL PLANNING came of age in the administration of President Franklin D. Roosevelt, the most important political leader in twentieth-century America. As inspirational head of the New Deal response to the crisis of the Great Depression of 1929–41, FDR led the most significant reform movement in modern America. As the national leader of the Democratic Party, he made possible the resurgence of his party, building a majority coalition that dominated national politics until at least 1968. As the president responsible for dealing with the wreckage of the Great Depression, FDR made possible the only experiment in public-sector national planning in U.S. history. Between 1933 and 1943 the National Planning Board, the National Resources Board, the National Resources Committee, and the National Resources Planning Board retained a remarkable continuity of direction from above. Bringing ideas, institutional support, and money from mainstream areas of American life, FDR's planners instituted a brief, stormy life for an advisory process of American national planning that moved beyond the voluntarism of nineteenth-century America but was never intended to create a European statist form of national planning. In a sense, New Deal planning proved to be an example of American exceptionalism compared with its counterparts elsewhere in fascist Italy, the Soviet Union, Nazi Germany, and a militarized Japan. Exceptionalism, however, should not be taken in an absolute sense, but rather needs clarification in a historical perspective too often missed in the theoretical abstractions of social science models. To fully understand New Deal planning requires the longer-term view made possible through the lens of historical focus, a

224

recognition of who the planners were, how they came to New Deal planning, and a close attention to the primary source records.

The origins of New Deal planning went back to the early twentieth century. Planning grew up as part of the creation of the modern organizational society that late twentieth-century Americans take for granted. Between 1900 and 1933 the groundwork was laid through the building of an organizational nexus for planning on a national scale. In the 1930s five men—all lifelong, independent Republicans—became FDR's planners, but they did not work alone. Before FDR's election in 1932 they had the support of complex hierarchical bureaucratic institutions first pioneered by the railroads and taken up soon enough by other industries. Eventually that model permeated associational life in modern America and made possible enormous advances in national economic growth while creating a variegated mix of political, social, and cultural institutions. Oftentimes, these institutions crossed between the lines that had separated private and public sectors for most of the nineteenth century, eventually leading to creation of what can be called the mixed, or cross-sectoral, institutions of twentieth-century America, which were private, public, and private/public. But the emergence of these modern American institutions entailed enormous costs as well, which were not immediately obvious to many.

Acceptance of the corporate model as *the* American way of life pushed aside older forms of voluntary cooperation. Farmer cooperatives first developed by the regional and national Farmers' Alliances in the late nineteenth century fell victim to the faith in continued progress based on an ideology stemming from the experiences of the managerial class. The older American sense of a tightly knit community of like-minded people broke down in the face of the successful corporate model. New sections of the upper class extended the corporate model beyond the confines of the business community into other areas of economic, social, political, and cultural life. As members of this new upper class, FDR's New Deal planners modified the corporate model to reinvigorate the tradition of voluntary action through corporatist associational activity. Moving beyond what they saw as the outmoded system of free-floating atoms miraculously interacting in a society based on competition and self-interested individuals, they helped to create the conditions for a distinctly American form of national planning in the course of their involvement in Progressive reform, mobilization for the Great War in 1917–18, and the efforts centered on Secretary of Commerce Herbert Hoover to build the associative state in New Era America. Like Hoover, they thought the experience gained from the Unemployment Conference of 1921 in response to the depression of 1920–21 would suffice to deal with the depression that began in 1929. But between 1929 and 1933 as the latest downturn in the business cycle became the Great Depression, with its attendant socioeconomic wreckage, the planners, unlike Hoover, proved willing to move forward into the New Deal. New possibilities for experimentation emerged from the changing conditions of Depression-era America: the collapsed economy, charismatic leadership by President Roosevelt with the support of Democratic majorities in Congress after 1932, and the rapid creation of new agencies in the early New Deal of 1933–34. Between 1934 and 1937 FDR's planners broadened their vision and sought to expand the promise of New Deal planning beyond the industrial, agricultural, and regional planning experiments of the National Recovery Administration, the Agricultural Adjustment Administration, the Tennessee Valley Authority, and the stillborn attempt to create other regional planning agencies on the model of the TVA. Caught in the crucible of recession, war, and postwar demobilization between 1937 and 1943, the planners played key roles in bringing forth what some scholars have begun to call the Third New Deal.[1] FDR's planners emphasized the significance of formulating workable economic policies in response to the recession of 1937, a streamlined executive branch through executive reorganization legislation, and the possibilities of postwar planning in the midst of the war against the overweening power of fascist states. Yet by the middle of World War II, New Deal planning fell victim to the changed conditions of the world's most powerful nation caught up in massive military and diplomatic efforts to defeat Germany, Italy, and Japan while engaging in a fragile Grand Alliance with the once powerful Great Britain and the emerging power of the Soviet Union. Internal differences among the planners, external constraints, limited resources, lagging support from FDR, fierce congressional opposition, growing tension between the executive and legislative branches of the federal government, a revived insistence on private-sector voluntarism, and the continued hold of a long-running tradition of antistatism led to what historian Alan Brinkley has termed the end of reform.[2]

The release of two extensive reports on postwar planning in 1943 along with the new economic and political environment of wartime combined to lead Congress to abolish the board. The hardening of congressional opposition to planning, Roosevelt's turn from Dr. New Deal to Dr. Win-the-War, and economic and military mobilization for World War II limited the planners in developing postwar plans for demobilization, a full employment economy, and expanded social welfare policies. Well-intentioned planners interested in building on the interwar organizational nexus of planning, voluntary cooperation among major interest groups, social science research, and social management came into increasing conflict with jealous executive-branch bureaucrats and politicians in Congress, which ended in abolition of the National Resources Planning Board. But the legacy of the NRPB carried over into the postwar world in the guise of the Council of Economic Advisers and a revived interest in postwar planning based on private, voluntary planning amid the changed conditions of postwar prosperity that made America the world's leading power. After abolition of the planning board in 1943, private-sector and cross-sectoral organizations took up planning in earnest that often drew on the examples set by FDR's planners, while returning to a more voluntarist form of planning and lesser state power in the post-1945 mixed economy, symbolized by the Employment Act of 1946.

FDR's planners now faced a number of constraints that limited their efforts at postwar planning. Events climaxed in the spring of 1943 with the nearly simultaneous release of the three-part report, congressional appropriations hearings, and blistering criticism of the NRPB in the midst of rising legislative-executive tension in the wake of the 1942 elections and the perception of executive-branch abuses of authority in the wartime mobilization. The planners continued to entertain an enormous amount of faith, admiration, and respect for President Roosevelt. Since the creation of the National Planning Board in July 1933, they had relied on him for guidance in the selection of their work, cooperation with other federal agencies, legal authority, and finances. Since 1939 Roosevelt had grown increasingly restive about expending political capital in their defense. The New Deal planners' conception of an advisory national planning evolving over time not only fit Roosevelt's shifting political inclinations but also left them open to congressional attack as agents of presidential ambition. After the 1939 reorganization placed the NRPB inside the Executive Office, Roosevelt went to the planning board when he wanted something specific done. His shift from Dr. New Deal to Dr. Win-the-War led to his slighting of the board and its domestic concerns amid the wartime emergency over the dire military and uncertain diplomatic conditions of a world war. By the spring of 1943 political circumstances had changed so dramatically since 1939 that Roosevelt gave only lackluster support to his own planning body.[3]

To educate the broader public about its postwar planning efforts, the

NRPB relied on the technique of publicity through liberal journals, press releases, and its pamphlet program.[4] Yet while its legal authority came from the president, its funding came from Congress. Created by executive order in August 1939, the NRPB received its operating monies from congressional appropriations for independent offices. Since 1935 the Congress had grown increasingly critical of national planning under FDR. Conservatives in Congress proved unwilling to recognize the emergence of cross-sectoral institutions which belied nineteenth-century rhetoric that sharply distinguished between activities in the "private" and the "public" sectors. Southern Democrats, old Progressives, and Republicans increasingly resisted what they considered the growth of "dictatorial" executive-branch power by Roosevelt and liberal reformers during both the New Deal and World War II. They gained in strength and influence in the wake of FDR's defeats on reorganization of the Supreme Court, the executive branch, and the Democratic Party and their own victories in the 1938 and 1942 congressional elections.[5] Conservative opposition to the 1943 postwar planning report and understandable concern with the military situation abroad brought a reaction against planning in the 1943 appropriations hearings.

About to be caught between the president and the Congress, the planners knew that things might go wrong in 1943. In the 1942 appropriations hearing, the House of Representatives had passed the Clark Amendment, specifically limiting board functions to those of the Federal Employment Stabilization Board (1931), which had been absorbed by the NRPB in the 1939 reorganization. President Roosevelt had granted the organization emergency war funds under his control for war planning. Delano and Merriam had premonitions that NRPB funds would be cut by a hostile Congress in the 1943 appropriations hearings. Yet they retained their ongoing faith that Roosevelt would help. Roosevelt, acting in political character, felt that his planners could take care of themselves. Between January and June 1943 the NRPB came to an inglorious end in a battle that closely resembled a comedy of errors. With the exception of wars and foreign policy making, scholars remain loath to accept the idea that historical actors do blunder and engage in irrational or seemingly contradictory behavior. Abolition of the planning board, however, involved blundering on the part of the planners, Franklin D. Roosevelt, Democratic floor leaders, and congressional critics from both parties.[6]

On January 11, 1943, board members appeared before the House Subcommittee on Independent Offices Appropriations to argue that the NRPB's war work and postwar planning required a small increase in funds from the previous year to $1.4 million. Representative Everett M. Dirksen (R-Ill.) criticized the board for shifting to the political left and hinted that Congress would be better off creating its own committee on postwar planning free from executive-branch control. One conservative southern Democrat joined the three Republicans on the subcommittee in a 4–3 vote to recommend that the NRPB be granted no funds for fiscal year 1944. Three days before the full House committee vote on February 9, Delano asked for an appointment with the president. Presidential aid Marvin McIntyre noted briefly on the request, "President said 'no sorry.'" The House committee reported that it recommended no monies for the NRPB.[7]

One day later, on February 10, Delano made a huge blunder in suggesting to the president that he release the 1943 report and *Security, Work, and Relief Policies* "in connection with the problem of our 1944 appropriations." Roosevelt at least waited until completion of debate in the House, but he did release the reports before the Senate subcommittee hearings. The House debate proved both vituperative and farcical. On February 8 Representative Frederick C. Smith (R-Ohio) stood in the House chambers to denounce the House subcommittee's granting of funds to the NRPB that it had refused to grant. Smith continued in an ideological tirade against the New Deal and Roosevelt, arguing that the 1942 elections constituted a "mandate" against growing governmental bureaucracy. Smith damned the NRPB on several counts: it had exceeded its legislative authority, it served as "the instrument" of the president, it had fully accepted the fiscal-spending policies of Alvin Hansen, and it had taken over congressional functions. In less polite language, Smith damned the board as fronting "a gigantic move to plan the new social order" in "this communistic program" aimed at invading "the domain of the sex life of our young people," while ultimately aiming at "the complete destruction of all free enterprise." The full House debate of May 15–17, 1943, did not improve on Smith's performance. When Representative Warren G. Magnuson (D-Wash.) rose to propose an amendment calling for $415,000 for the board, Representative Dirksen challenged the notion on a point of order, which the chairman upheld.[8]

The planners were concerned but kept their faith in Roosevelt. In the only major action on his part, Roosevelt wrote a polite letter of support drafted by NRPB director Charles W. Eliot II to Representative Clarence Cannon (D-Miss.) and Senator Carter Glass (D-Va.), chairmen of the House and Senate Committees on Appropriations.[9] On March 10, in another blundering move, Roosevelt submitted the two major postwar planning reports to the Congress. Under the prodding of Eliot, NRPB staff prepared extensive materials for the Senate subcommittee hearings, including analyses of how members might vote. The hearings on April 9 proceeded smoothly enough, but the subcommittee vote told another story. The Senate subcommittee granted the board $534,422, less than half its original request. Subcommittee members voted 5–5 twice before Gerald P. Nye (R–N.D.) switched his vote to yes. But a third-round 6–4 vote hid the confusion of party lines in both the subcommittees and the full Senate committee. The full committee deadlocked in a 10–10 vote and finally settled on a compromise recommendation of $200,000 to the full Senate.[10]

Debate in the Senate took even more twisted turns than in the House. In deference to an absent Robert A. Taft (R–Ohio), the chief opponent of the NRPB in the Senate, the debate was delayed twice. On May 27 Kenneth McKellar (D–Tenn.), acting chairman of the full Senate Committee on Appropriations, rose to offer an amendment asking for the $534,422 figure agreed on in subcommittee. Taft repeated the charges of his fellow Ohioan, Representative Smith, in noting that the NRPB "appears to be partly socialistic and partly the product of a dangerous financial imagination." Taft repeated the more substantive conservative charges aired in the House but ended in denouncing this "Utopia." After more than five hours of debate centered on McKellar's amendment, Senate conservatives demolished McKellar's presentation with continued interruptions and baseless charges. The Senate rejected the amendment by a vote of 43 nays, 31 ayes, and 22 not voting. The vote on the compromise $200,000 figure passed quickly 43–31.[11]

On June 14 House conferees refused to agree to the Senate's proposed appropriation for the board. Another damaging compromise was settled on—the NRPB would receive $50,000 to pay employees' back salaries, with the proviso that the board's functions would not be transferred to another agency, the NRPB would receive no monies from any other source, and its records would be deposited in the National Archives.[12] With such limited funds and stringent provisions, the NRPB could not hope to carry on even a small part of its work. Congress intended to end the planning agency permanently and to bury its history where few, if any, would ever find it.

Yet a number of questions remain for the historian. Did congressional conservative Democrats and Republicans mean their charges to be taken seriously? Was the NRPB's postwar planning program really the issue? Did these politicians oppose national planning on strict ideological grounds? Why had Roosevelt blundered so badly at the political game he usually played so well? What did the planners think of in the midst of this battle for survival? Most important, why really was the NRPB abolished?

During both the House and Senate debates, conservatives indicted the NRPB on a wide range of counts.[13] On the immediate, practical level, the charge of duplicating extant agencies' work missed the mark. The NRPB did draw on work done by various federal agencies, state and local planning boards, research institutes, and business groups. But as the supposed managerial arm of the presidency, it tried—unsuccessfully—to "coordinate" all this information. The charges of bureaucratic usurpation of authority had little meaning. Practically every major organized group—business, labor, agriculture—was guilty of the same thing. The most bruited-about charge—that the planning board represented socialism, communism, and fascism, often mentioned in the same political breath—reflected an increasingly common ploy used by both major parties in hope of electoral gain. Still the omnipresence of such ideological resistance suggests the powerful fear of fascism, communism, and any form of "collectivism" on the part of these representatives. Perceiving both the planning board and its postwar plans as representative of just these kinds of activity, political opponents successfully raised the specter of foreign-based ideas in the midst of wartime nationalism in such a way as to damn American national planning as a violation of a long-running tradition of fear of centralized power, distrust of the national state, and demonization of America's wartime enemies.

But in the congressional debate of 1943 even more serious charges were raised. The major ones centered on the acceptance of permanent fiscal-spending policy by the federal government and on executive-branch abuse of authority. Board members Delano, Merriam, Dennison, and Ruml all denied the allegation of being dangerous "spenders."[14] Their past involvement in national planning from its roots in the prewar years to the turning point in 1937–38 revealed the accuracy of their denials. At best, they hoped to use compensatory spending policy as a temporary tool in recession or depression to preserve economic balancing of production and consumption at high levels of employment and consequent growth in national income. The planners continually made clear that such policies would complement and sustain private investment. This was no statist assault on the redoubts of American capitalism.[15] There was no planners' conspiracy to replace American capitalism with fascist, communist, or socialist command economic planning. But conservative politicians in Congress refused to accept these honest disclaimers, arguing instead that such denials were subterfuges. Scholars who have since examined the ideological rhetoric of the debate unfortunately have accepted that political critique as accurate, in part by assuming that New Deal planning equated with statist, command-style planning combined with radical, costly expansion of the welfare state.

The crux of congressional hostility to national planning lay in the shift of executive-legislative power since 1933 attributed to the New Deal and war mobilization efforts of the Roosevelt administration. Even the most vociferous critics in Congress—Senator Robert A. Taft (R-Ohio), the leader of American conservatism, was the best example—accepted the necessity and value of postwar planning. They objected to executive-branch control of such planning. Even though the New Deal planners throughout the 1939–43 period publicly supported joint congressional-presidential postwar planning efforts, conservative politicians in Congress wanted exclusive control of those efforts.[16] Even before abolition of the planning board, the Senate had already established the Special Committee on Post-War Economic Planning headed by Walter L. George (D-Ga.), while the House soon created an equivalent committee under William M. Colmer (D-Miss.).[17]

Congressional critics were striking out at a false god—regimented, totalitarian state planning. No such beast existed in America. The planners' notion of advisory national planning did not contain the rigidities of fascist, Nazi, or Soviet command-style economic planning dominated by the state. Their idea of "democratic national planning" stemmed from an inordinate faith in the utility of expert knowledge based on social scientific research by participants in the organizational nexus built since the 1920s. The planners retained a disproportionate, at times almost irrational, faith in presidential power as exercised by Franklin D. Roosevelt. Liberal Democrats in the postwar period carried this faith in the presidency, little realizing the implicit dangers of what eventually came to be called the imperial presidency. In the wings, Roosevelt continued his game of playing administrators off against one another in the hope of compromising what at times could not be compromised. When necessary, FDR cut his political losses and left the people and institutions in trouble to fend for themselves. In the spring of 1943 he did just that with his planners on the NRPB.

The real issue in the planning debate of 1943 centered on the balance of power between Roosevelt as the president and the Congress. As such, the discussion of national planning that might have occurred never took place because of changed political circumstances and a series of complicated constraints. The confusions of the war, the ignorance of politicians, the political naïveté of the planners, the blundering strategy by Senator McKellar, and the indifference of Roosevelt precluded such a debate. The same problems resurfaced between 1944 and 1946 in the debate over the full employment bill.

Another element further complicated the debate over the continued existence of New Deal planning, one that the planners kept well under wraps. Internal disagreements abounded among and inside federal agencies. The NRPB unconsciously stepped on the toes of the powerful Rivers and Harbors Bloc favoring Army Corps of Engineers' planning. Federal agencies disliked the NRPB's "meddling" with their bureaucratic turf. Inside the planning board, field agents of the NRPB wanted more emphasis on their physical planning work, but the top-down approach of Frederic Delano and Charles Merriam remained dominant.[18] To worsen matters, NRPB director Charles Eliot sought to carve out his own niche in a reconstituted planning agency under his own direct control. At several key points in the 1943 appropriations battle, Eliot went to Roosevelt without authorization.[19] Incensed by the action, Merriam, Delano, and Yantis decided that Eliot would have to go, no matter what happened.[20] Eliot tried to convince various agencies to hire him and discussed his differences with Merriam with people in the field offices. These differences were over the means of national planning—whether the board should support long-range planning or more immediate piecemeal physical planning. Eliot stood on the side of narrowly defined physical planning. Personality clashes that had remained an undercurrent since the mid-1930s exacerbated the ideological cleavage within the planning board.

In some respects, then, the planning debate of 1943 remained a phony debate that completely missed the history of the planners and their institutional focus. Planning would continue, but without FDR's New Deal planners. By 1943 Henry Dennison's health had weakened from a December 7, 1941, heart attack. He had turned over the operation of the company to trusted managers.[21] Eighty-year-old Frederic Delano already had resigned as head of the National Capital Park and Planning Commission, took sick at the start of the appropriations process, and held little hope for continuance of the board. On June 1, 1943, Delano's wife, Matilda, died in the midst of the planning debate, adding personal grief to his political troubles.[22] By 1940 Charles Merriam had retired from the University of Chicago and taken up temporary teaching duties at Harvard. In a series of letters to his son Robert, a soldier serving in France,

Merriam indicated that he had planned to retire from the NRPB on September 1, 1943.[23] In setting August 31 as the last day of official operation for the NRPB, Congress beat him to the punch by one day. Merriam went on to write his magnum opus, *Systematic Politics* (1945), work for Truman's Loyalty Review Board, and write articles on the beginning of the atomic age. Eliot found a job with the Haynes Foundation in Los Angeles and later founded Resources for the Future, a research institute dedicated to work in physical planning and programming. The agency sponsored research and publication of Marion Clawson's *New Deal Planning* (1981), the second published history of the NRPB.[24]

In the same period, Ruml moved into the headlines for his only major public effort. In the summer of 1942 he had germinated the idea of a pay-as-you-go income tax that would forgive 1943 income taxes and institute a new payroll withholding tax to keep tax payments current rather than one year behind. His motivations were mixed. He publicized the plan after Treasury Department tax expert Randolph Paul nixed the idea and Roosevelt opposed the plan as a scheme to help the wealthy and hurt the lower classes. By the spring of 1943 Congress began work that resulted in partial acceptance of the plan. The idea involved implementing a tax cut to promote economic growth—the other half of the possible fiscal policy advocated by the NRPB in 1943. The idea did not receive official sanction until the triumph of the conservative variant of Keynesian economic policy with the 1964 tax cut. But the idea first arose in 1942 with Ruml, though he had not publicized the idea that clearly at the time. Rather, Ruml noted that the tax cut would be helpful to white-collar workers for such companies as Macy's Department Store, for which he was treasurer. From 1942 on, Ruml moved into work with the Committee for Economic Development and the National Planning Association, two of the many postwar planning groups that sprang up in 1943.[25]

By the summer of 1943 New Deal planning had reached its inglorious end. At a time when many Americans were becoming increasingly interested in domestic postwar planning, New Deal planning as a viable institution was killed by a vengeful Congress. But the planners' ideas lived on in the work of various executive-branch agencies, the House and Senate Committees on postwar planning, the work of research institutes, and the concerns of American business. In abolishing the NRPB, the conservative-dominated Congress fragmented national planning efforts by the executive branch, but Congress could not stem the planning tide. The postwar years saw the triumph of New Deal planning ideas in the form of a transformed modern American liberalism based on the policies of seeking a full employment economy and a mass consumption society. But that modern liberal consensus dominated postwar America in ways that neither New Deal Democrats nor Modern Republicans would have guessed during the wartime years. In the years after World War II Americans enjoyed a period of political consensus, economic growth, and social harmony similar to the New Deal planners' hopes for a prosperous economy and a mass consumption society of abundance for all. Yet those hopes did not work out in quite the way that any of the planners had intended.

Just as changing economic, political, and social conditions between 1900 and 1918 had led the planners into the national arenas of business, urban reform and city planning, the early years of rapidly emerging academic disciplines such as political science, economics, and psychology, so the years after 1945 saw new conditions that broke apart the New Deal planning nexus centered in the government-sponsored and government-financed boards of 1933–43. As the nation changed, so did the lives, ideas, and institutions of not only the planners but the people and institutions they had to deal with as supporters, rivals, and opponents. Between the accession to power of FDR and the Democratic Party through a new national political coalition and U.S. entry into World War II, national planning took a relatively more statist cast. In the years after 1943 it returned to a mixture of voluntarist and cross-sectoral organizations. Yet when viewed through the prism of private/public, voluntarist/statist, individualist/collectivist lenses, it seemed to have disappeared. The same thing had also happened in the 1920s after the dismantling of Great War mobilization agencies staffed by Wilsonians and Hooverians, who reappeared in many of the Hoover planning agencies of the 1920s. The next generation of American planners emerged from institutions built during the New Deal, the World War II mobilization, and the immediate postwar demobilization that reflected the complexity of cross-sectoral institutional life, just as had the Hooverians of the 1920s.

Between the 1890s and 1933 FDR's planners had helped to create the conditions for New Deal planning by building an organizational nexus for planning through a new kind of institutional voluntarism centered in the social and professional networks of the upper class. Comfortable family lives and social backgrounds combined with elite educations had placed each of them on a path toward planning that was neither inevitable nor self-conscious, but wartime mobilization work showed each the need for national perspective and ongoing institutional efforts at planning through the business firm, the city and region, the social sciences, a new generation of organized philanthropies, the new cross-sectoral institutions, and, when necessary, the federal government. Frederic Delano used his managerial experience in the railroad industry and city and regional planning in Chicago, Washington, and New York to arrive at a respected position by 1933 that made him a natural choice for his nephew Franklin Delano Roosevelt to select as chair of the New Deal planning agency. Charles Merriam's career in political science, Progressive reform, and social science management led to prominence not only at the University of Chicago and the American Political Science Association but also as founder and first leader of the Social Science Research Council. Economist Wesley Clair Mitchell, the nation's leading business-cycle expert, recognized during his war work that the country needed more, better, and better-organized economic knowledge, so he founded the National Bureau of Economic Research, which worked with various Hoover planning efforts throughout the New Era.

During the 1920s the five planners moved into a variety of associational circles that gradually brought their intellectual interests and organizational activities to a point of convergence, often through these new cross-sectoral institutions that could not be described by an older liberal ideological language. They learned to cross back and forth between private and public sectors, often working within settings that combined both. Leadership came from the Great Engineer, Herbert Hoover, in his role as secretary of commerce. Builders of Hoover's associative state in New Era America worked with committees growing out of the Unemployment Conference of 1921 that brought together the leadership of federal officials, the money of new philanthropies such as Ruml's LSRM, the social science expertise of SSRC leaders such as Merriam and Mitchell, and the practical business experience of such managers as Delano and Dennison. The President's Research Committee on Social Trends (1929–33) served both as culmination of the associational planning network of the New Era and as prologue to the New Deal planning emphasis on the predominant, but not exclusive, role of the positive state assisted by private-sector interest groups. Research director Wesley Clair Mitchell and vice chairman Charles Merriam wrote the introduction to the PRCST's final report, which called for a national planning agency. During the early New Deal, Mitchell and Merriam joined Delano as members of the nation's first governmental planning agency, the National Planning Board, while Dennison and Ruml gained experience as government advisers. When Mitchell resigned in late 1935, business leader Dennison and philanthropic manager cum policy adviser Beardsley Ruml took his place as representatives of the business community.

The Great Depression acted as catalyst to New Deal planning. The 1931–33 period saw the first major public debate over the possibilities of an American national planning directed by the state. Public commentators such as Gerard Swope, Charles A. Beard, George Soule, Stuart Chase, and Rexford Tugwell made dramatic—at times, sweeping— claims for national planning in public forums including most of the books and articles that later scholars used to write the earliest histories of New Deal planning. But the five individuals who actually planned, rather than talked about planning, were historically more significant than these social thinkers. As economic conditions worsened, unemployment rose and millions of Americans voted for FDR, the Democratic Party, and New Deal reform, thereby changing the political context in which planners might operate. Roosevelt's New Deal gave an entering wedge for governmental planning and coordination under Title II of the National Industrial Recovery Act of 1933. Serving on the new NPB, Delano, Merriam, and Mitchell prepared "A Plan for Planning," part 1 of the National Planning Board's 1934 *Final Report,* as a brief for a broad definition of national planning under the New Deal. Between 1934 and 1937 they gradually expanded the scope and content of planning to go beyond the narrow physical and natural resources planning that caught FDR's eye into the realm of socioeconomic planning and a permanent federal planning presence. Through a series of tenuous compromises, national planning began its fragile life tied to the executive branch and its charismatic leader Franklin Roosevelt but beholden to the jealousies of cabinet officials and, by the late 1930s, to the support of politicians in Congress.

As much of the New Deal wound down in the late 1930s, FDR's planners geared up to face the tests of recession, war, and postwar planning. Accepting the need for a temporary use of compensatory spending policy not related to the esoteric field of a still unknown Keynesian economics, the planners now had a vision with which to work. By the middle of 1939 these New Deal planners argued that the United States could create an economy of abundance through cooperation among interested groups mediated by the federal government. Full employment, economic growth, and the good society might be possible through investment in a high production, high consumption economy—a kind of New Era capitalism reborn in light of the lessons of worldwide depression. By the middle of wartime mobilization, they further developed this view through postwar planning work reflected in the wartime annual reports, especially the three-part 1943 report. The abundant society could be realized through government spending in times of recession or wartime to meet gaps left by the business and financial communities in the private sector. Only with such complementary state and voluntary action, argued Roosevelt's planners, could the American system of free enterprise survive after the war. In the process, they were developing a conception of modern liberalism that blurred the nineteenth-century distinctions between the private and the public sector—voluntarism had to change to meet the demands of modern organizational America, in which crosssectoral institutions played an increasingly important role. The 1942 and 1943 annual reports put forth a postwar vision of full employment, individual security made possible by an expanded and fully funded welfare state, and the guarantee of an Economic Bill of Rights for all citizens.

But a hostile Congress, changes in the planning board's structure and authority, and an ambivalent President Roosevelt led to the planning debate of 1943. Release of the postwar plan for economic growth alongside an extended and reformed Social Security system proved ill timed. In a fit of political jealousy masked in the ideological clothing of fear of rigid, statist planning seen in the ashes of the soon-to-be defeated fascist powers of Germany, Italy, and Japan and the perceived threat of a resurgent postwar communist threat from the Soviet Union, conservatives in Congress abolished the NRPB in the spring of 1943. Ideological fears, executive-legislative tensions, and the unwillingness of planners, the president, and Democratic leaders in Congress to engage in political infighting resulted in the tragicomic debate over postwar planning that abolished the planning agency, embarrassed FDR, and left two congressional postwar planning committees sitting in Congress wondering what to do next.

Ironically, interest in domestic postwar planning increased among the public at large just as Congress fired FDR's planners. Public-opinion polls revealed that organized groups as well as individual Americans feared postwar recession, loss of buying power through high unemployment, and the shift of an unbearable burden to private enterprise. From 1942 forward, postwar planning became a virtual national mania. In the letter releasing its 1943 report to Congress, the NRPB called for a national effort "to win the peace." Congress did not agree. Yet opinion polls revealed that, for most Americans, domestic concerns were much more important than foreign policy issues. Organized efforts at domestic postwar planning took off in 1943.[26]

These efforts were the immediate legacy of FDR's planners. While Congress declared a moratorium on executive-branch planning by mandating that all New Deal planning agency records be buried in the National Archives, planning for postwar America became more popular than ever. As a result of the abolition of the NRPB, planning broke apart into its constituent elements—governmental, professional, and interest group. The result was disconcerting in its variety and scope. Lacking coordination, planning became piecemeal and hard to trace.

In mid-1943 President Roosevelt created the Office of War Mobilization and Reconversion (OWMR) to plan for winding down of the war effort. Under director Harold Smith, the Bureau of the Budget took over some of the NRPB's work as it had tried to do since 1939. The reconversion debate proved an exercise in provincialism. OWMR director James F. Byrnes hired consultants Bernard Baruch, head of the War Industries Board in World War I, and John Hancock to report on reconversion. The two recommended a series of highly detailed measures for decontrol of the wartime machine. Pressures from employers, mothers, wives, lovers, and veterans quickly led President Harry S. Truman to accept rapid demobilization. In broader turns, the reconversion period saw a return to the voluntary efforts of an associative state, with predominant emphasis on the role of private-sector business and research groups. Interest-group power and political infighting led to the breakup of planning along organized group lines.[27]

During the debate over NRPB appropriations in the spring of 1943, even the most vocal opponents of the board supported postwar planning—but only under congressional direction. The George Committee in the Senate and the Colmer Committee in the House held hearings regarding postwar planning but never really accomplished much. Individual bills for postwar planning of public works programs by the states with federal matching grants did pass the Congress in 1944. The major effort came with the Servicemen's Readjustment Act of 1944, commonly known as the GI Bill of Rights, which grew out of the final efforts of the NRPB. In 1942 Delano asked Roosevelt to approve NRPB creation of the Conference on the Postwar Readjustment of Civilian and Military Personnel. Roosevelt privately approved the proposal, but he refused to sanction public discussion of the idea. NRPB consultant Leonard Outhwaite became research director of the committee. Outhwaite had worked with the War Industries Board in World War I, helped with postwar demobilization in 1918, and served with the Laura Spelman Rockefeller Memorial during the mid-1920s. In 1943 he got his chance. The NRPB committee recommended putting the Economic Bill of Rights into partial effect for one group of Americans—returning military veterans. Governmental assistance by way of mustering-out pay, extension of unemployment benefits, Veterans Administration loans for housing, and provision of educational benefits helped many veterans move into the society of abundance in the postwar years. After a complicated political process, the GI Bill of Rights led to governmental assistance in education, Veterans Administration (VA) home loans, and loan guarantees to start businesses and farms for millions of World War II veterans. Between 1945 and 1955 the federal government underwrote $33 billion in VA housing loans. By 1956 a total of $14.5 billion of taxpayer monies had been invested in educating and training 7.8 million of 15.6 million eligible veterans. Five and a half billion dollars of that educational assistance supported one of the most remarkable generations of college graduates in U.S. history, which included 450,000 engineers, 180,000 physicians, dentists, and nurses, 360,000 schoolteachers, 150,000 scientists, 243,000 accountants, 107,000 lawyers, and 36,000 clergy. The planners provided one of the clearest examples of the social utility of long-term human capital investment. Perhaps the most successful social welfare program in the nation's history, the GI Bill represented the best that government could offer millions of Americans in the postwar years. As one of the most popular pieces of federal legislation ever enacted, it helped to create the largest, best-educated, and highest-achieving middle-class generation in American history.[28]

Research institutes took up the challenge of postwar planning as well. Dennison and Filene's Twentieth Century Fund published long bibliographies on postwar planning materials as well as the six-volume series *When the War Ends* by popular economist Stuart Chase. The National Planning Association brought together representatives from business, labor, and agriculture to endorse the ideas of high employment, production, and consumption, which would increase the size of the American pie without redistributing power. Not surprisingly, Beardsley Ruml sat as a business representative on the National Planning Association.[29] A whole host of other research agencies conducted postwar planning, including the Brookings Institution. In the 1950s social science research moved into the circle of presidential advising, which carried through to the present. The names changed, the ideologies differed in degree, but the search for a national planning consensus dominated by the private sector united these efforts. As political, economic, and social conditions changed in the immediate postwar years, the balance between state and voluntary action swung back in favor of more emphasis on voluntarism, while a range of cross-sectoral planning organizations emerged.

The business community also proved eager to organize postwar planning efforts. The older and more conservative National Association of Manufacturers and the U.S. Chamber of Commerce followed the example of conservatives in Congress to argue that private enterprise should take up the task of building America. The more liberal and modern Committee for Economic Development (CED) began developing the tax-cut alternative to deficit spending first broached by Beardsley Ruml in 1938 and again during the wartime debate over his pay-as-you-go income tax plan in 1942. While adoption of Ruml's plan in the Current Tax Payment Act of 1943 raised the percentage of Americans who paid income tax from only 5 percent of the population in 1939 to 74.2 percent by 1945, it also allowed for current payments through the new payroll withholding tax and laid the foundation for what historian Robert Collins has called commercial Keynesianism—the conservative alternative to permanent deficit-spending policy—in the postwar years.[30] The CED began in the offices of the Department of Commerce, Herbert Hoover's institutional headquarters in creating the associative state of New Era America in the 1920s. Assistant Secretary of Commerce Wayne Taylor brought together businessmen such as Paul Hoffman and Beardsley Ruml in an effort to revive the dormant Business Advisory and Planning Council, on which Henry Dennison had served during the early New Deal. In the 1942–43 period, the CED actively cooperated with the NRPB. By the late 1940s, from his position as member of the Research Committee of the CED, Ruml extended the pay-as-you-go tax plan into a full-fledged alternative to permanent deficit spending. The tradition of associationalism from the 1920s lived on in the CED. The CED led the policy process in educating policy advisers in the Eisenhower, Kennedy, and Johnson administrations. This development culminated in the famous tax cut of 1964, which helped to fuel the economic growth of the 1960s.[31]

Franklin Delano Roosevelt's advisers had not forgotten the planners. In the fall of 1943 Roosevelt speechwriter Judge Samuel Rosenman solicited suggestions for campaign issues from Louis Brownlow, who brought out the NRPB's Economic Bill of Rights. Running for an unprecedented fourth term in 1944, Roosevelt incorporated the second Bill of Rights in his January 11, 1944, State of the Union address and in a Soldier's Field address in Chicago on October 28, 1944.[32] Historians still debate whether Roosevelt intended to reinstate the New Deal program of domestic reform after the war. If public-opinion polls done for the White House staff were any indication, had he lived, Roosevelt could have used postwar planning as an effective political message in the demobilization and reconversion period.[33]

Usually historians consider the abolition of the NRPB as one part of a more general dismantling of the New Deal in 1943. The Farm Security

Administration and other New Deal agencies came under attack in the same congressional session that abolished the NRPB.[34] Yet while abolition of the planning board resulted from ongoing executive-legislative branch tensions and Democratic/Republican partisan differences, the NRPB, unlike the other abolished New Deal agencies, carried on in spirit. The planners' postwar vision of a full employment economy and a society of abundance based on mass purchasing power did not disappear, as became evident in the debate over the employment bill in 1945 and 1946. Rather than reluctant planners' testifying to a critical Congress, this time more confident professionals, Keynesian economic experts, now testified to the need for a new managerial arm for the president, the Council of Economic Advisers, and a complementary one for the Congress, the Joint Economic Committee.[35] Passage of the bill marked partial victory for FDR's planners, although compromises in the final act meant the promise of an Economic Bill of Rights would have to wait for the long-term future.

Since the planning board no longer existed, postwar economic policy advice came from the professional economists who inherited Mitchell's concern for economic stabilization, but using the looser style of fiscal policy suggested by Alvin Hansen's work for the NRPB. The broader idea of socioeconomic planning raised between 1934 and 1943 now contracted to a more narrow, economic planning that made room for government, business, labor, agriculture, and other organized interest groups working in concert to achieve postwar abundance through industrial productivity, higher wages, and increases in mass purchasing power. This was not statist planning but the mixed economy of postwar America that institutionalized interest-group liberalism often through the work of cross-sectoral organizations that scholars are only beginning to study. Written into the final version of the Employment Act of 1946 was a provision that upheld part of the NRPB's 1943 postwar planning ideal: "The Congress hereby declares that it is the continuing policy and responsibility of the Federal Government to use all practicable means consistent with its needs and obligations and other essential considerations of national policy with the assistance and cooperation of industry, agriculture, labor, and State and local governments to coordinate and utilize all its plans, functions, and resources for the purpose of creating and maintaining, in a manner calculated to foster and promote free competitive enterprise and the general welfare, conditions under which there will be afforded useful employment, for those able, willing, and seeking to work, and to promote maximum employment, production, and purchasing power."[36] Scholars have debated the significance of the Employment Act of 1946, arguing that it revealed the strength of postwar American liberalism or the weakness of interest-group politicking. Yet consideration, debate, and voting on the act represented movement forward in the planners' bid to "win the peace." The Council of Economic Advisers carried on the economic planning efforts of FDR's planners in the postwar period, dependent on the wishes of each presidential administration. Use of social scientific expertise through a new corps of professional economists offering advice both to the president and the Congress meant that the idea of advisory national planning by experts working through the established political process had triumphed in the arena of economic policy making, but not in the broader arena of social policy.[37]

In the longer span of the years after World War II, policy makers—the new technocrats—overlooked the limitations of the New Deal planners' modern liberal ideology. Based in the ideology of upper-class professionals willing to expand use of the corporate model in the public service of the federal government, the planning ideal overlooked key areas of American life. The goal of full employment, they assumed, would take care of all the problems faced by working-class Americans, black Americans, and the growing number of women in the work force. Control from above looked beneficent to modern liberals interested in preserving the new American system with its mixed economy and weak welfare state. But what might happen to those individual citizens less privileged who were unable to join any influential organized group and make their views known in policy-making circles? Not until the 1960s did latter-day liberals in the Kennedy and Johnson administrations rediscover the social lag left in the modern American political economy. FDR's planners proved reluctant to participate actively in the political process of give-and-take between the president and the Congress, the Democratic majority and the Republican minority, policy-decision makers and interest groups, social science researchers and political activists, and the new cross-sectoral institutions of modern America and the older nineteenth-century political rhetoric of classical liberalism that so sharply distinguished between activity in the "private" and the "public" sectors. This modern liberalism marked a step forward from nineteenth-century liberalism, but it still left a range of economic and social issues untouched.

Coming from their social, educational, and institutional experiences of Progressive reform, wartime mobilization, Hoover's associative state, the recovery programs of the early New Deal, the policy proposals of the Third New Deal, and mobilization for World War II, FDR's planners had a constricted view of the democratic process that allowed room for organized, well-funded institutions and professional social scientific experts but left millions of ordinary citizens out of the policy-making process. The long-term trend of the continued concentration of economic power by the dominant business corporations backed by the rising tide of specialized experts in the social and natural sciences continued the inequality of access to wealth, power, influence, and control in America. FDR's planners had blind spots inherent in an elite vision of the affluent society. Recent evaluations of postwar U.S. history indicate that reliance on the ideology of pluralist consensus and the politics of economic growth set precedents for continued conflict under the surface of the homogenized society.[38]

From the 1960s forward, modern liberals tried to reinvigorate the planning ideal as seen in the debate over various full employment bills, the clarion call for a domestic security council finally heeded in the Nixon administration, and the passionate debate in the 1980s over the necessity of implementing industrial policy—a modernized version of industrial self-government akin to the NRA of Depression-era America.[39] To date, no American politician, party, profession, or interest group has reached beyond the limitations of the planning vision of the 1930s and the 1940s. The modern American liberalism that FDR's planners helped to create managed to forestall the possibility of revolution in hard times, but it also failed to deliver on what Herbert Croly in 1909 had called the promise of American life. The question haunting modern American national policy was whether Hamiltonian means could ever effect Jeffersonian ends.

In the broadest sense, the planners' techniques of managerial government through the advisory national planning process coordinated by social science experts in consultation with those in charge of the political process in cooperation with powerful private-sector groups more broadly undermined the American ideal of democratic governance and lost a sense of traditional American individualism.[40] Advocates of the modern organizational society, the planners, like other modern liberals, assumed that democracy and national policy making in twentieth-century America meant access to the political and economic system via organized group power. For interest groups in the business community, organized labor, the farm bloc, and the various professions, there was relative democracy. But there was no room for millions of unorganized individual Americans such as nonunion semiskilled and unskilled workers, black Americans moving north to escape racial segregation, the growing numbers of working women, the exploding population of American youth, the increasing numbers of white-collar employees, the forgotten poor whom social democrat Michael Harrington rediscovered in his *Other America* (1962), and other migrants to postwar American cities and suburbs. In 1944 James Patton, president of the National Farmers Union, the minority outpost of the vanishing family farmer, hauntingly addressed the limits of modern liberalism, including its variant represented by the New Deal planners:

> Special interests in America which demanded and obtained the abolition of the National Resources Planning Board are now making their own postwar plans for America. They are assembling a hand-picked coterie of special interests, so organized that people's organizations may be invited but submerged within the group, and so powerful that the people's government may be intimidated into accepting their dictation.
>
> If their effort succeeds, the democratic form of government in the United States will be set aside, and the foundations of our government will be undermined.
>
> . . . Our struggle to achieve the democratic way of life is doomed to fail—and the sacrifices of our boys' lives will be in vain—unless we arrive at action through constitutional, democratic processes, rather than action conceived and imposed by coalitions of powerful special interest groups.[41]

In the years after World War II, few thought about such issues, as many were caught up in the tide of prosperity made possible by a seemingly endlessly expanding economic pie. It took another generation of liberals in the 1960s to take up the challenge of enacting the Economic Bill of Rights in one of the most turbulent periods in U.S. history.

Although Congress sent the planning board's records to the National Archives to bury the planning ideal, FDR's planners and what they accomplished remained part of the emergence of modern America. They played a part in creating the new cross-sectoral institutions of the organized society that moved back and forth between private and public sectors in ways that scholars are only beginning to understand. They transformed the classical liberalism of the nineteenth century, based on the tenets of voluntarism, individualism, and community, replacing them with new values of associationalism, group organization, and the interest-group liberalism of the broker state that came under challenge after 1968. If for no other reason than the need to understand what we so casually take for granted, the history of New Deal planning deserves exhumation. In 1976 historian Otis L. Graham, Jr., author of the first comprehensive history of planning, *Toward a Planned Society: From Roosevelt to Nixon,* argued that American planning was best understood as a continuing process begun in the 1930s that eventually moved into the respectable arena of center-of-the-road politics. The history of FDR's planners shows that planning might have become respectable much earlier had politicians bothered to listen to the planners, and to have seen them as they saw themselves, as having emerged in the American context from the institutions of business, city and regional planning, the social sciences, organized philanthropy, and a new kind of governmental policy adviser. But American political culture had long feared centralized state power, while celebrating the innovative power of private, voluntary action. In times of national emergency or crisis, such as a depression or a war, piecemeal planning as found in the mobilization agencies of the two world wars and the New Deal agencies of the Great Depression found temporary acquiescence in relative increases in state power through the federal government. But political and economic circumstances changed over time. With the return of economic stability and prosperity and a shift in political-party power, political leaders, reflecting changes in public opinion, proved more comfortable returning to voluntarism and the less publicly known avenues found in the cross-sectoral institutions of modern America. During such times, Americans distrusted and feared the statist model, which in their eyes entailed a coercive use of public power often equated with the history and traditions of national planning in other countries. The historic American tradition of antistatism, the contemporary fear of fascism, and the emergence of postwar anticommunism in the early Cold War years forestalled the kind of historical understanding that there was an American tradition of national planning that had been created by the New Deal planners between the 1890s and 1943. Abolition of the NRPB in 1943, including the congressional mandate to send its records to dusty archival bins, allowed that tradition to be lost to the broader public. Recent public debates about balancing the federal budget over the course of the business cycle, the planning of public works to rebuild a rapidly aging infrastructure, and a renewed search for ways to spark productivity growth, increase mass purchasing power, and make the abundant society available to the mass of ordinary Americans suggest that the lessons of planning history remain, at best, only partially learned.

Abbreviations

CAM papers   President's Committee on Administrative Management Papers. Franklin D. Roosevelt Library, Hyde Park, N.Y.

CEM Papers   Charles E. Merriam Papers, Special Collections, Regenstein Library, University of Chicago, Chicago, Ill.

COHC   Columbia University Oral History Collection, New York.

CP   Commerce Papers, Herbert Hoover Papers, Herbert Hoover Presidential Library, West Branch, Iowa.

FAD Papers   Frederic Adrian Delano Papers, Franklin D. Roosevelt Presidential Library, Hyde Park, N.Y.

FDRL   Franklin D. Roosevelt Presidential Library, Hyde Park, N.Y.

HHP   Herbert Hoover Papers, Herbert Hoover Presidential Library, West Branch, Iowa.

HHPL   Herbert Hoover Presidential Library, West Branch, Iowa.

HSD Papers   Henry S. Dennison Papers, Baker Library, Harvard Graduate School of Business Administration, Boston, Mass.

LSRM   Laura Spelman Rockefeller Memorial Records, Rockefeller Archive Center, Pocantico Hills, North Tarrytown, N.Y.

NCPC   Records of the National Capital Planning Commission, Record Group 328, National Archives, Washington, D.C.

NRPB   Records of the National Resources Planning Board, Record Group 187. National Archives, College Park, Md.

OF   President's Official File, Franklin D. Roosevelt Papers. Franklin D. Roosevelt Library, Hyde Park, N.Y.

PPF   President's Personal File, Franklin D. Roosevelt Papers. Franklin D. Roosevelt Library, Hyde Park, N.Y.

PSF   President's Secretary File, Franklin D. Roosevelt Papers. Franklin D. Roosevelt Library, Hyde Park, N.Y.

RAC   Rockefeller Archive Center, Pocantico Hills, North Tarrytown, N.Y.

RF Records   Rockefeller Foundation Records, Record Group 1. 1. Rockefeller Archive Center, Pocantico Hills, North Tarrytown, N.Y.

UF   Unemployment File, Commerce Papers, Herbert Hoover Papers, Herbert Hoover Presidential Library, West Branch, Iowa.

Notes

1. The Origins of New Deal Planning

1. On the emergence of city and regional planning, see F. Adams, "Changing Concepts of Planning"; Adams and Hodge, "City Planning Instruction in the United States"; Hancock, "Planners in the Changing American City"; M. Scott, *American City Planning since 1890;* Birch, "Advancing the Art and Science of Planning"; McCarthy, "Chicago Businessmen and the Burnham Plan"; T. Hines, *Burnham of Chicago,* 312–45; Kantor, "Charles Dyer Norton and the Origins of the Regional Plan of New York."

2. Karl, *Charles E. Merriam and the Study of Politics;* Diner, *A City and Its Universities;* and Bulmer, "The Early Institutional Establishment of Social Science Research."

3. On Mitchell, see Hansen, "Wesley Mitchell, Social Scientist and Social Counselor"; Dorfman, "Wesley Clair Mitchell (1874–1948)"; essays in A. Burns, *Wesley Clair Mitchell;* F. Hill, "Wesley Mitchell's Theory of Planning." For the broader context of Mitchell's work in the economics profession, see Gruchy, *Modern Economic Thought,* 247–333; Dorfman, *The Economic Mind in American Civilization,* 3:455–73; Church, "Economists as Experts"; Grossman, "American Foundations and the Support of Economic Research"; and Alchon, *The Invisible Hand of Planning,* for a penetrating analysis.

4. McQuaid, "Henry S. Dennison and the 'Science' of Industrial Reform"; Heaton, *A Scholar in Action,* 98–138; McQuaid, "Corporate Liberalism in the American Business Community"; McQuaid and Berkowitz, *Creating the Welfare State,* 1–57.

5. Johnston, "The National Idea Man"; Kevles, "Testing the Army's Intelligence"; Baritz, *The Servants of Power;* Bulmer and Bulmer, "Philanthropy and Social Science in the 1920s"; Karl, "Philanthropy, Policy Planning, and the Bureaucratization of the Democratic Ideal"; Karl and Katz, "The American Private Philanthropic Foundation and the Public Sphere"; Coben, "Foundation Officials and Fellowships"; Kohler, "The Management of Science"; Kohler, "A Policy for the Advancement of Science"; and Kohler, *Partners in Science,* pp. 233–46.

6. On changes in the nature of American liberalism, see Louis Hartz, *The Liberal Tradition in America: An Interpretation of American Political Thought since the Revolution* (New York, 1955); Fine, *Laissez-Faire and the General Welfare State;* Gerber, *The Limits of Liberalism;* Mary O. Furner, "Knowing Capitalism: Public Investigation and the Labor Question in the Long Progressive Era," in *The State and Economic Knowledge,* ed. Furner and Supple, 241–86; Gary Gerstle, "The Protean Character of American Liberalism," *American Historical Review* 99 (October 1994): 1043–73; Lind, *The Next American Nation;* Sandel, *Democracy's Discontent;* A. Brinkley, *Liberalism and Its Discontents;* and Kloppenberg, *The Virtues of Liberalism.*

7. Schlesinger, Jr., *The Age of Roosevelt: The Coming of the New Deal,* 282–84; Conkin,

The New Deal, pp. 49, 52; Ekirch, Jr., *Ideologies and Utopias,* 36–71, 119; Lawson, *The Failure of Independent Liberalism,* 61–84; Pells, *Radical Visions and American Dreams,* 43–95; Westbrook, "Tribune of the Technostructure"; Shankman, "The Five-Day Plan and the Depression"; Kidd, "Collectivist Intellectuals and the Ideal of National Economic Planning"; Adelstein, "The Nation as an Economic Unit"; and Cooney, *Balancing Acts,* pp. 10, 40–50.

8. Graham, Jr., "The Planning Ideal and American Reality"; Graham, *Toward a Planned Society;* and Graham, Jr., "The Planning Idea From Roosevelt to Post-Reagan." For two useful complementary works on American national planning from a policy-analysis perspective, see D. Wilson, *National Planning in the United States* and *The National Planning Idea in U.S. Public Policy.* For historical references, see Patrick D. Reagan, "American Planning: A Bibliographical Essay," in *Voluntarism, Planning, and the State,* ed. Brown and Reagan, 141–62.

9. On the NRA, see Himmelberg, *The Origins of the National Recovery Administration;* Hawley, *The New Deal and the Problem of Monopoly,* 1–146; Ohl, *Hugh S. Johnson and the New Deal;* Brand, *Corporatism and the Rule of Law;* Bellush, *The Failure of the NRA;* Gordon, *New Deals;* Ellis W. Hawley, "Introduction to the 1995 Edition," in *The New Deal and the Problem of Monopoly,* xvii–xxxvii; Finegold and Skocpol, *State and Party in America's New Deal;* and Domhoff, *The Power Elite and the State* and *State Autonomy or Class Dominance?* On the Agricultural Adjustment Administration, see Hamilton, *From New Day to New Deal;* McConnell, *The Decline of Agrarian Democracy;* C. Campbell, *The Farm Bureau and the New Deal;* Kirkendall, *Social Scientists and Farm Politics in the Age of Roosevelt;* Perkins, *Crisis in Agriculture;* and Saloutos, *The American Farmer and the New Deal,* 35–38. On the TVA, see Hubbard, *Origins of the TVA;* Pritchett, *The Tennessee Valley Authority;* Selznick, *TVA and the Grass Roots;* McCraw, *TVA and the Power Fight;* Hargrove and Conkin, *TVA;* Creese, *TVA's Public Planning;* and Hargrove, *Prisoners of Myth.*

10. For the literature on the organizational society, see Galambos, "The Emerging Organizational Synthesis of Modern American History" and "Technology, Political Economy, and Professionalization"; James H. Soltow, "American Institutional Studies: Present Knowledge and Past Trends," *Journal of Economic History* 31 (1971): 87–105; Berkhofer, Jr., "The Organizational Interpretation of American History." Major works in this vein include Hays, *The Response to Industrialism;* Williams, *The Contours of American History,* pp. 320–425; Wiebe, *Businessmen and Reforms;* Kolko, *The Triumph of Conservatism;* Haber, *Efficiency and Uplift;* Wiebe, *The Search for Order;* Weinstein, *The Corporate Ideal in the Liberal State;* Israel, *Building the Organizational Society;* Chambers, *The Tyranny of Change;* Hawley, *The Great War and the Search for a Modern Order;* G. Nash, *The Crucial Era;* Galambos, *America at Middle Age;* and Galambos, *The New American State.* For some caveats about the organizational synthesis, see Fusfeld, "The Rise of the Corporate State in America"; Cuff, "American Historians and the 'Organizational Factor'"; Du Boff and Herman, "Alfred D. Chandler's New Business History"; Karl, *The Uneasy State;* A. Brinkley, "Writing the History of Contemporary America"; Livingston, "The Social Analysis of Economic History and Theory"; Higgs, *Crisis and Leviathan;* Balogh, "Reorganizing the Organizational Synthesis"; Dawley, *Struggles for Justice;* McGerr, "The Persistence of Individualism"; and Balogh, *Integrating the Sixties,* 1–33.

11. Chandler, Jr., and Galambos, "The Development of Large-Scale Economic Organizations in Modern America"; McCraw, "The Challenge of Alfred D. Chandler, Jr."; Chandler, Jr., *Strategy and Structure;* Chandler, *The Visible Hand;* Chandler and Daems, *Managerial Hierarchies;* McCraw, *The Essential Alfred Chandler;* Chandler, *Scale and Scope;* John, "Elaborations, Revisions, Dissents"; Porter, *The Rise of Big Business;* and Zunz, *Making America Corporate.*

12. A good summary of this literature is R. McCormick, "Public Life in Industrial America." Some of the best examples include Raymond A. Mohl, *The New City: Urban*

America in the Industrial Age, 1860–1920 (Arlington Heights, Ill., 1985); Hays, *Conservation and the Gospel of Efficiency;* Van Tine, *The Making of the Labor Bureaucrat;* Nelson, *Managers and Workers;* Rodgers, *The Work Ethic in Industrial America;* Montgomery, *Workers' Control in America;* Dubofsky, *Industrialism and the American Worker;* Montgomery, *The Fall of the House of Labor;* David Brody, "The American Worker in the Progressive Age," in *Workers in Industrial America,* 3–47; Alan M. Kraut, *The Huddled Masses: The Immigrant in American Society, 1880–1921* (Arlington Heights, Ill., 1982); John Bodnar, *The Transplanted: A History of Immigrants in Urban America* (Bloomington, Ind., 1985); William H. Harris, *The Harder We Run: Black Workers since the Civil War* (New York, 1982); Alice Kessler-Harris, *Out to Work: A History of Wage-Earning Women in the United States* (New York, 1982); Trachtenberg, *The Incorporation of America;* Rosenberg, *Spreading the American Dream.*

13. On the emergence and professionalization of academic social science in the United States, see Rudolph, *The American College and University,* 264–306, 329–72; Vesey, *The Emergence of the American University;* Bledstein, *The Culture of Professionalism;* Furner, *Advocacy and Objectivity;* Haskell, *The Emergence of Professional Social Science;* Haskell, *The Authority of Experts;* Edward T. Silva and Sheila A. Slaughter, *Serving Power: The Making of the Academic Social Science Expert* (Westport, Conn., 1984); Dorothy Ross, "The Development of the Social Sciences," in *The Organization of Knowledge in Modern America,* ed. Oleson and Voss, 107–38; Geiger, *To Advance Knowledge;* Ross, *The Origins of American Social Science;* Mary O. Furner, "Expert Advice: Constructing the Knowledge Base for Public Policy, 1880–1920," in *Intellectuals and Public Life,* ed. Fink, Leonard, and Reid, 145–81; Fink, *Progressive Intellectuals and the Dilemmas of Democratic Commitment;* and Silverberg, *Gender and American Social Science.*

On the growing importance of socioeconomic research in this period, see Baritz, *Servants of Power;* Eakins, "The Development of Corporate Liberal Policy Research in the United States"; Lyons, *The Uneasy Partnership;* Eakins, "The Origins of Corporate Liberal Policy Research"; Eakins, "Policy Planning for the Establishment"; McClymer, *War and Welfare;* Critchlow, *The Brookings Institution;* R. Smith, *The American Business System and the Theory and Practice of Social Science;* Converse, *Survey Research in the United States;* Bulmer, *Social Science Research and Government;* Fitzpatrick, *Endless Crusade;* J. Smith, *The Idea Brokers;* essays in Lacey and Furner, *The State and Social Investigation in Britain and the United States;* Jordan, *Machine-Age Ideology;* and Alchon, "Policy History and the Sublime Immodesty of the Middle-Aged Professor."

14. For key recent works dealing with Progressivism, see John D. Buenker, "The Progressive Era: A Search for a Synthesis," *Mid-America* 51 (1969): 175–193; Thelen, "Social Tensions and the Origins of Progressivism"; Peter G. Filene, "An Obituary for 'The Progressive Movement,'" *American Quarterly* 22 (1970): 20–34; David M. Kennedy, "Overview: The Progressive Era," *Historian* 37 (1975): 453–68; Robert H. Wiebe, "The Progressive Years, 1900–1917," in *The Reinterpretation of American History and Culture,* ed. William H. Cartwright and Richard L. Watson (Washington, D.C., 1973), 425–42; John D. Buenker, John C. Burnham, and Robert M. Crunden, *Progressivism* (Cambridge, Mass., 1977); Rodgers, "In Search of Progressivism"; Arthur S. Link and Richard L. McCormick, *Progressivism* (Arlington Heights, Ill., 1983); Richard L. McCormick, "Progressivism: A Contemporary Reassessment," in *The Party Period and Public Policy,* 263–88; Cooper, *Pivotal Decades;* Sklar, "Periodization and Historiography"; Chambers, *Tyranny of Change;* and Diner, *A Very Different Age.*

15. Williams, *The Contours of American History;* Kolko, *The Triumph of Conservatism;* Weinstein, *The Corporate Ideal in the Liberal State;* Fusfeld, "The Rise of the Corporate State in America"; Radosh and Rothbard, *A New History of Leviathan;* Noble, *America By Design;* Hawley, "The Discovery and Study of a 'Corporate Liberalism'"; Lustig, *Corporate Liberalism;* Sklar, *The Corporate Reconstruction of American Capitalism;* Berk, "Corporate

Liberalism Reconsidered"; and Collins, "American Corporatism," for an especially well-done case study.

Other reviews of this school with an emphasis on foreign policy include T. McCormick, "Drift or Mastery?" Gaddis, "The Corporatist Synthesis"; and Hogan, "Corporatism." Comparative perspectives on corporatism include Schmitter, "Still the Century of Corporatism?" and essays in Lehmbruch and Schmitter, *Patterns of Corporatist Policy-Making*. Ellis W. Hawley coined the term "associational state," in his "Herbert Hoover, the Commerce Secretariat, and the Vision of an 'Associative State'"; Ronald Schaffer uses the term "war welfare state" in *America in the Great War*, while Alan Dawley uses the term "parastate" in *Struggles for Justice*, 150, 296.

16. For significant works dealing with the wartime mobilization, see Porter, *War and the Rise of the State*, 269–75; Paxson, *American Democracy and the World War*; Koistinen, "The 'Industrial-Military Complex' in Historical Perspective"; Robert D. Cuff, "Business, the State, and World War I: The American Experience," in *War and Society in North America*, ed. Cuff and J. L. Granastein (Toronto, 1971), 1–19; Murray N. Rothbard, "War Collectivism in World War I," in *A New History of Leviathan*, ed. Radosh and Rothbard, 66–110; Cuff, *The War Industries Board*; Cuff, "We Band of Brothers"; Cuff, "Herbert Hoover, the Ideology of Voluntarism, and War Organization during the Great War"; Cuff, "Harry Garfield, the Fuel Administration, and the Search for a Cooperative Order during World War I"; Kennedy, *Over Here*; Vaughn, *Holding Fast the Inner Lines*; Conner, *The National War Labor Board*; McCartin, *Labor's Great War*; Hawley, "The Great War and Organizational Innovation"; Ferrell, *Woodrow Wilson and World War I*; Wynn, *From Progressivism to Prosperity*; Higgs, *Crisis and Leviathan*, 123–58; Schaffer, *America in the Great War*; Hawley, *The Great War and the Search for a Modern Order*; Himmelberg, "Business, Antitrust Policy, and the Industrial Board of the Department of Commerce"; Dawley, *Struggles for Justice*, 172–217; Robert D. Cuff, "War Mobilization, Institutional Learning, and State Building in the United States, 1917–1941," in *State and Social Investigation in Britain and the United States*, ed. Lacey and Furner, 388–425; and Koistinen, *Mobilizing for Modern War*.

17. Much of this recent research centers on the work of Herbert Hoover; the Department of Commerce, and efforts at promoting business-government cooperation as part of the economic policies of the Republican administrations in the 1920s. For the most important works, see J. Wilson, *Herbert Hoover*; Burner, *Herbert Hoover*; essays in *Herbert Hoover Reassessed*; Nash, *Understanding Herbert Hoover*; Ellis W. Hawley, Patrick G. O'Brien, Philip T. Rosen, and Alexander DeConde, *Herbert Hoover and the Historians* (West Branch, Iowa, 1989); R. Burns, *Herbert Hoover*; Lloyd, *Aggressive Introvert*; Best, *The Politics of Individualism*; Gelfand, *Herbert Hoover*; Runfola, "Herbert C. Hoover as Secretary of Commerce"; Hawley, *Herbert Hoover as Secretary of Commerce*; Hawley, "Secretary Hoover and the Bituminous Coal Problem"; Hawley, "Herbert Hoover, the Commerce Secretariat, and the Vision of an 'Associative State'"; Metcalf, "Secretary Hoover and the Emergence of Macroeconomic Management"; Himmelberg, *Origins of the National Recovery Administration*; Ellis W. Hawley, "Three Facets of Hooverian Associationalism: Lumber, Aviation, and Movies, 1921–1930," in *Regulation in Perspective*, ed. McCraw, 95–123; Keller, "Supply-Side Economic Policies during the Coolidge-Mellon Era"; Krog and Tanner, *Herbert Hoover and the Republican Era*; Metzger, "How New Was the New Era?"; Himmelberg, "Government and Business"; Alchon, *The Invisible Hand of Planning*; Ellis W. Hawley, "'Industrial Policy' in the 1920s and 1930s," in *The Politics of Industrial Policy*, ed. Barfield and Schambra, 63–86; Keller, "The Role of the State in the U.S. Economy during the 1920s"; Hawley, "Economic Inquiry and the State in New Era America"; essays in Himmelberg, *Business-Government Cooperation*.

18. The most persuasive works on the 1917–18 precedents for the New Deal include Leuchtenburg, "The New Deal and the Analogue of War," and Hawley, *The Great War and the Search for a Modern Order*.

19. Richard Hofstadter, "Herbert Hoover and the Crisis of American Individualism," in his *American Political Tradition* (New York, 1948); Degler, "The Ordeal of Herbert Hoover"; Murray N. Rothbard, "Herbert Hoover and the Myth of Laissez-Faire," in *A New History of Leviathan,* ed. Radosh and Rothbard, 111–45; P. Arnold, "Herbert Hoover and the Continuity of American Public Policy"; Hawley, Rothbard, Himmelberg, and Nash, *Herbert Hoover and the Crisis of American Capitalism;* Hawley, "Techno-Corporatist Formulas in the Liberal State"; Fausold and Mazuzan, *The Hoover Presidency;* Frank Freidel, "Hoover and Roosevelt and Historical Continuity," in *Herbert Hoover Reassessed,* 275–91; Fausold, *The Presidency of Herbert C. Hoover;* essays in Nash, *Understanding Herbert Hoover;* McElvaine, *The Great Depression: America,* 51–71; Lewis-Beck and Squire, "The Transformation of the American State."

20. For major interpretations of the New Deal, see Schlesinger, Jr., *The Age of Roosevelt,* 3 vols.; Graham, Jr., "Historians and the New Deal"; Leuchtenburg, *Franklin D. Roosevelt and the New Deal;* Howard Zinn, "Introduction," in *New Deal Thought,* ed. Zinn, xv–xxxvi; Conkin, *The New Deal;* Bernstein, "The New Deal"; Braeman, Bremner, and Brody, *The New Deal;* articles by Alan Brinkley, Bradford Lee, and William Leuchtenburg, *Wilson Quarterly* 6 (Spring 1982): 51–93; Romasco, *The Politics of Recovery;* Karl, *The Uneasy State;* McElvaine, *The Great Depression;* Cohen, *The Roosevelt New Deal;* Rosenof, "New Deal *Pragmatism* and Economic *Systems*"; Fraser and Gerstle, *The Rise and Fall of the New Deal Order;* Graham, Jr., *Soviet-American Dialogue on the New Deal;* Eden, *The New Deal and Its Legacy;* Badger, *The New Deal;* Biles, *A New Deal for the American People;* Parrish, *Anxious Decades;* Schwarz, *The New Dealers;* Gordon, *New Deals;* Finegold and Skocpol, *State and Party in America's New Deal;* A. Brinkley, *The End of Reform;* and Plotke, *Building a Democratic Political Order.*

Reviews of the recent literature on the New Deal include Kirkendall, "The New Deal as Watershed"; Auerbach, "New Deal, Old Deal, or Raw Deal"; Braeman, "The New Deal and the 'Broker State'"; Graham, Jr., "The New Deal"; Lowitt, "The New Deal"; Skocpol, "Political Response to Capitalist Crisis"; Gelfand and Neymeyer, *The New Deal Viewed from Fifty Years;* Skocpol, "Legacies of New Deal Liberalism"; Graham, Jr., "The Broker State"; Sitkoff, *Fifty Years Later;* Graham, Jr., and Wander, *Franklin D. Roosevelt;* Olson, *Historical Dictionary of the New Deal;* Cohen, *The Roosevelt New Deal;* Kidd, "Redefining the New Deal"; Braeman, "The New Deal"; A. Brinkley, "Prosperity, Depression, and War"; and the bibliographic sections in Badger, *The New Deal,* 313–64; Biles, *A New Deal for the American People,* 249–60; and Parrish, *Anxious Decades,* 490–502.

21. Jim F. Heath, "Domestic America during World War II: Research Opportunities for Historians," *Journal of American History* 58 (1971): 384–415; Polenberg, *War and Society;* Perrett, *Days of Sadness, Years of Triumph;* Blum, *V Was for Victory;* Philip Gleason, "Americans All: World War II and the Shaping of American Identity," *Review of Politics* 43 (1981): 483–518; Jeffries, "World War II and American Life"; Winkler, *Home Front, U.S.A.;* A. Brinkley, "The New Deal and the Idea of the State"; Katznelson and Pietrykowski, "Rebuilding the American State"; O'Neill, *A Democracy at War;* Adams, *The Best War Ever;* Sparrow, *From the Outside In;* and Jeffries, *Wartime America.*

22. Recent Marxist interpretations are considered in Skocpol, "Political Response to Capitalist Crisis"; Barrow, *Critical Theories of the State;* and Domhoff, *The Power Elite and the State* and *State Autonomy or Class Dominance?* Recent examples of radical interpretations of American national planning include Stabile, *Prophets of Order,* and Friedmann, *Planning in the Public Domain.* Libertarians challenge the Marxist view in LaVoie, *National Economic Planning,* and Higgs, *Crisis and Leviathan.*

23. These scholars have begun pointing to the importance of reassessing the role of the state in comparative historical contexts as a way of understanding national differences between administrative capacities to plan. Pioneering efforts are found in Skocpol and Finegold, "State Capacity and Economic Intervention in the Early New Deal"; Finegold, "From Agrarianism to Adjustment"; Skowronek, *Building a New American State;* Theda

Skocpol, "Bringing the State Back In: Strategies of Analysis in Current Research," in *Bringing the State Back In,* ed. Evans, Rueschemeyer, and Skocpol, 3–37; Gourevitch, *Politics in Hard Times;* Leuchtenburg, "The Pertinence of Political History"; Amenta and Skocpol, "Taking Exception"; Keller, "Role of the State in the U.S. Economy during the 1920s"; Brinkley, "The New Deal and the Idea of the State"; Katznelson and Pietry-kowski, "Rebuilding the American State"; Dubofsky, *The State and Labor in Modern America;* Finegold and Skocpol, *State and Party in America's New Deal;* Sparrow, *From the Outside In;* and Gillon, "The Future of Political History." For summaries and critiques of this approach, see Almond, "The Return to the State," and responses by Eric A. Nordlinger, Theodore J. Lowi, and Sergio Fabbrini in *American Political Science Review* 82 (September 1988): 853–901; Lewis-Beck and Squire, "The Transformation of the American State"; Farr, "The Estate of Political Knowledge"; Mitchell, "The Limits of the State"; Domhoff, "Class, Power, and Parties in the New Deal"; with responses by Richard S. Kirkendall, Ellis W. Hawley, William Graebner, Kenneth Finegold, and Jeff Manza in *Berkeley Journal of Sociology* 36 (1991): 1–49, 51–91; Katznelson, "The State to the Rescue?"; Robertson, "The Return to History and the New Institutionalism in American Political Science"; Koelble, "The New Institutionalism in Political Science and Sociology"; Gordon, review of *State and Party in America's New Deal,* by Skocpol and Finegold; papers by Gerald Gamm, Ira Katznelson, Brian R. Sala, and John Aldrich presented at the annual meeting of the Midwest Political Science Association, Chicago, April 11, 1997, published in *Political Methodologist: Newsletter of the Political Methodology Section, American Political Science Association* 8 (Fall 1997): 8–21; and Katznelson, "The Doleful Dance of Politics and Policy."

24. Commager, *Lester Frank Ward and the Welfare State,* xi–xxxviii; Fox, *The Discovery of Abundance;* Veblen, *The Engineers and the Price System;* Seckler, *Thorstein Veblen and the Institutionalists;* Gruchy, *Contemporary Economic Thought;* 19–87; Fine, *Laissez-Faire and the General Welfare State;* and Kent, "Planning for Abundance."

25. See works cited in n. 7.

26. Homan, "Economic Planning"; Chase, *A New Deal;* Soule, *A Planned Society;* Beard, *America Faces the Future;* Roosevelt, "Growing Up By Plan"; Fusfeld, *The Economic Thought of Franklin D. Roosevelt and the Origins of the New Deal;* Freidel, *Franklin D. Roosevelt: Launching the New Deal,* 60–101, 299–319, 408–35, 444–47; Tugwell, *The Brains Trust;* Rosen, "Roosevelt and the Brains Trust" and *Hoover, Roosevelt, and the Brains Trust;* Ekirch, *Ideologies and Utopias,* 105–40; Kirkendall, *Social Scientists and Farm Politics;* Cook, *Academicians in Government.*

27. Tugwell, "The Principle of Planning and the Institution of Laissez-Faire"; Tugwell, "The New Deal"; Tugwell, "The Progressive Orthodoxy of Franklin D. Roosevelt"; Tugwell, "The Sources of New Deal Reformism"; Fusfeld, "The Sources of New Deal Reformism"; Sternsher, *Rexford Tugwell and the New Deal;* Rosenof, "The Economic Ideas of Henry A. Wallace, 1933–1948."

28. Hawley, *The New Deal and the Problem of Monopoly,* 175–76. See the discussion on 169–86.

29. Karl, *Charles E. Merriam.*

30. L. Mitchell, *Two Lives;* Antler, *Lucy Sprague Mitchell;* and works cited in n. 3.

31. McQuaid, "Henry S. Dennison and the 'Science' of Industrial Reform"; Johnston, "The National Idea Man"; and Grattan, "Beardsley Ruml and His Ideas."

32. Merriam, "Planning Agencies in America" and "The National Resources Planning Board"; Gruchy, "The Concept of National Planning in Institutional Economics"; Clayton, "The Development of the Concept of National Planning in the United States"; Tugwell and Banfield, "Governmental Planning at Mid-Century"; Soule, *Planning U.S.A.,* a compendium of Soule's work about planning written since the 1930s; and the excellent discussion in Rosenof, *Dogma, Depression, and the New Deal,* 76–97.

33. Rockwell, "National Resources Planning" and "The Planning Function of the National Resources Planning Board"; Coyle, "The American National Planning Board"; Millett, *The Process and Organization of Government Planning,* 70–89 and 103–13; White, "The Termination of the National Resources Planning Board"; Seifert, "A History of the National Resources Planning Board"; Kalish, "National Resource Planning"; Warken, *A History of the National Resources Planning Board;* Clawson, *New Deal Planning;* and Beckman, "Federal Long-Range Planning."

34. Beckman, "Federal Long-Range Planning," 97.

35. Hynning, "Administrative Evolution of National Planning in the United States in the Pre-New Deal Era"; B. Jones, "A Plan for Planning in the New Deal"; Funigiello, "City Planning in World War II," later revised as "Urban Conservatism and the NRPB," in *The Challenge to Urban Liberalism,* 163–86; Lepawsky, "The Progressives and the Planners," "The New Deal at Mid-passage," "The Planning Apparatus," and "Style and Substance in Contemporary Planning."

36. Karl, *Executive Reorganization and Reform in the New Deal, Charles E. Merriam,* "The Power of Intellect and the Politics of Ideas," "Presidential Planning and Social Science Research," "Merriam's 'Continuously Planning Society,'" "Philanthropy, Policy Planning, and the Bureaucratization of the Democratic Ideal," *The Uneasy State,* and "Constitution and Central Planning."

37. Eakins, "The Development of Corporate Liberal Policy Research," "The Origins of Corporate Liberal Policy Research," and "Policy Planning for the Establishment"; Lyons, *The Uneasy Partnership;* Noggle, *Into the Twenties;* Brownlee, *Dynamics of Ascent,* chap. 14; and works cited in nn. 16 and 17.

38. Scholars have only begun to flesh out the history of these kinds of private/public institutions. In addition to the works cited in previous footnotes, for some of most thoughtful works in this area, see Rogin, "Voluntarism: The Political Functions of an Apolitical Doctrine"; McConnell, *Decline of Agrarian Democracy;* McConnell, *Private Power and American Democracy;* B. Smith, *The New Political Economy;* essays in Greenstone, *Public Values and Private Power in American Politics;* essays in Jeffreys-Jones and Collins, *The Growth of Federal Power in American History;* Alchon, *The Invisible Hand of Planning;* Domhoff, *The Power Elite and the State* and *State Autonomy or Class Dominance?;* Sklar, "Periodization and Historiography"; W. Scott, *Chester I. Barnard and the Guardians of the Managerial State;* Jordan, *Machine-Age Ideology.*

39. On the National Research Council, see Kevles, "George Ellery Hale, the First World War, and the Advancement of Science in America," "Hale and the Role of a Central Scientific Institution in the United States," and *The Physicists,* 111–18, 139–45. On the other research organizations, see Alchon, *The Invisible Hand of Planning* for the NBER; Berle, *Leaning Against the Dawn: An Appreciation of the Twentieth Century Fund;* Critchlow, *Brookings Institution;* J. Smith, *Brookings at Seventy-Five;* Hawley, "Economic Inquiry and the State in New Era America"; and Cuff, "War Mobilization, Institutional Learning, and State Building."

For the broader evolution of these kinds of research bodies, see J. Smith, *The Idea Brokers,* and Donald T. Critchlow, "Think Tanks, Antistatism, and Democracy: The Nonpartisan Ideal and Policy Research in the United States, 1913–1987," in *The State and Social Investigation in Britain and the United States,* ed. Lacey and Furner, 279–322.

40. For the postwar depression of 1920–21, see Soule, *Prosperity Decade,* 81–106; Hicks, *Rehearsal for Disaster;* Pilgrim, "The Upper Turning Point of 1920." McMullen, "The President's Unemployment Conference of 1921 and Its Results"; Grin, "The Unemployment Conference of 1921"; Metcalf, "Secretary Hoover and the Emergence of Macroeconomic Management"; Ellis W. Hawley, "Herbert Hoover and Economic Stabilization, 1921–22," in *Herbert Hoover as Secretary of Commerce,* ed. Hawley, 43–77; and Alchon, *The Invisible Hand of Planning.*

41. Correspondence between Robert M. Yerkes and Charles E. Merriam, Box 43, and correspondence between John C. Merriam and Charles E. Merriam, December 11 and 18, 1923, Box 35, CEM Papers; National Research Council—Human Migration Folders, Subseries 6, Series III, LSRM.

42. For an especially thoughtful discussion, see Milkis, *The President and the Parties.*

2. Frederic Adrian Delano

1. On the broader history of city planning, see Eugenie Ladner Birch, "Design, Process, and Institutions: Planning in Urban History," in *American Urbanism,* ed. Gillette and Miller, 135–54; Reps, *The Making of Urban America;* M. Scott, *American City Planning since 1890;* Adams and Hodge, "City Planning Instruction in the United States"; Hancock, "Planners in the Changing American City, 1900–1940"; Birch, "Advancing the Art and Science of Planning"; Krueckeberg, *The American Planner;* Fogelsong, *Planning the Capitalist City;* Schaffer, *Two Centuries of American Planning.*

2. Biographical sketches of Delano must be used with care, as factual information is often erroneous. For the best sources, see Delano, Frederic A.—Clippings, Tributes, Obituaries, Estate Papers, FAD Papers; D. Delano, *Franklin Roosevelt and the Delano Influence,* 185–89; Coyle, "Frederic A. Delano"; Memorial Committee, The Commercial Club of Chicago, "Frederic Adrian Delano: 1863–1953" (Chicago [1953], pamphlet); C[harles] W. E[liot II], "Frederic Adrian Delano: September 10, 1863–March 28, 1953," *Landscape Architecture* 43 (April 1953): 130–31; Peaslee, "Make No Little Planners" and "Commemoration"; obituaries in *Washington Post,* March 29, 1953, 14, and *New York Times,* March 29, 1953, 94; *National Cyclopedia of American Biography* 40 (1955): 564–65.

3. "The Reminiscences of M. L. Wilson," 1932, COHC; Frederic A. Delano, "Warren Delano (II) 1809–1898 and Catherine Robbins (Lyman) Delano 1825–1896: A Memoir" (1928), Delano Family Matters, FAD Papers; Reynolds, *Genealogical and Family History of Southern New York and the Hudson River Valley,* 3:1058–61; A. Johnson, *Franklin D. Roosevelt's Colonial Ancestors,* 102–17; Schriftgiesser, *The Amazing Roosevelt Family,* 196–99; Ward, *Before the Trumpet,* chap. 2. On Warren Delano II and the making of the family fortune, see Delano, *Franklin Roosevelt and the Delano Influence,* 157–71; Roosevelt, in collaboration with Samuel Duff McCoy, *Odyssey of an American Family,* 271–73; Freidel, *Franklin D. Roosevelt: The Apprenticeship,* 5–19; Frederic A. Delano, "Algonac: 1857–1931," Delano Family-Genealogy, Vertical File, FDRL; *Boston Sunday Globe,* June 28, 1908, 11; Dudden, *The American Pacific,* 3–11; Samuel Russell Company, FAD Papers; F. Grant, "Edward Delano and Warren Delano II"; Downs, "American Merchants and the China Opium Trade" and "Fair Game"; Geoffrey C. Ward, "'A Fair, Honorable, and Legitimate Trade': The Delanos in the Opium War," in *American Originals,* 203–21.

4. Liu, *Anglo-American Steamship Rivalry in China,* 1–26, and Delano, "Warren Delano (II)" and "Algonac."

5. Delano, "Warren Delano (II)."

6. Delano, "Algonac"; D. Delano, *Franklin Roosevelt and the Delano Influence,* 166–89; *Boston Morning Mercury,* September 11, 1920.

7. "Milestones in F. A. D.'s Career," Delano Family Matters, FAD Papers, and Warren Delano II to Franklin Hughes Delano, July 5, 1884, Delano Family Papers.

8. Warren Delano II to Franklin Hughes Delano, October 3, 1885, Delano Family Papers; Delano to My Dear Uncle, October 3, 1885, Warren Delano II to Franklin Hughes Delano, November 21, 1885, and Warren Delano II to F. A. Delano, December 2, 1885, and October 7, 1886, Family Papers, FAD Papers.

9. Cochran, *Railroad Leaders;* Chandler, "The Railroads"; Chandler, *The Railroads;* Chandler, *Strategy and Structure,* pp. 19–51, and Chandler, *The Visible Hand,* 79–187.

10. Larson, *Bonds of Enterprise,* 169.

11. On the link between the China traders and the western railroads, especially the Chicago, Burlington, and Quincy, see Cochran, *Railroad Leaders,* 40–44, 325; Johnson and Supple, *Boston Capitalists and Western Railroads,* 19–32, 156–80, 222–40, 264–86; Larson, *Bonds of Enterprise,* 5–24; *Boston Transcript,* April 22, 1905. For the CB&Q, see Overton, *Burlington Route,* 3–217. On Perkins, see Overton, "Charles Elliott Perkins"; Overton, *Perkins/Budd,* 1–78; Gagan, "The Railroads and the Public"; Larson, *Bonds of Enterprise,* 118–22, 173–76.

12. "Milestones in F. A. D.'s Career"; Warren Delano II to F. A. Delano, March 25 and April 14, 1886, FAD Papers.

13. Delano to Uncle [Franklin Hughes Delano], May 9, 1886, Family Correspondence, Franklin Hughes Delano Papers, Delano Family Papers (original spelling has been retained).

14. Delano to A. W. Newton, January 15, 1940, and Delano to Joe [?], July 2, 1944, Railroads, FAD Papers; Delano to Warren Delano II, December 5, 1886, attached to Warren Delano II to Franklin Hughes Delano, December 27, 1886, Franklin Hughes Delano Papers, Delano Family Papers; Delano to Warren Delano III, November 28 and December 5, 1886, Papers of Warren Delano III, Delano Family Papers.

15. "Milestones in F. A. D.'s Career"; *Boston Transcript,* October 25, 1931; *Boston Globe,* October 8, 1908; Delano, "Algonac"; *Daily Journal* (Newburgh, N.Y.), November 21, 1888; Overton, *Burlington Route,* 203, 239; *Chicago Times,* November 22, 1888; *New York Times,* June 1, 1943, 23; Warren Delano II to Delano, October 14, 1888, Family Papers, FAD Papers. On the 1888 strike, see Donald L. McMurry, *The Great Burlington Strike of 1888* (Cambridge, 1956), and Overton, *Burlington Route,* 206–14.

16. Delano to Warren Delano III, December 16, 1894, February and December 1896, March 28, April 3, and May 1, 1898, Warren Delano III Papers, Delano Family Papers.

17. Delano to Warren Delano III, March 20 and May 1, 1898, Warren Delano III Papers, Delano Family Papers.

18. Delano to Warren Delano, June 19, 1898, January 22, 1899, telegram of February 16, 1901, March 10, 1901, Warren Delano III Papers, Delano Family Papers; Thomas F. Sheridan to Delano, March 20, 1901, and George G. Yeomans to Delano, July 5, 1931, and Delano to Yeomans, July 13, 1931, Railroads, Subject File, FAD Papers; *Chicago Tribune,* June 24, 1901.

19. Gagan, "The Railroads and the Public"; Overton, *Burlington Route,* 181–83; Larson, *Bonds of Enterprise,* 171–95.

20. Delano to F. Haven Clark, February 28, 1934, Banking Reforms, Gold Standard, Economics, FAD Papers.

21. Draft of an article, Delano, "Cooperation in Railroad Work," January 1893, Speeches and Writings, FAD Papers, and "The Feast of Reason," *Burlington Hawkeye,* February 2, 1904.

22. "Address of Chairman F. A. Delano (Supt. of Motive Power) to the Members of the CB&Q and System Lines' Master Mechanics' Association at Minneapolis, April 19, 1900, Speeches and Writings, FAD Papers; Delano to Warren Delano III, December 21, 1900, February 7, 1901, May 25, June 17, and August 22, 1902, November 1, 1905, November 12 [1905?], October 7, 1906, Warren Delano III Papers, Delano Family Papers.

23. Delano to Warren Delano III, November 9, 1902, May 17, 1903, November 15, 1896, Delano Family Papers.

24. Overton, *Burlington Route,* 244–92; *New York Commercial,* January 9, 1905; Delano to Warren Delano III, January 2 and 6 and March 26, 1905, Warren Delano III Papers, Delano Family Papers.

25. Delano to Warren Delano III, April 13, 1905, Warren Delano III Papers, Delano Family Papers; *Chicago Interocean,* April 23, 1905; *New York Times,* April 26, 1905, 1, and

October 6, 1905, 1; *Boston Globe,* October 8, 1905; and biographical sketch in Delano, Frederic A . . . , Estate Papers, FAD Papers.

26. In 1908 Delano belonged to the American Society of Mechanical Engineers, the Western Society of Engineers, the Franklin Institute, the American Master Mechanic Association, the American Master Car Builders, the Association of International Railroads Congress, the Western Railroad Club, the Union League Club, the University Club, the Mid-Day Club, the Chicago Literary Club, the Commercial Club, and the Board of Directors of the Chicago Lying-In Hospital, *Boston Transcript,* April 22, 1905; *New York Tribune,* April 23, 1908, *New York Times,* April 23, 1908, 5.; *Portland Telegram,* May 17, 1908.

27. Delano took an active part in establishing the Harvard Business School, *Boston Globe,* October 8, 1908; Commercial Club of Chicago, "Frederic Adrian Delano"; Delano, "Railroading as a Profession," typescript of address, May 12, 1909, Speeches and Writings, FAD Papers.

28. Commercial Club of Chicago, "Frederic Adrian Delano."

29. "Milestones in F. A. D.'s Career"; Delano to John J. Glessner, February 7, 1922, Delano to Walter L. Moody, July 7, 1915, Delano to Walter H. Wilson, May 2, 1928, Chicago, FAD Papers; McCarthy, "Chicago Businessmen and the Burnham Plan"; Reps, *The Making of Urban America,* 497–525; T. Hines, *Burnham of Chicago,* 312ff.; Wacker, "Chicago Plan Is Heritage of World's Fair."

30. Delano to Wilson, May 2, 1928.

31. Wacker, "Chicago Plan"; Hines, *Burnham of Chicago,* 317–21; Walker, *The Planning Function in Urban Government* (1950), 17–19, 223–33.

32. F. Delano, "The Chicago Plan, with Particular Reference to the Railway Terminal Problem," 819.

33. Moody, *What of the City?* 326.

34. Early scholars of the Chicago Plan of 1909 praised it for its emphasis on commerce and industry, with some attention to beautifying parks for workers. See, for example, C. W. Eliot, "A Study of the New Plan of Chicago." Over time, scholars have become increasingly critical. See Lewis Mumford, *The Culture of Cities* (New York, 1938); D. Hill, "Lewis Mumford's Ideas on the City"; Walker, *The Planning Function in Urban Government;* M. Scott, *American City Planning since 1890,* 1–182; Michael P. McCarthy, "Businessmen and Professionals in Municipal Reform: The Chicago Experience, 1887–1920," in *The Age of Urban Reform,* ed. Ebner and Tobin, 43–54; D. White, *The Urbanists,* 68–76, 256–66; and Hines, *Burnham of Chicago,* 312–45.

35. Eliot, "Study of the New Plan of Chicago," 417, 418, 431.

36. Scott, *American City Planning since 1890,* 108.

37. Delano to Charles E. Merriam, March 22, 1944, CEM Papers.

38. Delano to F. A. Preston, December 9, 1925, Chicago, FAD Papers; Delano address to the Chicago Real Estate Board, January 25, 1906, and "Railway Terminals and Their Relation to City Planning," paper presented at the American Institute of Architects, December 16, 1909, Speeches and Writings, FAD Papers; Delano, "Consideration of the Various Suggestions Made for New Channels to Take the Place of the Present Narrow River," in Chicago Harbor Commission, *Report to the Mayor and Aldermen of the City of Chicago* (Chicago, 1909), 245–50.

39. Walker, *The Planning Function in Urban Government,* 235–74; Schlereth, "Burnham's *Plan* and Moody's *Manual.*"

40. Lubove, *The Urban Community,* 14; Charles E. Merriam, "City Planning in Chicago," address at City Planning Conference, May 9, 1917, Kansas City, CEM Papers.

41. Delano, "Authority and Responsibility," address before the Chicago Literary Club, January 31, 1910; "Choosing a Profession," address to the students of the University of Missouri, November 22, 1906; "Railroading as a Profession," Speeches and Writings, FAD Papers.

42. Delano, "Memories of the Great War: Its Problems and Its Triumphs," typescript volume, World War I Papers, and newspaper clipping dated June 1909 in Algonac Diary, October 1905-December 1909, Family Papers, FAD Papers. For his views on regulation, see Delano's speeches and testimony in *The Application of a Depreciation Charge in Railway Accounting* (Chicago, 1908); "Some Comments on the Public Regulation and Control of Railways," address before the Commercial Club of Hannibal, Missouri, March 25, 1909, Speeches and Writings, FAD Papers; Delano to Taft, November 20, 1909, Mississippi River Transportation, FAD Papers; "Railway Problems and Railway Rates," *World Today* 29 (1911): 159–65; *The Case for Increased Railroad Rates: Abstracts of Testimony and Arguments Presented to the Interstate Commerce Commission* (n.p., 1914), 19–32, 131–35; *The Railway Problem,* address before the Railway Business Association, January 16, 1917, New York City (New York, 1917).

43. Delano, *Questions of the Hour,* an address before the Toledo Transportation Club, November 24, 1911 ([Chicago], 1911), 13–14.

44. Croly, *The Promise of American Life,* 100–117, 315–98, and Walter Lippmann, *Drift and Mastery* (1914; Englewood Cliffs, N.J., 1961), 45–51, 91–100, 146–57. Cf. Forcey, *The Crossroads of Liberalism.*

45. Commission on Industrial Relations, FAD Papers; "Resume of Appointments to the Public Service of Frederic A. Delano," dated February 14, 1943, Delano, Frederic A . . . ., Estate Papers, FAD Papers; Kellogg, "The Industrial Relations Commission." For histories of the commission, see G. Adams, *Age of Industrial Violence;* Weinstein, *The Corporate Ideal in the Liberal State,* 172–213; and McCartin, *Labor's Great War,* 18–30.

46. Walsh to Joseph Tumulty, August 8, 1914, Woodrow Wilson Papers, Library of Congress, cited in G. Adams, *Age of Industrial Violence,* 62; correspondence in Commission on Industrial Relations, FAD Papers; Mrs. J. Borden Harriman, *From Pinafores to Politics* (New York, 1923), 137; "The Reminiscences of Mrs. Florence Jaffray Harriman (1950)," 28, COHC.

47. Delano to Dr. James Bryant Conant, October 30, 1935, Harvard University Committee on Regional Planning, FAD Papers; Delano is cited in John F. Sinclair, "Definite Object Essential to Success," *Omaha World Herald,* April 29, 1928.

48. Delano to Marriner Eccles, January 5, 1937, and copies of Delano's addresses and articles in Federal Reserve Board, Delano to Dr. Charles W. Eliot, October 14, 1916, Politics—Post Offices; and undated memorandum in Banking Reforms, Gold Standard, Economics, all in FAD Papers.

49. Delano to Harry A. Wheeler, October 21, 1937, and Delano, "The Federal Reserve System," December 13, 1931, Federal Reserve Board, FAD Papers; Delano, "The New Currency System and the Outlook for the Future," address before the Commercial Club of Chicago, October 12, 1914, Speeches and Writings, FAD Papers; Delano, *The Federal Reserve Act: The Place It Is to Occupy in American Finance,* address before the Baltimore Association of Credit Men, February 16, 1915 (Cleveland, 1915).

50. Delano to Dr. Charles W. Eliot, October 14, 1916, Delano, "Memories of the Great War," Delano to Atterbury, May 4, 1918, Delano to Secretary William McAdoo, June 6, 1918, Delano to Federal Reserve Board, June 21, 1918, Woodrow Wilson to Delano, June 24, 1918, all in Scrapbook re World War I, and George J. Seay to Woodrow Wilson, July 9, 1918, Federal Reserve Board, FAD Papers.

51. Delano, "Memories of the Great War"; James H. Graham to Delano, August 28, 1944, Railroads, FAD Papers; Dunn, "American Railway Forces in the Great War."

52. Hoover to Delano, May 22 and July 1 and 20, 1919, Delano to Colonel J. Logan, July 5, 1919, Delano to Hoover, July 21, 1919, "Important Dates and Landmarks," World War I Papers, FAD Papers; Hoover, *The Memoirs of Herbert Hoover,* 1:310–20; Burner, *Herbert Hoover,* 114–30.

53. Howard Elliott to Delano, July 3, 1920, Delano to Elliott, July 13, 1920, Delano to Daniel Willard, March 5, 1931, Railroads, FAD Papers; Delano, "The General Condi-

tions of the Railways in This Country Contrasted with Those of Europe," address to the Chamber of Commerce of the U.S., May 17, 1922, Speeches and Writings, FAD Papers. Cf. Kerr, *American Railroad Politics,* 228–29.

54. Red River Boundary Case File, FAD Papers; W. Clayton Carpenter, "The Red River Boundary Dispute," *American Journal of International Law* 19 (July 1925): 517–30; Correspondence (General), League of Nations Commission of Enquiry into Production of Opium in Persia File, FAD Papers.

55. During the 1920s Delano held membership in many associational groups: Metropolitan Club; Cosmos Club; chairman of the Board, Richmond, Virginia, Federal Reserve Bank; member (1913–25), president (1925–37), and chairman of the board (1937–43), American Civic Association, which merged with National Conference on City Planning in 1935 to form American Civic and Planning Association under Delano's urging; chairman, Committee of One Hundred on the Federal City, American Civic Association (1922–45); member (1926–29) and president (1929–42) National Capital Park and Planning Commission; chairman, Washington Housing Association; member of Board of Trustees, Brookings Institute of Economics; member of Board of Trustees, Russell Sage Foundation; chairman, New York Regional Planning Committee, Russell Sage Foundation; director, Regional Plan of New York and Its Environs; trustee, Carnegie Institute of Washington (1927–47); trustee, District of Columbia Institution for the Deaf; founder and first president, Washington City Community Chest. Information from sources cited in n. 1 above and material in FAD Papers. The growing literature on associational activities in the 1920s is best summarized in Hawley, *The Great War and the Search for a Modern Order.*

56. Commercial Club of Chicago, "Frederic Adrian Delano: (1863–1953): A Tribute," *Planning and Civic Comment* 19 (June 1953): 1–2, 15; Constance McLaughlin Green, *Washington: Capital City,* vol. 2, *1789–1950* (Princeton, 1963), 284–92.

57. Bureau of the Budget, Division of Administrative Management, "The National Capital Park and Planning Commission: A Study of the Organization for Planning the National Capital" (March 1944), copy in Box 96, Historical Data File 1929, NCPC Records; Major General Ulysses S. Grant, 3rd, "Washington—a Planned City in Evolution," in *American Planning and Civic Annual,* ed. Harlean James (1943), 62–73; Gutheim, consultant for the NCPC, *Planning for Washington,* 1–8; Gutheim, "The History: Washington Panorama; A Brief View of the Planned Capital City," in *The Federal City,* 40–50; Gutheim for the NCPC, *Worthy of the Nation,* 143–70; Horace W. Peaslee, "Backgrounds and Foregrounds of the American Planning and Civic Association's Committee of One Hundred on the Federal City," dated January 1, 1945, American Planning and Civic Association, Subject File, FAD Papers; F. Delano, "What the Inaugural Visitor Sees in Washington Today."

58. Charles F. Consul to the president, May 5, 1926, and Joshua Evans et al. to Delano, May 20, 1926, Delano, Frederic A . . . ., Estate Papers, FAD Papers; Gutheim, *Worthy of the Nation,* 186; interview with Charles W. Eliot II, Cambridge, Mass., November 27, 1979; Krueckeberg, "From the Backyard Garden to the Whole U.S.A."

59. Office Files of Chairman Frederic A. Delano, NCPC Records. Eliot regularly reported on the NCPC's work, for which see his "Progress on the Washington Plan," "A Great and Effective City," and "George Washington Memorial Parkway." Later developments were covered in the yearbook of the American Civic Association, *American Planning and Civic Annual.*

60. Delano, "Regional Planning Next." On the importance of regional planning in this period, see Birch, "Advancing the Art and Science of Planning," and D. Johnson, "Regional Planning for the Great American Metropolis."

61. Norton memorandum for the Russell Sage Foundation, January 31, 1921, Russell Sage Foundation, FAD Papers; "The Reminiscences of George McAneny (1949)," 16–

17, COHC; Kantor, "Charles Dyer Norton and the Origins of the Regional Plan of New York"; *Washington Evening Star,* March 28, 1953, B-14. The following section on the RPNY is based on material in Russell Sage Foundation, FAD Papers; Glenn, Brandt, and Andrews, *Russell Sage Foundation,* 1:438–51; M. Scott, *American City Planning,* 198–204, 223–27, 261–65, 289–94; D. Johnson, "Regional Planning for the Great American Metropolis."

62. M. Scott, *American City Planning,* 203–4.

63. T. Adams summarized the voluntary associational approach with the use of planning experts in "Regional Planning in Relation to Public Administration" and "The Social Objective in Regional Planning." The Russell Sage Foundation published a series of technical reports for the RPNY starting in 1928. For a summary of the work of the Regional Plan Association, see its *From Plan to Reality.*

64. Hoover's remarks of May 10, 1922, cited in frontispiece, *Major Economic Factors in Metropolitan Growth and Arrangement* (New York, 1928).

65. Beard, "Some Aspects of Regional Planning"; Mumford, "The Plan of New York," quotation from 153; Adams responded in "A Communication," see scholar's comment in M. Scott, *American City Planning,* 293.

66. Delano to Frederick P. Keppel, May 5, 1932, Frederick P. Keppel Papers, Columbia University, New York City.

67. M. Scott, *American City Planning,* 203. Scott served in one of the regional offices of the New Deal planning agency.

68. Glenn et al. *Russell Sage Foundation,* 2:464; material in Federated Societies 1925–1928, Leisure, Appropriations, LSRM; "Report of Conference and Project for Research and Instruction in City and Regional Planning" at Columbia University, May 3, 1928, in John Merriam Gaus, *The Graduate School of Design and the Education of Planners: A Report* (Cambridge, 1943), 48–50; interview with Eliot; Krueckeberg, "From the Backyard Garden to the Whole U.S.A."

69. Romasco, *The Poverty of Abundance,* 55–56, 143–50, 162–63; I. Bernstein, *The Lean Years,* 262–310.

70. Woods's introduction to E[rving] P[aul] Hayes, *Activities of the President's Emergency Committee for Employment* (Concord, N. H., 1936).

71. Delano address at committee meeting, February 19, 1931, District of Columbia folder, FAD Papers.

72. Correspondence and Delano, "A Proposal for a Volunteer Industrial Army," District of Columbia folder, FAD Papers; Delano to editor, *New York Times,* January 14, 1931, 16; Delano "An Army of the Unemployed," *Washington Star,* October 16, 1931; *Washington Evening Star,* February 28, 1933.

73. Delano to Thomas M. Hayes, October 5, 1931, Unemployment Relief, FAD Papers.

74. Delano to editor, *New York Times,* October 19, 1931, 26.

75. *Newburgh* (N.Y.) *News,* March 26, 1932; *New York Times,* March 18, 1932, 6, May 26, 1932, 24, May 31, 1932, p. 16; *Washington Star,* May 27, 1932.

76. Delano circular, April 2, 1929, Stable Money Association Folder, FAD Papers.

77. Correspondence in ibid.; Delano to the president, August 27, 1934, Roosevelt, Franklin D., FAD Papers; I. Fisher, *Stable Money.*

78. Delano to editor, *New York Times,* August 23, 1932, 18, and October 8, 1932, 18; Delano, "Our Recent Crisis and the Future," *Review of Reviews* 86 (December 1932): 27–29; Delano to University of Chicago Press, March 21, 1933, Chicago, FAD Papers.

79. Delano to Kassie, February 17, 1933, PPF 72, FDRL.

80. Delano telegram to Roosevelt, March 9, 1933, PPF 72, FDRL; Delano's response to a friend, November 25, 1935, Politics–Post Office Folder, FAD Papers; Laura D. Houghteling (Delano's daughter) to the editor, *New York Herald Tribune,* April 9, 1953.

81. Delano to Dr. Arnold Bennett Hall, April 21, 1933, FAD Papers.

82. Memorandum of Delano's remarks at Brookings Institution, May 19, 1933, Brookings Institution, FAD Papers.

83. On the origins of the Brookings Institution, see Eakins, "The Development of Corporate Liberal Policy Research in the United States," 105–10, 134–41, 170–72, 182–90, 197–99, 213–18, 314–16. On the growing shift away from support of New Deal policies, see Critchlow, *The Brookings Institution,* chap. 6; J. Smith, *Brookings at Seventy-Five,* 24–42. Delano's growing unease with the organization is evident in material in Brookings Institution Folder, FAD Papers.

84. Baruch to Delano, March 17, 1933, Unemployment Relief, FAD Papers; Delano to Colonel Louis Howe, April 7, 1933, PPF 72, FDRL; Delano, "Shifting Bureaus at Washington," *Review of Reviews,* May 1933, 33, 56–58; Delano to F. Haven Clark, February 28, 1934, Banking Reforms, Gold Standard, Economics, FAD Papers; Delano, "How Does Money Affect Prices?" *Review of Reviews,* January 1934, p. 13.

85. Leuchtenburg, "The New Deal and the Analogue of War."

86. Delano to F. Haven Clark, February 28, 1934, and Delano to David E. Lilienthal, January 1935, Tennessee Valley Authority, FAD Papers.

87. Delano to Hoover, August 23, 1922, and material in Coal, FAD Papers; Delano correspondence in OF 172, FDRL; Delano to editor, *New York Times,* August 22, 1933, 16. For the background to this effort, see Hawley, "Secretary Hoover and the Bituminous Coal Problem," and J. Johnson, *The Politics of Soft Coal.*

88. *New York Times,* July 7, 1933, 9; Delano Personnel File, Central Office Correspondence, NRPB Records.

89. "The Reminiscences of Gilmore D. Clarke (1959)," 123–25, and "The Reminiscences of M. L. Wilson (1956)," 1932–33, COHC; Harold L. Ickes to the president, April 26, 1941, OF 32, FDRL.

90. Roosevelt to Mrs. Caspar Whitney, December 8, 1930, Private Correspondence, Franklin D. Roosevelt Papers as Governor of New York, FDRL.

91. Roosevelt, "Growing Up by Plan"; Nixon, *Franklin D. Roosevelt and Conservation: 1911–1945;* Fusfeld, *The Economic Thought of Franklin D. Roosevelt and the Origins of the New Deal,* 50, 123–53, 239–40, 248–49, 254–57; Greer, *What Roosevelt Thought,* 65–67; Freidel, *Franklin D. Roosevelt: Launching the New Deal.*

92. Correspondence between Delano and Roosevelt, OF 72, FDRL; Delano to Walter Lippmann, August 2, 1935, FAD Papers; Delano memorandum for Mr. Eliot, August 30, 1943, 153.3 Personnel File, Central Office Correspondence, NRPB Records.

93. Delano to M. S. Sherman, August 3, 1933, Politics-Post Offices, FAD Papers.

94. Delano, "Conclusions Reached from Reading Mr. David Cushman Coyle's Pamphlet," September 20, 1933, OF 229, FDRL; F. Delano, "The Economic Implications of National Planning"; Delano, "Memorandum on National Planning," May 15, 1934, attached to minutes of National Planning Board, May 27–28, 1934, Box 169, CEM Papers; Delano untitled memorandum, January 19, 1935, attached to memorandum to the president, February 1, 1935, General, PPF 1820, FDRL; Delano, "Our Nation's Balance Sheet," December 26, 1935, Speeches and Writings, FAD Papers.

95. Delano to Harold Osgood, November 27, 1927, Banking Reform, Gold Standard, Economics Folder, FAD Papers.

3. Charles E. Merriam

1. See "Research in Political Behavior," *American Political Science Review* 46 (1952): 1004–5, and Dahl, "The Behavioral Approach in Political Science." Merriam placed his own work in perspective toward the end of his life in "Political Science in the United States."

2. For evaluations of Merriam's work by colleagues and students, see Leonard D. White, preface to *The Future of Government in the United States,* vi-vii; Truman, "The Impact on Political Science of the Revolution in the Behavioral Sciences"; Gabriel A. Almond, "Political Theory and Political Science," *American Political Science Review* 60 (1966): 869–79; Almond, "The Return to the State." Merriam's critics can be sampled in Easton, *The Political System,* 279–80, 292, 297–300; Somit and Tannenhaus, *The Development of Political Science,* 87–89, 109–28, 183–84; and the most incisive critique, Crick, *The American Science of Politics,* 108–9, 133–55, 176, 181.

3. Crick, *The American Science of Politics,* 139.

4. For the best biography of Merriam, see Karl, *Charles E. Merriam and the Study of Politics.* Richard Gordon Lindblad provides a good intellectual history of Merriam in "Progressive Politics and Social Change." Tang Tsou presents an interesting thesis concerning Merriam's methodological innovations in "A Study of the Development of the Scientific Approach in Political Studies in the United States," summarized in his "Fact and Value in Charles E. Merriam." For a sampling of evaluations over time, see those of a contemporary political scientist, Lindsay Rogers, "Notes on 'Political Science,'" *Political Science Quarterly* 79 (1964): 209–32; a college student, Eilene Marie Galloway, "Charles Edward Merriam, Jr."; and a Merriam student, Avery Leiserson, "Charles Merriam, Max Weber, and the Search for a Synthesis in Political Science." For the implication of Merriam as a manager of social science, see Karl, *Executive Reorganization and Reform in the New Deal,* chap. 2; Karl, "Merriam, Charles E.," *International Encyclopedia of the Social Sciences,* ed. David L. Sills (New York, 1968), 10:254–60; and Karl, "Charles Merriam Memorial Lecture." Karl extends the idea brilliantly in "The Power of Intellect and the Politics of Ideas" and "Philanthropy, Policy Planning, and the Bureaucratization of the Democratic Ideal." Other scholars hint at the idea in Orlans, "The Advocacy of Social Science in Europe and America," and Kuklick, "The Organization of Social Science in the United States."

Recognition of Merriam's work is noted in obituaries in *New York Times,* January 9, 1953, 29; *School and Society* 77 (January 17, 1953): 47; "The Merriam Political Legacy," *National Municipal Review* 42 (February 1953): 64, 66–67; *Public Management* 35 (February 1953): 26; *American Historical Review* 58 (1953): 793; *American Political Science Review* 47 (1953): 290–91; and *Social Service Review* 27 (1953): 218–19. Nicknames were found in correspondence in CEM Papers.

5. Unpublished shorter drafts of the autobiography, correspondence regarding publication, and tentative plans for a scholarly biography that never saw completion are in Boxes 2–3, CEM Papers. The published essay is in "The Education of Charles E. Merriam," in *The Future of Government in the United States,* ed. White, 1–24. Bibliographies of Merriam's published works are in ibid., 269–74, and Folder 1, Box 274, CEM Papers.

6. Karl, *Charles E. Merriam,* 1–21. The quotation is on p. 3.

7. Ibid., 7.

8. "Merriam: California and Lenox" and "Merriam's Early Experience as a Graduate Student of Political Science," fragments of typescript of "The Education of Charles E. Merriam," Box 3, CEM Papers.

9. Vesey, *The Emergence of the American University;* Furner, *Advocacy and Objectivity;* Bledstein, *The Culture of Professionalism;* Dorothy Ross, "The Development of the Social Sciences," in *The Organization of Knowledge in Modern America,* ed. Oleson and Voss, 107–38; Ross, *The Origins of American Social Science.* The quotation is from "Merriam's Early Experience as a Graduate Student of Political Science."

10. Herbst, *The German Historical School in American Scholarship,* esp. 99–128; Somit and Tannehaus, *The Development of Political Science,* 1–48; Hoxie et al., *A History of the Faculty of Political Science at Columbia University,* 3–75, 207–49, 256–83; "Merriam's Early Experience as a Graduate Student of Political Science."

11. "The Education of Charles E. Merriam"; Karl, *Charles E. Merriam,* 31–41; Lindblad, "Progressive Politics and Social Change," 14–24; "Merriam's Early Experience as a Graduate Student of Political Science."

12. J. G. Delano Roulhac Hamilton, introduction to *Truth in History and Other Essays,* by William A. Dunning; Merriam's memorial notice on Dunning in *American Political Science Review* 16 (1922): 692–94; Merriam to Howard W. Odum, May 11, 1925, Box 37, CEM Papers; Merriam, "Masters of Social Science: William Archibald Dunning," *Social Forces* 5 (September 1926): 1–8, later reprinted in *American Masters of Social Science,* ed. Odum, 131–45.

13. William R. Shepherd, "John William Burgess," in *American Masters of Social Science,* ed. Odum, 23.

14. Burgess, "Political Science and History," 407–8.

15. Burgess, *Reminiscences of an American Scholar* (New York, 1934); B. Brown, *American Conservatives,* 103–67; Loewenberg, "John William Burgess, the Scientific Method, and the Hegelian Philosophy of History"; Merriam, *American Political Ideas,* 379–81.

16. Goodnow, *Politics and Administration,* 20, 36–37; Merriam, *American Political Ideas,* 141, 162, 179, 222, 291, 389–92; "Merriam's Early Experience as a Graduate Student of Political Science"; Merriam's typescript review of John D. Lewis, *The Genossenschaft Theory of Otto von Gierke* (Madison, Wis., 1935), Box 273, and "Merriam on the Fringes of Administration," Box 3, CEM Papers; Merriam, *History of the Theory of Sovereignty Since Rousseau.*

17. M. White, *Social Thought in America,* 12, 3–46.

18. Storr, *Harper's University;* Karl, *Charles E. Merriam,* 39–60; Diner, *A City and Its Universities,* 3–75.

19. Merriam, *A History of American Political Theories,* esp. 305–33, and "Education of Charles E. Merriam."

20. "Merriam on the Fringes of Administration" and "Starting to Study Politics and Life—Theory and Practice," Box 3, CEM Papers; Merriam, "State Central Committees: A Study of Party Organization," *Political Science Quarterly* 19 (1904): 224–33; Merriam, "The Chicago Primary System," *Publications of the Michigan Political Science Association* 6 (March 1905): 118–24; Merriam, *Primary Elections: A Study of the History and Tendencies of Primary Election Legislation* (Chicago, 1908).

21. "An Intimate View of Urban Politics," unpublished version, Box 94, CEM Papers. Merriam later published a revised version, *Chicago: A More Intimate View of Urban Politics,* which summarized his observer-participant experiences in Chicago city politics.

22. Samuel Haber provides insight into the uses of efficiency ideology in his *Efficiency and Uplift,* esp. 51–116; Martin J. Schiesl confirms these insights for municipal reform in his *Politics of Efficiency,* esp. 112–23 on the New York Bureau of Municipal Research, as does Tropea, "Rational Capitalism and Municipal Government." Samuel P. Hays discusses the meaning of reform for the new middle class in his pioneering article "The Politics of Reform in Municipal Government in the Progressive Era." Diner, *A City and Its Universities,* pp. 33–35, 70–71, 89, 112, 128–29, 154–75, 180–81, provides detailed confirmation of Hays's view in emphasizing Merriam's role in Chicago.

23. Diner, *A City and Its Universities,* 155, 160–61.

24. Merriam, "Home Rule in Chicago's New Charter," *Voter* (Chicago), July 1907, 24–31; Merriam, "Chicago Charter Convention," *American Political Science Review* 2 (November 1907): 1–14; Flanagan, "Charter Reform in Chicago"; and Flanagan, *Charter Reform in Chicago.*

25. *Report of an Investigation of the Municipal Revenues of Chicago* (Chicago, 1906); Merriam, "City Planning in Chicago," typescript of address at City Planning Conference, Kansas City, May 9, 1917, Box 71, and Merriam to Graham Taylor, March 30, 1908, Box

13, CEM Papers. Karl, *Charles E. Merriam,* 61–83, gives the best account of Merriam's aldermanic tenure.

26. Chicago Harbor Commission, *Report to the Mayor and Aldermen of the City of Chicago* (Chicago, 1909); untitled and unsigned memo on Chicago Commission on City Expenditures, Folder 2, Box 82, CEM Papers; Merriam, "Work and Accomplishments of Chicago Commission on City Expenditures"; Merriam, "Investigations as a Means of Securing Administrative Efficiency"; Chicago Waste Commission, *Report* (Chicago, 1914); Merriam, "Budget Making in Chicago"; Chicago City Council Committee on Crime, *Report* (Chicago, 1915); Merriam, "Findings and Recommendations of the Chicago Council Committee on Crime."

27. Merriam's secretary to H. L. P., March 14, 1911, Folder 13, Box 24, CEM Papers; [Merriam], "'The People's Primaries' in Chicago," *Review of Reviews* 43 (1911): 466–68; Ickes, *The Autobiography of a Curmudgeon,* chap. 7; Ickes, "Chicago Mayoralty Campaign of 1911," unpublished memoir, Speeches and Writings File, Harold L. Ickes Papers; *Chicago Daily Tribune,* April 5, 1911; and McCarthy, "Prelude to Armageddon."

28. "Starting to Study Politics and Life—Theory and Practice Part II (The Bull Moose Campaign)," Box 3, CEM Papers; "Address of Charles E. Merriam Temporary Chairman State Convention—Progressive Party, August 3, 1912," typescript and other material, Box 73, CEM Papers; Merriam, "The Case for Home Rule," *Annals* 57 (January 1915): 170–74.

29. Diner, *A City and Its Universities,* 127–29; Merriam, "President Taft and President Hoover," Walgreen Lecture, University of Chicago, April 20, 1948, Folder 5, Box 4, Walgreen Foundation Records, University of Chicago Library; fragment of autobiography in Box 3, CEM Papers; *Chicago Tribune,* June 8–9, 1910.

30. *Chicago Tribune,* June 8, 1910, and Chicago Bureau of Public Efficiency, *Annual Reports* (Chicago, 1909–14).

31. Typescript of a dialogue between Charles and Robert Merriam [1953?], Box 275, CEM Papers.

32. Merriam, "City Planning in Chicago," 1. Merriam discussed similar ideas elsewhere in draft of Merriam to editor of *Chicago Tribune,* March 18, 1917, Box 14, CEM Papers; Diner, *A City and Its Universities,* 154; Merriam, "Outlook for Social Politics in the United States," *American Journal of Sociology* 18 (1913): 676–88; Merriam, "The City as a Problem in Government," in *Readings in Municipal Government,* ed. Chester C. Maxey (Garden City, N.Y., 1924), 1–8; Merriam, "Memoranda on Constitutional Convention," delivered before Illinois State Bar Association, June 2, 1917, typescript, Box 71, CEM Papers; Merriam, "Human Nature and Science in City Government."

33. Merriam, "City Planning in Chicago," 9–10.

34. Ibid.

35. Lindblad, "Progressive Politics and Social Change," 77.

36. Vaughn, *Holding Fast the Inner Lines;* Mock and Larson, *Words That Won the War,* 286–92; John R. Hearley, "Final Report—Rome Office Activities," Folder 5, Box 10, CEM Papers; Merriam, "American Publicity in Italy"; Merriam communication to CPI, October 2, 1918, Folder 5, Box 10, CEM Papers; "The Reminiscences of H. W. Schneider (1976)," 100 ff., COHC. One other source mentioned the alleged use of Rockefeller Foundation money but has been altered to delete this section.

37. "Merriam on the Fringes of Administration," Box 3, CEM Papers.

38. Merriam, *American Political Ideas.*

39. Ibid., 308–9.

40. Merriam, *The American Party System,* 382, 420.

41. Ibid. and Merriam, "Recent Tendencies in Political Thought," in *A History of Political Theories: Recent Times,* ed. Merriam and Harry Elmer Barnes (New York, 1924), 1–45.

42. Merriam, *Four American Party Leaders,* xi–xii.

43. Merriam, "The Present State of the Study of Politics," *American Political Science Review* 15 (1921): 173–85, and "Progress in Political Research," ibid. 20 (1926): 1–13, both reprinted in Merriam, *New Aspects of Politics.*

44. Merriam, *New Aspects of Politics,* 66.

45. Ibid., 66–67.

46. Ibid., 69, 71, 101, 246, 293, 314–15.

47. Ibid., 68–69.

48. Ibid., 83.

49. Karl, *Charles E. Merriam,* 140–68.

50. Correspondence in Folder 16, Box 17, Presidents' Papers, 1889–1925, University of Chicago Library; Merriam to President Max Mason, February 18, 1927, Folder 8, Box 107, Presidents' Papers, ca. 1925–1945, University of Chicago Library; drafts of memos on proposed Institute of Government, Box 122, CEM Papers.

51. Merriam, "The Next Step in the Organization of Municipal Research," *National Municipal Review* 11 (1922): 274–81; Merriam, "The Need for Business Executives in City Government," *City Manager Magazine* 8 (1926): 112–17; Merriam, "The Police, Crime, and Politics," *Annals* 146 (November 1929): 115–20; Merriam, *Chicago.* On the LCRC, see *Chicago: An Experiment in Social Science Research,* ed. T. V. Smith and Leonard D. White (Chicago, 1929); *Eleven Twenty-Six: A Decade of Social Science Research,* ed. Louis Wirth (Chicago, 1940); Bulmer, "The Early Institutional Establishment of Social Scientific Research"; Robert E. L. Faris, *Chicago Sociology: 1920–1932* (Chicago, 1970); and Bulmer, *The Chicago School of Sociology.*

52. Merriam and Gosnell's *Non-Voting* served as the initial volume in the LCRC's social science studies series, indicating that Merriam truly had caught up to Burgess's rank. On the PACH, see C. Herman Pritchett, "1313: An Experiment in Propinquity," typescript, Box 159, CEM Papers. "1313" was the successor to the PACH, which included the American Legislators' Association, the American Public Works Association, the Public Administration Service, the American Municipal Association, the International City Managers Association, the Municipal Finance Officers Association, the National Association of Housing, the National Municipal League, the Council of State Governments, and the PACH. Louis Brownlow headed the PACH in its early years, for which see his *Passion for Anonymity,* esp. 249–74.

53. Merriam, "The Present State of the Study of Politics," "Political Research," *American Political Science Review* 16 (1922): 315–21, and "The Significance of Psychology for the Study of Politics," ibid. 18 (1924): 469–88.

54. Merriam, Crane, Fairlie, and King, "Progress Report of the Committee on Political Research"; "Reports of the National Conference on the Science of Politics," *American Political Science Review* 18 (1924): 119–66; 19 (1925): 104–62; 20 (1926): 124–70; and Karl, *Charles E. Merriam,* 118–22, which discusses tensions within the committee.

55. Merriam, "The Present State of Politics in the United States," *American Review* 1 (1923): 269–76; Merriam, "Progress in Political Research," *American Political Science Review* 20 (1926): 1–13; John C. to Charles E. Merriam, March 20, 1926, Box 35, CEM Papers.

56. Merriam-Ruml correspondence, Box 39, CEM Papers.

57. Merriam, *The Making of Citizens.*

58. *Annual Report* of the American Historical Association (1925–29); Merriam, *Civic Education in the United States.* Karl, *Charles E. Merriam,* 186–200, gives an insightful view of differences among Merriam, Beard, and Counts. For philanthropic support, see University of Chicago—Civic Education 1927–33 Folder, Box 70, Subseries 6, Series III, LSRM.

59. Merriam to Ruml, June 5, 1923, Box 64, Subseries 6, Series III, LSRM, and "The Education of Charles E. Merriam," 10–11.

60. Merriam et al., "Progress Report of the Committee on Political Research"; Merriam, "News and Notes: Annual Report of the Social Science Research Council," *American Political Science Review* 20 (1926): 185–89; "News and Notes," *American Journal of Sociology* 28 (January 1923): 473–75 and 30 (July 1924): 90–92; Wesley Clair Mitchell and Horace Secrist, "Report of the Representatives of the American Economic Association on the Social Science Research Council," *American Economic Review* 14 supp. (March 1924): 174–76; Kuhlman, "The Social Science Research Council."

61. Merriam to Ruml, November 1 and 16, 1923, January 18 and 30 and March 24, 1924, and Yerkes to Merriam February 12, 1924, Box 64, Subseries 6, Series III, LSRM; Merriam-Yerkes correspondence from August 1921 to April 1924, Box 43, CEM Papers; John and Charles Merriam correspondence from November 1923 to March 1924, Box 194, John C. Merriam Papers; John C. Burnham, "Yerkes, Robert Mearns," *Dictionary of Scientific Biography,* ed. Charles Coulston Gillespie (New York, 1976), 14:549–51.

62. Merriam to Ruml, June 5, 1923, Edmund E. Day to Frank B. Stubbs, June 6, 1924, Arnold B. Hall to Ruml, November 11, 1924, Box 64, Subseries 6, Series III, LSRM; Ruml memo for Fosdick, July 16, 1923, Box 3, Series II, LSRM; Edmund E. Day for SSRC, Application for Funds, LSRM Docket, November 22, 1927, Box 4, Series I, LSRM.

63. Plans for initial financing were discussed in Merriam to Dr. Frederick P. Keppel, December 8, 1925, attached to Charles to John Merriam, December 9, 1925, Box 194, John C. Merriam Papers. The 1927 appropriations are in LSRM Docket, November 22, 1927. The extent of LSRM funding for social science research at the University of Chicago and the SSRC is noted in Social Sciences 1925–28 Folder, Box 63, University of Chicago, 1923–31 Folder, Box 70, University of Chicago—Social Science 1927–33 Folder, Box 72, all in Subseries 6, Series III, LSRM; *Final Report of the LSRM* (New York, 1933), 10–16. For the growing friendship between Merriam and Ruml, see correspondence in Box 3, Ruml Papers, and Box 56, Subseries 6, Series III, LSRM.

64. "A Decade of Council History: 1923–1933," typescript attached to Robert T. Crane to Merriam, February 23, 1934, Box 47, CEM Papers.

65. Correspondence between Charles and John Merriam, October 7, 9, and 31, 1926, and November 22, 1927, John C. Merriam Papers, and November 30 and December 3, 1926, December 22 and 25, 1927, Box 35, CEM Papers; Merriam to Dean Edmund E. Day, November 15, 1927, Day to Merriam, November 16, 1927, Merriam to Day November 18, 1927, Box 56, Subseries 6, Series III, LSRM; George E. Vincent to Merriam, March 14, 1929, Folder 3, Box 39, CEM Papers for the Rockefeller Foundation position. On the Rockefeller philanthropies work in Europe during this period, see Craver, "Patronage and the Directions of Research in Economics."

66. On the reorganization of the Rockefeller Foundation, see Coben, "Foundation Officials and Fellowships"; Kohler, "A Policy for the Advancement of Science"; Kohler, *Partners in Science,* 233–62. On Ruml's and Merriam's role in the Spelman Fund of New York, see [Merriam?], "Notes on Development of Spelman Fund Policy and Program," n.d., Folder 8, Box 157, and Merriam memo to Raymond Fosdick [1941?], Box 48, CEM Papers; Pritchett, "1313," 10–30; [Merriam], *Spelman Fund of New York.*

67. Merriam's proposals for such research centers can be found throughout the records of the LSRM and the Spelman Fund of New York. For examples, see drafts of "Memoranda on a Proposed Institute of Government Research," Box 122, CEM Papers; "Memorandum on Facilities for Research and Experiment for Governmental Officials, or Groups of Officials," attached to Merriam to Edmund E. Day, August 13, 1928, Box 56, Subseries 6, Series III, LSRM Papers; and drafts of various memoranda in Merriam, Charles, 1928–39 folder, Box 3, Series V, Spelman Fund of New York Collection.

68. "The Reminiscences of Guy Stanton Ford (1956)," 469–70, COHC. The summary volumes are *Recent Social Trends in the United States,* 2 vols. (New York, 1933). Specialized monographs are noted in the frontispiece. The account in the text is based

partially on Karl, "Presidential Planning and Social Science Research," and the revised version in Karl, *Charles E. Merriam,* 201–25.

69. Merriam to Robert S. Lynd, October 22, 1928, CEM Papers.

70. Albert Barrows to Robert S. Lind [*sic*], March 29, 1928, Lynd to Merriam, October 18, 1928, Lynd to Merriam, October 25, 1928, Box 34, CEM Papers.

71. Merriam to Colonel Arthur Woods, April 1, 1929, and Woods to Merriam, April 6, 1929, Box 43, CEM Papers.

72. Ogburn to Harrison, September 5, 1929, Ogburn to E. E. Day, September 5, 1929, Ogburn to Odum, September 6, 1929, and Odum to Ogburn, September 9, 1929, Ogburn Papers.

73. Hawley, "Herbert Hoover, the Commerce Secretariat, and the Vision of an 'Associative State,'" and essays in Hawley, *Herbert Hoover as Secretary of Commerce.*

74. Odum to Ogburn, September 21, 1929, Ogburn Papers; "MM's [Max Mason's] Visit at White House on President Hoover's Invitation, October 2, 1929" memorandum, Wesley Clair Mitchell to Hoover, October 21, 1929, Strother to Dr. George E. Vincent, October 22, 1929, memorandum to Day from Robert Lynd, October 22, 1929, Vincent to Strother, October 23, 1929, Strother to Vincent, December 9, 1929, Mitchell to Dean E. E. Day, December 19, 1929, all in Folder 3873, Box 326, Series 200S, RF Records; Ogburn to Strother, November 19, 1929, and Odum to Ogburn, November 21, 1929, Ogburn Papers; Committee minutes for December 6 and 14, 1929, Box 268, CEM Papers.

75. Karl, "Presidential Planning and Social Science Research," 388–94, 407–8. Hoover's attitude as presented by Hunt is in Hunt to Ogburn, January 15 and 27, 1930, Ogburn Papers; Hunt's remarks in Committee minutes, June 30, 1930, Folder 8, Box 32, CEM Papers. Merriam's objections are in Merriam to Mitchell, August 15, 1931, Box 36, CEM Papers; Merriam to Hunt, February 4, 1932, Box 32, CEM Papers; Merriam to Ogburn, February 4, 1932, Box 13, and Ogburn to Hunt, February 8, 1932, Box 12, Ogburn Papers; Committee minutes, March 5, 1932, Ogburn Papers. The committee finally accepted Merriam's argument and voted to begin publicity after the 1932 election, for which see committee minutes, March 14, 1932, Folder 8, Box 32, CEM Papers, and Ogburn to Mitchell, March 21, 1932, Ogburn Papers.

76. Merriam, "Government and Society," in *Recent Social Trends,* 2:1489–1541.

77. "A Review of Findings," in *Recent Social Trends,* 1:xi–lxxv, was unsigned as published. Karl, "Presidential Planning and Social Science Research," 394–95 discusses the revisions of Mitchell and Ogburn but remains unaware of Merriam's draft. Close comparison of *Recent Social Trends,* 1:xi, xii–xiii, lxiii, and lxx–lxxiv, and Merriam's "Tentative Draft of Committee Report" submitted June 15, 1932, Folder 3879, Box 326, Series 200S, RF Records, reveals how heavily Mitchell relied on Merriam's draft to revise his own. The following discussion and quotations are from Merriam's draft unless otherwise cited.

78. Merriam, "Tentative Draft of Committee Report," 3–4.

79. Ibid., 7–8.

80. Ibid., 70.

81. Ibid., 72–73.

82. Ibid., 75–78. Cf. *Recent Social Trends,* 1:lxxiii–lxxiv.

83. Merriam, "Tentative Draft of Committee Report," 75–77.

84. Ibid., 77–78.

85. Karl, "Presidential Planning and Social Science Research," 408.

86. John and Charles Merriam kept in close touch with Ickes, as seen in Charles to John Merriam, February 23, 1933, and John to Charles Merriam, March 9 and April 7, 1933, Box 122, John C. Merriam Papers. Merriam's views on Hoover are in his review of *The Challenge to Liberty,* by Hoover, and typescript of Merriam's address to the Univer-

sity of Chicago Planning Club, "Fifty Years of Planning Experience," April 17, 1950, Box 3, CEM Papers. For a perceptive view of Hoover's retreat from the implications of voluntarism, see Murray N. Rothbard, "Herbert Hoover and the Myth of Laissez-Faire," in *A New History of Leviathan,* ed. Radosh and Rothbard, 111–45. Merriam developed his ideas on politics, which led him to sympathize with the New Deal policies in *The Written Constitution and the Unwritten Attitude;* "Reducing Government Costs," *Minnesota Municipalities* 17 (1932): 231–36; "Government and Business"; and *Political Power.*

87. "Merriam on the Fringes of Administration," 18.

4. Wesley Clair Mitchell

1. The quotation is from Berle, Jr., "Wesley Clair Mitchell," 169, 172. Mitchell's reputation is based on his seminal work *Business Cycles* (1913). For evaluations of Mitchell's economic work, see Allen G. Gruchy, "The Quantitative Economics of Wesley C. Mitchell," in his *Modern Economic Thought,* chap. 4; Dorfman, *The Economic Mind in American Civilization,* 3:455–73 and 4:352–77; A. Burns, *Wesley Clair Mitchell;* and Vining, "Economic Theory and Quantitative Research." Mitchell's significance is best measured by the outpouring of professional commentary following his death, as seen in Remarks by William F. Ogburn at the Memorial Service for Wesley Clair Mitchell, Box 34, William F. Ogburn Papers, University of Chicago; Joseph H. Willits, "In Memoriam: Wesley Clair Mitchell, 1874–1948," *Science* 109 (February 25, 1949): 211–12; Kuznets, "Wesley Clair Mitchell, 1874–1948"; Mills, "Memorials: Wesley Clair Mitchell"; Dorfman, "Obituary: Wesley Clair Mitchell"; Hansen, "Wesley Mitchell, Social Scientist and Social Counselor"; and Schumpeter, "Wesley Clair Mitchell." For a bibliography of his life's works, see "List of Publications by Wesley C. Mitchell," in A. Burns, *Wesley Clair Mitchell,* 343–66.

2. Mitchell, "The National Bureau of Economic Research and Its Work," March 1, 1923, and Mitchell to Dr. Joseph H. Willits, December 29, 1941, Wesley C. Mitchell Papers, Columbia University; Mitchell, *The National Bureau's First-Quarter Century;* A. Burns, "Wesley Mitchell and the National Bureau"; "The Reminiscences of Leo Wolman (1961)," 14–16, COHC. Alchon, *The Invisible Hand of Planning,* best captures the significance of the NBER's work in the 1920s.

3. F. Hill, "Wesley Mitchell's Theory of Planning"; Hynning, "Administrative Evolution of National Planning in the United States in the Pre–New Deal Era"; Lyons, *The Uneasy Partnership,* 1–49; Grin, "The Unemployment Conference of 1921"; Runfola, "Herbert C. Hoover as Secretary of Commerce"; Hawley, "Herbert Hoover, the Commerce Secretariat, and the Vision of an 'Associative State'"; Metcalf, "Secretary Hoover and the Emergence of Macroeconomic Management"; Ellis W. Hawley, "Herbert Hoover and Economic Stabilization, 1921–22," in *Herbert Hoover as Secretary of Commerce,* ed. Hawley, 43–77; Alchon, *The Invisible Hand of Planning;* and Grossman, "American Foundations and the Support of Economic Research."

4. The President's Research Committee on Social Trends, *Recent Social Trends in the United States,* and Karl, "Presidential Planning and Social Science Research."

5. On the professionalization of economics in the late nineteenth-century United States, see Dorfman, *Economic Mind in American Civilization,* vol. 3; Church, "Economists as Experts"; Furner, *Advocacy and Objectivity;* A. W. Coats, "The Educational Revolution and the Professionalization of American Economics," in *Breaking the Academic Mould,* ed. Barber, 340–75; Ross, *The Origins of American Social Science.*

6. Biographical information on Mitchell comes primarily from L. Mitchell, *Two Lives,* 3–29, 55–93, and material cited in n. 1. Most of the sources cited in n. 1 emphasize Mitchell's role as an institutional economist specializing in study of business cycles and in developing new statistical series, the inductive method, and focus on historical develop-

ment of economic institutions such as business firms. Mitchell later summarized his early intellectual development in Mitchell to John Maurice Clark, August 9, 1928, cited in Clark, "Wesley C. Mitchell's Contribution to the Theory of the Business Cycles," 675–80.

7. L. Mitchell, *Two Lives,* 94–101, 162–80; Antler, *Lucy Sprague Mitchell;* Dorfman, *The Economic Mind in American Civilization,* 3:455–71; and Church, "Economists as Experts," which focuses specifically on Mitchell's career and the founding of the NBER in 1920 as emblematic of part of the profession by the 1920s.

8. Heaton, *A Scholar in Action,* 98–138; Cuff, *The War Industries Board;* Dorfman, *The Economic Mind in American Civilization,* 3:473–94; Potter, "The Central Bureau of Planning and Statistics"; and Cuff, "Creating Control Systems." Cf. Breen, "Foundations, Statistics, and State-Building."

9. Dorfman, *Economic Mind in American Civilization,* 4:360–77; Alchon, *The Invisible Hand of Planning,* 21–62; Mitchell, "Statistics and Government," reprinted with other articles strongly influenced by Veblenian ideas in Mitchell, *The Backward Art of Spending Money;* Allan G. Gruchy, "Institutional Economics prior to 1939," in his *Contemporary Economic Thought,* chap. 2.; Seckler, *Thorstein Veblen and the Institutionalists,* esp. chap. 8; L. Mitchell, *Two Lives,* 296–305. On the close fit between Mitchell and the NBER, see especially A. Burns, "Wesley Mitchell and the National Bureau," and the astute analysis in Alchon, *The Invisible Hand of Planning.*

10. President's Conference on Unemployment, Committee on Recent Economic Changes, *Recent Economic Changes in the United States,* and President's Research Committee on Social Trends, *Recent Social Trends in the United States.*

11. Cuff, "Herbert Hoover, the Ideology of Voluntarism, and War Organization during the Great War"; Gelfand, *Herbert Hoover;* Hawley, "The Great War and Organizational Innovation"; Hawley, *The Great War and the Search for a Modern Order;* essays in Hawley, *Herbert Hoover as Secretary of Commerce;* Hunt, *Conferences, Committees, Conventions and How to Run Them;* (New York, 1925); and Edward Eyre Hunt, "The Cooperative Committee and Conference System," memorandum to Hoover, December 14, 1926, CP-Hunt.

12. Hawley, "Herbert Hoover, the Commerce Secretariat, and the Vision of an 'Associative State'"; Hawley, "Secretary Hoover and the Bituminous Coal Problem"; J. Johnson, *The Politics of Soft Coal;* special issue on Hoover's agricultural policies in *Agricultural History* 51 (April 1977); Phillip T. Rosen, *The Modern Stentors* (Westport, Conn., 1980); Ellis W. Hawley, "Three Facets of Hooverian Associationalism: Lumber, Aviation, and Movies, 1921–1930," in *Regulation in Perspective,* ed. McCraw, 95–123; William G. Robbins, "Voluntary Cooperation vs. Regulatory Paternalism: The Lumber Trade in the 1920s," *Business History Review* 56 (1982): 358–79; and Clements, "Herbert Hoover and Conservation"; essays in Krog and Tanner, *Herbert Hoover and the Republican Era;* Hamilton, *From New Day to New Deal.*

13. On the continuing tension between nineteenth-century liberal republican values and the twentieth-century state, see the works of Ellis W. Hawley cited above; Karl, *The Uneasy State;* (Chicago, 1983); A. Brinkley, "Prosperity, Depression, and War"; Dawley, *Struggles for Justice.*

14. Paxson, *American Democracy and the World War;* Cuff, *The War Industries Board;* Cuff, "We Band of Brothers"; Cuff, "Herbert Hoover, the Ideology of Voluntarism, and War Organization during the Great War"; Kennedy, *Over Here,* esp. chaps. 2 and 6; Conner, *The National War Labor Board;* McCartin, *Labor's Great War;* Hawley, "The Great War and Organizational Innovation"; Ferrell, *Woodrow Wilson and World War I;* Schaffer, *America in the Great War;* and Schwartz, *The New Dealers,* 1–56.

15. Paxson, "The Great Demobilization"; Himmelberg, "Business, Antitrust Policy, and the Industrial Board of the Department of Commerce"; Noggle, *Into the Twenties;* Cuff, "Harry Garfield, the Fuel Administration, and the Search for a Cooperative Order

during World War I." For a contemporary view, see Elisha M. Friedman, *America and the New Era.*

16. U.S. Congress, Senate, Select Committee on Reconstruction and Production, *Reconstruction and Production, Hearings Pursuant to S. Res. 350,* 66th Cong., 2d sess., 1920, and *Reconstruction and Production,* S. Rept. No. 829 Pursuant to S. Res. 350, 66th Cong., 3d sess., 1921; Howenstine, "Public Works Program After World War I"; Lloyd, *Aggressive Introvert,* 59–72, 123–42; American Engineering Council, Committee on Elimination of Waste in Industry, Federated American Engineering Societies, *Waste in Industry* (New York, 1921); Hawley, "Herbert Hoover, the Commerce Secretariat, and the Vision of an 'Associative State'"; and Hawley, "Herbert Hoover and Economic Stabilization," for the reorganization of the Department of Commerce; and Brownlee, *Dynamics of Ascent,* chap. 14, for a good analysis of New Era capitalism.

17. Paul A. Samuelson and Everett E. Hagen, *After the War—1918–1920* (Washington, D.C., 1943); Soule, *Prosperity Decade,* 81–106; Hicks, *Rehearsal for Disaster;* Pilgrim, "The Upper Turning Point of 1920"; Wesley C. Mitchell's address to the American Economic Association, Pittsburgh, December 21, 1921, "The Crisis of 1920 and the Problem of Controlling Business Cycles." Statistics are from Pilgrim, "The Upper Turning Point of 1920," 276, and *Historical Statistics of the United States: Colonial Times to 1970* (Washington, D.C., 1975), part 1, Series D, 85–86, 135.

18. *The Memoirs of Herbert Hoover,* 2:44.

19. *Report of the President's Conference on Unemployment,* 15–16, and Sautter, *Three Cheers for the Unemployed,* 141–47.

20. Hoover telegram to J. H. Defrees, J. E. Edgerton, Ernest T. Trigg, T. DeWitt Cuyler, August 27, 1921, UF–Conference Members Suggested.

21. *Report of the President's Conference on Unemployment,* 7–14; chairman, Advisory Committee, to secretary of commerce, September 8, 1921, UF–Advisory Committee-Organization, Lists; and material in UF–Conference-Members and –Members Suggested; Brody, *Labor in Crisis,* 105, 115–28; Hurvitz, "Ideology and Industrial Conflict"; Wilson to Hoover, November 19, 1919, CP-Industrial Conference of March 6, 1920; Best, "President Wilson's Second Industrial Conference." Cf. Charles E. Harvey, "John D. Rockefeller, Jr., Herbert Hoover, and President Wilson's Industrial Conferences of 1919–1920," in *Voluntarism, Planning, and the State: The American Planning Experience, 1914–1946,* ed. Brown and Reagan, 25–46; Gerber, "Corporatism in Comparative Perspective"; and McCartin, *Labor's Great War,* 191–94.

22. Hoover to Gay, August 29, 1921, UF-Edwin F. Gay; Steuart to various economists, September 3, 1921, UF–Conference-Members; *Memoirs of Herbert Hoover,* 2:44; Edgar Rickard to C. C. Stetson, September 2, 1921, and lists for conference members dated September 2 and 3, 1921, UF–Conference-Members Suggested Misc.

23. "Advance Summary of Report of Economic Advisory Committee to the President's Unemployment Conference," September 22, 1921, UF–Advisory Committee Reports; Advisory Committee Reports and "Report of the Economic Advisory Committee to the Unemployment Conference," September 26, 1921, UF–Conference-Plans and Programs; *Report of the President's Conference on Unemployment,* 47–58, 66–69, 99–106, 161–67.

24. *Memoirs of Herbert Hoover,* 2:44.

25. "Advance Summary of Report of Economic Advisory Committee," 1–2.

26. Ibid.

27. *Report of the President's Conference on Unemployment* and Otto T. Mallery, "Draft Report of Sub-Committee No. 3 of the Advisory Committee to the Unemployment Conference, On Public Works," UF–Advisory Committee Reports. Mallery had served on the Industrial Board of Pennsylvania during the Great War, which developed a public works program that served as a model for later programs. Mallery was chairman of

the Public Works Committee at the Unemployment Conference, drafted several public works bills stemming from the work of the conference, and became the leading advocate of advance public works planning throughout the 1920s. See materials in UF–Mallery; Howenstine, "Public Works Policy in the Twenties"; Sautter, "North American Labor Agencies before World War I"; Sautter, "Unemployment and Government"; Sautter, "Government and Unemployment"; and Sautter, *Three Cheers for the Unemployed.*

28. Arthur Woods, "Putting the Servicemen Back to Work," *World's Work* 38 (August 1919): 396–99, and Howenstine, "Lessons of World War I."

29. *Report of the President's Conference on Unemployment,* 60–63; Woods to Mary Van Kleeck, November 9, 1921, UF–Mary Van Kleeck; Minutes of Woods' Committee meetings in UF–Public Works-Misc.; Colonel Arthur Woods, "Unemployment and You," typescript marked "for Sat. Evening Post," UF–Publicity-1922; Woods, "Unemployment Emergency," *North American Review* 215 (April 1922): 449–58; and materials in UF–Arthur Woods.

30. For Hoover aides' reactions, see Hunt memo to Hoover, May 22, 1923, Hunt draft of letter to John M. Glenn, May 22, 1923, and [R. S. Emmet] memo to Hunt, May 28, 1923, all in UF–Civic and Emergency Relief Commissions 1921–1923. On the problems in New York, Chicago, and Boston, see the appropriate sections in UF–Cities.

31. Van Kleeck to Woods, December 1 and 6, 1921, UF–Van Kleeck.

32. P. Klein, *The Burden of Unemployment.* Hoover admitted indirectly the limitations of the voluntary relief efforts in New York and Chicago in Hoover to the president, May 20, 1922, UF–1922, although that perspective changed by the time Hoover wrote about it in *Memoirs of Herbert Hoover,* 2:46.

33. Hoover to Hunt, June 5, 1922, UF.

34. Edward Eyre Hunt, "Action: An Account of the Measures That Have Arisen out of the President's Conference on Unemployment," *Survey,* December 17, 1921, 427–29; newspaper clippings in UF–Unemployment Facts; and Major R. L. Foster, "Publicity Report: The President's Conference on Unemployment," typescript dated May 8, 1922, UF–Publicity Report 1922; Hoover to the president, May 20, 1922, UF. For Hoover's use of public relations techniques throughout this period, see Lloyd, *Aggressive Introvert.*

35. On Hoover's piecemeal planning efforts, see references in n. 12; Himmelberg, *The Origins of the National Recovery Administration;* and Himmelberg, "Government and Business"; cf. Reich, *The Next American Frontier,* chap. 5.

36. Economic Advisory Committee resolution, September [15–19?] 1921, UF–Advisory Committee-Organization, Lists; E. E. Hunt to Mortimer Fleishhacker, October 29, 1921, and resolutions in UF–Standing Committee, 1921; Hoover to James M. Lee, November 3, 1921, UF–Advisory Committee-Corres.; Minutes of Standing Committee, November 7, 1921, UF–Business Cycles-1921. Cf. Vaughn Davis Bornet, "Herbert Hoover's Planning for Unemployment and Old Age Insurance Coverage, 1921 to 1933," in *The Quest for Security,* ed. John N. Schacht (Iowa City, Iowa, 1982), 35–71, and Nelson, *Unemployment Insurance.*

37. The description of the Hooverian committee and conference system in the text is drawn as a composite picture based upon study of the specialized investigations discussed below in the text. On the connections between organized philanthropy, social science research, and policy analysis in this period, see Lyons, *The Uneasy Partnership,* 1–49; articles by Ellis Hawley and Kim McQuaid in special issue on "corporate liberalism" in *Business History Review* 52 (Autumn 1978); Karl and Katz, "The American Private Philanthropic Foundations and the Public Sphere"; Grossman, "American Foundations and the Support of Economic Research"; Craver, "Patronage and the Directions of Research in Economics."

38. Lloyd, *Aggressive Introvert,* 61–62; Hunt files in Pre-Commerce Papers, Hoover Papers; F. M. Feiker to James H. McGraw, March 14, 1925, attached to Feiker to Hunt,

March 25, 1925, E. E. Hunt Collection, Hoover Library; and Hunt's drafts of articles in UF-Hunt. Biographical detail on Hunt can be found in the Hunt Collection, HHPL.

39. "Seasons and Business Cycles as Causes of Unemployment," UF–Advisory Committee Reports; "Unemployment and Business Cycles: Recommendation on Need for Cycle Study," memo marked "confidential—for conference members only," UF–Business Cycles-1921; Hunt to Hoover, October 21, 1921, UF–Business Cycles; and Hoover to Joseph Defrees, November 5, 1921, and Hunt to W. J. Myers, October 26, 1921, UF for the model from Waste in Industry.

40. Lloyd, *Aggressive Introvert,* 12, 53; Julius Barnes to Rickard, October 12, 1921; Rickard to Barry Smith, October 14, 1921; Rickard to R. A. Franks, October 14, 1921; Rickard to Christian Herter, November 16, 1921; Rickard to John M. Glenn, November 16, 1921; Hunt to Henry S. Pritchett, December 21, 1921; all in UF. For the Carnegie Corporation grant, see Pritchett to Hoover, February 14, 1922, UF–National Bureau of Economic Research.

41. Hoover to Rickard, November 14, 1921, UF.

42. Hoover to Rickard, November 18, 1921; Hunt to Defrees, Van Kleeck, and Woll, November 5, 1921; and Hoover to Defrees, November 5, 1921, all in UF. For background on Young, see McQuaid, "Young, Swope, and General Electric's 'New Capitalism'"; McQuaid, "Corporate Liberalism in the American Business Community"; Case and Case, *Owen D. Young and American Enterprise,*esp. 244, 266–68. On the concern for practical use, see Hunt to Young, February 13, 1922, UF–Business Cycles.

43. Mitchell to Hunt, October 20, 1921; Hunt to Hoover, October 21, 1921; Gay to Hoover, October 25, 1921; Hunt, "Plan of Follow-Up of Work of the President's Conference on Unemployment," November 2, 1921, all in UF–Business Cycles; Gay to Hoover, October 22, 1921, UF-NBER; Gay to Hunt, October 21, 1921, Hunt to Gay, October 27, 1921, Hunt memo to Hoover, February 13, 1922, all in UF; minutes of committee meetings and correspondence in UF-NBER for NBER-committee tensions; and for the final recommendations, see President's Conference on Unemployment, Committee on Business Cycles and Unemployment, *Business Cycles and Unemployment*.

44. Dorfman, *Economic Mind,* 4:367–68.

45. Donald J. Murphy, "John B. Andrews, the American Association for Labor Legislation, and Unemployment Reform, 1914–1929," in *Voluntarism, Planning, and the State,* ed. Brown and Reagan, 1–23.

46. Andrews to Hunt, July 26, 1922, UF-NBER.

47. Darwin J. Meserole to Hunt, April 24, 1923, UF–Business Cycles Report-Comments.

48. Feiker to Hunt, May 4, 1922; UF–Feiker; Hunt, "How Industry Can Avoid Summer Depression," *Printer's Ink,* May 18, 1922; Tead to Hunt, June 30, 1922, and committee resolution of July 18, 1922, UF–Business Cycle-Report-Publication of; committee minutes of meeting, July 18, 1922, UF–Business Cycles-1923-May-November; Hunt to Hoover, August 18, and publicity release dated April 2, 1923, UF; and Hunt, "The Long Look Ahead," *Survey,* July 1, 1923, 400–401.

49. Mitchell to Hunt, September 17, 1922, UF-Mitchell.

50. Hoover to Young, May 17, 1923, UF–Business Cycles.

51. Hunt to Hoover, December 29, 1926, UF.

52. Hunt to Mitchell, November 7, 1921, Mitchell to Hunt November 10, 1921, and attached memo to Hoover, all in UF-Mitchell; Hunt to General R. C. Marshall, December 5, 1921, UF-Marshall; Hunt to Edwin F. Gay, January 25, 1922, and Gay to Hunt, February 1, 1922, UF-Gay; Hunt to Pritchett, May 17, 1923, and Pritchett to Hoover, May 22, 1923, UF–Financing and Expenses of Conference.

53. Hoover to Trigg, May 28, 1923, CP–Seasonal Industries Investigation; and U.S.

Department of Commerce, Elimination of Waste Series, *Seasonal Operation in the Construction Industries* (Washington, D.C., 1924), v.

54. Hunt to Mitchell, May 7, 1923, and Mitchell to Hunt, May 8, 1923, UF–Mitchell; Hoover to Brookings, May 9, 1923, UF–Seasonal Stabilization.

55. Material in UF–Committee on Seasonal Operation in the Construction Industries-1923–1924, and Hoover to H. S. Pritchett, June 12, 1923, UF-Financing and Expenses of Conference.

56. Ernest T. Trigg to Hoover, March 6, 1924, CP–Seasonal Industries Investigation; *Seasonal Operation in the Construction Industries—Report and Recommendations of a Committee of the President's Conference on Unemployment* (New York, 1924); and U.S. Department of Commerce, Elimination of Waste Series, *Seasonal Operation*.

57. Gries to Hoover, October 16, 1924, UF–Seasonal Stabilization; Hoover speech before Associated General Contractors of America, January 12, 1925, Speech File, Hoover Library; Gries to Hoover, November 14, 1925, CP–Seasonal Industries Investigation; materials in UF-Mallery, UF–Public Works-Bills-1921–1923, and UF–Prosperity Reserve; Sautter, *Three Cheers for the Unemployed,* 197–202.

58. Hunt to Mitchell, October 26, 1923, UF–Mitchell; Hoover to Woods, September 26, 1924, CP–Rockefeller Foundation; Hunt, "Bases of Agreement in Industrial Disputes," memo, October 8, 1924, and Hunt to Willits, October 26, 1924, CP–Hunt; Hunt to Hoover, October 28, 1924, and Hoover to Woods, October 28, 1924, UF–Bases of Agreement in Industrial Disputes; Hunt to Ruml, October 31, 1924, CP–Hunt; Hoover to Woods, January 14, 1925, Hunt memo to Hoover, February 14, 1925, and Hunt memo to Hoover, May 14, 1926, CP–Rockefeller Foundation.

59. Hunt memo to Hoover, February 14, 1925, CP–Rockefeller Foundation.

60. "Industry's New Doctors," *New York Times,* June 4, 1922; Hoover to President Harding, March 17, 1923, copy from holdings in the Franklin D. Roosevelt Library, Hyde Park, N.Y., in the Franklin D. Roosevelt Collection, HHPL; "Meeting of the Board of Governors of the American Construction Council," May 16, 1923, American Construction Council file, Record Group 14, National Archives, Washington, D.C., copy in ibid.; Hoover to Roosevelt, June 12, 1923, from holdings in the Roosevelt Library, copy in Roosevelt Collection, Hoover Library.

61. Himmelberg, *Origins of the National Recovery Administration,* esp. 75–109.

62. Hunt, *Conferences, Committees, Conventions and How to Run Them;* Hunt, "Stabilizing Employment—the National Point of View," address to the Young Men's Christian Association, August 31, 1923, at Silver Bay Conference in Reprint File, HHPL; Hunt, "Conferences," mimeographed typescript dated December 1924, CP–Conferences; Hunt, "The Cooperative Committee and Conference System," memorandum to Hoover, December 14, 1926, CP–Hunt; "Planning," address before North Carolina Conference for Social Service, Raleigh, N. C., February 10, 1927, and Hunt, "Economic Investigations," May 19, 1927, memorandum for use of Sir Arthur Salter attached to memorandum to Mrs. Goodwin, June 17, 1927, Hunt Collection; Hunt, "Notes on Economic and Social Surveys"; Mitchell, *Business Cycles: The Problem and Its Setting,* as discussed in Dorfman, *Economic Mind,* 4:369–72.

63. The summary volumes were *Recent Economic Changes in the United States* and *Recent Social Trends in the United States*.

64. Hoover memo to Dr. Gries et al., March 17, 1927, UF.

65. *The Memoirs of Herbert Hoover,* 2:176, and 3:14–15; Hunt memo to Hoover, September 15, 1927, and Hoover to F. P. Keppel, October 26, 1927, UF–Business Cycles; Hoover to Henry M. Robinson, January 7, 1928, CP; Hunt memo to Hoover, December 17, 1927, Hoover to Woods, December 23, 1927, Ruml telegram to Hoover, December 29, 1927, and Hoover letters of invitation to serve on committee, January 6–7, 1928, all in CP–Committees-Economic Study-1927–1928; and Hunt to Paul Devinat, April 26, 1928, Hunt Collection.

66. Hunt, "America's Increasing Economic Stability," *Current History,* August 1929, 811–16; Hunt, *An Audit of America;* for a perceptive analysis of the committee, see Alchon, *The Invisible Hand of Planning,* 129–51.

67. *Recent Economic Changes,* 2:909–10.

68. Karl, "Presidential Planning and Social Science Research," and Karl, *Charles E. Merriam and the Study of Politics,* 118–39, 201–25.

69. Karl, "Presidential Planning and Social Science Research," emphasizes tensions within the committee.

70. For recent evaluations of New Era capitalism, see Holt, "Who Benefited from the Prosperity of the 1920s?"; Stricker, "Affluence for Whom?"; David Montgomery, "Thinking about American Workers in the 1920s," *International Labor and Working-Class History,* no. 32 (1987): 4–24; Fearon, *War, Prosperity, and Depression,* 18–86; McElvaine, *The Great Depression,* 25–50.

71. Henry S. Dennison, "Our Captains," an unpublished 1936 poem in possession of Elizabeth Dunker of Cambridge, Mass.

72. Mitchell's remarks published in *Authority and the Individual* (Cambridge, Mass., 1937), as cited in Hansen, "Wesley Mitchell, Social Scientist and Social Counselor," 252. Mitchell's ambivalence about national planning and government intervention is seen in Mitchell to Raymond Fosdick, January 18, 1927, and Mitchell to Joseph H. Willits, May 3, 1939, November 21, 1941, and May 22, 1942, all in Mitchell Papers.

5. Henry S. Dennison

1. For the nature and impact of changes in business, see works cited above in chap. 1, nn. 10 and 11. For some of the most challenging of these works, see the many works of Alfred D. Chandler, Jr.; Wiebe, *Businessmen and Reform;* Kolko, *The Triumph of Conservatism;* Weinstein, *The Corporate Ideal in the Liberal State;* Richard L. McCormick, "The Discovery That Business Corrupts Politics: A Reappraisal of the Origins of Progressivism," *American Historical Review* 86 (April 1981): 247–74; Sklar, *The Corporate Reconstruction of American Capitalism;* Cuff, *The War Industries Board;* Berkowitz and McQuaid, *Creating the Welfare State;* essays in Frese and Judd, *Business and Government;* Galambos and Pratt, *The Rise of the Corporate Commonwealth;* and essays in Himmelberg, *Business-Government Cooperation.* For a series of excellent case studies based on extensive research, see McQuaid, "A Response to Industrialism."

2. On the connection between business, research, and education, see Urwick and Brech, *The Making of Scientific Management,* 1:7–19, 165–77; Baritz, *The Servants of Power;* Noble, *America by Design;* R. Smith, *The American Business System and the Theory and Practice of Social Science;*and W. Scott, *Chester I. Barnard and the Guardians of the Managerial State.*

3. Galbraith, *A Life in Our Times,* 61. Biographical information on Dennison appears in Edmund Ware Smith, "H. S. D.—As His Family Knew Him," undated offprint in possession of Elizabeth Dunker, Cambridge, Mass.; J. Dennison, *Henry S. Dennison; Business Week,* December 17, 1949, 6, and February 15, 1964, 54; *New York Times,* March 1, 1952, 15; Urwick and Brech, *The Making of Scientific Management,* 1:112–25; Galbraith, "The Businessman as Philosopher"; *The National Cyclopedia of American Biography* 40 (1955): 52–53; and Duncan and Gullett, "Henry Sturgis Dennison." The best scholarly view is in McQuaid, "Henry S. Dennison and the 'Science' of Industrial Reform."

4. H. S. Dennison, *E. W. Dennison;* Heath, *Dennison Beginnings,* copy in possession of Elizabeth Dunker; Hayes, "History of the Dennison Manufacturing Company"; Carvein, "The Dennison Manufacturing Company."

5. J. Dennison, *Henry S. Dennison,* 8–9; interview with Elizabeth Dunker, Dennison's daughter, December 10, 1979, Cambridge, Mass.; *Harvard University Catalogue* (1899–1900); Henry S. Dennison, "The Harvard Graduate in the Business World," typescript, 1900–1915 file, HSD Papers.

6. J. Dennison, *Henry S. Dennison*, 10, and Vollmers, "Industrial Home Work of the Dennison Manufacturing Company of Framingham, Massachusetts."

7. Hayes, "History of the Dennison Manufacturing Company," 490–91.

8. Dennison memorandum, November 10, 1911, mimeograph copy of Dennison's recollections; Dennison, "1899—the Factory Manager Faces the Music," paper presented at Board of Directors meetings, Distribution Research Association, June 27, 1929, all in HSD Papers.

9. Dennison memorandum on National Cash Register Company, 1900, HSD Papers; for John H. Patterson's work at the National Cash Register Company, see Sealander, *Grand Plans*, esp. 18–42. On welfare capitalism, see Brandes, *American Welfare Capitalism*; Scheinberg, *Employers and Reformers*; David Brody, "The Rise and Decline of Welfare Capitalism," in his *Workers in Industrial America*, 48–81; Gitelman, "Welfare Capitalism Reconsidered."

10. Dennison memorandum on National Cash Register Company.

11. Dennison address to the 27th Street Store, October 30, 1908, Dennison, "Cooperation between the Selling Force and the Factory," talk at Boston Sales Managers' Club, April 27, 1910, Dennison talk to Sales Managers' Club of New York, March 1, 1929, all in HSD Papers.

12. Heath, "History of the Dennison Manufacturing Company," 164.

13. Ibid., 175–78; Dewhurst, "Something Better than Philanthropy"; *Boston Post*, April 9, 1915; Dennison, "The Principles of Industrial Efficiency Applied to the Form of Corporate Organization"; Dennison, "A Cooperative Industrial Experiment"; Forester, "A Promising Venture in Industrial Partnership." On the varied meanings of "industrial democracy" in this period, see Derber, *The American Idea of Industrial Democracy*, 111–95, and McCartin, *Labor's Great War*.

14. Dennison, "Christian Ethics and Business Management," lecture at Central Church, Worcester, Mass., May 9, 1927.

15. Dennison, "The Work of the Employment Department of Dennison Manufacturing Company, Framingham, Massachusetts," address at Boston Conference of Employment Managers, May 10, 1916, and "What the Employment Department Should Be in Industry," address at Employment Managers' Conference, April 2 and 3, 1917, Philadelphia, both in HSD Papers; Reilly, "Work of the Employment Department at the Dennison Manufacturing Company, Framingham, Massachusetts"; Nelson, *Unemployment Insurance*, 50–53.

16. J. Dennison, *Henry S. Dennison*, 14–15; interviews with James T. Dennison, December 12, 1979, Antrim, N. H., and Elizabeth Dunker, December 10, 1979, Cambridge, Mass.; Dennison typescript on old-age pensions dated 1915(?), HSD Papers; Heaton, *A Scholar in Action*, 89–91; Keyssar, *Out of Work*, 265–71. On the AALL, see Lubove, *The Struggle for Social Security*, and Donald J. Murphy, "John B. Andrews, the American Association for Labor Legislation, and Unemployment Reform, 1914–1929," in *Voluntarism, Planning, and the State*, ed. Brown and Reagan, 1–23.

17. *Boston Traveler*, June 13, 1919, 1; "The Reminiscences of George Rublee (1951)," 149–52, COHC; "Account of Dean Gay's World War I Work, 1919," Paul F. Cherington Papers; Heaton, *A Scholar in Action*, 98–138; Potter, "The Central Bureau of Planning and Statistics."

18. Cuff, "Creating Control Systems." On Baruch, see Baruch, *American Industry in the War*, 43–46, and Schwartz, *The Speculator*, 50–108.

19. Cuff, *The War Industries Board*, 5.

20. Berkowitz and McQuaid, *Creating the Welfare State*, 57–60; Cuff, "We Band of Brothers"; Cuff, "Herbert Hoover, the Ideology of Voluntarism, and War Organization during the Great War"; Kennedy, *Over Here*, 113–43; Schwartz, *The New Dealers*, 1–56.

21. Heath, "History of the Dennison Manufacturing Company," 182–83; J. Den-

nison, *Henry S. Dennison,* 16; Dennison, "Why I Believe in Profit Sharing"; Burritt, Dennison, Gay, Heilman, and Kendall, *Profit Sharing,* 119–24, 297–303; Dennison, "The Recognition of Fellowship," *Universalist Leader,* August 1919; Dennison to John P. Whitman, September 17, 1919, Organization file, HSD Papers; *Boston Sunday Advertiser,* September 28, 1919, 1; Dennison to William D. Smith, February 26, 1924, HSD Papers; Dennison, "The Proper Coordination of Capital and Labor," address before Stationers' Convention, October 1919, Richmond, Virginia, Notebooks, HSD Papers; Roland A. Gibson, "Three Experiments: An Interview with the Employers," *World Tomorrow* 8 (August 1925): 239–41.

22. Chenery, "The President's Industrial Conference"; Brody, *Labor in Crisis,* 105, 115–28; Hurvitz, "Ideology and Industrial Conflict"; Gerber, "Corporatism in Comparative Perspective"; and McCartin, *Labor's Great War,* 191–94.

23. Dennison, "Synopsis of Arguments in Support of Resolution concerning Plant Committee," October 6–23, 1919, HSD Papers.

24. Dennison, "Synopsis of Arguments in Support of Resolution concerning Control of Corporate Policy," October 6–23, 1919, and "Synopsis of Arguments in Support of Resolution on Collective Bargaining," October 16, 1919, HSD Papers.

25. Dennison, "The Washington Industrial Conference" memorandum, October 29, 1919, HSD Papers.

26. Dennison to Julius Rosenwald, December 1, 1919, and Dennison memorandum for managing editor of the *New York Evening Post,* December 30, 1919, HSD Papers; Dennison and Tarbell, "The President's Industrial Conference of October 1919."

27. McQuaid, "An American Owenite"; Berkowitz and McQuaid, *Creating the Welfare State,* 11–16; Urwick and Brech, *The Making of Scientific Management,* 1:116–19; Berle, *Leaning against the Dawn,* 3–24; Eakins, "The Development of Corporate Liberal Policy Research in the United States," 141–42, 179, 225–67.

28. Dennison, "A Dennisonian Proposition," *Bulletin of the Taylor Society* 5 (June 1920): 94–97; Dennison, "A Statement of the Problem," ibid. 5 ([August?] 1920): 200–202; Dennison, "Production and Profits," *Annals* 91 (September 1920): 160–61; Haber, *Efficiency and Uplift;* Nelson, *Frederick W. Taylor and the Rise of Scientific Management;* and Nelson, *A Mental Revolution.*

29. Dennison, "The Post Office," *Nation's Business* 11 (August 1923): 19–21; Dennison, "Basic Principles of Personnel Management in Government Economy"; 328–30; Post Office Department file, HSD Papers; Dennison address to the National Association of Postmasters, September 27, 1922, Washington, D.C., Notebook, HSD Papers; and Dennison address to National Association of Letter Carriers' Convention, September 4, 1923, Providence, R. I., HSD Papers.

30. Dennison, "How I Use the Business Cycle," *Nation's Business* 10 (February 1922): 9–10, 12; Rich, "Analyzing, Grading, and Value Operations of a Modern Manufacturing Organization"; 19–24; Bullard, "Can We Beat the Business Cycle?"; Heywood, "How the Dennison Manufacturing Company Meets the Slumps."

31. On private employers' efforts to promote unemployment plans, see Nelson, *Unemployment Insurance,* 28–36, 40–56, and Murphy, "John B. Andrews, the American Association for Labor Legislation, and Unemployment Reform, 1914–1929." On the Dennison Manufacturing Company, see Dennison, "Problems of Business Organization," *Administration: The Journal of Business Analysis and Control,* September 1921; Dennison, "Talk before Joint Meeting of Works Committee and Management," February 2, 1922, HSD Papers; "Job Security at Dennison's," *Survey* 47 (January 14, 1922): 595–96; Dennison, "Stabilizing Employment in a Diversified Seasonal Industry," *Proceedings of the Academy of Political Science* 9 (January 1922): 9–13; Dennison, "Regularization of Industry against Unemployment," *Annals* 100 (March 1922): 102–5; Dennison, "To Cut the Waste of Unemployment," *Nation's Business,* October 1924, 32–34; Martin Carpenter, "The

Unemployment Fund," U.S. Department of Labor, Bureau of Labor Statistics, *Bulletin No. 429* (Washington, D.C., 1927), 63–68; Dennison, "Unemployment within Employment: Paper," *Survey* 62 (April 1, 1929): 39–48; Dennison, "Unemployment Can Be Regularized," *American Federationist* 35 (1928): 1440–43; typescript of Dennison's talk to Sales Managers' Club of New York, March 1, 1929, HSD Papers; "Famous Firsts: Bringing Brainwork to the Fore," *Business Week,* December 17, 1949, 54. Figures for the unemployment rate are from Heywood, "How the Dennison Manufacturing Company Meets the Slumps," 75, while those on disbursements are from Dennison, "Unemployment within Employment," 46.

32. Dennison, "Methods and Results of the Unemployment Conference," typescript and Dennison memorandum, October 24, 1921, HSD Papers. See chap. 4 for a more extensive discussion of the Unemployment Conference of 1921.

33. Heald, "Business Thought in the Twenties"; McQuaid, "An American Owenite"; McQuaid, "Young, Swope and General Electric's 'New Capitalism'"; McQuaid, "Competition, Cartellization and the Corporate Ethic"; Case and Case, *Owen D. Young and American Enterprise;* McQuaid, "Corporate Liberalism in the American Business Community"; Metcalf, "Secretary Hoover and the Emergence of Macroeconomic Planning."

34. Dennison, "Planning Ahead," *Family,* April 1921; Dennison to Donham, April 20, 1921, Donham to Dennison, April 22, 1921, Dennison to Donham, May 11, 1921, Donham to Dennison, July 21, 1921, General Correspondence, Dean's Office Records, Graduate School of Business Administration Archives, Baker Library, Harvard University, Cambridge, Mass.; Dennison, "Depression Insurance"; interview with Elizabeth Dunker, December 10, 1979; Bruce Barton, "Business Is Better and Will Continue to Improve: An Interview with Henry S. Dennison," *American Magazine* 93 (March 1922): 8–9.

35. Dennison-Mitchell correspondence, Business Cycles file, HSD Papers; Dennison, "Management and the Business Cycle"; Dennison, "Methods and Results of the Unemployment Conference"; Dennison, "Credit Granting and the Business Cycle"; Dennison, "American Expansion and Industrial Stability," *Annals* 109 supp. (September 1923): 289–90; Dennison, "The Business Cycle," incomplete typescript written for *Boston Herald* but never published, January 1926, and Dennison statement for *Management Week,* 1926, HSD Papers; Dennison, "Unemployment Relief—a Burden or an Investment?" *System,* June 1926, 795–96; Dennison, "Tomorrow's Business," address at Chicago Association of Commerce, December 7, 1927, HSD Papers; Dennison statement in U.S. Senate, Committee on Commerce, 70th Cong., 1st sess., *Report No. 836 to Accompany S. 2475,* April 18, 1928; *Framingham News,* December 21, 1928.

36. Dennison, "Tomorrow's Business"; on Follett and Parker, see Urwick and Brech, *The Making of Scientific Management,* 1:48–70; Dennison, "An Employer's View of Property," *Annals* 103 (September 1922): 58–59; Dennison talk to the Worcester [Mass.] Rotary Club, April 23, 1924, Dennison to Whiting Williams, December 5, 1925, Dennison talk at Second Annual Connecticut Industrial Conference, Camp Hazen, Chester, Conn., June 26–27, 1926, all in HSD Papers; Dennison, "Employee Representation Plans and Labor Organizations," *Proceedings of the Academy of Political Science* 13 (July 1928): 141–45; Nelson, *Unemployment Insurance,* chaps. 6–8.

37. Dennison, "The Business of Government," address at Yale University, March 7, 1923, written for *New York Evening Post,* HSD Papers.

38. Dennison's lectures at the Bureau of Personnel Administration, New York City, HSD Papers; Dennison, "Business Management and the Professions," *Annals* 119 (May 1925): 143–47; Dennison, "The Essentials of a Profession," in *Business Management as a Profession,* ed. Henry C. Metcalf (Chicago, 1927), 24–37; and Dennison, *Incentives for Executives* (New York, 1928).

39. Hawley, "Secretary Hoover and the Bituminous Coal Problem"; *Framingham News,* May 21, 1929.

40. *Recent Economic Changes in the United States* and Alchon, *The Invisible Hand of Planning,* 129–51.

41. Dennison, "Management," in *Recent Economic Changes,* 2:495–546.

42. Dennison talk at Twelfth Quarterly Meeting of the New England Council, Manufacturers' Research Association, September 15, 1928, Lenox, Mass., HSD Papers. The records of the Manufacturers' Research Association are in the Graduate School of Business Administration Archives, Baker Library, Harvard University, Cambridge, Mass.

43. Notebook and clipping and J. A. G[arvey], "Memo on Junior Executives," n.d., in American Management Association File, HSD Papers; Urwick and Brech, *The Making of Scientific Management,* 1:116–19.

44. Dennison, "Management," in *Recent Economic Changes,* 2:497.

45. Minutes of Meetings, Committee on Problems and Policy, Social Science Research Council, August 27-September 3, 1926, Hanover, N. H., attached to Shelby Harrison to Beardsley Ruml, October 7, 1926, Box 64, Subseries 6, Series III, LSRM; entries for July 30 and August 15–21 1926, August 15–18 and 22–25, 1927, Office Diaries and E. E. Hunt to Miss Doris Piper, January 23, 1928, HSD Papers; "H. S. Dennison Is out for Hoover," *Boston Post,* October 25, 1928; *Framingham News,* July 12, 1929.

46. Unsigned and undated memorandum [probably W. J. Donald, early 1929] "Significance of Business Research," J[ohn] S. K[eir] memorandum on American Management Association for Dennison, September 30, 1929, Joe Willits to C. O. Ruggles, December 11, 1929, Willits to Dennison, December 11, 1929, Ruggles to Willits, December 14, 1929, [W. J. Donald] memorandum to Twentieth Century Fund [1929], Ruggles to Dennison, April 7, 1930, memorandums to Rockefeller Foundation [probably in early 1931], all in Business Research Council, 1929–1934 file, HSD Papers. The experiment occurred in the context of the Harvard Business School's use of social science research to professionalize business management and seek ways to stabilize labor-management relations under the leadership of Dean Wallace Donham, a longtime friend of Dennison's, for which see R. Smith, *American Business System,* and W. Scott, *Chester I. Barnard,* 40–60.

47. Memorandum to Rockefeller Foundation [probably in early 1931], Edmund E. Day to Dennison, April 1, 1931, Dennison to Edwin F. Gay, April 10, 1931, Ruggles to Dennison, April 27, 1931, Willits to Dennison, May 29, 1931, Evans Clark to Dennison, June 2, 1931, Dennison to Clark, June 3, 1931, Dennison to Edwin F. Gay, June 12, 1931, Dennison to Ruggles, November 20, 1933, Ruggles to Dennison, November 25, 1933, Office diary entry for October 15, 1934, and Donald R. Belcher to Dennison, January 21, 1935, all in Business Research Council, 1929–34 File, HSD Papers.

48. Dennison, "Reserves against Unemployment," address, December 26, 1930, in U.S. Department of Commerce, *Unemployment: Industry Seeks a Solution. A Series of Radio Addresses Given under the Auspices of the President's Emergency Committee for Employment, December 16, 1930,* 11–13.

49. Dennison, "Some Economic and Social Accomplishments of the Mechanization of Industry"; "slowly sucking maelstrom" is from Dennison, "Our Captains," unpublished 1936 poem in possession of Elizabeth Dunker, Cambridge, Mass.

50. Dennison, "Science of Management," address at Swarthmore College, March 7, 1930, Management file, HSD Papers; Dennison, "Social Self Control," *Annals* 149 (May 1930): 1–2; Dennison, "What Can Employers Do about It?" in Stanley B. Mathewson et al., *Restriction of Output Among Unorganized Workers* (New York, 1931), 183–95; Walton H. Hamilton, Henry S. Dennison, and Colonel Malcolm C. Rorty, *The Worldwide Depression: Ways Out, Addresses of 3 January 1931* (New York, 1931), 9–17; Dennison, "Experience Demonstrates Advantages of Unemployment Reserve Funds," *American Labor Legislation Review* 21 (March 1931): 29–32; "Our Economic Blood Pressure: An Interview by Roy Dickinson with Henry S. Dennison," *Printer's Ink* 155 (April 9, 1931); 3–4ff.

51. Vollmers, "Industrial Home Work of the Dennison Manufacturing Company,"

447, 465; Dennison, "Reserves Against Unemployment," 13; interview with Elizabeth Dunker, December 10, 1979; J. Dennison, *Henry S. Dennison,* 20–21.

52. Dennison to Tarbell, March 14, 1935, HSD Papers.

53. *Framingham News,* January 9, 1931.

54. McQuaid, "Young, Swope and General Electric's 'New Capitalism'" and "Competition, Cartellization and the Corporate Ethic." The Swope and Chamber of Commerce plans were reprinted in *America Faces the Future,* ed. Beard, 160–85, 196–264.

55. Dennison, *Organization Engineering;* Dennison, *Ethics and Modern Business* (Boston, 1932); Dennison, "The Need for the Development of Political Science Engineering."

56. Typescript, "Sermon Preached by H. S. Dennison in Jewish Synagogue-Boston," April 13, 1932, in possession of Elizabeth Dunker, Cambridge, Mass.

57. Dennison, "The Cycle 1927–1932," address to Boston Chapter of the National Cost Accounts Association, May 11, 1932, HSD Papers.

58. Dennison, "A Five-Year Plan for Planning," August 1932, 1–4, HSD Papers.

59. Ibid., 9–10.

60. Ibid., 10–13.

61. Ibid., 13–24; quotation is from 24.

62. Himmelberg, *The Origins of the National Recovery Administration;* Roper, *Fifty Years of Public Life,* 283–85; Kim McQuaid, "The Business Advisory Council of the Department of Commerce." Cf. Ronald Radosh, "The Myth of the New Deal," in *A New History of Leviathan,* ed. Radosh and Rothbard, 146–87, and Collins, "Positive Business Responses to the New Deal."

63. McQuaid, "The Business Advisory Council," 175.

64. Major works detailing the history of the NRA include Hawley, *The New Deal and the Problem of Monopoly,* 3–146; Brand, *Corporatism and the Rule of Law;* Ohl, *Hugh S. Johnson and the New Deal,* 92–254; and Bellush, *The Failure of the NRA.* For the changing context of business-government relations in this period, see Ellis W. Hawley, "The New Deal and Business," in *The New Deal,* ed. Braeman, Bremner, and Brody, 1:50–82; Hawley, "A Partnership Formed, Dissolved, and in Renegotiation"; Hawley, "The Corporate Ideal as Liberal Philosophy in the New Deal"; and Thomas K. McCraw, "The New Deal and the Mixed Economy," in *Fifty Years Later,* ed. Sitkoff, 37–67.

65. Entries for June 26, October 3, 18, 19, November 2, 3, 24, December 7, 12, 13, 17, 1933, Office Diaries, HSD Papers; Dennison, "Planning," memorandum for BAPC meeting of March 5, 1934, 153.3B, NRPB Records; *United States News* (Washington, D.C.), March 16, 1934, Extra NRA Edition, 11; Dennison, "The Future of the NRA: General Analysis," 1934, HSD Papers; Dennison, "Constructive Open Pricing vs. Destructive Price Cutting," *Paper Mill and Wood Pulp News,* January 19, 1935, 13–15; Dennison, "Subsidized Capital and How It Can Be Checked," *Printer's Ink,* March 14, 1935, 7, 10. On Swope, see McQuaid, "Competition, Cartellization, and the Corporate Ethic" and "The Business Advisory Council."

66. On the IAB, see McQuaid, "The Frustration of Corporate Revival during the Early New Deal." Dennison's appointment and participation are in October 2, 1933, and January–April 1934 entries, Office Diaries, HSD Papers. Dennison served as chairman of the IAB from March through April 1934.

67. Dennison, "Wagner Bill," typescript, 1935, probably written for the BAPC, HSD Papers. Brandes, *American Welfare Capitalism,* argues that these policies never took deep root with workers. In a slightly revised version of a 1968 article, David Brody argues that, but for the Depression, welfare capitalism might have become the dominant form of labor-management relations. For the original essay, see Braeman, Bremner, and Brody, eds., *Change and Continuity in Twentieth-Century America,* 146–78, and for the revision, see Brody, *Workers in Industrial America,* 48–81. Recent works include Nelson, "The Com-

pany Union Movement," and Gerald Zahavi, *Workers, Managers, and Welfare Capitalism: The Shoeworkers and Tanners of Endicott Johnson, 1890–1950* (Urbana, Ill., 1988). On the rise of the CIO, see Dubofsky and Van Tine, *John L. Lewis,* 181–279, and Zieger, *The CIO,* 1–89.

68. Dennison typescript, marked "Written for the Industrial Advisory Board 1934," and Dennison's address to the American Trade Association Executives' Dinner at the annual meeting of the U.S. Chamber of Commerce, May 2, 1934, HSD Papers; memorandum from Dennison to Mssrs. Hahn, Fahey, Leeds, Flanders, June 4, 1934, Dennison, "Suggestions for a Popular Presentation of Planning" [probably June 1934], Morris E. Leeds to Dennison, June 21, 1934, and Ralph E. Flanders to Dennison, June 22, 1934, all in Flanders Papers.

69. Dennison, "Suggestions for a Popular Presentation of Planning."

70. Merriam-Dennison correspondence, 1926–30, Box 28, and Delano to Merriam, May 31, 1934, and Merriam to Delano, June 6, 1934, Folder 8, Box 169, CEM Papers; Dennison memorandum to Hahn, Fahey, Leeds, Flanders, June 4, 1934, and Flanders to Dennison, June 22, 1934, Flanders Papers; Delano to Ickes, September 21 and December 2, 1935, Roper to Ickes, December 3, 1935, Ickes to Roosevelt, December 3, 1935, Dennison to Roosevelt, December 23, 1935, Roosevelt to Dennison, December 30, 1935, all in 153.3, NRPB Records; January 18, 1936 entry, Office Diaries, HSD Papers.

71. Dennison to Tarbell, March 14, 1935, HSD Papers.

72. Dennison, "Business and Government."

73. Entries in Office Diaries, HSD Papers for the 1936–43 period, show Dennison's active involvement at national planning agency meetings.

6. Beardsley Ruml

1. While no biography of Ruml exists, a brief chronology of his life is in Box 2, Series I, Ruml Papers. For the best information available, see Johnston, "The National Idea Man"; "Beardsley Ruml," *Fortune,* March 1945, 135–38ff.; Grattan, "Beardsley Ruml and His Ideas"; obituary in *New York Times,* April 19, 1960, 1–2; and Broadus Mitchell, "Ruml, Beardsley," in *Dictionary of American Biography,* ed. John A. Garraty, supp. 6, 1956–1960 (New York, 1980), 558–60.

2. Ruml's importance is hinted at in Stein, *The Fiscal Revolution in America;* Collins, "Positive Business Responses to the New Deal," 380–84; and Bulmer and Bulmer, "Philanthropy and Social Science in the 1920s."

3. Wren, "American Business Philanthropy and Higher Education in the Nineteenth Century"; Lyons, *The Uneasy Partnership,* 31–49; Grossman, "American Foundations and the Support of Economic Research"; D. Fisher, "The Role of Philanthropic Foundations in the Reproduction and Production of Hegemony"; the exchange between Donald Fisher and Martin Bulmer, "Debate"; Samelson, "Organizing for the Kingdom of Behavior"; 33–47; Alchon, *The Invisible Hand of Planning;* Hawley, "Economic Inquiry and the State in New Era America"; Coben, *Rebellion against Victorianism,* 60–68; D. Fisher, *Fundamental Development of the Social Sciences;* Jordan, *Machine-Age Ideology,* 110–84; and Sealander, *Private Wealth and Public Life.*

For philanthropic support of scientific research, see Kohler, "Science, Foundations, and American Universities in the 1920s"; Geiger, *To Advance Knowledge;* Coben, "Foundation Officials and Fellowships"; Kohler, "The Management of Science"; Kohler, "A Policy for the Advancement of Science"; Kohler, "Science and Philanthropy"; and Kohler, *Partners in Science.*

4. On the emergence of organized philanthropy, see Karl, "The Power of Intellect and the Politics of Ideas"; Karl, "Philanthropy, Policy Planning, and the Bureaucratization of the Democratic Ideal"; Karl and Katz, "The American Private Philanthropic Founda-

tion and the Public Sphere"; Karl, "Lo, the Poor Volunteer"; Karl and Katz, "Foundations and Ruling Class Elites." For some of the best recent case studies, see Wheatley, *The Politics of Philanthropy;* Lagemann, *Private Power for the Public Good;* Lagemann, *The Politics of Knowledge;* Jonas, *The Circuit Riders;* and Kohler, *Partners in Science.*

For good summaries of the direction of recent research, see comments by Katz, McCarthy, Kohler, and Karl in "Grantmaking and Research in the U.S."; articles in "Philanthropy, Patronage, Politics," special issue of *Daedalus* 116 (Winter 1987); Payton, Novak, O'Connell, and Hall, *Philanthropy: Four Views;* Hammack, "Private Organizations, Public Purposes"; Coon, *Money to Burn;* P. D. Hall, *Inventing the Nonprofit Sector.*

There is a huge literature on the history of American philanthropy. For the best overview, see Bremner, *American Philanthropy.* For further references, see Keele and Kiger, *Foundations;* Layton, *Philanthropy and Voluntarism;* and Kiger, *Historiographic Review of Foundation Literature.* For a sampling of the contemporary debate over the place, function, and role of philanthropy in America, see Nielsen, *The Big Foundations;* Nielsen, *The Golden Donors;* Arnove, *Philanthropy and Cultural Imperialism;* Peter Dobkin Hall, "Doing Well by Doing Good: Business Philanthropy and Social Investment, 1860–1984," in *Giving and Volunteering: New Frontiers of Knowledge,* ed. Virginia Hodgkinson (Washington, D.C., 1984), 27–73; P. D. Hall, "Reflections on the Nonprofit Sector in the Post-Liberal Era"; Karl and Katz, "The Unintended Logic of the Philanthropic Foundation"; Magat, *Philanthropic Giving;*and Odendahl, *Charity Begins at Home.*

5. On Carnegie, see Wall, *Andrew Carnegie,* and Livesay, *Andrew Carnegie and the Rise of Big Business.* For Rockefeller, see Fosdick, *John D. Rockefeller, Jr.;* Nevins, *A Study in Power;* Hawke, *John D.;* and John Ensor Harr and Peter J. Johnson, *The Rockefeller Century* (New York, 1988). For the change in philanthropic management, see Lindeman, *Wealth and Culture;* Coon, *Money to Burn;* Lagemann, *The Politics of Knowledge;* Gates, *Chapters in My Life;* Fosdick, *Chronicle of a Generation;* Fosdick, *The Story of the Rockefeller Foundation;* Flexner, *Funds and Foundations;* and Weaver, *U.S. Philanthropic Foundations.*

6. Nicknames cited were found in various articles cited above in n. 1. Merriam's descriptions of Ruml are in Merriam, "Impressions of the Second Hanover Conference," attached to Merriam to Ruml, September 8, 1927, Box 39, and Merriam to Ruml, May 11, 1945, Box 68, CEM Papers.

7. Hutchins cited in the *New Yorker,* February 10, 1945, 28.

8. Brownlow to C. Hartley Grattan, May 13, 1952, Ruml Papers.

9. "The Reminiscences of Frances Perkins (1955)," 450, which parallels the judgments found in "The Reminiscences of Guy Stanton Ford (1956)," 471, COHC; Robert M. Hutchins to Ruml, January 5, 1934, Folder 1, Box 110, Presidents' Papers, ca. 1925–1945, University of Chicago Library; Brownlow–Emmeline Nollen correspondence of March–April 1956 and Nollen-Ruml correspondence, Ruml Papers.

10. Johnston, "The National Idea Man," part 3, p. 36.

11. Biographical material on Ruml's early life comes from material cited in n. 1 above. Ruml often told interviewers that his parents were poor country farmers, although he told friends otherwise and more truthfully, as revealed in "The Reminiscences of Milburn L. Wilson (1956)," 703–4, and photographs in Wentzle and Salome Ruml Papers, State Historical Society of Iowa, Iowa City, Iowa. Ruml remained cagey and private about his personal life, as noted in Brownlow to C. Hartley Grattan, May 13, 1952, and Brownlow to Miss Nollen, April 25, 1956, Ruml Papers.

12. On Bingham, see his autobiographical essay in *A History of Psychology in Autobiography,* ed. Edwin G. Boring, Herbert S. Langfeld, Heinz Werner, and Robert M. Yerkes (1952; New York, 1968), 4:1–26.

13. Essays in Sokal, *Psychological Testing and American Society;* Angell's autobiographical essay in *A History of Psychology in Autobiography,* ed. Carl Murchison (Worcester, Mass., 1936), 3:1–38; Ruml's dissertation published in *Psychological Monographs* 24, no. 4 (1917);

"James Rowland Angell (1869–1949)," in Ernest R. Hilgard, *Psychology in America: A Historical Survey* (San Diego, 1987), 82–83; and "The Reminiscences of William Harold Cowley (1963)," 161–62, COHC, which details the rapid changes in Ruml's life during this period.

14. Kraus, *Personnel Research, History and Policy Issues;* Lynch, "Walter Dill Scott," later published in an expanded version as *Walter Dill Scott.*

15. Richard T. Von Mayrhauser, "The Manager, the Medic, and the Mediator: The Clash of Professional Psychological Styles and the Wartime Origins of Group Mental Testing," in *Psychological Testing and American Society,* ed. Sokal, 128–57; Von Mayrhauser, "Making Intelligence Functional"; Kevles, "Testing the Army's Intelligence"; Kevles, "George Ellery Hale, the First World War, and the Advancement of Science in America"; and Noble, *America by Design,* 207–8.

16. On the history and work of the CCPA, see U.S. Adjutant General's Department, Classification Division [successor title for the Committee on Classification of Personnel in the Army], *The Personnel System of the U.S. Army,* 1:39–112; Robert M. Yerkes, "How Psychology Happened Into the War" and "What Psychology Contributed to the War," in *The New World of Science, Development During the War,* ed. Yerkes, 351–89; and Kevles, "Testing the Army's Intelligence." On the continuity of industrial psychology from the prewar years through the 1920s, see Baritz, *The Servants of Power,* 3–95, and R. Smith, *The American Business System and the Theory and Practice of Social Science.*

17. *Personnel System of the U.S. Army,* 1:106, 361–70, 381–82, and secretary of war to Ruml, February 24, 1919, Folder 1, Box 1, Ruml Papers.

18. Ruml, "The Extension of Selective Tests to Industry"; Ruml and Paterson, "The Extension of Rating Scale Theory and Technique"; Ruml, "Notes on Applied Psychology," April 24, 1922, Ruml Papers. On the Scott Company, see Robert C. Clothier to Ruml, May 31, 1923, Folder 1, Box 1, Ruml Papers; Lynch, "Walter Dill Scott," 165–67; Baritz, *The Servants of Power,* 51–52.

19. Alfred D. Flinn to John D. Rockefeller, Jr., June 7, 1924, Robert I. Rees to Ruml, February 11, 1925, and W. V. Bingham to John D. Rockefeller, Jr., April 21, 1926, Personnel Research Federation Folders, Box 44, Civic Interests File, Records of John D. Rockefeller, Jr.; Baritz, *The Servants of Power,* 53–54, and Noble, *America by Design,* 228–31.

20. "The Reminiscences of Robert M. Lester (1968)," 24–31, COHC.

21. Ibid., 33–41; "The Reminiscences of Samuel S. Hall, Jr. (1968)," 27–34; "The Reminiscences of James W. Campbell (1968)," 55–57; "The Reminiscences of Morse Cartwright (1967)," 7, 21; "The Reminiscences of Henry Wriston (1969)," 18; "The Reminiscences of Francis Keppel (1967)," 5, all in COHC.

22. Raymond B. Fosdick to John D. Rockefeller, Jr., June 30, 1921, Box 62, Friends and Services File, Records of John D. Rockefeller, Jr.; Abraham Flexner to James R. Angell, November 18, 1921, Folder 1, Box 1, Ruml Papers; Fosdick to Rockefeller, Jr., December 3, 1921, LSRM, Inc. Folder, Box 57, Rockefeller Boards File, Records of John D. Rockefeller, Jr.; Angell to Ruml, December [22 or 23?], 1921, and Fosdick to Ruml, December 23, 1921, Folder 1, Box 1, Ruml Papers; Rockefeller, Jr., to Martin Ryerson, December 30, 1921, and Ryerson to Rockefeller, Jr., January 5, 1922, Fosdick Folder, Box 62, Friends and Services File, Records of John D. Rockefeller, Jr.; Leonard Outhwaite, "The Life and Times of the Laura Spelman Rockefeller Memorial," typescript, Outhwaite Papers, RAC; Collier and Horowitz, *The Rockefellers,* 98, 141–42; Harr and Johnson, *The Rockefeller Century,* 186–87.

23. Raymond B. Fosdick to John D. Rockefeller, Jr., December 2, 1921, LSRM, Inc. Folder, Box 57, Rockefeller Boards File, Records of John D. Rockefeller, Jr.

24. For a brief summary of the Rockefeller boards, see Nielsen, *The Big Foundations,* 47–60. Secondary accounts of three of the foundations include Corner, *A History of the Rockefeller Institute;* E. R. Brown, *Rockefeller Medicine Men;* Wheatley, *The Politics of Philan-*

thropy; Fosdick, *Adventure in Giving;* and Fosdick, *The Story of the Rockefeller Foundation.* Primary source materials for more detailed histories of these philanthropies exist at the RAC.

25. G. Adams, Jr., *Age of Industrial Violence;* Weinstein, *The Corporate Ideal in the Liberal State,* 172–212; McGovern and Guttridge, *The Great Coalfield War;* Gitelman, *Legacy of the Ludlow Massacre;* and Scheinberg, *Employers and Reformers,* 101–79.

26. Raymond B. Fosdick, who served as president of the Rockefeller Foundation from 1936 to 1948, provided an insider's account of the founding years in his *John D. Rockefeller, Jr.,* 121–22, and an analysis of the LSRM in his *Story of the Rockefeller Foundation,* 135–48, 192–209. For the changes in the early years of the memorial, see correspondence in LSRM, Inc. Folders, Box 58, Rockefeller Boards File, Records of John D. Rockefeller, Jr. A more recent view of the LSRM's work in the 1920s by two people who worked with the Rockefeller family and had access to unopened records is in Harr and Johnson, *Rockefeller Century,* 186–96.

27. Fosdick to Rockefeller, December 2, 1921.

28. Merriam cited in "Beardsley Ruml," *Fortune,* March 1945, 138.

29. Ruml's salary is noted in correspondence in LSRM, Inc. Folders, Boxes 57–58, Rockefeller Boards File, Records of John D. Rockefeller, Jr.

30. Ruml address to the Social Science Group, December 2, 1939, Ruml Papers.

31. Outhwaite, "The Life and Times of the Laura Spelman Rockefeller Memorial"; J. W. Ernst interview with Leonard Outhwaite, July 22, 1976, Newport, R. I., Outhwaite Papers; "The Reminiscences of Guy Stanton Ford (1956)," 473, COHC.

32. Ruml's memorandum to the board of trustees in Box 58, Rockefeller Boards File, Records of John D. Rockefeller, Jr. Selections from the memorandum are in Folder 8, Box 1, Series II, Ruml Papers, and Policy 1921–29 Folder, Box 2, Series II, LSRM. The following account is confirmed by Ruml's summary of the LSRM's work in LSRM, *Final Report,* and Fosdick, *The Story of the Rockefeller Foundation,* 192–202.

33. Quotations are from Ruml's memorandum to the board of trustees.

34. Ibid., emphasis in the original document.

35. Ibid., emphasis in the original document.

36. Ibid., emphasis in the original document.

37. Ruml memorandum for Fosdick, October 2, 1922, Policy 1921–29 Folder, Box 2, Series II, LSRM.

38. John D. Rockefeller, Jr., to Ruml, March 28, 1923, Dr. Ruml Corr. Folder, Box 57, Rockefeller Boards File, Records of John D. Rockefeller, Jr., and Fosdick, *The Story of the Rockefeller Foundation,* 195.

39. Annual financial statements in LSRM, *Report* (1923–28); reports in the LSRM Dockets, Boxes 1–4, Series I; individual organizational folders in Series II, LSRM; Johnson and Johnson, *Research in Service to Society;* Ogg, *Research in the Humanistic and Social Sciences,* which reviewed the research centers' efforts.

40. Bulmer, "The Early Institutional Establishment of Social Science Research"; University of Chicago Folders, Subseries 6, Series III, LSRM; for the memorial's support of Merriam's various projects, see Merriam, Charles E. 1925–27 Folder, ibid.; and for the Merriam-Ruml friendship, see correspondence in CEM Papers and Karl, *Charles E. Merriam and the Study of Politics,* 132–37.

41. Eakins, "The Development of Corporate Liberal Policy Research in the United States," 155–99; Alchon, *The Invisible Hand of Planning;* Hawley, "Economic Inquiry and the State in New Era America"; and Critchlow, *The Brookings Institution,* 62–81. For a broader perspective on the role of these kinds of private research institutions, see J. Smith, *The Idea Brokers,* and Donald T. Critchlow, "Think Tanks, Antistatism, and Democracy: The Nonpartisan Ideal and Policy Research in the United States, 1913–1987," in *The State and Social Investigation in Britain and the United States,* ed. Lacey and Furner, 279–322.

42. "The Reminiscences of Guy Stanton Ford (1956)," 469, and "The Reminiscences of Will W. Alexander (1952)," 350–54, COHC; E. Nollen interview with Louis Brownlow, April 13, 1956, Ruml Papers.

43. Merriam to Ruml, June 5, 1923, Social Science Research Council 1923–24 Folder, Subseries 6, Series III, LSRM; Ruml memorandum for Fosdick, July 16, 1923, Ruml Folder, Series II, LSRM; Dockets for November–December 1923, February 26, 1924, Series I, LSRM; Merriam-Yerkes correspondence, Box 43, CEM Papers. Information on the migration study is in National Research Council–Human Migration Folders and SSRC Folders, Subseries 6, Series II, LSRM; Charles and John Merriam correspondence, Box 194, John C. Merriam Papers; Merriam-Mitchell correspondence, Box 36, CEM Papers.

44. Merriam-Ruml correspondence in Box 39, CEM Papers; John to Charles Merriam, November 11, 1923, Box 194, John C. Merriam Papers; Charles to John Merriam, December 15, 1923, and John to Charles Merriam, December 18, 1923, Box 35, CEM Papers; Merriam to Mitchell, January 5, 1924, and Mitchell to Merriam, January 9, 1924, Merriam to Mitchell, February 6, 1924, Box 36, CEM Papers; Charles Merriam to Ruml, January 18, 1924, Box 39, CEM Papers.

45. Merriam to Ruml, October 24, 1924, Box 64, and Social Science Research Council–Fellowships Folders, Subseries 6, Series II, LSRM; Ruml to Merriam, October 27, 1924, Merriam to Ruml, October 29 and December 16, 1924, Box 39, CEM Papers; "The Reminiscences of Charles Dollard (1969)," 80, and "The Reminiscences of Gunnar Myrdal (1969)," 4–5, COHC.

46. Ruml to Robert McKennan, March 16, 1925, and other material in Hanover Conference Folders, and Social Science Research Council–Conference Folders, Subseries 6, Series III, LSRM. LSRM funding is noted in docket entries for March 11 and June 2, 1925, March 18 and December 9, 1926, February 17 and November 22, 1927, and November 8, 1928, Series I, LSRM. For a good description of the Hanover meetings, see Karl, *Charles E. Merriam,* 134–36.

47. Edmund E. Day for the SSRC, application for funds in docket entry, November 22, 1927, Series I, LSRM.

48. Merriam to Ruml, November 2, 1925, January 19 and March 1, 1926, Box 39, CEM Papers; Charles Merriam to Frederick P. Keppel, December 8, 1925, and Charles to John C. Merriam, December 9, 1925, Box 194, John C. Merriam Papers; the 96 percent figure is calculated from "Resources Available to Council," column in Social Science Research Council, *Decennial Report: 1923–1933* (New York, 1934), p. 105.

49. Percentage figures are derived from dollar amounts listed in "Appropriations for Social Science and Social Technology Made by the Laura Spelman Rockefeller Memorial up to December 1, 1927," Box 63, Subseries 6, Series III, LSRM.

50. John to Charles Merriam, May 6, 1926, Box 35, CEM Papers; Merriam to Mitchell, February 13 and September 25, 1928, and Mitchell to Merriam, November 10, 1928, Box 36, CEM Papers; docket entry, December 29, 1927, Series I, LSRM.

51. Ruml, "Each according to the Nature of His Own Experience," address before the SSRC, September, 1930, Ruml Papers; Ruml, "Memorandum: Conditions Affecting the Memorial's Participation in Projects in Social Science," June 1924, and correspondence in Policy 1921–29 Folder, Series II, LSRM; docket entry, July 10, 1924, Series I, LSRM; W. S. Richardson to John D. Rockefeller, Jr., June 20, 1924, Rockefeller Folder, Box 3, and Ruml to Fosdick, August 18, 1924, Ruml folder, Series II, LSRM; LSRM, *Final Report;* Fosdick, *Story of the Rockefeller Foundation,* 200–202; and Coben, "Foundation Officials and Fellowships."

52. For a view of the 1928 reorganization from the perspective of an older trustee, see Flexner, *Funds and Foundations,* 77–83, while Fosdick, *Story of the Rockefeller Foundation,* 134–44, 202–9, gives the modern corporate view, which is confirmed in Harr and Johnson, *Rockefeller Century,* 192–96. Nevins, *Study in Power,* 2:395–97, emphasizes the mana-

gerial concern for efficiency as the reason for the reorganization. The best studies of the internal conflict among the trustees are Robert E. Kohler's works, including "The Management of Science," "A Policy for the Advancement of Science," and *Partners in Science,* 233–62.

53. John D. Rockefeller, Jr., to John D. Rockefeller, April 9, 1926, and Rockefeller to Rockefeller, Jr., May 4, 1926, Rockefeller Folder, Series II, LSRM, reprinted in Joseph W. Ernst, ed., *"Dear Father"/"Dear Son": Correspondence of John D. Rockefeller and John D. Rockefeller, Jr.* (New York, 1994), 142–49.

54. For Day's appointment, see correspondence in LSRM Inc. Folder, Box 57, Rockefeller Boards File, Records of John D. Rockefeller, Jr., and "The Reminiscences of Guy Stanton Ford (1956)," 474–75.

55. T. M. Debevoise to Chauncey Belknap, November 26, 1928, Bertram Cutler to John D. Rockefeller, Jr., December 11, 1928, and Debevoise to Colonel Arthur Woods, December 26, 1928, LSRM, Inc. Folders, Boxes 57–58, Rockefeller Boards File, Records of John D. Rockefeller, Jr.; correspondence in Spelman Fund Folders, 237–39, Box 30, Series 100, Projects File, Record Group 1, Rockefeller Foundation Records.

56. Spelman Fund of New York, *Final Report* (New York, 1949); C. Herman Pritchett, "1313: An Experiment in Propinquity," typescript, Box 159, CEM Papers. "1313" was the street address and nickname for the umbrella group centered on the PACH. Karl, *Executive Reorganization and Reform in the New Deal,* 112–26; Ruml to Colonel Arthur Woods, December 19, 1930, Folder 5, Box 5, Series I, Ruml Papers; Spelman Fund-Dr. Charles E. Merriam Folders, Box 58, Rockefeller Boards File, Records of John D. Rockefeller, Jr.; Merriam to Ruml, November 5, 1948, Box V Series I, Ruml Papers, stresses the fund's achievements.

57. Karl, *Charles E. Merriam,* 159; Ruml to John D. Rockefeller, Jr., December 15, 1930, Box 58, Rockefeller Boards File, Records of John D. Rockefeller, Jr.; Dzuback, *Robert M. Hutchins,* 109–35; McNeill, *Hutchins' University,* 12, 33–34; Ruml, "The Chicago Plan," *Educational Record* 12 (1931): 359–68.

58. William F. Ogburn to Ruml, January 22, 1959, Box 4, Series I, Ruml Papers; Ruml to Hutchins, January 4, 1934, Ruml to Walter Dill Scott, January 10, 1934, Frank O. Lowden to Ruml, January 20, 1934, Ruml to Lowden, January 26, 1934, Folder 1, Box 1, Ruml Papers; E. Nollen interview with Louis Brownlow, April 13, 1956.

59. For recent works on agricultural policy in the 1920–35 period, see Hoffman and Libecap, "Institutional Choice and the Development of U.S. Agricultural Policies in the 1920s"; Hawley, "Economic Inquiry and the State in New Era America"; Finegold, "From Agrarianism to Adjustment"; Skocpol and Finegold, "State Capacity and Economic Intervention in the Early New Deal"; Hamilton, "Building the Associative State"; Hamilton, *From New Day to New Deal;* and Gilbert and Howe, "Beyond 'State vs. Society.'"

60. Historians have been aware that Ruml played some role in the evolution of farm relief policy in the early New Deal, but no one scholar has detailed that role. For brief mentions of Ruml's role in developing the domestic allotment plan, see Saloutos and Hicks, *Agricultural Discontent in the Middle West,* 453–54; Schlesinger, Jr. *The Age of Roosevelt,* 1:109–10 and 2:36–39; C. Campbell, *The Farm Bureau and the New Deal,* 49–50; Sternsher, *Rexford Tugwell and the New Deal,* 46, 170–93; Kirkendall, *Social Scientists and Farm Politics in the Age of Roosevelt,* 44; V. Perkins, *Crisis in Agriculture,* 27; Rosen, *Hoover, Roosevelt, and the Brains Trust,* 58–63, 178–94; Saloutos, *The American Farmer and the New Deal,* 35–38.

61. "The Reminiscences of Henry C. Taylor (1952)," 149–59, and "The Reminiscences of Milburn L. Wilson (1956)," 416–19, 452–69, COHC; Kirkendall, *Social Scientists and Farm Politics,* 11–15, 150; M. Wilson, "The Fairway Farms Project."

62. Henry C. Taylor to Arthur Woods, April 20, 1923, Ruml memorandum to

Woods, May 12, 1923, Ruml to Taylor, May 16, 1923, and Taylor to Ruml, October 14, 1923, all in Northwestern University–Institute for Research in Land Economics Folders, Subseries 6, Series III, LSRM; Taylor to Ruml, September 24, 1957, Ruml Papers; Montana Project 1923–24 Folder, Subseries 6, Series III, LSRM; Fairway Farms folders, Box 46, Business Interests file, Records of John D. Rockefeller, Jr.

63. For contemporary evaluations of the project, see H. R. Tolley to Dr. Woods, January 6, 1930, W. L. Stockton to Harold P. Fabian, February 20, 1930, Fabian to Woods, February 26, 1930, and M. L. Wilson to John D. Rockefeller, Jr., January 30, 1940, all Fairway Farms folders.

64. For the project's influence on the New Deal programs, see Huffman, "Montana's Contribution to New Deal Farm Policy." On the Farm Foundation, see material in Fairway Farms folder.

65. Kirkendall, *Social Scientists and Farm Politics,* 150. Hawley, "Economic Inquiry and the State in New Era America," contrasts the institutional strength of the Bureau of Agricultural Economics in the 1920s with the weakness of the NBER as an industrial planning body to argue that the roots of New Era state capacity for agricultural planning laid the groundwork for success in New Deal farm policy, while the institutional weakness of industrial planning in the 1920s may have contributed to the failure of the NRA as a form of industrial planning in the 1930s. Hawley addresses this issue more fully in Ellis W. Hawley, "'Industrial Policy' in the 1920s and 1930s," in *The Politics of Industrial Policy,* ed. Barfield and Schambra, 63–86.

66. Correspondence in Northwestern University–Institute for Research in Land Economics Folders, Subseries 6, Series III, LSRM. On the problems of the institute, see Rader, *The Academic Mind and Reform,* 204–22. Taylor later wrote to Ruml the "Rockefellers Saved My Career," in Taylor to Ruml, November 15, 1958, and attached draft of article for *Reader's Digest,* Ruml Papers. On Ruml's ideas, see "The Reminiscences of Milburn L. Wilson (1956)," 458, 586, COHC.

67. "The Reminiscences of Milburn L. Wilson," 502–3, 537–39, 585–87; correspondence in Agriculture Survey–Black 1928–30 Folder, Subseries 6, Series III, LSRM; Slichter, "Franklin D. Roosevelt and the Farm Problem"; Black, *Agricultural Reform in the United States,* chap. 10.

68. Lord, "M. L. Wilson" and "The Rebirth of Rural Life"; Rowley, "M. L. Wilson," later expanded as *M. L. Wilson and the Campaign for the Domestic Allotment.*

69. Tugwell confirmed this many times, as seen in his *Democratic Roosevelt,* 232; *The Brains Trust,* 200–210; and *Roosevelt's Revolution,* 48–58. Also see "The Reminiscences of M. L. Wilson (1956)," 698–704; "The Reminiscences of Oscar Clemen Stine (1957)," 182–85; and "The Reminiscences of Rexford Tugwell (1950)," 10–11, COHC; E. Nollen Interview with Louis Brownlow, April 13, 1956.

70. Rosenman, *The Public Papers and Addresses of Franklin D. Roosevelt,* 1:647–59.

71. Ibid., 693–711. For an excellent summary of the development of the farm speeches, see Slichter, "Franklin D. Roosevelt and the Farm Problem," 248–58.

72. In "The Reminiscences of Milburn L. Wilson (1956)," 705–6, Wilson recalled, "As I remember it, B. Ruml said [to Wilson], 'Push ahead on this. Somebody's got to take their clothes off and get in there. Maybe we could get a domestic allotment bill. I don't know about the political implications of this or about the frills on it; I'm interested in this rather simple core of making the tariff effective on the part that is domestically consumed.' 'But,' he said, 'legislation is somewhat of a compromise. If you have to have these frills, all right, but I don't want to get into the legislative end of it; I don't want to appear before any committees. Those kind of things I don't want to do.'"

73. "The Reminiscences of Rexford G. Tugwell (1950)," 25, 42–43.

74. Ruml, "Pulling Together for Social Service," *Social Service Review* 4 (March 1930): 1–10; Charles E. Merriam and Beardsley Ruml, "Observations on Trends and Opportu-

nities in Public Administration," October 1930, and material regarding the Reconstruction Trust Project, November 20, 1930, Ruml Papers; Hayes, *Activities of the President's Emergency Committee for Employment.*

75. Edith Abbott to Frederic Woodward, December 12, 1933, Folder 7, Box 84, Presidents' Papers, ca. 1925–1945, University of Chicago Library; Ruml, "Social Functions of Law and Lawyers," address before the Association of American Law Schools, December 28, 1933, Ruml Papers; "The Reminiscences of Frank Bane (1965)," 35, COHC; Ruml to Robert M. Hutchins, May 14, 1934, and June 1, 1935, in Folder 1, Box 126, Robert M. Hutchins Papers—Addenda, University of Chicago Library; [Ruml?], "The N.R.A. and the A. F. of L.," address before the Commercial Club of Cincinnati, Ohio November 30, 1934, Ruml Papers.

76. Memorandum Written Immediately after Congressional Elections of 1934, Ruml Papers.

77. Ibid.

78. Merriam to Delano, October 16, 1935, 153.3 NRPB Records.

79. Delano memorandum for Ickes, December 2, 1935, Ickes to the president, December 3, 1935, Roosevelt to Ruml, December 30, 1935, all in ibid.

80. Roosevelt to Ruml, December 18, 1935, Box 4, Series I, Ruml Papers.

7. The Organizational Nexus of New Deal Planning

1. Overviews include Karl, *The Uneasy State;* Chambers, *The Tyranny of Change;* Klein, *The Flowering of the Third America;* Hawley, *The Great War and the Search for a Modern Order;* Nash, *The Crucial Era.*

2. Koistinen, "The 'Industrial-Military Complex' in Historical Perspective"; Murray N. Rothbard, "War Collectivism in World War I" and "Herbert Hoover and the Myth of Laissez-Faire," in *A New History of Leviathan,* ed. Radosh and Rothbard, 66–110 and 111–45; Robert D. Cuff, "Business, the State, and World War I: The American Experience," in *War and Society in North America,* ed. Cuff and J. L. Granastein (Toronto, 1971), 1–19; Cuff, *The War Industries Board;* Cuff, "We Band of Brothers"; Cuff, "Herbert Hoover, the Ideology of Voluntarism, and War Organization during the Great War"; Cuff, "Harry Garfield, the Fuel Administration, and the Search for a Cooperative Order during World War I"; Hawley, *The Great War and the Search for a Modern Order;* Kennedy, *Over Here;* Hawley, "The Great War and Organizational Innovation"; Ferrell, *Woodrow Wilson and World War I;* R. Schaffer, *America in the Great War;* Dawley, *Struggles for Justice,* 172–217; Robert D. Cuff, "War Mobilization, Institutional Learning, and State Building in the United States, 1917–1941," in *The State and Social Investigation in Britain and the United States,* ed. Lacey and Furner, 388–425; and Koistinen, *Mobilizing for Modern War* and *Planning War, Pursuing Peace.*

3. For summaries of recent work on such changes, see Hawley, *The Great War and the Search for a Modern Order;* Karl, *The Uneasy State;* Fearon, *War, Prosperity, and Depression;* A. Brinkley, "Prosperity, Depression, and War"; Coben, *Rebellion against Victorianism;* Parrish, *Anxious Decades;* Dumenil, *Modern Temper.* For a more biographical perspective, see Gerber, *The Limits of Liberalism;* Schwarz, *The New Dealers;* Jordan, *Machine-Age Ideology.*

4. McCarthy, "Chicago Businessmen and the Burnham Plan"; Thomas Adams, "City and Town Planning," *Encyclopedia of the Social Sciences* (New York, 1930–34), 3:482–88; and John Nolen, "Regional Planning," ibid., 13:205–8; M. Scott, *American City Planning since 1890,* 1–311.

5. Adams and Hodge, "City Planning Instruction in the United States"; Hancock, "Planners in the Changing American City"; Birch, "Advancing the Art and Science of Planning."

6. Interview with Charles W. Eliot II, Cambridge, Mass., November 27, 1979; "Eliot, Charles William, 2nd," Biographical File, HUG 300, Harvard University Archives; Krueckeberg, "From the Backyard Garden to the Whole U.S.A." On the work of the NCPPC, see Gutheim, *Planning for Washington* and *Worthy of the Nation,* 143–70. The physical planning efforts can be examined in Record Group 328, Records of the National Capital Planning Commission.

7. Social Science Research Council, "A Decade of Council History," *Decennial Report: 1923–1933* (New York, 1934), 1–18; "Report of the History, Activities, and Policies of the Social Science Research Council," prepared by Louis Wirth for the Committee on Review of Council Policy, August 1937, Box 132, CEM Papers; Sibley, *Social Science Research Council;* D. Fisher, *Fundamental Development of the Social Sciences.*

8. For examples of some of the best recent work regarding the role of business leaders in this process, see McQuaid, "A Response to Industrialism"; McQuaid, "Corporate Liberalism in the American Business Community"; Berkowitz and McQuaid, *Creating the Welfare State,* 1–57; essays in Frese and Judd, *Business and Government;* and reprinted essays in Himmelberg, *Business-Government Cooperation.*

9. Karl, "The Power of Intellect and the Politics of Ideas" and "Philanthropy, Policy Planning, and the Bureaucratization of the Democratic Ideal"; Karl and Katz, "The American Private Philanthropic Foundation and the Public Sphere." For summaries of recent research on the second-generation philanthropies, see Patrick D. Reagan, introduction to the Transaction Edition of *Money to Burn,* by Horace Coon. For key works in the scholarly debate over this issue, see Arnove, *Philanthropy and Cultural Imperialism;* D. Fisher, "The Role of Philanthropic Foundations in the Reproduction and Production of Hegemony"; exchange between Donald Fisher and Martin Bulmer in "Debate"; Karl and Katz, "Foundations and Ruling Class Elites"; articles in "Philanthropy, Patronage, Politics," special issue of *Daedalus* 116 (Winter 1987); Payton, Novak, O'Connell, and Hall, *Philanthropy: Four Views;* Kohler, *Partners in Science;* P. D. Hall, *Inventing the Nonprofit Sector;* and Sealander, *Private Wealth and Public Life.*

10. P. Arnold, "Herbert Hoover and the Continuity of American Public Policy"; Runfola, "Herbert C. Hoover as Secretary of Commerce"; Hawley, "Herbert Hoover, the Commerce Secretariat, and the Vision of an 'Associative State'"; Alchon, *The Invisible Hand of Planning.* Recent evaluations of Hoover include essays in *Herbert Hoover as Secretary of Commerce,* ed. Hawley; in *Herbert Hoover Reassessed;* Krog and Tanner, *Herbert Hoover and the Republican Era;* Nash, *Understanding Herbert Hoover;* and Dodge, *Herbert Hoover and the Historians.* For more specific reference to the voluminous Hoover literature, see R. Burns, *Herbert Hoover.*

11. On these research centers, see Kevles, "George Ellery Hale, the First World War, and the Advancement of Science in America"; Alchon, *The Invisible Hand of Planning;* Hawley, "Economic Inquiry and the State in New Era America," for the NBER; Berle, *Leaning against the Dawn,* for the Twentieth Century Fund; Critchlow, *The Brookings Institution;* J. Smith, *Brookings at Seventy-Five.* On the related rise of the research university during this period, see Geiger, *To Advance Knowledge.*

For some of the best scholarly literature about these research institutes, see Eakins, "The Development of Corporate Liberal Policy Research"; Eakins, "The Origins of Corporate Liberal Policy Research"; Eakins, "Policy Planning for the Establishment"; Lyons, *The Uneasy Partnership;* Bulmer, *Social Science Research and Government;* essays in *The State and Economic Knowledge,* ed. Furner and Supple; Martin Bulmer, "The Decline of the Social Survey Movement and the Rise of American Empirical Sociology," in *The Social Survey in Historical Perspective,* ed. Bulmer, Bales, and Sklar, 291–315; J. Smith, *The Idea Brokers;* and Donald T. Critchlow, "Think Tanks, Antistatism, and Democracy: The Nonpartisan Ideal and Policy Research in the United States," in *The State and Social Investigation in Britain and the United States,* ed. Lacey and Furner, 279–322.

12. McMullen, "The President's Unemployment Conference of 1921 and Its Results"; Grin, "The Unemployment Conference of 1921"; Metcalf, "Secretary Hoover and the Emergence of Macroeconomic Management"; Ellis W. Hawley, "Herbert Hoover and Economic Stabilization, 1921–22," in *Herbert Hoover as Secretary of Commerce,* ed. Hawley, 43–77.

13. Hayes, *Activities of the President's Emergency Committee for Employment;* I. Bernstein, *The Lean Years,* 262–311; Romasco, *The Poverty of Abundance,* 55–56, 143ff.; Frank Bane, "Public Administration and the Public Welfare," an interview by James R. W. Leiby, 117–22, Regional Oral History Office, Bancroft Library, University of California, Berkeley, 1965; President's Emergency Committee for Unemployment 1930–31, Folder 787, Box 4, Series 5, Spelman Fund of New York Collection; President's Conference on Unemployment 1923–30, Folders 902–3, Subseries 7, Series III, LSRM; Mullins, *The Depression and the Urban West Coast.*

14. Mitchell and Merriam commented on the limitations of Hooverian ideology in Mitchell, "Mr. Hoover's 'The Challenge to Liberty,'" and Merriam's review in *American Political Science Review* 29 (1935): 131–33.

15. Wesley Clair Mitchell, "Institutes for Research in the Social Sciences," *Journal of Proceedings and Addresses of the Association of American Universities,* Thirty-First Annual Conference, November 7–9, 1929, 62–70; Mitchell, "Research in the Social Sciences"; Mitchell, "The Application of Economic Knowledge," and Charles E. Merriam, "The Relation of Government to Recent Social Change," both in *The Obligation of Universities to the Social Order* (Washington Square, N.Y., 1933), 169–76 and 239–57; Hynning, "Administrative Evolution of National Planning in the United States in the Pre-New Deal Era"; Tugwell and Banfield, "Governmental Planning at Mid-Century"; Graham, Jr., *An Encore for Reform,* 110–11; Lepawsky, "The Progressives and the Planners."

16. President's Research Committee on Social Trends, *Recent Social Trends in the United States,* 1:lxxiii.

17. Howard W. Odum to William F. Ogburn, February 13 and 21, 1933, and Ogburn to Odum, February 28, 1933, Box 13, Ogburn Papers; memorandum, February 25, 1933, Box 146, Robert T. Crane–Merriam correspondence, June–October 1933, Box 47, Merriam to George Soule, June 27, 1933, and Merriam to Ruml, July 10 and August 21, 1933, Box 56, undated memorandum from Merriam, Soule, and Ruml to SSRC, Box 132, all in CEM Papers; Franklin D. Roosevelt to Robert F. Crane, November 17, 1933, OF 868, FDRL; Harold F. Gosnell, "Commissions of Inquiry Appointed by the Social Science Research Council in 1933," July 24, 1935, Box 131, CEM Papers; "The Reminiscences of Guy Stanton Ford (1956)," 670ff., COHC; Social Science Research Council–Commission of Inquiry, 1933–35, File 382, Box 21, Subseries 1, Series 4, Spelman Fund of New York Collection.

18. Mallery, "A National Policy—Public Works to Stabilize Employment"; Howenstine, Jr., "Public Works Program After World War I"; Mallery, "The Long-Range Planning of Public Works"; Howenstine, Jr., "Public Works Policy in the Twenties"; Schlesinger, Jr., *Age of Roosevelt,* 1:85–87; E. E. Hunt to William F. Ogburn, January 27, 1932, Box 12, Ogburn Papers; Otto T. Mallery to Wesley Clair Mitchell, October 13, 1941, Mitchell Papers. For the broader context of Mallery's work, see Barber, *From New Era to New Deal,* and Sautter, *Three Cheers for the Unemployed.*

19. Rothbard, *America's Great Depression,* 172–78, 221–23, 234–36, 258–60; Hayes, *Activities of the President's Emergency Committee for Employment,* 38–64; I. Bernstein, *The Lean Years,* 267, 269–74; Frank W. Herring, "Public Works Construction as a Counter-Cyclical Instrument: 1930–1938," probably written for the National Resources Committee, Box 195, CEM Papers; Frederic A. Delano to the president, January 24, 1939, and Roosevelt to Colonel H. W. Waite, January 26, 1939, OF 1092, FDRL.

20. H. Warren, *Herbert Hoover and the Great Depression;* Romasco, *The Poverty of Abun-*

dance; Rothbard, "Herbert Hoover and the Myth of Laissez Faire"; Hawley, Rothbard, Himmelberg, and Nash, *Herbert Hoover and the Crisis of American Capitalism;* essays by Albert U. Romasco, Jordan A. Schwarz, and Ellis W. Hawley in *The Hoover Presidency,* ed. Fausold and Mazuzan, 69–119; Martin L. Fausold, "President Hoover's Farm Policies, 1929–1933," *Agricultural History* 51 (1977): 362–77; Hawley, *The Great War,* 177–86, 192–206. On the specifics of the public works, industrial recovery, and farm-relief programs, see J. Olson, *Herbert Hoover and the Reconstruction Finance Corporation;* Himmelberg, *The Origins of the National Recovery Administration;* and Hamilton, *From New Day to New Deal.*

21. For a juxtaposition of the extremes in the planning debate, see Harriman, "The Stabilization of Business and Employment," and Tugwell, "The Principle of Planning and the Institution of Laissez-Faire," with discussion, in *American Economic Review* 22 suppl. (1932): 62–104. Bernard Sternsher persuasively puts to rest the myth of "Red Rex" in *Rexford Tugwell and the New Deal.* Good overviews of the planning debate among intellectuals include Ekirch, Jr., *Ideologies and Utopias,* 36–71, 105–40, and Kidd, "Collectivist Intellectuals and the Ideal of National Economic Planning." Recent case studies include Westbrook, "Tribune of the Technostructure"; Shankman, "The Five-Day Plan and the Depression"; and Alchon, "Mary Van Kleeck and Social-Economic Planning." Major works in the planning debate included Chase, *A New Deal;* Soule, *A Planned Society;* Beard, *America Faces the Future,* which contained most of the best-known proposals; and Homan, "Economic Planning." For international comparative perspectives, see Garraty, *The Great Depression,* 140–51, 168–69, and Gourevitch, *Politics in Hard Times.* Recent appraisals by historians include Lawson, *The Failure of Independent Liberalism,* 61–84; Pells, *Radical Visions and American Dreams,* 43–95; Graham, Jr., *Toward a Planned Society,* 1–27; Warken, *A History of the National Resources Planning Board,* 4–37; Clawson, *New Deal Planning,* 21–36; and Cooney, *Balancing Acts,* 10, 40–50. A tripartite distinction among planners, business advocates, and antitrusters serves as the central theme in Hawley, *The New Deal and the Problem of Monopoly.*

On business-government relations during the 1930s, see Ellis W. Hawley, "The New Deal and Business," in *The New Deal,* ed. Braeman, Bremner, and Brody, 1:50–82; Hawley, "A Partnership Formed, Dissolved, and in Renegotiation"; Hawley, "The Corporate Ideal as Liberal Philosophy in the New Deal"; Hawley, "'Industrial Policy' in the 1920s and 1930s," in *The Politics of Industrial Policy,* ed. Barfield and Schambra, 63–86; Collins, *The Business Response to Keynes;* and McQuaid, *Big Business and Presidential Power,* chap. 1.

22. Hoover to Mitchell, October 26, 1934, reprinted in L. Mitchell, *Two Lives,* 370.

23. Mitchell to Hoover, December 24, 1934, cited in ibid., 372.

24. Conservation efforts before the New Deal are discussed in Hays, *Conservation and the Gospel of Efficiency,* esp. 1–4, 261–76; Swain, *Federal Conservation Policy,* esp. 160–70; Clements, "Herbert Hoover and Conservation"; Krog, "Organizing the Production of Leisure." Roosevelt's interest in conservation is detailed in Nixon, *Franklin D. Roosevelt and Conservation,* and is interpreted in comparative perspective in Cross, "Ideas in Politics." Roosevelt's ideas on planning are in Roosevelt to Mrs. Caspar Whitney, December 8, 1930, Private Correspondence, 1928–1932 File, Roosevelt as Governor Papers, FDRL; Roosevelt, "Growing Up by Plan"; Fusfeld, *The Economic Thought of Franklin D. Roosevelt and the Origins of the New Deal,* 45, 48–49, 123–53, 210–12, 254–56; Tugwell, "The Progressive Orthodoxy of Franklin D. Roosevelt."

25. On the continuities in public policy between Hoover and Roosevelt, see P. Arnold, "Herbert Hoover and the Continuity of American Public Policy"; Frank Freidel, "Hoover and Roosevelt and Historical Continuity," in *Herbert Hoover Reassessed,* 275–91; and essays in *Herbert Hoover and the Historians,* ed. Dodge.

26. Roosevelt, "The New Deal—An Interpretation," cited in Frank Freidel, *Franklin D. Roosevelt: Launching the New Deal,* 71.

27. The literature on the New Deal is immense and growing. For major interpreta-

tions, see Schlesinger, Jr. *The Age of Roosevelt;* Graham, Jr., "Historians and the New Deals"; Leuchtenburg, *Franklin D. Roosevelt and the New Deal;* Zinn, *New Deal Thought,* xv–xxxvi; Conkin, *The New Deal;* Bernstein, "The New Deal"; essays in *The New Deal,* ed. Braeman, Bremner, and Brody; articles by Alan Brinkley, Bradford Lee, and William Leuchtenburg, *Wilson Quarterly* 6 (Spring 1982): 51–93; Romasco, *The Politics of Recovery;* Karl, *The Uneasy State;* McElvaine, *The Great Depression;* Cohen, *The Roosevelt New Deal;* Rosenof, "New Deal *Pragmatism* and Economic *Systems*"; essays in *The Rise and Fall of the New Deal Order,* ed. Fraser and Gerstle; Graham, Jr., *Soviet-American Dialogue on the New Deal;* Eden, *The New Deal and Its Legacy;* Badger, *The New Deal;* Biles, *A New Deal for the American People;* Parrish, *Anxious Decades;* and Schwarz, *The New Dealers.*

Reviews of the recent literature on the New Deal include Kirkendall, "The New Deal as Watershed"; Auerbach, "New Deal, Old Deal, or Raw Deal"; Braeman, "The New Deal and the 'Broker State'"; Graham, Jr. "The New Deal"; Lowitt, "The New Deal"; Skocpol, "Political Response to Capitalist Crisis"; Gelfand and Neymeyer, *The New Deal Viewed from Fifty Years;* Skocpol, "Legacies of New Deal Liberalism"; Graham, Jr., "The Broker State"; Sitkoff, *Fifty Years Later;* Graham and Wander, *Franklin D. Roosevelt;* Olson, *Historical Dictionary of the New Deal;* Cohen, *The Roosevelt New Deal;* Kidd, "Redefining the New Deal"; Braeman, "The New Deal"; the bibliographic sections in Badger, *The New Deal,* 313–64; Biles, *A New Deal for the American People,* 249–60; Parrish, *Anxious Decades,* 490–502; and A. Brinkley, "Prosperity, Depression, and War."

28. Rexford G. Tugwell, "Comments," *Political Science Quarterly* 87 (1972): 561. Though Raymond Moley later moved to the right, at the time others took Tugwell's view, as seen in the literature on the Brain Trust: Tugwell, *The Brains Trust* and *Roosevelt's Revolution;* Schwarz, *Liberal: Adolf A. Berle;* Kirkendall, "A. A. Berle, Jr., Student of the Corporation"; Loftin, "The Political Theory of Adolf Augustus Berle, Jr."; Rosen, "Roosevelt and the Brains Trust" and *Hoover, Roosevelt, and the Brains Trust.*

29. There is a large body of works on Franklin D. Roosevelt, ranging from biographies to his role in coordinating reform efforts. Among the best of these works are Arthur M. Schlesinger, Jr., *The Age of Roosevelt,* 3 vols.; J. Burns, *Roosevelt: The Lion and the Fox* and *Roosevelt: The Soldier of Freedom;* Freidel, *Franklin D. Roosevelt: A Rendezvous with Destiny;* Kenneth S. Davis, *FDR,* 4 vols.; and Maney, *The Roosevelt Prescence.*

30. On the long-range organizational continuities, see Nash, "Experiments in Industrial Mobilization"; Leuchtenburg, "The New Deal and the Analogue of War"; Hawley, *The Great War,* esp. 213–29; Nash, *The Crucial Era,* 1–63; Freidel, "Hoover and Roosevelt and Historical Continuity"; Cook, *Academicians in Government from Roosevelt to Roosevelt.* Monographic studies of New Deal industrial and agricultural planning include Himmelberg, *Origins of the National Recovery Administration;* Hawley, *New Deal and the Problem of Monopoly;* Ohl, *Hugh S. Johnson and the New Deal;* Brand, *Corporatism and the Rule of Law;* Bellush, *The Failure of the NRA;* McQuaid, "The Frustration of Corporate Revival during the Early New Deal" and *Big Business and Presidential Power,* chap. 1; Kirkendall, *Social Scientists and Farm Politics in the Age of Roosevelt;* Saloutos, "New Deal Agricultural Policy" and *The American Farmer and the New Deal;* Skocpol and Finegold, "State Capacity and Economic Intervention in the Early New Deal"; and Finegold and Skocpol, *State and Party in America's New Deal.* Two model studies of lesser known New Deal planning efforts are Conkin, *Tomorrow a New World,* and J. Arnold, *The New Deal in the Suburbs.* The best summary of the planning for the NRA and AAA is Freidel, *Franklin D. Roosevelt: Launching the New Deal,* 60–101, 299–319, 408–35, 444–47. Perceptive comments on Roosevelt as politician and leader of the New Deal are in J. Burns, *Roosevelt: The Lion and The Fox;* Tugwell, *The Democratic Roosevelt;* and Conkin, *The New Deal,* chap. 1.

31. Ickes worked to create the hard-nosed image, as seen in his *Autobiography of a Curmudgeon.* Evaluations of Ickes include Lear, *Harold L. Ickes;* Harmon, "Some Contributions of Harold L. Ickes"; Trani, "Conflict or Compromise"; White and Maze, *Harold Ickes of the New Deal;* Watkins, *Righteous Pilgrim.*

32. Schlesinger, *The Age of Roosevelt*, 2:282–85; Ickes, *The Secret Diary of Harold L. Ickes*, 1:29, 34, 37, 53–57, 59–62, 66.

33. NPB minutes, July 30, 1933, Dr. N. I. Stone to Mitchell, August 29, 1933, Mitchell to Merriam, September 1, 1933, Merriam to Mitchell, November 4, 1933, Merriam to Malcolm Willey, December 4, 1933, all in CEM Papers; and B. Jones, "A Plan for Planning in the New Deal."

34. National Planning Board, *Final Report—1933–34* (Washington, D.C., 1934), 15–16.

35. Charles W. Eliot II to Merriam, February 12 and April 4, 1934, Delano to Merriam, May 31, 1934, Merriam to Delano, June 6, 1934, NPB minutes, April 23, 1934, all in Box 169, CEM Papers. Dennison arranged to review the final report with NPB members, as noted in Dennison memorandum to Mr. Hahn, Fahey, Leeds, and Flanders, June 4, 1934, Flanders Papers.

36. Roberts, "Demonstrating Neutrality"; Charles W. Eliot II to W. W. Campbell and R. T. Crane, April 24, 1934, and NPB minutes, May 4, 1934, Box 169, CEM Papers. The NAS and SSRC memoranda were included in NPB, *Final Report—1933–34*, 39–61. On the continued cooperation between the NPB and these organizations, see Delano to W. W. Campbell and R. T. Crane, February 14, 1935, Box 173, and Merriam to Edmund E. Day, March 30, 1935, Box 48, CEM Papers. For a different view of the social scientists' relationship with the federal government, see Lyons, *The Uneasy Partnership*, 1–79.

37. Auerbach, "Scientists in the New Deal."

38. Merriam's draft of May 24, 1934, attached to Charles W. Eliot II to J. C. Merriam, May 29, 1934, General Correspondence File, John C. Merriam Papers. The "Preliminary Draft of Report on National Planning," June 23, 1934, was presented to Roosevelt at his home in Hyde Park, N.Y., on June 25, 1934, for which see Box 263, 451.4, NRPB Records. The discussion in the text is based on the published version, "A Plan for Planning," NPB, *Final Report—1933–34*.

39. "A Plan for Planning," 18–29.

40. Ibid., 30–34.

41. Ibid., 35–38. Public and private pronouncements by Delano, Merriam, and Mitchell confirm the above textual analysis. For Delano, see "The Economic Implications of National Planning"; "Memorandum on National Planning," May 15, 1934, NPB minutes, May 27–28, 1934, Box 169, CEM Papers; memorandum to the president, February 1, 1935, Speech Material General File, Box 14, PPF 1820, FDRL; Delano to Walter Lippmann, August 2, 1935, and Delano to Dr. James Bryant Conant, October 30, 1935, Box 4, FAD Papers; Delano, "Our Nation's Balance Sheet," December 26, 1935, Speeches and Writings File, Box 24, FAD Papers.

Merriam presented the most complex view of planning and its relation to democracy, as seen in his speech before the joint meeting of the American Political Science Association and the American Sociological Association, December 26, 1934, Box 126, CEM Papers; Merriam review of *The Challenge to Liberty*, by Hoover, and in three books: *Civic Education in the United States, Political Power: Its Composition and Incidence,* and *The Role of Politics in Social Change*.

Mitchell discussed his ideas on planning in "Mr. Hoover's 'The Challenge to Liberty'"; L. Mitchell, *Two Lives*, 366–72; radio broadcast with Levering Tyson, November 29, 1934, Mitchell Papers; "The Social Sciences and National Planning," *Science*, January 18, 1935, 55–62; "Intelligence and the Guidance of Economic Evolution," in his *Authority and the Individual*, 3–36. Analysis of Mitchell's ideas appears in Tugwell, "Wesley Mitchell"; Gruchy, "The Concept of National Planning in Institutional Economics"; and F. Hill, "Wesley Mitchell's Theory of Planning."

42. NPB minutes, June 25, 1934, Box 169, CEM Papers.

43. Ibid.; Delano, Merriam, and Mitchell to the president, June 24, 1934; Delano,

Merriam, and Mitchell draft to Harold L. Ickes, June 27, 1934, never delivered; Delano to Merriam, Mitchell, and NPB, June 28, 1934; Delano to Ickes, July 2, 1934, and attached drafts dated June 29, 1934, all in Box, 169, CEM Papers; and diary entry for June 28, 1934, *The Secret Diary of Harold L. Ickes,* 1:171–72.

44. U.S. National Resources Board, *A Report on National Planning and Public Works in Relation to Natural Resources and Including Land Use and Water Resources with Findings and Recommendations.* The planners' concern with research is in Delano to Roosevelt, July 17, 1937, and Roosevelt to Delano, July 19, 1937, OF 1092, FDRL; U.S. National Resources Committee, *Research—A National Resource: Part 1, Relation of the Federal Government to Research; Part 2, Industrial Research; Part 3, Business Research* (Washington, D.C., 1938–41). In 1946 the National Archives prepared its *Preliminary List of Published and Unpublished Reports of the National Resources Planning Board, 1933–1943,* which still is used by researchers to consult NRPB Records. Clawson, *New Deal Planning,* 322–47 provides a convenient chronological listing of major reports by the planning board from 1933 through 1943.

45. Changes in administrative structure, authorization, and funding are summarized in Clawson, *New Deal Planning,* 39–51, 72–85, 189–98, 289–321; Rockwell, "National Resources Planning," 17–32; Kalish, "National Resource Planning," 87–105, 144–57.

46. Mitchell to Roosevelt, September 23, 1935, OF 1092, FDRL; Merriam to Ruml, September 27, 1935, Box 56, and Mitchell to Merriam, October 16 and November 27, 1935, Box 173, CEM Papers; Mitchell's draft notes for an address on Robert S. Lynd's *Knowledge for What?* Columbia Economics Club, May 2, 1939, Mitchell Papers; Mitchell's radio broadcast with Levering Tyson; Mitchell, "The Social Sciences and National Planning" and "Intelligence and Guidance of Economic Evolution"; F. Hill, "Wesley Mitchell's Theory of Planning," 111–12. For a different explanation of Mitchell's resignation, see Karl, "The Power of Intellect and the Politics of Ideas," 1027.

47. Organization charts in Baugh, *Preliminary Inventory of the Central Office Records of the National Resources Planning Board (Record Group 187),* 29–34.

48. Rockwell, "National Resources Planning"; Kalish, "National Resource Planning"; Warken, *A History of the National Resources Planning Board;* and Clawson, *New Deal Planning.*

49. Clawson, *New Deal Planning,* 77. Detailed narratives of the planning board's research are in Kalish, "National Resource Planning," 54–76, 105–15, 129–43, 157–83, 203–32, 245–98; Warken, *A History of the National Resources Planning Board;* 62–105; and Clawson, *New Deal Planning,* 107–75.

50. Rockwell, "National Resources Planning," 112–29; Clawson, *New Deal Planning,* 52–55, 208–13. Examples of Roosevelt's political maneuvering with the planning board are in Maury Maverick to Roosevelt, January 21, 1936, Roosevelt to Maverick, February 12, 1936, Business Advisory Council memorandum to Roosevelt, March 6, 1936, M. H. McIntyre memorandum for Assistant Secretary Draper, March 16, 1936, Delano to the president, April 17, 1936, Roosevelt memorandum to the heads of Executive Departments, Independent Establishments. . . , June 22, 1936, Roosevelt memorandum for acting director of the budget, June 8, 1936, all in OF 1092, FDRL. On the broader implications of this management style, see Hodgson, *All Things to All Men;* Milkis, *The President and the Parties.*

51. Leuchtenburg, "Roosevelt, Norris, and the 'Seven Little TVAs'"; Leuchtenburg, "Franklin D. Roosevelt's Supreme Court "Packing" Plan," in *The Walter Prescott Webb Memorial Lectures,* ed. Hollingsworth and Holmes, 69–115; and essays in Leuchtenburg, *The FDR Years.*

52. See material cited in n. 43; Henry Wallace, Harold Ickes, Frances Perkins, Harry Hopkins to the president, June 26, 1934, OF 1092, FDRL; diary entries for June 28, 1934, January 30 and April 10 and 30, 1935, *The Secret Diary of Harold L. Ickes,* 1:171–72,

281, 341, 354; diary entries for December 20, 1936, and January 10 and 30, 1937, ibid., 2:20–21, 38–45, 59; Clawson, *New Deal Planning,* 55–57, 199–207; Henry A. Wallace to the president, May 11, 1937, OF 1, FDRL; Harry L. Hopkins to Delano, April 11, 1935, OF 1092, FDRL.

53. Rockwell, "National Resources Planning," 132, summarizes the various planning bills in Congress in tabular form. Discussions of congressional opposition are in Kalish, "National Resource Planning," 183–202, 232–44; Rockwell, "National Resources Planning," 130–54; Clawson, *New Deal Planning,* 214–18.

8. The Crucible of Planning

1. Chapman, "Contours of Public Policy"; Karl, *The Uneasy State,* 155–81; Karl, "Constitution and Central Planning"; Jeffries, "The 'New' New Deal"; Baskerville, "Post-New Deal Economic Thought"; A. Brinkley, "The New Deal and the Idea of the State"; A. Brinkley, *The End of Reform;* Plotke, *Building a Democratic Political Order;* Jeffries, *Wartime America;* and Jeffries, "A 'Third New Deal'?"

2. Scholars have only begun to address this issue of growing internal conflict and external constraints on New Deal reform. Hints on this issue regarding New Deal planning are in John Hancock, "The New Deal and American Planning: The 1930s," in *Two Centuries of American Planning,* ed. Schaffer, 197–230. For political opposition, see Patterson, *Congressional Conservatism and the New Deal,* and Clyde P. Weed, *The Nemesis of Reform: The Republican Party during the New Deal* (New York, 1994), while Badger, *The New Deal,* 260–98, best summarizes the results of recent scholarship. For well-done case studies emphasizing constraints on New Deal reform, see Tweton, *The New Deal at the Grass Roots,* and Abrams, *Conservative Constraints.* Cf. McElvaine, *The Great Depression,* chap. 14, which argues that FDR and the New Deal had run out of ideas by 1937.

3. Rockwell, "National Resources Planning," 33–50; Kalish, "National Resource Planning," 203–314; Warken, *A History of the National Resources Planning Board,* 62–134; Clawson, *New Deal Planning,* 107–75. For the broadened focus, see the representative memorandum by Charles E. Merriam and Leon Henderson, "Emerging Industrio-Governmental Problems," November 9, 1939, Box 184, CEM Papers. For a good case study of one of the major studies, see Inouye and Susskind, "Technological Trends and National Policy."

4. Standard accounts of New Deal efforts at executive-branch reorganization include Karl, *Executive Reorganization and Reform in the New Deal,* and Polenberg, *Reorganizing Roosevelt's Government.* P. Arnold, *Making the Managerial Presidency,* and Milkis, *The President and the Parties,* place the issue in broader perspective.

5. The best overviews of the court plan are in William E. Leuchtenburg, "Franklin D. Roosevelt's Supreme Court 'Packing' Plan," in *Essays on the New Deal,* ed. Hollingsworth and Holmes, 69–115, and Leuchtenburg, *The Supreme Court Reborn.*

6. Ekirch, Jr., *Ideologies and Utopias;* James Holt, "The New Deal and the American Anti-Statist Tradition," in *The New Deal,* ed. Braeman, Bremner, and Brody, 1:27–49; McCraw, "The Historical Background"; and Hawley, "The New Deal State and the Anti-Bureaucratic Tradition."

7. For well-developed examples of the traditional account of the decline of New Deal reform in the late 1930s, see Leuchtenburg, *Franklin D. Roosevelt and the New Deal,* 197–324; Rosenof, *Dogma, Depression, and the New Deal;* Polenberg, *War and Society,* 73–98; and Richard Polenberg, "The Decline of the New Deal, 1937–1940," in *The New Deal,* ed. Braeman, Bremner, and Brody, 1:246–66. That account has been modified in more recent works such as McElvaine, *The Great Depression,* 306–22; Biles, *A New Deal for the American People,* 136–53; Parrish, *Anxious Decades,* 364–85, 437–76; K. Davis, *FDR: Into the Storm;* and A. Brinkley, *End of Reform.*

8. Polenberg, *War and Society;* Perrett, *Days of Sadness, Years of Triumph;* Blum, *V Was for Victory;* Winkler, *Home Front, U.S.A.;* O'Neill, *A Democracy at War;* Adams, *The Best War Ever;* Sparrow, *From the Outside In;* and Jeffries, *Wartime America.*

9. Brockie, "Theories of the 1937–38 Crisis and Depression," and Roose, *The Economics of Recession and Revival.*

10. The best descriptions of this economic policy crisis are in Hawley, *The New Deal and the Problem of Monopoly,* 283–403; Stein, *The Fiscal Revolution in America,* 91–130; Romasco, *The Politics of Recovery,* 216–40; May, "New Deal to New Economics"; and A. Brinkley, *End of Reform,* 23–136. Details of the debate from Eccles's and Morgenthau's perspectives can be traced in Eccles, *Beckoning Frontiers;* Hyman, *Marriner S. Eccles;* and John Morton Blum, ed., *From the Morgenthau Diaries* (Boston, 1959–67), a selection of material from the voluminous, very informative Morgenthau Diaries in the Henry Morgenthau, Jr., Papers, FDRL, Hyde Park, N.Y. Recent work has drawn attention to the significant roles of Corcoran and Cohen, for which see Lash, *Dealers and Dreamers,* 317–33, and Schwarz, *The New Dealers,* 138–56.

11. Stein, *The Fiscal Revolution in America,* uses "the struggle for the soul of FDR" as the title of chapter 6, on the response to the recession of 1937–38. The literature on the Keynesian school of economics is immense. For some representative and significant works, see Harris, *The New Economics;* Samuelson, "Economic Thought and the New Industrialism"; Barber, *From New Era to New Deal;* J. R. Davis, *The New Economics and the Old Economists;* Lekachman, *The Age of Keynes;* Critchlow, "The Political Control of the Economy"; and Barber, *Designs within Disorder.*

12. Kimmel, *The Federal Budget and Fiscal Policy,* 175–228; Sundelson, "The Emergency Budget of the Federal Government"; Sargent, "FDR and Lewis W. Douglas"; Browder and Smith, *Independent: A Biography of Lewis W. Douglas,* 84–116; entry for April 13, 1937, Morgenthau Diaries, Henry Morgenthau, Jr., Papers, FDRL.

13. Feis, "Keynes in Retrospect"; Harris, *John Maynard Keynes,* 73–79, 191–96; Lekachman, *Age of Keynes,* esp. 112–43; Stein, *The Fiscal Revolution,* 91–168; Stoneman, *A History of the Economic Analysis of the Great Depression in America;* William J. Barber, "Government as a Laboratory for Economic Learning in the Years of the Democratic Roosevelt," in *The State and Economic Knowledge,* ed. Furner and Supple, 103–37; and Walter S. Salant, "The Spread of Keynesian Doctrines and Practices in the United States," and Margaret Weir, "Ideas and Politics: The Acceptance of Keynesianism in Britain and the United States," both in *The Political Power of Ideas,* ed. P. A. Hall, respectively 27–51 and 53–86. Cf. Baskerville, "Post-New Deal Economic Thought," and Rosenof, *Economics in the Long Run.*

14. On the impact of Keynesian economists, see Sweezy, "The Kenyesians and Government Policy"; B. Jones, "The Role of Keynesians in Wartime Policy and Postwar Planning"; and Barber, *Designs within Disorder.* More specifically, economist Lauchlin Currie, who had joined Eccles at the Federal Reserve Board, worked closely with Leon Henderson and Isador Lubin, commissioner of labor statistics, in developing policy memoranda for Eccles and the spending faction in the midst of the policy debate, for which see B. Jones, "Lauchlin Currie, Pump Priming, and New Deal Fiscal Policy," and attached memorandums and comments by Lauchlin Currie, ibid., 525–48; B. Jones, "Lauchlin Curie and the Causes of the 1937 Recession"; and Currie, "Causes of the Recession."

15. Although no full-scale biography of Hansen has been written, there is a growing body of literature, including Seymour E. Harris, "Hansen, Alvin"; Galbraith, "How Keynes Came to America"; Bryant, Jr. "Alvin H. Hansen's Contribution to Fiscal Policy"; Breit and Ransom, "Alvin H. Hansen"; articles in *Quarterly Journal of Economics* 90 (1976): 1–37; Barber, "The Career of Alvin Hansen in the 1920s and 1930s"; Brazelton, "Alvin Harvey Hansen"; and scattered biographical information in the Alvin Hansen Papers, Harvard University Archives, Cambridge, Mass. The Hansen Papers contain a number

of letters to Hansen on his retirement in 1956 that reveal that many of the graduates of the Harvard seminar went into government service in the late 1930s and during World War II.

16. That Delano, Dennison, and Ruml were in the midst of the debate is not surprising, since all three had connections with the Federal Reserve Board. Delano had been on the original Board of Governors in 1914 until his service for the U.S. Army. He served as chairman of the Board of Governors and Federal Reserve agent of the Richmond, Virginia, Federal Reserve Bank from 1921 to 1936. Dennison became deputy chairman and director of the Federal Reserve Bank of Boston in January 1938 and served until 1945. In the summer of 1937 Marriner Eccles, chairman of the Board of Governors of the reorganized Federal Reserve Board in Washington, D.C., appointed Ruml a director of the Federal Reserve Bank of New York to replace Owen D. Young. From January 1941 through December 1946, Ruml served as chairman of the Board of Governors for the New York branch. Lowe, "New Deal to New Economics," 99–102, 202–4, 212–15, 220–22, and 229–32, briefly discusses Eccles's connection with the planners.

17. Over time, economists have placed increasingly less emphasis on the use and efficacy of fiscal spending policy by the New Deal, for which see Smithies, "The American Economy in the Thirties"; E. C. Brown, "Fiscal Policy in the Thirties"; Peppers, "Full-Employment Surplus Analysis and Structural Change"; and Adelstein, "The Nation as an Economic Unit."

18. Most scholars now accept the argument that spending policy would have come to the fore in the United States even without Keynes, as best seen in such works as Stein, *Fiscal Revolution in America;* Lowe, "New Deal to New Economics"; Stephen W. Baskerville, "Cutting Loose from Prejudice: Economists and the Great Depression," in *Nothing Else to Fear,* ed. Baskerville and Willett, 259–84; Baskerville, "Post-New Deal Economic Thought"; Weir, "Ideas and Politics."

19. Dennison, "Business and Government"; Dennison to Frank Murphy, April 1, 1937, HSD Papers; Dennison to McGraw-Hill Book Company, June 4, 1937, Mitchell Papers; various entries in Office Diary, HSD Papers; Galbraith, *A Life in Our Times,* 61–67. Collins, *The Business Response to Keynes,* 63–67, argues that these four came "to an essentially Keynesian analysis of the American economy and to a clear formulation of compensatory fiscal policy."

20. Dennison and Galbraith, *Modern Competition and Business Policy;* Berle and Means, *The Modern Corporation and Private Property;* Kirkendall, "A. A. Berle, Jr."; Schwarz, *Liberal: Adolf A. Berle and the Vision of an American Era,* 55–68; McCraw, "In Retrospect: Berle and Means"; and Lee, "From Multi-Industry Planning to Keynesian Planning."

21. Dennison, Filene, Flanders, and Leeds, *Toward Full Employment.*

22. Office Diary entries for August 7 and 10, 1936, November 18, 1937, and May 12, 1938, HSD Papers; "The Reminiscences of Paul Appleby (1952)," 143ff., COHC. Ruml's work for Macy's can be seen in Macy's Training Squad, 1936–40, Box 1, Series II, Ruml Papers.

23. E. Nollen interview with Louis Brownlow, April 13, 1956, Box 1, Ruml, "Business Outlook," October 28, 1937, and Ruml memorandum dated February 5, 1938, Series II, all in Ruml Papers; Ruml to Professor Charles Rist, February 15, 1938, and Ruml to Merriam, March 29, 1938, Box 56, Ruml memorandum, Box 179, CEM Papers; Ruml, "Warm Springs Memorandum," April 1, 1938, Box 1, Series II, Ruml Papers; Ruml to Jacob Viner and to Arthur F. Burns, February 25, 1958, Folder 5, Box 4, Series I, Ruml Papers; Ruml to Arthur Schlesinger, Jr., February 25, 1957, Folder 4, Box 4, Series I, Ruml Papers; Aubrey Williams to Ruml, September 14, 1938, Gladys E. Campbell to Arline Smith, October 13, 1938, and attached, Williams to Ruml, January 2, 1940, and Ruml to Williams, January 1940, all in R Personal File, Williams Papers, FDRL; Harry L. Hopkins to David Lynch, November 10, 1942, F.D.R.—Monopoly Message,

1938 File, Hopkins Papers, FDRL; "Leon Henderson in the Lion's Den," undated newspaper clipping in L-H Speeches—Etc—Postwar File, War Production Board papers, Henderson Papers, FDRL; Memorandum of E. N. [Emmeline Nollen], Conversation with Leon Henderson for B. R. Memoirs, undated, Folder 3, Box 1, Ruml Papers; and Eccles, *Beckoning Frontiers,* 246.

24. Ruml, "Warm Springs Memorandum."

25. Ibid.; Leon Henderson to Ruml, November 1, 1946, Box 3, Ruml Papers.

26. Reagan, "The Withholding Tax, Beardsley Ruml, and Modern American Public Policy."

27. Rosenman, *The Public Papers and Addresses of Franklin D. Roosevelt,* vol. for 1938, pp. 221–48. Cf. 226 and Ruml, "Warm Springs Memorandum."

28. The full text is in *FDR's Fireside Chats,* ed. Buhite and Levy, 112–23; the quotation is on 115.

29. Delano to the president, April 15, 1938, Fireside Chat on Economic Conditions, April 1938 File, Rosenman Papers, FDRL; Delano, "Comments Re Article in New York Times on Subject of 'Spending Never Stops,'" April 23, 1938, Politics-Post Offices File, Box 5, Series 1, and Delano, "Memorandum in regard to the Budget," in Banking Reforms, Gold Standard, Economics File, Box 2, FAD Papers; Delano to secretary of the treasury April 12, 1938, and attached memorandum "Where Are We?" April 9, 1938, Morgenthau Diaries, Book 120, pp. 181–209, FDRL.

30. Delano to Morgenthau, April 27, 1938, and Morgenthau to Delano, April 28, 1938, Morgenthau Diaries, Book 121, pp. 208, 212–14, FDRL; Delano memorandum to the president, June 6, 1938, Folder 33, Box 1, Series II, Ruml Papers; Charles W. Eliot II, "Confidential Memorandum of Conference with the President, June 6, 1938," Box 174, CEM Papers; and Delano to the president, August 12 and December 19 and 20, 1938, Folder 4, Box 4, Series I, Ruml Papers.

31. The Morgenthau Diaries contain complete transcripts of meetings of the Fiscal and Monetary Advisory Board from its first meeting on October 20, 1938, until its gradual disappearance. They clearly indicate that Morgenthau remained uncomfortable about the idea and continually made sarcastic remarks about it in private policy planning sessions of the Treasury group immediately under Morgenthau. Lowe, "New Deal to New Economics," 244–48, gives a brief description of the board. Albert Lepawsky, a staff member of the planning agency, later wrote a history of the board, arguing that it served as a transition group to carry over the New Deal reforms into the war period; see Lepawsky, "The New Deal at Mid-passage."

32. Key researchers for the NRC's Industrial Policy Committee included Gardiner Means, Isador Lubin, Leon Henderson, Lauchlin Currie, Herbert Feis, and Mordecai Ezekiel. On the committee, see Gruchy, "The Economics of the National Resources Committee"; Hawley, *The New Deal and the Problem of Monopoly,* 172–78, 398–99; Warken, *A History of the NRPB,* 90–96, 145–49. The committee's most important study, *The Structure of the American Economy: Part 1, Basic Characteristics,* and *Part 2, Toward Full Use of Resources* (Washington, D.C., 1939–40), brought together the ideas of Means, D. E. Montgomery, J. M. Clark, Hansen, and Ezekiel without endorsing any one of them. For recent analysis of the committee's work, see Lee, "Gardiner C. Means and the Origins of His Doctrine of Administered Prices," "A New Dealer in Agriculture," and "From Multi-Industry Planning to Keynesian Planning."

33. For a representative sampling of the planners' ambivalence to permanent spending, see Delano to Raymond L. Buell, February 9, 1939, Box 173, CEM Papers; Dennison's testimony on May 22, 1939, in U.S. Congress, Temporary National Economic Committee, *Hearings, Part 9; Savings and Investment* (Washington, D.C., 1940), pp. 3774–89; Delano to the President, May 22, 1939, PPF 72, FDRL; Ruml untitled paper in Folder 33, Box 1, Series II, and Ruml, "Remarks by way of Introduction to the CED Tax and Fiscal Proposal of 1947," Box 2, Series I, Ruml Papers.

34. A. E. Buck memorandum "Financial Management by the President," September 9, 1936, File D-II, Papers of the President's Committee on Administrative Management, 1936–37, FDRL; Merriam's testimony before the Joint Congressional Committee on Reorganization of Government Departments, March 8, 1937, Box 266, and Merriam, "Administrative Management," January 30, 1939, Folder 9, Box 263, CEM Papers; Merriam, "Public Administration and Political Theory"; Marx, "The Bureau of the Budget"; Berman, *The Office of Management and Budget and the Presidency,* 3–15; and Lowe, "New Deal to New Economics," 38–47. For the origins of executive reform, Arnold, *Making the Managerial Presidency,* is the best account.

35. Merriam, "Planning Agencies in America," *American Political Science Review* 29 (1935): 197–211; Merriam, "Governmental Planning in the United States"; Merriam, "Planning in a Democracy," *American Planning and Civic Annual* (1940) (Washington, D.C., 1940), 1–12; Merriam, "The National Resources Planning Board," *Public Administration Review* 1 (1940–41): 116–21; Merriam, "The National Resources Planning Board," in *Planning for America,* ed. George Galloway et al., 489–506; Karl, "Merriam's 'Continuously Planning Society'"; and for a somewhat different view, see Karl, *Charles E. Merriam and the Study of Politics,* 226–70.

36. E. Nollen interview with Louis Brownlow; Minutes of the Problems and Policy Committee, SSRC, February 25, 1933, Box 146, CEM Papers; Howard Odum to William F. Ogburn, February 13 and 21, 1933, and Ogburn to Odum, February 28, 1933, Box 13, Ogburn Papers; Robert T. Crane telegram to Merriam, June 19, 1933, and Merriam to Crane, August 3, 1933, Box 47, Merriam to George Soule, June 27, 1933, Box 56, Merriam to Ruml, July 10, 1933, and Merriam, Soule, Ruml Memorandum to SSRC [July 1933?], Box 56, Merriam to Crane, August 21, 1933, and other correspondence, Box 47, all in CEM Papers; [Crane] memorandum to Problems and Policy Committee, SSRC, October 24, 1933, and Crane to Ruml, October 18, 1933, SSRC Commissions 1934 File, Box 26, Ogburn Papers; Crane to Roosevelt [November 1933], Roosevelt to Crane, November 17, 1933, Roosevelt memorandum for Mac [M. H. McIntyre], December 24, 1934, and McIntyre to Gulick, December 27, 1934, OF 868, FDRL.

37. R. B. Fosdick to John D. Rockefeller, Jr., December 20, 1933, Box 58, Rockefeller Boards File, Records of John D. Rockefeller, Jr.; "Notes on Development of Spelman Fund Policy and Program," 14, Box 157, CEM Papers.

38. Roosevelt Memorandum to secretary of the interior, December 28, 1933, Merriam to Ickes, November 1, 1933, January 2 and March 7, 1934, and Ickes to Merriam, March 9, 1934, Correspondence with Friends File, Secretary of Interior File, Ickes Papers, Library of Congress; *The Secret Diary of Harold L. Ickes,* 1:136; Merriam to Professor W. Y. Elliot, January 22, 1934, Box 47, and Harold F. Gosnell, "Commissions of Inquiry Appointed by the Social Science Research Council in 1933," Box 131, CEM Papers; SSRC Commission of Inquiry on Public Service Personnel, *Better Government Personnel* (New York, 1935); File A-II-5, Papers of the President's Committee on Administrative Management, FDRL, Hyde Park, N.Y.; Merriam to Bruce Bliven, April 15, 1938, Box 45, and Merriam to Delano, October 4, 1935, Box 173, CEM Papers; cross-reference of Ickes to Roosevelt, December 20, 1935, OF 1092, FDRL; Ickes to Roosevelt, December 20, 1935, OF 285, Merriam to My Dear Count [Guy Moffett], December 13, 1935, Merriam, Charles 1928–39 File, Box 3, Series 5, Spelman Fund of New York Records.

39. On Gulick, see Karl, *Executive Reorganization,* 127–65. On Hansen's work, see scrapbook of clippings on Commission of Inquiry on National Policy in International Economic Relations, HUG(B)-H145.80F, Hansen Papers; SSRC Commission of Inquiry on National Policy in International Relations, *Report: International Economic Relations* (Minneapolis, 1934); Wesley Clair Mitchell to Merriam, May 18, 1934, Box 169, CEM Papers. For Hansen's initial work with the NRC, see memorandum of Henry S. Dennison–Harold Merrill phone conversation of June 16, 1938, and Merrill to Hansen, June 17, 1938, 153.3 NRPB Records. Material from NRPB Records will be cited by

the numerical classification system described in Baugh, *Preliminary Inventory of the Central Office Records of the National Resources Planning Board.* Unless otherwise identified, the material is from the Central Office Correspondence File.

40. Eliot memorandum for Mr. Delano, March 19, 1936, OF 1092, FDRL.

41. Ickes to president, February 8, 1936, and Merriam to Brownlow, February 20, 1936, Box 173, CEM Papers; Memorandum on Conference with the President, March 4, 1936, File A-II-7, Papers of the President's Committee on Administrative Management; Louis Brownlow, "Management Study," March 16, 1936, and Charles W. Eliot II notes re conference with president, March 16, 1936, Box 178, CEM Papers.

42. Congressional resistance to the reorganization bill centered on provisions for a permanent planning board, for which see Roosevelt to Lindsey Warren, February 7, 1939, and Warren to Roosevelt, February 10, 1939, Eliot's memorandum for the Advisory Committee April 5, 1939, Delano to Ickes, April 6, 1939, Ickes to Delano, April 11, 1939, Delano to Roosevelt, April 11, 1939, Roosevelt to Delano, April 21, 1939, all in OF 1092, FDRL; and Polenberg, *Reorganizing Roosevelt's Government,* 134–35, 138, 163.

43. Material in n. 35; special issue on the Executive Office, *Public Administration Review* 1 (Winter 1941); Rockwell, "National Resources Planning," 86–129. For a perceptive analysis of the long-term implications of reorganization, see Milkis, *The President and the Parties.*

44. Rockwell, "National Resources Planning," 130–54; Kalish, "National Resource Planning," 298–314; Clawson, *New Deal Planning,* 214–18.

45. On the importance of this broader international comparative perspective on liberal thinking, see F. Warren III, *Liberals and Communism;* Ekirch, *Ideologies and Utopias,* 208–44; Alexander, *Nationalism and American Thought,* 164–89; Pells, *Radical Visions and American Dreams,* 292–368; Garraty, *The Great Depression,* 182–257; and A. Brinkley, *End of Reform,* 137–74. Merriam's correspondence in CEM Papers reflected this concern.

46. Biographical information on Yantis is based on Yantis, George F. File, 153.2-A, NRPB Records; Merriam-Yantis correspondence, Box 59, CEM Papers; correspondence in Yantis Papers, University of Washington Library, Seattle, Wash. NRPB reports and internal correspondence indicate Yantis's interest in regional natural resources planning. For a general account of one of the major projects, see McKinley, *Uncle Sam and the Pacific Northwest,* and Voeltz, "Genesis and Development of a Regional Power Agency in the Pacific Northwest." On the broader importance of these kinds of infrastructure projects for the New Deal, see Schwarz, *The New Dealers.*

47. NRPB minutes, September 4–6, 1939, 103.71, NRPB Records; Delano to the president, September 5, 1939, OF 1092, FDRL; H. M. Waite to Delano, September 8 and November 29, 1939, 667.43 and 667.1, NRPB Records; Delano to the president, November 2, 1939, OF 1092; NRPB minutes, June 14–15, 1940, 103.71, NRPB Records; Delano Memorandum on Democracy and Planning in Crisis, 104.1, NRPB Records. Warken, *A History of the NRPB,* 135–81, and Clawson, *New Deal Planning,* 177–81 provide summaries of the NRPB's post-defense planning efforts.

48. Memorandum of Conference with the President, October 8, 1940, 104.1, NRPB Records; Delano memorandum to the president, November 12, 1940, NRPB minutes, November 10–12, 1940, 103.71, NRPB Records; Industrial Location Section, NRPB, "Industrial Location and National Policy" typescript, March 1941, OF 1092, FDRL; and various items in NRPB minutes, 103.71, NRPB Records. The NRPB Records are filled with various reports concerning plant-site location.

49. On Roosevelt and the confusion of mobilization agencies, see Catton, *The War Lords of Washington;* Janeway, *The Struggle for Survival;* Polenberg, *War and Society,* 5–36; Perrett, *Days of Sadness, Years of Triumph,* 67–74; Blum, *V Was for Victory,* 117–46; Winkler, *Home Front, U.S.A.,* 1–23; D. Brinkley, *Washington Goes to War;* O'Neill, *A Democracy at War,* 75–103; and A. Brinkley, *End of Reform,* 175–200.

50. NRPB Records and OF 1092, FDRL, contain copies of the quarterly economic-trends reports. Roosevelt's unwillingness to approve the NRPB's idea for a public productivity conference was noted in Delano memorandum for the president, August 29, 1941, and Roosevelt memorandum for Delano, September 1, 1941, in PSF for NRPB, FDRL; NRPB minutes, September 29–30 and October 21–23, 1941, 103.71, NRPB Records.

51. Sumner Welles to the president, October 18, 1941, OF 4351, FDRL; Delano to Vice President Henry A. Wallace, October 25, 1941, NRPB Minutes, October 21–23, 1941, NRPB Records.

52. NRPB minutes, March 17–19, 1942, 103.71, NRPB Records. Merriam's published works in this period dealt with the relationship between foreign affairs and domestic fear of the destruction of democracy, as seen in *On the Agenda of Democracy* and *What Is Democracy?*

53. Publicity efforts are noted in various files of Records of Post-War Agenda Section, NRPB Records.

54. U.S. NRPB, *Development of Resources and Stabilization of Employment in the United States;* NRPB, *Progress Report: 1940–1941;* NRPB, *Our Public Works Experience;* NRPB, *National Resources Development Report for 1942.*

55. Trattner, "Progressivism and World War I"; Hirshfield, "Nationalist Progressivism and World War I"; Knoles, "American Intellectuals and World War I"; Cywar, "John Dewey"; Bourcke, "The Status of Politics"; A. Davis, "Welfare, Reform, and World War I"; R. Schaffer, *America in the Great War,* 64–126; Shapiro, "The Twilight of Reform."

56. For convincing accounts of the failure of reform during World War II, see Polenberg, *War and Society,* 73–98; Perrett, *Days of Sadness, Years of Triumph,* 325–56; David Brody, "The New Deal and World War II," in *The New Deal,* ed. Braeman, Bremner, and Brody; Blum, *V Was for Victory,* 221–45; Winkler, *Home Front, U.S.A.,* 84–97; and A. Brinkley, *End to Reform,* 175–271.

57. John McDiarmid, "The Mobilization of Social Scientists," in *Civil Service in Wartime,* ed. L. White, 74–80; Rockwell, "National Resources Planning," 155–206, on the 1940 reorganization; Brady, "Toward Security," 30–169, for the best discussion of NRPB postwar planning efforts.

58. Merriam to Gulick, February 20, 1941, Box 59, CEM Papers; Eliot, "Status of Work" February 28, 1941, NRPB minutes, March 6–7, 1941, 103.71, NRPB Records; Gulick, *Administrative Reflections from World War II,* x; Gulick, "Preliminary Tabulation of Appropriate Post-Defense Measures," July 22, 1941, attached to Eliot to Merriam, July 29, 1941, Box 47, CEM Papers; Gulick and Eliot memorandum for NRPB, June 10, 1942, 830.5, NRPB Records; Gulick memorandum to NRPB, August 12, 1941, NRPB minutes, August 15–17, 1941, 103.71, NRPB Records; Lloyd George memorandum for Mr. Eliot, August 27, 1941, NRPB minutes, August 29, 1941, 103.71.

59. The NRPB published a whole series of educational pamphlets that often summarized more technical and lengthy works, for which see *After Defense What? Full Employment, Security, Upbuilding America, Post-Defense Planning* (Washington, D.C., August 1941); Alvin H. Hansen, *After the War: Full Employment, Post-War Planning* (Washington, D.C., January, 1942); Charles S. Ascher, *Better Cities, Building America* (Washington, D.C., April 1942); Miles L. Colean, *Role of Housebuilding Industry, Building America* (Washington, D.C., July 1942); *After the War, Toward Security* (Washington, D.C., September 1942); *Post-War Planning, Full Employment, Security, Building America* (Washington, D.C., September 1942); *Future of Transportation, Building America* (Washington, D.C., September 1942); *Post-War Agenda, Full Employment, Security, Building America* (Washington, D.C., November 1942); Alvin H. Hansen, *After the War* (1943 revision); *Post-War Plan and Program* (Washington, D.C., February 1943); Lawrence K. Frank, with the assistance of Louise K. Kiser, *Human Conservation, Story of Our Wasted Resources* (Washington, D.C., March 1943).

Clawson, *New Deal Planning,* 333–346 lists the major pamphlets. NRPB Records contain a complete set of these pamphlets. For a particularly revealing unpublished pamphlet, see Ralph J. Watkins, "The Framework for an Economy of Plenty," November 27, 1942, Box 229, CEM Papers. For the NRPB's urban planning work during the war, see Funigiello, *The Challenge to Urban Liberalism,* 163–86.

60. NRPB reports and minutes emphasized the need for economic balance and stabilization. For some representative examples, see "A Plan for Post-Defense Planning," prepared by NRPB staff under the direction of John Millett, July 18, 1941, NRPB minutes, July 21–23, 1941, and "Proposed Federal Programs for Urban Redevelopment and Housing," NRPB minutes, August 15–17, 1941, both in 103.71, NRPB Records.

61. Gulick to Johnson, February 18, 1943, 830.31, NRPB Records.

62. Delano to the president, August 19, 1939, NRPB minutes of meeting, August 19, 1939, 103.71, and Delano memorandum to the president, July 31, 1940, 104.1, NRPB Records; for the Four Freedoms speech, see Rosenman, *The Public Papers and Addresses of Franklin D. Roosevelt,* vol. for 1941, pp. 663–72; Luther Gulick, "Preliminary Considerations on Post-Defense Planning," March 6, 1941, NRPB minutes, March 1941, 103.71, NRPB Records; Eliot Memorandum for the NRPB, May 23, 1941, Box 238, CEM Papers; NRPB Minutes, June 28–30, 1941, 103.71, NRPB Records.

63. "Notes on Conference with the President," June 29, 1941, 104.1, NRPB Records; "Proposed Messages to Congress on Post-War Security (Social Security Board and National Planning Commission)," October 1, 1941, OF 1092, FDRL; "Interviews with Louis Brownlow and Luther Gulick, June 1, 1949," Box 1, General Correspondence File, Rosenman Papers; Rosenman, *Working with Roosevelt,* 424–26.

64. NRPB, *National Resources Development Report for 1943,* part 1, *Post-War Plan and Program* (Washington, D.C., January 1943), 3.

65. Scholars have only begun to address the nature of American politics and culture in the 1940s, especially in regard to the emergence of this new liberalism, as noted in Reagan, "Fighting the Good War at Home." John Morton Blum argues in *V Was for Victory* that the fundamental conservatism of Depression-era America carried over into the war years, but he does not develop the point fully. Two of Blum's students provide different perspectives; see Winkler, *Home Front, U.S.A.,* and Jeffries, *Wartime America.* Chafe, *The Unfinished Journey,* and Boyer, *Promises to Keep,* begin to suggest the implications of this new liberalism, while A. Brinkley, "The New Deal and the Idea of the State"; A. Brinkley, *End of Reform,* 227–71; and Kloppenberg, *The Virtues of Liberalism,* 100–123, 137–41, are the most recent treatments of the subject. Cf. Graebner, *The Age of Doubt.*

66. Eliot memorandum for NRPB, "A Six Months 'Must' Program," May 20, 1942, NRPB minutes, May 25–27, 1942, 103.71, NRPB Records; Eliot memorandum for the staff, June 2, 1942, NRPB minutes, June 12–13, 1942; "Notes on Conference with Mr. John Maynard Keynes," NRPB minutes, June 3–6, 1941; NRPB minutes, December 16–17, 1941, for conference with Treasury economists and Budget Director Harold Smith; NRPB minutes, June 12–13, 1942, for acceleration of postwar planning; NRPB minutes, August 11–14, 1942, for cooperation with Federal Reserve Board; NRPB minutes, October 5–9, 1942, for meeting with Keynesian economists before finalizing draft of 1943 report.

67. NRPB minutes, October 5 and November 9 and 20–21, 1939, 103.71, NRPB Records; Delano to Mrs. Franklin D. Roosevelt, November 14, 1939, OF 1092, FDRL.

68. "The Reminiscences of E. M. Burns (1965)," 56–67, COHC; Vera Shlakman, "Eveline M. Burns: Social Economist," in *Social Security in International Perspective,* ed. Jenkins, 3–25; interview with Dr. Eveline Burns, New York City, October 1, 1979, copy in COHC; E. Burns, *Toward Social Security;* L. Jones, *Eveline M. Burns and the American Social Security System,* 27–30, 71–78, 94–98.

69. "The Reminiscences of E. M. Burns," 104–12; interview with Dr. Burns; Delano

memoranda for the president, October 2 and 8, 1941, Delano to General Edwin M. Watson, October 15, 1941, Delano to the president, December 4, 1941, all in OF 1092, FDRL; NRPB to the president, January 16, 1942, NRPB minutes, January 7, 1942, 103.71, NRPB Records; Merriam to Burns, December 10, 1942, Box 217, CEM Papers; E. Burns, "The Beveridge Report"; L. Jones, *Eveline M. Burns*, 107–8.

70. K. Olson, "The American Beveridge Plan." Cf. James T. Patterson, "Comparative Welfare History: Britain and the United States, 1930–1945," in *The Roosevelt New Deal*, ed. Cohen, 125–43, and Edwin Amenta and Theda Skocpol, "Redefining the New Deal: World War II and the Development of Social Provision in the United States," in *The Politics of Social Policy in the United States*, ed. Weir, Orloff, and Skocpol, 81–122.

71. During the war, Hansen published a number of articles and books dealing with compensatory spending policy that put him in the public eye, including those referred to in n. 59. For one sample of NRPB "cold feet" about Hansen's recommendations, see memorandum for Stephen Early, August 12, 1941, OF 1092, FDRL. For differences in the NRPB recommendations, cf. Hansen's pamphlets cited above in n. 59 with U.S. NRPB, *National Resources Development Report for 1943*, part 1, pp. 13, 27–30. NRPB differences with Hansen came out in the open during the congressional debate over the 1943 appropriations.

72. U.S. NRPB, *National Resources Development Report for 1943: Part 1, Postwar Plan and Program; Part 2, Wartime Planning for War and Post War;* and *Part 3, Security, Work, and Relief Policies*.

73. Ibid.; Reagan, "The Withholding Tax, Beardsley Ruml, and Modern American Public Policy"; Collins, *Business Response to Keynes*, 115–209; Collins, "American Corporatism"; Wolfe, *America's Impasse*.

Epilogue: The Abolition and Legacy of New Deal Planning

1. Karl, *The Uneasy State*, 155–81; Karl, "In Search of National Planning"; Karl, "Constitution and Central Planning"; Jeffries, "The 'New' New Deal"; and Jeffries, "A 'Third New Deal'?"

2. A. Brinkley, *The End of Reform*. On constraints facing the New Deal and the legacy of reform, see William E. Leuchtenburg, "The Achievement of the New Deal," in *Fifty Years Later*, ed. Sitkoff, 211–31; Frank B. Freidel, "The New Deal: Laying the Foundation for Modern America," in *The Roosevelt New Deal*, ed. Cohen, 3–18; Badger, *The New Deal*, 260–98; Hawley, "The New Deal State and the Anti-Bureaucratic Tradition"; Hamby, *Liberalism and Its Challengers;* and Leuchtenburg, *In the Shadow of FDR*.

This body of work hints at the need for more work carrying the analysis through the years 1937–45, such as implied in Richard Polenberg, "The Decline of the New Deal, 1937–1940," and David Brody, "The New Deal and World War II," both in *The New Deal*, ed. Braeman, Bremner, and Brody, 246–66 and 267–309; Jeffries, "World War II and American Life"; Skocpol, "Legacies of New Deal Liberalism"; A. Brinkley, "Writing the History of Contemporary America"; Baskerville, "Post-New Deal Economic Thought"; Katznelson and Pietrykowski, "Rebuilding the American State"; McElvaine, *The Great Depression*, 306–22; A. Brinkley, "The New Deal and the Idea of the State"; essays in Grant, Nekkers and Waarden, *Organising Business for War;* Polenberg, "The Good War?"; Jeffries, *Wartime America;* Plotke, *Building a Democratic Political Order;* and Sparrow, *From the Outside In*.

3. Roosevelt's attitude toward planning always had been ambivalent, as noted in shorthand notes on a number of NRPB-related materials in OF 1092, FDRL. Yet Roosevelt covered his own tracks by sending noncommittal letters to people inquiring about planning, such as Roosevelt memorandum for Delano, September 9, 1942, in OF 1092, FDRL; materials in NRPB minutes, October 24–28, 1942, 103.71, NRPB Records;

William Green to Roosevelt, October 26, 1942, and Roosevelt to Green, November 5, 1942, OF 1710, FDRL.

4. In January 1943 director Charles W. Eliot II began limited distribution of a mimeograph sheet called "Planning Now" to update information on postwar planning for those people who inquired. NRPB Records contain copies of these materials. Press coverage of the NRPB increased immensely from late 1942 to early 1943, as seen in the best-known piece on the subject by Bliven, Lerner, and Soule, "Charter for America." For excellent summaries of the NRPB's postwar planning efforts and awareness of them, see Nelson Thomas Whyatt, "Planning for the Postwar World: Liberal Journalism during World War II" (Ph.D. diss., University of Minnesota, 1971), 1–207, and Brady, "Toward Security: Postwar Economic and Social Planning in the Executive Office, 1939–1946," 1–169.

5. Patterson, *Congressional Conservatism and the New Deal;* Clyde P. Weed, *The Nemesis of Reform: The Republican Party during the New Deal* (New York, 1994), 169–203; McCoy, "Republican Opposition during Wartime"; Moore, "The Conservative Coalition in the United States Senate." Congressional opposition to the NRPB can be followed in detail in the massive materials in 201–5, NRPB Records.

6. Delano to Merriam, February 23, 1943, 203; Merriam to Delano, August 21, 1942, NRPB minutes, August 1942, 103.71; Delano to the president, October 14, 1942, NRPB minutes, October 1942; NRPB minutes, December 16–17, 1942, all in NRPB Records. Histories of the NRPB all deal with the abolition of the board in 1943. For the best history, see P. White, "The Termination of the National Resources Planning Board." For other accounts, see Seifert, "A History of the National Resources Planning Board"; Warken, *A History of the National Resources Planning Board,* 225–45; Clawson, *New Deal Planning,* 213–41; and planner Merriam's own account, "The National Resources Planning Board: A Chapter in American Planning Experience."

7. U.S. Congress, House, Committee on Appropriations, *Hearings before the Subcommittee on Independent Offices Appropriations Bill for 1944,* 50–76; Clarence Cannon to Delano, February 15, 1943, Box 218, CEM Papers; Charles W. Eliot II memorandum for NRPB, February 20, 1943, 203, NRPB Records; U.S., Congress, House, Representative Richard B. Wigglesworth speaking on NRPB appropriations, 78th Cong., 1st sess., February 16, 1943, *Congressional Record* 89:979–80; Eliot, "Status of Work," March 9, 1943, NRPB minutes, March 8–10, 1943, 103.71, NRPB Records; Delano memorandum for Colonel Marvin H. McIntyre, February 6, 1943, OF 1092, FDRL; U.S., Congress, House, *Independent Offices Appropriations, 1944,* 22.

8. Delano memorandum for the president, February 10, 1943, NRPB minutes, February 1943, 103.71, NRPB Records; U.S. Congress, House, Representative Frederick C. Smith speaking on the NRPB, 78th Cong., 1st sess., February 8, 1943, *Congressional Record* 89:717–21 and 978–79, 1014–18, 1030–32, 1041–49, 1072, 1977, 4380–82, A1146, A1183–84, and A1612–14 for the debate; Eliot memorandum for NRPB, February 18, 1943, 203, NRPB Records.

9. Merriam to Delano, February 17, 1943, Box 218, and Merriam to George Yantis, February 19, 1943, Box 217, CEM Papers; Merriam to Delano, February 19, 1943, 103.72, NRPB Records; Roosevelt to Uncle Fred, February 22, 1943, OF 1092, FDRL; Delano to Merriam, February 23 and 26, 1943, Box 218, CEM Papers; Eliot memorandum for the president, March 2, 1943, OF 1092; NRPB draft of letter to Senator Glass, NRPB minutes, March 8–10, 1943, 103.71; Roosevelt to Glass, March 15, 1943, and James F. Byrnes to Roosevelt, March 12, 1943, OF 1092; Roosevelt to Glass and Roosevelt to Clarence Cannon, March 24, 1943, 203, NRPB Records.

10. U.S. Congress, Senate, Committee on Appropriations, *Hearings before Subcommittee, Independent Offices Appropriations Bill for 1944,* 189–240; Eliot memorandum for NRPB, April 9, 1943, Eliot memorandum for Delano, May 12, 1943, Delano memoran-

dum for the president, May 20, 1943, 203, NRPB Records; U.S. Congress, Senate, *Independent Offices Appropriations Bill, 1944,* 2; Eliot memorandum for NRPB, May 24, 1943, NRPB minutes, June 11–12, 1943, 103.71, NRPB Records.

11. U.S. Congress, Senate, *Congressional Record* 89:4671–72, 4784–85, 4919, 4924–30, 4942–66 for the Senate debate; NRPB minutes, May 17–21, 1943, 103.71, NRPB Records for a number of documents, including letters to various senators printed in the *Congressional Record* in response to criticisms; Eliot memoranda for NRPB, May 20 and 24, 1943, and Delano memorandum for the president, May 28, 1943, all in 203, NRPB Records; Merriam to Ruml, June 2, 1943, Box 217, CEM Papers.

12. Merriam to Delano, May 29, 1943, Box 218, CEM Papers; U.S. Congress, House, Committee on Appropriations, *Independent Offices Appropriations Bill, 1944;* Kenneth McKellar to Delano, May 31, 1943, and Eliot memoranda for NRPB, June 4, 16, 17, 18, 1943, 203, NRPB Records; U.S. Congress, House of Representatives and Senate, various speakers on monies for the NRPB, 78th Cong., 1st sess., June 16 and 18, 1943, *Congressional Record* 89:5937–39, 6044–45.

13. The NRPB was aware of the nature of congressional criticisms, on which it kept tabs in "Summary of Arguments against the NRPB" [April 3–5, 1943?], Victor M. Cutter to Eliot, April 5, 1943, and "Questions concerning the National Resources Planning Board," April 7, 1943, all in 203, NRPB Records.

14. Denials of advocating permanent spending policy are in Eliot to Charles E. Hofrichter, January 20, 1942, S Correspondence File and John D. Millett memorandum for Mr. Miller, April 24, 1942, Interoffice Memoranda, Box 9, Records of the Post-War Agenda Section, NRBP Records; Beardsley Ruml, "Business Organizes to Look Ahead," address to Vancouver Board of Trade, March 12, 1943, Series II, Ruml Papers; Eliot to Victor Cutter, March 30, 1943, 433.1, NRPB Records; Henry S. Dennison to Roderic Olzendam, April 20, 1943, HSD Papers; Delano to Robert A. Taft, May 20, 1943, Box 218, CEM Papers; Merriam to Alben K. Barkley and Robert A. Taft, May 20, 1943, NRPB minutes, May 1943, and Delano to Charles L. McNary, May 26, 1943, 103.71, NRPB Records; Delano to Lister Hill, May 27, 1943, 765, NRPB Records. Three of these letters were read into U.S. Congress, Senate, debate over NRPB monies, 78th Cong., 1st sess., May 27, 1943, *Congressional Record* 89:4672, 4925, 4954.

15. New Deal opponent Raymond Moley, in "What Beveridge Really Said," *Wall Street Journal,* December 23, 1942, noted the reliance on "free enterprise" implicit in these plans, while New Deal advocate Ernest K. Lindley, in "How the Postwar Reports Came to Be," *Newsweek,* March 22, 1943, 27, noted that the NRPB's postwar plans were "essentially conservative."

16. For NRPB support of joint executive-congressional postwar planning, see notes on Delano's and Eliot's conference with Senator Robert F. Wagner, NRPB minutes, March 27–28, 1941, Delano to Mary T. Norton, June 25, 1941, and Delano to Robert Ramspeck, June 28, 1941, NRPB minutes, June 28–30, 1941, 103.71, NRPB Records; Delano to Senator Robert F. Wagner, January 9, 1942, Box 219, CEM Papers; Eliot memorandum re Conference with the President, February 23, 1943, 104.1, NRPB Records; George F. Yantis to Merriam, February 23, 1943, and Merriam to Yantis, February 26, 1943, Box 217, CEM Papers; Ralph J. Watkins to Raymond B. Gibbs, March 2, 1943, 203, NRPB Records. For NRPB members' comments on congressional hostility, see E. M. Burns to Virginia Thompson, March 14, 1947, General Correspondence File, Burns Papers; Henry S. Dennison to Virginia Thompson, May 8, 1947, 1940–45 File, HSD Papers.

17. Scholars have yet to examine the role of the Senate Special Committee on Post-War Economic Policy and Planning (the George Committee) and the House Special Committee on Post-War Economic Policy and Planning (the Colmer Committee) in postwar and demobilization planning.

18. The Washington-Field Section tension is best noted in B. H. Kizer to George F. Yantis, February 17, 1943, and Roy [?] to Merriam, February 18, 1943, Box 217, CEM Papers.

19. Eliot memorandum for NRPB, June 2, 1943, NRPB minutes, June 2 and 11–12, 1943, 103.71, NRPB Records; C. W. E[liot] to Wayne Coy, June 2, [1943], Post War Planning Folder, Alphabetical File, Wayne Coy Papers, FDRL; Victor Cutter to Eliot, June 1, 1943, Eliot to Cutter, June 3, 1943, and Cutter to Eliot, June 5, 1943, 203, NRPB Records; Merriam to Delano, August 19, 1943, 104.1, NRPB Records; Eliot memorandum for General E. M. Watson, September 1, 1943, Watson memorandum for the president, September 1, 1943, and Roosevelt memorandum for Delano, and Delano to Watson, September 25, 1943, OF 1092, FDRL; Merriam to Delano, September 16, 1943, Box 218, CEM Papers; Eliot memorandum for Watson, September 25, 1943, OF 1092; Merriam, Delano, Eliot correspondence, September–October 1943, 103.73, NRPB Records; Merriam to Delano, January 4, 1944, Box 61, CEM Papers; Eliot to William Hassett, November 1, 1944, OF 5584-C, FDRL; Merriam to Delano, November 15, 1944, Box 61, CEM Papers. Eliot denied these ambitions in an interview, November 27, 1979, Cambridge, Mass.

20. Merriam was the most vocal critic of Eliot's work, but Delano, Yantis, and Dennison sided with Merriam; however, Eliot continued to hold to the view that only Merriam was involved. Eliot assumed that he and Delano maintained friendly relations throughout the period from 1926 to 1943, but numerous documents show otherwise, as seen in Merriam to Delano, November 9, 1935, Box 173; Merriam to Thomas C. Blaisdell, April 18, 1940, Box 217; George B. Galloway to Merriam, June 10, 1941, Box 48; Merriam to Yantis, September 19, 1942, Box 217; Merriam to Delano, February 24, 1943, Box 218; Merriam to Yantis, February 26, 1943, and Yantis to Merriam, March 20, 1943, Box 217; Merriam to Delano, February 27, April 20, and October 8, 1943, Box 218; Merriam to Luther Gulick, April 29, 1943, Box 49; all of the above in CEM Papers; Delano to General Edwin M. Watson, March 5, 1943, OF 1092, FDRL.

21. Office Diary entries, HSD Papers.

22. On Delano's resignation from the NCPPC, see OF 32, FDRL, and for his decision to leave the planning board, see Delano to John B. Hughes, February 22, 1943, 203, and NRPB minutes, June 29–30, 1943, 103.71, NRPB Records.

23. Merriam's letters to his son are in Box 2, CEM Papers, while his decision to leave the board is in Charles to John C. Merriam, October 15, 1943, Box 53, CEM Papers.

24. Eliot to the president, December 7, 1943, PPF 8592, FDRL; interview with Eliot, November 27, 1979.

25. Reagan, "The Withholding Tax, Beardsley Ruml, and Modern American Public Policy." Ruml continued to advocate business-government cooperation, as noted in his *Government, Business, and Values,* based on lectures given at the University of Omaha, March 25–26, 1943, while his work with the Committee for Economic Development is placed in context in Collins, "American Corporatism."

26. Opinion polls in Climate of Opinion File, General Post-War Planning File, A–F, Records of the Post-War Agenda Section, NPRB Records; polls in Public Opinion Polls Subject File, PSF, FDRL; Domestic–Post War File, Box 60, Oscar Cox Papers, FDRL. "To Win the Peace" is from Roosevelt's fireside chat following the declaration of war on December 9, 1941, in Rosenman, *The Public Papers and Addresses of Franklin D. Roosevelt,* vol. for 1941, 522–30. The NPRB letter to Congress of December 16, 1942, is in U.S. NRPB, *National Resources Development Report for 1943, Part 1, Post-War Plan and Program,* iii.

27. For the Bureau of the Budget's efforts, see Brady, "Toward Security," 170–233. On the OWMR, see Somers, *Presidential Agency: OWMR;* Baruch and Hancock, *Report on War and Post-War Adjustment Policies;* Schwarz, *The Speculator: Bernard M. Baruch in Washington,* 453–66; and Ballard, *The Shock of Peace.* On the reconversion debate, see

B. Bernstein, "The Truman Administration and Its Reconversion Wage Policy"; Bernstein, "The Removal of War Production Board Controls on Business"; Bernstein, "The Debate on Industrial Reconversion"; Bernstein, "America in War and Peace: The Test of Liberalism," in *Towards a New Past: Dissenting Essays in American History,* ed. Bernstein, 289–321; and Shepard, "Reconversion, 1939–1946."

28. Materials on the various postwar public works planning bills are in scattered sections of NRPB Records and in the Robert F. Wagner Papers, Georgetown University Library, Washington, D.C. Study of House and Senate committee reports and the *Congressional Record* would give more materials for a history of this effort. NRPB efforts for the GI Bill are noted in Minutes, July 7–8, 1942, 103.71, NRPB Records; materials in OF 1092-D, FDRL; U.S. NRPB, *Demobilization and Readjustment;* Reeves, "Planning for Postwar Readjustment"; Joseph Ernst interview with Leonard Outhwaite, July 22, 1976, in Outhwaite Papers. The NRPB's efforts are placed in perspective in Davis Ross, *Preparing for Ulysses,* 52–63, while the impact of the GI Bill is discussed in Blum, *V Was for Victory,* 333–340; K. Olson, *The G. I. Bill, the Veterans, and the Colleges;* Mosch, *The G. I. Bill;* Reagan, "Roosevelt Signs the G. I. Bill"; Skocpol, "Delivering for Young Families"; and Reagan, "Fighting the Good War at Home."

29. Twentieth Century Fund File, Organization Correspondence File, Records of the Post-War Agenda Section, NRPB Records; *Postwar Planning in the United States;* Stuart Chase's volumes published by the Twentieth Century Fund in the "When the War Ends" series: *The Road We Are Traveling: 1914–1942* (1942), *Goals for America: A Budget of Our Needs and Resources* (1942), *Where's the Money Coming From? Problems of Postwar Finance* (1943), *Democracy under Pressure: Special Interests vs the Public Welfare* (1945), *Tomorrow's Trade: Problems of Our Foreign Commerce* (1945), and *For This We Fought* (1946). No history of the National Planning Association has yet been written, but for some insight, see Eakins, "The Development of Corporate Liberal Policy Research in the United States," 274–496, which compares the NPA, the NRPB, and the Committee for Economic Development.

30. Reagan, "The Withholding Tax"; Collins, *The Business Response to Keynes;* and Wolfe, *America's Impasse.*

31. Schriftgiesser, *Business Comes of Age* and *Business and Public Policy;* Eakins, "Business Planners and America's Postwar Expansion"; McQuaid, "The Business Advisory Council of the Department of Commerce" and "Corporate Liberalism in the American Business Community"; Collins, "Positive Business Responses to the New Deal" and "American Corporatism."

32. Rosenman, *Working with Roosevelt,* 424–26, and *The Public Papers and Addresses of Franklin D. Roosevelt,* vol. for 1944–45, pp. 32–42 and 369–78.

33. Hinchey, "The Frustration of the New Deal Revival"; Polenberg, *War and Society,* 73–98; and A. Brinkley, *End of Reform.*

34. Perrett, *Days of Sadness, Years of Triumph,* 325–56; Brody, "The New Deal and World War II"; Blum, *V Was for Victory,* 221–300 and 323–32.

35. Bailey, *Congress Makes a Law;* Colm, *The Employment Act Past and Future;* Leon H. Keyserling, "Discussion," *American Economic Review* 62 (May 1972): 134–38; Millet, *The Process and Organization of Government Planning;* James L. Sundquist, Bertram R. Gross, Leon H. Keyserling, and Walter S. Salant, "The Employment Act of 1946," in *Economics and the Truman Administration,* ed. Heller, 97–109; Robert M. Collins, "The Emergence of Economic Growthmanship in the United States: Federal Policy and Economic Knowledge in the Truman Years," in *The State and Economic Knowledge,* ed. Furner and Supple, 138–70; Flash, *Economic Advice and Presidential Leadership;* Naveh, "The Political Role of Academic Advisers"; Rosenof, *Economics in the Long Run.*

36. The quotation is from the Employment Act of 1946, cited in Bailey, *Congress Makes a Law,* 228.

37. Scholars have begun to analyze the failure of wartime and postwar social welfare policy making, as seen in James T. Patterson, "Comparative Welfare History: Britain and the United States, 1930–1945," in *The Roosevelt New Deal,* ed. Cohen, 125–43; Patterson, *America's Struggle against Poverty;* essays in Critchlow and Hawley, *Federal Social Policy;* essays in Fraser and Gerstle, *Rise and Fall of the New Deal Order;* essays in Weir, Orloff, and Skocpol, *The Politics of Social Policy in the United States;* Margaret Weir, "Ideas and Politics: The Acceptance of Keynesianism in Britain and the United States," in *The Political Power of Economic Ideas: Keynesianism Across Nations,* ed. P. A. Hall, 53–86; Kloppenberg, "Who's Afraid of the Welfare State?"; Berkowitz, *America's Welfare State;* Margaret Weir, "Ideas and the Politics of Bounded Innovation," in *Structuring Politics,* ed. Steinmo, Thelen, and Longstreth, 188–216; Skocpol, *Social Policy in the United States;* and Kloppenberg, *The Virtues of Liberalism,* 100–123.

38. No historian has really written about the role of organizational groups in policy making in the post-1945 period, but for thought-provoking works on the period, see Hodgson, *America in Our Time;* (Garden City, New York, 1976); Norman A. Graebner, *The Age of Global Power: The United States since 1939* (New York, 1979); Wolfe, *America's Impasse;* Galambos, *America at Middle Age;* Chafe, *The Unfinished Journey;* Boyer, *Promises to Keep;* and Patterson, *Grand Expectations.* Suggestive case studies can be found in McQuaid, *Big Business and Presidential Power;* McQuaid, *Uneasy Partners;* essays in *American Society,* ed. Knowlton and Zeckhauser; essays in *The New American State,* ed. Galambos; and essays in *Integrating the Sixties,* ed. Balogh.

39. Graham, Jr., *Toward a Planned Society,* details the postwar efforts at reviving the planning ideal, while Clawson, *New Deal Planning,* tries to make a case for revival of at least part of the NRPB experience. On the industrial policy debate of the 1980s, see Reich, *The Next American Frontier;* Rohatyn, *The Twenty-Year Century;* C. Johnson, *The Industrial Policy Debate;* Barfield and Schambra, *The Politics of Industrial Policy;* and the definitive history of the subject in Graham, Jr., *Losing Time.* Representative democratic left proposals for planning can be sampled in Bowles, Gordon, and Weiskopf, *Beyond the Waste Land,* and Alperovitz and Faux, *Rebuilding America,* while libertarian critiques are found in Lavoie, *National Economic Planning,* and Higgs, *Crisis and Leviathan.* A more balanced account from a historical perspective is B. Campbell, *The Growth of American Government,* which emphasizes the complexity of the American federal system of government and the necessity of examining change over time.

40. McConnell, *Private Power and American Democracy,* and Lowi, *The End of Liberalism.*

41. James Patton, "Resolution on Post-War Planning," National Farmers' Union, *Minutes* (1944), National Farmers' Union Headquarters, Denver, Colo. I would like to thank Roy T. Wortman of Kenyon College for bringing this document to my attention. Also see Patton telegram to Roosevelt, March 1, 1944, OF 899, FDRL.

Bibliography

Primary Sources

MANUSCRIPT COLLECTIONS

Burns, Eveline M. Papers. Columbia University Library, New York.

Cherington, Paul F. Papers. Harvard Graduate School of Business Administration Archives, Baker Library, Harvard University, Cambridge, Mass.

Columbia Oral History Collection. Columbia University, New York. Reminiscences of Will Alexander, Paul Appleby, Frank Bane, Eveline Burns, James W. Campbell, Morse Cartwright, Gilmore D. Clarke, William Harold Cowley, Charles Dollard, Isadore S. Falk, Guy Stanton Ford, Samuel S. Hall, Jr., Alvin H. Hansen, Mrs. Florence Jaffray Harriman, Robert M. Lester, George McAneny, Gunnar Myrdal, Frances Perkins, George Rublee, Oscar Clemen Stine, Henry C. Taylor, Rexford G. Tugwell, Henry A. Wallace, Milburn L. Wilson, Leo Wolman, and Henry Wriston.

Cox, Oscar. Papers. Franklin D. Roosevelt Library, Hyde Park, N.Y.

Delano, Frederic Adrian. Papers. Franklin D. Roosevelt Library, Hyde Park, N.Y.

Delano Family. Papers. Franklin D. Roosevelt Library, Hyde Park, N.Y.

Dennison, Henry S. Papers. Harvard Graduate School of Business Administration Archives, Baker Library, Harvard University, Cambridge, Mass.

Eliot, Charles W., II. Biographical File, HUG 300. Harvard University Archives, Cambridge, Mass.

Flanders, Ralph E. Papers. Syracuse University Library, Syracuse, N.Y.

General Correspondence, Dean's Office Records. Graduate School of Business Administration Archives, Baker Library, Harvard University, Cambridge, Mass.

Hansen, Alvin Harvey. Papers. Harvard University Archives, Cambridge, Mass.

Henderson, Leon. Papers. Franklin D. Roosevelt Library, Hyde Park, N.Y.

Hoover, Herbert. Commerce Papers. Herbert Hoover Library, West Branch, Iowa.

Hopkins, Harry L. Papers. Franklin D. Roosevelt Library, Hyde Park, N.Y.

Hunt, Edward Eyre. Papers. Herbert Hoover Library, West Branch, Iowa.

Hutchins, Robert M. Papers. University of Chicago Regenstein Library, Chicago.

Ickes, Harold L. Papers. Library of Congress, Washington, D.C.

Laura Spelman Rockefeller Memorial Collection. Rockefeller Archive Center, Pocantico Hills, North Tarrytown, N.Y.

Manufacturers' Research Association Papers. Harvard Graduate School of Business Administration Archives, Baker Library, Harvard University, Cambridge, Mass.

Merriam, Charles E. Papers. University of Chicago Regenstein Library, Chicago.

Merriam, John Campbell. Papers. Library of Congress, Washington, D.C.

Mitchell, Wesley Clair. Papers. Columbia University Library, New York.

Morgenthau, Henry, Jr. Papers. Franklin D. Roosevelt Library, Hyde Park, N.Y.

National Capital Planning Commission. Records. Record Group 328. National Archives, Washington, D.C.

National Resources Planning Board. Records. Record Group 187. National Archives, College Park, Md.

Ogburn, William Fielding. Papers. University of Chicago Regenstein Library, Chicago.

Outhwaite, Leonard. Papers. Rockefeller Archive Center, Pocantico Hills, North Tarrytown, N.Y.

President's Committee on Administrative Management. Papers. Franklin D. Roosevelt Library, Hyde Park, N.Y.

Presidents' Papers. 1889–1925 and ca. 1925–1945. University of Chicago Regenstein Library, Chicago.

Rockefeller, John D., Jr. Records. Record Group 2. Private Archives of the Messrs. Rockefeller, New York.

Rockefeller Foundation. Records. Record Group 1. 1. Rockefeller Archive Center, Pocantico Hills, North Tarrytown, N.Y.

Roosevelt, Franklin D. Papers. President's Official File. Franklin D. Roosevelt Library, Hyde Park, N.Y.

———. President's Personal File. Franklin D. Roosevelt Library, Hyde Park, N.Y.

———. President's Secretary File. Franklin D. Roosevelt Library, Hyde Park, N.Y.

Rosenman, Samuel I. Papers. Franklin D. Roosevelt Library, Hyde Park, N.Y.

Ruml, Beardsley. Papers. University of Chicago Regenstein Library, Chicago.

Ruml, Wentzle and Salome. Papers. State Historical Society of Iowa, Iowa City.

Spelman Fund of New York Collection. Rockefeller Archive Center, Pocantico Hills, North Tarrytown, N.Y.

Wagner, Robert F. Papers. Georgetown University, Washington, D.C.

Williams, Aubrey. Papers. Franklin D. Roosevelt Library, Hyde Park, N.Y.

Yantis, George Franklin. Papers. University of Washington Library, Seattle.

INTERVIEWS

Burns, Eveline M. New York, October 1, 1979.

Dennison, James T. Antrim, N. H., December 12, 1979.

Dunker, Elizabeth. Cambridge, Mass., December 10, 1979.

Eliot, Charles W., II. Cambridge, Mass., November 27, 1979.

Secondary Sources

BOOKS

Abrams, Carl. *Conservative Constraints: North Carolina and the New Deal.* Jackson: University of Mississippi Press, 1992.

Adams, Graham, Jr. *Age of Industrial Violence, 1910–15: The Activities and Findings of the United States Commission on Industrial Relations.* New York: Columbia University Press, 1966.

Adams, Michael C. C. *The Best War Ever: America and World War II.* Baltimore: Johns Hopkins University Press, 1994.

Alchon, Guy. *The Invisible Hand of Planning: Capitalism, Social Science, and the State in the 1920s.* Princeton: Princeton University Press, 1985.

Alexander, Charles C. *Nationalism in American Thought, 1930–1945.* Chicago: Rand McNally, 1969.

Alperovitz, Gar, and Jeff Faux. *Rebuilding America: A Blueprint for the New Economy.* New York: Pantheon Books, 1984.

Antler, Joyce. *Lucy Sprague Mitchell: The Making of a Modern Woman*. New Haven: Yale University Press, 1987.

Arnold, Joseph L. *The New Deal in the Suburbs: A History of the Greenbelt Town Program, 1935–1954*. Columbus: Ohio State University Press, 1971.

Arnold, Peri E. *Making the Managerial Presidency: Comprehensive Reorganization Planning, 1905–1980*. Princeton: Princeton University Press, 1986.

Arnove, Robert F., ed. *Philanthropy and Cultural Imperialism: The Foundations at Home and Abroad*. Boston: G. K. Hall, 1980; Bloomington: Indiana University Press, 1982.

Ash, Mitchell G., and William R. Woodward, eds. *Psychology in Twentieth-Century Thought and Society*. New York: Cambridge University Press, 1987.

Ashmore, Harry S. *Unseasonable Truths: The Life of Robert Maynard Hutchins*. Boston: Little, Brown, 1989.

Badger, Anthony. *The New Deal: The Depression Years, 1933–1940*. New York: Noonday Press, 1989.

Bailey, Stephen Kemp. *Congress Makes a Law: The Story behind the Employment Act of 1946*. New York: Columbia University Press, 1950.

Ballard, Jack Stokes. *The Shock of Peace: Military and Economic Demobilization after World War II*. Washington, D.C.: University Press of America, 1983.

Balogh, Brian, ed. *Integrating the Sixties: The Origins, Structures, and Legitimacy of Public Policy in a Turbulent Decade*. University Park: Pennsylvania State University Press, 1996.

Barber, William J. *Designs within Disorder: Franklin D. Roosevelt, the Economists, and the Shaping of American Economic Policy, 1933–1945*. New York: Cambridge University Press, 1996.

———. *From New Era to New Deal: Herbert Hoover, the Economists, and American Economic Policy, 1921–1933*. New York: Cambridge University Press, 1985.

———, ed. *Breaking the Academic Mould: Economists and American Higher Learning in the Nineteenth Century*. Middletown, Conn.: Wesleyan University Press, 1988.

Barfield, Claude E., and William A. Schambra, eds. *The Politics of Industrial Policy*. Washington, D.C.: American Enterprise Institute for Public Policy, 1986.

Baritz, Loren. *The Servants of Power: A History of Social Science in American Industry*. Middletown, Conn.: Wesleyan University Press, 1960.

Barrow, Clyde W. *Critical Theories of the State: Marxist, Neo-Marxist, Post-Marxist*. Madison: University of Wisconsin Press, 1993.

———. *Universities and the Capitalist State: Corporate Liberalism and the Reconstruction of American Higher Education, 1894–1928*. Madison: University of Wisconsin Press, 1990.

Baruch, Bernard. *American Industry in the War: A Report of the War Industries Board (March 1921)*. New York: Prentice-Hall, 1941.

Baruch, Bernard, and John M. Hancock. *Report on Post-War Adjustment Policies*. Washington, D.C.: Government Printing Office, 1944.

Baskerville, Stephen W., and Ralph Willett, eds. *Nothing Else to Fear: New Perspectives on America in the Thirties*. Manchester: Manchester University Press, 1985.

Baugh, Virgil E., comp. *Preliminary Inventory of the Central Office Records of the National Resources Planning Board (Record Group 187)*. Washington, D.C.: Government Printing Office, 1953.

Beachley, Charles E. *History of the Consolidation Coal Company, 1864–1934*. New York: Consolidation Coal Company, 1934.

Beard, Charles A., ed. *America Faces the Future*. New York: Vanguard, 1932.

Bellush, Bernard. *The Failure of the NRA*. New York: W. W. Norton, 1975.

Bender, Thomas, ed. *The University and the City: From Medieval Origins to the Present*. New York: Oxford University Press, 1988.

Bensel, Richard Franklin. *Yankee Leviathan: The Origins of Central State Authority in America, 1859–1877.* New York: Cambridge University Press, 1990.

Berkowitz, Edward D. *America's Welfare State: From Roosevelt to Reagan.* Baltimore: Johns Hopkins University Press, 1991.

Berkowitz, Edward D., and Kim McQuaid. *Creating the Welfare State: The Political Economy of Twentieth-Century Reform.* New York: Praeger Publishers, 1980; Lawrence: University Press of Kansas, 1992.

Berle, Adolf A. *Leaning Against the Dawn: An Appreciation of the Twentieth Century Fund.* New York: Twentieth Century Fund, 1969.

Berle, Adolf A., and Gardiner C. Means. *The Modern Corporation and Private Property.* New York: Macmillan, 1932.

Berman, Larry. *The Office of Management and Budget and the Presidency, 1921–1969.* Princeton: Princeton University Press, 1979.

Bernstein, Irving. *The Lean Years: A History of the American Worker, 1920–1933.* Boston: Houghton Mifflin, 1960.

Best, Gary Dean. *The Politics of Individualism: Herbert Hoover in Transition, 1918–1921.* Westport, Conn.: Greenwood Press, 1975.

The Best of Planning: Two Decades of Articles from the Magazine of the American Planning Association. Chicago: University of Chicago Press, 1989.

Biles, Roger. *A New Deal for the American People.* DeKalb: Northern Illinois University Press, 1991.

Black, John D. *Agricultural Reform in the United States.* New York: McGraw-Hill, 1929.

Bledstein, Burton J. *The Culture of Professionalism: The Middle Class and the Development of Higher Education in America.* New York: W. W. Norton, 1976.

Blum, John Morton. *V Was for Victory: Politics and American Culture during World War II.* New York: Harcourt Brace Jovanovich, 1976.

———, ed. *Roosevelt and Morgenthau: A Revision and Condensation of From the Morgenthau Diaries.* Boston: Houghton Mifflin, 1972.

Bowles, Samuel, David M. Gordon, and Thomas E. Weisskopf. *Beyond the Waste Land: A Democratic Alternative to Economic Decline.* Garden City, N.Y.: Anchor Press/Doubleday, 1983.

Boyer, Paul. *Promises to Keep: The United States Since World War II,* 2nd ed. Boston: Houghton Mifflin, 1999.

Braeman, John, Robert H. Bremner, and David Brody, eds. *Change and Continuity in Twentieth-Century America: The 1920s.* Columbus: Ohio State University Press, 1968.

———. *The New Deal.* 2 vols. Columbus: Ohio State University Press, 1975.

Braeman, John, Robert H. Bremner, and Everett Walters, eds. *Change and Continuity in Twentieth-Century America.* Columbus: Ohio State University Press, 1964.

Brand, Donald R. *Corporatism and the Rule of Law: A Study of the National Recovery Administration.* Ithaca: Cornell University Press, 1988.

Brandes, Stuart D. *American Welfare Capitalism, 1880–1940.* Chicago: University of Chicago Press, 1976.

Breit, William, and Roger L. Ransom. *The Academic Scribblers.* Rev. ed. Chicago: Dryden Press, 1982.

Bremner, Robert H. *American Philanthropy.* Chicago: University of Chicago Press, 1960, 1988.

———. *From the Depths: The Discovery of Poverty in the United States.* New York: New York University Press, 1956.

Brinkley, Alan. *The End of Reform: New Deal Liberalism in Recession and War.* New York: Alfred A. Knopf, 1995.

———. *Liberalism and Its Discontents.* Cambridge, Mass.: Harvard University Press, 1998.

Brinkley, David. *Washington Goes to War.* New York: Alfred A. Knopf, 1988.

Brody, David. *Labor in Crisis: The Steel Strike of 1919.* Philadelphia: J. B. Lippincott, 1965.

————. *Workers in Industrial America: Essays on the Twentieth Century Struggle.* 2d ed. New York: Oxford University Press, 1993.

Browder, Robert Paul, and Thomas G. Smith. *Independent: A Biography of Lewis W. Douglas.* New York: Alfred A. Knopf, 1986.

Brown, Bernard E. *American Conservatives: The Political Thought of Frances Lieber and John W. Burgess.* New York: Columbia University Press, 1951.

Brown, E. Richard. *Rockefeller Medicine Men: Medicine and Capitalism in America.* Berkeley: University of California Press, 1979.

Brown, Jerold E., and Patrick D. Reagan, eds. *Voluntarism, Planning, and the State: The American Planning Experience, 1914–1946.* Westport, Conn.: Greenwood Press, 1988.

Brown, JoAnne. *The Definition of a Profession: The Authority of Metaphor in the History of Intelligence Testing, 1890–1930.* Princeton: Princeton University Press, 1992.

Brown, JoAnne, and David K. van Keuren, eds. *The Estate of Social Knowledge.* Baltimore: Johns Hopkins University Press, 1991.

Brown, Richard D. *Knowledge Is Power: The Diffusion of Information in Early America, 1700–1865.* New York: Oxford University Press, 1989.

Brownlee, W. Elliot. *Dynamics of Ascent: A History of the American Economy.* 2d ed. New York: Alfred A. Knopf, 1979.

Brownlow, Louis. *A Passion for Anonymity: The Autobiography of Louis Brownlow.* 2 vols. Chicago: University of Chicago Press, 1958.

Buck, Paul, ed. *The Social Sciences at Harvard, 1860–1920.* Cambridge, Mass.: Harvard University Press, 1965.

Buhite, Russell D., and David W. Levy, eds. *FDR's Fireside Chats.* Norman: University of Oklahoma Press, 1992.

Bulmer, Martin. *The Chicago School of Sociology: Institutionalization, Diversity, and the Rise of Sociological Research.* Chicago: University of Chicago Press, 1984.

————, ed. *Social Science Research and Government: Comparative Essays on Britain and the United States.* Cambridge: Cambridge University Press, 1987.

Bulmer, Martin, Kevin Bales, and Kathryn Kish Sklar, eds. *The Social Survey in Historical Perspective, 1880–1940.* New York: Cambridge University Press, 1991.

Burgess, John W. *Reminiscences of an American Scholar: The Beginnings of Columbia University.* New York: Columbia University Press, 1934.

Burritt, Arthur, Henry Dennison, Edwin F. Gay, Ralph E. Heilman, and Henry P. Kendall. *Profit Sharing: Its Principles and Practice.* New York: Harper & Brothers, 1918.

Burner, David. *Herbert Hoover: A Public Life.* New York: Alfred A. Knopf, 1979.

Burns, Arthur F. *The Frontiers of Economic Knowledge.* Princeton: Princeton University Press, for National Bureau of Economic Research, 1954.

————, ed. *Wesley Clair Mitchell: The Economic Scientist.* New York: National Bureau of Economic Research, 1952.

Burns, Eveline M. *Toward Social Security: An Explanation of the Social Security Act and Survey of the Larger Issues.* New York: Whittlesey House, 1936.

Burns, James MacGregor. *Roosevelt: The Lion and the Fox.* New York: Harcourt, Brace & World, 1956.

————. *Roosevelt: The Soldier of Freedom.* New York: Harcourt Brace Jovanovich, 1970.

Burns, Richard D., comp. *Herbert Hoover: A Bibliography of His Times and Presidency.* Wilmington, Del.: Scholarly Resources, 1991.

Campbell, Ballard C. *The Growth of American Government: Governance from the Cleveland Era to the Present.* Bloomington: Indiana University Press, 1995.

Campbell, Christiana M. *The Farm Bureau and the New Deal: A Study of the Making of National Farm Policy, 1933–1940.* Urbana: University of Illinois Press, 1962.

Campbell, John L., J. Rogers Hollingsworth, and Leon Lindberg, eds. *Governance of the American Economy*. New York: Cambridge University Press, 1991.

Case, Josephine Young, and Everett Needham Case. *Owen D. Young and American Enterprise*. Boston: David Godine, 1982.

Castles, Francis G., ed. *The Comparative History of Public Policy.* New York: Oxford University Press, 1989.

Catton, Bruce. *The War Lords of Washington*. New York: Harcourt, Brace, 1948.

Chafe, William H. *The Unfinished Journey: America Since World War II*. 4th ed. New York: Oxford University Press, 1999.

Chambers, John Whiteclay, II. *The Tyranny of Change: America in the Progressive Era, 1890– 1920*. 2d ed. New York: St. Martin's Press, 1992.

Chandler, Alfred D., Jr. *The Railroads: The Nation's First Big Business*. New York: Harcourt, Brace & World, 1965.

———. *Scale and Scope: The Dynamics of Industrial Capitalism*. Cambridge, Mass.: Harvard University Press, Belknap Press, 1990.

———. *Strategy and Structure: Chapters in the History of the American Industrial Enterprise*. Cambridge, Mass.: MIT Press, 1962.

———. *The Visible Hand: The Managerial Revolution in American Business*. Cambridge, Mass.: Harvard University Press, Belknap Press, 1977.

Chandler, Alfred D., Jr., and Herman Daems, eds. *Managerial Hierarchies: Comparative Perspectives on the Rise of the Modern Industrial Enterprise*. Cambridge, Mass.: Harvard University Press, 1980.

Chase, Stuart. *A New Deal*. New York: Macmillan, 1932.

Christie, Jean. *Morris Llewellyn Cooke: Progressive Engineer*. New York: Garland Publishing, 1983.

Clarke, Jeanne Nienaber. *Roosevelt's Warrior: Harold L. Ickes and the New Deal*. Baltimore: Johns Hopkins University Press, 1996.

Clawson, Marion. *New Deal Planning: The National Resources Planning Board*. Baltimore: Johns Hopkins University Press, for Resources for the Future, 1981.

Cleland, David Ira. *The Origin and Development of a Philosophy of Long-Range Planning in American Business*. New York: Arno Press, 1976.

Coats, A. W., ed. *Economists in Government: An International Comparative Study*. Durham, N.C.: Duke University Press, 1981.

Coben, Stanley. *Rebellion against Victorianism: The Impetus for Cultural Change in 1920s America*. New York: Oxford University Press, 1991.

Cochran, Thomas C. *Railroad Leaders, 1845–1890: The Business Mind in Action*. Cambridge, Mass.: Harvard University Press, 1953.

Cohen, Wilbur J., ed. *The Roosevelt New Deal: A Program Assessment Fifty Years After*. Austin, Tex.: Lyndon B. Johnson School for Public Affairs, 1986.

Collier, Peter, and David Horowitz. *The Rockefellers: An American Dynasty*. New York: New American Library, 1977.

Collins, Robert M. *The Business Response to Keynes, 1929–1964*. New York: Columbia University Press, 1981.

Colm, Gerhard, ed. *The Employment Act Past and Future: A Tenth Anniversary Symposium*. Washington, D.C.: National Planning Association, 1956.

Commager, Henry Steele, ed. *Lester Ward and the Welfare State*. Indianapolis: Bobbs-Merrill, 1967.

Commercial Club of Chicago, Memorial Committee. *Frederic Adrian Delano: 1863–1953*. Chicago: Commercial Club, 1953.

Conkin, Paul. *The New Deal*. 3d ed. Arlington Heights, Ill.: Harlan Davidson, 1992.

———. *Tomorrow a New World: The New Deal Community Program*. Ithaca: Cornell University Press, for the American Historical Association, 1959.

Conner, Valeri Jean. *The National War Labor Board: Stability, Social Justice, and the Voluntary State in World War I.* Chapel Hill: University of North Carolina Press, 1983.

Converse, Jean M. *Survey Research in the United States: Roots and Emergence, 1890–1960.* Berkeley: University of California Press, 1987.

Cook, Paul B. *Academicians in Government from Roosevelt to Roosevelt.* New York: Garland Publishing, 1982.

Coon, Horace. *Money to Burn: Great American Foundations and Their Money.* Reprint, with new introduction by Patrick D. Reagan. New Brunswick: Transaction Publishers, 1990.

Cooney, Terry A. *Balancing Acts: American Thought and Culture in the 1930s.* New York: Twayne Publishers, 1995.

Cooper, John Milton, Jr. *Pivotal Decades: The United States, 1900–1920.* New York: W. W. Norton, 1990.

Copeland, Melvin T. *And Mark an Era: The Story of the Harvard Business School.* Boston: Little, Brown, 1958.

Corner, George W. *A History of the Rockefeller Institute, 1901–1953: Origins and Growth.* New York: Rockefeller Institute Press, 1962.

Creese, Walter L. *TVA's Public Planning: The Vision, the Reality.* Knoxville: University of Tennessee Press, 1990.

Crick, Bernard. *The American Science of Politics: Its Origins and Conditions.* London: Routledge & Keegan Paul, 1959.

Critchlow, Donald T. *The Brookings Institution, 1916–1952: Expertise and the Public Interest in a Democratic Society.* DeKalb: Northern Illinois University Press, 1985.

Critchlow, Donald T., and Ellis W. Hawley, eds. *Federal Social Policy: The Historical Dimension.* University Park: Pennsylvania State University Press, 1988.

Croly, Herbert. *The Promise of American Life.* 1909; New York: Capricorn Books, 1964.

Cruikshank, Jeffrey L. *A Delicate Experiment: The Harvard Business School, 1908–1925.* Cambridge, Mass.: Harvard Business School Press, 1987.

Cuff, Robert D. *The War Industries Board: Business-Government Relations during World War I.* Baltimore: Johns Hopkins University Press, 1973.

Davis, J. Ronnie. *The New Economics and the Old Economists.* Ames: Iowa State University Press, 1971.

Davis, Kenneth S. *FDR: The Beckoning of Destiny, 1882–1928.* New York: G. P. Putnam's Sons, 1972.

———. *FDR: The New York Years, 1928–1932.* New York: Random House, 1985.

———. *FDR: The New Deal Years, 1933–1937.* New York: Random House, 1986.

———. *FDR: Into the Storm, 1937–1940.* New York: Random House, 1993.

Dawley, Alan. *Struggles for Justice: Social Responsibility and the Liberal State.* Cambridge, Mass.: Harvard University Press, 1991.

Delano, Daniel Webster, Jr. *Franklin Roosevelt and the Delano Influence.* Pittsburgh: J. S. Nudi Publications, 1946.

Dennison, Henry S. *E. W. Dennison: A Memorial.* Boston: D. B. Updike, Merrymount Press, 1909.

———. *Organization Engineering.* New York: McGraw-Hill, 1931.

Dennison, Henry S., Lincoln Filene, Ralph E. Flanders, and Morris E. Leeds. *Toward Full Employment.* New York: Whittlesey House, 1938.

Dennison, Henry S., and John Kenneth Galbraith. *Modern Competition and Business Policy.* New York: Oxford University Press, 1938.

Dennison, James T. *Henry S. Dennison (1877–1952): New England Industrialist Who Served America!* New York: Newcomen Society in North America, 1955.

Derber, Milton. *The American Idea of Industrial Democracy: 1865–1965.* Urbana: University of Illinois Press, 1970.

Diner, Steven J. *A City and Its Universities: Public Policy in Chicago, 1892–1919.* Chapel Hill: University of North Carolina Press, 1980.

———. *A Very Different Age: Americans of the Progressive Era.* New York: Hill & Wang, 1998.

Dodge, Mark M., ed. *Herbert Hoover and the Historians.* West Branch, Iowa: Herbert Hoover Presidential Library Association, 1989.

Domhoff, G. William. *The Power Elite and the State: How Policy is Made in America.* New York: Aldine de Gruyter, 1990.

———. *State Autonomy or Class Dominance? Case Studies on Policy Making in America.* New York: Aldine de Gruyter, 1996.

Donahue, John D. *The Privatization Decision: Public Ends, Private Means.* New York: Basic Books, 1989.

Dorfman, Joseph. *The Economic Mind in American Civilization.* 5 vols. New York: Viking Press, 1949–59.

Dubofsky, Melvyn. *Industrialism and the American Worker, 1865–1920.* 3d ed. Arlington Heights, Ill.: Harlan Davidson, 1996.

———. *The State and Labor in Modern America.* Chapel Hill: University of North Carolina Press, 1994.

Dubofsky, Melvyn, and Warren Van Tine. *John L. Lewis: A Biography.* New York: Quadrangle, 1977.

Dudden, Arthur Power. *The American Pacific: From the Old China Trade to the Present.* New York: Oxford University Press, 1992.

Dumenil, Lynn. *Modern Temper: American Culture and Society in the 1920s.* New York: Hill & Wang, 1995.

Dunning, William A. *Truth in History and Other Essays.* New York: Columbia University Press, 1937.

Dzuback, Mary Ann. *Robert M. Hutchins: Portrait of an Educator.* Chicago: University of Chicago Press, 1991.

Easton, David. *The Political System: An Inquiry into the State of Political Science.* New York: Alfred A. Knopf, 1953.

Ebner, Michael, and Eugene Tobin, eds. *The Age of Urban Reform: New Perspectives on the Progressive Era.* Port Washington, N.Y.: Kennikat Press, 1977.

Eccles, Marriner S. *Beckoning Frontiers.* New York: Alfred A. Knopf, 1951.

Eden, Robert, ed. *The New Deal and Its Legacy: Critique and Reappraisal.* Westport, Conn.: Greenwood Press, 1989.

Ekirch, Arthur A., Jr. *Ideologies and Utopias: The Impact of the New Deal on American Thought.* Chicago: Quadrangle Books, 1969.

Elkins, Stanley, and Eric McKitrick, eds. *The Hofstadter Aegis: A Memorial.* New York: Alfred A. Knopf, 1974.

Ernst, Joseph W., ed. *"Dear Father"/"Dear Son": Correspondence of John D. Rockefeller and John D. Rockefeller, Jr.* New York: Fordham University Press, in cooperation with Rockefeller Archive Center, 1994.

Evans, Peter, Dietrich Rueschmeyer, and Theda Skocpol, eds. *Bringing the State Back In.* New York: Cambridge University Press, 1985.

Fausold, Martin L. *The Presidency of Herbert C. Hoover.* Lawrence: University Press of Kansas, 1985.

———, and George T. Mazuzan, eds. *The Hoover Presidency: A Reappraisal.* Albany: State University of New York Press, 1974.

Fearon, Peter. *War, Prosperity and Depression: The U.S. Economy, 1917–45.* Lawrence: University Press of Kansas, 1987.

Ferrell, Robert H. *Woodrow Wilson and World War I, 1917–1921.* New York: Harper & Row, 1985.

Fine, Sidney. *Laissez Faire and the General-Welfare State: A Study of Conflict in American Thought, 1865–1901.* Ann Arbor: University of Michigan Press, 1956.

Finegold, Kenneth, and Theda Skocpol. *State and Party in America's New Deal.* Madison: University of Wisconsin Press, 1995.

Fink, Leon. *Progressive Intellectuals and the Dilemmas of Democratic Commitment.* Cambridge, Mass.: Harvard University Press, 1997.

———, Stephen T. Leonard, and Donald M. Reid, eds. *Intellectuals and Public Life: Between Radicalism and Reform.* Ithaca: Cornell University Press, 1996.

Fisher, Donald. *Fundamental Development of the Social Sciences: Rockefeller Philanthropy and the United States Social Science Research Council.* Ann Arbor: University of Michigan Press, 1993.

Fisher, Irving. *Stable Money: A History of the Movement.* New York: Adelphi, 1934.

Fitzpatrick, Ellen. *Endless Crusade: Women Social Scientists and Progressive Reform.* New York: Oxford University Press, 1990.

Flanagan, Maureen A. *Charter Reform in Chicago.* Carbondale: Southern Illinois University Press, 1987.

Flash, Edward. *Economic Advice and Presidential Leadership: The Council of Economic Advisors.* New York: Columbia University Press, 1965.

Flexner, Abraham. *Funds and Foundations: Their Policies Past and Present.* New York: Harper & Brothers, 1952.

Foglesong, Richard E. *Planning the Capitalist City: The Colonial Era to the 1920s.* Princeton: Princeton University Press, 1986.

Foner, Eric, ed. *The New American History.* Rev. ed. Philadelphia: Temple University Press, 1997.

Forcey, Charles. *The Crossroads of Liberalism: Croly, Weyl, Lippmann, and the Progressive Era, 1900–1925.* New York: Oxford University Press, 1961.

Fosdick, Raymond B. *Adventure in Giving: The Story of the General Education Board.* New York: Harper & Row, 1962.

———. *Chronicle of a Generation: An Autobiography.* New York: Harper, 1958.

———. *John D. Rockefeller, Jr.: A Portrait.* New York: Harper & Brothers, 1956.

———. *The Story of the Rockefeller Foundation.* New York: Harper & Brothers, 1952.

Fox, Daniel M. *The Discovery of Abundance: Simon N. Patten and the Transformation of Social Theory.* Ithaca: Cornell University Press, for the American Historical Association, 1967.

Fraser, Steve, and Gary Gerstle, eds. *The Rise and Fall of the New Deal Order, 1930–1980.* Princeton: Princeton University Press, 1989.

Freidel, Frank. *Franklin D. Roosevelt: The Apprenticeship.* Boston: Little, Brown, 1952.

———. *Franklin D. Roosevelt: Launching the New Deal.* Boston: Little, Brown, 1973.

———. *Franklin D. Roosevelt: A Rendezvous with Destiny.* Boston: Little, Brown, 1990.

Frese, Joseph R., and Jacob Judd, eds. *Business and Government: Essays in 20th-Century Cooperation and Confrontation.* Tarrytown, N.Y.: Sleepy Hollow Press and Rockefeller Archive Center, 1985.

Friedman, Elisha M., ed. *America and the New Era: A Symposium on Social Reconstruction.* New York: E. P. Dutton, 1920.

Friedmann, John. *Planning in the Public Domain: From Knowledge to Action.* Princeton: Princeton University Press, 1987.

Funigiello, Philip J. *The Challenge to Urban Liberalism: Federal-City Relations during World War II.* Knoxville: University of Tennessee Press, 1978.

Furner, Mary O. *Advocacy and Objectivity: A Crisis in the Professionalization of American Social Science, 1865–1905.* Lexington: University Press of Kentucky, 1977.

Furner, Mary O., and Barry Supple, eds. *The State and Economic Knowledge: The American and British Experiences*. New York: Woodrow Wilson International Center for Scholars and Cambridge University Press, 1990.

Fusfeld, Daniel R. *The Economic Thought of Franklin D. Roosevelt and the Origins of the New Deal*. New York: Columbia University Press, 1956.

Galambos, Louis. *America at Middle Age: A New History of the U.S. in the Twentieth Century.* New York: New Press/McGraw-Hill, 1982.

———, ed. *The New American State: Bureaucracies and Policies since World War II*. Baltimore: Johns Hopkins University Press, 1987.

Galambos, Louis, and Joseph Pratt. *The Rise of the Corporate Commonwealth: U.S. Business and Public Policy in the Twentieth Century.* New York: Basic Books, 1988.

Galbraith, John Kenneth. *A Life in Our Times: Memoirs.* Boston: Houghton Mifflin, 1981.

Galloway, George, et al., eds. *Planning for America.* New York: Henry Holt, 1941.

Garraty, John A. *The Great Depression: An Inquiry into the Causes, Course, and Consequences of the Worldwide Depression of the Nineteen-Thirties as Seen by Contemporaries and in the Light of History.* New York: Harcourt Brace Jovanovich, 1986.

Gates, Frederick T. *Chapters in My Life.* New York: Free Press, 1977.

Geiger, Roger L. *To Advance Knowledge: The Growth of American Research Universities, 1900–1940.* New York: Oxford University Press, 1986.

Gelfand, Lawrence E., ed. *Herbert Hoover: The Great War and Its Aftermath, 1914–23.* Iowa City: University of Iowa Press, 1979.

Gelfand, Lawrence E., and Robert J. Neymeyer, eds. *The New Deal Viewed from Fifty Years: Papers Commemorating the Fiftieth Anniversary of the Launching of President Franklin D. Roosevelt's New Deal in 1933.* Iowa City: Center for the Study of the Recent History of the United States, 1983.

Gerber, Larry G. *The Limits of Liberalism: Josephus Daniels, Henry Stimson, Bernard Baruch, Donald Richberg, Felix Frankfurter and the Development of the Modern American Political Economy.* New York: New York University Press, 1983.

Gilbert, James. *Another Chance: Postwar America, 1945–1968.* New York: Alfred A. Knopf, 1981.

———. *Designing the Industrial State: The Intellectual Pursuit of Collectivism in America, 1880–1940.* Chicago: Quadrangle, 1972.

Gillette, Howard, Jr., and Zane L. Miller, eds. *American Urbanism: A Historiographical Frontier.* New York: Greenwood Press, 1987.

Gitelman, Howard M. *Legacy of the Ludlow Massacre: A Chapter in American Industrial Relations.* Philadelphia: University of Pennsylvania Press, 1988.

Glenn, John M., Lilian Brandt, and F. Emerson Andrews. *Russell Sage Foundation: 1907–1946.* 2 vols. New York: Russell Sage Foundation, 1947.

Goodnow, Frank. *Politics and Administration.* New York: Macmillan, 1900.

Gordon, Colin. *New Deals: Business, Labor, and Politics in America, 1920–1935.* New York: Cambridge University Press, 1994.

Gourevitch, Peter. *Politics in Hard Times: Comparative Responses to International Economic Crises.* Ithaca: Cornell University Press, 1986.

Graebner, William S. *The Age of Doubt: American Thought and Culture in the 1940s.* Boston: Twayne Publishers, 1991.

Graham, Otis L., Jr. *An Encore for Reform: The Old Progressives and the New Deal.* New York: Oxford University Press, 1967.

———. *Losing Time: The Industrial Policy Debate.* Cambridge, Mass.: Harvard University Press, 1992.

———. *Toward a Planned Society: From Roosevelt to Nixon.* New York: Oxford University Press, 1976.

———, ed. *Soviet-American Dialogue on the New Deal.* Columbia: University of Missouri Press, 1989.

Graham, Otis L., Jr., and Meghan Robinson Wander, eds. *Franklin D. Roosevelt, His Life and Times: An Encyclopedic View*. Boston: G. K. Hall, 1985.

Grant, Wyn, Jan Nekkers, and Frans van Waarden, eds. *Organising Business for War: Corporatist Economic Organisation during the Second World War*. New York: Berg Publishers, 1991.

Greenstone, J. David, ed. *Public Values and Private Power in American Politics*. Chicago: University of Chicago Press, 1982.

Greer, Thomas H. *What Roosevelt Thought*. East Lansing: Michigan State University Press, 1958.

Gruchy, Allen G. *Contemporary Economic Thought: The Contribution of Neo-Institutional Economics*. Clifton, N.J.: Augustus M. Kelley, 1972.

———. *Modern Economic Thought: The American Contribution*. New York: Prentice-Hall, 1947.

Gulick, Luther. *Administrative Reflections from World War II*. University: University of Alabama Press, 1948.

Gutheim, Frederick. *The Federal City: Plans and Realities*. Washington, D.C.: Smithsonian Institution Press, 1976.

———. *Planning for Washington, 1924–1976: An Era of Planning for the National Capital and Environs*. Washington, D.C.: National Capital Planning Commission, 1976.

———. *Worthy of the Nation: The History of Planning for the National Capital*. Washington, D.C.: Smithsonian Institution Press, 1977.

Haber, Samuel. *Efficiency and Uplift: Scientific Management in the Progressive Era, 1890–1920*. Chicago: University of Chicago Press, 1964.

———. *The Quest for Authority and Honor in the American Professions, 1750–1900*. Chicago: University of Chicago Press, 1991.

Hall, Peter A., ed. *The Political Power of Economic Ideas: Keynesianism across Nations*. Princeton: Princeton University Press, 1989.

Hall, Peter Dobkin. *Inventing the Nonprofit Sector, and Other Essays on Philanthropy, Voluntarism, and Nonprofit Organizations*. Baltimore: Johns Hopkins University Press, 1992.

———. *The Organization of American Culture, 1700–1900: Private Institutions, Elites, and the Origins of American Nationality*. New York: New York University Press, 1984.

Hamby, Alonzo L. *Beyond the New Deal: Harry S. Truman and American Liberalism*. New York: Columbia University Press, 1973.

———. *Liberalism and Its Challengers: From F.D.R. to Bush*. 2d ed. New York: Oxford University Press, 1992.

———. *Man of the People: A Life of Harry S. Truman*. New York: Oxford University Press, 1995.

Hamilton, David E. *From New Day to New Deal: American Farm Policy from Hoover to Roosevelt, 1928–1933*. Chapel Hill: University of North Carolina Press, 1991.

Hargrove, Erwin C. *Prisoners of Myth: The Leadership of the Tennessee Valley Authority, 1933–1990*. Princeton: Princeton University Press, 1994.

Hargrove, Erwin C., and Paul K. Conkin, eds., *TVA: Fifty Years of Grass-roots Bureaucracy*. Urbana: University of Illinois Press, 1983.

Harris, Seymour E. *John Maynard Keynes: Economist and Policy Maker*. New York: Charles Scribner & Sons, 1955.

———, ed. *The New Economics: Keynes' Influence on Theory and Public Policy*. New York: Alfred A. Knopf, 1947.

Haskell, Thomas L. *The Emergence of Professional Social Science: The American Social Science Association and the Nineteenth-Century Crisis of Authority*. Urbana: University of Illinois Press, 1977.

————, ed. *The Authority of Experts: Studies in History and Theory*. Bloomington: Indiana University Press, 1984.

Hatch, Nathan O., ed. *The Professions in American History*. Notre Dame, Ind.: University of Notre Dame Press, 1988.

Hawke, David F. *John D.: Founding Father of the Rockefellers*. New York: Harper & Row, 1980.

Hawley, Ellis W. *The Great War and the Search for a Modern Order: A History of the American People and Their Institutions, 1917–1933*. New York: St. Martin's Press, 1979, 1992.

————. *The New Deal and the Problem of Monopoly: A Study in Economic Ambivalence*. Princeton: Princeton University Press, 1966; New York: Fordham University Press, 1995.

————, ed. *Herbert Hoover as Secretary of Commerce, 1921–1928: Studies in New Era Thought and Practice*. Iowa City: University of Iowa Press, 1981.

Hawley, Ellis W., Murray N. Rothbard, Robert F. Himmelberg, and Gerald Nash. *Herbert Hoover and the Crisis of American Capitalism*. Cambridge, Mass.: Schenkman, 1972.

Hayek, Friedrich A. *The Road to Serfdom*. Chicago: University of Chicago Press, 1944.

Hayes, E. P. *Activities of the President's Emergency Committee for Employment (October 17, 1930-August 19, 1931)*. Concord, N.H.: Rumford Press, 1936.

Hays, Samuel. *Conservation and the Gospel of Efficiency: The Progressive Conservation Movement, 1890–1920*. New York: Atheneum, 1969.

————. *The Response to Industrialism: 1885–1914*. Chicago: University of Chicago Press, 1957.

Heath, Charlotte. *Dennison Beginnings: 1840–1878*. N.p.: privately printed, 1928.

Heaton, Herbert. *A Scholar in Action: Edwin F. Gay*. Cambridge, Mass.: Harvard University Press, 1952.

Heller, Francis H., ed. *Economics and the Truman Administration*. Lawrence: Regents Press of Kansas, 1981.

Herbert Hoover Reassessed: Essays Commemorating the Fiftieth Anniversary of the Inauguration of Our Thirty-First President. Washington, D.C.: Government Printing Office, 1981.

Herbst, Jurgen. *The German Historical School in American Scholarship: A Study in the Transfer of Culture*. Ithaca: Cornell University Press, 1965.

Hicks, John D. *Rehearsal for Disaster: The Boom and Collapse of 1919–1920*. Gainesville: University of Florida Press, 1961.

Hidy, Ralph W., and Paul E. Cawein, eds. *Individual Enterprise and National Growth*. Boston: D.C. Heath, 1967.

Higgs, Robert. *Crisis and Leviathan: Critical Episodes in the Growth of American Government*. New York: Oxford University Press, 1987.

Himmelberg, Robert F. *The Origins of the National Recovery Administration: Business, Government, and the Trade Association Issue, 1921–1933*. New York: Fordham University Press, 1976.

————, ed. *Business-Government Cooperation, 1917–1932: The Rise of Corporatist Policies*. Vol. 5 of *Business and Government in America since 1870*. New York: Garland Publishing, 1994.

Hines, Thomas S. *Burnham of Chicago: Architect and Planner*. Chicago: University of Chicago Press, 1979.

Hines, Walker. *War History of American Railroads*. New Haven: Yale University Press, 1928.

Hodgson, Godfrey. *All Things to All Men: The False Promise of the Modern American Presidency from Franklin D. Roosevelt to Ronald Reagan*. New York: Simon & Schuster, 1980.

————. *America in Our Time, from World War II to Nixon: What Happened and Why.* Garden City, N.Y.: Doubleday, 1976.

Hollingsworth, Harold M., and William F. Holmes, eds. *Essays on the New Deal: The Walter Prescott Webb Memorial Lectures.* Austin: University of Texas Press, for University of Texas at Arlington, 1969.

Hoogenboom, Ari, and Olive Hoogenboom. *A History of the ICC: From Panacea to Palliative.* New York: W. W. Norton, 1976.

Hoover, Herbert. *The Memoirs of Herbert Hoover.* 3 vols. New York: Macmillan, 1951–52.

Horowitz, David, ed. *Corporations and the Cold War.* New York: Monthly Review Press, 1970.

Hoxie, R. Gordon, et al. *A History of the Faculty of Political Science at Columbia University.* New York: Columbia University Press, 1955.

Hubbard, Preston J. *Origins of the TVA: The Muscle Shoals Controversy, 1920–1932.* Nashville: Vanderbilt University Press, 1961.

Hunt, Edward Eyre. *An Audit of America: A Summary of Recent Economic Changes in the United States.* New York: McGraw-Hill, 1930.

————. *Conferences, Committees, Conventions and How to Run Them.* New York: Harper & Brothers, 1925.

Hyman, Sidney. *Marriner S. Eccles: Private Entrepreneur and Public Servant.* Stanford, Calif.: Stanford University Graduate School of Business, 1976.

Ickes, Harold L. *The Autobiography of a Curmudgeon.* 1943; Chicago: Quadrangle, 1969.

————. *The Secret Diary of Harold L. Ickes.* 3 vols. New York: Simon & Schuster, 1953–54.

Israel, Jerry, ed. *Building the Organizational Society: Essays on Associational Activities in Modern America.* New York: Free Press, 1972.

Janeway, Eliot. *The Struggle for Survival.* New Haven: Yale University Press, 1951.

Jeffries, John W. *Wartime America: The World War II Home Front.* Chicago: Ivan R. Dee, 1996.

Jeffries-Jones, Rhodri, and Bruce Collins, eds. *The Growth of Federal Power in American History.* DeKalb: Northern Illinois University Press, 1983.

Jenkins, Shirley, ed. *Social Security in International Perspective: Essays in Honor of Eveline M. Burns.* New York: Columbia University Press, 1969.

Johnson, Alvin Page. *Franklin D. Roosevelt's Colonial Ancestors: Their Part in the Making of American History.* Boston: Lathrop, Lee & Shephard, 1933.

Johnson, Arthur M., and Barry E. Supple. *Boston Capitalists and Western Railroads: A Study in the Nineteenth-Century Railroad Investment Process.* Cambridge, Mass.: Harvard University Press, 1967.

Johnson, Chalmers, ed. *The Industrial Policy Debate.* San Francisco: Institute for Contemporary Studies, 1984.

Johnson, Guy Benton, and Guion Griffis Johnson. *Research in Service to Society: The First Fifty Years of the Institute for Research in Social Science.* Chapel Hill: University of North Carolina Press, 1980.

Johnson, James P. *The Politics of Soft Coal: The Bituminous Industry from World War I through the New Deal.* Urbana: University of Illinois Press, 1979.

Jonas, Gerald. *The Circuit Riders: Rockefeller Money and the Rise of Modern Science.* New York: W. W. Norton, 1989.

Jones, Linda R. Wolf. *Eveline M. Burns and the American Social Security System, 1935–1960.* New York: Garland Publishing, 1991.

Jordan, John M. *Machine-Age Ideology: Social Engineering and American Liberalism, 1911–1939.* Chapel Hill: University of North Carolina Press, 1994.

Karl, Barry D. *Charles E. Merriam and the Study of Politics.* Chicago: University of Chicago Press, 1974.

————. *Executive Reorganization and Reform in the New Deal: The Genesis of Administrative*

Management, 1900–1939. Cambridge, Mass.: Harvard University Press, 1963; Chicago: University of Chicago Press, 1979.

————. *The Uneasy State: The United States from 1915 to 1945.* Chicago: University of Chicago Press, 1983.

Keele, Harold M., and Joseph C. Kiger, eds. *Foundations.* Westport, Conn.: Greenwood Press, 1984.

Kennedy, David M. *Over Here: The First World War and American Society.* New York: Oxford University Press, 1980.

Kerr, K. Austin. *American Railroad Politics, 1914–1920: Rates, Wages, Efficiency.* Pittsburgh: University of Pittsburgh Press, 1968.

————. *Organized for Prohibition: A New History of the Anti-Saloon League of America.* New Haven: Yale University Press, 1986.

Kettl, Donald F. *Leadership at the Fed.* New Haven: Yale University Press, 1986.

Kevles, Daniel J. *The Physicists: The History of a Scientific Community in America.* New York: Alfred A. Knopf, 1977.

Keyssar, Alexander. *Out of Work: The First Century of Unemployment in Massachusetts.* New York: Cambridge University Press, 1986.

Kiger, Joseph C. *Historiographic Review of Foundation Literature: Motivations and Perceptions.* New York: Foundation Center, 1987.

Kimball, Bruce A. *The "True Professional Ideal" in America.* Cambridge, Mass.: Blackwell, 1992.

Kimmel, Lewis. *The Federal Budget and Fiscal Policy, 1789–1959.* Washington, D.C.: Brookings Institution, 1959.

Kirkendall, Richard S. *Social Scientists and Farm Politics in the Age of Roosevelt.* Columbia: University of Missouri Press, 1966.

Klein, Maury. *The Flowering of the Third America: The Making of an Organizational Society, 1850–1920.* Chicago: Ivan R. Dee, 1993.

Klein, Philip. *The Burden of Unemployment: A Study of Unemployment Relief in Fifteen American Cities, 1921–22.* New York: Russell Sage Foundation, 1923.

Kloppenberg, James T. *The Virtues of Liberalism.* New York: Oxford University Press, 1998.

Knowlton, Winthrop, and Richard Zeckhauser, eds. *American Society: Public and Private Responsibilities.* Cambridge, Mass.: Ballinger Publishing, 1986.

Kohler, Robert E. *Partners in Science: Foundations and Natural Scientists, 1900–1945.* Chicago: University of Chicago Press, 1991.

Koistinen, Paul A. C. *The Military-Industrial Complex: A Historical Perspective.* New York: Praeger Publishers, 1980.

————. *Mobilizing for Modern War: The Political Economy of American Warfare, 1865–1919.* Lawrence: University Press of Kansas, 1997.

————. *Planning War, Pursuing Peace: The Political Economy of American Warfare, 1920–1939.* Lawrence: University Press of Kansas, 1998.

Kolko, Gabriel. *The Triumph of Conservatism: A Reinterpretation of American History, 1900–1916.* Chicago: Quadrangle, 1967.

Kraus, Michelle P. *Personnel Research: History and Policy Issues: Walter Van Dyke Bingham and the Bureau of Personnel Research.* New York: Garland Publishing, 1987.

Krog, Carl E., and William R. Tanner, eds. *Herbert Hoover and the Republican Era: A Reconsideration.* Lanham, Md.: University Press of America, 1984.

Krueckeberg, Donald A., ed. *The American Planner: Biographies and Recollections.* New York: Methuen, 1983.

————, ed. *Introduction to Planning History in the U.S.* New Brunswick, N.J.: Rutgers University, Center for Urban Policy Research, 1983.

Krushal, William H., ed. *The Social Sciences: Their Nature and Uses. Papers Presented at the*

50th Anniversary of the Social Science Research Building, the University of Chicago, December 16–18, 1979. Chicago: University of Chicago Press, 1982.

Lacey, Michael J., and Mary O. Furner, eds. *The State and Social Investigation in Britain and the United States.* New York: Woodrow Wilson Center Press and Cambridge University Press, 1993.

Lagemann, Ellen Condliffe. *The Politics of Knowledge: The Carnegie Corporation, Philanthropy, and Public Policy.* Middletown, Conn.: Wesleyan University Press, 1989.

———. *Private Power for the Public Good: A History of the Carnegie Foundation for the Advancement of Teaching.* Middletown, Conn.: Wesleyan University Press, 1983.

Larson, John Lauritz. *Bonds of Enterprise: John Murray Forbes and the Burlington Route in America's Railway Age.* Cambridge, Mass.: Harvard University Press, 1984.

Larson, Magali S. *The Rise of Professionalism: A Sociological Analysis.* Berkeley: University of California Press, 1977.

Lash, Joseph P. *Dealers and Dreamers: A New Look at the New Deal.* New York: Doubleday, 1988.

Laura Spelman Rockefeller Memorial. *Annual Report.* New York: Laura Spelman Rockefeller Memorial, 1922–33.

Lavoie, Don. *National Economic Planning: What Is Left?* Cambridge, Mass.: Ballinger Publishing, 1985.

Lawson, Alan. *The Failure of Independent Liberalism, 1930–1941.* New York: Capricorn Books, 1971.

Layton, Daphne Niobe. *Philanthropy and Voluntarism: An Annotated Bibliography.* New York: Foundation Center, 1987.

Lear, Linda J. *Harold L. Ickes: The Aggressive Progressive, 1873–1933.* New York: Garland Publishing, 1981.

Lehmbruch, Gerhard, and Philippe C. Schmitter, eds. *Patterns of Corporatist Policy-Making.* Beverly Hills, Calif.: Sage Publications, 1982.

Lekachman, Robert. *The Age of Keynes.* New York: McGraw-Hill, 1966.

Leuchtenburg, William E. *The FDR Years: On Roosevelt and His Legacy.* New York: Columbia University Press, 1995.

———. *Franklin D. Roosevelt and the New Deal: 1932–1940.* New York: Harper & Row, 1963.

———. *In the Shadow of FDR: From Harry Truman to Bill Clinton.* 2d ed. Ithaca: Cornell University Press, 1993.

———. *The Perils of Prosperity, 1914–32.* Chicago: University of Chicago Press, 1958.

———. *The Supreme Court Reborn: The Constitutional Revolution in the Age of Roosevelt.* New York: Oxford University Press, 1995.

Lind, Michael. *The Next American Nation: The New Nationalism and the Fourth American Revolution.* New York: Free Press, 1995.

Lindeman, Eduard D. *Wealth and Culture: A Study of One Hundred Foundations and Their Operations during the Decade 1921–1930.* New York: Harcourt, Brace, 1936.

Lindley, Ernest K. *Franklin D. Roosevelt: A Career in Progressive Democracy.* New York: Blue Ribbon Books, 1931.

Linowes, David F. *Privatization: Toward More Effective Government. Report of the President's Commission on Privatization.* Urbana: University of Illinois Press, 1988.

Liu, Kwang Ching. *Anglo-American Steamship Rivalry in China, 1862–1874.* Cambridge, Mass.: Harvard University Press, 1962.

Livesay, Harold. *Andrew Carnegie and the Rise of Big Business.* Boston: Little, Brown, 1975.

Livingston, James. *Origins of the Federal Reserve System: Money, Class, and Corporate Capitalism, 1890–1913.* Ithaca: Cornell University Press, 1986.

Lloyd, Craig. *Aggressive Introvert: Herbert Hoover and Public Relations Management, 1912–1932.* Columbus: Ohio State University Press, 1972.

Lowi, Theodore. *The End of Liberalism.* New York: W. W. Norton, 1969, 1979.

Lubove, Roy. *The Struggle for Social Security, 1900–1935.* Cambridge, Mass.: Harvard University Press, 1968.

————. *The Urban Community: Housing and Planning in the Progressive Era.* Englewood Cliffs, N.J.: Prentice-Hall, 1967.

Lustig, R. Jeffrey. *Corporate Liberalism: The Origins of Modern American Political Theory, 1880–1920.* Berkeley: University of California Press, 1982.

Lynch, Edmund C. *Walter Dill Scott: Pioneer in Personnel Management.* Austin: University of Texas, Bureau of Business Research, 1968.

Lyons, Gene M. *The Uneasy Partnership: Social Science and the Federal Government in the Twentieth Century.* New York: Russell Sage Foundation, 1969.

Magat, Richard, ed. *Philanthropic Giving: Studies in Varieties and Goals.* New York: Oxford University Press, 1989.

Maier, Charles S. *Recasting Bourgeois Europe: Stabilization in France, Germany, and Italy in the Decade after World War I.* Princeton: Princeton University Press, 1975.

————, ed. *The Changing Boundaries of the Political: Essays on the Evolving Balance between the State and Society, Public and Private in Europe.* Cambridge: Cambridge University Press, 1987.

Maney, Patrick J. *The Roosevelt Presence: A Biography of Franklin Delano Roosevelt.* New York: Twayne Publishers, 1992.

May, Dean Lowe. *From New Deal to New Economics: The Liberal Response to the Recession of 1937.* New York: Garland Publishing, 1981.

Mayer, Milton. *Robert Maynard Hutchins: A Memoir.* Berkeley: University of California Press, 1993.

McCartin, Joseph A. *Labor's Great War: The Struggle for Industrial Democracy and the Origins of Modern American Labor Relations, 1912–1921.* Chapel Hill: University of North Carolina Press, 1997.

McClymer, John F. *War and Welfare: Social Engineering in America, 1890–1925.* Westport, Conn.: Greenwood Press, 1980.

McConnell, Grant. *The Decline of Agrarian Democracy.* Berkeley: University of California Press, 1953.

————. *Private Power and American Democracy.* New York: Alfred A. Knopf, 1966.

McCormick, Richard L. *The Party Period and Public Policy: American Politics from the Age of Jackson to the Progressive Era.* New York: Oxford University Press, 1986.

McCraw, Thomas K. *TVA and the Power Fight, 1933–1939.* Philadelphia: J. B. Lippincott, 1971.

————, ed. *The Essential Alfred Chandler: Essays toward a Historical Theory of Big Business.* Boston: Harvard Business School Press, 1988.

————. *Regulation in Perspective.* Cambridge, Mass.: Harvard University Press, 1981.

McElvaine, Robert S. *The Great Depression: America, 1929–1941.* 2d ed. New York: Times Books, 1993.

McGovern, George, and Leonard F. Guttridge. *The Great Coalfield War.* Boston: Houghton Mifflin, 1972.

McKinley, Charles. *Uncle Sam and the Pacific Northwest: Federal Management of Natural Resources in the Columbia River Valley.* Berkeley: University of California Press, 1952.

McNeill, William H. *Hutchins' University: A Memoir of the University of Chicago, 1929–1950.* Chicago: University of Chicago Press, 1991.

McQuaid, Kim. *Big Business and Presidential Power: From FDR to Reagan.* New York: William Morrow, 1982.

————. *Uneasy Partners: Big Business in American Politics, 1945–1990.* Baltimore: Johns Hopkins University Press, 1994.

Merkle, Judith A. *Management and Ideology: The Legacy of the International Scientific Management Movement.* Berkeley: University of California Press, 1980.

Merriam, Charles E. *The American Party System: An Introduction to the Study of Political Parties in the United States.* New York: Macmillan, 1922.

——. *American Political Ideas: Studies in the Development of American Political Thought, 1865–1917.* New York: Macmillan, 1920.

——. *Chicago: A More Intimate View of Urban Politics.* New York: Macmillan, 1929.

——. *Civic Education in the United States.* New York: Charles Scribner's Sons, 1934.

——. *Four American Party Leaders.* New York: Macmillan, 1926.

——. *A History of American Political Theories.* New York: Macmillan, 1903.

——. *History of the Theory of Sovereignty since Rousseau.* New York: Columbia University Press, 1900.

——. *The Making of Citizens: A Comparative Study of Methods of Civic Training.* Chicago: University of Chicago Press, 1931.

——. *New Aspects of Politics.* 3d ed., with Introduction by Barry D. Karl. 1925, 1931; Chicago: University of Chicago Press, 1970.

——. *On the Agenda of Democracy.* Cambridge, Mass.: Harvard University Press, 1941.

——. *Political Power: Its Composition and Incidence.* New York: Whittlesey House, McGraw-Hill, 1934.

——. *The Role of Politics in Social Change.* Washington Square, N.Y.: New York University Press, 1936.

[——.] *Spelman Fund of New York: Final Report.* New York: Spelman Fund, 1949.

——. *Systematic Politics.* Chicago: University of Chicago Press, 1945.

——. *What Is Democracy?* Chicago: University of Chicago Press, 1941.

——. *The Written Constitution and the Unwritten Attitude.* New York: Richard R. Smith, 1931.

Merriam, Charles E., and Harold Gosnell. *Non-Voting: Causes and Methods of Control.* Chicago: University of Chicago Press, 1924.

Milkis, Sidney M. *The President and the Parties: The Transformation of the American Party System since the New Deal.* New York: Oxford University Press, 1993.

Miller, Arthur S. *The Modern Corporate State: Private Governments and the American Constitution.* Westport, Conn.: Greenwood Press, 1976.

Millett, John D. *The Process and Organization of Government Planning.* New York: Columbia University Press, 1947.

Mitchell, Lucy Sprague. *Two Lives: The Story of Wesley Clair Mitchell and Myself.* New York: Simon & Schuster, 1953.

Mitchell, Wesley Clair. *The Backward Art of Spending Money and Other Essays.* New York: McGraw-Hill, 1937.

——. *Business Cycles.* Berkeley: University of California Press, 1913.

——. *Business Cycles: The Problem and Its Setting.* New York: National Bureau of Economic Research, 1927.

——, ed. *The National Bureau's First Quarter-Century.* New York: National Bureau of Economic Research, 1945.

Mock, James R., and Cedric Larson. *Words That Won the War: The Story of the Committee on Public Information.* Princeton: Princeton University Press, 1939.

Montgomery, David. *The Fall of the House of Labor: The Workplace, the State, and American Labor Activism, 1865–1925.* New York: Cambridge University Press, 1987.

——. *Workers' Control in America: Studies in the History of Work, Technology, and Labor Struggles.* New York: Cambridge University Press, 1979.

Moody, Walter D. *What of the City?* Chicago: A. C. McClurg, 1919.

Morgenthau, Henry, III. *Mostly Morgenthaus: A Family History.* New York: Ticknor & Fields, 1991.

Morrison, Samuel Eliot. *Three Centuries of Harvard, 1636–1936.* Cambridge, Mass.: Harvard University Press, Belknap Press, 1946.

Mosch, Theodore R. *The G. I. Bill: A Breakthrough in Educational and Social Policy in the United States.* Hicksville, N.Y.: Exposition Press, 1975.

Mosher, Frederick C. *"The President Needs Help": Proceedings of a Conference Held on January 15, 1987 to Celebrate the Fiftieth Anniversary of the Report on the President's Committee on Administrative Management and the Presentation of the Annual Burkett Miller Award for Distinguished Public Service.* Lanham, Md.: University Press of America, 1988.

Mullins, William H. *The Depression and the Urban West Coast, 1929–1933: Los Angeles, San Francisco, Seattle, and Portland.* Bloomington: Indiana University Press, 1991.

Muncy, Robyn. *Creating a Female Dominion in American Reform, 1890–1935.* New York: Oxford University Press, 1991.

Nash, Gerald D. *The Crucial Era: The Great Depression and World War II. Organizing America, 1933–1945.* 2d ed. New York: St. Martin's Press, 1992.

Nash, Lee, ed. *Understanding Herbert Hoover: Ten Perspectives.* Stanford, Calif.: Hoover Institution Press, 1987.

Nelson, Daniel. *Frederick W. Taylor and the Rise of Scientific Management.* Madison: University of Wisconsin Press, 1980.

———. *Managers and Workers: Origins of the New Factory System in the U.S., 1880–1920.* Madison: University of Wisconsin Press, 1975, 1996.

———. *Unemployment Insurance: The American Experience, 1915–1935.* Madison: University of Wisconsin Press, 1969.

———, ed. *A Mental Revolution: Scientific Management since Taylor.* Columbus: Ohio State University Press, 1992.

Nevins, Allan. *A Study in Power: John D. Rockefeller, Industrialist and Philanthropist.* New York: Charles Scribner's Sons, 1953.

Nielsen, Waldemar. *The Big Foundations.* New York: Columbia University Press, for the Twentieth Century Fund, 1972.

———. *The Golden Donors: A New Anatomy of the Great Foundations.* New York: E. P. Dutton, 1989.

Nixon, Edgar B., ed. *Franklin D. Roosevelt and Conservation, 1911–1945.* 2 vols. Hyde Park, N.Y.: Franklin D. Roosevelt Library, 1957.

Noble, David F. *American by Design: Science, Technology, and the Rise of Corporate Capitalism.* New York: Alfred A. Knopf, 1977.

Noggle, Burl. *Into the Twenties.* Urbana: University of Illinois Press, 1974.

Odendahl, Teresa. *Charity Begins at Home: Generosity and Self-Interest among the Philanthropic Elite.* New York: Basic Books, 1990.

Odum, Howard W., ed. *American Masters of Social Science.* New York: Henry Holt, 1927.

Ogg, Frederic Austin. *Research in the Humanistic and Social Sciences: Report of a Survey Conducted for the American Council of Learned Societies.* New York: Century, 1928.

Ohl, John Kennedy. *Hugh S. Johnson and the New Deal.* DeKalb: Northern Illinois University Press, 1985.

Oleson, Alexandra, and John Voss, eds. *The Organization of Knowledge in Modern America, 1860–1920.* Baltimore: Johns Hopkins University Press, 1979.

Olson, James S. *Herbert Hoover and the Reconstruction Finance Corporation, 1931–1933.* Ames: Iowa State University Press, 1977.

———. *Saving Capitalism: The Reconstruction Finance Corporation and the New Deal, 1933–1940.* Princeton: Princeton University Press, 1988.

———, ed. *Historical Dictionary of the New Deal: From Inauguration to Preparation for War.* Westport, Conn.: Greenwood Press, 1985.

Olson, Keith W. *The G. I. Bill, the Veterans, and the Colleges.* Lexington: University Press of Kentucky, 1974.

O'Neill, William L. *A Democracy at War: America's Fight at Home and Abroad in World War II.* New York: Free Press, 1993.

Overton, Richard C. *Burlington Route: A History of the Burlington Lines.* New York: Alfred A. Knopf, 1965.

———. *Perkins/Budd: Railway Statesmen of the Burlington.* Westport, Conn.: Greenwood, 1982.

Parrish, Michael E. *Anxious Decades: America in Prosperity and Depression, 1920–1941.* New York: W. W. Norton, 1992.

Patterson, James T. *America's Struggle against Poverty, 1900–1980.* Cambridge, Mass.: Harvard University Press, 1981.

———. *Congressional Conservatism and the New Deal: The Growth of the Conservative Coalition in Congress, 1933–1939.* Lexington: University of Kentucky Press, 1967.

———. *Grand Expectations: The United States, 1945–1974.* Vol. 10 of *Oxford History of the United States.* New York: Oxford University Press, 1996.

Paxson, Frederic L. *American Democracy and the World War.* 3 vols. Boston: Houghton Mifflin, 1936–48.

Payton, Robert, Michael Novak, Brian O'Connell, and Peter Dobkin Hall. *Philanthropy: Four Views.* New Brunswick, N.J.: Transaction Publishers, 1988.

Pells, Richard. *Radical Visions and American Dreams: Culture and Social Thought in the Depression Years.* New York: Harper & Row, 1973.

Perkins, Frances. *The Roosevelt I Knew.* New York: Viking Press, 1946.

Perkins, Van L. *Crisis in Agriculture.* Berkeley: University of California Press, 1969.

Perrett, Geoffrey. *Days of Sadness, Years of Triumph: The American People, 1939–1946.* 1973; Baltimore: Penguin Books, 1974.

Plotke, David. *Building a Democratic Political Order: Reshaping American Liberalism in the 1930s and 1940s.* New York: Cambridge University Press, 1996.

Polenberg, Richard. *One Nation Divisible: Class, Race, and Ethnicity in the United States since 1938.* New York: Viking Press and Pelican Books, 1980.

———. *Reorganizing Roosevelt's Government: The Controversy over Executive Reorganization, 1936–1939.* Cambridge, Mass.: Harvard University Press, 1966.

———. *War and Society: The United States, 1941–1945.* Philadelphia: J. B. Lippincott, 1972.

Porter, Bruce D. *War and the Rise of the State: The Military Foundations of Modern Politics.* New York: Free Press, 1994.

Porter, Glenn. *The Rise of Big Business, 1860–1920.* 2d ed. Arlington Heights, Ill.: Harlan Davidson, 1992.

Postwar Planning in the United States: An Organization Directory. 2 vols. New York: Twentieth Century Fund, 1942.

President's Conference on Unemployment. *Report of the President's Conference on Unemployment.* Washington, D.C.: Government Printing Office, 1921.

———. Committee on Business Cycles and Unemployment. *Business Cycles and Unemployment.* New York: McGraw-Hill, 1923.

———. Committee on Recent Economic Changes. *Recent Economic Changes in the United States.* 2 vols. New York: McGraw-Hill, 1929.

President's Research Committee on Social Trends. *Recent Social Trends in the United States.* 2 vols. New York: McGraw-Hill, 1933.

Pritchett, Charles Herman Pritchett. *The Tennessee Valley Authority: A Study in Public Administration.* Chapel Hill: University of North Carolina Press, 1943.

Rader, Benjamin. *The Academic Mind and Reform: The Influence of Richard T. Ely in American Life.* Lexington: University of Kentucky Press, 1966.

Radosh, Ronald, and Murray N. Rothbard, eds. *A New History of Leviathan: Essays on the Rise of the American Corporate State.* New York: E. P. Dutton, 1972.

Regional Plan Association. *From Plan to Reality.* 3 vols. New York: Regional Plan Association, 1933–42.

Reich, Robert B. *The Next American Frontier.* New York: Times Books, 1983.

Reps, John W. *The Making of Urban America: A History of City Planning in the United States.* Princeton: Princeton University Press, 1965.

————. *Washington on View: The Nation's Capital since 1790.* Chapel Hill: University of North Carolina Press, 1991.

Reynolds, Cuyler, comp. *Genealogical and Family History of Southern New York and the Hudson River Valley.* New York: Lewis Historical Publishing, 1914.

Rice, Stuart, ed. *Methods in the Social Sciences.* Chicago: University of Chicago Press, 1931.

Rodgers, Daniel T. *The Work Ethic in Industrial America: 1850–1920.* Chicago: University of Chicago Press, 1978.

Rohatyn, Felix G. *The Twenty-Year Century: Essays on Economics and Public Finance.* New York: Random House, 1983.

Romasco, Albert V. *The Politics of Recovery: Roosevelt's New Deal.* New York: Oxford University Press, 1983.

————. *The Poverty of Abundance: Hoover, the Nation, the Depression.* New York: Oxford University Press, 1965.

Roose, Kenneth. *The Economics of Recession and Revival: An Interpretation of 1937–38.* New Haven: Yale University Press, 1954.

Roosevelt, Hall, in collaboration with Samuel Duff McCoy. *Odyssey of an American Family: An Account of the Roosevelts and Their Kin as Travelers from 1613 to 1930.* New York: Harper, 1939.

Roper, Daniel C. *Fifty Years of Public Life.* 1941; Westport, Conn.: Greenwood Press, 1968.

Rosen, Elliot. *Hoover, Roosevelt, and the Brains Trust: From Depression to New Deal.* New York: Columbia University Press, 1977.

Rosenberg, Emily S. *Spreading the American Dream: American Economic and Cultural Expansion, 1890–1945.* New York: Hill & Wang, 1982.

Rosenof, Theodore. *Dogma, Depression, and the New Deal: The Debate of Political Leaders over Economic Recovery.* Port Washington, N.Y.: Kennikat Press, 1975.

————. *Economics in the Long Run: New Deal Theorists and Their Legacies, 1933–1993.* Chapel Hill: University of North Carolina Press, 1997.

Rosenman, Samuel. *Working with Roosevelt.* New York: Harper & Brothers, 1952.

————, comp. *The Public Papers and Addresses of Franklin D. Roosevelt.* 13 vols. New York: Harper & Brothers, 1938–50.

Ross, Davis R. B. *Preparing for Ulysses: Politics and Veterans during World War II.* New York: Columbia University Press, 1969.

Ross, Dorothy. *The Origins of American Social Science.* New York: Cambridge University Press, 1991.

Rothbard, Murray. *America's Greatest Depression.* 3d ed. Kansas City: Sheed & Ward, 1975.

Rowley, William D. *M. L. Wilson and the Campaign for the Domestic Allotment.* Lincoln: University of Nebraska Press, 1970.

Rudolph, Frederick. *The American College and University: A History.* New York: Alfred A. Knopf, 1962.

Ruml, Beardsley. *Government, Business, and Values.* New York: Harper & Brothers, 1943.

Saloutos, Theodore. *The American Farmer and the New Deal.* Ames: Iowa State University Press, 1982.

Saloutos, Theodore, and John D. Hicks. *Agricultural Discontent in the Middle West: 1900–1939.* Madison: University of Wisconsin Press, 1951.

Salzman, Jack, ed. *Philanthropy and American Society: Selected Papers.* New York: Columbia University, Center for American Culture Studies, 1987.

Samuels, Warren J., and Steven G. Medema. *Gardiner C. Means: Institutionalist and Post-Keynesian.* Armonk, N.Y.: M. E. Sharpe, 1990.

Sandel, Michael J. *Democracy's Discontent: America in Search of a Public Philosophy.* Cambridge, Mass.: Harvard University Press, Belknap Press, 1996.

Sandilands, Roger J. *The Life and Political Economy of Lauchlin Currie: New Dealer, Presidential Adviser, and Development Economist.* Durham, N.C.: Duke University Press, 1990.

Sargent, James E. *Roosevelt and the Hundred Days: Struggle for the Early New Deal.* New York: Garland Publishing, 1981.

Saunders, Charles B., Jr. *The Brookings Institution: A Fifty-Year History.* Washington, D.C.: Brookings Institution, 1966.

Sautter, Udo. *Three Cheers for the Unemployed: Government and Unemployment before the New Deal.* New York: Cambridge University Press, 1991.

Savage, Sean J. *Roosevelt: The Party Leader, 1932–1945.* Lexington: University Press of Kentucky, 1991.

Schaffer, Daniel, ed. *Two Centuries of American Planning.* Baltimore: Johns Hopkins University Press, 1988.

Schaffer, Ronald. *America in the Great War: The Rise of the War Welfare State.* New York: Oxford University Press, 1991.

Scheinberg, Stephen J. *Employers and Reformers: The Development of Corporation Labor Policy, 1900–1940.* New York: Garland Publishing, 1986.

Schiesl, Martin J. *The Politics of Efficiency: Municipal Administration and Reform in America, 1880–1920.* Berkeley: University of California Press, 1977.

Schlesinger, Arthur M., Jr. *The Age of Roosevelt.* Vol. 1, *The Crisis of the Old Order: 1919–1933.* Boston: Houghton Mifflin, 1957.

———. *The Age of Roosevelt.* Vol. 2, *The Coming of the New Deal.* Boston: Houghton Mifflin, 1959.

———. *The Age of Roosevelt.* Vol. 3, *The Politics of Upheaval.* Boston: Houghton Mifflin, 1960.

Schlesinger, Arthur M., Jr., and Morton White, eds. *Paths of American Thought.* Boston: Houghton Mifflin, 1963.

Schriftgiesser, Karl. *The Amazing Roosevelt Family, 1613–1942.* New York: W. Funk, 1942.

———. *Business and Public Policy: The Role of the Committee for Economic Development, 1942–1967.* Englewood Cliffs, N.J.: Prentice-Hall, 1967.

———. *Business Comes of Age: The Impact of the Committee on Economic Development, 1942–1960.* New York: Harper & Brothers, 1960.

Schultz, Stanley K. *Constructing Urban Culture: American Cities and City Planning, 1800–1920.* Philadelphia: Temple University Press, 1989.

Schwartz, Bonnie Fox. *The Civil Works Administration, 1933–1934: The Business of Emergency Employment in the New Deal.* Princeton: Princeton University Press, 1984.

Schwarz, Jordan A. *Liberal: Adolf A. Berle and the Vision of an American Era.* New York: Free Press, 1987.

———. *The New Dealers: Power Politics in the Age of Roosevelt.* New York: Alfred A. Knopf, 1993.

———. *The Speculator: Bernard M. Baruch in Washington, 1917–1965.* Chapel Hill: University of North Carolina Press, 1981.

Scott, Mel. *American City Planning since 1890.* Berkeley: University of California Press, 1969.

Scott, William G. *Chester I. Barnard and the Guardians of the Managerial State.* Lawrence: University Press of Kansas, 1992.

Sealander, Judith. *Grand Plans: Business Progressivism and Social Change in Ohio's Miami Valley, 1890–1929.* Lexington: University Press of Kentucky, 1988.

———. *Private Wealth and Public Life: Foundation Philanthropy and the Reshaping of American Social Policy from the Progressive Era to the New Deal.* Baltimore: Johns Hopkins University Press, 1997.

Seckler, David. *Thorstein Veblen and the Institutionalists: A Study in the Social Philosophy of Economics.* Boulder: Colorado Associated University Press, 1975.

Selznick, Philip. *TVA and the Grass Roots: A Study of Politics and Organization.* Berkeley: University of California Press, 1949.

Sibley, Elbridge. *Social Science Research Council: The First Fifty Years.* New York: Social Science Research Council, 1974.

Silva, Edward T., and Sheila A. Slaughter. *Serving Power: The Making of the Academic Social Science Expert.* Westport, Conn.: Greenwood Press, 1984.

Silverberg, Helene, ed. *Gender and American Social Science: The Formative Years.* Princeton: Princeton University Press, 1998.

Sitkoff, Harvard, ed. *Fifty Years Later: The New Deal Evaluated.* New York: Alfred A. Knopf, 1985.

Sklar, Martin J. *The Corporate Reconstruction of American Capitalism, 1890–1916: The Market, the Law, and Politics.* New York: Cambridge University Press, 1987.

———. *The United States as a Developing Country: Studies in U.S. History in the Progressive Era and the 1920s.* New York: Cambridge University Press, 1992.

Skocpol, Theda. *Social Policy in the United States: Future Possibilities in Historical Perspective.* Princeton: Princeton University Press, 1995.

Skowronek, Stephen. *Building a New American State: The Expansion of National Administrative Capacities, 1877–1920.* New York: Cambridge University Press, 1982.

Smith, Bruce L. R., ed. *The New Political Economy: The Public Use of the Private Sector.* New York: Wiley, 1975.

Smith, Dennis. *The Rise of Historical Sociology.* Philadelphia: Temple University Press, 1991.

Smith, James A. *Brookings at Seventy-Five.* Washington, D.C.: Brookings Institution, 1991.

———. *The Idea Brokers: Think Tanks and the Rise of the New Policy Elite.* New York: Free Press, 1991.

Smith, Robert M. *The American Business System and the Theory and Practice of Social Science: The Case of the Harvard Business School, 1925–1945.* New York: Garland Publishing, 1986.

Social Science Research Council. *Decennial Report: 1923–1933.* New York: Social Science Research Council, 1934.

———. Commission of Inquiry on Public Service Personnel. *Better Government Personnel.* New York: McGraw-Hill, 1935.

Sokal, Michael M., ed. *Psychological Testing and American Society, 1890–1930.* New Brunswick, N.J.: Rutgers University Press, 1987.

Somers, Herman. *Presidential Agency: OWMR, The Office of War Mobilization and Reconversion.* Cambridge, Mass.: Harvard University Press, 1950.

Somit, Albert, and Joseph Tannenhaus. *The Development of Political Science: From Burgess to Behavioralism.* Boston: Allyn & Bacon, 1967.

Soule, George. *A Planned Society.* New York: Macmillan, 1934.

———. *Planning U.S.A.* New York: Bantam, 1968.

———. *Prosperity Decade: From War to Depression, 1917–1929.* New York: Holt, Rinehart & Winston, 1947.

Sparrow, Bartholomew H. *From the Outside In: World War II and the American State.* Princeton: Princeton University Press, 1996.

Stabile, Donald. *Prophets of Order: The Rise of the New Class. Technocracy and Socialism in America.* Boston: South End Press, 1984.

Stein, Herbert. *The Fiscal Revolution in America.* Chicago: University of Chicago Press, 1969.

———. *Presidential Economics: The Making of Economic Policy from Roosevelt to Reagan and Beyond.* New York: Simon & Schuster, 1984.

Steinmo, Sven, Kathleen Thelen, and Frank Longstreth, eds. *Structuring Politics: Historical Institutionalism in Comparative Analysis*. New York: Cambridge University Press, 1992.

Sternsher, Bernard. *Rexford Tugwell and the New Deal*. New Brunswick, N.J.: Rutgers University Press, 1964.

Stoneman, William E. *A History of the Economic Analysis of the Great Depression in America*. New York: Garland Publishing, 1979.

Storr, Richard J. *Harper's University: The Beginnings*. Chicago: University of Chicago Press, 1966.

Streeck, Wolfgang, and Phillipe C. Schmitter, eds. *Private Interest Government: Beyond Market and State*. Newbury Park, Calif.: Sage Publications, 1985.

Swain, Donald C. *Federal Conservation Policy, 1921–1933*. Berkeley: University of California Press, 1963.

Trachtenberg, Alan. *The Incorporation of America: Culture and Society in the Gilded Age*. New York: Hill & Wang, 1982.

Tugwell, Rexford G. *The Battle for Democracy*. New York: Columbia University Press, 1935.

———. *The Brains Trust*. New York: Viking Press, 1968.

———. *The Democratic Roosevelt*. Garden City, N.Y.: Doubleday, 1957.

———. *Roosevelt's Revolution: The First Year—a Personal Perspective*. New York: Macmillan, 1977.

———. *To the Lesser Heights of Morningside: A Memoir*. Philadelphia: University of Pennsylvania Press, 1982.

Twentieth Century Fund. *Postwar Planning in the United States: An Organization Directory*. 2 vols. New York: Twentieth Century Fund, 1942.

Tweton, Jerome. *The New Deal at the Grass Roots: Programs for the People in Otter Tail County, Minnesota*. St. Paul: Minnesota Historical Society Press, 1988.

Urwick, L., and E. F. L. Brech. *The Making of Scientific Management*. 2 vols. London: Management Publications Trust, 1949.

U.S. Adjutant General's Department, Classification Division. *The Personnel System of the U.S. Army*. Vol. 1, *History of the Personnel System*. Washington, D.C.: Committee on Classification of Personnel in the Army, 1919.

U.S. Congress. House. Committee on Appropriations. *Hearings before the Subcommittee on Independent Offices Appropriations Bill for 1944*. 78th Cong., 1st sess., 1943.

———. *Independent Offices Appropriations, 1944*. H. Rept. 109 to Accompany HR 1762. 78th Cong., 1st sess., 1943.

———. *Independent Offices Appropriations Bill, 1944*. H. Rept. 552 to Accompany HR 1762. 78th Cong., 1st sess., 1943.

U.S. Congress. Senate. Committee on Appropriations. *Hearings before Subcommittee, Independent Offices Appropriations Bill for 1944*. 78th Cong., 1st sess., 1943.

———. *Independent Offices Appropriations Bill, 1944*, S. Rept. 247 to Accompany HR 1762. 78th Cong., 1st sess., 1943.

U.S. Congress. House and Senate. *Congressional Record*. 78th Cong., 1st sess., 1943, vol. 89.

U.S. National Planning Board. *Final Report—1933–34*. Washington, D.C.: Government Printing Office, 1934.

U.S. National Resources Board. *A Report on National Planning and Public Works in Relation to National Resources and Including Land Use and Water Resources, with Findings and Recommendations*. Washington, D.C.: Government Printing Office, 1934.

U.S. National Resources Committee. Industrial Committee. *The Structure of the American Economy*. 2 vols. Washington, D.C.: Government Printing Office, 1939–40.

———. *Research—A National Resource*. Vol. 1, *Relation of the Federal Government to Research*. Washington, D.C.: Government Printing Office, 1938.

U.S. National Resources Planning Board. *Demobilization and Readjustment: Report of the Conference on Postwar Readjustment of Civilian and Military Personnel.* Washington, D.C.: Government Printing Office, 1943.

————. *Development of Resources and Stabilization of Employment in the United States.* 3 vols. Washington, D.C.: Government Printing Office, 1941.

————. *National Resources Development Report for 1942.* Washington, D.C.: Government Printing Office, 1942.

————. *National Resources Development Report for 1943: Parts 1–3.* Washington, D.C.: Government Printing Office, 1943.

————. *Our Public Works Experience.* Comp. John Kenneth Galbraith and G. Griffith Johnson. Washington, D.C.: Government Printing Office, 1941.

————. *Progress Report: 1940–1941.* Washington, D.C.: Government Printing Office, 1941.

————. *Research—A National Resource.* Vol. 2, *Industrial Research;* Vol. 3, *Business Research.* Washington, D.C.: Government Printing Office, 1940–41.

Van Tine, Warren R. *The Making of the Labor Bureaucrat: Union Leadership in the United States, 1870–1920.* Amherst: University of Massachusetts Press, 1973.

Vaughn, Stephen L. *Holding Fast the Inner Lines: Democracy, Nationalism, and the Committee on Public Information.* Chapel Hill: University of North Carolina Press, 1980.

Veblen, Thorstein. *The Engineers and the Price System.* 1919, 1921; New York: Harcourt, Brace & World, 1963.

Vesey, Lawrence R. *The Emergence of the American University.* Chicago: University of Chicago Press, 1965.

Walker, Robert Averill. *The Planning Function in Urban Government.* Chicago: University of Chicago Press, 1941, 1950.

Wall, Joseph Frazier. *Andrew Carnegie.* 2 vols. New York: Oxford University Press, 1970.

Ward, Geoffrey C. *American Originals: The Private Worlds of Some Singular Men and Women.* New York: HarperCollins, 1991.

————. *Before the Trumphet: Young Franklin Roosevelt, 1882–1905.* New York: Harper & Row, 1985.

————. *A First-Class Temperament: The Emergence of Franklin D. Roosevelt.* New York: Harper & Row, 1989.

Ware, Alan. *Between Profit and State: Intermediate Organizations in Britain and the United States.* Princeton: Princeton University Press, 1989.

Warken, Philip W. *A History of the National Resources Planning Board, 1933–1943.* New York: Garland Publishing, 1979.

Warren, Frank, III. *Liberals and Communism: The "Red Decade" Revisited.* Bloomington: Indiana University Press, 1966.

Warren, Harris G. *Herbert Hoover and the Great Depression.* New York: Oxford University Press, 1959.

Watkins, T. H. *Righteous Pilgrim: The Life and Times of Harold L. Ickes, 1874–1952.* New York: Henry Holt, 1990.

Weaver, Warren. *U.S. Philanthropic Foundations.* New York: Harper & Brothers, 1952.

Weinstein, James. *The Corporate Ideal in the Liberal State: 1900–1918.* Boston: Beacon Press, 1968.

Weinstein, James, and David W. Eakins, eds. *For a New America: Essays in History and Politics from Studies on the Left, 1959–1967.* New York: Random House, 1970.

Weir, Margaret, Ann Shola Orloff, and Theda Skocpol, eds. *The Politics of Social Policy in the United States.* Princeton: Princeton University Press, 1988.

Wheatley, Steven C. *The Politics of Philanthropy: Abraham Flexner and Medical Education.* Madison: University of Wisconsin Press, 1988.

White, Dana F. *The Urbanists, 1865–1915.* Westport, Conn.: Greenwood Press, 1989.

White, Graham, and John Maze. *Harold Ickes of the New Deal: His Private Life and Public Career.* Cambridge, Mass.: Harvard University Press, 1985.

White, Leonard D., ed. *Civil Service in Wartime.* Chicago: University of Chicago Press, 1945.

———. *The Future of Government in the United States: Essays in Honor of Charles E. Merriam.* Chicago: University of Chicago Press, 1942.

White, Morton. *Social Thought in America: The Revolt against Formalism.* 1949; Boston: Beacon Press, 1957.

Wiebe, Robert. *Businessmen and Reform: A Study of the Progressive Movement.* Chicago: Quadrangle, 1968.

———. *The Search for Order: 1877–1920.* New York: Hill & Wang, 1967.

Williams, William Appleman. *The Contours of American History.* Chicago: Quadrangle, 1966.

Wilson, David E. *The National Planning Idea in United States Public Policy: Five Alternative Approaches.* Boulder, Colo.: Westview Press, 1980.

———, comp. *National Planning in the United States: An Annotated Bibliography.* Boulder, Colo.: Westview Press, 1979.

Wilson, Joan Hoff. *Herbert Hoover: Forgotten Progressive.* Boston: Little Brown, 1975.

Winkler, Allan M. *Home Front, U.S.A.: America During World War II.* Arlington Heights, Ill.: Harlan Davidson, 1986.

Wolfe, Alan. *America's Impasse: The Rise and Fall of the Politics of Growth.* New York: Pantheon Books, 1981.

Wynn, Neil A. *From Progressivism to Prosperity: World War I and American Society.* New York: Holmes & Meier, 1986.

Yerkes, Robert M., ed. *The New World of Science: Its Development during the War.* New York: Century, 1920.

Zieger, Robert H. *The CIO, 1935–1955.* Chapel Hill: University of North Carolina Press, 1995.

Zinn, Howard, ed. *New Deal Thought.* Indianapolis: Bobbs-Merrill, 1966.

Zunz, Olivier. *Making America Corporate, 1870–1920.* Chicago: University of Chicago Press, 1990.

ARTICLES

Adams, Frederick J. "Changing Concepts of Planning." *American Journal of Economics and Sociology* 15 (1956): 245–51.

Adams, Frederick J., and Gerald Hodge. "City Planning Instruction in the United States, 1900–1930." *Journal of the American Institute of Planners* 31 (1965): 43–51.

Adams, Thomas. "A Communication: In Defense of the Regional Plan." *New Republic,* July 6, 1932, 207–10.

———. "Regional Planning in Relation to Public Administration." *National Municipal Review* 15 (January 1926): 35–42.

———. "The Social Objective in Regional Planning." *National Municipal Review* 15 (February 1926): 79–87.

Adelstein, Richard P. "'The Nation as an Economic Unit': Keynes, Roosevelt, and the Managerial Ideal." *Journal of American History* 78 (June 1991): 160–87.

Ahmad, Salma. "American Foundations and the Development of the Social Sciences between the Wars: Comments on the Debate between Martin Bulmer and Donald Fisher." *Sociology* 25 (August 1991): 511–20.

Alchon, Guy. "Mary Van Kleeck and Social-Economic Planning." *Journal of Policy History* 3 (1991): 1–23.

———. "Policy History and the Sublime Immodesty of the Middle-Aged Professor." *Journal of Policy History* 9 (1997): 358–74.

Aldrich, John. "Does Historical Political Research Pose Any Special Methodological Concerns?" *Political Methodologist* 8 (Fall 1997): 17–21.

Almond, Gabriel A. "The Return to the State." *American Political Science Review* 82 (September 1988): 853–74.

Amenta, Edwin, and Theda Skocpol. "Taking Exception: Explaining the Distinctiveness of American Public Policies in the Last Century." In *The Comparative History of Public Policy,* ed. Francis G. Castles, 292–333. New York: Oxford University Press, 1989.

Arnold, Peri Ethan. "Herbert Hoover and the Continuity of American Policy." *Public Policy* 20 (1972): 522–44.

Ashford, Douglas E. "The Whig Interpretation of the Welfare State." *Journal of Policy History* 1 (1989): 24–43.

Auerbach, Jerold S. "New Deal, Old Deal, or Raw Deal: Some Thoughts on New Left Historiography." *Journal of Southern History* 35 (November 1969): 18–30.

Auerbach, Lewis E. "Scientists in the New Deal: A Pre-War Episode in the Relations between Science and Government in the United States." *Minerva* 3 (1965): 457–82.

Balogh, Brian. "Reorganizing the Organizational Synthesis: Federal-Professional Relations in Modern America." *Studies in American Political Development* 5 (Spring 1991): 119–72.

Barber, William J. "The Career of Alvin H. Hansen in the 1920s and 1930s: A Study in Intellectual Transformation." *History of Political Economy* 19 (Summer 1987): 191–205.

Baskerville, Stephen W. "Post-New Deal Economic Thought, Government, and Society, 1937–1941." *Storia Nordamericana* (Italy) 6 (1989): 57–68.

Beard, Charles A. "Some Aspects of Regional Planning." *American Political Science Review* 20 (1926): 273–83.

"Beardsley Ruml." *Fortune,* March 1945, 135–38ff.

Beckman, Norman. "Federal Long-Range Planning: The Heritage of the National Resources Planning Board." *American Institute of Planners Journal* 26 (May 1960): 89–97.

Berk, Gerald. "Corporate Liberalism Reconsidered: A Review Essay." *Journal of Policy History* (1991): 70–84.

Berkhofer, Robert F., Jr. "The Organizational Interpretation of American History: A New Synthesis." *Prospects* 4 (1979): 611–29.

Berle, Adolf Augustus, Jr. "Wesley Clair Mitchell: The Economic Scientist." *Journal of the American Statistical Association* 48 (June 1953): 169–75.

Bernstein, Barton J. "The Debate on Industrial Reconversion: The Protection of Oligopoly and Military Control of the War Economy." *American Journal of Economics and Sociology* 26 (1967): 159–72.

———. "The New Deal: The Conservative Achievements of Liberal Reform." In *Towards a New Past: Dissenting Essays in American History,* ed. Barton J. Bernstein, 263–88. New York: Vintage, 1969.

———. "The Removal of War Production Board Controls on Business, 1944–1946." *Business History Review* 39 (1965): 243–60.

———. "The Truman Administration and Its Reconversion Wage Policy." *Labor History* 6 (1965): 214–31.

Best, Gary Dean. "President Wilson's Second Industrial Conference, 1919–1920." *Labor History* 16 (1975): 505–20.

Birch, Eugenie Ladner. "Advancing the Art and Science of Planning: Planners and Their Organizations, 1909–1980." *Journal of the American Planning Association* 46 (January 1980): 22–49.

Bliven, Bruce, Max Lerner, and George Soule. "Charter for America: A Special Section." *New Republic,* April 19, 1943, 523–42.

Bourcke, Paul F. "The Status of Politics, 1901–1919: *The New Republic,* Randolph Bourne, and Van Wyck Brooks." *Journal of American Studies* 8 (1974): 171–202.

Braeman, John. "The New Deal and the 'Broker State': A Review of the Scholarly Literature." *Business History Review* 46 (1972): 409–29.

———. "The New Deal: The Collapse of the Liberal Consensus." *Canadian Review of American Studies* 20 (Summer 1989): 41–80.

Brazelton, W. Robert. "Alvin Harvey Hansen: Economic Growth and a More Perfect Society: The Economist's Role in Defining the Stagnation Thesis and in Popularizing Keynesianism." *American Journal of Economics and Sociology* 48 (October 1989): 427–40.

Breen, William J. "Foundations, Statistics, and State-Building: Leonard P. Ayres, the Russell Sage Foundation, and U.S. Government Statistics in the First World War." *Business History Review* 68 (1994): 451–82.

Breit, William, and Roger L. Ransom. "Alvin H. Hansen—The American Keynes." In *The Academic Scribblers,* rev. ed., 81–104. Chicago: Dryden Press, 1982.

Bremer, William W. "'Along the American Way': The New Deal's Work Relief Programs for the Unemployed." *Journal of American History* 62 (December 1975): 636–52.

Brinkley, Alan. "Liberals and Public Investment: Recovering a Lost Legacy." *American Prospect,* Spring 1993, 81–86.

———. "The New Deal and the Idea of the State." In *The Rise and Fall of the New Deal Order, 1930–1980,* ed. Steve Fraser and Gary Gerstle, 85–121. Princeton: Princeton University Press, 1989.

———. "The Problem of American Conservatism." *American Historical Review* 99 (April 1994): 409–29.

———. "Prosperity, Depression, and War, 1920–1945." In *The New American History,* rev. ed., ed. Eric Foner for American Historical Association, 133–58. Philadelphia: Temple University Press, 1997.

———. "Writing the History of Contemporary America: Dilemmas and Challenges." *Daedalus* 113 (1984): 121–41.

Brinkley, Alan, Bradford A. Lee, and William E. Leuchtenburg. "The New Deal." *Wilson Quarterly* 6 (Spring 1982): 50–97.

Brockie, Melvin D. "Theories of the 1937–38 Crisis and Depression." *Economic Journal* 60 (1950): 292–310.

Bronfenbrenner, Martin. "Early American Leaders—Institutional and Critical Traditions." *American Economic Review* 75 (1985): 13–27.

Brown, E. Cary. "Fiscal Policy in the Thirties: A Reappraisal." *American Economic Review* 46 (1956): 857–79.

Bullard, Arthur. "Can We Beat the Business Cycle?" *World's Work,* December 1923, 211–16.

Bulmer, Martin. "The Early Institutional Establishment of Social Science Research: The Local Community Research Committee at the University of Chicago, 1923–1930." *Minerva* 18 (1980): 51–110.

———. "The Methodology of Early Social Indicator Research: William Fielding Ogburn and 'Recent Social Trends,' 1933." *Social Indicators Research* 13 (1983): 109–30.

———. "Quantification and Chicago Social Science in the 1920s: A Neglected Tradition." *Journal of the History of the Behavioral Sciences* 17 (1981): 312–31.

Bulmer, Martin, and Joan Bulmer. "Philanthropy and Social Science in the 1920s: Beardsley Ruml and the Laura Spelman Rockefeller Memorial, 1922–29." *Minerva* 19 (Autumn 1981): 347–407.

Burgess, John W. "Political Science and History." *American Historical Review* 2 (1897): 401–8.

Burns, Arthur F. "Wesley Mitchell and the National Bureau." In *Twenty-Ninth Annual Report,* 3–55. New York: National Bureau of Economic Research, 1949.

Burns, Eveline. "The Beveridge Report." *American Economic Review* 33 (1943): 512–33.

Campbell, John L., and Leon N. Lindberg. "The State and the Organization of Economic Activity." In *Governance of the American Economy,* ed. John L. Campbell, J. Rogers Hollingsworth, and Leon N. Lindberg, 356–95. New York: Cambridge University Press, 1991.

Carvein, Paul E. "The Dennison Manufacturing Company." In *Individual Enterprise and National Growth,* ed. R. W. Hidy, 1–28. Boston: D.C. Heath, 1967.

Chandler, Alfred D., Jr. "The Railroads: Pioneers in Modern Corporate Management." *Business History Review* 39 (1965): 26–40.

Chandler, Alfred D., Jr., and Louis Galambos. "The Development of Large-Scale Economic Organizations in Modern America." *Journal of Economic History* 30 (1970): 201–17.

Chenery, William L. "The President's Industrial Conference: The First Fortnight." *Survey,* October 26, 1919, 35–37.

Christie, Jean. "The Mississippi Valley Committee: Conservation and Planning in the Early New Deal." *Historian* 32 (1969–70): 449–69.

Church, Robert L. "Economists as Experts: The Rise of an Academic Profession in the United States, 1870–1920." In *The University In Society,* ed. Lawrence Stone, 2:571–609. Princeton: Princeton University Press, 1974.

Clark, John Maurice. "Wesley C. Mitchell's Contribution to the Theory of Business Cycles." In *Methods in Social Science: A Case Book,* ed. Stuart A. Rice, 662–80. Chicago: University of Chicago Press, 1931.

Clements, Kendrick A. "Herbert Hoover and Conservation, 1921–33." *American Historical Review* 89 (1984): 67–88.

Coben, Stanley. "Foundation Officials and Fellowships: Innovation in the Patronage of Science." *Minerva* 14 (Summer 1976): 225–40.

Collins, Robert M. "American Corporatism: The Committee for Economic Development, 1942–1964." *Historian* 44 (1982): 151–73.

———. "Positive Business Responses to the New Deal: Roots of the Committee for Economic Development." *Business History Review* 52 (1978): 369–91.

Coyle, David Cushman. "The American National Planning Board." *Political Quarterly* 16 (1945): 246–52.

———. "Frederic A. Delano: Catalyst." *Survey Graphic,* 35 (July 1946): 252–54.

Craver, Earlene. "Patronage and the Directions of Research in Economics: The Rockefeller Foundation in Europe, 1924–1928." *Minerva* 24 (Summer–Autumn 1986): 205–22.

Critchlow, Donald T. "The Political Control of the Economy: Deficit Spending as a Political Belief, 1932–1952." *Public Historian* 3 (Spring 1981): 5–22.

Cross, Whitney R. "Ideas in Politics: The Conservation Policies of the Two Roosevelts." *Journal of the History of Ideas* 14 (1953): 421–38.

Cuff, Robert D. "American Historians and the 'Organizational Factor.'" *Canadian Review of American Studies* 4 (Spring 1973): 19–31.

———. "Creating Control Systems: Edwin F. Gay and the Central Bureau of Planning and Statistics, 1917–1919." *Business History Review* 63 (1989): 588–613.

———. "Harry Garfield, the Fuel Administration, and the Search for a Cooperative Order during World War I." *American Quarterly* 30 (1978): 39–53.

———. "Herbert Hoover, the Ideology of Voluntarism, and War Organization during the Great War." *Journal of American History* 64 (September 1977): 358–72.

————. "We Band of Brothers—Woodrow Wilson's War Managers." *Canadian Review of American Studies* 5 (Fall 1974): 135–48.

Currie, Lauchlin B. "Causes of the Recession [1 April 1938]." *History of Political Economy* 12 (Fall 1980): 316–35.

————. "Comments on Pump Priming." *History of Political Economy* 10 (Winter 1978): 525–33.

————. "Comments on Pump Priming," "Federal Income-Increasing Expenditures, 1932–1935," and "Comments and Observations." *History of Political Economy* 10 (1978): 525–48.

Currie, Lauchlin, and Martin Krost. "Federal Income-Increasing Expenditures, 1932–1935." Ca. November 1935; reprinted in *History of Political Economy* 10 (Winter 1978): 534–40.

Cywar, Alan. "John Dewey: Toward Domestic Reconstruction, 1915–1920." *Journal of the History of Ideas* 30 (1969): 385–400.

Dahl, Robert A. "The Behavioral Approach in Political Science: Epitaph for a Monument to a Successful Protest." *American Political Science Review* 55 (1961): 763–72.

Davis, Allen F. "Welfare, Reform, and World War I." *American Quarterly* 19 (1967): 516–33.

Degler, Carl N. "The Ordeal of Herbert Hoover." *Yale Review* 52 (Summer 1963): 563–83.

————. "In Pursuit of an American History." *American Historical Review* 92 (February 1987): 1–12.

Delano, Frederic A. "The Chicago Plan with Particular Reference to the Railway Terminal Problem." *Journal of Political Economy* 21 (1913): 819–31.

————. "The Economic Implications of National Planning." *Proceedings of the American Philosophical Society* 74 (1934): 21–28.

————. "Regional Planning Next." *National Municipal Review* 13 (March 1924): 141–48.

————. "Shifting Bureaus at Washington." *Review of Reviews,* May 1933, 33, 56–58.

————. "What the Inaugural Visitor Sees in Washington Today." *Sunday Star* (Washington, D.C.), March 5, 1933, 24–25, 33.

Dennison, Andrew. "The Dennison Manufacturing Company." In *Individual Enterprise and National Growth,* ed. Ralph W. Hidy and Paul E. Cawein, 1–28. Boston: D.C. Heath, 1967.

Dennison, Henry S. "Basic Principles of Personnel Management in Government Economy." *Annals* 113 (May 1924): 328–30.

————. "Business and Government." *Michigan Alumnus Quarterly Review* 41 (Summer 1935): 295–305.

————. "A Cooperative Industrial Experiment." In *Business and the Church,* ed. Jerome Davis, 191–203. New York: n. p., 1926.

————. "Credit Granting and the Business Cycle." *Credit Monthly,* February 1922.

————. "Depression Insurance: A Suggestion to Corporations for Reducing Unemployment." *American Labor Legislation Review* 12 (March 1922): 31–36.

————. "Management." In President's Research Committee on Social Trends, *Recent Economic Changes in the United States,* 2:495–546. New York: McGraw-Hill, 1929.

————. "Management and the Business Cycle." *Journal of the American Statistical Association* 18 (March 1922): 20–31.

————. "The Need for the Development of Political Science Engineering." *American Political Science Review* 26 (1932): 241–55.

————. "The Principles of Industrial Efficiency Applied to the Corporate Organization." *Annals* 61 (September 1915): 183–86.

————. "Some Economic and Social Accomplishments of the Mechanization of Industry." *American Economic Review* 20 supp. (March 1930): 152–53.

————. "Why I Believe in Profit Sharing." *Factory,* March 1918, 424.

"Dennison, Henry S." *National Cyclopedia of American Biography* 40 (1955): 152–53.

Dennison, Henry S., and Ida Tarbell. "The President's Industrial Conference of October 1919." *Bulletin of the Taylor Society* 5 (April 1920): 79–92.

Dewhurst, Mary. "Something Better than Philanthropy." *Outlook,* September 1, 1915, 48–51.

Domhoff, G. William. "Class, Power, and Parties in the New Deal: A Critique of Skocpol's State Autonomy Theory." *Berkeley Journal of Sociology* 36 (1991): 1–49.

Dorfman, Joseph. "Obituary: Wesley C. Mitchell (1874–1948)." *Economic Journal* 59 (September 1949): 448–58.

Downs, Jacques M. "American Merchants and the China Opium Trade, 1800–1840." *Business History Review* 42 (1968): 418–42.

————. "Fair Game: Exploitive Role Myths and the American Opium Trade." *Pacific Historical Review* 41 (1972): 133–49.

Drury, Michael. "Ruml." *Life,* April 12, 1943, 35–38.

Du Boff, Richard B., and Edward S. Herman. "Alfred Chandler's New Business History: A Review." *Politics and Society* 10 (1980): 87–110.

Dugger, William M. "An Institutionalist Theory of Economic Planning." *Journal of Economic Issues* 21 (December 1987): 1649–75.

Duncan, W. Jack, and C. Ray Gullett. "Henry Sturgis Dennison: The Manager and the Social Critic." *Journal of Business Research* 2 (April 1974): 133–46.

Dunn, Samuel O. "American Railway Forces in the Great War." *Railway Age,* January 3, 1919, 7–23.

Eakins, David W. "Business Planners and America's Postwar Expansion." In *Corporations and the Cold War,* ed. David Horowitz, 143–71. New York: Monthly Review Press, 1969.

————. "The Origins of Corporate Liberal Policy Research, 1916–1922: The Political-Economic Expert and the Decline of Public Debate." In *Building the Organizational Society: Essays on Associational Activities in Modern America,* ed. Jerry Israel, 163–79. New York: Free Press, 1972.

————. "Policy Planning for the Establishment." *A New History of Leviathan: Essays on the Rise of the American Corporate State,* ed. Ronald Radosh and Murray N. Rothbard, 188–205. New York: E. P. Dutton, 1972.

Eliot, Charles W. "A Study of the New Plan of Chicago." *Century Magazine,* January 1910, 417–31.

Eliot, Charles W., II. "George Washington Memorial Parkway." *Landscape Architecture* 22 (April 1932): 190–200.

————. "A Great and Effective City." *American Magazine of Art,* August 1931, 130–36.

————. "Progress on the Washington Plan." *Landscape Architecture* 20 (October 1929): 28–32.

Erd, Rainer. "Why Is There No Corporatism in the United States?" In *The Crisis of Modernity: Recent Critical Theories of Culture and Society in the United States and Germany,* ed. Gunter H. Lenz and Kurt L. Shell, 83–89. Frankfurt am Main: Center for North American Studies and Research, 1986.

Farr, James. "The Estate of Political Knowledge: Political Science and the State." In *The Estate of Social Knowledge,* ed. Joanne Brown and David K. van Keuren, 1–21. Baltimore: Johns Hopkins University Press, 1991.

Feis, Herbert. "Keynes in Retrospect." *Foreign Affairs* 29 (1951): 564–77.

Feldman, H. "The Outstanding Features of Dennison Management." Parts 1–3. *Industrial Management* 64 (1922): 67–73, 145–50, 225–30.

Finegold, Kenneth. "From Agrarianism to Adjustment: The Political Origins of New Deal Agricultural Policy." *Politics and Society* 11 (1982): 1–27.

Fisher, Donald. "The Role of Philanthropic Foundations in the Reproduction and Pro-
    duction of Hegemony: Rockefeller Foundations and the Social Sciences." *Soci-
    ology* 17 (1983): 206–33.
Fisher, Donald, and Martin Bulmer. "Debate." *Sociology* 18 (1984): 573–87.
Flanagan, Maureen A. "Charter Reform in Chicago: Political Culture and Urban Pro-
    gressive Reform." *Journal of Urban History* 12 (1986): 109–40.
Forester, Robert F. "A Promising Venture in Industrial Partnership." *Annals* 44 (Novem-
    ber 1912): 97–103.
Friedmann, John, and Robin Bloch. "American Exceptionalism in Regional Planning,
    1933–2000." *International Journal of Urban and Regional Research* (Great Britain)
    14 (1990): 576–601.
Funigiello, Philip J. "City Planning in World War II: The Experience of the National
    Resources Planning Board." *Social Science Quarterly* 53 (June 1972): 91–104.
Fusfeld, Daniel. "The Rise of the Corporate State in America." *Journal of Economic Issues*
    6 (1972): 1–22.
———. "The Source of New Deal Reformism: A Note." *Ethics* 65 (April 1955): 218–19.
Gaddis, John Lewis. "The Corporatist Synthesis: A Skeptical View." *Diplomatic History* 10
    (1986): 357–62.
Gagan, David P. "The Railroads and the Public, 1870–1881: A Study of Charles Elliott
    Perkins' Business Ethics." *Business History Review* 39 (Spring 1965): 41–56.
Galambos, Louis. "The Emerging Organizational Synthesis of Modern American His-
    tory." *Business History Review* 44 (Autumn 1970): 279–90.
———. "Technology, Political Economy, and Professionalization: Central Themes of the
    Organizational Synthesis." *Business History Review* 57 (Winter 1983): 471–93.
Galbraith, John Kenneth. "The Businessman as Philosopher." *Perspectives USA*, no. 13
    (Autumn 1955): 57–69.
———. "How Keynes Came to America." *New York Times Book Review*, May 16, 1965,
    1, 34–39. Reprinted in *A Contemporary Guide to Economics, Peace, and Laughter*,
    1971; New York: New American Library, 1972.
Gamm, Gerald. "Buried Treasure: Theory and Historical Data." *Political Methodologist* 8
    (Fall 1997): 8–11.
Garnett, E. B. "Beardsley Ruml Has Never Worked Except with His Mind." *Kansas City
    Star*, December 5, 1948, C1–2.
Gerber, Larry G. "Corporatism in Comparative Perspective: The Impact of the First
    World War on American and British Labor Relations." *Business History Review*
    62 (1988): 93–127.
Gilbert, Jess, and Carolyn Howe. "Beyond 'State vs. Society': Theories of the State and
    New Deal Agricultural Policies." *American Sociological Review* 56 (April 1991):
    204–20.
Gillon, Steven M. "The Future of Political History." *Journal of Policy History* 9 (1997):
    240–55.
Gitelman, H. M. "Welfare Capitalism Reconsidered." *Labor History* 33 (Winter 1992):
    5–31.
Glad, Paul W. "Progressives and the Business Culture of the 1920s." *Journal of American
    History* 53 (June 1966): 75–89.
Gordon, Colin. "New Deal, Old Deck: Business and the Origins of Social Security,
    1920–1935." *Politics and Society* 19 (1991): 165–208.
———. Review of *State and Party in America's New Deal*, by Kenneth Finegold and Theda
    Skocpol. *Journal of Economic History* 56 (June 1996): 529–30.
Graham, Otis L., Jr. "The Broker State." *Wilson Quarterly* 8 (Winter 1984): 86–97.
———. "Historians and the New Deal, 1944–60." *Social Studies* 44 (1963): 133–40.
———. "The New Deal." In *American Politics and Government: Party, Ideology, and Reform*

in American History, ed. Hugh Davis Graham, 329–38. New York: Harper & Row, 1975.

———. "The Planning Idea From Roosevelt to Post-Reagan." In *The New Deal Viewed from Fifty Years,* ed. Lawrence E. Gelfand and Robert J. Neymeyer, 1–19. Iowa City: Center for the Study of the Recent History of the United States, 1983.

———. "The Planning Ideal and American Reality: The 1930s." In *The Hofstadter Aegis,* ed. Stanley Elkins and Eric McKitrick, 257–99. New York: Alfred A. Knopf, 1974.

Grattan, C. Hartley. "Beardsley Ruml and His Ideas." *Harper's Magazine,* May 1952, 78–86.

Griffith, Robert. "Dwight D. Eisenhower and the Corporate Commonwealth." *American Historical Review* 87 (1982): 87–122.

Grin, Carolyn. "The Unemployment Conference of 1921: An Experiment in National Cooperative Planning." *Mid-America* 55 (1973): 83–107.

Grossman, David M. "American Foundations and the Support of Economic Research, 1913–29." *Minerva* 20 (Spring–Summer 1982): 59–82.

Gruchy, Alan G. "The Concept of National Planning in Institutional Economics." *Southern Economic Journal* 6 (October 1939): 121–44.

———. "The Economics of the National Resources Committee." *American Economic Review* 29 (1939): 60–73.

Hall, Peter Dobkin. "Reflections on the Nonprofit Sector in the Post-Liberal Era." In *Philanthropy and American Society: Selected Papers,* ed. Jack Salzman, 17–45. New York: Columbia University, Center for American Studies, 1987.

Hamilton, David E. "Building the Associative State: The Department of Agriculture and American State-Building." *Agricultural History* 64 (Spring 1990): 207–18.

Hammack, David C. "Private Organizations, Public Purposes: Nonprofits and Their Archives." *Journal of American History* 76 (June 1989): 181–91.

Hancock, John L. "Planners in the Changing American City, 1900–1940." *Journal of the American Institute of Planners* 33 (1967): 290–304.

Hansen, Alvin. "The New Crusade against Planning." *New Republic,* January 1, 1945, 9–12.

———. "Wesley Mitchell, Social Scientist and Social Counselor." *Review of Economics and Statistics* 31 (1949): 245–55.

Harmon, M. Judd. "Some Contributions of Harold L. Ickes." *Western Political Quarterly* 7 (1954): 238–52.

Harriman, Henry I. "The Stabilization of Business and Employment." *American Economic Review* 22 supp. (1932): 62–74.

Harris, Seymour E. "Breaking a Lance with Mr. Hayek." *New York Times Book Review,* December 9, 1945, 3, 14, 16.

———. "Hansen, Alvin." In *International Encyclopedia of the Social Sciences,* ed. David L. Sill, 6:319–23. New York: Macmillan, and Free Press, 1968.

Hawley, Ellis W. "Antitrust and the Association Movement, 1920–1940." In Federal Trade Commission, *National Competition Policy,* 97–141. Washington, D.C.: Government Printing Office, 1981.

———. "The Corporate Ideal as Liberal Philosophy in the New Deal." In *The Roosevelt New Deal: A Program Assessment Fifty Years After,* ed. Wilbur J. Cohen, 85–103. Austin, Tex.: Lyndon B. Johnson School of Public Affairs, 1986.

———. "The Discovery and Study of a 'Corporate Liberalism.'" *Business History Review* 52 (1978): 309–20.

———. "Economic Inquiry and the State in New Era America: Anti-Statist Corporatism and Positive Statism in Uneasy Coexistence." In *The State and Economic Knowledge: The American and British Experiences,* ed. Mary O. Furner and Barry Supple, 287–324. New York: Woodrow Wilson International Center for Scholars, and Cambridge University Press, 1990.

————. "Herbert Hoover, the Commerce Secretariat, and the Vision of an 'Associative State,' 1921–1928." *Journal of American History* 61 (June 1974): 116–40.

————. "The New Deal State and the Anti-Bureaucratic Tradition." In *The New Deal Legacy,* ed. Robert Eden, 77–92. Westport, Conn.: Greenwood Press, 1989.

————. "A Partnership Formed, Dissolved, and in Renegotiation: Business and Government in the Franklin D. Roosevelt Era." In *Business and Government: Essays in 20th-Century Cooperation and Confrontation,* ed. Joseph Frese and Jacob Judd, 187–219. Tarrytown, N.Y.: Sleepy Hollow Press, 1985.

————. "Secretary Hoover and the Bituminous Coal Problem, 1921–1928." *Business History Review* 42 (1968): 247–70.

Hayes, E. P. "History of the Dennison Manufacturing Company." Part 1. *Journal of Economic and Business History* 1 (August 1929): 467–502.

Hays, Samuel. "The Politics of Reform in Municipal Government in the Progressive Era." *Pacific Northwest Quarterly* 55 (1964): 157–69.

Heald, Morrell. "Business Thought in the Twenties: Social Responsibility." *American Quarterly* 13 (1961): 126–36.

Heath, Charlotte. "History of the Dennison Manufacturing Company." Part 2. *Journal of Economic and Business History* 2 (November 1929): 163–202.

Heywood, Johnson. "How the Dennison Manufacturing Company Meets the Slumps." *Advertising and Selling Fortnightly,* March 11, 1925, 15–16, 72–75.

Hill, David R. "Lewis Mumford's Ideas on the City." *Journal of the American Planning Association* 51 (Autumn 1985): 407–21.

Hill, Forest G. "Wesley Mitchell's Theory of Planning." *Political Science Quarterly* 72 (1957): 100–118.

Himmelberg, Robert F. "Business, Antitrust Policy, and the Industrial Board of the Department of Commerce, 1919." *Business History Review* 42 (1968): 1–23.

————. "Government and Business, 1917–1932: The Triumph of 'Corporate Liberalism'?" In *Business and Government: Essays in 20th-Century Cooperation and Confrontation,* ed. Joseph R. Frese and Jacob Judd, 1–23. Tarrytown, N.Y.: Sleepy Hollow Press, 1985.

Hirschfield, Charles. "Nationalist Progressivism and World War I." *Mid-America* 45 (1963): 139–56.

Hobson, Wayne K. "Professionals, Progressives, and Bureaucratization: A Reassessment." *Historian* 39 (1977): 639–58.

Hoffman, Elizabeth, and Gary D. K. Libecap. "Institutional Choice and the Development of U.S. Agricultural Policies in the 1920s." *Journal of Economic History* 51 (June 1991): 397–411.

Hogan, Michael J. "Corporatism: A Positive Appraisal." *Diplomatic History* 10 (1986): 363–72.

Holt, Charles. "Who Benefited from the Prosperity of the 1920s?" *Explorations in Economic History* 14 (July 1977): 277–89.

Homan, Paul T. "Economic Planning: The Proposals and the Literature." *Quarterly Journal of Economics* 47 (November 1932): 102–22.

Howenstine, E. Jay. "Lessons of World War I." *Annals* 238 (March 1945): 180–87.

————. "Public Works Policy in the Twenties." *Social Research* 13 (1946): 479–500.

————. "Public Works Program after World War I." *Journal of Political Economy* 51 (1943): 523–37.

Huffman, Roy E. "Montana's Contribution to New Deal Farm Policy." *Agricultural History* 33 (October 1959): 164–67.

Hunt, Edward Eyre. "Notes on Economic and Social Surveys." *Bulletin of the Taylor Society* 13 (February 1928): 3–11.

Hurvitz, Haggai. "Ideology and Industrial Conflict: President Wilson's First Industrial Conference of October 1919." *Labor History* 18 (1977): 509–24.

Hynning, Clifford J. "Administrative Evolution of National Planning in the United States in the Pre-New Deal Era." *Plan Age* 5 (June 1939): 157–89.

Inouye, Arlene, and Charles Susskind. "'Technological Trends and National Policy, 1937': The First Modern Technology Assessment." *Technology and Culture* 18 (1977): 593–621.

"James R. Angell." In *A History of Psychology in Autobiography,* ed. Carl Murchison, vol. 3, 1–38. Worchester, Mass.: Clark University Press, 1936.

Jeffries, John W. "The 'New' New Deal: FDR and American Liberalism." *Political Science Quarterly* 105 (Fall 1990): 397–418.

———. "A 'Third New Deal'?: Liberal Policy and the American State, 1937–1945." *Journal of Policy History* 8 (1996): 387–409.

Jensen, Richard. "The Causes and Cures of Unemployment in the Great Depression." *Journal of Interdisciplinary History* 19 (Spring 1989): 553–83.

John, Richard R. "Elaborations, Revisions, Dissents: Alfred D. Chandler, Jr.'s *The Visible Hand* after Twenty Years." *Business History Review* 71 (1997): 151–200.

Johnson, David A. "Regional Planning for the Great American Metropolis: New York between the Wars." In *Two Centuries of American Planning,* ed. Daniel Schaeffer, 167–96. Baltimore: Johns Hopkins University Press, 1988.

Johnston, Alva. "The National Idea Man." Parts 1–3. *New Yorker,* February 10, 17 and 24, 1945, respectively 28–32ff., 26–30ff., and 30–34ff.

Jones, Byrd L. "Lauchlin Currie and the Causes of the Recession of 1937." *History of Political Economy* 12 (Fall 1980): 303–15.

———. "Lauchlin Currie, Pump Priming, and New Deal Fiscal Policy, 1934–1936." *History of Political Economy* 10 (Winter 1978): 509–24.

———. "A Plan for Planning in the New Deal." *Social Science Quarterly* 50 (1969): 525–34.

———. "The Role of Keynesians in Wartime Policy and Postwar Planning, 1940–1946." *American Economic Review* 62 (May 1972): 125–33.

Kantor, Harvey A. "Charles Dyer Norton and the Origins of the Regional Plan of New York." *Journal of the American Institute of Planners* 39 (1973): 35–42. Reprinted in *The American Planner: Biographies and Recollections,* ed. Donald A. Krueckeberg, 179–95. New York: Methuen, 1983.

Karl, Barry D. "Charles Merriam Memorial Lecture." *Public Administration Review* 35 (1975): 538–41.

———. "Constitution and Central Planning: The Third New Deal Revisited." *Supreme Court Review* 6 (1988): 163–201.

———. "Lo, the Poor Volunteer: An Essay on the Relations between History and Myth." *Social Service Review* 58 (1984): 493–522.

———. "Merriam's 'Continuously Planning Society.'" *University of Chicago Magazine* 67 (Summer 1975): 36–39.

———. "Philanthropy, Policy Planning, and the Bureaucratization of the Democratic Ideal." *Daedalus* 105 (Fall 1976): 129–49.

———. "The Power of Intellect and the Politics of Ideas." *Daedalus* 97 (1968): 1002–35.

———. "Presidential Planning and Social Science Research: Mr. Hoover's Experts." *Perspectives in American History* 3 (1969): 347–409.

Karl, Barry D., and Stanley N. Katz. "The American Private Philanthropic Foundation and the Public Sphere, 1890–1930." *Minerva* 19 (Summer 1981): 236–70.

———. "Foundations and Ruling Class Elites." *Daedalus* 116 (Winter 1987): 1–40.

———. "The Unintended Logic of the Philanthropic Foundation: Foundations and Ruling Class Elites." In *Philanthropy and American Society: Selected Papers,* ed. Jack Salzman, 63–86. New York: Columbia University, Center for American Culture Studies, 1987.

Katz, Stanley, Kathleen D. McCarthy, Robert E. Kohler, and Barry D. Karl. "Grant-Making and Research in the U.S., 1933–1983." *Proceedings of the American Philosophical Society* 129 (March 1985): 1–19.

Katznelson, Ira. "The Doleful Dance of Politics and Policy: Can Historical Institutionalism Make a Difference?" *American Political Science Review* 92 (1998): 191–97.

———. "Reflections on History, Method, and Political Science." *Political Methodologist* 8 (Fall 1997): 11–14.

———. "The State to the Rescue? Political Science and History Reconnect." *Social Research* 59 (1992): 719–37.

Katznelson, Ira, and Bruce Pietrykowski. "Rebuilding the American State: Evidence from the 1940s." *Studies in American Political Development* 5 (Fall 1991): 301–39.

Keller, Robert R. "The Role of the State in the U.S. Economy during the 1920s." *Journal of Economic Issues* 21 (June 1987): 877–84.

———. "Supply-Side Economic Policies during the Coolidge-Mellon Era." *Journal of Economic Issues* 16 (September 1982): 773–90.

Kellogg, Paul U. "The Industrial Relations Commission." *Survey,* December 28, 1912, 386.

Kevles, Daniel. "George Ellery Hale, the First World War, and the Advancement of Science in America." *Isis* 59 (Winter 1968): 427–37.

———. "Hale and the Role of a Central Scientific Institution in the United States." In *The Legacy of George Ellery Hale,* ed. Helen Wright, Joan N. Warnow, and Charles Weiner, 273–82. Cambridge, Mass.: MIT Press, 1972.

———. "Testing the Army's Intelligence: Psychologists and the Military in World War I." *Journal of American History* 55 (December 1968): 565–81.

Kidd, Stuart. "Collectivist Intellectuals and the Ideal of National Economic Planning, 1929–33." In *Nothing Else to Fear: New Perspectives on America in the Thirties,* ed. Stephen W. Baskerville and Ralph Willett, 15–35. Manchester: Manchester University Press, 1985.

———. "Redefining the New Deal: Some Thoughts on the Political and Cultural Perspectives of Revisionism." *Journal of American Studies* 22 (1988): 389–415.

Kirkendall, Richard S. "A. A. Berle, Jr., Student of the Corporation, 1917–1932." *Business History Review* 35 (1961): 43–58.

———. "The New Deal as Watershed: The Recent Literature." *Journal of American History* 54 (1968): 839–52.

Kloppenberg, James T. "Who's Afraid of the Welfare State?" *Reviews in American History* 18 (September 1990): 395–405.

Knoles, George H. "American Intellectuals and World War I." *Pacific Northwest Quarterly* 59 (1968): 203–15.

Koelble, Thomas A. "The New Institutionalism in Political Science and Sociology." *Comparative Politics* 27 (1995): 231–43.

Kohler, Robert E. "The Management of Science: The Experience of Warren Weaver and the Rockefeller Foundation Programme in Molecular Biology." *Minerva* 14 (Autumn 1976): 279–306.

———. "A Policy for the Advancement of Science: The Rockefeller Foundation, 1924–29." *Minerva* 16 (Winter 1978): 480–515.

———. "Science and Philanthropy: Wickcliffe Rose and the International Education Board." *Minerva* 23 (1985): 75–95.

———. "Science, Foundations, and American Universities in the 1920s." *Osiris* 3 (1987): 135–64.

Koistinen, Paul A. C. "The 'Industrial-Military Complex' in Historical Perspective." *Business History Review* 41 (1967): 367–403.

Krog, Carl E. "'Organizing the Production of Leisure': Herbert Hoover and the Conservation Movement in the 1920s." *Wisconsin Magazine of History* 67 (Spring 1984): 199–218.

Krueckeberg, Donald A. "From the Backyard Garden to the Whole U.S.A.: A Conversation with Charles W. Eliot, 2nd." *Journal of the American Planning Association* 46 (October 1980): 440–48. Reprinted in *The American Planner: Biographies and Recollections,* ed. Donald A. Krueckeberg, 350–65. New York: Methuen, 1983.

Kuhlman, A. F. "The Social Science Research Council: Its Origins and Objects." *Social Forces* 6 (June 1928): 583–88.

Kuklick, Henrika. "The Organization of Social Science in the United States." *American Quarterly* 28 (1976): 124–41.

Kuznets, Simon. "Wesley Clair Mitchell, 1874–1948." *Journal of the American Statistical Association* 44 (1949): 126–31.

Lee, Frederic S. "From Multi-Industry Planning to Keynesian Planning: Gardiner Means, the American Keynesians, and National Economic Planning at the National Resources Committee." *Journal of Policy History* 2 (1990): 186–212.

Leiserson, Avery. "Charles E. Merriam, Max Weber, and the Search for a Synthesis in Political Science." *American Political Science Review* 69 (1975): 175–85.

Lepawsky, Albert. "The New Deal at Midpassage." *University of Chicago Magazine* 67 (Summer 1975): 29–35.

———. "The Planning Apparatus: A Vignette of the New Deal." *Journal of the American Institute of Planners* 42 (January 1976): 16–32.

———. "The Progressives and the Planners." *Public Administration Review* 31 (May/June 1971): 297–303.

———. "Style and Substance in Contemporary Planning: The American New Deal's National Resources Planning Board as a Model." *Plan Canada* 18 (September-December 1978): 153–87.

Leuchtenburg, William E. "The Historian and the Public Realm." *American Historical Review* 97 (February 1992): 1–18.

———. "The New Deal and the Analogue of War." In *Change and Continuity in Twentieth-Century America,* ed. John Braeman, Robert H. Bremner, and Everett Walters, 81–143. Columbus: Ohio State University Press, 1964. Reprinted in Leuchtenburg, *The FDR Years: On Roosevelt and His Legacy,* 35–75. New York: Columbia University Press, 1995.

———. "The Pertinence of Political History: Reflections on the Significance of the State in America." *Journal of American History* 73 (December 1986): 585–600.

———. "Roosevelt, Norris, and the 'Seven Little TVAs.'" *Journal of Politics* 14 (August 1952): 418–41.

Lewis-Beck, Michael S., and Peverill Squire. "The Transformation of the American State: The New Era-New Deal Test." *Journal of Politics* 53 (February 1991): 106–21.

Livingston, James. "The Social Analysis of Economic History and Theory: Conjectures on Late Nineteenth-Century American Development." *American Historical Review* 92 (February 1987): 69–95.

Loewenberg, Bert James. "John William Burgess, the Scientific Method, and the Hegelian Philosophy of History." *Mississippi Valley Historical Review* 42 (1955): 490–509.

Loftin, Bernadette K. "The Political Theory of Adolf Augustus Berle, Jr." *Southern Quarterly* 9 (October 1970): 93–106.

Lohoff, Bruce A. "Herbert Hoover, Spokesman of Humane Efficiency: The Mississippi Flood of 1927." *American Quarterly* 22 (Fall 1970): 690–700.

Lord, Russell. "M. L. Wilson: Pioneer." *Survey Graphic,* October 1941, 507–12.

———. "The Rebirth of Rural Life." *Survey Graphic,* December 1941, 687–91.

Lowitt, Richard. "The New Deal: An Essay Review." *Pacific Northwest Quarterly* 68 (1977): 25–30.

Lynch, Edmund. "Walter Dill Scott: Pioneer Industrial Psychologist." *Business History Review* 42 (1968): 149–70.

Mallery, Otto M. "The Long-Range Planning of Public Works." In President's Conference on Unemployment, Committee on Business Cycles and Unemployment, *Business Cycles and Unemployment,* chap. 14. New York: McGraw-Hill, 1923.

———. "A National Policy—Public Works to Stabilize Employment." *Annals* 81 (January 1919): 56–61.

"Man behind the Ruml Plan: Government Reform as a Hobby." *United States News,* May 7, 1943, 18–19.

Marx, Fritz Morstein. "The Bureau of the Budget: Its Evolution and Present Role." Parts 1 and 2. *American Political Science Review* 39 (1945): 653–84 and 869–98.

McCarthy, Michael P. "Chicago Businessmen and the Burnham Plan." *Journal of the Illinois State Historical Society* 63 (Autumn 1970): 228–56.

———. "Prelude to Armageddon: Charles E. Merriam and the Chicago Mayoral Election of 1911." *Journal of the Illinois State Historical Society* 67 (1974): 505–18.

McCormick, Richard L. "Public Life in Industrial America, 1877–1917." In *The New American History,* rev. ed., ed. Eric Foner for American Historical Association, 107–32. Philadelphia: Temple University Press, 1997.

McCormick, Thomas J. "Drift or Mastery? A Corporatist Synthesis for American Diplomatic History." *Reviews in American History* 10 (1982): 318–30.

McCoy, Donald R. "Republican Opposition during Wartime, 1941–1945." *Mid-America* 49 (1967): 174–89.

McCraw, Thomas K. "The Historical Background." In *American Society: Public and Private Responsibilities,* ed. Winthrop Knowlton and Richard Zeckhauser, 15–42. Cambridge, Mass.: Ballinger Publishing, 1986.

———. "In Retrospect: Berle and Means." *Reviews in American History* 18 (1990): 578–96.

McGerr, Michael. "The Persistence of Individualism." *Chronicle of Higher Education,* February 10, 1993, A48.

———. "The Price of the 'New Transnational History.'" *American Historical Review* 96 (October 1991): 1056–67.

McQuaid, Kim. "An American Owenite: Edward A. Filene and the Parameters of Industrial Reform, 1890–1937." *American Journal of Economics and Sociology* 35 (1976): 77–94.

———. "The Business Advisory Council of the Department of Commerce, 1933–1961: A Study in Corporate/Government Relations." *Research in Economic History* 1 (1976): 171–97.

———. "Competition, Cartellization and the Corporate Ethic: General Electric's Leadership during the New Deal Era, 1933–40." *American Journal of Economics and Sociology* 36 (1977): 417–28.

———. "Corporate Liberalism in the American Business Community, 1920–1940." *Business History Review* 52 (1978): 342–68.

———. "The Frustration of Corporate Revival during the Early New Deal." *Historian* 41 (1979): 682–704.

———. "Henry S. Dennison and the 'Science' of Industrial Reform, 1900–1950." *American Journal of Economics and Sociology* 36 (1977): 79–98.

———. "Young, Swope and General Electric's 'New Capitalism': A Study in Corporate Liberalism, 1920–33." *American Journal of Economics and Sociology* 36 (1977): 323–34.

Merriam, Charles E. "American Publicity in Italy." *American Political Science Review* 13 (1919): 541–55.

———. "Budget Making in Chicago." *Annals* 62 (November 1915): 270–76.

———. "Findings and Recommendations of the Chicago Council Committee on Crime." *Journal of Criminal Law and Criminology* 6 (1915): 345–62.

———. "Government and Business." *Journal of Business* 6 (1933): 181–90.

———. "Human Nature and Science in City Government." *Journal of Social Forces* 1 (1923): 459–64.

———. "Investigations as a Means of Securing Administrative Efficiency." *Annals* 41 (May 1912): 281–303.

———. "The National Resources Planning Board." *Public Administration Review* 1 (1940–41): 116–21.

———. "The National Resources Planning Board: A Chapter in American Planning Experience." *American Political Science Review* 38 (1944): 1075–88.

———. "Planning Agencies in America." *American Political Science Review* 29 (1935): 197–211.

———. "Political Science in the United States." In *Contemporary Political Science: A Survey of Methods, Research, and Teaching,* 233–48. Paris: UNESCO, 1950.

———. "Public Administration and Political Theory." *Journal of Social Philosophy* 5 (1939–40): 293–308.

———. Review of Herbert Hoover, *The Challenge to Liberty. American Political Science Review* 29 (1935): 131–33.

———. "Work and Accomplishments of Chicago Commission on City Expenditures." *City Club Bulletin* 4 (1911): 195–208.

Merriam, Charles E., Robert F. Crane, John A. Fairlie, and Clyde L. King. "Progress Report of the Committee on Political Research." *American Political Science Review* 17 (1923): 274–312.

Metcalf, Evan. "Secretary Hoover and the Emergence of Macroeconomic Management." *Business History Review* 49 (1975): 60–80.

Metzer, Jacob. "How New Was the New Era? The Public Sector in the 1920s." *Journal of Economic History* 45 (March 1985): 119–26.

Milkis, Sidney M. "The New Deal, Administrative Reform, and the Transcendence of Partisan Politics." *Administration and Society* 18 (February 1987): 433–72.

Mills, Frederick C. "Memorials: Wesley Clair Mitchell, 1874–1948." *American Economic Review* 39 (1949): 730–42.

Mitchell, Timothy. "The Limits of the State: Beyond Statist Approaches and Their Critics." *American Political Science Review* 85 (March 1991): 77–96.

Mitchell, Wesley C. "The Application of Economic Knowledge." In *The Obligation of Universities to the Social Order.* Washington Square, N.Y.: New York University Press, 1933.

———. "The Crisis of 1920 and the Problem of Controlling Business Cycles." *American Economic Review* 12 supp. (March 1922): 20–32.

———. "Mr. Hoover's 'The Challenge to Liberty.'" *Political Science Quarterly* 49 (1934): 599–614.

———. "The Social Sciences and National Planning." *Science,* January 18, 1935, 55–62.

———. "Statistics and Government." *Quarterly Publications of the American Statistical Association* 16 (March 1919): 223–36.

———. "Research in the Social Sciences." In *The New Social Science,* ed. Leonard D. White, 4–15. Chicago: University of Chicago Press, 1930.

Moore, John Robert. "The Conservative Coalition in the United States Senate, 1942–1945." *Journal of Southern History* 33 (1967): 368–76.

Mucciaroni, Gary. "Political Learning and Economic Policy Innovation: The United States and Sweden in the Post-World War II Era." *Journal of Policy History* 1 (1989): 391–418.

Mumford, Lewis. "The Plan of New York." Parts 1 and 2. *New Republic,* June 15 and 22, 1932, 121–26 and 146–54.

Nash, Gerald D. "Experiments in Industrial Mobilization: WIB and NRA." *Mid-America* 45 (July 1963): 157–74.

Naveh, David. "The Political Role of Economic Advisers: The Case of the U.S. President's Council of Economic Advisers, 1946–1976." *Presidential Studies Quarterly* 11 (1981): 492–510.

Nelson, Daniel. "The Company Union Movement, 1900–1937: A Reexamination." *Business History Review* 46 (1982): 335–58.

Nordlinger, Eric A., Theodore J. Lowi, and Sergio Fabbrini. "The Return to the State: Critiques." *American Political Science Review* 82 (September 1988): 875–901.

O'Brien, Patrick G. "Hoover and Historians: Revisionism since 1980." *Annals of Iowa* 49 (1988): 394–402.

O'Brien, Patrick G., and Philip T. Rosen. "Hoover and the Historians: The Resurrection of a President." Parts 1 and 2. *Annals of Iowa* 46 (1982): 25–42, 83–99.

Olson, Keith W. "The American Beveridge Plan." *Mid-America* 65 (1983): 87–99.

Orlans, Harold. "The Advocacy of Social Science in Europe and America." *Minerva* 14 (Spring 1976): 6–32.

Overton, Richard C. "Charles Elliott Perkins." *Business History Review* 31 (1957): 292–309.

Patterson, James T. "The Rise of Presidential Power before World War II." *Law and Contemporary Problems* 40 (Spring 1976): 39–57.

Paxson, Frederic L. "The Great Demobilization." *American Historical Review* 44 (1939): 237–51.

Peaslee, Horace W. "Commemoration." *American Institute of Architects Journal* 20 (October 1953): 190–92.

———. "Make No Little Planners: The Work of an Institute Honorary Member, Frederic A. Delano, 1936–1953." *American Institute of Architects Journal* 20 (September 1953): 136–39.

Peppers, Larry. "Full-Employment Surplus Analysis and Structural Change: The 1930s." *Explorations in Economic History* 10 (Winter 1973): 197–210.

"Philanthropy, Patronage, and Politics." Special issue of *Daedalus* 116 (Winter 1987).

Pilgrim, John D. "The Upper Turning Point of 1920: A Re-Appraisal." *Explorations in Economic History* 11 (1974): 271–98.

Polenberg, Richard. "The Good War? A Reappraisal of How World War II Affected American Society." *Virginia Magazine of History and Biography* 100 (1992): 295–322.

Porter, Amy. "Pay-As-You-Go Ruml." *Collier's Weekly,* March 6, 1943, 13, 63.

Potter, Z. L. "The Central Bureau of Planning and Statistics." *Publications of the American Statistical Association* 16 (March 1919): 275–85.

Reagan, Patrick D. "Fighting the Good War at Home." *Reviews in American History* 25 (September 1997): 481–87.

———. "Republicans and Realignment: The New Deal Years." *Reviews in American History* 24 (March 1996): 132–37.

———. "Roosevelt Signs the G. I. Bill." In *Great Events from History: Business and Commerce,* ed. Frank N. Magill, 845–50. Pasadena, Calif.: Salem Press, 1994.

———. "The Withholding Tax, Beardsley Ruml, and Modern American Public Policy." *Prologue* 24 (Spring 1992): 18–31.

Reeves, Floyd W. "Planning for Postwar Readjustment." *Public Management* 26 (1944): 330–36.

Reilly, Philip J. "Work of the Employment Department at the Dennison Manufacturing Company, Framingham, Massachusetts." *Annals* 65 (May 1916): 87–94.

Rich, A. B. "Analyzing, Grading, and Value Operations of a Modern Manufacturing Organization." *Annals* 100 (March 1922): 19–24.

Roberts, Alisdair. "Demonstrating Neutrality: The Rockefeller Philanthropies and the Evolution of Public Administration, 1927–1936." *Public Administration Review* 54 (1994): 221–28.

Robertson, David Brian. "The Return to History and the New Institutionalism in American Political Science." *Social Science History* 17 (1993): 1–36.

Rockwell, Landon G. "The Planning Function of the National Resources Planning Board." *Journal of Politics* 7 (1945): 169–78.

Rodgers, Daniel T. "In Search of Progressivism." *Reviews in American History* 10 (December 1982): 113–32.

Rogin, Michael. "Voluntarism: The Political Functions of an Apolitical Doctrine." *Industrial and Labor Relations Review* 15 (1962): 521–35.

Roosevelt, Franklin D. "Growing Up by Plan." *Survey,* February 1, 1932, 483–85, 506–7.

———. "The New Deal—An Interpretation." *Liberty,* December 10, 1932, 7–8.

Rosen, Elliot A. "Roosevelt and the Brains Trust: An Historiographical Overview." *Political Science Quarterly* 87 (1972): 531–63.

Rosenof, Theodore. "The Economic Ideas of Henry A. Wallace, 1933–1948." *Agricultural History* 41 (1967): 143–53.

———. "Freedom, Planning, and Totalitarianism: Reception of F. A. Hayek's *Road to Serfdom.*" *Canadian Review of American Studies* 5 (1974): 149–65.

———. "New Deal *Pragmatism* and Economic *Systems:* Concepts and Meanings." *Historian* 49 (1987): 368–82.

Rowley, William D. "M. L. Wilson: 'Believer' in the Domestic Allotment." *Agricultural History* 43 (1969): 277–87.

Ruml, Beardsley. "The Extension of Selective Tests to Industry." *Annals* 181 (January 1919): 38–46.

———. "Pulling Together for Social Service." *Social Service Review* 4 (March 1930): 1–10.

———. "The Reliability of Mental Tests in the Division of an Academic Group." *Psychological Monographs* 24, no. 4 (1917).

———. "Some Notes on Nostalgia." *Saturday Review of Literature,* June 26, 1946, 7–9.

Ruml, Beardsley, and Donald G. Paterson. "The Extension of Rating Scale Theory and Technique." *Psychological Bulletin* 17 (February 1920): 80–81.

Sala, Brian R. "The New Institutionalism and the Study of Old Institutions." *Political Methodologist* 8 (Fall 1997): 14–17.

Saloutos, Theodore. "New Deal Agricultural Policy: An Evaluation." *Journal of American History* 51 (September 1974): 394–416.

Samelson, Franz. "Organizing for the Kingdom of Behavior: Academic Battles and Organizational Policies in the Twenties." *Journal of the History of the Behavioral Sciences* 21 (1985): 33–47.

Samuelson, Paul A. "Economic Thought and the New Industrialism." In *Paths of American Thought,* ed. Arthur M. Schlesinger, Jr., and Morton White, 24–67. Boston: Houghton Mifflin, 1963.

Sargent, James E. "FDR and Lewis W. Douglas: Budget Balancing and the Early New Deal." *Prologue* 6 (1974): 33–43.

Sautter, Udo. "Government and Unemployment: The Use of Public Works before the New Deal." *Journal of American History* 73 (June 1986): 59–86.

———. "North American Government Labor Agencies before World War I: A Cure for Unemployment?" *Labor History* 24 (1983): 366–93.

———. "Unemployment and Government: American Labor Exchanges before the New Deal." *Histoire sociale/Social History* 18 (1986): 335–58.

Schlereth, Thomas J. "Burnham's *Plan* and Moody's *Manual:* City Planning as Progressive Reform." *Journal of the American Planning Association* 47 (1981): 70–82. Reprinted in *The American Planner: Biographies and Recollections,* ed. Donald A. Krueckeberg, 75–99. New York: Methuen, 1983.

Schmitter, Phillipe C. "Still the Century of Corporatism?" *Review of Politics* 36 (1974): 85–131.

Schumpeter, Joseph A. "Wesley Clair Mitchell (1874–1948)." *Quarterly Journal of Economics* 64 (1950): 139–55.

Secrist, Horace. "Statistics of the United States Shipping Board." *Journal of the American Statistical Association* 16 (March 1919): 236–47.

Shankman, Arnold. "The Five-Day Plan and the Depression." *Historian* 43 (May 1981): 393–409.

Shapiro, Stanley. "The Twilight of Reform: Advanced Progressives after the Armistice." *Historian* 33 (1971): 349–64.

Sklar, Martin J. "Periodization and Historiography: Studying American Political Development in the Progressive Era, 1890s-1916," and discussion with Steven Hahn. *Studies in American Political Development* 5 (1991): 173–223.

Skocpol, Theda. "Delivering for Young Families: The Resonance of the GI Bill." *American Prospect,* September-October 1996, 66–72.

———. "Legacies of New Deal Liberalism." *Dissent* 30 (Winter 1983): 33–44.

———. "The Narrow Vision of Today's Experts on Social Policy: Specialists give too little thought to building political coalitions and expanding electoral support." *Chronicle of Higher Education,* April 15, 1992, B1–2.

———. "Political Response to Capitalist Crisis: Neo-Marxist Theories of the State and the Case of the New Deal." *Politics and Society* 10 (1980): 155–201.

Skocpol, Theda, and Finegold, Kenneth. "State Capacity and Economic Intervention in the Early New Deal." *Political Science Quarterly* 97 (1982): 255–78.

Skowronek, Stephen. "Franklin Roosevelt and the Modern Presidency." *Studies in American Political Development* 6 (Fall 1992): 322–58.

Slichter, Gertrude Almy. "Franklin D. Roosevelt and the Farm Problem, 1929–32." *Mississippi Valley Historical Review* 43 (September 1956): 238–47.

Smithies, Arthur. "The American Economy in the Thirties." *American Economic Review* 36 supp. (1946): 11–27.

Stricker, Frank. "Affluence for Whom? Another Look at Prosperity and the Working Classes in the 1920s." *Labor History* 24 (1983): 5–33.

Sundelson, J. W. "The Emergency Budget of the Federal Government." *American Economic Review* 24 (1934): 53–68.

Sweezy, Alan. "The Keynesians and Government Policy, 1933–1939." *American Economic Review* 62 (May 1972): 116–24.

Thelen, David P. "Social Tensions and the Origins of Progressivism." *Journal of American History* 56 (1969): 323–41.

Trani, Eugene P. "Conflict or Compromise: Harold Ickes and Franklin D. Roosevelt." *North Dakota Quarterly* 36 (1968): 19–29.

Trattner, Walter I. "Progressivism and World War I: A Re-Appraisal." *Mid-America* 44 (1962): 131–45.

Tropea, Joseph. "Rational Capitalism and Municipal Government: The Progressive Era." *Social Science History* 13 (Summer 1989): 137–58.

Truman, David B. "The Impact on Political Science of the Revolution in the Behavioral Sciences." In *Research Frontiers in Politics and Government,* 202–31. Washington, D.C.: Brookings Institution, 1955.

Tsou, Tang. "Fact and Value in Charles E. Merriam." *Southwestern Social Science Quarterly* 36 (1955–56): 9–26.

Tugwell, Rexford G. "The New Deal: The Progressive Tradition." *Western Political Quarterly* 3 (1950): 390–427.

———. "The Principle of Planning and the Institution of Laissez-Faire." *American Economic Review* 22 supp. (1932): 75–92.

———. "The Progressive Orthodoxy of Franklin D. Roosevelt." *Ethics* 64 (October 1953): 1–23.

————. "The Sources of New Deal Reformism." *Ethics* 64 (July 1954): 249–76.

————. "Wesley Mitchell: An Evaluation." *New Republic,* October 6, 1937, 238–40.

Tugwell, Rexford G., and E. C. Banfield. "Governmental Planning at Mid-Century." *Journal of Politics* 13 (May 1951): 133–63.

Tyrrell, Ian. "American Exceptionalism in an Age of International History." *American Historical Review* 96 (October 1991): 1031–55.

Vining, Rutledge. "Economic Theory and Quantitative Research: A Broad Interpretation of the Mitchell Position." *American Economic Review* 41 (May 1951): 106–18.

Voeltz, Herman C. "Genesis and Development of a Regional Power Agency in the Pacific Northwest, 1933–43." *Pacific Northwest Quarterly* 53 (1962): 65–76.

Vogel, David. "Why Businessmen Distrust Their State: The Political Consciousness of American Corporate Executives." *British Journal of Political Science* 8 (1978): 45–78.

Vollmers, Gloria. "Industrial Home Work of the Dennison Manufacturing Company of Framingham, Massachusetts, 1912–1935." *Business History Review* 71 (1997): 444–70.

Von Mayrhauser, Richard T. "Making Intelligence Functional: Walter Dill Scott and Applied Psychological Testing in World War I." *Journal of the History of the Behavioral Sciences* 25 (January 1989): 60–72.

Wacker, Charles C. "Chicago Plan Is Heritage of World's Fair." *Chicago Commerce,* October 6, 1923, 23–24.

Walcott, Charles, and Karen M. Hult. "Management Science and the Great Engineer: Governing the White House during the Hoover Administration." *Presidential Studies Quarterly* 20 (Summer 1990): 557–79.

"Walter Van Dyke Bingham." In *A History of Psychology in Autobiography,* ed. Edwin G. Boring, Herbert S. Langfeld, Heinz Werner, and Robert M. Yerkes, vol. 4, 1–26. 1952; New York: Russell & Russell, 1968.

Westbrook, Robert B. "Tribune of the Technostructure: The Popular Economics of Stuart Chase." *American Quarterly* 32 (1980): 382–408.

Wilson, M. L. "The Fairway Farms Project." *Journal of Land and Public Utility Economics* 2 (1926): 156–71.

Wolman, Leo. "Statistical Work of the War Industries Board." *Journal of the American Statistical Association* 16 (March 1919): 248–60.

Wren, Daniel A. "American Business Philanthropy and Higher Education in the Nineteenth Century." *Business History Review* 57 (1983): 321–46.

Wright, Gavin. "The Political Economy of New Deal Spending: An Econometric Analysis." *Review of Economics and Statistics* 56 (February 1974): 30–38.

Young, Allyn A. "National Statistics in War and Peace." *Journal of the American Statistical Association* 16 (March 1919): 873–85.

Zeckhauser, Richard. "The Muddled Responsibilities of Public and Private America." In *American Society: Public and Private Responsibilities,* ed. Winthrop Knowlton and Richard Zeckhauser, 45–77. Cambridge, Mass.: Ballinger Publishing, 1986.

Zieger, Robert H. "Herbert Hoover: A Reinterpretation." *American Historical Review* 81 (1976): 800–810.

UNPUBLISHED MATERIALS

Anmad, Salma P. "Institutions and the Growth of Knowledge: The Rockefeller Foundations' Influence on the Social Sciences between the Wars." Ph.D. diss., University of Manchester, 1987.

Brady, Patrick George. "Toward Security: Postwar Economic and Social Planning in the Executive Office, 1939–1946." Ph.D. diss., Rutgers University, 1975.

Bryant, Keith, Jr. "Alvin H. Hansen's Contribution to Fiscal Policy." Ph.D. diss., University of Alabama, 1967.

Chapman, Richard Norman. "Contours of Public Policy, 1939–1945." Ph.D. diss., Yale University, 1976.

Clayton, Glenn L. "The Development of the Concept of National Planning in the United States." Ph.D. diss., Ohio State University, 1948.

Collins, Robert M. "The Persistence of Neo-Corporatism in Postwar Business-Government Relations." Paper delivered at convention of the Organization of American Historians, Detroit, Mich., April 1981.

Eakins, David W. "The Development of Corporate Liberal Policy Research in the United States, 1885–1965." Ph.D. diss., University of Wisconsin, 1966.

Eliot, Charles W., II, and Harold E. Merrill. "Guide to the Files of the National Resources Planning Board and Predecessor Agencies." Typescript dated December 31, 1943. Record Group 187, National Archives, College Park, Md.

Galloway, Eileen Marie. "Charles E. Merriam, Jr." B.A. thesis, Swarthmore College, 1928.

Grant, Frederic D., Jr. "Edward Delano and Warren Delano II: Case Studies in American China Trade Attitude toward the Chinese, 1834–1844." B.A. thesis, Bates College, 1976.

Grossman, David Michael. "Professors and Public Service, 1885–1925: A Chapter in the Professionalization of the Social Sciences." Ph.D. diss., Washington University, 1973.

Hawley, Ellis W. "The Great War and Organizational Innovation: The American Case." Unpublished paper, University of Iowa, 1984.

———. "Techno-Corporatist Formulas in the Liberal State, 1920–1960: A Neglected Aspect of America's Search for a New Order." Unpublished paper, University of Iowa, 1974.

Hinchey, Mary Hedge. "The Frustration of the New Deal Revival, 1944–1946." Ph.D. diss., University of Missouri, 1965.

Jeffries, John W. "World War II and American Life: A Watershed." Paper delivered at convention of the Organization of American Historians, Cincinnati, Ohio, April 1983.

Kalish, Richard. "National Resource Planning: 1933–1939." Ph.D. diss., University of Colorado, 1963.

Karl, Barry D. "Herbert Hoover and the Progressive Myth of the Presidency." Address at the Herbert Hoover Seminar, Herbert Hoover Presidential Library, West Branch, Iowa, August 1974.

———. "In Search of National Planning: The Case for a Third New Deal." Paper delivered at convention of the Organization of American Historians, Cincinnati, Ohio, April 1983.

Kent, James Robert. "Planning for Abundance: Capitalism and American Ideas of National Planning, 1880–1920." Ph.D. diss., University of Kansas, 1983.

Lee, Frederic S. "Gardiner C. Means and the Origin of His Doctrine of Administered Prices." Unpublished paper, Roosevelt University, 1987.

———. "A New Dealer in Agriculture: G. C. Means and the Writing of *Industrial Prices*." Unpublished paper, Roosevelt University, 1987.

Lindblad, Richard Gordon. "Progressive Politics and Social Change: The Political Ideas of Charles E. Merriam." Ph.D. diss., University of Minnesota, 1972.

May, Dean Lowe. "New Deal to New Economics: The Response of Henry Morgenthau, Jr. and Marriner S. Eccles to the Recession of 1937." Ph.D. diss., Brown University, 1974.

McCarthy, Michael. "Businessmen and Professionals in Municipal Reform: The Chicago Experience, 1877–1920." Ph.D. diss., Northwestern University, 1970.

McMullen, Joseph H. "The President's Unemployment Conference of 1921 and Its Results." M.A. thesis, Columbia University, 1922.

McQuaid, Kim. "A Response to Industrialism: Liberal Businessmen and the Evolving Spectrum of Capitalist Reform, 1886–1960." Ph.D. diss., Northwestern University, 1975.

Merrill, Harold E., comp. "Guide to the Files of the National Resources Planning Board and Predecessor Agencies." Washington, D.C.: National Archives, 1943.

Rockwell, Landon G. "National Resources Planning: The Role of the National Resources Planning Board in the Process of Government." Ph.D. diss., Princeton University, 1942.

Runfola, Ross Thomas. "Herbert C. Hoover as Secretary of Commerce, 1921–1923: Domestic Planning in the Harding Years." Ph.D. diss., State University of New York, Buffalo, 1973.

Sautter, Udo. "American Unemployment Policy: The Planning, 1920–1933." Paper delivered at convention of the Organization of American Historians, Cincinnati, Ohio, December 30, 1988.

Seifert, Robert L. "A History of the National Resources Planning Board, 1939–1943." M.A. thesis, Ohio State University, 1959.

Shepard, David Hugh. "Reconversion, 1939–1946: Images, Plans, Realities." Ph.D. diss., University of Wisconsin, 1981.

Tsou, Tang. "A Study of the Development of the Scientific Approach in Political Studies in the United States, with Particular Emphasis on the Methodological Aspects of the Works of Charles E. Merriam and Harold D. Lasswell." Ph.D. diss., University of Chicago, 1951.

White, Philip L. "The Termination of the National Resources Planning Board." M.A. thesis, Columbia University, 1949.

Whyatt, Nelson Thomas. "Planning for the Postwar World: Liberal Journalism during World War II." Ph.D. diss., University of Minnesota, 1971.

Index